News Writing
and Reporting
for Today's Media

News Writing
and Reporting
for Today's Media

Bruce D. Itule

Arizona State University

Douglas A. Anderson

Arizona State University

McGraw-Hill, Inc.

New York   St. Louis   San Francisco   Auckland
Bogotá   Caracas   Lisbon   London   Madrid
Mexico City   Milan   Montreal   New Delhi
San Juan   Singapore   Sydney   Tokyo   Toronto

This book was set in Palatino by The Clarinda Company.
The editors were Hilary Jackson, Fran Marino, and Susan Gamer;
the production supervisor was Denise L. Puryear.
The cover was designed by Robin Hoffmann.
The photo researcher was Elyse Rieder.
R. R. Donnelley & Sons Company was printer and binder.

News Writing and Reporting for Today's Media

This book is printed on acid-free paper.

Permissions and credits appear on pages 695–696, and on this page by reference.

1 2 3 4 5 6 7 8 9 0   DOC   DOC   9 0 9 8 7 6 5 4 3

ISBN 0-07-032415-8

Library of Congress Cataloging-in-Publication Data

Itule, Bruce D., (date).
   News writing and reporting for today's media / Bruce D. Itule,
Douglas A. Anderson.—3rd ed.
     p.   cm.
  Includes index.
  ISBN 0-07-032415-8 (acid-free paper)
  1. Reporters and reporting.   2. Journalism—Authorship.
I. Anderson, Douglas A.   II. Title.
PN4781.I78   1994   93-14829
070.4'3—dc20

Photo by Ethan Miller.

Photo by Frank Hay.

Bruce D. Itule

Douglas A. Anderson

Bruce D. Itule is director of student publications at Arizona State University, where he also is a clinical associate professor in the Walter Cronkite School of Journalism and Telecommunication. Before moving to ASU, he was night city editor of the *Chicago Tribune*. He has been a reporter or copy editor at the *Arizona Daily Star* in Tucson, *The Phoenix* (Ariz.) *Gazette*, the *Boulder* (Colo.) *Daily Camera*, the *Denver Post*, the *Minneapolis Star* and the *Montrose* (Calif.) *Ledger*. Mr. Itule is the coauthor of *Contemporary News Reporting, News Writing and Reporting for Today's Media, Writing the News* and *Visual Editing*. He has also written articles on journalism for professional journals, including *The Quill, Journalism Educator, Grassroots Editor* and *APME News*, and he frequently contributes articles to regional and national magazines.

Douglas A. Anderson is a professor and director of the Walter Cronkite School of Journalism and Telecommunication at Arizona State University. He is author or coauthor of *A "Washington Merry-Go-Round" of Libel Actions, Contemporary Sports Reporting, Electronic Age News Editing, Contemporary News Reporting, News Writing and Reporting for Today's Media* and *Writing the News*. He has also written articles that have appeared in such academic and professional publications as *Journalism Quarterly, Newspaper Research Journal, American Journalism, APME News, Journalism Educator* and *Grassroots Editor*. His teaching specialties are reporting, communication law and editing, and he was formerly managing editor of the *Hastings* (Neb.) *Daily Tribune*. Professor Anderson was a graduate fellow at Southern Illinois University, where he received his Ph.D.

Contents

The authors of this book have asked me to jot down a few thoughts on being a reporter. A few thoughts is just about the appropriate number, since I've never considered news reporting to be a craft or a trade or—as some romantics called it when I first began—a racket that requires much explanation.

What a reporter does is get news stories. Simple enough?

A reporter is the basic unit of the news business, just as the infantryman is the basic unit of the war business. Editors and generals are paid more, travel better and wield great power. But without the reporter or grunt, nothing much is going to be done.

So what does it take to be a reporter?

Assuming you are reasonably literate, have no felonious habits and can show up for work sober and clear-headed, here are minimal qualities.

- *You have to be smart.* Many of the people you will be covering, whether they are local politicians, White House aides, business executives or something in between, will be very smart. And since many of them will try to spin you like a top, you have to be bright enough to recognize and resist being conned.

- *It helps to have a sense of humor.* That's because so much news reflects the chronic silliness of human beings, and if you can't occasionally laugh at what you see, you will start developing holes in your stomach lining. If you happen to lack a sense of humor but insist on getting into news work, then you should direct you career toward an executive job, in which a serious, even ponderous, manner can be an asset because people will be deluded into believing you are a deep thinker.

- *You must be resourceful, imaginative and able to think quickly on your feet.* Much news is routine, predictable, easy to gather and write. But much of it must be sniffed out, and there are no set guidelines for how to do it. You have to devise them on the spot or along the way. Try this. If it doesn't work, try that. If the front door doesn't open, there's always the back door. Or bang on the window.

- *You should have a strong streak of skepticism.* People are going to lie to you. Presidents lie, members of Congress lie, campaign managers lie, business executives lie, public relations people lie, crooks lie and even their victims lie. A reporter hears more lies than anybody in our society except maybe a divorce court judge. You need wit and patience as well as the technical skills to sift though the bunk. You need to double-check and triple-check until you have something resembling facts, if not great truths. As Arnold Dornfeld, the legendary night editor of the Chicago City News Bureau, loved to tell quivering cub reporters: "Laddie, if your mother says she loves you, check it out."

- *You have to have news sense.* If you do not have it, you don't belong in news work. You will be like a tone-deaf musician or a color-blind artist. But what is news sense? I'm really not sure. It's like trying to define what's funny. An editor once told me that it's an instinct for knowing what makes people's jaws drop and eyes pop open when they hear or read about something. A little self-test: When you tell your friends or family about something you saw or heard, do their eyes glaze, do they yawn, do they drift to another part of the room? Chances are, you do not have news sense. But if they listen intently, if they lean forward in anticipation for the punch line, maybe you have it. Look, it's like rhythm. If you got it, you know it.

- *You have to have energy, a second wind, a finishing kick.* Reporting can be hard work. Stories don't always break or develop for the convenience of the 9-to-5 commuter. They can require long hours, tedious legwork. Covering a long political campaign is an almost endless string of 18-hour work days. An investigation into local sewer contracts can mean weeks of poring over specifications, bids and contracts. The best reporters are never clock watchers.

- *A thick hide helps.* Despite the illusion created by a TV press conference, many people do not want to answer a reporter's questions. They will slam the door, hang up the telephone, tell you to bug off. Rejection is part of the job, and you can't take it personally or let it wear you down. Nor can you let it make you vindictive and malicious. There's nothing in any lawbook that says somebody has to talk to a guy with a notebook or a microphone in hand. Maybe journalism schools should require every student to spend a few weeks selling door-to-door.

- *Which leads to personality.* You do not have to act like a game show host, but if strangers are going to respond, if sources are going to be trusting, if public figures are going to be open, it doesn't hurt to have a polite, civilized, even amiable personality. There's more to reporting than chasing somebody up the jailhouse steps and shouting, "How does it feel to be charged with slaying your mom with an ax?"

- *You have to be fair.* That means giving people a chance to tell their side of a story and presenting it accurately. It means not baiting, taunting, or goading people into an intemperate response. It means not putting words in their mouths. It means checking and rechecking, even if getting all the facts in a story could cause the story to vanish. Those are people, remember, and they have friends, families and reputations. Pencils have erasers, but printing presses and TV screens don't.

There's more to it, I suppose, but that's what the rest of this book is for.

Mike Royko

Chicago, Illinois

Preface

We wrote *News Writing and Reporting for Today's Media,* Third Edition, to show students what it is like to be a news reporter and writer. Our aim was to write an all-encompassing text and make it lively. We wanted to make the drama of news reporting come alive, to kindle excitement while painting a realistic picture.

Our book teaches students to write a story in the newsroom while sitting at a computer terminal. It also takes them out on the beat and into the press box, the council chamber, the courthouse, the wire-service bureau and the press conference. It introduces them to current issues and to reporters and editors who provide down-to-earth advice. We want students to learn the basics while examining the work of professionals.

Students will be with the *Topeka* (Kan.) *Capital-Journal* reporter Roger Aeschliman as he covers a major fire, *Chicago Tribune* reporters Gary Washburn and Ann Marie Lipinski on the scene of an air crash in Texas, *Mesa* (Ariz.) *Tribune* reporter Mike Padgett at a murder trial, *Chicago Sun-Times* feature writer Mary Gillespie as she interviews Miss Illinois, *Omaha* (Neb.) *World-Herald* sportswriter Lee Barfknecht at a University of Nebraska football game, consumer reporter David Horowitz on the air in Los Angeles, investigative reporter Charlie Zdravesky as he prepares a radio piece in Albuquerque, N.M., reporter Dawn Garcia as she covers minority affairs for the *San Francisco Chronicle,* and *Chicago Tribune* environment reporter Casey Bukro on assignment. And these are only a few of the reporters who have been gracious enough to participate in making this book possible.

Our focus is on real reporters in real situations, but this storytelling does not cloud the lessons of the text. We have woven the experiences of journalists into the pedagogical fabric of our book. The reporters provide anecdotes; they also serve as instructional models. In this edition we have, whenever needed, updated our examples or introduced new reporters and stories.

One thing we learned as this book went through the review process is that virtually every school has a unique approach to teaching news writing and reporting. Some schools, for example, require a text and workbook for an entire semester before turning their students loose for in-the-field reporting. Other schools do not use workbooks; they send students into the field at the beginning of the first writing course while concurrently exposing them to the basics of news writing. Some schools teach writing for the print media only; others also introduce students to broadcast writing. Because the approaches are so diverse, we wrote a textbook that is flexible enough to meet the needs of most institutions and instructors.

We have also learned through experience that students will not trudge through a densely written text. At the same time, however, instructors will not use superficial texts. Therefore, we wanted to write a text that would be both as readable and as complete as we could make it.

KEY FEATURES

News Writing and Reporting for Today's Media has several important features:

- *First-person accounts from reporters and editors.* We enhance the practical aspects of the text by bringing students into actual reporting situations. We show how concepts and principles work in real situations, and we explore the problems, philosophical questions and issues that journalists face on the job.

- *Integrated sections on broadcast writing.* The text is primarily about writing and reporting for newspapers, but throughout it we provide examples of how broadcasters cover the news and write their stories. We point out differences between print and broadcast reporting and writing but also examine the many similarities.

- *Numerous current examples of stories from a wide range of newspapers and broadcast stations.* We use examples of stories from large metros, medium-circulation dailies, small-circulation dailies and student newspapers along with broadcast examples from geographically diverse markets of all sizes.

- *Detailed, comprehensive discussions of the rudiments of news writing and reporting.* We provide chapters on leads, story organization, developing a news story from day to day, interviewing, quotes and attribution, qualities of good writing and gathering information.

- *Comprehensive discussions of special kinds of reporting.* After we set forth the rudiments of writing, reporting and gathering information, we provide chapters on writing obituaries and press releases as well as covering press conferences and speeches, weather and disasters, multicultural developments and issues, police and fire departments, local government, courts, sports and business and consumer news.

- *Thorough instruction in areas that often receive only cursory treatment in other texts.* We discuss the use of survey methods to gather information for news stories, electronic retrieval strategies, wire-service reporting and legal and ethical issues.

We have also written an accompanying Workbook that gets away from "Springdale, U.S.A."-type exercises. As far as possible, our exercises are based on real news events. In addition to providing writing exercises, each chapter of the Workbook contains review questions for the corresponding chapter in the text.

ABOUT THE THIRD EDITION

This third edition continues to emphasize real reporters and stories, which serve as instructional models. We have, however, updated the first-person accounts and provided fresh examples of stories throughout.

We have also revised, expanded and reorganized many sections; and we have updated the Workbook and Instructor's Manual.

In addition to these changes, the third edition features:

- *A new chapter on developing a news story.* As part of our section on the rudiments of news writing and reporting, we have written a new chapter to show students how to develop a story from day to day and week to week. Many stories are worth more than a single day of coverage; this chapter explains how reporters cover such stories and organize their writing.

- *A new chapter on multicultural reporting and sensitivity.* This chapter goes beyond telling students how important it is for reporters to be sensitive to different cultures, ethnic groups, religions and lifestyles. The chapter emphasizes the importance of consistent, accurate and systematic coverage of the issues and events brought about largely by the rapidly changing demographics of the United States. The chapter also outlines trends in multicultural reporting and provides examples of minority-affairs coverage.

- *Several new sections reflecting changes in recent years.* For example, we have updated our chapter on the use of electronic data bases in the reporting process. We have also added environmental reporting and science and medical writing to our chapter on specialty reporting.

ORGANIZATION OF THE TEXT

News Writing and Reporting for Today's Media can be used in one-semester courses in news writing, in second-semester courses in reporting or in two-semester courses in news writing and reporting. Because each chapter is self-contained, instructors can use any combination of chapters they wish.

PART ONE: THE FOURTH ESTATE

Part One, The Fourth Estate, introduces students to contemporary news media, provides an overview of jobs in the media and examines how news is viewed by newspaper and broadcast reporters and editors.

1 The opening chapter emphasizes that writers can find employment at newspapers, the wire services, television and radio stations, magazines, public relations firms and advertising agencies and in photojournalism. It then explores how reporters cover the news and examines the primary jobs held by print and broadcast reporters.

2 Chapter 2 describes the evolution of news treatment. It outlines the traditional criteria of newsworthiness, examines the factors that affect news treatment, presents guidelines for pitching news stories to editors and explores editorial decision making at three newspapers.

PART TWO: THE RUDIMENTS

Part Two, The Rudiments, is the heart of the text. It provides instruction on writing summary and special leads, organizing stories, developing stories, quoting and attributing, and the qualities of good writing.

3 In Chapter 3, students are shown how to write summary leads. In the first section of this chapter, the underlying principles—including the primary elements *who, what, why, when, where and how*—are explained. In the second section, specific guidelines for lead paragraphs are given.

4 Chapter 4 discusses alternatives to the summary lead, explaining and providing examples of narrative, contrast, staccato, direct address, question, quote and "none of the above" leads. It also gives specifics on writing these leads, emphasizing the need for strong, vivid verbs and ending with an illustration of how several different leads could be written for the same story.

5 The fifth chapter shows students how to organize news stories. It describes the steps involved in writing inverted-pyramid stories and also takes a look at the hourglass style—in which a writer presents the major news in the first few paragraphs before using a transitional paragraph to introduce a chronology of events. Chapter 5 ends with a look at organizing broadcast stories.

6 Chapter 6 discusses the development of a news story from day to day or week to week. It explains how editors and reporters determine which stories should or should not be developed beyond a single item, and it describes the phases of a developing story. As an example, the chapter uses a massive manhunt for an escaped convict, which dragged on for 55 days and brought hundreds of police and reporters into Arizona's mountain forests.

7 Students learn from Chapter 7 that strong, vivid quotations can make an ordinary news story special. This chapter describes types of quotations—direct, partial and indirect—and discusses when and how to quote. It also takes up attribution and punctuation of quotations.

8 Chapter 8 features advice on writing from Roy Peter Clark and Donald Fry of the Poynter Institute for Media Studies in St. Petersburg, Fla. Clark takes a look at traits of good writers, and Fry gives practical guidelines for constructing clear, "open" sentences. Then, examples are used to illustrate each of Robert Gunning's "Ten Principles of Clear Writing."

PART THREE: GATHERING INFORMATION

Part Three, Gathering Information, gives students instruction in the basics of the reporting process. The chapters in this section explain how to use library sources and electronic data bases, how to interview and how to use surveys to gather information.

9 Chapter 9 covers standard sources of information in newsrooms and libraries, emphasizing that background information is essential to good reporting and writing. It also takes up government as an information source, discussing the federal Freedom of Information Act and various state laws on open records and open meetings.

10 Electronic data bases are the newest tools journalists can use in searching for information. Chapter 10—written by Professor Roy Halverson of Arizona State University—shows students how they can strengthen their stories through electronic retrieval of information, examines the types of electronic sources now available to reporters and provides instruction on how to use them.

11 Chapter 11 underscores the importance of interviewing; it covers doing the related research, setting up interviews and conducting interviews for news stories, features and investigative stories. It shows students how to structure the interview, ask the right questions at the right times, establish rapport, take notes and so on.

12 Chapter 12 takes up the important concept of "precision journalism," examining the growth of survey research as a way of gathering information for news stories. This chapter addresses basic considerations involved in conducting surveys: formulating and testing questions, developing samples, collecting and analyzing data and writing the story. Chapter 12 also presents rules for reporting polls.

PART FOUR: BASIC ASSIGNMENTS

Part Four, Basic Assignments, takes up fundamental stories that reporters often encounter: obituaries, rewrites of press releases, weather, disasters, press conferences and speeches.

13 Chapter 13 stresses that obituaries are among the best-read items in newspapers and that reporters should strive not only to provide the basic facts but also to humanize obits with anecdotes and quotations. This chapter outlines the information typically given in obituaries and examines policies of various newspapers regarding names, nicknames, courtesy titles, ages, addresses and causes of death.

14 Chapter 14 discusses press releases and gives tips on evaluating them—deciding if they are of interest to the audience—and on rewriting them. The chapter also offers tips to students who are interested in a career in public relations.

15 In Chapter 15, the student is given a front-row seat at a press conference and a speech by the lawyer F. Lee Bailey. This chapter explains how to prepare for press conferences and speeches, how to cover them and how to organize the information into a coherent story.

16 Chapter 16 provides guidelines for writing about weather and disasters. It describes types of weather stories: forecasts, travel conditions and closings, record-breaking weather, unusual weather and seasonal and year-end coverage. It also takes a look at AP style for weather stories. The chapter illustrates disaster coverage by examining reporting of the crash of an airliner in Texas.

PART FIVE: BEATS

Part Five, Beats, takes a look at the writing and reporting techniques that are necessary for covering typical beats: multicultural affairs, city government, police and fire departments, courts and sports.

17 Chapter 17 stresses how important it is for students to be sensitive to cultures, ethnic groups, religions and lifestyles different from their own. Reporters and editors provide plenty of useful advice on how journalists can improve coverage of minority affairs.

18 In Chapter 18, coverage of city government is explored. This chapter describes forms of municipal governments (mayor-council, council-manager and commission), emphasizes the importance of getting a feel for the people in power and provides advice on covering city council meetings and the city budget process.

19 Chapter 19 presents strategies for effective coverage of police and fire departments. It emphasizes the importance of understanding how these organizations are structured, developing sources within them and reading and using departmental records. Advice on writing stories about arrests, burglaries, accidents and rapes is given. A reporter's day on the police and fire beat—a day that includes coverage of a major fire—is described. Chapter 19 ends with suggestions for beat reporters.

20 Our next beat is the courts. In Chapter 20, students are introduced to the federal and state judicial systems and to the importance of mastering judicial structures, learning terminology and writing stories in understandable language. The basic criminal process and the basic civil process are described, and a criminal case is traced, step by step, from arrest to verdict. Advice is given on reporting both criminal and civil cases.

21 The final beat in Part Five is sports. Chapter 21 explores the evolution of sports writing and contemporary trends in sports coverage and writing styles. It gives practical advice on reporting sports—working with statistics and writing games up for print and broadcast—but it emphasizes that sports writing extends beyond merely reporting games to coverage of contract negotiations, courtroom battles and boardroom decisions.

PART SIX: ADVANCED ASSIGNMENTS

Part Six, Advanced Assignments, looks at features, in-depth and investigative reporting, business and consumer news and other specialized reporting.

22 Chapter 22 begins by distinguishing between hard news and soft news and describing types of features: personality profiles, human interest stories, trend stories, in-depth stories and backgrounders. It points out that the main function of features is to humanize, add color, educate, entertain, illuminate and analyze. It then provides advice on writing features: finding a theme, developing the story, using effective transitions, and so forth.

23 Chapter 23 explains that in-depth and investigative articles provide comprehensive accounts that go well beyond a basic news story. Students are shown, first, how to investigate these stories—how to "smell" a story, research it, conduct interviews and if necessary go undercover. Then they are shown how to write the story—how to find the best lead, how to use anecdotes and observations and how to tie the story together with a logical thread.

24 Chapter 24 explores business and consumer reporting. Students are given instruction on writing both news and feature stories and are also shown how to read annual reports so as to transform a maze of numbers into an understandable story. The chapter lists some important sources for consumer stories and provides tips on consumer reporting.

25 Today more than ever before, print and electronic news media are hiring specialty reporters. Chapter 25 examines four specialized areas—science and medicine, environment, religion and legal affairs—and reporters who cover them. It also gives advice for aspiring specialty reporters.

PART SEVEN: WRITING FOR RADIO, TELEVISION AND THE WIRES

The chapters in Part Seven, Writing for Radio, Television and the Wires, describe similarities and differences between reporting and writing for newspapers and for broadcasting and the wire services.

26 Chapter 26 stresses that, although broadcast writing differs in several respects from print writing, the same principles of clarity and conciseness apply to both. This chapter looks at the basics of broadcast style and broadcast writing and illustrates how to write for radio and television. It also features advice from working professionals.

27 Chapter 27 introduces students to the wire services—primarily The Associated Press. The chapter describes how wire services operate and how their reporters write stories for morning and afternoon cycles. It also describes how wire services are used: how wire stories are rewritten to emphasize local angles and how wire sources are combined for roundup stories.

PART EIGHT: BEYOND THE WRITING

Part Eight, Beyond the Writing, examines legal and ethical ramifications of reporting.

28 Chapter 28 introduces students to several legal issues that are of particular concern to reporters. After a discussion of the First Amendment and the press, it considers libel, newsroom searches, protection of sources, invasion of privacy, infliction of emotional distress and the question of fair trial versus free press. Landmark cases are discussed, and practical guidelines are provided.

29 Our final chapter—Chapter 29—focuses on journalistic ethics; it stresses that, increasingly, society is calling for accountability in journalism. This chapter begins with a discussion of authoritarian and libertarian press systems and the "social responsibility" theory, and then takes up public criticism of the press and the response of the press to that criticism. It examines codes of ethics and some of the most important ethical issues facing journalists today: fairness and objectivity, misrepresentation by reporters, privacy versus the public's right to know, conflicts of interest and journalistic arrogance.

APPENDIXES

We provide three important features as appendixes. *Appendix A* gives many of the style rules of The Associated Press. *Appendix B* gives some excerpts from representative codes of journalistic ethics. And the *Glossary* (*Appendix C*) defines key terms used in the text.

ACKNOWLEDGMENTS

Some of the journalists interviewed for this book have moved to other jobs. References to them, however, remain within the context of their jobs at the time their articles were published or broadcast or at the time they were interviewed.

Many people contributed to the research and preparation of our text through their insights, advice and willingness to provide examples. They include the entire staff of the *Chicago Tribune,* and in particular, environment reporter Casey Bukro; Managing Editor Dick Ciccone, who allowed us to use whatever stories and resources we needed; Mitch Dydo, a consummate copy editor; Jim Warren; Bill Recktenwald; Mary Wilson; Bill Parker; Milt Hansen; Jerry Crimmins; Bill Garrett; Joe Tybor; Neil Mehler; Barbara Sutton; Tom Hardy; Ellen Soeteber; Greg Gerdes; Dennis Ginosi; Gary Washburn; Mike Tackett; Pat Reardon; Ann Marie Lipinski; and Jerry Thornton.

Others who were particularly helpful include assistant managing editor Howard Finberg and reporter David Cannella of *The Arizona Republic;* Associated Press Detroit Bureau Chief Charles Hill; *Birmingham* (Ala.) *News* Managing Editor Thomas Bailey; *Beaumont* (Texas) *Enterprise* Managing Editor William Mock; Ted Murphy, senior vice president and general manager of Bozell Public Relations in Minneapolis; Chicago freelance writer Katherine Rodeghier; Mary Beth Sammons, Chicago business writer; *Chicago Sun-Times* feature writer Mary Gillespie; Marlene Desmond, communications director of the Colorado Lottery; *Colorado Springs* (Colo.) *Gazette Telegraph* Managing Editor Ben Wood; *Denver Post* photographer Brian Brainerd; Kenneth Bowling, news editor, *Dallas Morning News; Detroit News* editor and publisher Robert H.

News Writing
and Reporting
for Today's Media

one

The
Fourth Estate

Associated Press staffers Jeff Baenen and Paula Froke work on a story.
(Photo by Jim Mone, The Associated Press)

1

The Modern Media

Opportunities abound for good writers. These

writers can showcase their talents at newspapers,

the wire services, television stations, radio

stations, magazines, public relations firms and

advertising agencies. A well-rounded college

education, combined with professional experience,

can help prepare today's graduates for work in the

media. This chapter provides an overview of news

media before examining how reporters cover the

news. The chapter closes with descriptions of key

jobs in both newspaper and broadcast newsrooms.

Assignment. Cover the mayor's press conference; write a 300-word news story for the morning edition of the newspaper.

Assignment. Cover the mayor's press conference; write a 200-word wire-service story.

Assignment. Cover the mayor's press conference; write a 100-word story for the 6 o'clock television news.

Assignment. Cover the mayor's press conference; write a 75-word story for a 5 o'clock radio newscast.

Assignment. Cover the mayor's press conference; write a 1,000-word feature for a city magazine on behind-the-scenes preparation by his staff members.

Assignment. Attend the mayor's press conference. Write a 500-word news release for a public relations agency that has been retained to advise and handle publicity for the incumbent, who is seeking re-election. Work in background on the mayor's wife, who has agreed to head a local fund-raising drive for needy families.

Assignment. Attend the mayor's press conference. See if you can get some ideas for copy to be included in an advertisement. Your advertising agency has been retained to handle advertising for the incumbent's re-election campaign.

Assignment. Photograph the mayor's press conference. Make certain that the visuals produced are integrated with the written words.

The market for people who want to pursue writing careers is broad and diverse. Three decades ago, a majority of students coming out of journalism schools used their talents primarily at newspapers. Today, many students still look for newspaper jobs, but others seek and find work at outlets such as television, radio, public relations and advertising.

This book is aimed primarily at students who want to be news writers and reporters. But it is important to realize that many of the skills necessary to function as a news writer and reporter are required in a variety of other fields. Clear, concise, accurate writing is important in all media-related jobs. It takes skill to phrase a memo to an advertising client clearly, just as it does to write an understandable story for tens of thousands of newspaper readers or radio listeners.

Regardless of the medium for which they work, writers must be able to gather information, find the most important elements, put the story together and communicate it effectively within the parameters of the medium.

TODAY'S MEDIA

NEWSPAPERS

There are about 1,585 daily and 8,300 weekly newspapers in the United States, and at one time or the other each of them is looking for a skilled news writer and reporter. Some newspapers will hire only people who have had experience at other dailies or weeklies; others will hire people right out of college.

Qualified people who want to write for newspapers can usually find a job, if they are willing to go anywhere and work for a newspaper of any size. Metropolitan daily newspapers have more than enough applicants for the few jobs that open up each year, and they are able to choose their employees from a pool of people. Smaller dailies and weeklies, however, do not have as many applicants, and the competition for jobs at these papers is not as fierce.

Every week, *Editor & Publisher*, the journalism trade magazine, publishes help-wanted advertisements in the classified section. The available jobs may range from executive editor at a major newspaper to beginning reporter at a community daily. Newspapers also post job notices in journalism schools and departments. Some newspaper editors visit schools to try to recruit reporters and copy editors. More than three-fourths of the entry-level reporting jobs today go to graduates of journalism schools.

Of course, it is still possible to find a job at a newspaper without a journalism degree. Many reporters at newspapers majored in history, political science or another field. People with law degrees or other specialized degrees are becoming reporters; and some people without degrees still become newspaper reporters, although that is becoming more of a rarity.

Today, newspapers of all sizes are looking for qualified reporters who have combined a college education with actual writing experience. They want people who have read the books and are also "street-smart." This means that the people getting the jobs first are those who have done well in college and probably have worked for their campus newspaper and served an internship.

Writing for a newspaper is exciting. It enables reporters to wear many hats, to meet all types of people, to create, to live vicariously and to be where the news is happening. But it is a tough life:

The hours are often crummy; news does not happen only from 8 a.m. to 5 p.m., Monday through Friday. It often occurs on holidays, in the middle of the night and on weekends.

The pressure is severe; every reporter has a deadline, and every reporter tries to beat the competition.

No story is definitive; the deadline will not permit it. Often, the story is old news by the time the newspaper is in the reader's hands.

Many of the stories deal in human suffering. There is death, rape, squalor. Name it, and a newspaper reporter will eventually see it.

Still, it is rewarding to be a newspaper writer. The work is seldom dull, and it does not it have to be routine. There is a great sense of accomplishment in interviewing people and telling their stories. There is nothing quite like a byline on the front page; a mother and father saying thanks for helping find a blood donor for their seriously ill 3-year-old; a politician admitting that he has indeed embezzled public funds.

For most reporters, it all starts in journalism school. "Journalism school taught me how to focus the talent I already had," said Zeke Wigglesworth, travel editor of the *San Jose* (Calif.) *Mercury News*. "Writing is like any other talent. It's like painting. You are born with it, but it needs to be developed. A journalism school or a good newspaper will help you develop your talent."

Wigglesworth's beat is the world. As a reporter for the *Minneapolis Star* and now as travel editor for the *Mercury News*, he has interviewed farmers in the backwoods of Minnesota and yuppies in a restored California mining town. He has talked to shopkeepers in Asia, traced his own roots to England and covered a murder in South America. He writes *news stories* that chronicle the *who, what, where, when, why* and *how* of timely occurrences. He writes *feature stories* that analyze the news, entertain an audience or describe people, places or things in or out of the news.

Wigglesworth, who holds a bachelor's degree in journalism, is a highly skilled professional journalist who is able to communicate with his readers in clear, concise sentences. "Anyone can be trained to go out and find *who, what, where, when, why* and *how* and write a basic news story," he said. "If you have talent, you can go beyond that."

WIRE SERVICES

The two major wire services in the United States, The Associated Press (AP) and United Press International (UPI), transmit news of local, regional, national and international importance. Perhaps Mark Twain said it best: "There are only two forces that can carry light to all corners of the globe—the sun in the heavens, and the Associated Press down here."

According to "Associated Press: Reporting the World," published by the wire service, the AP reaches more than 1 billion people each day through 15,000 news outlets. In its Washington bureau alone, the AP transmits an average of 200,000 words and 300 photographs each day. More than 1,600 reporters, editors and photographers work for the AP, and it is always looking for new talent.

Charles Hill, the AP chief of bureau in Detroit and former chief of bureau in Minneapolis, wrote in *The Rip-Saw*, a publication of the Minnesota Press Club, about his first experience with the wire service: "When I walked into the basement of an office building in Charlotte, N.C., to begin working for the world's oldest and largest news cooperative, I was amazed. Because that Associated Press bureau was in charge of news coverage in North Carolina and South Carolina, I expected legions of reporters and editors. I found three or four news people.

"Make that three or four *busy* news people."

Indeed, when hiring news people, Hill looks for journalists who have "initiative, imagination and the desire to work hard." Hill said: "AP staffers must be able to write accurately, clearly and quickly. AP work is physically demanding. The pace is fast. You have to concentrate every minute. You are exhausted at the end of the day."

AP policy is that "applicants for full-time, regular news jobs should have a minimum of 18 months of full-time news experience on a daily newspaper or broadcast station. For people who lack the 18-month minimum experience requirement, the AP has a limited number of temporary openings that sometimes lead to a regular position." Journalists interested in any AP jobs can apply at the bureau nearest them. Applicants are given tests in vocabulary and news writing. Also, the bureau chief conducts an interview.

Hill, who holds a journalism degree, noted that the temporary news jobs open to less experienced journalists don't necessarily lead to regular AP employment but sometimes do. For example, Hill worked in several temporary jobs in bureaus in North Carolina before joining the AP as a regular staffer in Connecticut. Temporary staffers sometimes fill in for staffers who are on leave or help out when other news people are pulled away from their regular duties because of vacations or legislative sessions.

The AP also hires *stringers,* part-time correspondents who cover a specific subject or geographical area. Work as a stringer can occasionally lead to full-time employment.

While solid news skills and versatility are essential for AP news people, specialized backgrounds can also be useful. Hill mentioned two reporters he hired while in Minneapolis: Tony Kennedy, an AP business writer; and Mike Nadel, an AP sportswriter. Kennedy had been a business reporter for the *St. Cloud Daily Times* and for *The Milwaukee Journal* before being hired by the AP, where his duties have included desk work, government reporting and spot news reporting. His business expertise has also helped him win assignments to produce a weekly business news feature and cover major breaking stories such as the merger of Northwest Airlines and Republic Airlines. Nadel, whose coverage of University of Wisconsin sports for the AP helped prepare him for promotion to Minnesota AP sports editor, still covers high school and collegiate sports. However, his experience has also given him the opportunity to cover the World Series, the Winter Olympics, the National Football League playoff games and the National Hockey League's Stanley Cup championships.

"The AP is a wonderful place to start a career, and it also offers many rewarding opportunities to keep our staffers challenged and fulfilled throughout their careers," Hill said. "Wire service staffers must be versatile. On any given day, they might do straight news writing, or sports writing or broadcast writing. They might do editing work on the desk. Or they might report from the scene of a major news event. The variety of work and the pace of the job are attractive to a lot of staffers. There's always something that needs to be done right now."

TELEVISION

While newspapers have gone out of business or merged in many cities, television stations have expanded their news departments to compete with other stations. In many areas of the United States, where there may be only one metropolitan newspaper, the intense competition is among broadcast journalists. Competition is just as fierce at the network level.

There are about 1,488 television stations in the United States. That includes 556 commercial VHF and 575 commercial UHF stations and 124 educational VHF and 233 educational UHF stations. There also are about 10,900 cable systems.

Viewers can now see news as it is happening anyplace in the world. The electronic gadgetry of broadcast journalism has brought everything from wars to famines to harvests into everyone's living room.

This rapid expansion can last only so long, though. Local stations and the networks will do what they can in the 1990s to trim some of the immense costs of delivering the news. In many cases, advertising revenues have not kept pace with the high costs of expansion. Some local stations have started to look at their news operations and are cutting back.

Network news is changing, too. Besides feeling the pinch of financial cutbacks, the networks are facing a barrage of competition. They no longer have a monopoly in covering national and foreign news. Local stations in the largest markets are sending reporters throughout the nation and the world, competing directly with network correspondents. Many local stations have expanded their news shows to an hour or more, both before and after the network news. This means that television viewers are getting much of their national and foreign news from their local stations before the network news shows begin.

The networks are also being squeezed by cable. Ted Turner's 24-hour, all-news Cable News Network and Headline News have brought profound changes to American broadcast journalism. CNN and Headline News are now available throughout the United States and are expanding rapidly into other countries. Viewers no longer have to wait for the morning or nightly news. If they have cable, they can turn their televisions on at any hour and learn what is happening in the world.

In a speech at the annual awards banquet of the Los Angeles Chapter of the Society of Professional Journalists, Turner said: "My background was not journalism. I got into the broadcast business by buying a station in Atlanta [which he built into the superstation WTBS]. We didn't have any news. Now I feel as if I have 48 hours of news a day. It proves you can do anything. Everyone said we couldn't do it and we proved we could."

Ann Nykanen, special projects producer at WBBM-TV, a station in Chicago owned and operated by CBS, has worked in both print and broadcast news.

After she earned her bachelor's degree in journalism, Nykanen worked as a reporter for nearly five years at *The Arizona Republic* in Phoenix before she moved to Chicago.

"A newspaper cannot take you somewhere live," she said. "If there is a fire raging at 5 p.m., we'll go live. We'll have our reporter there. The viewer will see the flames and activity. People may see firefighters carrying people out. This is the type of dramatic story where we have newspapers beat."

Of course, there are advantages to newspaper reporting, Nykanen said. "We cannot cover as much news as a newspaper, because we don't have as many reporters on the street," she said. "Even if we could, it wouldn't fit on our broadcast."

RADIO

There has been a serious traffic accident at Third Street and Central Avenue. Reporters from a newspaper, a television station and a radio station arrive at the scene at the same time and begin gathering facts.

They all get the same information, but the newspaper reporter must wait for the next edition before his or her work is seen. That is hours away.

The television reporter must consider the visuals of the story and wait for a camera crew. The story is not serious enough for the reporter to break into regular programming.

With only a microphone in hand, the radio reporter goes on the air almost immediately, advising listeners that there has been an accident and warning motorists of the traffic congestion in the area.

"To me, radio news is the ideal medium to work in," said Patrice Bingham, news director of KOLO, the NBC radio affiliate in Reno, Nev. "It's the immediacy factor. The adrenalin really flows when you are doing a breaking story. No other medium can go on the air immediately and let you know what is happening. TV can't do it as quickly; it has to be pretty. TV needs equipment and all the people to do it. On radio, all you need is a telephone or microphone. When something major happens, it is easy for us to break into the programming or wait for the next newscast, since they occur so often."

There are about 11,024 radio stations in the United States. Of those, about 4,988 are commercial AM stations, 4,539 are commercial FM and 1,497 are educational FM stations.

KOLO is a commercial AM country music station in a medium-size market. There are three full-time journalists—Bingham and two others—in its newsroom. Each of them has reporting and anchoring responsibilities from 6 a.m. to 6 p.m. Monday through Friday and is on call 24 hours a day. They also do public affairs programming on the weekend. During the week, they produce 2½ minutes of local news twice an hour—at 25 and 55 minutes after the hour—to go with 2½ of national and international news from the network.

"When I hire somebody, I look for a person with a college degree," said Bingham, who has a bachelor's degree in journalism and also completed graduate course work in journalism. "It need not necessarily be a journalism degree if the person has experience in journalism or broadcasting.

"I feel that a journalism education is important because I don't have time to teach people the history and legal ramifications of the business they are entering. If they can't write, can't put a sentence together or don't know grammar, they don't have a place in this newsroom."

Bingham said her station emphasizes local news. Besides the usual government meetings, accidents and fires, she and the other two reporters cover lifestyle and business stories in Reno and Nevada. They often look behind the scenes and explore community and state problems. "We have two mobile-equipped news cars," she said. "We can go anywhere and transmit live."

Because they have so little time on the air, they must condense their stories into little more than headlines. A long story would run 60 seconds; many stories run only 20 to 40 seconds. "Radio news is necessarily a headline service," Bingham said. "Newspaper people say that we read and rewrite their stories. I say that often they hear one of our stories and then work on it. We complement each other. We depend on each other."

Radio reporters need the same basic reporting skills as news gatherers in other media. "You must know whom to go to and what to ask," said Bingham, who worked as an intern at a newspaper and a television station before going into radio. "Interning at a newspaper is very important. A person who wants to go into broadcasting should not intern at a station only. Once you have learned the basics, then you can translate that into a conversational style for broadcast writing."

MAGAZINES

There are thousands of magazines in the United States. They range from small-circulation publications that serve special-interest groups to national magazines for mass audiences.

There are magazines for collectors of antique cars, baseball cards or almost anything else, for every religion, for every philosophy and on and on. There are quarterlies, monthlies and weeklies. At many magazines the staff consists of one person; at others it consists of only a handful. At some—*Newsweek, Time, National Geographic, Better Homes and Gardens*—there are hundreds of people on the staff.

Some magazine writers are highly trained professional journalists; some are not. The large-circulation national magazines can hire the best people because they offer the highest salaries and the biggest exposure. A small, special-interest magazine is more likely to hire people who want only to write about that special field or who have no experience and want to learn how to write.

While newspaper reporters must limit most of their stories to 10 or 12 inches, magazine writers often compose in-depth articles that may run 50 or more inches. That gives them more room for creativity.

"At a magazine you have the time to really explore a subject because the deadline pressure is much different from that at a newspaper," said Mary Kathryn Glassner, a layout editor at *National Geographic.* "Because a magazine story can be more in-depth, there is a wider range of things a writer can do."

Glassner, who studied journalism in college, worked at *Newsday, The Denver Post* and the *Mesa* (Ariz.) *Tribune* before she joined *National Geographic,* one of the world's most respected magazines. "I think in the industry *National Geographic* is the pinnacle," she said. "It's the place that has the most resources. It gives journalists the opportunity to do complete coverage. There are no holds barred. It doesn't matter what the story costs; we want the best story a writer can get, and the best pictures—and we want the truth."

Glassner said that aspiring journalists who want to work at a national magazine should start at a small newspaper where they can learn all the basics of creating an editorial product. "If you can be an integral part of the editorial product—writing stories, captions or headlines, or editing copy—you will have the foundation to grow into larger papers where you will face new challenges," she added. "You need to keep challenging yourself. That will keep you sharp and growing.

"The great thing about journalism is that your career can keep growing. There are so many things you can do. If you focus on what you want to do in journalism and you keep sharpening your skills, eventually you will end up in the national magazine arena."

PUBLIC RELATIONS

The stereotype of the public relations practitioner slapping a client on the back with one hand while juggling a drink with the other is fast disappearing.

Ted Murphy, senior vice president and general manager of Bozell Public Relations in Minneapolis, said that one of his pet peeves is the applicant who says, "Hey, I like people, so I'm just right for this job."

"Hey, great," said Murphy. "I like people, too, but other qualities—such as being able to write—are more important."

Murphy, who holds a master's degree in public relations, said the ability to write is a "basic tool" for the public relations practitioner. "If you're in PR and you can't write, you're as effective as a carpenter who can't drive a nail."

Murphy's 10 employees all have writing backgrounds. In fact, he gives a three-hour writing test to job applicants. It consists of four parts. Applicants must write a news release from a speech; they must edit another speech; they must outline a brochure; and they must write a five-paragraph "new product" release that contains technical information.

"The test shows me how applicants work under pressure and how they handle a variety of writing assignments," Murphy said.

Murphy also looks for employees who are highly motivated, intelligent and outgoing. "They should possess excellent oral communication skills and they should have confidence in their abilities," he said.

Thousands of journalism school graduates seek jobs in public relations each year. Robert T. Reilly, journalism professor emeritus at the University of Nebraska at Omaha, estimated there are more than 100,000 public relations practitioners in America. Reilly, author of "Public Relations in Action," said that perhaps 20 percent of the practitioners work for the 1,600 private consulting public relations firms. The remainder work in public relations departments at corporations and other institutions.

ADVERTISING

The ability to write effectively for various media is vitally important for employees and executives of advertising agencies. When preparing a commercial for radio, writers have to create images with words and sounds. When preparing television commercials, however, writers must select words to supplement what the audience sees. In developing ads for print, writers must remember that their words, which are not accompanied with sound or moving pictures, must work hard to attract, inform and persuade the audience.

"We place a great emphasis on writing skills at our agency," said Charles Kelly, vice president, director of client services for Kerker and Associates in Minneapolis. The firm employs 35 people.

"Naturally, copywriters need writing skills," Kelly said. "But these skills are also important in account management."

Writing skills are important, for example, when dealing with clients. "In writing plans for our clients we focus on the objectives, strategies and creative rationales," Kelly said. "Account managers must prepare and write these plans. How the plans are written certainly contributes to development of a perception of the agency and how capable its people are.

"Also, it's important to be able to express a point of view to a client in regard to the value of an idea or to justify a particular budget. Often this must be in writing. You must be both expressive and persuasive."

Kelly, who holds a master's degree in journalism, noted that words are at a premium when writing advertising copy. "It's vital that each word does as much as it can to convey the message," he said. "A 30-second commercial could consist of 60 words or fewer. Print ads vary, depending on the space, but you must be clear and persuasive. The right words must be chosen to give the right message. You don't get a second chance."

There are about 10,000 advertising agencies in the United States, ranging from one-person agencies to major firms. About one-third of them employ more than 10 people. Graduates of journalism schools are more likely to find employment at these larger firms than at the smaller operations. In addition, many corporations and institutions have in-house advertising departments.

"Turnover is 15 to 20 percent a year at a lot of agencies," Kelly said. "People seem to have a loyalty to the profession but not necessarily to an agency. This is especially true in the creative department, where copywriters and art directors work."

PHOTOJOURNALISM

American journalism is undergoing a visual revolution. Newspaper pages that 25 years ago were gray columns of type broken by black-and-white pictures have been transformed into well-designed packages that integrate words, photographs, illustrations, graphics and color.

This integration of words and visuals has created great opportunities for photojournalists, many of whom are trained in journalism schools. Photojournalists are becoming equal partners with word journalists in newsrooms throughout the country, as publishers and editors have come to understand the important role visuals play in telling stories and attracting audiences.

Black-and-white and color images of events and people are being "captured" around the world on film or digitally by *electronic cameras,* filmless cameras that record pictures on a video floppy disk. Thanks to advances in photo reproduction and printing processes, high-quality images can be presented more quickly than ever, and less expensively.

"Everyone is still working on getting more and more color into the newspaper," said Brian Brainerd, a photographer for *The Denver Post.* "Color has changed the content of photography because there is more temptation to set up pictures to make the color right. As photographers get more comfortable with color, it will be easier to get more candid shots."

As a newspaper photographer, Brainerd must use news judgment whenever he is on assignment. "To get the great pictures, a newspaper photographer has to be there," he said. "On many stories a reporter can get all of the facts over the telephone if it is not possible to be there, but a photographer can't. Newspaper photographers have to predict the news, in a way. They have to know what news events will yield the best pictures."

Brainerd, who has a bachelor's degree in broadcast journalism, said he most enjoys taking pictures that are unusual, offbeat or funny. "The thing I like about features is that you are not in a pack situation," he added. "I don't think I could be a presidential photographer in a pack, where you get off the bus, go do your shoot and then get back on the bus."

HOW REPORTERS COVER THE NEWS

Often, when young journalists who want to work for a newspaper or in radio or television think of where they would like to work, they think of the huge papers and stations or networks that pay the best wages and have scores of "specialists" traveling around the world. But the truth is that most reporters will never work in New York, Chicago, Los Angeles or Washington, D.C. The majority will work for the hundreds of community newspapers and small broadcast outlets throughout the United States. Some reporters use their first job as a springboard to a medium-size metropolitan newspaper or station; then they will move up to a major American city. Others will spend their careers in a small community, learning every aspect of journalism. They will cover social club meetings; they will interview presidential candidates in town for a whirlwind tour; they even may sell ads, do production work and answer the telephone.

Reporting takes three forms:

- General assignment
- Beats
- Specialties

Each of these areas has distinct characteristics, but their borders are fuzzy. News stories simply do not fall neatly into a single category. They tend to spill over into all three. That means that good reporters must be able to operate effectively in any of these areas.

GENERAL ASSIGNMENT REPORTING

General assignment reporters cover breaking news or feature stories as they come up. Assignments for general assignment reporters usually come directly from an editor or from assistants who have read something in the mail, on the wires or in another publication or who have heard about a story from a public relations person, another editor or reporter or someone who telephones the newsroom.

General assignment reporters—they are called GAs for short—mainly cover *spot news*, which is news occurring now. They are important to any newsroom operation because they are there when a story breaks. For example, there may be a report on the radio that protesters are marching on a suburban Town Hall to demonstrate against an increase in water rates. A GA is sent to the scene immediately. Later in the day, the same GA may cover a parade downtown, then a community meeting in which political candidates are questioned.

The most successful GAs are excellent and quick writers who know their communities well. The stories they write range from crime to crops, from weather to widgets. They must know what is going on and who the main players are around town.

WORKING A BEAT

Beat reporters cover breaking news and features in specific geographic and subject areas every day, such as police and fire departments; county and federal courts; and city, county and state governments. They generally come up with their own story ideas, based on knowledge of their beats and constant contact with sources. They may also be given assignments by their editors or news directors. Beat reporters usually write at least one story a day.

"I'm responsible for any spot news that occurs on my beat while I'm at work," said Kym Fox, one of three reporters who cover the court beat for the *San Antonio* (Texas) *Express-News*. "I roam the halls of the County Courthouse, going from courtrooms to attorneys' offices. I check with them to see if I missed anything. I have my favorite sources in every office whom I can call on whenever I hear anything."

Fox is a typical beat reporter. She is responsible for letting her newsroom know when a story breaks. She comes up with her own ideas and usually covers the stories she chooses. Her newspaper relies heavily on her; she cannot afford to miss a story.

"Beat reporting is more stressful than general assignment," said Fox, who was a GA when she first came to the *Express-News*. "GAs never are accused of missing something. They are reacting to the city editor. If something happens on the court beat and the competition gets it and I don't, it's my butt."

Fox knows that the key to being a successful beat reporter is covering as much of the beat as possible each day. Beat reporters have to budget their time carefully. Besides covering spot news and features, they must constantly cultivate sources and potential sources.

"Beat reporters make sure a newspaper is getting all the news," Fox said. "If we didn't have someone in the courthouse, City Hall and the police station who knew all the important people, things would get by. You would never know if something was wrong."

SPECIALTY REPORTING

Specialty reporters cover breaking news and features in even more specialized areas than beat reporters, such as transportation, energy, medicine, the environment, education, law and aviation. Like beat reporters, they are responsible for finding and writing the stories that originate in their areas.

Their story ideas come from contacting sources and from public relations people, the wires and other editors, reporters and publications. While general assignment and beat reporters are concerned with spot news, specialty reporters are often interested in long-range stories, the roots of problems and the reasons behind the news. This means that they often operate under the most flexible deadlines.

For instance, if there is serious contamination in the largest lake in town, the environmental reporter will first write a spot news story reporting it. Then the reporter may go on to study the problem in depth over a period of time to find out what caused the contamination, how it will affect the community in years to come, what can be done about it and what lessons it has taught city officials.

Specialty reporters have to talk to experts in a specialized field and then write stories in language readers will understand. Thus they must be experts as well as skilled news writers.

They must also be excellent reporters who can cross over into many areas. In the story on the contamination of the lake, the environmental reporter would have to talk to people at city hall to find out why it happened, sources in the medical field to check on its health effects, police and fire officials who are keeping people away from the lake and researchers who are studying long-term effects of water pollution.

THE NEWSPAPER NEWSROOM

PEOPLE IN THE NEWSROOM

Most newspaper newsrooms are structured the same way. At the top is the *editor*, whose role changes depending on the size of the paper. At a community newspaper the editor also may be a publisher, a business manager, a reporter, a photographer and an advertising salesperson. At a metro the editor may have nothing to do with the day-to-day editorial process; the *managing editor* is in charge.

At the other end of the ladder are the beginning reporters, who are trying to make their mark on the profession and hoping to get their names on front-page stories—that is, to get a *byline*. The number of newsroom personnel between the beginning reporter and the top editor is determined by the circulation of the newspaper and its budget.

Managing Editor

At most newspapers the *managing editor* runs the newsroom. It is his or her job to make sure that the newspaper is out on time each day and that costs are kept within a budget. The managing editor is usually responsible for hiring and firing newsroom personnel and serves as a spokesperson for the paper. At smaller newspapers the managing editor is also involved in selecting stories, photos and graphics; making assignments; laying out pages; and editing copy and writing headlines.

In a typical newsroom the managing editor has a number of subeditors, each responsible for one facet of putting out the paper.

News Editor and Copy Desk

The *news editor* is in charge of the *copy desk*, where *makeup editors* and *copy editors* work. Their job is to dummy (lay out) pages and write headlines for the wire copy and the locally written stories that go on the news pages each day.

At larger papers there is a national copy desk that handles stories from other cities, a foreign copy desk that edits copy from other countries and a local copy desk that handles stories by "cityside" reporters. Individual departments, such as sports and lifestyle, may also have their own copy desks. Some newspapers have a "universal copy desk," which edits stories from every department.

Most daily newspapers are members of The Associated Press (AP) and subscribe to United Press International (UPI) and several supplemental news services, which give them a steady flow of stories from cities and battlefields throughout the United States and the world. Once the news editor decides which "wire stories" and which cityside stories go into the paper, they are sent to a makeup editor, who positions them on a page and assigns the size and style of the headline. Then each story is sent to the *slot editor* on the copy desk. The slot editor distributes the story to a copy editor who edits it and writes the headline. The copy desk is the last desk to handle the story before it appears in print.

City or Metropolitan Editor

The *city editor* runs the city (or metropolitan) desk and is in charge of the city-side general assignment, beat and specialty reporters. Assistant city editors may help hand out assignments and review stories. Reporters come to the city desk for ideas, with ideas, for counseling and with stories ready for editing.

It is the city editor's job to make sure that the news in the city (or metropolitan area) is covered and as many local stories as possible get into each edition. There is only so much space between the first and last pages of a newspaper, and ads fill up much of that space. What is left is called the *editorial news hole.* The city editor and the other subeditors at the paper are hoping to fill as much of the editorial news hole as possible with stories or photographs from their staffs; thus much of their time is spent trying to sell their material to the managing and news editors.

The number of reporters reporting to the city editor is determined by the size of the newspaper. Major metropolitan newspapers have hundreds of reporters; community newspapers may have only a few.

State Editor

The *state editor*—alternatively called the *area* or *suburban editor*—supervises reporters who cover communities and areas outside the city in which the newspaper is published. At a big newspaper, reporters may staff bureaus in communities throughout the state. They write news and feature stories about events and people in those communities, then call them in or send them by computer to the state editor, who edits the stories and finds space for them in the newspaper. Even small newspapers have state or area desks, but instead of covering the entire state, they often cover only other communities in the county or in the circulation area of the paper. Coverage of neighboring communities or other cities in the state is important to newspapers because they always are trying to increase their circulation and advertising base.

National and Foreign Editors

Metropolitan newspapers usually have *national* and *foreign editors* who work much like the state editor, but they supervise reporters in bureaus throughout the country or the world. Some newspapers may have reporters in Washington and New York. Others may have fully staffed bureaus in Washington, New York and other major American cities. They may also have reporters in London, Rome, Moscow, Beijing and other major foreign cities. Community newspapers generally do not have national and foreign correspondents; they depend on the wire services to supply them with national and foreign news and features.

Photo Editor

The *photo editor* supervises a newspaper's photographers. At many papers the photo editor sits at or near the city desk, assigning photographers to accompany reporters on news and feature assignments. Some papers have one photographer who handles everything, including pictures for advertisements. Others have several who divide assignments; a few have dozens who are specialized in the types of events they cover.

Graphics Editor

The *graphics editor* serves as the liaison between reporters, editors, photographers, artists and designers to coordinate the production of maps, charts, diagrams, illustrations and other informational graphics that accompany stories. Most metropolitan newspapers have had a graphics editor for years, and now some community newspapers have added this important position to their staffs. At papers where there is no graphics editor, the photo editor or news editor is usually responsible for the graphics. An artist or staff of artists works for the graphics editor.

Sports Editor

The *sports editor* is in charge of sportswriters and the desk people who process their copy. The writers cover sports events and features in a community's high schools and colleges. They also cover professional sports in their area. The desk people on the sports staff edit stories and lay out the daily sports pages. The sports editor often writes a column.

Lifestyle Editor

The *lifestyle editor*, who might also be called a *feature editor*, heads what is usually a paper's main feature section. The section may include articles by lifestyle writers, a food editor, an entertainment writer, a drama critic, a television writer and other reviewers and critics. It may include engagement and wedding announcements. The lifestyle editor, like the sports editor, is also responsible for editing and laying out pages each day.

Editors at the *San Jose Mercury News* gather to decide what stories and photos will be included in the day's editions. *(Photo by Michael Rondou)*

Financial Editor

The *financial editor* is in charge of the business news that goes into the newspaper. Most papers have a business page or business section each day, and many have a staff of financial reporters who cover area businesses. Financial news has grown in popularity in recent years, and many papers are expanding their staffs to cover it. Newspapers have always printed closing stock averages and press releases on business openings, expansions and closings, but now they are assigning their own reporters to cover financial news as aggressively as any other news.

THE NEWS HUDDLE

At least once each day, the foreign, national, state, city, news, photo and graphics editors meet with the managing editor in what may be called a *news huddle, doping session, news conference, editors' meeting* or *editorial conference*. In this meeting they discuss the top foreign, national, state and local stories and photographs. They decide which stories will make it into the paper and which of those stories will be on the front page. A breaking news story could change their plans, but after about 20 minutes of give and take, these editors have determined what their readers will get that day. The sports, lifestyle and financial editors also meet with the managing editor each day, and they will be called into the meeting if they have stories that are being considered for the news section.

A.M. AND P.M. COVERAGE

Morning newspapers are called *A.M.s.* They report news that breaks on the *A.M. cycle,* generally from noon to midnight, as well as other non-breaking stories. Their news huddles are held in the late afternoon because deadlines are in the evening and the papers are printed and delivered during the night, while most people are sleeping. Beat reporters for an A.M. generally work during the day, but many staff members work during the evening.

Evening newspapers are called *P.M.s,* and the *P.M. cycle* runs from about midnight to noon. Editors at P.M.s hold their news huddles in the morning because their deadlines are usually before noon. P.M.s try to get the latest news to their readers, but they realize that by the time the paper is printed and distributed in the afternoon, most of their readers will have had a chance to hear the news on radio or watch it on television. Therefore, they try to offer their readers a bigger and more comprehensive news report and more local feature stories than radio or television can. Larger evening papers also have more than one edition each day, which helps them deliver the latest news possible.

Evening newspapers are fighting an uphill battle, however. P.M.s still outnumber A.M.s in the United States—most newspapers in small, one-paper cities are P.M.s—but many have shut down or switched to A.M. (People still like to look at their morning newspaper before work each day, while they are drinking coffee, to find out what happened since they went to bed the night before.) There are many complicated reasons for the decline of evening newspapers, but it can be attributed partly to changing lifestyles. In most households today both the man and the woman are wage earners, and they are bombarded by radio and television throughout the day. When they get home, they often want to use their leisure time in some other way than reading an evening newspaper.

Work on an evening paper is done primarily during the day, and by late afternoon, when the last edition is out, many of the staffers are off work.

For the most part, morning and afternoon newspapers cover the same news events, but the writing angles are different. Traditionally, a morning newspaper is a *paper of record,* offering straightforward news accounts of what happened in the world, nation, state and community since the last edition. A paper of record also is a source for future historical reference. It often prints texts of speeches or court decisions that other papers summarize briefly.

Reporters at A.M.s generally cover newsworthy events that break during the day or night before the next morning's edition. Readers who open their newspaper first thing in the morning might not know anything about the event; they want to know the essential ingredients, the *who, what, where, when, why* and *how.* Therefore, A.M.s usually report the news firsthand.

By contrast, reporters working for afternoon newspapers are generally covering events that occur after their deadlines for that day's paper. This means that news which breaks in the afternoon or evening must be reported the following afternoon, after morning newspapers and radio and television have already provided the essential ingredients. Because they are writing about events that already have been well covered, reporters for P.M.s often write comprehensive stories that encompass not only the essential ingredients but also a unique angle. Their accounts should not be a rehash of what was already reported. They often have time to analyze events and look for angles not covered in A.M.s or by the electronic media.

When several wildfires broke out in western Arizona, coverage by the morning *Tempe* (Ariz.) *Daily News Tribune* and the afternoon *Phoenix Gazette* illustrated how A.M.s and P.M.s typically handle a story. The *Tribune* carried an Associated Press story that reported the breaking news. It began:

> At least six wildfires burned parts of Arizona Monday, including two blazes north of Yuma that had blackened 4,800 acres of California and Arizona desert along the Colorado River.

When the *Gazette* reported the story, it took a different approach. Instead of merely recapping the number of fires and how many acres had been burned, the writer, Steve Cheseborough, concentrated on a unique angle: smoke had drifted 150 miles from the fire and had cast a thick haze over the Phoenix area. His story began:

> There is plenty of smoke but no fire. Not here, anyway.
> The thick haze that hung over the Valley this morning traveled 150 miles to get here from two huge wildfires along the Colorado River.
>
> The fires started Sunday on the California side of the Colorado and spread to Arizona north of Yuma, where they consumed about 4,800 acres by Monday night.

Stories do not always break on the A.M. cycle, of course. When they occur early in the morning, on the P.M. cycle, afternoon newspapers are the first to report them. In these cases, reporters for A.M.s would look for a different angle.

COMPUTERS IN THE NEWSROOM

Computers have brought great changes to American newsrooms, and it appears that even bigger changes will occur during the 1990s.

Pagination: Computerized Layouts

Computers are being used in today's newsrooms for more than just writing and editing. At many newspapers a computerized layout process called *pagination* is being used. In pagination, the stories, photographs, graphics, cutlines and headlines that make up a page are assembled electronically on a computer screen. Once the electronic page is complete, it is sent to a computerized typesetter that translates the information into the images and words which make up a page.

Electronic Cameras

Computerized cameras are beginning to replace the 35mm cameras that have been used by news photographers for more than 20 years. An *electronic camera* looks like a standard 35mm camera, but it uses no film. Instead, pictures are recorded on a video floppy disk that resembles a computer floppy disk.

To make a picture, the photographer points the camera at a subject in the usual way. A sensor inside the camera records the image by electronic signal. The images can be viewed on a television monitor or can be printed out in color. They can also be transmitted over telephone lines to receiving stations. Because everything is done electronically, darkrooms, chemicals and the time it takes to process and print film are eliminated.

THE BROADCAST NEWSROOM

Broadcast reporters gather news somewhat differently from print reporters. They must think about aural and visual possibilities before they cover a story, and they write fewer words. But they are reporters, and they have the same goals every day as print reporters:

- They want to get the news across in an interesting, concise and direct way.
- They want to serve and keep their audience.
- They want to beat their competition and be the best in their market.

"TV and print are trying to do the same thing, but the tools are different and each side has its advantages," said Ann Nykanen, a broadcast producer at WBBM-TV in Chicago. "In TV the visual and audio impact and its immediacy are an advantage. Its pictures and sounds will arrest your attention.

"But we cannot give the in-depth information that print can provide. We can't explain the entire city budget in two minutes. If you want to know all those details, you have to read the paper.

"The TV reporter will tell the story differently but still needs to cover it and understand it like the newspaper reporter. And technically, the coverage is much more complicated for us. A newspaper reporter needs a pad and pen. For us there is equipment, cables and being in the right place to beam back signals to the station."

PEOPLE IN THE BROADCAST NEWSROOM

There also are similarities and differences in the hierarchy of broadcast and print newsrooms. Job titles in a broadcast newsroom are different from those at a newspaper, but the jobs are not. And, like a newspaper, the size of the broadcast newsroom, whether it is radio or television, is related to the size of the station and the market it serves.

News Director

At the top of the newsroom is the *news director,* who reports to a station manager or general manager and does many of the jobs that a managing editor of a newspaper does. The news director is responsible for the entire news operation, including what goes on the air, the newsroom budget and hiring and firing most reporters and other personnel.

At larger stations there also is an assistant news director, who helps in the business and editorial areas and may be used in long-range planning of news coverage.

In a typical television newsroom a number of people work under the news director to produce the television newscast.

Executive Producer

The *executive producer* runs the newsroom. He or she is responsible for story content, reading and editing reporters' scripts as they come in from the field, long-range planning and scheduling and countless other decisions that require quick management-level decisions. At a smaller station the executive producer may also make assignments and decide the layout of each news show.

Assignment Editor

Many stations have two *assignment editors* (or *assignment managers*), one working during the day and the other at night. They run the "desk," the reporter's contact with the newsroom. They coordinate all assignments, keep track of crews in the field, listen to police and fire radios, make follow-up calls for reporters and take incoming calls. They also call out camera crews or reporters whenever needed on breaking stories and do local follow-ups on national stories that move over the wires.

At larger stations there also may be a *planning editor* (also called a *metro editor*) working on the desk who is responsible for long-term planning of coverage of future events, such as trials or elections. This person also plans special projects such as series to be used during "sweeps" (ratings) periods and is responsible for specialty reporters who cover areas such as consumer, financial and medical news. One or more researchers may work on the desk along with the planning editor.

Broadcast Producers

Broadcast producers put the newscasts together. If a station has newscasts at noon, 6 p.m. and 10 p.m., it may also have three broadcast producers. They are responsible for their own shows, choosing which stories to use, in what order to use them, how long to make them and what production style (how much videotape of a scene, interviews, etc.) will be appropriate. The producers also edit scripts, which the anchors will read, for content, style and continuity. They work closely with the assignment editors to decide which reporters will cover which stories, and they work with the news director and executive producer to decide which stories will make it onto the air. Once the newscast is on the air, the broadcast producer goes into the control room to make sure that the show begins and ends on time. The producer will often have to kill a story at the end of the show because the newscast is running long or will have to ask the anchors to stretch a story because the newscast is running short.

Associate Producer

Associate producers help the broadcast producers lay out their news shows. There is usually one associate producer for each broadcast producer. If the station is a network affiliate, the associate producers will monitor the *feeds,* tapes sent to the stations by satellite from the network's headquarters. They also write scripts, provide wire stories to reporters, take calls and help the assignment editor. At most stations the associate producers are in charge of the tapes that are fed back to the stations by local crews in the field. They make sure that all the tapes to be used in a newscast are edited and ready to go once the show begins.

Reporters and Photographers

At any given time a station might have several *reporters* and *camera crews* out covering beats or breaking news. A station may also have specialty and investigative reporters. Television and radio stations report more stories each day than they have reporters cover because many stories come from the wires or are local stories that do not require a reporter to "package" them with narration. Stories such as these may be covered by the desk and written by news writers or producers, who give them to the anchor to read. At many stations the reporter is also a *field producer,* who decides which shots the camera crew will make. In larger operations a field producer accompanies the reporters and photographers and directs the news gathering.

Anchors

Each newscast usually has one or two *anchors,* the on-camera people who read the scripts. They may be part- or full-time reporters who also anchor the news, or they may be full-time anchors who do no reporting at all. They may write their own scripts or read only what the reporters and desk staff have written.

News Writers

Only the largest television stations in the country have *news writers,* people who write all the scripts the anchors will read and edit tapes before they go on the air. At most stations, anchors and reporters write their own scripts, and technical crews edit the tapes.

DECIDING WHAT GOES ON THE AIR

Newspaper editors decide what will be in the day's editions during their daily editorial conferences. Broadcast executives do the same during editorial meetings that are held several times throughout the day. In these meetings the news director meets with the top producers and editors to decide which stories will be covered on which newscasts.

Ann Nykanen, who produces the 5 o'clock news each weeknight on WBBM-TV in Chicago, begins her workday at 8:30 a.m., a half-hour before her first editorial meeting of the day. That gives her a chance to look at the daily newspapers for stories of interest and make notes of stories that may be of interest to her station. She also reads a list of possible stories made up for her by her planning editor.

"Before the meeting we all are getting ready for our own jobs," she said. "The assignment manager is in early, getting reporters and crews out on stories and reviewing a lengthy list prepared the day before of all the things that we know are going on. By the time we meet, she has boiled down the list to something reasonable and has tentatively assigned reporters to the various stories."

Nykanen said that at the meeting the list is reviewed and discussed by the news director, assistant news director, assignment manager, metro editor, executive producer and broadcast producers. "We almost always have to prioritize coverage because we can't cover everything," she said. "On an average day, we have 10 crews on the street (each crew is two people, a camera operator and a sound technician). If the U.S. attorney has scheduled a news conference, we may not have a reporter to cover it but we'll decide to send a crew to shoot it. When the tape comes back, a news writer will watch it, cut it and write the story.

"At the meeting, we also try to come up with the angles we want to cover on a given story. We talk about how we can make the story advance from the day before, what kind of follow-up or reaction we ought to get, whether we should try to get a newsmaker to appear live on one of the shows and which stories merit live coverage at 5 and 6 p.m. A political fund-raiser that is happening during the dinner hour is a natural for a live shot at 6 o'clock."

Nykanen said many of the decisions made during the morning meeting are changed during the day as stories break or change. "The meeting takes about a half-hour to 45 minutes; then we go about our separate responsibilities," she added. "It's the last time we'll all sit around together for the day. When the stories break, and things change, the decisions will be made in a more impromptu fashion by the executive producer, the broadcast producers and the assignment manager."

Clearly, journalists at all media in America face fast-paced, never ending challenges as they write and process the news of the day.

Chapter

2

Ingredients
of News

Editors at *The Detroit News* decide on the stories, photos and art
that will be included in the next edition.
(Photo by Dale Young)

Ingredients of News

Each day, journalists in print and electronic media

decide which news stories they will disseminate.

These journalists select stories that are most

relevant and interesting to readers and listeners.

There is no scientific formula for measuring news

value, but traditional elements of news help to

guide reporters and editors who make the

selections.

In 1957 the Supreme Court held that obscenity is not protected by the First Amendment. That decision placed a burden on the court: it had to define *obscenity*. Over the years, the court has attempted to structure a workable definition. Justice Potter Stewart, in 1964, summarized the court's frustration. He said that obscenity might be difficult to define, but "I know it when I see it."

A definition of *news* is equally elusive. The stock answers are easy: news is "man bites dog"; news is something you haven't heard before; news is what editors and reporters say it is.

One thing is clear: news is different things to different people. Certainly, geography plays a role. News of unemployment in the steel industry will be on the front page in Pittsburgh but might not receive a mention in Great Bend, Kan. Conversely, a 15-cent increase in wheat prices will get front-page treatment in Great Bend but might not rate even a brief mention in Pittsburgh.

WHAT IS NEWS TREATMENT?

People have always been hungry for news. Colonial Americans hurried to meet arriving ships, to pick up letters and newspapers from Europe. The first attempt to publish a colonial newspaper was on Sept. 25, 1690, when Benjamin Harris of Boston issued *Publick Occurrences Both Foreign and Domestick*. His unauthorized paper was shut down by Massachusetts Bay officials after the first issue—and the next newspaper in the colonies was not printed until 1704—but *Publick Occurrences* began a wave of American newspapers that over the last three centuries has brought readers news of diverse happenings.

In *Publick Occurrences* Harris said that he would furnish his readers "with an account of such considerable things as have arrived unto our notice."

HARD NEWS AND SOFT NEWS

In today's media-conscious world, news comes from many print and broadcast fronts. Sometimes news is bad; sometimes it is good. It can be hard; it can be soft.

Hard news events, such as killings, city council meetings and speeches by leading government officials, are timely and are reported almost automatically by most newspapers, radio stations and television outlets.

Soft news events, such as a lunch to honor a retiring school custodian or a car wash by fourth-graders to raise money for a classmate with cancer, are not usually considered immediately important or timely to a wide audience. These events still contain elements of news, however, and the media often report them. (A more complete discussion of hard and soft news appears in Chapter 22.)

In 1978 a researcher, Ruth Clark, reported the results of a study she conducted for the American Society of Newspaper Editors (ASNE) and United Press International. The study, "Changing Needs of Changing Readers," reported that readers wanted more local news and "how-to" pieces "to help them cope" with day-to-day activities. They also wanted the material presented in an easy-to-read form that did not demand too much of their time.

In the mid-1980s, when Clark was again commissioned by ASNE and UPI to determine what readers wanted on their news pages, she found that readers' desires had changed. She reported that readers wanted more hard news and less emphasis on the softer lifestyle pieces they had favored little more than a half decade earlier. According to an article in *Editor & Publisher* magazine, Clark told ASNE: "When people were asked what they like best about newspapers, 73 percent said keeping up with the news. Only 27 percent said they preferred interesting stories about people, places and things to do."

Clearly, there is a place for hard news and soft news in newspaper, television and radio reports. Most media strive to present both.

THE GATEKEEPING PROCESS

Selection of news for print or broadcast, like a pass-interference call in football, is subjective. Communication researchers refer to people who make news decisions as *gatekeepers*. These editors, news directors and reporters can open the gate to let news flow; they can close the gate to keep news from oozing out. Of course, sources can also be considered gatekeepers. If they refuse to supply information, possibly there will be no story.

David M. White was the first researcher to study the gatekeeping process at newspapers. His case studies of the early 1950s have been replicated many times; the findings show that gatekeepers are alive and well at American newspapers and electronic news media.

One person seldom has complete control over all the gates in the process of disseminating news. For example, the managing editor of a newspaper reads a story in a national news magazine about contemplated congressional action to cut benefits to military veterans. While mulling the possibility of developing a local angle, the managing editor notices that The Associated Press has just moved a similar national story. Seeing the AP story reinforces the editor's belief that it should be further developed by a reporter.

The managing editor then talks to the news editor about assigning the story to a reporter. The managing editor suggests that the reporter interview some local veterans for their reactions to the contemplated cutbacks. The news editor, however, has just seen a local television interview with an American Legion official about the possible cutbacks. The news editor says that the interview was not enlightening, that the local official did not know enough about the issue to say anything more than, "We all fought for our country, and nobody should try to take our benefits away."

The news editor suggests that, rather than putting together a quick local story based on off-the-cuff emotional reactions, a reporter first conduct some interviews with state congressional representatives and review the specific proposals. Then, the reporter could get reactions from local residents. The story would have to be held a day or so, but the managing editor agrees that a stronger article would be worth the delay.

The news editor checks to see which reporters are available to write the story. There are three to choose from: one is a veteran of the Korean War; another was a conscientious objector during the Vietnam War; the third has been out of college for only three years and has had no contact with the military. The news editor decides—subjectively, of course—that the third reporter might approach the story more objectively than the other two. Accordingly, the young reporter, who doesn't know a general from a corporal, gets the assignment.

The gatekeeping process continues: The reporter must decide whom to interview and what to ask, which answers to include in the story, which element to play up in the lead and which sources are the most knowledgeable and quotable.

After making these decisions, the reporter writes the story and turns it in to an assistant city editor for review. The assistant city editor thinks that more emphasis should be placed on comments made by a veteran's widow who was interviewed. The reporter obliges. The news editor determines that the story should run 20 inches and be given a four-column headline. It is to be a front-page story.

A copy editor reads the story and removes some of the material the assistant city editor asked the reporter to add. The reporter rants and raves about the cut. An assistant managing editor is called on to resolve the dispute. A compromise is reached; the widow's comments are left in the story, but because the article must still be cut, a comment from an American Legion member who says that a local congressman is antimilitary is deleted. The assistant managing editor says that the publisher is a good friend of the congressman, but that this is not a factor in the decision to delete the remark.

Thirty minutes before deadline, a reporter calls the city desk to say that the superintendent of schools has just been fired by the board of education. This story will run 20 inches. The news editor decides to take the story on veterans off the front page and move it to an inside news section. The managing editor intervenes, saying that it should remain on the front page, where readership is highest. The managing editor then orders an international story to be shifted from the front page to an inside page.

This scenario could be extended, but the point is clear: There is no scientific formula for deciding what is news and where it should be placed in a newspaper. At several junctures in the process of gathering and writing news, decisions to include or exclude information are made. Reporters and editors, consciously or unconsciously, often rely on time-honored news elements to help them make these decisions.

WHAT MAKES NEWS?

CRITERIA FOR NEWSWORTHINESS

For decades, textbooks on reporting have discussed the classic elements of news. Criteria most often considered as determining newsworthiness include these:

- *Timeliness.* Is it a recent development, or is it old news?
- *Proximity.* Is the story relevant to local readers?
- *Conflict.* Is the issue developing, has it been resolved or does anybody care?

- *Eminence and prominence.* Are noteworthy people involved? If so, that makes the story more important.
- *Consequence and impact.* What effect will the story have on readers?
- *Human interest.* Even though it might not be an earth-shattering event, does it contain unique, interesting elements?

Some examples will illustrate these classic criteria.

Timeliness

Freshness strengthens a news story. For example, when a storm hits, readers immediately need to know its effects. The first two paragraphs from an article in *The Evansville* (Ind.) *Press* illustrate the timely nature of such a story:

Tri-State roads called "hazardous at best" by the National Weather Service won't improve until at least tomorrow when sunny skies, temperatures near freezing and drying winds should help road clearing work.

Police throughout the Tri-State urged residents to stay home as drifting snow closed roads throughout the Evansville area. Some could remain closed for days, weather officials said.

When a 25-year-old patient suffered a series of mild strokes after receiving an artificial heart, a search was accelerated to find a donor heart. When one was located, United Press International led its story with:

TUCSON, Ariz.—A medical team flew to Texas Friday to fetch a donor heart to replace the Jarvik 7 mechanical organ that has kept a young Arizona man alive for more than a week.

Breaking news stories command space at most newspapers and more air time at most radio and television outlets. Readers and listeners want to know what is happening *now.*

Proximity

Events close to home are naturally of interest to the news media. Note the following lead paragraph from *The Gleaner,* Henderson, Ky.:

The city's stormwater management consultant Monday night unveiled a proposal designed to handle Henderson's stormwater problems and estimated cost of the plan at $26 million.

Henderson's stormwater problems might not be of interest to readers in Biloxi, Miss., or Laramie, Wyo., but they deserve front-page treatment in Henderson.

Unemployment was running above the national average in Beaumont, Texas, and so it was big news when Beaumont was in the running for a new automobile plant. The story in *The Beaumont Enterprise* began:

> Southeast Texas civic leaders are joining a crowd of suitors for a futuristic General Motors plant that offers 6,000 jobs.
>
> General Motors officials are looking for a place to build their planned Saturn subcompact car, and state Rep. Al Price said he hopes community leaders could unite to bring the carmaker to the Beaumont area.

The lead on a story published in the *Colorado Springs Gazette Telegraph* would not have raised an eyebrow among readers anywhere else. But it was news in Colorado Springs.

> Two people who had been expected to run for the Colorado Springs City Council District 1 seat said Tuesday they will not be candidates.

Local economic developments are naturally of significant interest to readers. One story in the *Plano* (Texas) *Star Courier* led with:

> The Plano Chamber of Commerce initiated a program Wednesday to emphasize to local consumers and merchants the importance of spending money within the city.

Conflict

Conflict—whether it involves people, governmental bodies or sports teams—is often considered newsworthy. For example, note the lead on a story published in *The Star-Herald* of Scottsbluff, Neb.:

> A request from Nebraska Western College to install a storm sewer along the north side of East 27th Street was denied by the Scottsbluff City Council Monday night based on opposition from property owners in the area.

Here is another lead from *The Gleaner* in Henderson, Ky.:

> Efforts to block the city's purchase of land that could be used to expand the city landfill appeared this weekend to be headed for defeat at Tuesday's city commission meeting.

The *Tempe* (Ariz.) *Daily News Tribune* recognized the news value in action taken by the Arizona Board of Regents in response to apartheid practices in South Africa:

> The Arizona Board of Regents Friday voted 4–3 to cut financial ties with South Africa "as soon as possible."

Eminence and Prominence

Some happenings are newsworthy simply because well-known people are involved. Thousands of people chop firewood in this country each year. That generally would not be considered to be worth a news story. Nearly every time Ronald Reagan split a log at his California vacation home during his presidency, however, it made the news.

Stabbings in metropolitan areas normally do not receive front-page treatment—unless the victims are prominent. The lead paragraph from an *Evansville Press* story follows:

> A former Indiana State University Evansville basketball player was fatally stabbed and another ex-player was seriously hurt in a fight early today at the North Park Village parking lot.

Newspapers routinely publish obituaries. Only when a person of particular prominence dies, however, does the story make news in papers around the country. Here's the lead on a UPI story that was widely published:

> Robert W. Woodruff, the millionaire philanthropist who turned Coca-Cola from a drugstore novelty to a soft drink known around the world, died last night at the age of 95.

Consequence and Impact

Few developments hit a community as hard—economically and emotionally—as mass layoffs by major employers. It is not surprising, then, that media give prominent play to these occurrences. Here are the first two paragraphs of a story published in *The Gleaner*, Henderson, Ky.:

> Alcan Aluminum Corp. announced Thursday it will shut down one of three potlines at its Sebree smelter, resulting in the layoff of about 250 employees.
>
> "Alcan has no proposed date when the employees might be called back," the company said in a statement.

The impact of layoffs is not limited to the employees and their families. An economic domino effect is felt throughout the area. Readers are always interested in stories that have considerable impact on their communities.

Projects that would involve millions of dollars naturally have a major impact on an area. Recognizing this, *The Evansville Press* led a story with:

> A group of western Kentucky businessmen quietly is planning to build a Tri-State airport that would replace commercial airports in Evansville and Owensboro.

Far-from-home news events can also have a strong impact on local readers. Note this lead from a story published in the *Plano Star Courier:*

> Former Plano resident Steven J. Welden, 24, was one of 47 sailors killed Wednesday morning in the explosion of the Navy ship *USS Iowa* 300 miles off the coast of Puerto Rico.
>
> Welden, who grew up in Plano and attended Meadows Elementary, Armstrong Middle and Williams High schools, had just completed a four-year tour of duty with the Navy and re-enlisted and was transferred to the *USS Iowa* battleship in January, said his father, Frank Hacker of Plano.

An action taken by the County Commission in Birmingham, Ala., would eventually have an impact on residents there, as emphasized in the first two paragraphs of a story in *The Birmingham News:*

> In two to three weeks, Jefferson County's Family Court complex should be a safer place.
>
> The County Commission Tuesday gave tentative approval to stationing security guards at the entrance of the Family Court building while it is open and at the entrance to the county's detention center around-the-clock.

Human Interest

It may be a cliché that there are a lot of interesting people in the world, but it is a fact that newspaper readers and television viewers like to hear about them. Human interest stories often appeal to the emotions of readers, pulling them into the lives of others or into subjects of broad concern. Bob Dvorchak wrote a story for The Associated Press that undoubtedly captured the interest of his readers in the first two paragraphs. The story was about an aide to a Pennsylvania state senator:

> On weekdays, Dennis Sciabica toils in politics as an aide to a state senator. In his free time, he's a professional cowboy, wrestling steers and riding snorting bulls.
>
> "Both are high risk businesses," Sciabica says. "I've had people tell me that I sling the bull during the week and ride it on weekends."

Longtime school principals in Midwestern towns touch a lot of lives. Undoubtedly readers had considerable interest in a story published in *The Hastings* (Neb.) *Tribune* that began:

Kenneth Wiederspan moved to Hastings in 1967 where he assumed his first—and last—job in an elementary school.

"I started here and I've been here ever since," the Longfellow School principal said. "I wouldn't give up the elementary to go back to high school. I love kids, love elementary."

After 22 years at Longfellow, Wiederspan is retiring.

Do you ever wonder what happens to old soldiers who are nearly broke and who have medical problems? Chet Barfield of the *Mesa* (Ariz.) *Tribune* did. He found that they often end up in Veterans Administration Domiciliaries. He ventured to Prescott, Ariz., to a domiciliary and lured his readers into his story with this lead paragraph:

This is where they come, the old soldiers—sick, crippled, destitute and homeless. When there's no place else, they come here, to this sanctuary in the pine-covered hills.

OTHER FACTORS AFFECTING NEWS TREATMENT

In addition to the classic criteria of newsworthiness, other factors influence whether a story should be done. These include:

- *Instincts of editors and reporters.* To paraphrase Justice Stewart: They know news when they see it.
- *Audience.* Would inner-city residents of Los Angeles, for example, be interested in the death of a former governor of North Carolina?
- *"News holes."* Depending on available space, some stories could make the paper one day, but be left out on another.
- *Availability of news.* Depending on what is happening locally and in the world, there are simply more stories to choose from on some days. On slow news days, editors and reporters will scratch for stories of borderline value. On heavy news days, some good stories don't merit dissemination.
- *Philosophy of the medium.* The business-oriented *Wall Street Journal*, for example, selects stories on the basis of criteria different from those of a metropolitan arts and entertainment publication.
- *Pressure from the publisher.* Most publishers try not to interfere openly with the news process, but most editors and reporters are aware of the political and social leanings of owners.
- *Influence of advertisers.* Usually it is a subtle consideration, but some editors might think twice, for example, about giving prominent space to the formation of a "committee for decency in movies" if local theaters are major advertisers.

- *News mix.* News media often strive to balance hard news with soft news and to provide local, national and international stories.

- *Competition among media.* To some extent, morning and afternoon newspapers supplement each other, as do the print and electronic media. Each medium has its strengths and weaknesses in coverage of news. But most media try to keep one step ahead of the competition, and this sometimes affects handling of news.

- *Changing demographics.* Demographics—the distribution, density, size and composition of the American population—are changing, and the nation's media need to adjust their news coverage accordingly.

An elaboration of these factors follows.

Instincts of Editors and Reporters

William Mock, managing editor of *The Beaumont* (Texas) *Enterprise* (circulation: 70,000 weekdays), said that "gut instincts and common sense" often take over when making news decisions: "We have to second-guess what our readers really want to know."

If, for example, local teachers are threatening to strike and the wire services move a story about a school strike 2,000 miles away, the assumption is that local readers will be interested. If local teachers were not poised for a walkout, the instinct of the editor would probably be that local readers are not interested in the far-from-home strike story.

Experienced editors and reporters develop a sense of what readers want. Readership surveys and demographic breakdowns, of course, provide editors and reporters with background information that can help hone their instincts.

The Audience

"To determine news value, editors and reporters should put themselves in the reader's easy chair," Mock said. "You have to keep in mind that the reader probably is going to listen to the radio driving to and from work and very likely will watch some television news." According to Mock, when readers pick up the newspaper in the morning, they already have an idea of what is going on in the world. When they are getting ready for work or school, the *Enterprise* must compete for their attention. It must compete not only with the radio and television news readers have heard in the last 12 hours but with scrambled eggs, bacon, toast, spilled orange juice and kids jockeying for position in the bathroom. The readers may know what they saw on television the night before and what they heard on the radio that morning, but they may be confused about the details. The *Enterprise* has to tell readers what is behind the news—put it into perspective for them.

Mock makes it a point to know his readers. Beaumont, a city of 125,000, has "a fairly good mix of socioeconomic demographics," according to Mock. The area is heavily dependent on the petrochemical industry. "Developments that in any way touch this industry, nationally or internationally, ripple down to many of our readers," Mock said. "Our unemployment rates often run above the average. When a company closes in Beaumont, that is a big story. It means more people will be out there competing for scarce jobs. The closing of a company might not be a big deal in areas with relatively low unemployment rates, but it means a lot to our readers and to our economy."

Mike Moscardini, assistant managing editor of the *St. Petersburg* (Fla.) *Times* (circulation: 360,000 weekdays), noted that many of his readers are elderly. "We naturally take an intense interest in such things as proposals to adjust Social Security benefits," Moscardini said. He also pointed out that knowledge of the audience allows editors and reporters to consider more subtle factors when making news decisions. "We'll carry a story on a sailboat accident in Europe, for example, simply because a lot of people around here have sailboats and might be interested," Moscardini said.

The News Hole

The size of the *news hole*—the number of column inches available for news—varies at most publications from day to day. On days when the pages are *wide open* (when there are comparatively few advertisements and many column inches are available for news) stories of borderline importance might be published. When pages are *tight* (if comparatively little space is available for news), stories that would be published on a day when even average space is available simply cannot be worked into the news hole.

The Gleaner in Henderson, Ky., is an 11,000-circulation Tuesday-through-Sunday publication. On most days, the paper runs 20 to 24 pages (with the equivalent of 10 to 12 full pages available for news); on Sundays, it averages 42. In a year, *The Gleaner* devotes about 48 percent of its total space to news.

At some daily papers, when the news side is given the *dummy*—a page-by-page mark-up that has ads with specific sizes keyed in—editors are locked into the assigned space. At *The Gleaner*, however, the editor, Ron Jenkins, has authority to get additional space when it is necessary.

"On a lot of days, it seems that we have 10 gallons of water to put in a 5-gallon bucket," Jenkins said. "When the news hole is really tight, the emphasis in our paper is on local news. We do a lot of cutting on national and international stories on those days. If we have five significant wire stories, but room to run only three of them, we'll slice all five at the bottom just to get them in the paper. On tight news days, we run a lot of national and international news briefs [capsulized accounts of longer news stories]."

Availability of News

Some days are slower than others in terms of available news stories. News stories that would not merit publication on relatively brisk news days might make their way into print in a Saturday afternoon paper. Saturdays are often slow news days because government offices and other news-making institutions are closed. Newspapers stockpile non-timely features and trend stories for use on these days.

Major-market electronic media and large-circulation newspapers naturally have more resources for gathering news than smaller operations do. A large-circulation newspaper, for example, has scores of reporters and editors for gathering and processing news. It also subscribes to a wide variety of news services in addition to The Associated Press, United Press International or both. For a fee, newspapers can subscribe to any number of supplemental news services, such Knight-Ridder, Gannett and the New York Times News Service. (See Chapter 27 for a discussion of supplemental services.) Because of budget restrictions, smaller newspapers do not subscribe to several supplemental services. Instead, they rely primarily on one of the major wire services and a skeleton news staff. Thus, available resources limit how news media gather and handle the news.

Philosophy of the Medium

Some newspapers, such as *The New York Times,* consider themselves papers of record. It is not unusual for the *Times* to devote a full page to the text of a public official's speech or to verbatim excerpts from a significant Supreme Court decision. Most newspapers do not have the space to provide such detail. Instead, most American dailies would publish a story highlighting the speech or the court case.

Radio and television stations emphasize breaking news and stories where sound and film are logical supplements. These media are technologically well suited to keep pace with breaking news stories; newspapers are not. Radio can literally update stories by the minute. Television does not update stories as often as radio, but if a story merits it, a television station is in a position to interrupt regular programming to do so.

Pressure from the Publisher

Warren Breed, in an early research study of socialization in the newsroom, found that newspaper publishers have much to say in both long-term and immediate news policy decisions. His study, which was published in an article in *Social Forces* in 1955, concluded that many publishers hesitate to issue direct commands to slant a news story. It is logical, however, to assume that some subtle influence is always present, and low-key inferences or suggestions by publishers are philosophically and ethically more acceptable than open commands.

Managing editors of daily newspapers in Kansas and Nebraska perceive little direct pressure from their publishers when making news and editorial decisions, according to a mail questionnaire survey in the two states. The study, which was reported in the *Nebraska Newspaper* magazine, noted, however, that editors often respond to subtle suggestions from their publishers. The study showed a tendency on the part of managing editors to consider the same persons (on the basis of occupation) influential in the community as they believe their publishers consider influential.

The study showed that editors of daily newspapers in Kansas and Nebraska enjoy some management autonomy—far greater freedom than that of "middle management" employees in other businesses. Still, there is a limit to an editor's management freedom when the most difficult decisions must be made: it often extends, in those cases, only to the publisher's door.

Publishers seldom pressure reporters directly about how to handle a news story. If they are pressured, however, reporters must react on a case-by-case basis. Naturally, their response depends on several factors. For example, does the publisher have a reputation for applying pressure to reporters? If so, how have other reporters dealt with it? What is the working relationship of the publisher, editors and reporters at the newspaper? Is the publisher one who might admire reporters who stand by their opinions in the teeth of pressure? Or is the publisher one who would just as soon fire reporters as look at them?

Possibly the best way for reporters to deal with pressure from publishers, or advertisers, is to seek advice from experienced editors, who have probably encountered similar situations.

Influence of Advertisers

The potential always exists for advertisers to influence the dissemination of news. Theoretically, however, the news side of any medium is independent of the advertising arm; and most of the time, it works out that way.

Editors and reporters instinctively bristle at the thought of an advertiser's attempt to blackmail the newspaper into running—or not running—a story. News organizations that would give in to blackmail are few and far between—particularly if a significant story hangs in the balance. Suppression of major news events because of pressure from advertisers is unlikely. For example, it is difficult to imagine a newspaper, television station or radio station spiking a story about an investigation into alleged bid rigging by a local contractor simply because the contractor is a big advertiser.

The potential for spiking a story about a minor news event, however, is probably greater. An editor, for example, might exercise "news judgment" (by rationalizing that "no one really cares") not to publish a story if the same contractor was convicted of first-offense drunken driving. Also, few newspapers or electronic news media delve deeply into consumer news reporting about local products and services. Some larger newspapers and television stations do, but they are in the minority. Reporters are generally more aggressive in tackling government issues than business issues.

Still, newspaper editors and reporters, for the most part, make every effort to avoid any appearance of catering to advertisers. This noble stand, of course, is economically less risky at large-circulation newspapers (where a single advertising account would not make a crucial profit-loss difference) than at smaller dailies and weeklies, where one large account could contribute a disproportionate share of overall revenue.

The News Mix

Most newspapers, radio stations and television stations strive for a *news mix*—a combination of hard news stories and lighter feature pieces. Also, these outlets present a combination of local, regional, national and international news.

Ron Jenkins, editor of *The Gleaner,* said that his newspaper uses a "smorgasbord approach" to the presentation of news. "We've had readership surveys show that the appetite among readers is spread fairly evenly among local, national and international news," he said.

The Gleaner emphasizes local news, but Jenkins reported that the newspaper hopes to add a half page of national news each day. "We hope the advertising growth will allow us to do that," he said.

Editors at the *St. Petersburg Times* use news sections to divide the content of their newspaper systematically. The first section is almost exclusively national and international; the second section is reserved for state and local news; the third section is sports; the fourth section displays features. "We want our readers to know where to look for certain types of news," the assistant managing editor, Mike Moscardini, said.

Competition among Media

Competition has an effect on news coverage by various outlets. In Henderson, Ky. (population: 27,000), for example, the editor, Ron Jenkins, has to look over his shoulder at the newspapers of metropolitan Evansville, Ind., a city of 121,000 just 6 miles away.

"We must provide our readers with the news that they won't get in the Evansville newspaper," Jenkins said. "Our policy is to keep the design of our newspaper simple, clean and inviting. But, when you open up the package, there has to be some substance in it."

For example, *The Gleaner* publishes major stories at the end of every month about the number of building permits that were issued locally. "Following the trend in building permits is a way of monitoring our local economy," Jenkins said. "Sometimes the stories are played on Page 1—if there is a significant upward or downward movement—but usually we play the story on the business page." The Evansville papers would be unlikely to carry the story at all.

Clearly, editors and reporters at local media react to one another in making their news judgments. It is common for reporters and editors to monitor not only other newspapers but electronic news media as well. Some events, such as a press conference at which the mayor announces his or her intention to seek re-election, would naturally be covered by the print and electronic media.

Occasionally, however, a newspaper will cover an event that it normally would not simply because a television station is giving the event substantial attention. For example, a television station might do updates on its 6 p.m. and 10 p.m. newscasts about a 14-year-old who is attempting to break the world's record for sit-ups. Because television is giving so much attention to the event, a newspaper might also carry a picture and short story. Editors would not want readers to believe that the newspaper was missing a "big" story. Editors and reporters at the newspaper might have felt that the teenager doing sit-ups wasn't really newsworthy, but because television gave it so much coverage, the newspaper had to provide some.

Changing Demographics

Many newspapers across the United States are expanding and enhancing their coverage of the many cultures that make up the population. In 1990, for example, the *Los Angeles Times* published a four-part series, written by the media critic David Shaw, that examined multiculturalism in American newsrooms and minority coverage by the nation's newspapers. In that series, Shaw noted that the demographics of the United States had changed dramatically during the past decade. He cited some staggering statistics:

- The percentage of blacks in the population increased significantly; the black population has grown at twice the rate of the white population.
- The Latino population has grown at almost six times the rate of whites.
- The Asian-American population has grown at more than 10 times the rate of whites.
- In the 1990s, 87 percent of the country's population growth will be among minorities.

Clearly, news coverage must be responsive to these significant changes. It is increasingly imperative for journalists to be sensitive to and knowledgeable about racial and social diversity. In fact, the United States is fast becoming a country where virtually any group can call itself a "minority." Newspapers, in particular, must alter their traditional patterns of coverage if they are to paint consistently accurate portraits of various ethnic groups and to examine, on a day-to-day basis, the impact of cultural trends and changing demographics on society. (See Chapter 17 for a more complete discussion of milticultural reporting.)

PITCHING NEWS STORIES TO EDITORS

Competition for space in a newspaper or time on a news broadcast is fierce. Reporters must compete aggressively for valuable inches or minutes. Those who develop the knack of ferreting out stories and effectively presenting their ideas often win the favor of their supervisors. A reporter who has good news judgment will capture the attention of an editor. These reporters are acknowledged and appreciated because good story ideas take some of the pressure off busy editors who are always seeking them.

Following are some ingredients in the successful pitching of stories.

SPECIFICITY

When approaching an editor with a story idea, don't just name the subject. Do not, for example, tell an editor that you would like to do a story on a star volleyball player who is ready to return to the team after sitting out from competition for a season. That general idea, in itself, has some merit. But it will probably generate the most common comeback of editors: "That's interesting, but what's the angle?"

Always go to your editor with a proposed angle. In the case of the story about the volleyball player, for instance, the reporter might emphasize that the player had to sit out her junior year because of pregnancy and that the article would explore her feelings about making it back into the sport and the hard work she went through to get into physical and mental condition to play. But this does not mean that, on the basis of further interviews and research, the angle could not change. Reporters should guard against having such a firm fix on one angle that they would not react to new material. Reporters should not be bound to a preconception.

If you have done a good job preparing your story pitch, you have virtually written your lead. Obviously, the key to submitting a solid story proposal is to conduct sufficient preliminary research. It does not take much effort to make an extra telephone call to a source, to consult the clip file or to check a reference book. Taking these steps before you pitch the story enables you to be more precise.

SUCCINCTNESS

Editors are busy. They have other reporters and stories competing for their attention. Do not waste the editor's time with a long-winded story proposal.

For example, assume that you want to do a story about pick-up basketball games that take place in your school's gymnasium during noon hours on weekdays. It would be unwise to saunter up to an editor and say: "You know, there are about 50 students, dropouts, faculty members and alumni who gather at the gymnasium on weekday noons to play basketball. I stopped by there the other day, and it looked as though they were having a lot of fun. I think it is interesting that a lot of people from various stations in life skip lunch to play basketball. You know, I even saw a couple of our varsity players over there the other day. I think this is more than a sports story. I think it's a good story about people who enjoy playing games to break up the tension of the day. What do you think? Shall I give it a try?"

In all likelihood, the editor would shut you off before you reached the fourth sentence. Remember: You are trying to sell the merits of your proposal. You will not do that by boring the editor to the point of frustration.

Get to the point: "Each weekday noon, about 50 students, dropouts, faculty members and alumni play basketball in the school's gymnasium. This is an unusual group. You can find 45-year-old nationally known physicists and department administrators out there trading elbows, glares and high fives with students half their age. These people form a subculture of sorts on the campus. I want to interview several of them to find out what brings them together."

ENTHUSIASM

If you are not enthusiastic about your story idea, chances are your editor will not be. Editors want meat and bone on story ideas—not generalities. If you excite your editor about the story, you will probably be given the time and support to explore it fully. If the editor is not interested in the idea—if you cannot sell the story—chances are you will be discouraged from writing it. Editors often make decisions to go with stories on the basis of the effectiveness of a reporter's pitch. If you are blasé about the story, you can't expect your editor to get excited about it.

An editor will know if you are just throwing out ideas without adequate thought. Go to the editor with a game plan. Explain not only the specific angles you intend to pursue but also how long you think it will take to write the story and how long you think the story will run.

MONITORING THE MEDIA

Editors sometimes complain that reporters are interested only in reading the stories they write themselves. Don't fall into this trap. Read the newspaper from cover to cover; listen to newscasts on television and radio. National stories might trigger local possibilities. For example, assume that there is a serial rapist on the rampage in California. What are the tendencies of this rapist and others like him? Are there certain high-risk situations that women should avoid? Local law enforcement officials and psychologists could help you develop an angle. Stories like this are both current and timely. They are timely because a series of rapes is taking place now in another state—and that, in itself, is newsworthy. They are current in the sense that this is a topic which has been and remains on the minds of many. So many of these stories have been written that the subject has acquired a news value independent of whether such a serial rape might have occurred the previous night. In addition, the topic has impact and involves conflict.

Don't forget that old local stories can trigger new ones, called *follows*. Such stories are often appropriate and newsworthy. For example, assume that you read an article about a radiation leak in the life sciences building on your campus. The building was evacuated. Check to see if classes were held in the building the next day; check to see if additional precautions will be taken to prevent future leaks; check to see if the leak posed a danger to nearby buildings. The possibilities are almost limitless. Make notes of stories you think might generate a logical follow. Don't hesitate to pitch the follow to your editor.

A LOOK AT THE SELECTION OF NEWS

Because of the factors discussed in the previous sections, newspapers and electronic media treat the news in different ways. This section illustrates the variety in news selection by newspapers of various circulations in geographically diverse areas. Editors at *The Gleaner* in Henderson, Ky., and at the *San Jose* (Calif.) *Mercury News* discuss the decision making that led to their front pages for the same day: Tuesday, Jan. 5, 1993. To illustrate the perpetual evolution of news and the constant discussion of how it should be presented, editors at *The Detroit News* describe their preparation for editions of Jan. 6.

The Gleaner is a morning newspaper; its circulation is 11,000 Tuesday through Saturday and 14,000 on Sunday. The *San Jose Mercury News* is an all-day newspaper; its circulation is 270,000 Monday through Friday, 255,000 on Saturday mornings and 330,000 on Sundays. *The Detroit News* is an all-day newspaper; its circulation is 445,000 Monday through Friday (*The Detroit News and Free Press* circulates 912,000 on Saturday mornings and 1,202,000 on Sundays).

As you review the content of these newspapers, note the distinct differences in story selection—which are based, to some extent, on many of the factors discussed earlier in this chapter.

THE GLEANER

David Dixon, the managing editor, explained the decision-making process that was followed in putting together the front page of *The Gleaner*.

"As a community newspaper, local news is our bread and butter. If a state, national or world story *demands* Page 1 treatment it gets such treatment. If all things are equal and nothing screams from the wire for Page 1 play, we go local.

"Intense local coverage is what my readers expect and get from *The Gleaner*, and what they don't get elsewhere, especially from our most direct competition, two nearby metro dailies.

"With that in mind, Page 1 of Jan. 5 fell into place rather easily. I will comment briefly on each selection:

"The 'Deep Wound' story is an automatic selection for the front page. On the Sunday after Christmas a pickup truck carrying six local teens crashed into a tractor-trailer truck that was backing across the highway in front of them. Two very active and popular 16-year-olds were killed, and the truck driver was charged with manslaughter. This story recounted the community memorial service for the dead teens; speakers included some survivors of the wreck.

"Overwhelming community interest and very strong art dictated that this be played prominently on Page 1.

"The need for and location of a new county jail has been a growing controversy for some years. The current jail is overcrowded, was designed for a different era and does not meet state standards. At the urging of community leaders and the newspaper, and in the face of an ultimatum from the state, the reluctant county government started to plan for a new jail.

"The debate as to location, architect's costs and the burden on the taxpayers has grown more feverish as the actual construction of a jail has become a distinct reality. This story put the lid on the number of sites that would be considered, and indeed a final site decision was made the next day.

"The jail issue is one that will see the top of *The Gleaner*'s front page many times in the months ahead.

"The story on the EDC director is probably the first concrete report on what has been a growing sense of aimlessness in the local industrial recruitment effort. Economic development is an intensely competitive endeavor from community to community. There has been much off-the-record comment and informal discussion that maybe Henderson has not been doing as well as it should.

"This story is the first official indication that at least one head will roll.

"The report on candidates filing to run for office received routine play for such stories. It is our feeling that someone who has officially entered a race for a local government position deserves an introduction on Page 1. At the same time we are aware of the need to treat such filings in more or less the same way, so that all candidates—whether 'major' or 'minor'—get fair treatment in beginning their campaigns for local office.

TUESDAY Lady Cols whip Union Co. B1

the gleaner

JANUARY 5, 1993 HENDERSON, KENTUCKY © 20 pages; No. 4, 108th year 35¢

'A deep wound'

400 gather to remember teens lost in accident

By S. KAYE SUMMERS
of The Gleaner staff

Friendship and faith.

Those were the treasures shared with a crowd of about 400 gathered Sunday at Henderson County High School to say goodbye to two teen-agers killed in a highway accident.

As Ira Hancock spoke softly from the lectern at the community memorial service in the school's gym, he told of the 16-year-olds he called his closest friends — Denise Elliott and Brandon Abell.

"They both made me realize something I knew all along —these people loved Jesus Christ and because of that, they knew there was a plan."

A week ago Sunday, Miss Elliott, Abell, Hancock and three friends piled into Hancock's truck. The six teen-agers were headed to Miss Elliott's house to watch a movie.

On that foggy and rainy night, the pickup truck collided with a tractor-trailer that had backed across their lane on U.S. 41-Alternate near Cairo.

Ms. Elliott and Abell, both popular Henderson County High student-athletes, were killed. "It hurts me a lot because they were both good friends of mine," said Hancock, 17.

Hancock's feelings for his cousin Abell and Miss Elliott were mirrored in the messages of several others during Sunday's service. Fifteen friends, coaches and pastors paid their respects with a gift of words.

Beth Bantly, one of the accident's four survivors, said "it was an honor for me to say that she (Miss Elliott) called me her best friend."

The two were inseparable. "We did almost everything together. We not only had a friendship; we had a friendship in the Lord."

With her arm in a cast and a few scratches on her face, Miss. Bantly, 16, told the crowd that the accident should serve as a reminder.

"This should teach everyone to live each day as if it was their last one."

Miss Bantly's sister, Jennie Bantly, 15, who also survived the accident, was listed in fair condition Monday night at Deaconess Hospital. Another passenger in the pickup truck, Chris Head, 16, was released early last week from Community Methodist Hospital.

David Latham, chaplain of CMH, said sharing memories of the two is part of the healing process.

"Everyone is trying to make believable the unbelievable," he said. "The loss of someone we care for is like a deep wound" that needs to heal. "That process is already beginning to occur as each of us tell our stories."

Latham recommended that the audience talk about their feelings. And if one can't find another to open up to, he said to write down the frustrations, pray or "go to the woods and scream and cry."

Latham also addressed members of the crowd who never knew the families of Miss Elliott or Abell. "Even if you didn't know them, what has happened has affected you," he said.

He also remembered Scotty G. Brown, "the truck driver who bears the burden that will be a never-ending nightmare."

Along with feelings of sorrow will also be anger, Latham said.

"We want to believe that only bad things happen to bad people," he said. "There'll be anger at the truck driver or at ourselves ... But eventually we've got to let go of it or the anger will eat us up."

Prentis Ragland, assistant football coach at County High, said he's chosen a light-hearted remembrance of Abell.

Ragland described one of the

See SERVICE, back page

Beth Bantly, who was injured but survived an accident that killed two Henderson County High School students, is comforted by her mother, Mary Lou Bantly, Sunday during a memorial service at the school. Fifteen-year-old Jennie Bantly was also injured in the accident and remains hospitalized. (Gleaner photo by Cathy Clarke)

Court's list of jail sites rises to 15

By FRANK BOYETT
of The Gleaner staff

Henderson Fiscal Court now has up to 15 sites to choose from in building a proposed new jail.

Monday was the deadline for submittal of proposals from people interested in selling land to the county for a new jail. But that call for proposals resulted in only two new offers, according to Jay Smith, the architect on the project, and Judge-executive Paul Herron Jr.

Henderson Fiscal Court set the deadline before Christmas, in an effort to keep new potential sites from cropping up and slowing down the selection process. Landowners were given until Monday to present information about their land, such as price, size, location and the availability of utilities.

"Just two is all we have gotten," Herron said. "We had one formal offer and another lady called. I don't have anything about one of those pieces — just a telephone call."

Herron declined to say where those sites are located, or who was offering them.

The court had earlier been considering about a dozen different sites.

"But most of them are undermined (with old coal mines) or are in the floodplain," Herron said.

He added that information about the new sites has been turned over to the architect, and that a presentation is expected to be made to fiscal court this morning.

The architect said there are

See JAIL, back page

EDC director may be ousted

By CHUCK STINNETT
of The Gleaner staff

The Henderson Area Economic Development Council may soon be looking for a new executive director.

Officials confirmed Monday that there is a move on the EDC board to oust Mitch Robinson, who has served as the executive director since the spring of 1988.

The position, which pays $43,250 annually, involves carrying out the day-to-day duties of the EDC, the lead agency here for seeking out new industries and helping existing industries.

While final action is up to the EDC's 16-member board of directors, sources say the board's five-member executive committee wants to replace Robinson.

"The executive committee will probably recommend that his contract not be renewed at the end of April," Mayor William L. Newman, who chairs the EDC, said when contacted Monday.

Besides Newman, the EDC's executive committee includes insurance agent Tom Latta; bankers John Daniel and Jerry Wischer; and attorney Bill Branaman.

Newman confirmed that there was some dissatisfaction among board members with Robinson's job performance, primarily concerning "the self-motivation."

"I don't know whether the full board will concur or not," the mayor said. The full 16-member

See EDC, back page

Robinson

Clary seeks re-election; McCormick enters race

Gleaner staff report

Sheriff Dennis Clary filed Monday for re-election, and Donald "Hugh" McCormick filed to make another run for the 4th District magistrate's seat on Henderson Fiscal Court.

Clary has been sheriff since 1986 and was the first Henderson County sheriff to be elected to a second consecutive term. That distinction was due mostly to timing, however, since prior to his election sheriffs could not seek a second consecutive term. A constitutional amendment lifted that prohibition.

Clary joined the sheriff's department in 1974 and was a deputy for 10 years before seeking the sheriff's job in the 1985 election. His experience is his main qualification, he said.

"I'm familiar with the insides and outs of this office," he said. "There's a lot more to it than just the law enforcement. There's a lot of administration.'

The only other candidate to file for sheriff so far is William "Bob" Wilson.

Clary said he wants to be re-elected so he can ensure the new deputy merit system is fully implemented and "to make sure the additional training is initiated."

Clary, 53, is a graduate of Henderson County High School and has attended a number of law enforcement training seminars.

He lives at 120 S. Barren Church Road. He has three adult children and four granddaughters.

McCormick ran in second place in 1989, when he first sought Magistrate Willie Nunley's seat. So far, Nunley and Bill Sheffer have also filed for the seat.

"It's time for new leadership and ideas in this county and my district," he said. "I feel our county is just sitting on the back burner and we need some new fresh people to light the fires and get us going in a positive direction."

He said he wants new jobs so young people won't have to leave Henderson County to work. He said he is also interested in dealing with issues such as a new jail, surface mining and an administrative code.

McCormick, 35, is an auxiliary operator at Big Rivers Electric Corp. and is a graduate of Henderson City High School.

He and his wife, Lynn, live at 36 S. Alvasia St. with their two children.

Clary McCormick

Whirlpool recalling workers

Gleaner staff report

Whirlpool Corp.'s refrigerator plant in Evansville recalled 292 workers on Monday and plans to bring back another 397 on March 1, spokeswoman Debby Castrale said.

"Plus we'll be hiring some number" that will also start work on March 1, Mrs. Castrale said. "It will probably be a couple hundred anyway. It depends on how many don't come back from layoff" and have to be replaced.

Whirlpool laid off 689 workers in October and November, saying they would be recalled in 1993.

Some were idled so the plant could modernize refrigerator assembly Line 2; those recalled on Monday will work on that line.

Others were laid off because of a seasonal slowdown in refrigerator sales.

When all are recalled, the plant's hourly workforce will exceed 3,600.

The plant's salaried workforce and a group of some 300 Whirlpool corporate employees will bring the total to some 4,300, not counting workers hired in March.

Approximately 4,000 people submitted applications in late November for the upcoming job openings.

Applications are no longer being accepted.

Green Coal Co. lays off 24

Gleaner staff report

Green Coal Co. laid off 24 people late last week in reaction to decreased production at its Henderson County mine.

"Production levels had declined and we had to bring employment levels into line with production levels to stay in the black," explained company spokesman Jim Grise. "Hopefully it will be a temporary situation."

Grise explained that recent wet weather is "primarily" responsible for the layoffs, in that it has slowed down mining operations.

"We experience it every winter," he said. "It slows production rates and you have to make certain adjustments. But this is the first (layoff) of this magnitude."

The mine had employed about 175 people before the layoff but is now down to about 150, he said.

Index

Opinion	A4
Sports	B1-3
Business	B5
Advice	A6
Comics	B4
Movie times	A6
People	A6
Nation-World	A5
Local-Region	A3
Deaths	A2
Classified	B6-8

Cooling off

Partly cloudy today; high in the low 40s. Colder tonight; low in the mid-20s. Cloudy Wednesday; high in the mid-40s. Dry Thursday; high in the low 40s and low in the mid-20s. Chance of rain Friday. **More on Page A7.**

The air quality index for Monday was 18 (good). The leading pollutant was sulfur dioxide.

Murderer Westley Dodd

■ Killer set to be hanged A8

■ Serbs block peace plan A5

■ Fair health plan urged A2

■ Crash kills 25 tourists A5

Legislators return today

Kentucky legislators gather today for an organizational session that follows months of turmoil stemming from an FBI corruption probe, and the 103rd U.S. Congress also gets under way this afternoon.

In Washington, Congress' largest freshman class since 1949 will be sworn in.

For the state legislature, Majority Whip Kenny Rapier, D-Bardstown, said he expects this session to be a "mending process."

Stories on A3, A5

The Gleaner's front page on Jan. 5, 1993.

"We always encourage participation in the democratic process, and we always strive for fairness.

"The little package of worker callbacks and layoffs in the lower right earned that position mostly on the meat-and-potatoes nature of the subject and an underwhelming wire report. In particular, one company mentioned is one of the largest employers in the area, offering some of the most sought-after jobs. In the other case, what has been a controversial strip-mining operation announced some layoffs.

"Perhaps one way to look at the treatment of these stories would be to harken to Bill Clinton's campaign headquarters slogan: 'The economy, stupid.'

"Things that were 'on the bubble' and ran elsewhere:

"Another in a series of somewhat indefinite stories about a state effort toward health-care reform. This is, of course, a can't-miss issue and one that has seen and will see much Page 1 treatment. But in this case we had another news media event by another coalition with very little specifics except a call to treat all income levels fairly. This story topped Page 2.

"The U.S. Congress and the state legislature were both to convene the next day. Both important stories; both with much predicting and little breaking news. These stories topped their respective state and national pages inside.

"We also considered the daily roundup from Somalia. This ran at the top of the back page, our 'second front.'

"The only other story that received any consideration as a possible Page 1 piece was an account of a local man who foiled the theft of his truck by jumping into the bed and hanging on for a rather wild ride. We ended up running this story on the back page, mainly because it was several days old owing to delay in getting confirmation from the police department in the neighboring city where this occurred. Also—and this is hard to explain—the incident, which occurred in the pre-dawn hours of New Year's Day, had something of a faint scent about it."

SAN JOSE MERCURY NEWS

The deputy managing editor, David Yarnold, explained the decision-making process behind the front page of the *San Jose Mercury News*.

"Today's front page was a mixture of good enterprise, reaction and planning.

"We try, whenever possible, to identify a central question or topic. We think that's one of the most effective ways we can reflect readers' interests and touch a nerve.

"We've suffered through six years of drought. Water rationing affects everyone. Weeks of steady rain and snow in the Sierra have led the average person to wonder if the drought is over. It's a newsroom joke that reporters routinely insert a phrase into every weather story that reads: 'Forecasters said today's storm will do little to end the drought.' So it was news when officials said maybe, just maybe, the drought will be broken. We decided after our first news meeting, held at 11:15 in the morning, to point our metro reporting staff, the art department and the photography department toward a weather centerpiece—answering the question of the day.

SCIENCE & MEDICINE
COMPUTERS SEND RADIOLOGY IMAGES
Systems linking doctors/1E

LIVING **MYTH OF TEEN ANGST**
Perception of 'typical' adolescent challenged/1C

INSIDE **IBM OUTSELLS APPLE**
Late spurt helps firm regain lead in PC sales/6D

San Jose Mercury News

MORNING FINAL ★★★C
85 CENTS

Serving Northern California Since 1851

···· TUESDAY
JANUARY 5, 1993

Stewart Boxer
He avoids the spotlight and never gives interviews.

❛We're sort of like any other couple you ever met.❜
— *Richard Blum, husband of U.S. Sen. Dianne Feinstein, D-Calif.*

Richard Blum
Dianne Feinstein's spouse has been called 'Mr. Feinstein.'

The men behind Boxer and Feinstein

BY LINDA GOLDSTON
Mercury News Staff Writer

One is an investment banker who doesn't mind the spotlight and even held his wife's purse while she was interviewed. The other, an attorney, is fiercely private and avoids the press at all costs.

Life may never be quite the same

for either.

They are the men behind two of California's most high-profile women, the newest members of a still fledgling club of male political spouses. But as the husbands of the state's first two female U.S. Senators, Richard Blum and Stewart Boxer are bound to receive more

scrutiny than most.

"You do have to appreciate the fact that you're married to somebody of interest or notoriety," said Jim Schroeder, husband of long-time Congresswoman Pat Schroeder, D-Colo., and the dean of male political spouses in Washington. "There haven't been very many of us so

there really aren't many guidelines. The first thing you do is take a back seat to your wife's career and try to stay out of trouble."

Neither Blum, who is married to Sen. Dianne Feinstein, nor Boxer, who shares his name with former Marin County Congresswoman Bar-

See HUSBANDS, Back Page

Court lets child killer die by hanging

Ruled 'not cruel,' it's nation's first since '65

WALLA WALLA, Wash. (AP) —Three-time child killer Westley Allan Dodd, who asked that he be afforded the same treatment he gave one of his victims, was executed early today in the nation's first hanging in 28 years.

The 31-year-old shipping clerk died just after midnight when a prison official pushed a button that opened a trap door and Dodd dropped the 7-foot-1-inch length of his gallows rope.

The state Supreme Court cleared the way for the execution when it issued a one-sentence ruling late Monday rejecting a bid by 26 Washington residents to halt the hanging as cruel and unusual punishment. The vote was 7-1.

It was Washington state's first execution since 1963.

Dodd had decided to drop all appeals. He had said he must die because "I will kill and rape again.

See HANGING, Page 3A

Alcohol-related accidents fall 39% in county

BY GINA BOUBION
Mercury News Staff Writer

A dramatic drop in alcohol-related accidents made this holiday season the safest on Santa Clara County's roads in more than a decade.

Police on Monday credited the decrease in accidents and arrests to harsher penalties, greater public awareness and rigorous law enforcement efforts.

Drunken driving arrests were down throughout the state, according to the California Highway Patrol. In Santa Clara County, alcohol-related injury accidents dropped 39 percent this year, from 74 during the 1991-'92 holiday season to 45 this year — the lowest figure in 12 years. In San Mateo County, the decline

See ALCOHOL, Page 5A

Snowboard bindings implicated in deaths

BY BILL SUNDERLAND AND MIKE CASSIDY
Mercury News Staff Writers

The doctor who tried to save one of two snowboarders suffocated in deep snow at a Sierra ski resort questioned Monday whether pressure-release bindings could have saved both victims' lives.

The bindings, which are common on skis and can come off in a fall, also were cited as a possible problem in the deaths at Homewood ski resort by officials at Heavenly Valley and Sugar Bowl ski resorts. Snowboard bindings must be released by hand, a complication that could have hindered the victims' efforts to

See SNOWBOARD, Page 4A

THE WET WINTER OF '93

Hopes rise for end of drought

It might as well be real Even though the snow on the ground is artificial, Monday's air was chilly enough for John Fuller to bundle up for the cleanup of Christmas in the Park at San Jose's Plaza Park.

RICK E. MARTIN — MERCURY NEWS

■ **Snowpack:**
Supplies in the Sierra are a third above normal.

■ **Reservoirs:**
Runoff is expected to replenish state's water system.

BY FRANK SWEENEY
Mercury News Staff Writer

For the first time in years, California's water suppliers have some hope that the drought at last could be ending after the Pacific storms that buried Sierra Nevada and Siskiyou Mountains communities with the heaviest snow in more than six years.

The Sierra snowpack on average now holds a third more water than normal for this time of year, according to officials of the state Department of Water Resources.

Although the big reservoirs that form the heart of the state's water supply system contain only half of what they should in the first week in January, big things are expected when all that snow starts to melt.

The amount of water available from the State Water Project, the Central Valley Project and San Francisco's Hetch Hetchy system is critical to Santa Clara County.

In a normal year, the county gets half its water from those systems, which are fed by the rain and snow in the Sierra Nevada and Siskiyou Mountains. The rest comes from local reservoirs and the valley's ample groundwater reserve.

With the latest storms, the Santa Clara Valley Water District reservoirs are finally starting to fill, too. The 10-reservoir system was nearly a quarter full Monday morning.

"We're really excited," said water district spokeswoman Teddy Morse. "Let's face it, back-to-back storms this early in winter are needed, and we're just getting

See WATER, Page 5A

Double-whammy on way: rain, snow

BY FRANK SWEENEY
Mercury News Staff Writer

A powerful Alaskan storm and a warm, subtropical Pacific system are expected to collide over central California today, bringing heavy rain south of the Bay Area and more snow to the Sierra.

Wednesday could be even wetter, and rain or showers could continue into the weekend.

Despite its arctic origin, the storm front from the north is expected to end the bone-chilling

Despite its arctic origin, the latest storm front is expected to end the bone-chilling nights for the time being.

nights for the time being. After climbing into the 50s today, temperatures are expected to drop only into the high 30s tonight.

It plummeted to a freezing 29 degrees in San Jose early Monday, coating cars and houses with a sheen of frost. Lows in the 20s also were reported in Fremont, Gilroy and Morgan Hill, while

other Bay Area readings were in the low 30s.

In the Santa Cruz Mountains, freezing temperatures formed "black ice" — a coating nearly impossible to see on the pavement — on parts of Highway 17. One northbound lane was closed south of Old Santa Cruz Highway

See WEATHER, Back Page

SAN JOSE RAINFALL

As of
Monday

Season to
date: 6.49
inches

Latest storm:
1.29 inches

Normal to
date:
5.38
inches

GAO sees waste in space toilet

Cost overruns compounded by tricky engineering

BY KATHY SAWYER
Washington Post

WASHINGTON — To begin to understand the challenges of going to the bathroom in space, suggests NASA engineer Henry Pohl, imagine removing the commode in your house from its niche on the floor and bolting it to the ceiling. And then trying to use it.

The comparison is not exact, of course. Upside down on the ceiling, you still have gravity — it's just pulling the wrong way. Pohl's point is that humans tend to take gravity for granted when conducting their bodily functions, and this is a luxury that astronauts and space toilet engineers do not have.

The "how do you go to the bathroom in space?" question is of intense and perennial interest to schoolchildren — and, recently, to federal auditors focusing on government waste.

The General Accounting Office's October report on NASA's new, improved shuttle toilet — scheduled for its first flight test in mid-January — found that vague instructions, misunderstandings and unneeded changes had boosted the project's original price tag by 900 percent — to $30 million.

"Costs increased primarily because NASA accepted a number of contractor-recommended improvements to the original

See TOILET, Back Page

WEATHER

■ Cloudy with rain likely in the afternoon; highs about 50. Rain tonight and Wednesday. PAGE 2B

Young is offensive player of the year

■ 49ers quarterback honored by AP
PAGE 1D

Copyright 1993
San Jose Mercury News

Front page of the *San Jose Mercury News,* Jan. 5, 1993.

"Good old-fashioned enterprise turned up two of our front-page stories.

"Two snowboarders died over the long weekend in similar, freakish accidents. When we asked if something was inherently unsafe about snowboarding, we learned that the bindings may have prevented at least one of the victims from digging himself out of fresh powder. We were the first to report on the hazards posed by those bindings and we came back two days later with a feature in our outdoors subsection on safe snowboarding.

"The other piece of enterprise grew out of a routine countywide report on a decline in the number of deaths and arrests attributable to drunken driving. At the suggestion of an editor, the reporter broadened the story to include Bay Area and state figures. We haven't hesitated to put countless stories on the front page about the hazards of—and tragedies caused by—drunk drivers, so why not put the good news on the front page, too?

"There was some debate about putting the Washington hanging execution on the front page, but Paul Van Slambrouck, assistant managing editor/news, and I felt the case had received enough attention to merit the front page and it would be new to readers in the morning, since the execution took place just past midnight. The story made our first chase edition.

"We put the story about the space shuttle toilet on the front because any toilet that costs $30 million deserves to be on anyone's front page.

"The other planned part of the front page was our strip story on the men behind California's two women senators. This story ran the morning both were sworn in and was a natural for this day. It talked about the pressure on the spouse of a senator and about the relationships these men have with their high-profile wives. We're working hard to display more prominently stories we know will be of interest to women as well as men. That made our decision to strip this story an obvious one.

"The teasers were decided upon in our 11:15 news meeting and were selected because the Science and Medicine section has a tremendous following here in Silicon Valley and the story on myths about teenagers helps us appeal to an audience we're all trying harder to reach."

THE DETROIT NEWS

Dale Peskin, assistant managing editor, and Beth Valone, afternoon news editor, explained the decision-making process leading to the front pages of *The Detroit News*.

"*The Detroit News* begins selecting content for its front pages by asking two questions: What do our readers need to know? What interests our readers?

"Those questions are asked throughout a news cycle that begins at about 9 a.m. and ends about 7 a.m. the following morning. *The Detroit News* is unusual among American newspapers in its commitment to aggressive overnight staffing and coverage. Between editions, *The News* does extensive remakes of front pages and many inside pages, striving for fresh and lively products that differ significantly in the A.M. and P.M. cycles. Its pages embody an around-the-clock strategy that factors in the needs of readers in both cycles and the ability to zone extensively for late home delivery. There is no agenda for selecting stories, no formula for displaying them. The editors simply look at the news of the day and talk about it. A lot.

Wednesday
January 6, 1993

34°
20°
Mostly cloudy
Overcast and cold, with highs in the mid-30s.
Details, 10F

25¢   50¢ outside 6-county metropolitan area

Final Scores

Miserable first half dooms Pistons
■ Miami Heat capitalize on ice-cold Detroit shooting, then hold on for an 89-83 victory. **Sports, 1C**

Mr. October heads for Cooperstown
■ Jackson is elected to baseball's Hall of Fame
Page **1C**

The Detroit News

'Mommy's gone': Kids found in filth

By Corey Williams
THE DETROIT NEWS

■ **Like 'a skeleton':** Crack-addicted prostitute's 3 children rescued while she works the streets.

New oil spill recalls '89 Valdez disaster

DETROIT NEWS WIRE SERVICES

LONDON — An abandoned oil tanker lay grounded on a rocky island shore today, battered by mountainous waves and threatening to spill 25 million gallons of crude into a wildlife refuge of northern Scotland.

Howling winds and rough seas Tuesday hampered efforts to contain oil spilling from the tanker Braer. The accident near Scotland threatens to become an environmental disaster.

On the rocks
The Braer accident threatens to become a major environmental catastrophe. Here's why.

Shetland Islands

No public school for 1st Family in D.C.

By Richard A. Ryan
NEWS WASHINGTON BUREAU

WASHINGTON — When First Daughter Chelsea Clinton arrives for her first day at Sidwell Friends School later this month, Ashley Bullock thinks chances are good that she will take the locker next to hers.

Clinton tries to avert flood of Haitians

DETROIT NEWS WIRE SERVICES

WASHINGTON — Worried that a human tide of Haitians may flee for America around Inauguration Day, President-elect Bill Clinton is expected to make a public statement this week to persuade the refugees it might be better for them to stay home.

Young conquers the World (Book, that is)

By Vivian S. Toy
THE DETROIT NEWS

INSIDE

Auto Show '93: Coverage in Business, Pages 1-2F

The morning, single-copy sales edition of *The Detroit News*'s front page on Jan. 6, 1993. Note the late-sports billboard above the flag, and the bold type for the impact headline.

"Four general meetings are held to help shape news coverage and to coordinate efforts of a large and far-flung staff.

"The first meeting, held at 12:30 p.m., provides an early blueprint for the next day's editions. The meeting is chaired by a deputy managing editor, with eight departments represented—national/international, state, local, business, features, sports, photo and graphics. Editors discuss and react to the early news reports, ferret out problems and develop a plan of action for reporters, photographers and artists.

"The first decisions about content and the presentation of stories occur about 5 hours later at a 5:30 p.m. meeting. At this time editors work from an 8- to 10-page news 'budget' that contains summaries of top stories from each department. Editors propose stories for Page 1 and discuss plans for department section fronts. A deputy or assistant managing editor chairs this meeting, questioning editors about stories, sometimes requesting additional reporting, photography or graphics. All editors at the meeting are encouraged to offer opinions or suggestions about stories and their play to ensure a full and open discussion of issues, problems, pressure points.

"The preliminary story selections at the 5:30 meeting are geared for *The Detroit News* morning edition. This single-copy, street-sale edition is designed and edited to attract attention in newsstands and honor boxes. When all is said and done, its front page should say 'Buy Me.'

"These nine stories from the Jan. 5 budget were offered for 1A in the morning edition of Jan. 6.

"*From the national desk:*

"Haitians—A boatload of Haitian refugees arrives in Florida, signaling a potential crisis for the new Clinton administration. Facing the prospect that a human tide of Haitian refugees may flee for America, the president-elect is pressured to act swiftly to develop a policy.

"Chelsea—The First Daughter is enrolled in private school in Washington.

"Oil spill—Tanker grounded off Shetland Islands near Scotland leaks oil, threatening a wildlife refuge.

"Fleetwood Max—The rock group that provided the generational theme for Bill Clinton's campaign will reunite to perform at his inauguration.

"*From the metro desk:*

"Abandon—After neighbors hear their screams, three children, the oldest of which is 3 years old, are found alone, malnourished and living in filth at their home.

"Baby—A Michigan judge backs a local couple's bid to keep their 2-year-old adopted child. An Iowa court previously had ordered the couple to return the child to its biological parents, who gave the child up for adoption.

"Mayor—Detroit Mayor Coleman Young becomes only the seventh mayor of an American city to be listed in the World Book Encyclopedia.

"Israel guns—Report from our staff reporter in Israel on an ex-Detroit couple coping with violence in Israel, but refusing to buy a gun for protection.

"*From the business desk:*

"Auto show—Our columnist previews a major Detroit event, the International Auto Show, with a column on GM scaling back its profile at the show because of hard times.

"Editors raised several question about the 1A candidates. These were the most significant:

"Oil spill—How serious was the spill? Did it compare in size with the Exxon Valdez spill? Would it develop during the night to our advantage? How much information would we get through the cycle? Could we do an informational graphic to make the story more understandable? Are good wire photos available?

"Abandon—Was this a 'Home Alone' story? Would we distort it by calling it a 'Home Alone' story? How serious is the problem of child neglect in Metro Detroit? Where are the parents? What is the family's history with social agencies? Are we prepared for the possible arrest of parents through the night? Is there a map of the neighborhood? Photos?

"Mayor—Why was the mayor picked for the encyclopedia? When would the book be published? What other public figures had been given prominence?

"Fleetwood Max—Does anyone really care that this group is reuniting?

"Jackie Thomas, the news editor, and Dale Peskin, assistant managing editor, agreed on these six stories as likely for Page 1—Oil Spill, Chelsea, Haitians, Abandon, Mayor and Baby. They planned to use a photo and index package on the Auto Show instead of the column.

"Their tentative decisions were reviewed and discussed at a post-meeting conference with Managing Editor Christy Bradford. She thought three of the five were strong stories: Abandon, Oil Spill and Chelsea.

"The three discussed sensitivity questions regarding a story about abandoned, malnourished children living in squalor, but agreed that it was compelling and focused public attention on a serious problem. They also discussed local TV coverage of the story, and how *The Detroit News* could provide a more thorough account. Bradford suggested additional reporting to document the seriousness of child neglect in Detroit. She suggested that the story might lead the front page because many readers would be interested in it and the public policy questions it raised were important.

"Bradford also requested additional reporting on the Chelsea story. She contacted Deb Price, an editor in *The Detroit News* Washington Bureau, and asked that a reporter locate and interview students at the private school where Chelsea would enroll.

"Bradford also asked about the extent of the oil spill and the availability of photos or graphics. They adjourned to further reassess stories, new developments, photos and graphics before their final decisions.

"Between 6 and 8 p.m., News Editor Thomas reviewed stories and Peskin began developing a design for the front page. City desk reporters supplemented the Abandon story with details from the scene and statistics showing the prevalence of child neglect. A reporter from the Washington Bureau interviewed one of Chelsea Clinton's new schoolmates, giving our story a fresh angle and a staff byline. The photo desk arranged for The Associated Press to take a photograph of students at Chelsea's new school.

"Meantime, the national desk and the graphics department worked on an informational graphic explaining the oil spill, which by 8 p.m. had grown in size. Peskin ordered a color graphic for the front page and worked with the graphics editor on its sizing and content.

"At the 8 p.m. meeting, Thomas made these final calls for the front page: Abandon, Oil Spill, Chelsea, Mayor and Haitians. Baby, a compelling but continuing legal saga, was moved to the Metro section front because editors thought its widespread play throughout the day did not favor our news cycle. The Fleetwood Mac story was moved to a 'Hot Story' position on Page 2A. This spot is saved for a quick-read story that may have no lasting significance, but is interesting as a talker.

"Additionally, Thomas chose to promo a late Detroit Pistons' basketball game and the selection of Reggie Jackson to baseball's Hall of Fame in our sports-oriented, above-the-flag billboard.

"In addition to the billboard, the front page was designed to display the three top 'sell' stories—Abandon, Oil Spill and Chelsea—above the fold.

"As this group of editors worked to produce the first edition, another group began planning a new front page for the second edition. If the morning front page says 'Buy Me,' the front page of the second edition, primarily an afternoon home-delivered edition, says 'Read me.' Its design is more restrained, its content tailored to local readers who receive their newspapers at their home in the afternoon. Sometimes it is driven by overnight or morning news. On other days editors must anticipate how their decisions fulfill the needs of readers who will see the paper 18 hours later.

"Beth Valone, afternoon news editor, begins considering changes for the afternoon edition at about 10 p.m., eight hours before her edition closes.

"She begins by reviewing the budgets from the 8 p.m. news meeting, which include specific stories intended for the P.M. cycle. She then looks for new stories from originating desks (primarily the city desk) and from the wires. The city desk usually offers at least one new enterprise story for the P.M. paper or a story that can be zoned in the key suburban areas of Oakland and Macomb counties, or both. Valone's mission is to press the afternoon strategy through the night, seeking out second-day leads and headlines, late sports, pushing for nut graphs that anticipate and interpret, scouring for fresh news developments and directing the news desk and city desk to react. At her 1 a.m. news meeting she coordinates the overnight staff to follow through.

"For editions of Jan. 6, Valone, Bradford and Deputy Managing Editor Gatti decided that three stories on the front page remained relevant and interesting throughout our cycle and should remain on the front page for afternoon readers: Abandon, Oil Spill and Chelsea.

"For the lead, she kept the Abandon story because of its compelling detail and the overnight arrest of the children's mother. She also kept Oil Spill but changed the play because the story would be at least 30 hours old by the time afternoon readers got their papers. She kept Chelsea partly because *The News* version included the student interview that she found in no other versions, wire or broadcast.

"She put the story about the study of passive smoke on the front page because the findings validated suspicions about the carcinogenic effects which, in turn, suggested to her a P.M. lead on the serious potential for limiting legislation. She was right on. This angle was the lead in the follows of many newspapers a full day later.

25¢

50¢ outside 5-county metropolitan area

The Detroit News

15

Wednesday, JANUARY 6, 1993

TONIGHT'S LOW: 20°
TOMORROW'S HIGH: 32°
Weather, 10F

N E

Oakland
Macomb
EDITION

'Mommy's gone': Kids found in filth

■ **Like 'a skeleton':** Crack-addicted prostitute's 3 children rescued while she works the streets.

By Corey Williams
THE DETROIT NEWS

Roaches crawled on 11-month-old Martell Collier and "when he looked at me, I thought I was looking at a skeleton with eyes," said a horrified neighbor, Doreen Burns.

"I ran out of there screaming."

Martell and his sisters, Sharmae, 3, and Shivon, who will be 2 on Friday, were malnourished when they were rescued Monday night from their malodorous apartment in the Herman Gardens housing project, where their crack-addicted mother often left them alone, police said.

The mother, an admitted prostitute, was walking on Joy Road in Detroit soliciting customers when she was arrested about 11 p.m. Monday, police said.

The children were taken from the apartment after Burns, 39, also a resident of the housing project on Detroit's west side, reported their incessant crying to police.

The children's mother, Tara Michelle Austin, 30, was expected to be arraigned today in 36th District Court on charges of third-degree child abuse and two counts of neglect.

Tuesday, Burns, who was familiar with the cries of hunger, sickness and loneliness from the apartment in the 8500 block of Rutland, said she called police because she knew the children needed help.

"Something just got in me to the point that I wasn't going to take it any more," Burns said. "I got tired of preaching to Tara and telling her to quit leaving those babies.

"I kept telling her, 'The way you leave and stay gone hours at a time, anything can happen.' She would

laugh it off. All Tara does is walk the streets day and night."

At 9 p.m. Monday, a friend told Burns the children were standing in the window, crying.

"The 2-year-old was standing in the window with a bottle sticking out of her mouth," said Burns, who went to check on the children. "The milk was so cloudy it looked like butter. I asked her where Tara was at. She said, 'Mommy's gone.' "

Please see Rescued, 5A

Please see Rescued, 5A

Township slams door on solicitors

By Rebecca Powers
THE DETROIT NEWS

IN OAKLAND

Winter's early evening darkness and Bloomfield Township's soliciting ordinance are interfering with freedom of speech, according to a Lansing-based environmental group.

Michigan Environmental Defense, a citizens' lobbying and educational organization, has sued the township, claiming its rules governing solicitors violate constitutional rights.

The legal complaint, filed in U.S. District Court in Detroit, argues that early curfews for door-to-door canvassers — and a requirement that they submit to criminal background checks — inhibit their rights to political discussion.

The lawsuit stems from a 1992 incident in which canvassers were threatened with ticketing or arrest because they had not complied with the rules. The township's ordinance bans soliciting after 5 p.m. during winter and after 7 p.m. during daylight savings time.

Please see Suit, 2A

Please see Suit, 2A

ASSOCIATED PRESS
Chelsea Clinton: Attending posh school riles some.

Clintons select private school for Chelsea

By Richard A. Ryan
NEWS WASHINGTON BUREAU

WASHINGTON — When Chelsea Clinton arrives for her first day at Sidwell Friends School later this month, Ashley Bullock thinks chances are good that she will take the locker next to hers.

Although she hasn't had much time to think about it yet, Ashley, also a 12-year-old seventh-grader, has a feeling about what she may say to Chelsea.

"I'll probably say 'Hi, how are you doing,' " Ashley said. "How do you like being the president's daughter?' "

Then, Ashley said, she will tell Chelsea "you will have to study a lot here. The teachers are nice,

Please see Chelsea, 9A

Please see Chelsea, 9A

■ **'Horrendous scene':** Howling winds and rough seas batter the abandoned tanker leaking 25 million gallons of crude oil. The spreading slick threatens a wildlife refuge.

REUTER
High winds and rough seas Tuesday off the Shetlands hampered efforts to contain the spill.

Ship gushing oil off Scotland likely to rival Exxon Valdez as worst spill

DETROIT NEWS WIRE SERVICES

LONDON — An abandoned oil tanker lay grounded on a rocky island shore today, battered by mountainous waves and threatening to spill 25 million gallons of crude into a wildlife refuge off northern Scotland.

The oil — more than twice the amount lost from the Exxon Valdez when that ship ran aground in Alaska in 1989 — reportedly was already gushing from two holes in the Braer.

Authorities worried that the Liberian-registered vessel would break up completely.

The smell of oil was heavy in the night air several miles from the scene, and police closed off the immediate area in fear of an explosion as gales blew oil and fumes up and over the clifftops.

The tanker was abandoned after its engines failed during a storm. The winds then forced the vessel among the Shetland Islands where it ran aground on a rocky beach at Main-

Please see Braer, 8A

Please see Braer, 8A

What's threatened

Bird nesting areas, seal colonies and salmon farms along the west coast of the Islands are at risk. Here are some of the water fowl at risk.

Loon
Eider duck
Puffin
Black shug

Other animals
Killer whales, porpoises, black guillemots, long-tailed ducks

Shetland Islands

25 miles
25 km

Spill's direction
Fitful Head
Braer
Sumburgh Head

SCOTLAND
North Sea
GREAT BRITAIN
FRANCE

THE DETROIT NEWS

METRO

Candid for cable

A Farmington Hills cable TV company held a video contest to inspire community programing and it went to the dogs. Page 8B

New face on Macomb

The Macomb County Board has undergone a major transformation. Its new chairman seeks bipartisan harmony — and more federal money for highway projects. Page 3B

Kathy Osery walks along a Jerusalem street on Tuesday.

A different country

Kathy and Yefat Osery recently returned to Israel after three years in Metro Detroit. They worry for their safety, but draw the line at carrying a gun. Page 6A

Passive smoking deadly, too, EPA says

■ **Carcinogen:** Approval of report is likely to trigger wider regulations.

AP AND WASHINGTON POST

WASHINGTON — An EPA report to be released Thursday will blame 3,000 deaths a year on secondhand cigarette smoke, and health advocates say it is likely to force wider regulation of smoking in public facilities and workplaces.

Environmental Protection Agency officials said Tuesday that the long-delayed report will indict "passive" smoke as a human carcinogen that causes lung cancer in adults and greatly increases the risk of respiratory illnesses, such as pneumonia and bronchitis, in children.

EPA administrator William Reilly's endorsement of the report by a panel of scientific advisers to the agency will end a contentious two-year review of the issue during which the panel's evidence and conclusions have been denounced repeatedly by the tobacco industry.

The EPA has no authority to regulate indoor air pollution. However, the move could influence how local governments and the federal Occupational Safety and Health Administration (OSHA) adopt and enforce workplace anti-smoking rules.

The EPA's scientific advisory panel approved the report that concluded environmental tobacco smoke is a "Class A" human carcinogen — a group that includes asbestos, arsenic and benzene. The panel estimated secondhand smoke annually causes the lung cancer death of approximately 3,000 U.S. adults.

The report also blames secondhand smoke for hundreds of thousands of cases of childhood bronchitis and pneumonia and for increasing the severity of asthma attacks in children.

Public health advocates hailed the news that the EPA would take the final step in endorsing the scientific panel's conclusions.

"This really puts the EPA imprimatur on something the public has known for a long time — that is, that secondhand smoke is dangerous, that tobacco smoke, whether inhaled from one's own cigarette or someone else's cigarette, is basically the same product," said Alfred Munzer, a Washington area lung specialist and the incoming president of the American Lung Association. "We believe this will motivate state governments and local governments to enact further regulations limiting smoking in public places."

SPORTS

Big hit in the Hall

Reggie Jackson was elected to baseball's Hall of Fame on Tuesday. Page 1C

INSIDE

Accent	1D	Essentials	10F
Autos	1E	Horoscope	8F
Business	1F	Lottery	10F
Classified	7E	Movies	6B
Class./Auto	2E	Obituaries	9C
Comics	8F	Sports	1C
Crossword	9F	Stocks	3F
Deaths	9C	TV	10D
Editorials	10A	Weather	10F

The Detroit News
Michigan's No. 1 Newspaper

A GANNETT Newspaper
119th Year No. 133
Copyright, 1993 The Detroit News, Inc.

Home Delivery/
222-NEWS
Classified Ads/
877-7500

Wheelin' into the auto show

■ **When:** Saturday through Jan. 17 in Cobo Center.

■ **Tickets:** At door or in advance at Ticket-Master. Adults $7; 65 and over $3; 12 and under free with parent, otherwise $3

■ **Inside:** Ford increases share of U.S. market; Olds hopes Aurora changes its fortunes; GM's influence fades. Page 1F

"One of her zone/enterprise stories centered on an Oakland County community being sued by a lobbying group over an ordinance that limits hours for door-to-door soliciting, an annoyance for suburb dwellers everywhere.

"She pushed back Haitians because the second-day angle predicted that a Clinton statement was still days away.

"She also pushed Mayor back to the Metro front.

"She retained a down-sized refer package to the auto show coverage.

"All in all, it was a rather routine news day, with routine developments between editions. Front-page changes from morning to afternoon were less dramatic than on many days.

"By the time Valone went home at 10 a.m., *The Detroit News* already was in the next day's news cycle."

Clearly, an examination of the decision-making procedures that went into the production of these front pages shows that editors do not make decisions in a vacuum. They have a feel for news value and knowledge of their readers' interests.

two

The Rudiments

When reporters cover a breaking news event such as a protest in front of a federal building, they will probably begin their stories with summary leads.
(Photo by Irwin Daugherty)

3

Summary Leads

A summary lead gives an audience the gist of a story in the first paragraph. It is terse, with generally no more than 35 words in one sentence, and summarizes the major elements of a newsworthy event. Summary leads are usually used on hard news stories so that readers do not have to guess or wait to find out what is going on.

Reporters are the eyes and ears of their audiences. When reporters cover a breaking news event, their first stories summarize what happened, to whom, where, when, why and how. More in-depth stories may be written later about people and things touched by the event, but initially, reporters are there to gather the essential facts and write their stories as quickly and as near their deadlines as possible.

Such hard news stories usually begin with a *summary lead*, a terse opening paragraph that provides the gist of the story and invites readers inside. Summary leads are used on news stories because they give the major points of the story immediately. That way, people do not have to guess or wait to find out the news. Most people do not have time to read a newspaper from start to end. Because they spend so little time with the news and often do not read entire articles, they demand the most important points at the start of the story.

CONCEPTS: PRINCIPLES OF SUMMARY LEADS

THE INVERTED PYRAMID

A summary lead generally tops a traditional writing form called an *inverted pyramid*, in which the news is stacked in paragraphs in order of descending importance. The lead summarizes the principal items of a news event. The second paragraph and each succeeding paragraph contain secondary or supporting details in order of decreasing significance. All the paragraphs in the story contain newsworthy information, but each paragraph is less vital than the one before it. This writing form puts the climax of a story at the beginning, in the lead, and so it is different from a form often used for novels, short stories and drama—and for some news features—in which an author begins with background and works to a climax.

Examples of the inverted-pyramid form can be found in writing done before the mid-19th century, but most journalism historians say that the concept was developed during the American Civil War. Newspaper correspondents in the field sent their dispatches by telegraph. Because they were afraid that the system would malfunction or the enemy would cut the wires, the correspondents squeezed the most important information into the first few sentences. Wire services, which used telegraphers to transmit stories until computers were introduced in the early 1970s, have continued to use the inverted pyramid as their staple form of reporting. That enables the wire services to move stories quickly in small chunks and their customers to use the stories in whatever lengths they need.

Newspapers also adopted the inverted-pyramid form because it capsulizes the news quickly. It gives readers the convenience of grasping the news of the day by simply skimming lead paragraphs. The form allows readers to decide whether they want to continue reading a story or leave it after any one of its paragraphs. An inverted pyramid can also be trimmed from the bottom, which makes it easier to fit it into the tight news holes of a newspaper. (Inverted-pyramid style is discussed in more detail in Chapter 5.)

A reporter writing a summary lead tries to get the gist of the story in a terse sentence of generally no more than 35 words. *(Photo by Alan Carey/The Image Works)*

THE FIVE W'S AND H

A summary lead, generally in no more than 35 words, tells an audience the most important of the six primary elements of an event, the *five W's and H.* They are:

- *Who* the event happened to or who acted on whom
- *What* happened or will happen
- *Where* the action occurred
- *When* it happened
- *Why* the action took place; the reason behind it
- *How* it happened

Reporters look for these six elements whenever they cover a news event. It makes no difference how big or small the story is. Reporters gather the facts to answer *who, what, where, when, why* and *how;* they rate the importance of each fact; then they are ready to write a lead and news story.

The most important of the six elements go into a summary lead. The less important elements go into the second and succeeding paragraphs. In most cases it would take too many words to try to put all six elements into one lead paragraph.

Identifying the W's and H

For example, this is what could occur after a press conference at City Hall. The name and the situation are not real, but they are typical. In the press conference, the mayor—we will call her Kathy Riedy—announces that there will be no increase in property taxes this year, even though the city will lose more than $3 million in community development grants from the federal government. She says:

> There will be no increase in property taxes this year. We are not going to ask our residents to pay for the cuts they are suffering because of slashes in the federal budget. We had planned to spend $3 million in community development block grants to rebuild sidewalks that are crumbling in the downtown area, but those funds have been cut. These sidewalks were built during the Depression, and we need to replace them. We will go ahead with the sidewalk project this year, but increased property taxes will not fund it. If we cannot find alternative federal funds, we will attempt to raise the city sales tax, at least for a year, to pay for this vital project.

While taking notes, a reporter for the local newspaper decides that *what* the mayor has said about the sidewalk project is the most important point of the press conference; therefore, that will become the top of the inverted pyramid. Riedy has covered several topics during the press conference, but she concentrated on the tax issue. Although the mayor says that property taxes will not be increased, she also says that sales taxes may be. In a nice political way, Riedy says that the city will not take any money out of one pocket; it will try to take it out of another pocket.

While taking notes, the reporter highlights the five W's and H. That will make it easier to find them while the story is being written. The reporter notes:

Who. Mayor Kathy Riedy.

What. Downtown sidewalks will be rebuilt this year, without an increase in property taxes and even though federal funds are being cut.

Where. City Hall press conference.

When. Monday.

Why. Cuts in federal budget will cost the city $3 million in community block grants.

How. Look for alternative federal funds or increase sales tax.

Rating the W's and H

After the five W's and H are identified, they must be rated according to their importance. This is not always easy for beginning reporters, but here are three principles that will help:

- *Conduct research.* If possible, do not cover a news event without researching the subject and the people involved. That will make it easier to spot the freshest news, the key issues, the elements that have been reported before and the embellishments.

- *Try to identify the five W's and H during the reporting process.* A news story is based on the six primary elements; look and listen for them. While taking notes, highlight them with an asterisk. Underline or put a double asterisk on those that are the most important.
- *Talk to editors.* They will often say what direction they want a story to take.

THE THOUGHT PROCESS BEHIND THE LEAD

Reporters all say the same thing about news writing: while they are interviewing a source, covering a speech or working at the scene of a traffic accident, they are thinking about their leads and stories. This thought process begins even before they start taking notes and continues until their stories are completed. They often have their leads in mind before they actually write their stories.

Several factors can influence how a reporter thinks about a story:

- *What has been reported in the past.* Reporters are always looking for something new. In our example, if Mayor Riedy has given six speeches this week in which she has discussed exactly the same things about the sidewalk project, the reporter will probably quit thinking about that as the best lead.
- *How the reporter feels about the subject.* Reporters take their own prejudices and emotions into every story they cover. Reporters concerned about the city's sidewalks will probably concentrate on what the mayor says about them.
- *How the audience feels about the subject.* If the sidewalk project has been an ongoing and controversial issue in the city, reporters should know this. They will want to keep their readers, viewers or listeners informed on the latest developments.
- *Instructions from an editor.* If the boss says, "Get a lead on the sidewalks," the reporter will probably concentrate on this issue.

As the mayor talks, the reporter begins thinking about a lead, perhaps in this way:

> "The mayor says no increase in property taxes this year. Sounds like rhetoric. What does she mean? She's going ahead with the sidewalk project. How is she going to pay for it? Bingo! No new property taxes, but she's willing to raise the sales tax. This means that ultimately the taxpayers are going to pay for it. Get as much as possible on that."

In the newsroom, composing the story at a computer terminal, the reporter has to decide how many of the W's and H can be put into the lead while still keeping it brief and easy to understand. *Who* is important because whenever the mayor speaks, everyone in the city can be affected. *When* she spoke, *what* she said and the reason behind what she said (*why*) are also critical in summarizing the story. *Where* she said it and her solution to the problem are also important, but the reporter decides that these elements are not vital to the summary and can appear in the second paragraph.

The first lead the reporter writes emphasizes *what* and *why:*

> The city will not increase property taxes this year but still will rebuild downtown sidewalks, even if it loses $3 million in federal community development funds, Mayor Kathy Riedy said Monday.

The second paragraph provides *how* and *where:*

> However, the mayor said that the city sales tax may need to be increased to pay for the project. "If we cannot find alternative federal funds, we will attempt to raise the city sales tax, at least for a year," Riedy said in a City Hall press conference.

Like any journalist, the reporter looks over the initial lead. It is not wrong, but it should have emphasized both the property tax and the sales tax. By moving up *how* and then putting the sidewalk project in the second paragraph, the reporter can make the lead stronger. The rewritten lead also begins with *who,* rather than ending with it, to emphasize who is saying "no new taxes here, but new taxes there."

The new lead:

> Mayor Kathy Riedy said Monday that the city will not increase property taxes this year to pay for federal funding cuts, but it may have to increase sales taxes.

Second paragraph:

> "We had planned to spend $3 million in community development block grants to rebuild sidewalks that are crumbling in the downtown area," Riedy said in a City Hall press conference. "We will go ahead with the sidewalk project this year, but increased property taxes will not fund it."

The reporter can write still other summary leads on the story that emphasize other W's or H. The lead can emphasize *how:*

> The city sales tax may be increased this year if the city cannot find alternative funding sources for a project to rebuild sidewalks, Mayor Kathy Riedy said Monday.

Why can be emphasized:

> A $3 million cut in federal community block grants will not stop the city from rebuilding downtown sidewalks this year, Mayor Kathy Riedy said Monday.

What and *where* can be emphasized:

> Downtown sidewalks will be rebuilt this year without an increase in property taxes, Mayor Kathy Riedy said Monday during a City Hall press conference.

By giving the five W's and H in the beginning paragraphs, the reporter has summarized the entire inverted pyramid. All the key elements are reported in terse paragraphs; they are not crammed into one. Every paragraph in the story should be less important than the one before it, either giving additional details of Riedy's statements on taxes and the sidewalk project or reporting other things she said.

MULTIPLE-ELEMENT LEADS

The lead on Riedy that combined the property and sales taxes is an example of a *multiple-element lead* or *double-barreled lead.* Such a lead gives equal rating to two or more of the primary elements in a story and informs the audience immediately that more than one major event is occurring.

Here is another example of a news story topped by a multiple-element summary lead. The story ran in the *Chicago Tribune.*

The lead:

> A 31-year-old motorist was killed and 900 customers in Hammond lost electrical power Thursday after a commuter train plowed into the motorist's car and the wreckage hit a power pole, police said.

This 34-word lead answered four of the W's and H:

Who. A 31-year-old motorist (he or she is still unnamed) and 900 electricity customers.
What. Was killed and lost electrical power.
Where. Hammond.
When. Thursday.
How. The train hit the car, which then hit a power pole

The lead summarized the news event. It also informed readers that two major events had occurred: a motorist was killed, and 900 customers lost their power. It could have been shortened by moving the power outage information into the second paragraph, but because the reporter considered the motorist and the outage equally important, he wrote a multiple-element lead.

Second paragraph:

> Killed was Ray Carey, of 749 118th St., Hammond, a steelworker, said Sgt. John Pohl of the traffic division of the Hammond Police Department.

Names are usually not used in the lead paragraph of a news story unless the person is (like Mayor Riedy) well-known. In this case, therefore, it was necessary to put the name of the motorist—and answer *who* —in the second paragraph. This paragraph also provided the victim's home address and the source of the information.

SUMMARY LEADS ON FEATURES

Summary leads can also be used on *feature* stories. A *feature*—an umbrella term for a variety of stories written on soft news events—is usually not structured as an inverted pyramid, and writers will often top it with a special lead (special leads will be discussed in Chapter 4). However, that does not preclude a summary lead on a feature.

Feature writers design their leads to invite readers into their stories, not to report breaking news. If they are writing about a person or an occurrence connected with a news event, the breaking news has probably been reported earlier or elsewhere. Thus the most important of the five W's and H do not have to appear in a feature lead. They can be reported somewhere else in the story.

A feature lead can be a narrative, a contrast or a question. It may talk directly to the reader or be written in the first person. Or it may summarize the thrust of the story. The point is that feature writers have many types of leads they can use; the summary is one of their options.

For example, here is a summary lead on a feature story about the ordeal a father went through to recover his kidnapped son:

> SCITUATE, R.I.—Thirteen-year-old Robert C. Smith, abducted from his California home 21 months ago, buried his face in his father's arms in a dramatic family reunion yesterday morning outside the State Police barracks here. (*The Boston Globe*)

Here is a summary lead on a feature about how nurses who are frustrated with life in hospitals and clinics are shifting their skills to jobs in the business or legal world:

> Tighter regulations and skimpy medical insurance reimbursements are prompting American nurses to quit their jobs to launch or work in a range of profitable health-care-related businesses. (*Los Angeles Times*)

Experienced reporters covering the same news event or interviewing the same people will usually come up with the same basic leads because they are able to determine which of the W's and H are the most important. This does not mean that the wording of their leads will be the same. It means that the key elements of the story will be presented in one form or another in the opening paragraph.

For instance, here are two summary leads from two writers on the same event:

CHICAGO (UPI)—A grand jury indicted 18 people Thursday on charges they bilked homeowners, most of them elderly, out of more than $200,000 through home-repair schemes—including charging an elderly man $50,000 to unplug his toilet. (United Press International)

CHICAGO (AP)—A grand jury investigating home-repair schemes on Thursday indicted 18 people, including a contractor whose company charged an 84-year-old widow $50,000 to fix a leaky toilet. (Associated Press)

Both leads emphasized the *what* of this story—grand jury indictments. *Who* was mentioned partially (18 people), but the names were listed later because none of those charged was well known to most readers and 18 names would take up too much space in the lead. *Where* and *when* (Chicago, Thursday) and *why* (for charging people too much) were in the leads.

There were differences, however. The 35-word UPI lead told readers that the 18 indicted people allegedly bilked people out of more than $200,000, and one of those bilked was an elderly man. The 29-word AP lead contained fewer words and concentrated on another person who allegedly was bilked, an 84-year-old woman. It was more specific because it gave the woman's age and used *widow*, a descriptive word.

Of the two wire-service leads, the shorter AP lead, which included the 84-year-old widow, was more inviting and probably enticed more readers to continue.

GUIDELINES: WRITING A SUMMARY LEAD

HOW MANY WORDS?

A summary lead should contain no more than 35 words. Of course, there will be times when more words are needed to summarize a story; but the longer the lead, the greater the risk that it will be difficult to read or understand. The general rule to follow when writing a summary lead is: *Use a single sentence of no more than 35 words to summarize an event.*

Usually, a lead can be shortened by cutting out unnecessary adjectives. For example, here is a 44-word lead:

Two women were injured and part of Michigan Avenue was closed for nearly seven hours Saturday when a three-alarm fire at a high-rise construction site set off a series of explosions that sent metal and other debris flying across the Magnificent Mile. (*Chicago Tribune*)

This lead was long because it contained multiple elements and tried to get too much information into a single sentence. It reported that two people were injured and that explosions sent metal and other debris across Michigan Avenue, which is one of Chicago's busiest streets and is called the Magnificent Mile. Even with multiple elements, however, leads can normally be written in 35 words or fewer. Here is the lead again, with nine words that could have been trimmed indicated by brackets:

Two women were injured and part of Michigan Avenue was closed [for nearly seven hours] Saturday when a [three-alarm] fire at a high-rise construction site set off a series of explosions that sent [metal and other] debris flying across the Magnificent Mile.

Leads with more than 35 words can often be tightened into easier-to-read sentences. The following 38-word lead has been rewritten in 25 words. The shorter lead would have given readers a tighter and smoother summary. Original lead:

A man suspected of shooting a Dallas police officer who responded to a burglary in a North Dallas neighborhood Friday night was charged with attempted capital murder Saturday, but officials have been unable to identify him. (*Dallas Times Herald*)

Rewritten lead:

An unidentified suspect accused of shooting a police officer who responded to a North Dallas burglary was charged with attempted capital murder Saturday, police said.

Here are two summary leads that summarized news in single, brief sentences. The first one did it in 24 words and the second in 29.

Williston moved into its fourth day of below-zero temperatures today, after a low temperature of 27 degrees below zero was recorded Sunday night. (*Williston, N.D., Daily Herald*)

CHICAGO (AP)—The Chicago Mercantile Exchange has expelled and levied a fine of $100,000 against a member who police believe was associated with a multimillion-dollar commodity scam in the Northwest. (Associated Press)

AVOIDING CLUTTER LEADS

It's tough to try to cram the five W's and H into a 35-word sentence. Why try? Doing so usually makes for an awkward and difficult-to-understand summary lead, which means lost readers and howling editors. The general rule to follow is: *Put the most important primary elements in the lead. Do not clutter it with all of them. Save the remaining elements for the second, third, fourth and, if needed, later paragraphs.*

Following this rule will help avoid a *clutter lead* such as this one, which ran in a university daily:

> An 11-year-old boy who has less than a year to live is doing "remarkably well" after doctors implanted radioactive "seeds" on his cancerous brain tumor last week, the first time such a treatment has been used, a University Medical Center spokesman said.

The writer simply tried to cram too much into this 44-word multiple-element lead. *The first time such a treatment has been used* should have been saved for the second paragraph. And there was no reason to put the *last week* time element in the lead. Why tell readers that a major element of the story is several days old? The time of the operation should have been used in the second or third paragraph.

AVOIDING BURIED LEADS

If the most important element of a news story is not in the summary lead, the writer has probably *buried* it in another paragraph, which means that readers have to hunt for the news. This is not good. A summary lead should provide the key point immediately; it should not keep readers guessing.

A beginning reporter handed this story to the city editor:

> Police Chief John Jones discussed the city's crime problem with interested townspeople at a meeting Monday night.
>
> Jones agreed to meet with residents who have grown increasingly concerned about the safety of their neighborhoods.
>
> The chief said that there were more serious crimes reported here in the last 12 months than during any other year in the city's history.

The editor scolded the reporter for "burying" the lead in the third paragraph. The most important element of this story was obviously the police chief's revelation that crime in the city was at its highest level ever, not the fact that he had discussed the problem. Citizens knew the topic of the meeting before it was held.

The lead should have read:

> Police Chief John Jones said Monday night that there were more serious crimes reported here last year than during any other 12 months in the city's history.

Here is the lead paragraph of a lengthy story about a university radio station:

> Saturday marked the first anniversary of Pitt's radio station, WPTS-98.5 FM, and to celebrate, a party was held on the William Pitt Union lawn.

The story was not about the party, however. It was about the problems of running a professional radio station at a university. The fourth paragraph switched to the problems, and the rest of the story dealt with them. The problems should have been in the lead. The party could have been mentioned in the second, third or fourth paragraph.

Here is another example of a lead that failed to report the news:

> Faculty members and school administrators will have a chance to reflect on academic issues in an informal manner this weekend.

Reflect on academic issues and *in an informal manner* mean nothing to readers. The second paragraph told the news. It said that the Academic Senate would hold a retreat at a downtown hotel to discuss its structure, purpose and future. *That* should have been the lead.

DETERMINING THE FOCAL POINT

A reporter directs the focus of a summary lead by choosing which of the W's and H to emphasize. If a well-known person is involved in the story, *who* may be the most important element. In that case, *who* becomes the *focal point* of the lead, and the story would probably start with a name:

> NICOSIA, Cyprus (AP)—Danielle Mitterrand, wife of French President Francois Mitterrand, narrowly escaped a car bomb attack today that killed four people in northern Iraq. (Associated Press)

Manning Marable is resigning as chairman of the Black Studies Department at Ohio State to become professor of political science and sociology at the University of Colorado at Boulder. (*The Lantern,* Ohio State University)

If a person who is not well known does something newsworthy, the *what* element may be the focal point of the lead:

FORT WORTH—A firefighter was critically injured Sunday when a wall fell on him as he fought a poolhall blaze three blocks from the station where he had worked for 17 years. (*The Dallas Morning News*)

Noblesville, Ind.—A 12-year-old Noblesville boy was killed Saturday morning when a rifle he took to his room after watching a horror movie accidentally discharged. (*The Indianapolis Star*)

If *where, when, why* and *how* are the most important elements, one of them should be the focal point of the summary lead. In this lead, *where* is the focal point:

HARRISBURG—Ten state and federal investigators fanned out yesterday across south-central Pennsylvania searching poultry farms for signs that an outbreak of potentially devastating avian influenza in Maryland had come from or spread to this state. (*The Philadelphia Inquirer*)

In this lead, *when* is the focal point:

From December to February, the Earth's frigid underbelly, Antarctica, makes itself habitable. (*The Dallas Morning News*)

In this lead, *why* is the focal point:

Faced with a potential windfall of $30 million in utility tax revenue over the next five years, Kansas City officials on Thursday outlined several spending options that also offer some of the most significant tax reductions in years. (*Kansas City Times*)

In this lead, *how* is the focal point:

> Arson was blamed for a fire at the Flatbush Ave. station of the Long Island Rail Road yesterday that spread heavy smoke into nearby subway lines, delaying hundreds of thousands of commuters and straphangers. (*New York Daily News*)

Generally, the reporters covering a news event decide which of the elements are most important. Sometimes most of the elements can be put into the lead; at other times only one or two may be appropriate.

POSITIONING THE TIME ELEMENT

The *time element*, the *when* of a story, is an important part of most summary leads because it conveys immediacy to the reader. It needs to be placed so that it does not disturb the flow of the sentence.

Option 1: Time Element after the Verb

Usually, the best position for the time element is immediately after the verb:

> An 8-year-old west Phoenix girl was killed Monday morning when a car jumped a curb and ran her down as she stopped to pick up a schoolbook from the sidewalk. (*The Arizona Republic*)

> More than 400 people met Sunday to kick off a volunteer campaign in support of a $195.5 million bond election for the Dallas Independent School District, although officials said certain sections of town may not support the package. (*The Dallas Morning News*)

Option 2: Time Element after the Object

The time element may follow the object of the verb:

> Firefighters in Oregon battled a forest fire Monday that threatened 150 homes, and in California crews tried to contain a forest and brush fire that forced the evacuation of three communities. (Associated Press)

Option 3: Time Element after an Adverb or Prepositional Phrase

The time element may follow an adverb or prepositional phrase:

> Interest rates on short-term Treasury securities rose slightly Monday to the highest level in three weeks. (Associated Press)

CAPE CANAVERAL, Fla. (AP)—
The Columbia space shuttle broke
through the clouds and roared into
orbit Thursday on a marathon 13-day
mission that is expected to lead to even
longer stays in space. (Associated
Press)

Option 4: Time Element in a "Comfortable" Spot

Sometimes, the time element cannot follow the verb directly because it reads awkwardly in that position. Therefore, it must be moved to a "comfortable" spot in the sentence:

The Colorado Springs City Council on Tuesday approved the route of an electrical transmission line near the city's eastern edge, despite objections by landowners who wanted the project relocated. (*Colorado Springs Gazette Telegraph*)

In this lead the time element was placed between the subject and the verb, which most grammarians would say not to do. It would be awkward, however, to say that the council "approved Tuesday." And the time element would not fit comfortably anywhere else in the sentence. Therefore, in this case, the subject and verb were split to make the sentence read more smoothly.

Option 5: Time Element at the End

Sometimes the time element is put at the end of the sentence:

KINGMAN—A chair lift-type "aerial gondola" to convey people across the Colorado River between Bullhead City and Laughlin officially received the support of the Mohave County Supervisors Monday. (*Mohave Valley News*, Bullhead City, Ariz.)

WRITING IN THE ACTIVE VOICE

Whenever possible, write summary leads (or any other leads or paragraphs) in the active voice rather than the passive voice. In the active voice the subject acts upon an object; in the passive voice the subject is acted upon.

Editors and news directors consider the active voice more direct and vigorous than the passive voice. Here are some examples:

Like the biting Arctic wind that whips across Northwestern's campus, the onset of winter depression numbs many students. (*The Daily Northwestern*, Northwestern University)

NAPLES, Fla. (AP)—Three major fires and dozens of smaller ones, many of them set by arsonists, rampaged across Florida today after killing a rookie firefighter and devouring about 50,000 acres of woodland dried by cold weather. (Associated Press)

The passive voice should be used only when the person or thing receiving the action is more important than the person or thing doing the acting, as in these examples:

> Five Northwestern students were arrested Thursday at Scott Hall as more than 70 people protested recruiting on campus by the CIA. (*The Daily Northwestern,* Northwestern University)

> Williston teachers were told at an informal forum Wednesday that they can pass or fail the four District 1 House candidates in the Nov. 6 general election. (*Williston,* N.D., *Daily Herald*)

In many cases, a lead written in the passive voice should be rewritten into the active voice. For example, here was the first lead written on a robbery story:

> A downtown jewelry store was robbed on Saturday of $50,000 to $100,000 by a "well-dressed" gunman, police said.

It was rewritten as follows:

> A "well-dressed" gunman stole $50,000 to $100,000 from a downtown jewelry store Saturday, police said.

Writing in the active voice does not mean that stories should be written in the present tense. Because news stories generally describe events that have already occurred, the sentences should be written in the past tense. Voice and tense are two different things and should not be confused.

PROVIDING ATTRIBUTIONS

Attribution tells an audience who gave information to a reporter. It adds authenticity and authority to a story. An audience looks at or hears what the sources say and then evaluates the worth of their statements. (Attribution will be discussed more fully in Chapter 7.) There are three guidelines to follow in deciding whether to use attribution in summary leads.

Attributing Facts

Attribution is not needed when a fact—something that has actually happened or is obviously true—is reported:

An argument that began at a gourmet restaurant in Kansas City's State Line Road antique district Saturday night ended in the shooting deaths of an owner, a cook and an employee as well as the wounding of a passerby. (*Kansas City Star*)

Or:

A free public ceremony commemorating the 56th anniversary of the birth of slain civil rights leader Dr. Martin Luther King will be at 1 p.m. Monday in the Union Bazaar on the University of Wisconsin-Parkside campus. (*Kenosha*, Wis., *News*)

Attributing Opinions

Attribution is needed when a reporter is repeating the voiced opinion of a source, as happens in most stories, and it usually identifies the source by name or title:

STORRS, Conn.—The swashbuckling escapades of movie hero Indiana Jones do a good job of promoting the profession of archeology but distort its true purpose, a state archeologist said. (United Press International)

Or:

NEW YORK—Baby-boom "yuppies" get more publicity, but older, more cautious investors have by far a bigger impact on Wall Street, a new survey shows. (*USA Today*)

Vague Attributions

Vague attributions can be used if a source is speaking on behalf of a governmental or private agency:

WASHINGTON—Seldane, a prescription drug used by millions for hay-fever and allergy problems, may be fatal for patients with liver problems or if taken with some antibiotics, the Food and Drug Administration warned Tuesday. (Reuters)

The number of Americans delinquent on their mortgage payments hit a record high level in the third quarter, the Mortgage Bankers Association of America said. (*Kenosha*, Wis., *News*)

REVISING THE LEAD:
SUMMARIZING THE STORY AND ENTICING READERS

Summary leads should do two things:

1 *Summarize the story.*
2 *Invite readers inside.*

Putting the most important of the W's and H into the opening paragraph will summarize the story. Using the strongest possible words will entice readers.

The trick to writing a summary lead that summarizes and entices, rather than one that simply wraps up the story, is to continue working on the lead until the best possible combination of words is used. This means:

- *Do not go with the first lead.* After writing an acceptable lead, rewrite it to improve it. Keep saying, "I can make this lead better."
- *Avoid superfluous words.*
- *Avoid gobbledygook.*
- *Write clearly and concisely.*
- *Use vivid verbs.*
- *Use colorful words.*

For example, this lead was written for a story about the traits women seek in their mates:

> Women are likely to be disappointed in their choice of a permanent mate, a study shows.

The lead did summarize the story, but it was dull. It did not sing. Readers could have taken a look at it and said, "So what?" The writer needed to work on the lead more, to use a better combination of words to better summarize the story.

Here was the rewritten version:

> Women want permanent mates who are sensitive, self-assured and warm, but they usually come up cold, a sociologist's report shows.

The rewritten lead used five more words than the original lead, but it was still concise. It did a better job of telling the story. It used more colorful words, which meant that readers could "see" the story better. It also identified the source more clearly. *A study* means nothing to readers unless they know who conducted it. *A sociologist's report* gave the lead authority; it told readers that an expert in the field was the source.

Here is another lead that needed a boost:

> Help has arrived for some of the students whose class times conflict
> with their favorite soap operas.

This lead was not wrong; it just needed punch. It summarized the story (students could call a number in town to get a soap-opera update), but it did not entice.

With a little more work, the writer came up with:

> Help has arrived for soap-opera fans who choose to attend class even
> though they would rather dote over daytime dramas.

Writers can often improve a lead if they read it out loud after writing it. This lead was written on a story about a new freeway in town:

> Proposition 300 is a "dream list" of poorly researched proposals for
> a freeway system that would not benefit taxpayers who are paying for
> it but do not use it, a resident said Tuesday.

There are so many short words in this lead that readers would have tripped over them. They would have had to read the sentence two or three times to figure out what it was saying. And who is this resident making such a profound statement?

The writer worked harder on the lead, coming up with:

> Proposition 300 is a "dream list" of poorly researched proposals for
> a freeway system that would not benefit the residents who pay for it,
> an opponent of the measure said Tuesday.

Journalists from newspapers and the electronic media descend on major sports events
such as the NCAA championship basketball games.
(Reuters/Bettman)

Special Leads

A brief summary lead is best for breaking hard

news stories. However, today's daily print and

electronic media do not cover only breaking

stories. Their daily reports include non-breaking

news and feature stories on a myriad of topics.

These stories go beyond merely reporting the who,

what, where, when, why *and* how *of an event;*

their leads are written to tease and to entice.

Whenever they are about to write, journalists ask themselves, "What is the best lead for this story?" Unfortunately, there is no easy answer.

Chapter 3 focused on the summary lead, which gives readers the gist of an entire story in a single paragraph. A summary of no more than 35 words is the most appropriate lead on a breaking hard news story—such as a fire, an accident or a speech by a government official—because readers want to know the news. They want the *who, what, where, when, why* and *how* of a breaking news event, and they demand the most important of those W's and H in the first paragraph.

Today's media, however, do not cover only breaking news. Both newspapers and the electronic media use non-breaking stories such as this year's forecast for farm prices or a report on how one neighborhood is fighting crime. They use personality profiles that describe interesting people in or out of the news, and "how to" stories, such as repairing household appliances or cooking Thanksgiving turkeys. There are interpretative and analytical pieces that detail the weaknesses in this year's legislature or explore how the city might go about developing parkland. There are sports, business, consumer, travel, fashion, entertainment and other special-interest stories.

This chapter will discuss alternatives to the summary lead. On some news stories and on most features, the best lead may not be a one-paragraph summary. Instead, the beginning may invite readers into a story. It may tease them, put them in the middle of the action, talk directly to them, ask them a question or set them up for a climax.

TYPES OF SPECIAL LEADS

Leads that are not summaries usually fall into one of the following categories:

- *Narrative*
- *Contrast*
- *Staccato*
- *Direct address*
- *Question*
- *Quote*
- *"None of the above"*

NARRATIVE LEADS

Elements of the Narrative Lead

A *narrative lead* is the most popular lead on features and non-breaking news stories. It draws people into a story by putting them, suddenly, in the middle of the action. It should entice a person to continue reading or listening.

Lead block   Although a narrative lead can be written in a single paragraph, it is usually written in a lead block, two or more paragraphs that build up to a paragraph that tells readers the major point of the story. Like any journalistic writing, the lead block is constructed with terse sentences.

Because a narrative lead often involves a person, it is acceptable to use that person's name in the opening paragraph. This is usually not done in a summary lead, unless the person is well known, but using a name right away in a narrative allows an audience to identify more quickly with a major player in the story.

Here is a two-paragraph narrative lead block from *The Daily Northwestern*, the campus paper at Northwestern University. The story was about an annual contest sponsored by a sorority. In the first paragraph, the writer, Sarah Okeson, introduced a young man, allowing readers to feel some emotional attachment to him and, Okeson hoped, to the story. The opening paragraph also began in the middle of the action:

> Peter Spears swiveled his hips to the tune of "Neutron Dance," turned his back to the audience and ripped off his jacket, revealing a shirt opened to the waist.

The second paragraph continued the narrative. It painted a picture, drawing readers deeper into the story:

> Spears strutted to the beat and slowly tossed off his shirt and pants. Still wearing a black bow tie and black bikini swimsuit, he dove into the Patten Gymnasium pool.

By now, the writing should have caught the readers' interest. Okeson used vivid words—"swiveled," "ripped," "revealing," "strutted," "tossed off," "black bikini"—to paint a colorful picture. By the end of the second paragraph, readers should have felt as if they were in the action, emotionally tied somehow to Peter Spears.

A summary lead could have been written on the story, saying:

> A freshman Sigma Nu member won the Mr. Anchor Splash title Sunday in the fourth annual contest sponsored by Delta Gamma sorority.

But the narrative worked better. The contest was not a hard news event. Readers might not have been interested in how sorority and fraternity members spent this Sunday. The narrative was used to entice them.

Nut graph   After two or three paragraphs of narrative, it is time to use a *"so what" paragraph*, telling readers precisely what the story is about. (Narrative is used to entice readers; it should not dominate the story.) The common name for the explanatory paragraph that follows the introductory narrative is *nut graph*. It explains the significance of a story or gives its *news peg*, which links the story to previously reported news. The nut graph should be placed fairly high in the story—the third, fourth or fifth paragraph.

Here is Okeson's nut graph, which was the third paragraph of the story:

> Spears, a CAS (College of Arts and Sciences) freshman and Sigma Nu member, won the Mr. Anchor Splash title Sunday in the fourth annual competition sponsored by Delta Gamma sorority.

Writing a Narrative Lead

Using observation　The key to writing an effective narrative lead is to write it around observation, what you as a reporter see, hear, smell, taste or touch while working on a story. When interviewing people it is critical to make notes on:

- How they move
- What they are doing during the interview
- What they are wearing and the color of their clothes
- How loudly or softly they speak
- How long it takes them to answer a question
- Smells and sights around them
- Anything that makes them unusual

These observations are extremely important in stories; they are vital to a narrative lead. Okeson would not have been able to write her narrative on the Mr. Anchor Splash contest if she had not observed the action herself.

An observation is used to begin a narrative, as in this lead from the *Montrose* (Calif.) *Ledger:*

> Anderson L. Brooks was about to leave home for another day at work. He adjusted his black, narrow necktie the way he had for 40 years. He slipped on his favorite brown hat, the one with the sweat ring showing through the band. He lit a cigarette and left for downtown Los Angeles.

In another narrative lead, Barbara Brotman of the *Chicago Tribune* used observation to paint a vivid picture of a Romanian immigrant who drives a taxicab in Chicago. In the first two paragraphs, Brotman put readers inside the cab, just as the driver was taking a call. In the third paragraph, her nut graph, she told readers that this is the story of a cab driver who put a mobile telephone in his car. Readers could not help wanting to know more about the cabbie after reading the opening paragraphs:

The phone rings in Constantin Gogu's office, which he has pulled over to a curb on North Michigan Avenue. Gogu picks it up.

"Hello," he says. "To pick you up in 20 minutes?" The office is open for business, and business has been so good that it must seem to this Romani-an immigrant that the Statue of Liberty is lifting her lamp beside the door of Checker Cab No. 4468.

Gogu's place of business is the 1983 Chevrolet Impala taxicab he owns. One month ago, Gogu spent nearly $2,000 to install a mobile telephone in the taxi.

Keeping the story going Additional observations and narrative should be used later and throughout the story, not only about the person in the lead but about other characters. This should keep readers so emotionally attached to the main players that they would want to read the entire story, no matter how long. For example, in the story on Constantin Gogu, Brotman used this paragraph in the middle of the story to introduce three paragraphs on Gogu's first year in the United States:

It is a wonderful job, it is a marvelous country. Gogu, whose nickname is George, pulls out a wad of his morning's take—about $130—buys coffee in a downtown McDonald's and explains.

Developing raw materials into a narrative lead Tom Blodgett, a reporter for the *State Press,* the daily at Arizona State University, had plenty of material from which to work when he was ready to write his story about Valentina Vega, an ASU volleyball player and a single parent. He had interviewed the woman extensively. He had talked with her teammates and coach. He also watched her interact with her 6-month-old son during a study-hall session in the arena where the team competes.

Deciding on the lead was not easy. Blodgett wanted to make certain that the beginning paragraphs would set the stage for the entire story. There was no need for a summary; this story was not breaking news. Many earlier stories had reported that the woman had to miss a year of play because she was pregnant. This story would update readers, telling them how an unmarried mother is coping with school, her baby and her attempt to be a star volleyball player once again.

Blodgett's first lead was:

Every collegiate athlete faces the challenge of balancing school and sport.

All single mothers know what it is like to juggle a career and parenting.

Perhaps only ASU volleyball player Valentina Vega knows what it is like when the two divergent lives are fused together through circumstances.

Dull, isn't it? The three paragraphs use some important buzz words—"balancing school and sport," "juggle a career and parenting," "divergent lives are fused" (*fused together* is a redundancy)—but they do not project an image; they do not paint a picture that will draw readers into the story. After three paragraphs, readers still have little idea what the story is about, nor do they feel that they are part of any action.

Blodgett went back to work, looking over his notes in search of a better lead. One of the things that he remembered was the study-hall session. In his observations he had made a note on Vega, sitting at a table studying math with her son at her side, propped up against a chair in the arena.

Can there be a better way to show readers sports, school, mom and child? This single observation became the basis of Blodgett's new lead, a narrative that put readers in the middle of the action:

> Valentina Vega sat in the Activity Center studying math with her teammates on the ASU volleyball team.
>
> At her side, propped against a chair, was her newest teammate, the one who changed the way she thinks about sports, school and her life.
>
> Vega, a 21-year-old junior, redshirted last season when she learned she was pregnant. In April, she gave birth to a boy, Brandon Michael Vega.
>
> She has remained single.

The rewrite was a typical narrative lead block. It was simple and easy to understand. It painted a picture in the first two paragraphs so that readers could see the young mother and volleyball player studying with her son at her side. The third paragraph was the nut graph, which told readers the reason for the story.

CONTRAST LEADS

Elements of the Contrast Lead

A *contrast lead* compares or contrasts one person or thing with another, or several people or things with one another. These "old and new," "short and tall" or "yesterday and today" leads tell an audience the way something was and now is. They can be used on any type of news or feature story. Here is an example from the *Williston* (N.D.) *Daily Herald:*

> When Buster Jones took over the little bar on Main Street in Williston, his hair was the color sometimes referred to as "fire in the woodshed."

The opening paragraph told readers that this story would be about Buster Jones, who opened a bar on Main Street when he was a young man. The second paragraph brought them up to date:

> Now there's "snow on the rooftop," and next January Buster will celebrate his 40th year in business at the same little bar. He took a little time Wednes- day to reflect on some of the changes in Buster's Old Inn since he went into business for himself.

Most contrast leads are written in two-paragraph blocks. The first paragraph sets the stage, explaining a past event or perception. The second paragraph brings the audience up to date. There is no reason to keep bouncing readers back and forth before giving them the news peg. It may even be possible to write the contrast lead in a single paragraph, as in this example from the *Milwaukee Sentinel*:

> A baby who was so small at birth that, if she had died, she would have been considered a miscarriage, this week reached 4 pounds and is thriving at St. Joseph's Hospital, physicians and nurses said.

Writing a Contrast Lead

Using observation As in a narrative lead, observation can make a contrast lead crackle. It can help convince an audience to stay with a story until the end.

Here is a three-paragraph contrast lead from the *Los Angeles Times* that used observations in the first two paragraphs:

> One of the things that strikes motorists about the Santa Ana Freeway in downtown Los Angeles is the sharp turn it makes just east of the Civic Center to swing around a big, bulky building emblazoned with the words *Home of Brew 102*.
>
> Each day, thousands of motorists in the freeway's eastbound lanes pass within a few feet of the landmark plant, which was around long before the freeway was built in the mid-1950s.
>
> The old Maier Brewery building, reportedly unused for 13 years, was a formidable obstacle when the freeway was laid out. Now, 30 years later, state highway planners are preparing to bypass it again, as they prepare to build a downtown extension of the San Bernardino Freeway busway along the freeway's north side, next to Union Station.

Using "turn words" Strong *turn words* should be used to introduce the second half of the contrast. The most common turn words are *but, now, today* and *yesterday*. However, there is plenty of opportunity to be creative. For instance, in the above lead on the Los Angeles freeway, the turn word in the third paragraph was *now*. It did not have to be. Instead, the writer could have left out the word and simply started the sentence with *Thirty years later*. Or the paragraph could have started: *Highway planners are hoping the beer plant won't brew trouble again as they prepare to build a downtown extension . . .*

Just a little bit of creativity, often a single word, may mean a larger audience. There's no need to be overly cute; it is just better to avoid the standard words, to avoid being trite. Here is an example from *The News-Sun* in Waukegan, Ill.:

> Anton Kolb, the 51-year-old Libertyville chauffeur who is the state's newest Lotto millionaire, hasn't had a vacation in 12 years.
> He may take a few days off now.

Using a contrast lead for a hard news story   A contrast lead is not reserved for features only. Because it often reports breaking news, it is an effective alternative to a summary lead on a hard news story. As in the above examples, contrasts can be used on news stories about babies who beat the odds and survive and new construction on freeways.

Here are two more examples of hard news stories topped by contrast leads, the first from the *San Jose* (Calif.) *Mercury News* and the second from *The Birmingham* (Ala.) *News:*

> It now takes an hour to drive from San Jose to Palo Alto when commuter traffic clogs Highway 101.
> By the end of this century, it could take twice that long, and Santa Clara County transportation planners are trying to head off that commuter's nightmare.

> On Tuesday, the federal government put a temporary ban on the import of foreign-made assault rifles in the wake of concerns about their availability.
> By Wednesday, stacks of fliers asking people to call their congressmen on April 19 to protest anti-gun laws were being distributed at Birmingham-area gun shops.

Good and bad contrast leads: Two examples   Here is a two-paragraph contrast lead from the *Chicago Sun-Times:*

> When Gloria Jean Wilson was arrested on murder charges last April, police were only able to piece together the first name of the deaf mute woman, so they nicknamed her "Gloria Swanson" in honor of the legendary actress.
> Yesterday, following months of language training so she could tell her story in court, Gloria was found not guilty in the April 25 murder of Wilbert Taylor by Criminal Court Judge Earl Strayhorn. Gloria was convicted of involuntary manslaughter and sentenced to one year probation.

Although this lead was wordy (both the first and second paragraphs could have been tightened), it is much better than another contrast lead on the same story, this one from the *Chicago Tribune:*

She is a deaf mute, and she survives by collecting aluminum cans on the Near West Side.

She lives by her wits and knows only a crude sign language of the streets. When she was arrested and charged with fatally stabbing a transient in April, she refused to give police her last name and, for a month, she sat in jail.

Her name is Gloria, and, somewhere along the line, prosecutors began referring to her as Gloria Swanson. Although they were trying her for murder, they admired her work ethic.

"Gloria is one of those people that slipped through the cracks," said Assistant State's Atty. Thomas Roche. "She has some education, but she mainly walks the streets. We had no choice but to charge her."

On Wednesday, with the help of an interpreter, Gloria Wilson, who is 24 and lives at 2710 W. Cortez St., told her story for the first time.

After a short hearing, in which she testified that the man she stabbed sought to rape her, Criminal Court Judge Earl Strayhorn found her guilty of involuntary manslaughter and sentenced her to 12 months' probation.

In this second example, readers are not given the news peg until the sixth paragraph. As in the first story, the writer attempted to contrast Gloria as she was then to as she is now, but the readers were left hanging too long. They should have been told in the second paragraph—as they were in the *Sun-Times* lead—that Gloria was cleared of murder charges but found guilty of involuntary manslaughter. Most of the material in the second, third, fourth and fifth paragraphs of the *Tribune* story should have been used later, after readers were told the news.

STACCATO LEADS

Elements of the Staccato Lead

A *staccato lead* is made up of a short burst of phrases that carry an audience into a story by dangling some of its key elements in front of them. It is meant to tease readers and to set the mood for the story, as in these examples:

Friday. The night the music stopped.

The first day of his prison term. 3,649 to go.

The staccato lead can be used on newspaper news and feature stories, but it is most commonly used in television news stories. For example, on a story about a reunion of Vietnam War veterans, an Independent News Network story began with tape of a veteran saying:

"THIS IS BEAUTIFUL. THIS IS GREAT."

Then, the voice-over from the reporter told viewers:

IT WAS A HAPPY REUNION FOR VIETNAM WAR VETERANS.

On the same day, *The New York Times,* using a summary news lead for the same event, reported on the front page:

> Vietnam veterans accepted New York City's thanks yesterday at a bittersweet tickertape parade through the canyons of lower Manhattan.

The staccato is also often used in magazine stories, as in this example from *Rolling Stone:*

> "Sherman McCoy, 816 Park Avenue." At the instant the detective on the other end of the line, Martin, mentioned the name and the address, Larry Kramer happened to be leaning back in his swivel chair looking at a plastic cup of coffee on Ray Andriutti's desk.

Writing a Staccato Lead

After the short phrase or burst of phrases, a sentence or paragraph must tell the audience the news peg of the story. Readers or viewers should not have to wait to find out what the story is about.

An *Orlando Sentinel* story on color schemes for apartments began with a staccato lead:

> Off-white or beige walls. Brown or gray carpet. Beige vinyl kitchen floors.

The phrases should have brought readers into the story quickly. In the second paragraph they were told the reason for the story, which was about using something other than natural colors in decorating an apartment:

> These are the staples of apartment decor. Which is fine if you are into earth tones and neutrals. But what if you have a brighter color scheme in mind and the rules forbid any change?

The *Orlando Sentinel* also used a staccato lead in a story about a new play that would be performed on the roof of a downtown parking garage. It began:

> Sixth floor, Orlando City Parking Garage, 53 W. Central Blvd., downtown Orlando.

In the second paragraph, readers were told:

> Things are happening on the roof of the city parking garage, but not what the place's builders had in mind—there are hardly any cars in sight. In their place are a unicyclist, a roller skater, a rock band, a handful of parents and some three dozen kids, putting in one of their last rehearsals for the original young people's musical "Stack 'Em in the Streets."

Elements of the Direct-Address Lead

In a *direct-address lead*, the news or feature writer communicates directly with the audience by using the word *you* in the lead. These leads give writers an opportunity to reach out to their audience, to include them as individuals in a story. Instead of telling how experts say spark plugs should be changed, a writer tells an individual reader or viewer: This is how you should change your spark plugs. The direct-address lead can be effective because it works like a recruiting poster, telling readers, "we want you" to take the time to complete this story.

A direct-address lead is usually one paragraph long. The second paragraph of the story provides the news peg, as in this example from the *Orange County* (Calif.) *Register:*

> MIAMI—Your corner gas station—and the entire U.S. oil industry—is about to change more dramatically than ever in the 100-year history of the car, experts say.
>
> Gas prices, which have been creeping up, are on the way to a nearly 20-cent jump, a leading oil analyst said. A sizable number of oil refineries face extinction, according to the federal government. Spot gas shortages are likely. And some motorists will start hearing their engines knock annoyingly.

A direct-address lead can also string readers along for two or three paragraphs before the nut graph is written. Here is an example from the *Mohave Valley News* in Bullhead City, Ariz.:

> Imagine you're in Lake Havasu High School basketball coach Chuck Taylor's place.
>
> Your team is rated No. 3 in the Arizona Republic's Class AA top five poll; it's off to a rocketing 7–2 start and it has won the Parker Christmas Tournament for the first time ever.
>
> You're opening AA-Conference action tonight—but not against No. 4-ranked Kingman High. Your team is playing in Bullhead City against 2–8 Mohave High, a team long on hard luck, short on experience and short on height. What do you tell your players before they take the floor at 7 p.m.?
>
> "We're looking at the game like we're going against Kingman," said Taylor. "It's a conference game. It's an important game and I expect a lot of intensity from the kids. We aren't taking Mohave lightly."

This lead on a sports story was effective because it put readers in Coach Taylor's place. Then it let him talk directly to readers and also give the news peg of the story. Along with involving readers in the story, the first three paragraphs also provided the following essential information:

Lake Havasu's record and rating.

Conference play is opening.

Mohave's record and weaknesses.

Time the game starts.

Writing a Direct-Address Lead

Use direct-address leads sparingly   Direct address is not for every story. It is not appropriate on breaking news, where it is necessary to give a brief summary of the event without becoming personally involved with an audience.

If there is a fire and three people are killed, the lead would probably say:

> Three people were killed today in a fire on West 35th Street.

It would not say:

> Imagine what you would have seen if you were walking down West
> 35th Street today.

As the sports lead from the *Mohave Valley News* illustrates, however, writers can weave the news into direct-address leads.

Be prepared to rewrite direct-address leads   Some editors dislike direct-address leads because they believe that reporters should never talk directly to readers. Editors also argue that direct-address leads are often aimed at a narrow segment of the readership or generalize in a way that would anger readers, as in:

> You wouldn't think this city could come up with such a creative plan,
> but . . .

If a direct-address lead is the best for the story, discuss it with an editor and defend it if necessary. Editors who say that they do not like direct-address leads can often be talked into running them if the writer makes a good enough case. Otherwise, be prepared to rewrite.

The next leads to be discussed—question leads, quote leads and "none of the above"—are the toughest ones to get into print. The reason: Editors want the news high in the story. They do not want their writers to flimflam the audience.

QUESTION LEADS

Elements of Question Leads

Some editors would say that *question leads*—which begin a story by asking an audience a question or a series of questions—are never acceptable because they rarely work, are overused or force people to look for answers that should have been in the opening paragraph. Also, editors contend that writers sometimes rely on question leads as crutches, using them when they cannot decide what the key point is. Despite the obstacles, questions can be used effectively to begin news and feature stories. Just be sure to use them sparingly and appropriately.

Answer the question quickly   The key to writing a question lead is to answer the question as quickly as possible. Ideally, the question should be answered in the first paragraph; if not, it must be answered in the second. Do not leave an audience hanging, trying to figure out what the story is about.

For example, here is a question lead by a UPI writer, Iris Krasnow, that worked. Notice how she answered her brief staccato questions immediately, rather than asking them all before giving the answers:

WASHINGTON   (UPI)—Waltzing? It's in. Bedhopping? Out. Miss Manners etiquette? In. Raunchy locker room talk? Out.

Marriage? In. Non-commitment? It's sweet history.

Seems all that is left to the torrid sexual revolution is the faint smoke of candlelit romance, one on one. Even rocker Linda Ronstadt has turned to vintage torch songs—what's going on?

In this question lead from *The Wall Street Journal*, the writer, Christopher Conte, waited until the second paragraph to give his readers answers:

FAIRFAX   COUNTY,   Va.—Every weekday morning, Gretchen Davis drives down Fairfax Farms Road on the way to work at the Ayr Hill Country Store in nearby Vienna. Sounds pastoral, doesn't it?

But a short way down the road, Mrs. Davis reaches Route 50, a major arterial highway through this Washington, D.C., suburb. There, a river of cars

roars through the suburban calm. "Sometimes you have to wait 20 minutes just for a gap in the traffic big enough to get out—and even then you have to take a chance," the shopkeeper says. For Mrs. Davis, stop-and-go traffic often stretches what used to be a pleasant 20-minute commute into a nerve-wracking hour.

Tease the audience   Conte's question lead was effective because it teased readers, telling them to read the next paragraph to find the answer. The story began in the peaceful setting of the suburbs, but told readers almost immediately that suburbia has grown so rapidly that it is facing the same traffic nightmares plaguing big cities. Although it could have started with a summary lead telling readers that years of explosive and unplanned growth have flooded the suburbs with too many cars, it used a question instead to move readers from peaceful image to stark reality.

Combine question leads with direct address   Question leads can use direct address to ask readers, individually, a question. In his story on the great number of clubs in the United States Bill Marvel of *The Dallas Morning News* wrote:

Say you're fed up with the state of affairs in Washington. But Ross Perot isn't running. Why not secede from the union? Join the Free Territory of Ely-Chatelain, a group of households each of which has declared itself to be a sovereign and independent nation.

When *The Daily Northwestern* at Northwestern University ran a story on demands by women to be paid the same as men for comparable jobs, it began:

> Okay, you're the boss. Who's worth more to you—your secretaries or your truck drivers? Your librarians or your electricians? Your carpenters or your nurses?

QUOTE LEADS

Elements of Quote Leads

A *quote lead* allows a central character to begin a news or feature story by talking directly to the audience. The quotation may be the most powerful one in the story, or it may set the tone for what is to follow.

Writing a Quote Lead

General guidelines for quote leads Use the quote lead sparingly. Most newspaper editors ban quote leads on breaking news stories because quotations may not provide the major points of the story.

Quote leads are particularly effective in broadcasting, where a story begins with tape of a central character speaking dramatically and then switches to the reporter, who ties the quotation to the news event. An example of this was given in the previous discussion of staccato leads, where the broadcast story began with Vietnam War veterans saying, "This is beautiful. This is great."

When writing a quote lead for print, put the attribution in the first paragraph so that readers do not have to wait to find out who is speaking. Do not write a long quotation in the opening paragraph and then begin the second paragraph with *Those were the words of . . . .* Also, try to incorporate some elements of news with the quotation in the first paragraph. If this is not possible, put some news in the second paragraph.

Avoid carrying a quote lead for more than a paragraph or two. There is no need to keep an audience hanging before attributing the quotation and giving the news peg. Use more quotations after the news is reported.

Here are three examples of quote leads. The first one is from the *New York Daily News,* with the attribution at the beginning; the second is from the *College Heights Herald* of Western Kentucky University, with the attribution at the end; and the third is from the *Mohave Valley News* in Bullhead City, Ariz., with the attribution in the middle:

> As Yogi Berra would say: "It ain't over till it's over." But yesterday it was over—at least for now.

> "Dumb jocks are not being born, they are being systematically created," Dr. Harry Edwards said at a lecture Tuesday night in Garrett Auditorium.

> "It was bedlam," smiled George Burden. "It really was. My teammates told me I looked a little white in the face and that I should sit down."

Don't misrepresent in a quote lead   Before writing a quote lead, make sure it is powerful enough to draw in an audience or significant enough to set the tone of the story. Also, be careful that the quotation, if used out of context, does not misrepresent the speaker's point.

For example, the mayor might say: "I'm the boss. I'm the person who ultimately has to decide if we are going to spend all that money on the downtown renewal project. Of course, the voters can change my mind." In this case, a reporter would be misrepresenting the mayor's point if a news story began:

> "I'm the boss," the mayor said today.

Beware of libel when using a quote lead   Before using a quotation, screen it carefully for libel. The fact that someone said something does not allow a writer to use it worry-free. In this story from the *Kenosha* (Wis.) *News*, a potentially damaging quotation was used in the lead:

> "I'm glad he's in custody so he can stop killing people," said Vernita Wheat's brother, Anthony, 18, when he was told Friday the man accused of killing his sister had been taken into custody.

The suspect was later found guilty, and the chances were slim that he would take action against the paper, but the writer should have been more careful. Reporters do not have license to use anything uttered by a source.

"NONE OF THE ABOVE" LEADS

When Is a Lead "None of the Above"?

Sometimes, a lead is "none of the above." It simply will not fit into one of the categories described here. It may be a combination of several of the categories, or it may be what some editors call a "freak lead," which defies definition. It may be lines from a published poem or song that introduce a news or feature story. It may be a poem or song that the writer makes up, as in:

Today is Tuesday.

A day to sail.

Tomorrow is Wednesday.

Beware of a gale.

This example points out the fundamental problems with "none of the above" leads: they may be too cute; they may be difficult to understand; or they may turn readers off.

Still, if they are used sparingly and appropriately, these leads can work, as in this story from the *Milwaukee Sentinel:*

> Dear God,
>
> Things are rather confused here at the State Senate in Madison.
>
> On Monday morning, Senate President Fred Risser (D-Madison) was quoted as saying senators had abandoned their formal opening prayer at the beginning of each session.

Combining Several Types of Leads

"None of the above" leads probably work best when they consist of a combination of several categories of leads, rather than a poem, a song or some other type of strange beginning. Here is a lead from the *New York Daily News* on a story about an 18.6-mile walk to raise money for the March of Dimes and a 36-mile bicycle tour. It is a summary; it's an anecdote; and it also has a touch of music in it.

> Over hills, over dales, 40,000 people hit the city trails yesterday for charity and fun.

For a story about a new reference book on fashion in China, Lenore Magida, a correspondent for the *San Francisco Examiner,* used a lead block that combined quotations, a narrative, a direct address, a question and a strong nut graph:

> SHANGHAI—"Bikinis are out!" yells Lo Chaotian.
>
> "Bikinis are out!" cries Wang Jianhua, who asks that you please call her Patty.
>
> "Bikinis are out!" they shout in unison.
>
> The message is believable. But the messengers?
>
> Lo and Wang are colleagues at the Shanghai Translation publishing house. They do dictionaries and other reference volumes.

For his story on women's chances in politics in Arizona, Steve Yozwiak of *The Arizona Republic* used a lead block that contained staccato, question and direct address:

> McCain. Rhodes. Stump. Kyl. Kolbe.
>
> Do these names look familiar?
>
> You may be seeing them in the newspapers for two more years—or even longer.
>
> In the "Year of the Woman" and in an atmosphere of anti-incumbent fever, Arizona voters may buck a national trend in November and return those six men to Congress.

This unusual, creative photograph of three collegiate swimmers is the visual counterpart of a special lead that uses creative writing to draw readers into the story.
(Photo by Sean Openshaw)

CREATING EFFECTIVE LEADS

USING STRONG VERBS IN LEADS

Reporters must write sentences that are concise, accurate and easy to understand. A strong, colorful verb in each of these sentences will make the writing even better. This is particularly important in special leads, which may not provide the main news of the story right away. In these cases, the words, rather than the news, draw an audience inside.

A vivid verb can animate a sentence, as in, "The hostages snaked their way along the dusty road to freedom." Words can paint a picture. Sentences can describe a snowstorm, a riot, a trial or a parade so accurately that an audience can see the event.

Here is a narrative lead on a story that appeared in the *Des Moines Sunday Register.* By using vivid verbs in his narrative, the writer, Bob Shaw, effectively drew his readers into the story.

MESQUAKIE SETTLEMENT, IA.— It was still dark when the 7-year-old boy was awakened by rustling mice beneath the tattered sofa that served as his bed. His little sister, still groggy and struggling with the zipper on her coat, lurched past. Judging from the wind hissing through the window cracks, the outhouse seat would be cold.

"Look at this place," the father muttered, as the seven-member family stirred to life in the condemned two-bedroom house just before dawn.

Imagine how dull Shaw's lead would have been if he had used dismal verbs:

MESQUAKIE SETTLEMENT, IA.—Mice under his bed woke up the 7-year-old boy. His tired sister went past him. There was wind coming through the window cracks, which meant that the outhouse seat would be cold.

"Look at this place," their father said as the seven-member family got up in their two-bedroom house before dawn.

Here is a summary lead from *The Washington Post. Grew* could have been used as the verb of the sentence, but *picked up steam* was used instead. The difference between the verbs is subtle, but the more vivid verb painted a better picture for readers.

Seven persons, including a Maryland congressman and four demonstrators in New York, were arrested today as an ongoing protest against apartheid in South Africa spread to a second city and picked up steam with the announcement of similar demonstrations today in Boston and Los Angeles.

In a *Kenosha* (Wis.) *News* story on an authorization by the Wisconsin Public Service Commission to withdraw party-line telephone service in areas where it is seldom used, the lead was:

Wisconsin Bell is hanging up on the party line.

And a colorful verb was used in the lead of this story in the *Milwaukee Sentinel* about a possible tax increase in Wisconsin on packages of cigarettes. (The unusual spelling of *cigarette* in the story is *Sentinel* style.)

There's a catch in Gov. Earl's new budget that will have Wisconsin cigaret smokers continuing to cough up 41 cents a pack in taxes even if 8 cents of the federal tax expires as scheduled Oct. 1.

When writing the lead, or any other paragraph in a story, it is important to pick the most precise verb, the one that enhances each sentence and makes the scene clearer to an audience. This does not mean that writers should try to surprise or shock their audiences with a spectacular verb in each sentence. When a 17-year-old boy is shot and killed by a shotgun blast, the lead should simply say that he was shot and killed, not, "A 17-year-old boy was blown away today."

Be accurate and colorful, not cute, sensational or shoddy.

CHOOSING A LEAD: WHICH LEAD, AND WHEN?

The nice thing, but sometimes the most annoying thing, about writing leads is that there is really no "best" lead or "most correct" lead for a news or feature story. Tradition and time—either the time people spend reading or viewing news or the limited time and space journalists have to present it—still dictate that summary leads are the best on hard news stories. However, there are exceptions.

For instance, if a story breaks in time for a noon broadcast, the lead may be:

THREE FIREFIGHTERS WERE INJURED TODAY WHEN FIRE RACED
THROUGH THE 16-STORY FIRST NATIONAL BANK BUILDING, THE
CITY'S TALLEST.

On the 6 p.m. news, the lead of the story will probably be changed, even if there are no new developments. The hard news will still be reported, but this time the lead may be:

FOR YEARS CITY OFFICIALS HAVE COMPLAINED THAT THE FIRE
DEPARTMENT DOES NOT HAVE ENOUGH EQUIPMENT FOR FIGHTING
HIGH-RISK FIRES.
THEIR FEARS WERE REALIZED TODAY WHEN FIRE RACED
THROUGH THE 16-STORY FIRST NATIONAL BANK BUILDING.

The only real rule in writing leads is that there really are no rules. Writers do not sit at their computer terminals and say to themselves, "I'm going to write a summary lead on this story" or "This story deserves a contrast lead or a narrative lead." They usually write the lead before the story, although sometimes they construct the story before writing what they think is the best lead.

Several things help writers decide on the lead:

- *Their own creativity.* It is always nice to be different from everyone else, as long as the audience understands the final product.
- *What their sources said.* Writers have to work with what their sources said or did. They cannot make up quotations or narrative to enhance their stories.
- *Their observations.* Writers are limited by what they see, hear, smell and touch during an interview. They are not allowed to embellish or obfuscate.
- *Tradition.* Reporters usually know when to write a summary lead and when to steer away from it.
- *Their editors and news directors.* Face it. Reporters write for editors and news directors. Some bosses like only summaries; some will also accept narrative and contrast leads but no others; and some think that quote leads are fine.
- *Space.* A reporter may come up with a terrific three-paragraph lead that takes up 2 inches. But if an editor says, "You have only 8 inches of space," that wonderful lead will probably be abandoned.

To illustrate how it is possible to write different leads on a single story, here is part of a news story from the *Chicago Tribune:*

BRADFORD, England—Police said Sunday that the final death toll could exceed 85 in a fire that engulfed the main grandstand at a soccer stadium in this city in northern England Saturday.

On a day that civic celebrations had been planned to honor the championship Bradford City soccer club, flags flew at half-staff to mourn what Sports Minister Neil Macfarlane called "the worst tragedy we have ever seen in English football (soccer)."

Some spectators died in their seats as the flames jumped through the wooden stands within four minutes. Other spectators, their clothes and hair aflame, were crushed to death in a stampede to escape through padlocked gates.

As police began trying to identify 52 bodies recovered so far from the charred wreckage, a spokesman said 24 people remained unaccounted for and 12 of the 211 injured in the blaze were fighting for their lives.

Although the cause of the fire remained unknown, West Yorkshire Chief Constable Colin Sampson said that arson could not be ruled out. But he added, "The early indication is that it was not a deliberate criminal act."

The fire began late in the first half of a game between Bradford City and Lincoln City, of the English Football League's Third Division.

Many bodies were burned beyond recognition and Sampson said they would have to be identified through teeth and personal possessions.

Members of the crowd of 12,000 told horrifying stories of how spectators were burned.

"The place was full of children, families and old people. I saw a man on fire and I don't want to see anything like that again," said John Waite.

This story is a *follow-up*, which provides the latest news of a story that broke—was reported—earlier. In this case, the breaking story on Saturday would have reported the fire, probably with a summary lead, and given the preliminary death count. The follow-up, also with a summary lead, says that the final toll may reach 85. (For a complete discussion on writing follow-ups, see Chapter 6.)

The story could also have started with any of the special leads except "none of the above," which simply would not have been appropriate on such a hard news story. Here are some examples.

First, a narrative lead:

> The flags flew at half-staff in Bradford City as West Yorkshire Chief Constable Colin Sampson and others dug through the rubble of the burned soccer club and hunted for clues and bodies.

Second, a contrast lead:

> It started as a day of celebration to honor the championship Bradford City soccer club in its game against Lincoln City.
>
> It ended in tragedy as fire engulfed the main grandstand in the city's soccer stadium, killing as many as 85 and injuring 211.

Third, a staccato lead:

> Soccer on Saturday. A tradition. A celebration. Now, a nightmare.

Fourth, a direct-address lead:

You cannot comprehend the nightmare of Bradford City until you have walked through the charred wreckage, where spectators, their clothes and hair aflame, were crushed to death in a stampede.

Fifth, a question lead:

Was it arson or was it accident that sparked the tragic fire at the Bradford City soccer stadium?

Finally, a quote lead:

"I saw a man on fire, and I don't want to see anything like that again," a spectator, John Waite, said Sunday as he recalled the horror of the fire at the Bradford City soccer stadium.

When there is a chemical spill and workers are injured,
reporters will probably write inverted-pyramid news stories
about the event.
(Photo by Sean Openshaw)

5

Organizing
a News Story

Organizing a news or feature story effectively is

important. If the lead draws readers or viewers

into the story, what follows must interest them to

the end. To do this, reporters must write in a clear

style that flows from paragraph to paragraph.

In this chapter . . .

Inverted-Pyramid Style
An Example of the Inverted Pyramid: Covering a Suicide Attempt | Organizing an Inverted Pyramid: Guidelines to Follow | Improving an Inverted-Pyramid Story: An Example of Revision

Hourglass Style
Advantages of the Hourglass Style | An Example of Hourglass Style: A Bizarre Accident | Organizing an Hourglass | When to Use the Hourglass

Organizing A Broadcast News Story
Basic Considerations | An Example of Organizing a Broadcast Story: A Shooting in Indianapolis

When the call came in, it seemed almost unbelievable. At about the time extra police and fire units were being summoned over the police radio, which is monitored in the newsroom, a hysterical woman telephoned the city desk to say that someone was dangling upside down outside a window of a high-rise apartment building.

Within seconds, reporters and photographers were in action. If someone was indeed dangling out of a high-rise, it could be a major news story, either of the person falling to his or her death or of a dramatic rescue by firefighters and police officers. Reporters never know what they will find when they are sent to the scene of an emergency, where news is breaking, but this is where they must be at their best. Every second will be critical.

In this case there indeed was someone dangling out of the window, 16 floors above a busy street in Chicago. She was a 49-year-old woman who reportedly had swallowed sleeping pills and ammonia and had slit her throat before diving out the window. However, somehow her heavy pullover robe had snagged on the window, which slammed shut, leaving her dangling upside down. As about 100 onlookers and scores of firefighters and police gathered beneath her, she kicked frantically to free the robe so that she could complete her attempt at suicide.

Two of the reporters assigned to the story were Lauren Silverman and Mark Eissman of the *Chicago Tribune*. While Silverman raced to the scene, Eissman worked the phones from the newsroom. It was also Eissman's job to write the story.

Because activity at the scene was over within minutes, most of the work of gathering information for the story had to be done over the phone. "All we really knew was that some woman apparently was attempting to commit suicide and somehow dangled out the window for about 10 minutes before being rescued," Eissman said.

INVERTED-PYRAMID STYLE

When reporters cover news, they are always thinking of the stories they must write. They usually write the lead first, often composing it mentally while interviewing sources or checking records. When they write the story, they must present the news in a clear style that flows from paragraph to paragraph.

Most breaking news stories are written in *inverted-pyramid* style, in which the most important of the five W's and the H are in the lead (as described in Chapter 3). What comes after the lead is also important. The lead should interest readers; the *body*, or middle, of the story should hold them until the conclusion.

AN EXAMPLE OF THE INVERTED PYRAMID: COVERING A SUICIDE ATTEMPT

The story that Eissman wrote on the woman dangling from the window illustrates a typical inverted pyramid with a beginning, middle and conclusion. The *who, what, where, when, why* and *how* of the event were high in the story,

which could have been trimmed from the bottom. Along with the hard news facts, transitions and quotations were used to keep the story flowing and readers reading. And it ended with news, albeit the least important, which was an effective way to conclude the story without saying "the end." There were even a couple of things the writers should have avoided, which will be discussed as the story is analyzed paragraph by paragraph.

Preliminaries

How should a suicide be covered? Despite a policy at the *Tribune* not to run stories of suicides or suicide attempts, Eissman said that his editors wanted to print this story because of the drama of the attempt and the rescue. However, they decided not to reveal the woman's name or address.

The *Tribune*'s policy on suicide or suicide-attempt stories is not unusual. Most newspapers choose not to run such stories because of sensitivity to the feelings of families or other survivors. Most follow the same general guideline: they do not report a suicide or an attempt unless it is unusual or involves a well-known person.

In fact, only a minority of newspapers even use the word *suicide* in obituaries. A national survey of 165 newspaper managing editors selected at random found that 62 percent of the newspapers never use the word *suicide* in obituaries, even if it is determined to be the cause of death. The word is sometimes used by 21 percent of the newspapers and always used by 17 percent. Of the editors who said that they use the word, 91 percent insist that attribution be made to an official source such as a coroner. (The writing of obituaries is covered in Chapter 13.)

"After we finished, I thought one last time about our decision to write the story the way we did," Eissman said. "I thought the work of the fire department should be highlighted. I was comfortable about our decision to say as little about the woman as possible."

Gathering the facts To cover the story adequately, Eissman had to telephone many people before his deadline, and he ran into the same obstacles that all reporters face. "I called the head of the fire department battalion that had responded to the call and was told he'd call me back shortly," Eissman said. "I tried to reach a relative of the woman, but there was no answer."

He was able to talk to a spokesperson at the hospital where the woman was taken, who gave him her age and told him that she was in fair condition. Next he checked a *Haines Criss-Cross Directory*, which reporters use to find names and phone numbers when they know only addresses. A directory is a big help in covering breaking news because reporters often know only *where* something is happening. By looking up an address in the directory, they can find the identity and phone number of the person at the address.

Eissman wanted to find the names and phone numbers of the woman's neighbors so that he could try to find people who knew the woman and who could perhaps provide insight into why she was trying to kill herself.

"Most said they didn't know the woman," the reporter said. "Finally one of the neighbors said she knew quite a bit about the woman but didn't really want to talk about it. I asked her why not, and she said she did not like to talk about her neighbor's business. I asked her if she would talk to me if I didn't use her name, and she said yes."

Eissman said that he had no problem speaking to the neighbor off the record because the story was more about the rescue attempt than about the woman herself. Still, he was trying to find out what would make this woman want to kill herself.

"The neighbor said the woman had been despondent over the recent breakup of her second marriage and was suffering from a life-threatening disease," Eissman said. "I called back the hospital spokesman to try to confirm what the neighbor had told me. He said he was aware that the woman had been suffering from a life-threatening disease. The information about the disease and a recently failed marriage was later confirmed by another neighbor and the woman's relatives."

Finally, the battalion chief who directed the rescue returned Eissman's call. The reporter said:

"He told me the rescue attempt was the most dramatic he'd ever seen. I asked him every question I could think of about the incident. I asked him how the department was alerted to the call, and he said he wasn't sure but would check. He then told me the woman had ingested ammonia and sleeping pills, had slit her wrists and had jumped out the window.

"He said her robe snagged on the bottom part of the window, and the window slammed shut, leaving her dangling in midair."

Writing the Story

The lead   Eissman wrote a summary lead for the story, which carried his and Silverman's byline. It emphasized *what* and *how:*

> For 10 heart-stopping minutes Saturday morning, a 49-year-old woman dangled upside down outside the 16th-floor window of her Lake Shore Drive apartment, saved from falling only by a heavy pullover robe that had snagged on a window part.

The lead also told readers *when* (Saturday morning), *who* (a 49-year-old woman) and *where* (Lake Shore Drive apartment). It was strong because it contained vivid descriptions and verbs:

For 10 heart-stopping minutes
Heavy pullover robe
Dangled
Saved
Snagged

The lead was not as crisp as it could have been, though. It would have been stronger if the writer and his editors had pared it to 35 or fewer words and had eliminated the introductory phrase. They could have retained the W's and the vivid descriptions and verbs by writing:

A 49-year-old woman dangled upside down outside the 16th floor of her Lake Shore Drive apartment for 10 minutes Saturday, saved from falling by a pullover robe that snagged on a window part.

The body of the story   After the lead—from the second to the final paragraph—an inverted-pyramid story is structured to present the news in order of descending importance. It is usually not built chronologically. The most important of the W's and H are put in the lead. The second most important are in the second paragraph, the third most important in the third paragraph and so on. Each paragraph further explains or complements the ones before it.

In their second paragraph, Eissman and Silverman answered the *why* of the story. By combining information that Eissman gathered over the phone with Silverman's observations at the scene, the paragraph told readers that the woman wanted to commit suicide. This information was kept out of the lead because the writers and their editors wanted to stress that this story was about how the woman was saved, not about her intention to die.

> The woman, who reportedly had swallowed sleeping pills and ammonia and slit her throat and wrists before diving out the window, kicked frantically to free the robe and complete the suicide attempt while more than 100 onlookers gathered and firefighters broke down seven doors in trying to find her apartment.

"As we wrote the story, additional questions about details of the incident came to mind," Eissman said. "The chief called back to tell me that a 9-year-old boy had called from a nearby building and had alerted firefighters about the suicide attempt."

Eissman said that even while his editors were reading the story, he again called Michael Hughes, the battalion chief, to get additional details.

"I asked what kind of robe she was wearing," Eissman said. "Hughes had to ask others involved in the rescue before he could answer. I asked him why he picked the firefighter he did to rescue the woman, which was done by tying a safety belt around her leg and pulling her in through the window. Hughes said, 'That guy was skinny enough to fit through the opening of the window.'

"I confirmed other details we were using in the story. I covered many elements of the story again to be sure they were accurate. I questioned Hughes about every part of the window until I could figure out how the woman's robe got caught."

Hughes was introduced in the third paragraph. He was the source for most of the story; therefore, he needed to be introduced early. As in most inverted pyramids, the opening paragraphs provided the W's and H and enticed readers into the story. Now it was time to introduce the main sources and to explain the primary elements:

> "Her body was entirely, totally out of the window," said 1st Battalion Chief Michael Hughes, who directed the rescue from the ground. "Her head stretched down to the 15th floor."

In the fourth through seventh paragraphs, Hughes was allowed to tell the story through a series of *direct quotations,* which tell readers precisely what a source said, and *paraphrases,* which provide the essence of what a source said. To keep stories from reading like speeches, writers should avoid long strings of direct quotations.

The bottom of the woman's full-length, red velvet robe was knotted on an 8-inch metal opening mechanism of a transom-type window, Hughes said. The floor-level window had snapped up as the woman jumped off it, catching the robe, he said.

"My heart was pounding," he said. "She could have gone at any second. It was a miracle. I've been on the job for 31 years, and this was the most dramatic rescue I've ever seen."

Firefighters were called to the 29-story condominium on North Lake Shore Drive at about 9 a.m. by a boy in a nearby building, Hughes said.

"When we got there, the hardest part was telling what floor she was on. At first we thought she was on the 24th. We had about 27 guys search and search until we found the right apartment."

During the telephone interview, Hughes gave Eissman the names of the firefighters who pulled the woman to safety. The reporter talked to one of them briefly, and now he wanted to introduce the man. To do this, Eissman had to write a *transitional paragraph,* which told readers that the story was passing from one area to another. By beginning the eighth paragraph with a transition—*Once inside the apartment*—the story moved readers from outside the building to inside the apartment, where firefighters rescued the woman:

Once inside the apartment, Hughes said, firefighters slid a safety belt through an 18-inch opening between the window and the frame and lassoed the woman's leg as she resisted fiercely.

"If we opened the window (any farther), she would have fallen," said fire-

fighter Rory O'Shea, who did the lassoing. Firefighter George Beary helped pull the woman in.

O'Shea, 40, who is 5 feet 7 inches tall and weighs 145 pounds, was selected for the task "because he was skinny enough to fit through the opening of the window," Hughes said.

Now, through another transition, readers were moved from inside the apartment to the street below:

Below, four civilians joined 11 firefighters in holding out a 16-foot circular safety net.

"Right there I had to give them a crash course on how to hold it," Hughes said. "I was yelling for them to keep their feet forward and their arms away from their bodies so they wouldn't break their ribs if she fell."

Hughes said firefighters had tried to reach the woman with a hydraulic ladder that was too short, so they had to resort to the lasso maneuver.

As the woman was pulled to safety, applause erupted from the street and other battalion units where firefighters were listening to the ordeal, Hughes said.

The conclusion   Writers do not conclude news stories by telling readers "the end." They simply quit writing after they have reported all the pertinent information they can get into the allocated space. They often conclude a story with a direct quotation, letting a source talk directly to readers. The quotation should tie readers emotionally to the story, reminding them that the writing has ended but that the story and the people involved in it have not. For example, a story on a town hit by a tornado could end with a local homeowner saying, "We won't let this drive us out. We will rebuild."

The final paragraph can also report additional facts, which remind readers that only the writing—not the story—is ending. This is how Eissman and Silverman's story ended. The last paragraph described the woman further and updated her condition, reminding readers that this person's story was not over. If the story had been about a woman's attempted suicide, the information in the last paragraph would have been much higher. But since the story was about a heroic rescue, the description of the woman and her condition, although important, was used at the end:

> The woman, described by relatives and neighbors as despondent over a failed second marriage and a life-threatening disease, was listed in fair condition Saturday evening in Rush-Presbyterian Hospital.

ORGANIZING AN INVERTED PYRAMID: GUIDELINES TO FOLLOW

Every story is different, but there are some basic guidelines that should generally be followed in organizing an inverted pyramid.

Guideline 1: Write a Terse Lead

Write a brief lead paragraph of no more than 35 words that gives the major news of the story. Write a second paragraph providing major points of the news event that would not fit in the opening paragraph.

Guideline 2: Provide Background

Use the third paragraph, and more paragraphs if necessary, to provide *background*, which explains things for readers. Background can come from a source, who explains something technical; or from the reporter, to make a story clearer. Even breaking news stories need background paragraphs to explain what has happened before. For example, in a story on the first day of a murder trial, the writer may use the third, fourth and fifth paragraphs to give details of the crime.

If there is more than one major element, use background paragraphs high in the story to wrap them all up. Then each one can be developed later.

Guideline 3: Present News in Order of Descending Importance

Continue reporting news of the story using paragraphs in order of descending importance. Inverted pyramids are seldom constructed chronologically. When reporters want to write a chronology, they often use another writing form, the hourglass, which will be explained later in this chapter.

Guideline 4: Use Quotations Throughout

A good time to introduce direct quotations is after the audience has been given the major news and background information. Separate direct quotations by using supplementary news and paraphrases. Sprinkle quotations throughout the story rather than string them together. Remember, quotations are useful because they let people in the news communicate directly to an audience.

Guideline 5: Use Transitions

A paraphrase, a background paragraph, a paragraph with additional news or even a direct quotation can be used as transition to move readers smoothly from one paragraph to another. Transition alerts an audience that a shift or change is coming up.

Transitions can be developed in several ways:

- *Numerically*—first, second, third, etc.
- *By time*—at 3 p.m., by noon, three hours later, etc.
- *Geographically*—in Tucson, outside the home, District 3 voters, etc.
- *With words*—also, but, once, meanwhile, therefore, in other action, however, below, above, etc.

Guideline 6: Do Not Editorialize

Reporters are eyewitnesses to news. Their job is to tell an audience what they saw and what other people said. They should not include their personal opinions. If they think that something is rotten, they let the direct quotations from people involved in the story support, and rebut, their own opinion.

Guideline 7: Avoid "The End"

Continue reporting news until the end. This helps readers know that even though the writing has stopped, the story has not. An effective way to conclude a news story is with a direct quotation.

IMPROVING AN INVERTED-PYRAMID STORY: AN EXAMPLE OF REVISION

Not every story is as exciting to cover and to write as that of a woman dangling upside down from a high-rise apartment. Many of the stories that reporters cover deal with more routine occurrences, such as traffic accidents, speeches by politicians and actions by governmental bodies. To keep their audiences interested in these stories, reporters must avoid bland and disorganized writing. They must write crisply and vividly.

Initial Version

Here is a story written for a university daily. It is used to illustrate the process that a reporter often goes through to come up with a story that is well written and well organized. The story is real, but some of the writing is changed to avoid using the name of the school and the sources.

A $151 million state university appropriations request may be cut because of monetary demands from other state programs, the chairman of the Senate's Education Committee said Saturday.

Sen. William Delgado, D-Mainsville, said the budget proposal, which represents a $13 million increase over last year's request, may be limited owing to demands on lawmakers to fund new programs for the chronically mentally ill.

The appropriations request, which was approved unanimously by the Board of Regents Friday, totals $151,298,342. Last year's request was $138,298,356.

"It's kind of like a kid asking for an allowance," Delgado said, adding that the Legislature will have to determine how much money is available before approving the budget requests.

"There is just so much money to go around," Delgado said. "First of all we have to take a look and see what we have extra. I feel we may not have enough."

Delgado said the governor has been pushing for programs for the mentally ill, and the Legislature may have to consider funding those programs before allocating funds to the university.

The Legislature will begin discussion on the budgets in January, when its regular session reconvenes.

In other matters, the university will lose 22 faculty positions next year because of a decline in its full-time student equivalent counts. The regents made the announcement at their meeting on campus Friday because they said FTE decreased by 499 this year.

The Legislature provides one faculty member for every 22 FTE.

Jim Horan, associate director of university budgets, said the decline in enrollments may be attributed to increasing enrollments at state community colleges.

The regents also approved new policies for the training of graduate teaching assistants at the university.

The new policies, which were prompted by complaints from students, require that foreign teaching assistants be required to pass a proficiency test of written and spoken English before teaching.

Analysis: What's Wrong with It?

The initial version of the story missed the boat for several reasons:

Lead. The lead was wrong.

Writing style. The writing was dull and loose.

Organization. The story was not organized effectively. There are three major elements—the appropriations request, the loss of faculty and the testing of foreign teaching assistants—yet two of them are buried at the end.

First, let's consider the lead. In the initial story, readers were told that the Legislature may cut the university's budget request. This is not news. Budget requests are wish lists. It would be news if a budget were approved exactly as proposed.

The lead also reported that something *may* happen. Avoid writing *may* leads. They are hypothetical. The action that they are reporting may or may not happen. An audience wants something definite.

The lead of this story should have been that the university is going to lose faculty members next year because of declining enrollment. Twenty-two people are going to lose their jobs, or departments that were hoping for new faculty members are not going to get them.

Next, let's look at the writing. Throughout the initial version, the writing was dull and loose. It needed tightening and sharpening.

For example, in the second paragraph the writer said that the budget proposal "may be limited owing to demands on lawmakers to fund new programs for the chronically mentally ill." The writing could have been crisper:

The budget proposal may be pared because lawmakers are being pushed to fund new programs for the chronically mentally ill.

The sixth paragraph reported that the governor has been pushing for the new programs and that the Legislature "may have to consider funding those programs before allocating funds to the university."

Why not say this?

The Legislature will yield to the governor's demands for the mentally ill before it funds the university, Delgado said.

Finally, consider the organization. The story should be topped with the 22 cuts in the faculty. The new tests for foreign teaching assistants and the threat of budget cuts should also be mentioned high in the story. Then each can be explained later.

There are several holes in the story. FTEs need to be explained better, as do the reasons for the new tests for foreign teaching assistants. Readers also need to be told in what areas the faculty positions would be lost.

The Rewrite

The rewritten story read:

> The university will lose 22 faculty positions next year because of declining enrollments.
>
> Funding for the positions is based on full-time equivalent counts, FTEs, which decreased by 499 this year. The Board of Regents announced the decrease during its meeting on campus Friday.
>
> FTEs are the total number of hours being taken by all students divided by 12, a normal full-time load.
>
> At their meeting, the regents also:
>
> • Approved new policies for the training of foreign-born graduate teaching assistants at the university.
>
> • Approved a $151 million budget request for next year, an increase of $13 million over last year.
>
> Jim Horan, associate director of university budgets, blamed the decline in students here on the increasing enrollments at state community colleges.
>
> "We cannot compete with them for first- and second-year students," Horan said. "They're easier to get into, smaller and half the price."
>
> The Legislature uses a ratio of one faculty member to every 22 full-time equivalents, or FTEs, when it appropriates salaries.
>
> University officials said that they will try to avoid laying off any faculty members. Instead, the 22 positions will be made up by attrition, they added.
>
> The issue of training foreign graduate students came up after students in the math and history departments complained that they could not understand their instructors.
>
> The new policies require that foreign teaching assistants pass a proficiency test of written and spoken English before they can teach.
>
> The request for an increased budget was approved unanimously by the regents. It totals $151,298,342, an amount that Sen. William Delgado, D-Mainsville, called wishful thinking, "like a kid asking for an allowance."

Delgado, chairman of the Senate's Education Committee, said that the proposal may be pared because the governor is pushing lawmakers to fund new programs for the chronically mentally ill.

"There is just so much money to go around," Delgado said. "First we all have to take a look and see what we have extra."

The Legislature will begin debate on the budget in January, when its regular session reconvenes.

Analysis: Why Is the Rewrite Better?

For a number of reasons, the rewritten and reorganized version of the regents story was better than the initial version:

The lead was stronger. It reported substance rather than something that may or may not be. After reading the initial lead, someone was likely to say, "So what?" After the second lead, a reader was likely to say, "Wow! Who is going to be fired?"

The story was better organized. By using *bullets*—bold dots that begin and highlight paragraphs—the writer introduced other major elements early in the story. After six paragraphs, readers knew what the article was about. In the initial version, the three major elements were stacked on top of each other, which meant that readers did not know all of them until the end. In the rewrite, the major elements were introduced right away, and the two least important ones were developed later.

The writing was tighter. More vivid verbs were used.

Holes were filled. FTEs were defined. Readers were told from where the 22 faculty positions would come, why community colleges are taking away students and which students complained about foreign-born teaching assistants.

HOURGLASS STYLE

Most news stories are written in the traditional inverted pyramid, but there are alternatives. "When we are writing stories on deadline, we have to depend on strategies that have proved themselves," said Roy Peter Clark, dean of the faculty at The Poynter Institute for Media Studies in St. Petersburg, Fla. "We have to reach into our toolbox and pull out our handy gadgets that help us organize our thinking and communicate to readers. I think that the problem with some writers is that they have a single form that they go back to over and over again, and they don't have at their fingertips a variety of forms out of which they can find just the right one to tell a particular story."

Clark is an advocate of a writing form called the *hourglass style*, which is often used by reporters covering trials or police and fire news. In this form, the writer provides the major news in the first few paragraphs of the story. The paragraphs are written in order of descending importance, just like in an

Hourglass style works well in a news story in which the reporter wants to provide the details in chronological order. One example would be a story on a major crime involving a police SWAT team.
(Photo by Irwin Daugherty)

inverted pyramid. Then the writer uses a turn, a transitional paragraph to introduce a chronology of the events of the story. Transitional paragraphs include: *Police gave the following account of the accident, The victim told the jury what happened* and *Johnson said that he was attacked shortly after he left work.* After the turn, the rest of the details of the story are told in chronological order.

ADVANTAGES OF THE HOURGLASS STYLE

Clark said that the hourglass style offers these advantages:

- The important news is presented high in the story.
- The writer can take advantage of narrative.
- The most important information is repeated in the narrative so that readers have a chance to absorb it.
- Unlike the top-heavy inverted pyramid, the hourglass has a balanced structure.
- It keeps readers in the story and leads up to a real conclusion.
- It discourages editors from slashing from the bottom.

"The hourglass is a natural way to tell a story," Clark said. "You blurt out the more important information right away, and then someone says, 'That was fascinating. How did it happen?' I've seen it on an interesting range of stories, including governmental meetings in which the writer tells the news at the top of the story and then recounts how the events took place in a chronological order. I think the hourglass opens up the reporter to a level of reporting that the pyramid sometimes discourages."

AN EXAMPLE OF HOURGLASS STYLE: A BIZARRE ACCIDENT

The news story from the *Philadelphia Inquirer* that follows was written by Reid Kanaley in the hourglass style. It was the story of a truck slamming into an office building and killing a man working at his desk.

The first six paragraphs of the story were written in typical inverted-pyramid style, with the most important points first. The turn came in the seventh paragraph, where the story said, *Anderson gave the following account of the accident.* Then the narrative followed.

A Delaware County businessman died yesterday morning after a tractor-trailer careened into a busy Chester County intersection and slammed through the office where he was sitting at his desk.

The truck driver was seriously injured in the 8:09 a.m. accident at Route 202 and Brinton's Bridge Road in Birmingham Township. There were no other injuries, officials said.

Police said the brakes of the tractor-trailer, a flatbed loaded with coiled steel, apparently had failed. The truck veered across lanes of oncoming traffic, hitting a van, plowing through the office building and into a parked van before coming to a stop, according to Birmingham Police Chief Wade L. Anderson.

The businessman, James E. Dever, 50, of Stonebridge Road, Thornton, died during emergency surgery at Chester County Hospital in West Chester about 10:30 a.m., hospital spokeswoman Donna Pennington said. She described Dever's injuries as "multiple trauma."

The truck driver, Steven Rowe, 26, of Chesapeake, Ohio, was taken to Chester County Hospital with multiple injuries. He was listed in satisfactory condition last night.

Dever was a salesman for the Logan Co., a conveyor manufacturer, according to his son, Thomas Dever, of West Chester.

Anderson gave the following account of the accident:

Rowe's tractor-trailer was northbound on Route 202. At Brinton's Bridge Road, the truck, apparently unable to stop for a red light, crossed the southbound lanes and struck the front end of a van making a left turn onto the road. The driver of the van, Joseph A. Koskoszka of New Castle, Del., was not injured.

The truck continued past the cross street and up a grade into the parking lot of the Birmingham Professional Building on the northwest corner of the intersection. Dever was the only person in the two-story building at the time. He was at his desk in a first-floor corner office when Rowe's truck crashed through the office and into a parked van owned by Anderson. The impact demolished two walls of Dever's office and pinned him under the debris.

The van rolled onto its side and smashed the front window of the neighboring building, the Patterson Schwartz real estate office.

Anderson said he had just left his office in the basement of the Birmingham Professional Building and was sitting in a patrol car when Rowe's truck skidded by.

"I could see it was out of control, and the driver was making every attempt to miss anything," he said. "He did a fantastic job. He missed me; he missed the cars. He thought the lesser of the evils would be hitting the building, but, of course, it didn't work out that way."

Anderson estimated damages of $75,000. No charges have been filed, but the accident remains under investigation, Anderson said.

Besides his son Thomas, Dever is survived by his wife, Barbara; two daughters; and two other sons.

ORGANIZING AN HOURGLASS

The 30-word lead on Kanaley's story clearly summarized the event: A man was killed when a truck crashed into his office. In the second paragraph readers found out the time of the accident and that the truck driver was injured. Then in succeeding paragraphs (until the seventh) readers were told:

- *How* the accident occurred
- *Who* was killed
- *Who* was injured
- *Where* the dead man worked

This story could have been concluded after the sixth paragraph; instead, a transitional paragraph was written that invited the audience to read a blow-by-blow account of the accident. Readers had the option of stopping or continuing.

The second half of the hourglass should not repeat the first half word for word. Obviously, some facts will be repeated, but the second half of the story should make the succession of events clearer. For instance, the second paragraph of the truck-crash story said that the accident occurred at Route 202 and Brinton's Bridge Road. The eighth paragraph reported that the tractor-trailer was northbound on Route 202 and was apparently unable to stop for a red light at Brinton's Bridge Road. The paragraph repeated the location of the accident, but it provided additional details.

WHEN TO USE THE HOURGLASS

An hourglass cannot be used in every news story. It would be impractical, for example, when writing a personality profile, a weather story, an obituary or an advance on a holiday celebration. But in a story that has a succession of events, such as a trial, a meeting or a police or fire story, the hourglass style can be used effectively. "A story form does not have to be a straitjacket," Clark said. "It should be a liberating device. Reporters need to look for the best structure to tell the best possible story. I would call the hourglass a way of reconciling two essential values for the writer: (1) getting the news high up and not wasting the readers' time, and (2) telling a good story in a narrative style."

ORGANIZING A BROADCAST NEWS STORY

BASIC CONSIDERATIONS

Radio and television reporters cover a news event just like print reporters. They look for the news, hope to get the best lead before deadline and try to beat their competition. Because one medium is based on what an audience hears, another on what it sees and the other on what it reads, what is broadcast on a radio or television news show is different from what is printed in a newspaper, but the reporting techniques are the same. A television reporter may write only 100 words for a story illustrated by dramatic videotape. A newspaper reporter may write 1,000 words on the same topic, and a single photograph might accompany the story. But how these two reporters gather the news is the same. They both do their homework, so that they are familiar with the topic; they probably ask the same sources the same questions; and their leads may even be the same. However, because of the differences between their media with regard to style, time and production, there will be differences in how their stories are organized and presented to their audiences.

AN EXAMPLE OF ORGANIZING A BROADCAST STORY: A SHOOTING IN INDIANAPOLIS

Julie Carey, education reporter for WTHR-TV, the NBC affiliate in Indianapolis, was at home, about to drink her first cup of coffee. At the same time more than 200 high school students were standing on a busy downtown corner on a rainy morning, waiting to change buses for rides to school. The morning ritual was part of a court-ordered desegregation plan in Indianapolis schools.

"There had been some fights and other minor incidents on the corner before, but nothing serious," Carey said. "Merchants had long complained about vandalism and rowdiness, and they feared worse. On this morning, those fears were realized. The usual morning chatter of the students was silenced by a shotgun blast. A 15-year-old had packed a shotgun along with his schoolbooks that day. His target, a 17-year-old, lay critically wounded on the sidewalk."

Covering the Story

In the WTHR newsroom, the assignment editor heard about the shooting on police radios. The editor sent a photographer to the scene within minutes of the shooting. The photographer captured on videotape the tragic moment of paramedics pounding on the victim's chest as they carried him to an ambulance.

"The story fell to me as education reporter because it involved high school students and the busing plan," Carey said.

"My first step was a phone call to the hospital emergency room to confirm that the 17-year-old was dead. The next phone call, to homicide detectives, was fruitless. They were too busy questioning witnesses."

Carey said that she and the same photographer who shot the original videotape then headed for the police station, hoping to get an interview. It's uncommon for a photographer to accompany a reporter until an interview is firmly set, but exceptions are made in a high-profile story such as this one, Carey added.

"We were under a tight deadline," she said. "It was after 10 a.m., and we had to have our story reported, photographed and edited for the noon news. We were shut out again at the police station and told to come back later in the afternoon.

"We had just about an hour until deadline and needed a 'soundbite,' a taped interview for the noon story."

Carey said that she and the photographer picked up the victim's address from the police report on the shooting. Their next stop was the boy's neighborhood, where they could get tape of his home setting.

"It was drizzling, and the street was bare when we arrived at the victim's inner-city neighborhood of broken buildings scarred by gang graffiti," Carey said. "We began shooting tape. I stood outside, hoping someone would come along who knew the victim. I approached a woman who was hurrying across the street and asked her if she knew the victim.

"Finally, our luck changed. The woman was the victim's aunt, and she was willing to talk to us on camera. The camera acted like a magnet, and others came out, willing to talk. The victim's cousin, a witness to the shooting, came first. Then the victim's sister came out and, finally, a gang member, who talked about getting revenge.

"The photographer captured it all, standing behind me, panning from face to face, picking up words and expressions of anger and confusion."

The First Version

By now it was 11:30 a.m., a half hour before the news show was to begin. "I wrote the story in my notebook in the car, listening to my quotes on a microcassette recorder," Carey said. "I typed it quickly when I got back to the newsroom. We had about 10 minutes until the show started. We put together a hastily edited version."

Carey wrote about 100 words to accompany the videotape that was shot during the morning. Her story was given 1 minute and 30 seconds, and it was presented early in the newscast. Her story began with a summary lead:

> A 17-YEAR-OLD MANUAL HIGH SCHOOL STUDENT WAS SHOT AND KILLED THIS MORNING AS HE WAITED TO CHANGE BUSES AT A DOWNTOWN BUS STOP.

Carey wrote her story in inverted-pyramid style, but she had to build it around the videotape that was used. Unlike a print reporter, she had to make certain that her words were compatible with the tape.

Now the tape of the paramedics at work was shown. As viewers watched the emotional scene, Carey's story continued:

> ELI LEWIS WAS RUSHED TO WISHARD HOSPITAL AFTER BEING SHOT SEVERAL TIMES. DOZENS OF OTHER STUDENTS WERE ALSO AT THE STOP. POLICE ARE NOW INTERVIEWING A NUMBER OF EYE-WITNESSES AND HAVE DEVELOPED A STRONG LEAD ABOUT WHO THE SUSPECT MIGHT BE. RELATIVES BELIEVE LEWIS IS THE VICTIM OF A GANG-RELATED DISAGREEMENT . . . BUT THEY DON'T BELIEVE THE SHOTS WERE INTENDED FOR HIM.

For the next 25 seconds, a portion of the videotape of the interviews with friends and family was shown. Then the anchor concluded the story with:

> THE VICTIM'S FRIENDS AND RELATIVES SAY ELI LEWIS WAS NOT A GANG MEMBER, BUT MAY HAVE BEEN MISTAKEN FOR SOMEONE ELSE.

The Follow-Up

Carey still had more reporting to do on her story about the slaying of the 17-year-old high school student. She still had to interview police to find out if the shooting was indeed gang-related and if a suspect had been arrested and charged with the crime.

The reporter said: "In the early afternoon we shot our final on-camera interview, with a police captain who told us, 'This is the truest gang slaying I've seen in recent years.' Those words became the lead to our story for the 6 o'clock show."

Carey was back in the newsroom by midafternoon, reviewing her quotations and writing her follow-up. The lead of her noon story had reported the shooting; now she needed to write a follow-up lead reporting the developments in the last few hours.

She said: "I recorded my *voice track* [her part of the report that would accompany the anchor's words and the videotape]. It is the photographer's job to electronically mix the voice track with the videotape."

Next, Carey had to make more phone calls to additional sources. "One call was to an assistant police chief who added important information: the shooting had spurred a joint meeting among school, bus and police officials to study the crowd problem," she said.

"I made a final call, less than an hour before news time, and found out that a 15-year-old had turned himself in and would be charged with murder. [He later was convicted.] We had a new lead to the story."

Carey said that her story for the 6 o'clock news attempted to document a tragic death, both visually and in words. "We tried to go beyond the spot news element of the story and show why one teen-ager would kill another, why it could happen again and what officials could do to head off more violence."

The Broadcast

For the 6 o'clock news show, Carey's story was given 1 minute and 45 seconds. It began with terse sentences read by an anchor:

> A 15-YEAR-OLD WASHINGTON HIGH SCHOOL STUDENT IS IN JAIL TONIGHT, AND A 17-YEAR-OLD MANUAL HIGH SCHOOL STUDENT IS DEAD FOLLOWING A SHOOTING AT A BUSY DOWNTOWN BUS STOP THIS MORNING. JOHN MITCHEM IS CHARGED WITH MURDER IN WHAT A POLICE CAPTAIN CALLS "THE TRUEST GANG SLAYING" IN RECENT YEARS. JULIE CAREY REPORTS.

Carey continued her story as a narrative, carefully weaving her words around the videotape:

ELI LEWIS WAS WAITING TO CHANGE BUSES ALONG WITH DOZENS OF OTHER STUDENTS WHEN HE WAS GUNNED DOWN . . . HE DIED SHORTLY AFTERWARDS FROM A WOUND TO HIS CHEST. HIS COUSIN WAS WITH HIM.

Now the cousin was shown on camera, standing in the gang's graffiti-scarred neighborhood where the victim had lived. The cousin's remarks included this quotation:

"ALL I SEEN WAS THIS GUY'S SHOTGUN."

Then Carey appeared on camera, standing in the street in the neighborhood:

FRIENDS, RELATIVES AND POLICE TELL A SIMILAR STORY ABOUT WHY THE SHOOTING OCCURRED . . . A TEEN-AGER FROM A GROUP KNOWN AS THE 30TH STREET GANG IS ALLEGEDLY RESPONSIBLE . . . POLICE SAY HE WAS AVENGING AN EARLIER SCUFFLE WITH THE 24TH STREET GANG, WHICH MARKS OFF LEWIS' NEIGHBORHOOD AS ITS TURF. BUT LEWIS' RELATIVES SAY HE RESISTED GANG INVOLVEMENT.

After more videotape of police and relatives, the camera switched back to the anchor, who wrapped up the report with:

THE SHOOTING BROUGHT ANOTHER ISSUE TO A HEAD—THE CONGESTION OF DOWNTOWN CORNERS CREATED BY THE HUNDREDS OF STUDENTS ROUTED THROUGH THE AREA EACH DAY. MERCHANTS AND DOWNTOWN WORKERS HAVE COMPLAINED LOUDLY AND THE POLICE DEPARTMENT HAS BEEN PUSHING FOR SOME CHANGE. A POLICE DEPARTMENT ASSISTANT CHIEF SAYS TODAY'S VIOLENCE HAS PROMPTED ACTION. METRO AND I.P.S. [INDIANAPOLIS PUBLIC SCHOOLS] OFFICIALS HAVE AGREED TO MEET NEXT WEEK TO STUDY WAYS STUDENTS COULD BE MORE DIRECTLY TRANSPORTED TO SCHOOL.

Obviously, Carey could not develop her story as a print reporter would. Her words were supplemental to the dramatic videotape, which meant that the words she used had to be organized to enhance the pictures.

Judi Villa, a reporter for *The Phoenix* (Ariz.) *Gazette,* interviews a Phoenix
police officer after a downtown shooting and bank robbery.
(Photo by Tom Tingle)

Developing
a News Story

Many stories are more than one day's worth of

fleeting news. These stories develop from day to

day, from week to week, and reporters covering

them have to follow certain guidelines as they

organize their writing.

Some stories develop over time, and reporters covering them have to follow certain guidelines to guarantee that:

- The latest news is reported and the story is advanced from day to day.
- Readers, viewers or listeners who may not know about earlier occurrences are given adequate background to bring them up to date.
- Observations, narrative and anecdotes are reported.

DECIDING WHICH STORIES TO DEVELOP

Even in a local market on a routine day, the media must decide continually whether stories should or should not be developed beyond a single item. Some local news events—a train derailment, a major fire, a head-on collision, the search for a new college president, the hunt for an escaped convict—may be worth developing into several stories. Others—the naming of a bank president, a minor fire or fender bender with no injuries, the closing of a business, a vacation Bible school—are worth only one.

A STORY'S IMPACT

A story is developed from day to day when reporters and their editors or news directors feel that it is newsworthy; that is, the news event itself, its aftermath or the news it generates has a continuing impact on an audience. Of course, the fact that reporters stop covering a story does not mean that the story stops developing. It simply means that there is room each day for only so many stories, and judgments about their newsworthiness or human interest determine which ones are continued and which ones are dropped.

For example, a truck carrying a load of potatoes into town skids off the highway, overturns and spills the cargo all over the road. That is certainly worth a story. If the truck driver is not injured, the mess is cleaned up quickly and the truck leaves town two hours later, the news event deserves only a single story reporting the unusual crash. But if the driver is critically hurt and then dies, or a reporter finds out that the potatoes were stolen, or several residents are arrested with shopping bags full of potatoes, the story may be developed for days.

OTHER FACTORS INFLUENCING COVERAGE

Other factors besides the impact on an audience help the daily news media decide whether or not to continue developing a story. These factors include:

- *Prejudices of reporters, editors and news directors.* Obviously, if a reporter or a news executive has a particular interest in a story, it tends to be given more attention than other stories.
- *Size of the market.* The daily media in large markets are more likely to have enough resources and staff members to cover a story in depth for many days. Reporters in small markets, where everyone is doing a little

bit of everything and moving from story to story, usually do not have that luxury.

- *Pressure for exclusivity.* Every news organization would like to be the only one in town with a story. An exclusive news story or feature article means more readers, listeners or viewers.

- *What the competition is doing.* All the media are highly interested in what their competition is printing or putting on the air. A newspaper reporter will often go after a story because of what was reported by a television or radio reporter; broadcast reporters will often chase stories being developed by print reporters.

- *What other stories are developing.* If another major story breaks, it will be given priority. This means that reporters may be pulled off the stories that began developing earlier.

COVERING DEVELOPING STORIES

PHASES OF A DEVELOPING STORY

Whenever a major news event occurs, all the daily media strive to keep their audiences as up to date as possible. A story can be developed for hours or for months, and it is usually covered in four phases:

- *Phase 1.* The story first breaks. Journalists rush to the scene to report the news as it is happening, or they work the phones to put together an initial breaking story. They work on the story full time, and their primary function is to tell their audiences *what* happened, *when, where* and to *whom.* The story is front-page news. Reporters will usually write *mainbars,* primary stories that report the *breaking news;* and *sidebars,* supplemental stories that explain the news or report the human element.

- *Phase 2.* Journalists try to explain the *why* and *how* of the story, but they also continue to report late-breaking developments, such as cleanup operations or a final casualty count. This means that the story is likely to remain front-page news. *Second-day stories,* which report the latest news as well as summarize the earlier news, and sidebars are written to put the news into perspective for an audience.

- *Phase 3.* The story is no longer front-page news, unless something unusual happens to warrant front-page treatment, but reporters are still covering it full time or routinely. They look for something fresh, but they also analyze and continue to humanize the story. Follow-ups and features may be written for days afterward.

- *Phase 4.* Few reporters are working on the story full time any longer, but there may be a few pursuing specific angles. Reporters still make routine checks. Weeks or months later, there may be a major development as officials release their findings or investigative reporters come up with something. The story could become front-page news again.

Whenever reporters cover a developing story, their primary consideration is their deadline. They can stretch their coverage as much as possible, but the ever-present deadline must be met. When the time comes to phone in their notes or to push the button on their stories, reporters must go with what they've got. This means that no story they write can be definitive. All they can do is report the latest and most reliable information available at the time they write their stories. There will always be more information to gather and another story to write the next day, in a week, in a month or next year.

CHRONOLOGY OF A MAJOR STORY

An Escaped Convict: The Story Begins

When Danny Ray Horning escaped from the maximum-security Central Unit of the Arizona State Prison at Florence, newspapers and broadcast outlets hardly noticed. At most the escape received a few paragraphs on an inside page or near the end of a broadcast.

Things changed rapidly, however. Fifty-five days later, when Horning was captured nearly 200 miles away from the prison, his story had been front-page news for weeks. He had become one of the biggest stories of the year as he eluded search dogs and hundreds of police in Arizona's mountain forests. How reporters covered this story illustrates how stories are developed from day to day.

Horning had escaped by donning a medical worker's clothes and simply walking out of the prison. He was serving four life sentences for robbing a bank and was a suspect in the killing and dismembering of a California man.

At that time, Judi Villa was covering the police beat for *The Phoenix* (Ariz.) *Gazette,* an evening paper with a circulation of 90,000. Like other reporters in the Phoenix area, Villa did not begin covering the story on a daily basis until about a month after Horning's escape. By then, Horning, a wilderness survivalist, had managed to hide from everyone trying to hunt him down. There had been massive searches in several counties, but they were called off as authorities ran out of leads.

Reporting the First Big Break

A big break in the story came when a northern Arizona county announced that it was considering hiring a survivalist to help search for Horning. Villa, who had been working the story by phone as part of her daily routine, turned her full-time attention to Horning when the announcement about the survivalist was made. She interviewed the survivalist, who told her that there were only a few places where Horning could hide for a long period. He told Villa that Horning was probably living off crayfish, fish and plants in the Clear Creek area of northern Arizona, which is filled with chasms and caves.

In her story on the survivalist Villa reported the latest news in her opening paragraphs:

Law enforcement
officers in the
Grand Canyon
search car trunks
for the escaped
convict Danny Ray
Horning.
*(Photo by Tom Tingle,
The Phoenix Gazette)*

Coconino County authorities are considering using a noted wilderness survivalist to help search for escaped convict and California murder suspect Danny Ray Horning.

Larry Olsen, 52, who operates an outdoor treatment program for youths and was asked to participate in the 1987 hunt for Idaho fugitive killer Claude Dallas, said he offered to help in the northern Arizona search for Horning.

The number of searchers was cut in half, from 80 to 40, over the weekend, and authorities said they were running out of leads on Horning.

As is typical in developing stories, the lead block that reported the latest news was followed by background—a report of earlier news to bring readers up to date. Villa's fourth paragraph provided this background:

Horning, 33, escaped May 12 from the maximum-security Central Unit of the Arizona State Prison at Florence by disguising himself as a medical worker. Last Wednesday, a former Corrections Department employee spotted Horning near Clint Wells, 45 miles southeast of Flagstaff, helping three youths with their truck. As authorities approached, Horning fled into the Mogollon Rim country, where he is believed to have survived for nearly a month.

After the background material is presented, a developing story should return to the latest occurrences. Villa's story did precisely that. It went on to report more information on Olsen, the survivalist, and how he thought he could help capture Horning. Additional background is usually presented near the end of the story.

Advancing the Story

The day after she wrote the story on Olsen, Villa was sent to northern Arizona to continue working on her story. Her task was straightforward: Continue advancing the story each day. Report the latest developments in news stories, and also look for feature stories that emphasize *color*, observations, narrative or anecdotes to give an audience a clearer picture of a person or event.

"I had covered the story over the phone initially, but then it was only a prison escape," Villa said. "The story was beginning to develop into something bigger, however, as Horning eluded police."

Villa started work at 8 a.m. on the day her city editor sent her and a photographer into the field on the Horning story. She would work until 11:30 p.m. that day, the first of many 12- to 16-hour days she would spend on a quickly developing story.

She said the first stop for her and the photographer, Dana Leonard, was the command post that had been set up "in the middle of nowhere" by authorities. "We were 23 miles from a phone," Villa said. "We asked for a briefing. I had been talking to the command post on the phone before we went there (about 90 miles southeast of Flagstaff)."

Villa's first day in the field produced little news. Horning was elusive and the authorities were frustrated. She knew there was no real breaking news to report, and so she wrote a piece that emphasized color. It began:

Glendale resident Leota Jarrel has spent many of her summers as host at Double Springs campground at Mormon Lake, where escaped convict and California murder suspect Danny Ray Horning is believed to be hiding.

This summer is no different.

"Every day in Phoenix the same kind of people (as Horning) are running up and down the streets," Jarrel said Wednesday.

In her next paragraph Villa "backgrounded" her readers with the same information that had been presented in her earlier stories. Then her 20-inch story turned back to Jarrel. She used more background later in her story.

Keeping up with the news   Two days later, the search for Horning was called off, but Villa did not quit working on the story. She followed it by phone. Horning was spotted a week later; this produced another flurry of stories, but the search was called off after three days.

The developing story was rekindled later in the month when Horning took hostages and shot at law enforcement officers at the Grand Canyon. This happened in a national park in the summer, a peak time for tourists. Now the story would develop from minute to minute.

"The assistant metro editor called me at home at 9 a.m. Sunday and asked me if I wanted to go to the Grand Canyon," Villa said. "I said 'sure,' and he said to be at the newsroom in an hour. He told me to plan to stay overnight. I wasn't prepared for five days. We (Villa and a photographer) left so quickly that I didn't think to bring along a portable computer. I had to phone in everything.

"As before, we started at the command post, trying to figure out who was who. There were 12 or 13 agencies involved—FBI, county sheriffs, the National Park Service, the state Department of Corrections, dog teams, the Border Patrol—and each had its own area. You wanted to know someone from each one. Each had its own little system, and their efforts weren't all that together. Some agencies didn't know things that the other agencies knew. There were four main spokespeople."

Providing background Villa's first story from the Grand Canyon was filled with color based on her observations and interviews. The only news she had to report was that Horning had not yet been captured. Instead of filing a one-sentence story reporting that nothing had happened, Villa spent the day meeting people and visiting with them. Her writing illustrated how a variety of color stories or sidebars can be written as a major story develops and how important it is to "background" readers continually. A reporter can never assume that readers have been following a story from the first day.

Here is much of Villa's first story; the annotations on the right show how her writing followed a pattern typical to developing stories.

Prison escapee Danny Ray Horning continued to elude more than 200 searchers in the Grand Canyon, but park business went on as usual and visitors said they were not afraid of the convict.	*The latest news in a summary lead*
"My son has a water gun, so we are safe," said Melitta Trautvietter, a visitor from Germany who was at the canyon on Sunday with her son, Nils, 13, and daughter, Dana, 10.	*Introduction of key source with strong quote; color*
"We were a little scared when we first came here," Nils said. "But now it's fine. We think they lost him."	
Today, officials planned door-to-door searches of residential areas around the canyon.	*News*
Horning, 33, was spotted Friday night at the Grand Canyon after taking two hostages from Flagstaff on Thursday afternoon. He tried to kidnap a family at Babbitt's, a general store in the Grand Canyon's South Rim Village, just before 9 p.m. Friday. The family escaped when the teenage son started screaming, frightening Horning, who fled with the couple he already held hostage.	*Background*
After firing three to five rounds at pursuing officers, Horning abandoned the vehicle, turned the couple loose on the West Rim between Hopi and Mohave points and fled into the woods. Backpackers reported spotting Horning hiking down the Bright Angel trail Saturday.	

Joyce Patterson of New Jersey said she heard the shots Friday night.

"We kind of wrote it off as someone doing something stupid like shooting an animal," said Patterson, who was visiting the park with her husband, 6-year-old son and 11-year-old daughter. She said the family avoided the park Saturday but chose to return Sunday and finish their vacation.

"We figured they would keep people away if it wasn't safe," Patterson said.

Second source; more color

The sightings sparked a third large-scale manhunt for Horning since he escaped May 12 from the maximum-security unit at the Arizona State Prison at Florence.

Two attempted break-ins Saturday night—one at the Maswik Lodge and one at a residential mobile home—also may be tied to Horning, said Jim Tuck, public affairs officer for Grand Canyon National Park.

Background

"After those, dogs picked up some pretty strong scents," Tuck said, but officers couldn't positively link Horning to the scenes.

Three leads turned up no signs of Horning on Sunday.

A woman entering the park shortly before noon reported seeing a man matching Horning's description in a valley 35 miles south of the park.

News

Villa's story continued for several more paragraphs. She introduced another law enforcement source, who provided more information on the search.

Persisting   As the week wore on, Villa continued to interview people and to keep up with the latest information from authorities. She was also in constant contact with her newsroom.

"Mobile phones and pagers don't work at the canyon," she said. "I called in three or four times a day from the pay phones at the command post. The *Gazette* has an 800 number."

Initially, Villa had been sent to the Grand Canyon for only a day, but she said: "After the first night I wanted to stay. We just knew he was there. My editors left it up to me from day to day if I should stay. They called my husband and asked him to pack some more clothes for me."

She also had the challenge of finding a bed each night in a national park with limited hotel rooms.

"We had to move every night," Villa said. "Tourists with reservations got their rooms. Then law enforcement people got rooms. What was left went to us. Journalists had to stand in line each day, waiting for rooms."

When Villa first got to the canyon, there was only one other reporter from Phoenix. Within a few days, however, newspapers and television stations from throughout the state had sent reporters and photographers. Horning also had become national news, and journalists from throughout the country began arriving at the Grand Canyon.

"By Thursday the law enforcement people started calling regular press conferences two times a day because there were so many reporters," Villa said. "Before that it was easy to get to people.

"It got really difficult to find a new lead every day. There were a couple of days where there was real newsy stuff. A couple of days I looked for features, for things that the other papers weren't getting."

Villa had three deadlines each morning, at 6:15, 8:45 and 10. "I didn't get much in the morning that I didn't have the night before," she said. "Horning was a person who moved at night when no one could see him. I usually called in my stories at about 10 p.m., before I went to bed. Then I would be back out at 6 a.m., checking for things that I could add to my story. The search teams worked 12-hour shifts starting at 6 a.m., so 6 to 10 a.m. was a good time to talk to the new teams."

Villa was called back to Phoenix five days after she arrived at the Grand Canyon. The story was dragging, and a second *Gazette* reporter was at the canyon covering another story. Her editors decided that Villa would be the one to come home.

Three days later, Horning was captured about 110 miles south of the Grand Canyon. He was seized early in the morning, which means that the morning newspapers got the break on the story. The *Mesa* (Ariz.) *Tribune* reported:

> A defiant and unremorseful Danny Ray Horning smugly cracked jokes after being captured early Sunday near Sedona, 55 days after escaping from the state prison at Florence and embarking on a kidnapping and robbery spree while eluding scores of police.

Even after the capture, the story continued to develop. The afternoon *Phoenix Gazette* could not merely report that Horning had been caught 12 hours earlier. Michael Murphy, who replaced Villa at the Grand Canyon, had to advance the story. Here is how his story began:

> In the end, it wasn't Rambo that inspired Danny Ray Horning's nearly two-month run from the law across Arizona's high country, but a film titled "Death Hunt."
>
> "I enjoy excitement," an unbowed Horning said Sunday as he was led in shackles to a Coconino County courtroom where he faced 12 felony counts, including three counts of attempted murder. Bond was set at $2 million.
>
> Grinning from ear to ear, the crafty robber whose escapades left Arizona lawmen with red faces told reporters of his survival in the outdoors and how he wanted to win a $1 million ransom and "get the hell out of this area."

Villa said she was greatly disappointed that she was not in northern Arizona when Horning was caught, but she still had a terrific experience. "It was a total adrenalin high," she said. "I talked about it for weeks when I got back. I slept four hours a night for five days and I wasn't tired.

"I saw dog searches, door-to-door searches, guns drawn, painted faces, weapons. It was like being there when a city is under siege.

"The most exciting day was Monday, when Horning stole a car at gunpoint. We (Villa and a photographer) got there before the barricade went up. We were nearby and heard it on our police scanner. That happened at 5 or 6 at night. I was up until 1 or 2 that night."

Reporting the news and capturing the mood   As Villa covered the Horning story at the Grand Canyon, she had two major goals: report the latest news first while providing readers with necessary background, and capture the mood of what was going on at the canyon.

"We had to be careful of spoon-fed stuff," she said. "The authorities held press conferences that weren't important."

She gave the following tips for covering a developing story:

- *Look more in-depth.* "You have to look at things that might not seem important when you first hear them. You have to think a lot to come up with every angle."
- *Make a conscientious effort to work with sources.* "Talk to as many people as you can. I made friends with the officials. I talked to them other than just for business. I made myself a fixture. I paid a lot of attention to visitors and what people at the next table were talking about."
- *Look for the unique.* "That's how we scooped the other papers."

Carrying on the Coverage

The Horning story entered its final phases after the convict was captured and returned to prison. Stories were written for months, but only the major stories made it to the front page or the beginning of a newscast. Reporters were no longer covering the story full time, though they were on the lookout for further developments. For example, within a month of Horning's capture, journalists reported the following:

Horning pleaded not guilty to 12 felony counts.

The state had spent more than $1 million in its largest-ever manhunt.

Horning went right through a roadblock at the Grand Canyon because police failed to recognize him.

California prosecutors were planning to seek Horning's extradition from Arizona so that they could pursue a conviction and death sentence against him in the slaying and dismemberment of a 39-year-old man.

The guard who let Horning out of the state prison was fired, a deputy warden was demoted and four other prison employees were disciplined for security breakdowns that led to Horning's escape.

Weeks after Horning was returned to prison, Hollywood's initial interest in turning the manhunt into a television "movie of the week" was fading.

Obviously, the Horning story could continue to develop for months or years. As long as there is interest in him, as long as reporters are checking out leads, there could be further stories on the convict who truly had a great time for nearly two months.

A CHECKLIST FOR DEVELOPING STORIES

The steps that reporters followed in covering the Horning story as it unfolded are typical in any developing story:

- *Report the latest news first.* The first stories report the breaking news. Follow-up stories should report the latest developments first.

- *Report the original breaking news high in any follow-ups.* Even in a major occurrence such as the crash of an airliner, reporters cannot assume that their audiences have read or heard about the event. Reporters must still provide background of the original breaking news, although it does not have to be in the lead. In the early follow-ups, the original news should be in the second, third or fourth paragraph. It can be lower in later follow-ups but it should still be high in the story.

- *Advance each follow-up.* Reporters do not cover a developing story merely to report the old news over and over. They must continually search for fresh developments. Each story they write should move into a new phase.

- *Find as many sources as possible.* When a major story first breaks, there is usually pandemonium as law enforcement officials, gapers, family members and the media rush to the scene. Sources may be easy to find in the beginning, but they may not be reliable. As more and more reporters arrive, and as the officials in charge gain better control, sources will tend to dry up. It is important to get to as many sources as possible, but it also is important to toss out the unreliable information.

- *Get color.* Major developing stories affect people, which means that stories must reflect the human element. Audiences want to hear from as many of the players as possible. They want to know what trouble the police are having or how the search dogs are trained or how difficult it is to fly a helicopter over the scene. Color can be used throughout a main news story, after the major news is reported. It can also be used in a sidebar or feature, where the color itself may become the lead and the news is supplemental.

- *Handle continuing deadline pressure.* Reporters covering developing stories cannot quit working once the first deadline passes. They know that there will be more news to report at their next deadline, in an hour, later in the day or tomorrow. They can report only the latest news possible at their deadlines; their stories are never definitive.

- *Cooperate with other reporters.* Journalists often trade information. Of course, they do not give away their leads or key information that they gathered exclusively, but they often help each other find sources or identify developments.

Print and broadcast reporters rush to the scene of a major fire because they know
that is where they will find witnesses and victims who can provide them
with colorful quotes.
(Photo by Bruce D. Itule)

Quotations and Attribution

Strong, vivid quotations can make a flat story

bristle; they can supplement generalities with

specifics; and they can pull a reader emotionally

into a story. Through quotations, sources can

communicate directly to readers. To achieve their

maximum impact, however, quotations must be

handled carefully and logically; and quotations

must be attributed.

Quotations can be more than strings of words with punctuation marks surrounding them. They can generate emotion; they can provide vivid description, anecdotes and explanatory or exclusive material. Quotations can be the soul of a news story or feature. They can bring a dull story to life; and they can make a good story even better. Even ordinary statements, when placed in the context of a story, can send tingles down a person's back.

Writing for the *Independent Florida Alligator*, Greg Lamm, a journalism major at the University of Florida, quoted the convicted killer James Dupree Henry, who was about to be put to death:

> "My final words are 'I am innocent,'" Henry said softly after he was strapped in the oak chair at 7:02 a.m., two minutes before he was jolted with 2,000 volts of deadly current. He was pronounced dead at 7:09 a.m.

Lamm went on to quote Florida's governor:

> Gov. Bob Graham, on the other end of an open telephone line, told prison Superintendent Richard Dugger at 7:03 that no stay would be granted. Graham ended the conversation by saying, "God bless us all."

The short direct quotations selected by Lamm enhance the narration. Lamm's description of the minutes leading up to the electrocution is vivid, but the quotation—"My final words are 'I am innocent'"—makes readers realize that there is more to the death scene than a lethal electrical charge. A life is being taken, and a person is being given a last chance to reflect on his death. The human angle is further emphasized in the governor's "God bless us all."

Quotations can make a reader want to continue with a story. The challenge is learning how and when to use them.

USING QUOTATIONS

TYPES OF QUOTATIONS

Statements can be handled as:

- Complete direct quotations
- Partial quotations
- Indirect or paraphrased quotations

Assume that, during an interview, an attorney, John Jones, says:

Quotations packed with such feeling do not come along in every story. When they do, make the most of them.

Use direct quotations to capture personality Kelly Frankeny wrote a story about Dr. "Red" Duke, a native of Texas and professor of surgery at the medical school of the University of Texas in Houston. Duke offers free medical advice in his news health reports on television. Note the third paragraph of Frankeny's story, which was published in *The Daily Texan*:

He's Dr. "Red" Duke.
A television star?
"Shit no. I have a hard time with that," says the 56-year-old doctor who's taken to the airwaves to promote "wellness." "I call myself an over-exposed old man."

The story went on to say that Duke wanted to pass along health information to his viewers like an "old country schoolteacher." The quotations help to paint a picture of Duke's personality. (See "Observing Taste in Quotations," on pages 140–141, for a discussion on the use of profanities in direct quotations.)

Use direct quotations to supplement statements of fact In a story about Monte Johnson, athletic director of the University of Kansas, Matt DeGalan wrote in the *Daily Kansan* what Johnson said about the firing of basketball coach Ted Owens and football coach Don Fambrough: that it was difficult. But the reporter knew that such a statement should not stand by itself. DeGalan followed up with these direct quotations from Johnson:

"In my case it was extremely painful, because I cared about those people just like I would about one of my friends," he said. "I think the only thing that probably allows you to survive something like that is that you have to believe what you are doing is right.
"There's still emotion involved in it. There's still frustration involved in it and there's still mixed reaction to it, but I just have to go ahead and put my head on the pillow at night and say I made the most conscientious decision I could make with the facts I had available, and nobody will give you total credit for that."

Use direct quotations for dialogue In a personality profile on the television investigative reporter John Camp, Donna Moss of Louisiana State University's *Daily Reveille* used dialogue to illustrate how Camp got into the business. Moss recounted an early career exchange between Camp and the manager of a small radio station:

"Camp, you ever done any news?"
"Nope," he quickly shot back.
"You ever want to do any news?"
"Nope."
"Well, you're going to do the news."
"Okay."

Use direct quotations to reduce attributions Assume, for example, that Kareem Abdul-Jabbar, retired star of the Los Angeles Lakers and the leading scorer in the history of the National Basketball Association, said this after a Laker victory over the Boston Celtics in a championship series game:

> I am uncomfortable with the threatening talk by players from both teams, with the escalation of rugged play in the games and with the possibility of a brawl at any time. I think basketball is to be played as a game of beauty, not as an exhibition of brawn. But if someone brings a tire iron to the game, I am forced to respond in kind.

If Jabbar's statement is handled as a direct three-sentence quotation, it would read like this (with attribution following only the first sentence):

> "I am uncomfortable with the threatening talk by players from both teams, with the escalation of rugged play in the games and with the possibility of a brawl at any time," Kareem Abdul-Jabbar said. "I think basketball is to be played as a game of beauty, not as an exhibition of brawn. But if someone brings a tire iron to the game, I am forced to respond in kind."

If Jabbar's statement is used as an indirect quotation, attribution would have to be provided for every sentence. This could get cumbersome. It does help, however, to vary the writing by alternating the placement of the attribution. For example:

> Kareem Abdul-Jabbar said that he is not comfortable with the talk, the escalation of rugged play and the promise of a brawl. Basketball is a game of beauty, not brawn, he said. But if tire iron tactics are used by the opposition, he said he will respond in kind.

Pitfalls to Avoid in Quoting

Reporters can easily fall into traps when quoting sources. Here are some guidelines to consider:

Beware of inaccuracies in quotations Reporters should verify quotations that sound suspect. If, for example, there is a bad connection or background noise when interviewing by telephone, always verify the quotation. This will reduce the chance of error. It is easy to say: "I was distracted by the noise on the line. Could you repeat that for me, please?" Or: "Let me make sure I have that comment right. Could I read it back to you?"

Reporters should check further if a remark that the source verifies still sounds suspect. For example, the manager of a local factory said: "My company employs 250 people—more than any other firm in town." The reporter asks for verification; and the manager confirms the quotation. However, the Chamber of Commerce figures show that his firm employs 200 workers—and there are 12 companies in town that employ more.

If follow-ups reveal that the quotation is inaccurate, the reporter could call the source back to ask if there is an explanation for the discrepancy, or the quotation could be left out.

Beware of rambling quotations   Some sources love to hear themselves talk. If their long, drawn-out *rambling quotations* bore the reporter, chances are they will also bore the audience. Assume that a judge has said:

> Because of the sensationalism surrounding the trial, I want to make sure that the accused receives a fair hearing. Now, of course, I understand that the press will want to cover the trial extensively. And, according to *Richmond Newspapers* v. *Virginia*, the press has a right to attend public trials, absent overriding considerations. Now, good members of the press, you won't find a more fervent defender of First Amendment rights than I am, but, as a judge sworn to perform my duties fairly, let me tell you that I will do everything in my power to see to it that the accused receives a fair trial, for he, too, has basic Sixth Amendment rights that guarantee him as much.

The judge might have said all this—and the reporter might have dutifully written it down. But getting accurate direct quotations does not carry with it a license to bore readers unnecessarily. Under these circumstances, paraphrase the statement and possibly supplement it with some partial quotations.

Beware of incomprehensible quotations   When reporters interview lawyers, physicians, engineers or research scientists, chances are that some of the quotations gathered will not be understandable to lay readers. In these instances, reporters must work diligently to paraphrase the quotation into understandable terms, to get the source to rephrase it or to supplement it with an explanatory paragraph.

Edward Sylvester, a journalism professor at Arizona State University and the author of three books based on science research and extensive interviews with scientists, said: "Science writing may be one of the few areas of reporting in which writers frequently show long quotes and even whole stories to sources before publication. The reason is that the material is often so complex and shades of meaning can change intention so much that even a close associate might put a statement in a way the source would consider quite wrong. On the other hand, as a popular writer/reporter, you cannot quote technical material in the precise yet dense language of the science specialty. The result of these two demands—for precision yet simplicity—is often a 'negotiated settlement,' in which the writer attempts to translate a difficult quote on the spot: 'Could we say that . . .?' Or, 'In other words, you've found that . . . .' Often as not, the answer is no, with an attempt to elucidate by the scientist and a reattempt to interpret by the reporter.

"This process is all the more important when you consider how often the words 'breakthrough,' or 'major discovery' or, most value-loaded of all, 'cure' appear in the press. It is extremely important to the public's interest and its perception of science that such words be used with the greatest care. To further complicate matters, the journalist who has just checked technical information and quotations with a source may in the future be in an adversarial relationship with the same source and be unwilling to reveal all information in hand until publication."

Do not reconstruct partial quotations Do not add things to a quotation to make it better or to cover up your failure to get the entire quotation. Use it merely as a partial quotation or as an indirect quotation. Do not take a partial quotation (an incomplete sentence) and add your words to make it a complete sentence.

Avoid using fragmentary quotations *Fragmentary quotations*—quotations used in extremely small parcels that are spread throughout a paragraph—serve no purpose. When set in type, they will look confusing:

> Sen. Johnson said that he wanted to take care of the problem "immediately." He said that it was a "pressing issue" that should not be put "on hold." According to the senator, the issue will "come before the Legislature" before the week "is half over." He said that he is "anxious" to go about "settling" the matter.

The best advice on using fragmentary quotations is: Don't.

Avoid illogicalities in presenting quotations Assume that a source has said: "I intend to pursue this matter with all the energy I can summon." Do not write: Sen. Johnson said that he will "pursue this matter with all the energy he can summon." Instead, write: Sen. Johnson said, "I intend to pursue this matter with all the energy I can summon." Or: "I intend to pursue this matter with all the energy I can summon," Sen. Johnson said. Remember: Quotation marks mean that you are using the precise words of the speaker. The speaker would not have referred to himself as "he" in a direct quotation.

Observing Taste in Quotations

The Associated Press Stylebook addresses the use of obscenities, profanities and vulgarities: "Do not use them in stories unless they are part of direct quotations and there is a compelling reason for them."

Handling offensive language The AP always alerts editors to stories that contain profanities, indicating that the language might be offensive to some readers. Editors can then decide whether to leave it in or to delete it. The AP also tries to limit the offensive language to paragraphs that can be deleted easily.

The AP Stylebook further notes:

> In reporting profanity that normally would use the words *damn* or *god,* lowercase *god* and use the following forms: *damn, damn it, goddamn it.* Do not, however,

change the offending words to euphemisms. Do not, for example, change *damn it* to *darn it*.

If a full quote that contains profanity, obscenity or vulgarity cannot be dropped but there is no compelling reason for the offensive language, replace letters of an offensive word with a hyphen. The word *damn,* for example, would become *d*—— or ——.

The *Washington Post*'s Deskbook on Style notes that the test of whether to use an obscenity should be "'why use it?' rather than 'why not use it?'" The *Post*'s stylebook urges reporters to check individual cases with appropriate editors. The *Post* advocates, when a profanity must be used, the "s—— form, which serves the purpose of communicating without jarring sensibilities any more than necessary."

Policies on the use of profanity can vary among news media. Always check with a supervising editor if you are unsure of how to handle a quotation.

Handling dialect   The use of dialect can also be a matter of taste; dialect often appears to ridicule the subject in a condescending way. The AP Stylebook points out that dialect—"the form of language peculiar to a region or a group, usually in matters of pronunciation or syntax"—should not be used "unless it is clearly pertinent to a story."

The *New York Times* Manual of Style and Usage advises: "Unless a reporter has a sharp ear and accurate notes he would do well to avoid trying to render dialect."

ATTRIBUTING QUOTATIONS

WHEN AND HOW TO ATTRIBUTE

Attribution tells readers the source of information. Not every piece of information, however, requires attribution. In the following lead paragraphs, it is assumed that a reliable source—either an individual or a government entity—provided the factual information and that the reporters knew beyond a reasonable doubt that what they were writing was true:

> Evansville will earmark $750,000 or more for resurfacing and repairing city streets this year, several times the amount spent last year. (*Evansville,* Ind., *Press*)

> The drought in south central Nebraska has forced some area cattlemen to partially liquidate their herds or find alternative feed supplies. (*The Hastings,* Neb., *Tribune*)

Attribution for some factual information would be ludicrous:

Omaha Burke blasted Lincoln High 81–54 in a non-conference high school basketball game Friday night, according to the team's statistician.

Attribution is needed, however, when opinions or other information subject to change or controversy is cited. For example:

> The Trans Alaska Pipeline may have to be shut down temporarily so that a sagging section of pipe under the Dietrich River can be bypassed, according to the line's operators. (*Fairbanks*, Alaska, *Daily News-Miner*)

Verbs of Attribution

Because *said* is a neutral verb, it should nearly always be used in the attribution for news stories. *Added* can also be used because it, too, is an *objective verb of attribution.* Susan Sheehan, writing in *The New York Times Magazine,* noted that syndicated columnist Jack Anderson often allowed subjective perception to dictate his choice of verbs of attribution. She wrote: "Anderson's characters rarely have something to say, state or comment upon; they whine, huff, snort, grump, mutter, bare their fangs or worse." Such a style might be appropriate for opinion columnists such as Anderson or in some feature stories, but it is not appropriate for reporters who write straight news stories.

Using *said* as the verb of attribution might seem repetitive and unimaginative, but reporters do not have to bombard readers with it after every sentence. Some newspapers continue to follow the rule that loose-hanging quotations (quotations without an attributive tag) are unacceptable. Other newspapers allow them, however, if a source is quoted in two or more consecutive paragraphs. Here, attribution at the end of the first paragraph effectively tells readers who the speaker is:

> "I think that the budget will be approved at our next meeting," council member Susan Long said.
>
> "I am sure that the special-interest groups will be out in force. We'll have to weigh both sides carefully.
>
> "I'm confident that we'll arrive at the correct decision."
>
> Long added that she thought this year's budget was the most explosive issue the council had dealt with in four years.

Here are some verbs of attribution that should generally be avoided:

asserted	demanded	opined
bellowed	emphasized	stated
contended	hinted	stammered
cried	harangued	stressed
declared	maintained	

Because verbs of attribution refer to speech and not to conduct or action, they should *not* be used in ways that suggest physical impossibilities:

"This is the best day of my life," Jones smiled.

"It will be a difficult task," Johnson grimaced.

The reporter should write:

"This is the best day of my life," Jones said with a smile.

"It will be a difficult task," Johnson said with a grimace.

Verbs of attribution can be found in most stories. A portion of an article by Emil Venere, published in the *Tempe* (Ariz.) *Daily News Tribune,* is reprinted below. The verbs of attribution are italicized.

Democratic gubernatorial hopeful Bill Schulz *told* a group of supporters Saturday that inferior education for poor people and prison overcrowding are tied together and must be solved by first improving inner-city school programs.

Schulz, 54, also *said* the state has failed to provide care for chronically depressed people, another factor associated with the failure to rehabilitate jail inmates and help indigent children on the road to success.

The as-yet-unofficial Democratic candidate for governor spoke to about 75 members of the East Valley Democratic Breakfast Club during a regular 8 a.m. meeting in Mesa. The founder and former president of WRS Investments, an apartment-management firm in Arizona, *said* he intends to formally announce his candidacy in September.

Schulz has toured eight states, speaking to governors and officials about pressing economic problems, he *said,* and expects to visit two more by the end of this year.

"How can one person be really equipped to deal with all of them (issues)?" he *asked.*

By studying the ways in which other states have dealt with the same kinds of problems, he *answered.*

"We have got nothing in this state that can't be fixed," he *said.*

Calling high costs for prison operation and inmate overcrowding a horrendous problem, he *said,* "We're going to have to raise taxes just to operate our prisons."

Arizona is spending roughly $140 million, including special appropriations, to run its prisons this fiscal year. Next year, including all legislative appropriations, that figure will be closer to $167 million, he *said.*

"We're getting a lousy return," he *said.* At an average annual cost of $18,000 an inmate, prisoners who are not rehabilitated are a constant drag on the state's economy, while many students from indigent families are likely to become dropouts and end up in jail because of Phoenix's poor inner-city school programs.

"They're going to be tax users rather than tax producers," he *said.* "The people who need the education the most are getting the worst education."

Identification in Attributions

Seldom is a person so well known that his or her name will stand by itself in a lead. Thus, attribution usually identifies the source by title and name. For example:

Parking fees at the Fairbanks International Airport are scheduled to become a reality by early summer, according to airport manager Doyle Ruff. (*Fairbanks, Alaska, Daily News-Miner*)

Measures ordered Monday by a federal judge to prevent suicide at the El Paso County Jail were already being taken or were being planned, Sheriff Bernard Berry said Thursday. (*Colorado Springs Gazette Telegraph*)

Sometimes, to streamline the writing, only the title of the person is used in the lead. The person's name is used in a subsequent paragraph. For example:

A mining company in the Circle Mining District was fined and forced to shut down its operation last summer not because it violated regulations anymore than other miners, but because it dared to point it out, according to its Fairbanks attorney.

Lynette and Dexter Clark were forced by the Environmental Protection Agency to shut down work at their mine last August after they refused to apply for a discharge permit. The EPA and the Clarks' attorney, William Satterberg, settled the dispute in December, but Satterberg said he is dissatisfied with the outcome. (*Fairbanks, Alaska, Daily News-Miner*)

Titles should also be used for attribution in leads when an opinion has been expressed by more than one person. Note also that when attributing statements to more than one person, direct quotations are not used:

Steps have been taken to improve leadership, morale and communications within the Colorado Springs Police Department in the past year, but internal problems have not disappeared, five City Council members said Monday. (*Colorado Springs Gazette Telegraph*)

Attribution in leads can lack specificity if a spokesperson is repeating an official position:

An explosion and fire killed two crewmen on the aircraft carrier *USS America*, the Navy said Sunday. (Associated Press)

In paragraphs that follow the lead, first-reference attribution should contain the person's name and title or some other means of identification. For example:

"I didn't know her well, but I thought that she was a wonderful person," said a neighbor, Helen Johnson.

"She was one of the finest students I ever taught," said Gerald Sylvester, a geography professor at State University.

Reporters also need to be aware of what some editors call "hearsay attribution." This occurs when a statement is made to sound as though it came from one source, but it actually came from another. For example: *Smith said that he knocked one mugger down and then chased the other man two blocks before bringing him to the ground with a diving tackle.* Actually, the reporter was relying on a police report and had never talked to Smith. It is dangerous, as well as misleading, to write a sentence that merely implies attribution. If the statement sounds like a good angle, check with the source. In this case, the reporter should have given Smith a call, or the sentence should have read: *Police said Smith told them that he . . . .*

Placement of Attributions: Six Guidelines

Attribution usually *follows* the information because what is said is normally more important than who said it. For example:

Soviet armored units killed more than 1,000 men, women and children in attacks on a dozen villages in Afghanistan suspected of helping guerrillas fighting the communist government, Western diplomats said Tuesday. (Associated Press)

What appears to be an important advance in developing an X-ray laser space weapon powered by a nuclear bomb has been made by scientists at the Lawrence Livermore National Laboratory, federal scientists said Tuesday. (*The New York Times*)

Building more prisons is only a short-term solution to a problem that needs to be attacked at its roots—the poverty conditions that breed crime, Nebraska Attorney General Robert Spire said Thursday. (*The Hastings, Neb., Tribune*)

Sometimes, however, the attribution can be of such significance or relevance that it *precedes* the information. For example:

An Illinois Central Gulf Railroad official assured Henderson and area businessmen that industries served by that company will continue to have rail service. (*The Gleaner,* Henderson, Ky.)

Financial experts believe Beaumont city officials ignored some standard practices that might have saved the city's investment when a securities firm through which it invested collapsed. (*Beaumont,* Texas, *Enterprise*)

The guidelines on the following pages should be considered when handling attribution for direct quotations.

Guideline 1 *If a single sentence is quoted directly, attribution usually follows the quotation.* Thus:

"The prices will continue to escalate," he said.

It is permissible, however, to introduce the sentence with its attribution:

He said, "The prices will continue to escalate."

Guideline 2 *If multiple sentences are quoted directly, attribution normally follows the first sentence.* The reader should not have to meander through two or more complete sentences before being told who the speaker is. Note how confusing the following is:

"The proposal to change school district boundaries needs to be put into operation immediately. This change is necessary to distribute students evenly throughout the various schools in our system," Superintendent Henry Smith said.

"School district boundary lines do not have to be changed. Many of the building principals are merely afraid that their teachers will have to work harder if enrollments at their schools increase. The whole proposal is the self-serving idea of a handful of principals," said school board member Ben Johnson.

Guideline 3 *When speakers change, new attribution should be placed before the first quoted sentence.* Note the confusion in the following example:

"We must raise tuition to generate funds to pay adjunct professors so we can open up new course sections," said Susanne Graham, a member of the board of regents. "It's the only way we can meet the needs of our students."

"An increase in tuition is the last thing students need," said senior class President Lisa Kelly.

The change of speakers should have been noted immediately. For example:

"We must raise tuition to generate funds to pay adjunct professors so we can open up new course sections," said Susanne Graham, a member of the board of regents. "It's the only way we can meet the needs of our students."

Senior class President Lisa Kelly said, "An increase in tuition is the last thing students need."

Often, though, a transition sentence is the most effective way to let readers know when speakers change:

"We must raise tuition to generate funds to pay adjunct professors so we can open up new course sections," said Susanne Graham, a member of the board of regents. "It's the only way we can meet the needs of our students."

Senior class President Lisa Kelly saw it differently.

"An increase in tuition is the last thing students need," she said.

Guideline 4 *Attribution can precede a multiple-sentence direct quotation (although many editors prefer that attribution always follow the first sentence).* When this occurs, the attribution should be followed by a colon:

Council member John P. Jones said: "We expect to ratify the new budget at our next meeting. We think we have worked out all the problems. It has been a difficult four weeks."

Guideline 5 *Attribution to the same speaker should not be used more than once in a quotation, even if the quotation continues for several paragraphs.* This construction should be avoided:

"We expect to ratify the new budget at our next meeting," council member John P. Jones said. "We think we have worked out all the problems," he noted. "It has been a difficult four weeks," he observed.

Guideline 6 *If a partial quotation is followed by a complete direct quotation, use attribution between them.* Thus:

No decision has been made on whether Israel will attack "with all we have," Eitan said. "We are sitting and waiting."

ANONYMOUS SOURCES

Each time reporters conduct interviews, they face the risk that their sources will request anonymity. Therefore, reporters in any market must learn how to deal with people who are willing to provide information only if their names are not used in the story. Because every story is different, there are no hard and fast rules on dealing with requests for anonymity, but there are general guidelines to follow.

Guidelines for Reporters

Be up-front with the source. Establish rules for the interview *before* it begins. Then there should be no misunderstanding about how the material can be used. Never assume that sources, particularly sources who are not accustomed to working with the media, understand the established conventions that deal with the use of material.

These conventions are:

- *On the record.* All material can be used, complete with the name of the source and his or her identification. For example: "We expect a quick settlement of the strike," said John P. Johnson, secretary of labor.
- *Off the record.* The material cannot be used. Period. Reporters must decide whether the information they could potentially gain under these circumstances is worth it. Often, reporters refuse to accept information off the record, choosing instead to ferret it out from another source.
- *On background.* The material can be used, but attribution by name cannot be provided. For example: "We expect a quick settlement of the strike," a high-ranking Labor Department official said.
- *On deep background.* The material can be used, but not in direct quotations. Also, the material cannot be attributed to the source. For example: *A quick settlement of the strike is expected.* Reporters can, however, seek verification from other sources for material on deep background and possibly get these other sources to agree to being quoted. If no verification can be found, the reporter must decide whether to take a chance on using the material. Editors or news directors should also be consulted in these circumstances. If the material proves false or incorrect, the reporter and the newspaper or broadcast medium are left holding the bag.

It is a good practice to tell the source immediately, "I am a reporter working for the *River City News.*" Then it is the source's responsibility to practice self-control, because he or she should realize that everything that is said will be on the record, unless other arrangements have been worked out before the interview.

Case-by-Case Decisions

Some sources know that they are talking to a reporter and still ask for anonymity after they have talked too long and too much. When this happens—and it does happen quite often—reporters must decide whether to use the name anyway or to respect the source's wishes.

In making this decision, reporters must consider the importance of the story, the value of the source and the editorial policies of their employers.

For example, suppose that a prosecuting attorney in a murder case calls to tell you that the defendant has agreed to plead guilty to a charge of killing a 22-year-old woman. The attorney gives you the information, but then says, "The judge has told us not to discuss this, so don't use my name—this is on deep background."

You could say, "Look, you've worked with reporters before; you can't establish a non-attribution ground rule after you've given me the information." Or, you could reason that you will need the attorney again as a source. It is just as easy to make a few more calls to confirm the information as it is to use the attorney's name in the story and risk getting your source into trouble or losing your source. Once the material is checked with other reliable sources, your lead can say (without attribution):

> A Brookfield man has agreed to plead guilty to a charge of killing a
> 22-year-old woman.

Or you can use this construction:

> A Brookfield man has agreed to plead guilty to a charge of killing a
> 22-year-old woman, according to sources close to the case.

Developing a strong network of reliable sources is one key to being an effective reporter; this means that you will sometimes have to acquiesce when a source requests anonymity.

Sometimes anonymous sources are government or corporate officials who do not want their names used because they believe that their bosses or the institutions for which they work should have credit for the statement. For instance, "City Hall said today" may be the mayor's top aide discussing the police department's negotiations with City Hall for additional funding. The reporters know who said it, but they use the nameless attribution because this was the condition for the interview.

Anonymous sources are also valuable because they can lead you to other sources; do not turn them off simply because they do not want their names used. Explain to them the policies of the particular newspaper or radio or television station regarding the use of anonymous sources and the importance of their being identified in the story. Often people can be persuaded to go on the record if they realize how vital the story is and that without an identified source it may never be printed. If nothing works, look for other sources, using the unnamed source for guidance.

Quill published a story by John Doe, a person who the magazine said wanted "to remain anonymous, mostly because his bosses don't approve of anonymous sources, and he'd like to preserve his job." The magazine said that Doe covered stories of "national and international importance."

Doe wrote: "In these days of the credibility gap, decent, clean-living reporters are supposed to abhor . . . nameless sources. But if they never quoted one, their copy would lose much of its value."

Doe said that reporters for large news media, in order to gain access to and publish certain information, routinely use anonymous sources. "Refusal to do so would deprive the public of much information it needs to form opinions about national and world affairs," he wrote. Doe emphasized, however, that "a conscientious reporter has to judge the reliability of the source, the facts that the source is professing to give and especially whether or not the source has a motive to distort the facts for a cause or for personal gain."

Reporters
occasionally meet
in out-of-the-way
places with sources
who want to remain
anonymous.
(Photo by Don Empie).

Policies on Anonymous Sources

Naturally, policies on the use of anonymous sources will vary. The policies discussed in this section, however, are typical.

"Reporters must name the source of information in every story whenever possible," the *Denver Post's* policy states. "Exceptions must be thoroughly discussed with editors and house counsel." The paper also tells its reporters to avoid using unnamed sources if possible and, when confronted with them, to seek alternative sources and documentation.

The *Bangor* (Maine) *Daily News* instructs its reporters: "If reporter and editor see clear need for confidentiality, the reason for anonymity should be explained in the story as fully as possible short of identification. If the reason isn't good, scrap the source and the quote." The newspaper goes on to say: "Information from an anonymous source should be used only if at least one source substantiates the information."

At the *Detroit Free Press,* reporters are not allowed to promise news sources absolute confidentiality on their own. At least one editor must know the identity of the source, and it is up to a supervising editor, in consultation with the reporter, to decide whether or not to use the unnamed source.

RULES FOR PUNCTUATING QUOTATIONS
AND ATTRIBUTIONS IN PRINT

Punctuation often plagues reporters who deal with quotations and attributions. Here are some guidelines.

Rule 1 *When introducing a direct quotation with attribution, place a comma after the verb and before the opening quotation marks.* Thus:

Jones said, "We will be there tomorrow."

Rule 2 *When introducing an indirect quotation with attribution, do not place a comma after the verb.* Thus:

Jones said that he would be there Wednesday.

Rule 3 *When ending an indirect quotation with attribution, place a comma before the attribution.* Thus:

He will be there Wednesday, Jones said.

Rule 4 *Always place commas and periods inside closing quotation marks.* Do not, for example, write:

"All of our transcontinental flights are full", she said.

Instead, write:

"All of our transcontinental flights are full," she said.

Do not write:

She said, "All of our transcontinental flights are full".

Instead, write:

She said, "All of our transcontinental flights are full."

Rule 5 *Always place colons and semicolons outside the closing quotation marks.* Thus:

Coach Jones said that it was his "dumbest mistake": deciding to start an untested freshman at quarterback.

And:

> Coach Jones said that it was his "dumbest mistake"; he should not have started an untested freshman at quarterback.

Rule 6 *Placement of a question mark depends on whether it belongs to the quotation or to the surrounding sentence.* Because the question mark belongs to the quoted passage—and not to the surrounding sentence—the following example is incorrect:

> Coach Jones asked his team, "Can we win this game"?

It should be punctuated like this:

> Coach Jones asked his team, "Can we win this game?"

Because the question mark belongs to the surrounding sentence—and not to the quotation—the following example is incorrect:

> Did the coach say, "We'll have to wait and see?"

It should be punctuated like this:

> Did the coach say, "We'll have to wait and see"?

Because the question mark belongs to the quoted passage—and not to the surrounding sentence—the following example is incorrect:

> "Will we continue to win"? asked the coach.

It should be punctuated like this:

> "Will we continue to win?" asked the coach.

Because the question mark belongs to the surrounding sentence—and not to the quoted passage—the following example is incorrect:

> Why does every coach say, "We're going to win this game?"

It should be punctuated like this:

> Why does every coach say, "We're going to win this game"?

Remember: If the quoted passage itself asks the question, the question mark should appear *inside* the quotation marks; if the surrounding sentence asks the question, the question mark should appear *outside* the quotation marks.

Rule 7   *A quotation within a quotation should be set off in single quotation marks.* The following example is incorrect:

> "Johnson's plea to "win this game for the community" really fired us up," Smith said.

It should be punctuated like this:

> "Johnson's plea to 'win this game for the community' really fired us up," Smith said.

Or like this:

> "Johnson made a plea to 'win this game for the community,'" Smith said.

If you use a quotation within a quotation that quotes a third party, that quotation should be in double marks. For example:

> "I was shocked," the parent added, "when coach Johnson screamed, 'As my predecessor said, "Let's kill 'em."'"

Rule 8   *Remember to insert closing quotation marks.* When facing a deadline, it is easy to forget to provide closing quotation marks. Note the following:

> "We're so enthusiastic about this project that we can't stop thinking about it, Jones said.

It should be punctuated like this:

> "We're so enthusiastic about this project that we can't stop thinking about it," Jones said.

Rule 9   *Closing quotation marks are not used at the end of a paragraph if the same speaker continues directly to the next paragraph.* The following is incorrect:

> "We're so enthusiastic about this project that we can't stop thinking about it," Jones said. "We look forward to getting council approval."
> "We hope that will come at the next meeting," Jones added.

It should be punctuated like this:

> "We're so enthusiastic about this project that we can't stop thinking about it," Jones said. "We look forward to getting council approval.
> "We hope that will come at the next meeting."

Rule 10 *When a quotation is interrupted by its attribution, remember to insert additional marks.* Note the following incorrect example:

> "Get in there now," the coach said, before I make you run extra laps."

It should be punctuated like this:

> "Get in there now," the coach said, "before I make you run extra laps."

Rule 11 *When reporting dialogue, start a new paragraph with each change of speakers.* For example:

> "I think it is wise to lengthen the school year," Smith said.
> "It would be ludicrous to do so," Johnson said.
> "I think the only ludicrous thing around here is you," Smith said.
> "Let's keep this discussion on a higher plateau," Johnson said.

Do not run the dialogue into a paragraph such as this:

> "I think it is wise to lengthen the school year," Smith said. "It would be ludicrous to do so," Johnson said. "I think the only ludicrous thing around here is you," Smith said. "Let's keep this discussion on a higher plateau," Johnson said.

RULES FOR QUOTATIONS AND ATTRIBUTIONS IN BROADCASTS

Guidelines that govern quotations and attributions for broadcast are similar to those for print in that the audience must be told where the information came from and when the precise words of the speaker are used. But differences are dictated by the unique qualities of each medium. Professor Ben Silver of Arizona State University, a former CBS newsman, made the following observations.

Rule 1 *Broadcast journalists should normally avoid the print style of placing attribution after a sentence.* For example, a newspaper would say:

> "North Ward elementary students scored higher on the Iowa Test of Basic Skills than pupils at any other school in the community," Principal Jason Smith said.

A broadcast journalist, however, should give attribution *before* a quotation:

> PRINCIPAL JASON SMITH SAID, "NORTH WARD ELEMENTARY STUDENTS SCORED HIGHER ON THE IOWA TEST OF BASIC SKILLS THAN PUPILS AT ANY OTHER SCHOOL IN THE COMMUNITY."

Providing attribution before the quotation lets the listeners know immediately that it is a quotation from the newsmaker and not from the broadcaster. Also, attribution before the quotation sounds more conversational and natural. For example, if you were talking to a classmate, you would probably say, "Professor Jones said that there will be no class tomorrow." You would probably not say to the classmate, "There will be no class tomorrow, said Professor Jones."

Attribution before the quotation is used almost exclusively in broadcast style. Occasionally, however, attribution can be placed in the middle of a quotation. For example:

"PRICES ON CARS WILL GO UP AN AVERAGE OF 11 PERCENT NEXT YEAR." THAT'S ACCORDING TO SECRETARY OF COMMERCE RALPH REILLY, WHO ADDS: "AND THE END IS NOT IN SIGHT."

Broadcast writers should opt for attribution between sentences only when particular emphasis is to be placed on what is said—for instance, car prices are going up 11 percent—rather than on who said it.

Rule 2 *Do not use quotations that contain a personal pronoun without first providing attribution.* For example, avoid this construction:

"I AM ECSTATIC THAT OUR NORTH WARD STUDENTS SCORED HIGHER ON THE IOWA TEST OF BASIC SKILLS THAN ANY OTHER ELEMENTARY PUPILS IN THE ENTIRE COMMUNITY." THOSE ARE THE WORDS OF PRINCIPAL JASON SMITH.

Listeners need to be told immediately who the speaker using the personal pronoun is. Otherwise, if the person reading the news starts out with, "I am ecstatic that . . . ," listeners would logically assume that the broadcast journalist was expressing his or her personal opinion. Remember: Listeners cannot see the quotation marks around sentences—as readers of newspapers and magazines can. Thus, when writing for broadcast, attribution must be clear and straightforward.

For example, Smith's quotation above could have been handled as follows for broadcast:

NORTH WARD PRINCIPAL JASON SMITH IS PLEASED WITH THE SCORES ON A STANDARDIZED TEST THAT HIS STUDENTS RECENTLY TOOK. HE PUT IT THIS WAY: "I AM ECSTATIC THAT OUR NORTH WARD STUDENTS SCORED HIGHER ON THE IOWA TEST OF BASIC SKILLS THAN ANY OTHER ELEMENTARY PUPILS IN THE ENTIRE COMMUNITY."

Rule 3 *If the source's title is important and recognizable, it is often natural to use the title to start the attribution.* For example:

> SECRETARY OF COMMERCE RALPH REILLY SAID TODAY THAT
> PRICES ON CARS WILL GO UP AN AVERAGE OF 11 PERCENT NEXT
> YEAR.

Rule 4 *Make quotations short.* Long quotations bog down stories written for broadcast. They are difficult for the newscaster to read and for the listener to comprehend. Of course, if a 35-word direct quotation is particularly vivid and strong, use it. But it should be broken up with attribution. If the 35-word direct quotation is not particularly vivid and strong, boil it down. Broadcasters should use more paraphrases than direct quotations.

Rule 5 *Because the listener cannot see quotation marks, broadcast reporters must frequently set up a quotation through words.* For example:

> HE PUT IT THIS WAY . . .

Or:

> THESE ARE HIS EXACT WORDS . . .

Rule 6 *Because the listener cannot see quotation marks, voice inflection can also help indicate a direct quotation.* For example:

> JONES SAID, "<u>THIS</u> IS A <u>FANTASTIC</u> DAY."

Rule 7 *When writing for broadcast, insert quotation marks when appropriate even though the listener cannot see them.* This makes it easier for the anchor or the reporter who is reading the material to recognize it as a quotation.

Qualities of Good Writing

Don Fry.
(Courtesy of The Poynter Institute for Media Studies, St. Petersburg, Florida)

Qualities of Good Writing

8

Writing is hard work. After gathering

information, the best writers draft, rewrite and

edit their stories. During the writing process, they

spend additional time just thinking about their

stories. Good writers take pride in their work.

They realize that not every story will be a

blockbuster, but they always do their best to serve

their readers.

Newspaper editors are placing more emphasis on good writing today than ever before. Seminars, workshops and conventions often feature sessions on how reporters can improve their writing. Some newspapers designate editors to serve as in-house writing coaches; other newspapers import writing coaches to work with reporters who need to polish their skills.

This chapter, then, will present guidelines for good writing by three acknowledged experts.

ROY PETER CLARK: FOURTEEN TRAITS OF GOOD WRITERS

Roy Peter Clark, who may be the best known writing coach in the United States, described one of his first days in the newsroom of the *St. Petersburg* (Fla.) *Times.*

It was more than 15 years ago; Clark had left behind a comfortable niche as a university professor to become a writing coach. Most of the reporters in the newsroom were not particularly impressed with his Ph.D. in English literature. He knew little of the day-to-day practicalities of journalism.

Writing in the *Washington Journalism Review,* Clark recalled the need he felt "to interview every reporter on the staff to learn much more than I could hope to teach." He told of an early experience:

> One day, I found myself sitting beside Howell Raines, then political editor in St. Petersburg, now a Washington reporter for the *New York Times.* Howell had written a series of political profiles that became legendary in the newsroom. They were powerful and influential character studies so well written that other reporters could quote passages verbatim.
>
> The week I interviewed Howell, *two* of his books had been published, a terrific novel called "Whiskey Man," and an oral history of the civil rights movement, "My Soul Is Rested." I felt humbled at the prospect of coaching him. What could I tell him, "Use more active verbs in your next novel, Howell"?
>
> I decided to become student instead of teacher, and asked Howell a dozen questions about political reporting. I recorded his responses. Howell described how to write about politicians as human characters and not just authority figures. He got down to nitty-gritty matters of interviewing and lead writing.

Clark used portions of the interview in his in-house newsletter; it was well received. It occurred to him that advice from respected writers could be both instructional and inspirational to reporters.

Clark served as writing coach at the *St. Petersburg Times* for two years, worked as a reporter and then joined the staff of the Modern Media Institute, which in 1983 became the Poynter Institute for Media Studies. Nelson Poynter, publisher of the *St. Petersburg Times* and *Evening Independent,* willed the controlling stock of the Times Publishing Co. to the institute. Clark, who continues to function as a writing coach, serves as dean of the faculty at the institute, which serves students of all ages and professionals from all over the nation.

Roy Peter Clark.
*(Courtesy of The Poynter Institute for Media
Studies, St. Petersburg, Florida)*

In his article in the *Washington Journalism Review,* Clark told how he had interviewed dozens of reporters during writing seminars at the institute and during his years as editor or co-editor of "Best Newspaper Writing," which is published each year by the institute. The book features award-winning stories in the American Society of Newspaper Editors' annual writing contest.

Clark began to see similar qualities in the outstanding reporters he interviewed. In turn, he developed a list of 14 qualities often shared by good writers.

Here is Clark's discussion of the common traits, adapted from the article in *Washington Journalism Review.*

TRAIT 1

Good writers see the world as their journalism laboratory, a storehouse of story ideas. If they can get out of the office, they can find a story. In fact, they can't walk down the street or drive to the mall or watch television without finding something to write about.

TRAIT 2

Good writers prefer to discover and develop their own story ideas. They have an eye for the off-beat and may find conventional assignments tedious. They appreciate collaboration with good editors but spend more time avoiding bad editors and what they perceive to be useless assignments.

TRAIT 3

Good writers are voracious collectors of information. This usually means that they take notes like crazy. They are more concerned with the quality of information than with flourishes of style. They more often describe themselves as reporters than writers.

TRAIT 4

Good writers spend too much time and creative energy working on their leads. They know that the lead is the most important part of their work, the passage that invites the reader into the story and signals the news. They are inclined to describe how they rewrote a lead a dozen times until they "got it right."

TRAIT 5

Good writers talk about "immersing themselves" in the story. They live it, breathe it and dream it. They plan and rehearse the story all day long, writing it in their heads, considering their options, talking it over with editors, always looking for new directions and fresh information.

TRAIT 6

Most good writers are bleeders rather than speeders. When they write, in the words of the great *New York Times* sportswriter Red Smith, they "open a vein." This is because their standards are so high that their early drafts seem painful and inadequate. But when deadline comes or a big story breaks, adrenalin kicks them into a different warp factor. They can speed when they have to.

TRAIT 7

Good writers understand that an important part of writing is the mechanical drudgery of organizing the material, what the AP's Saul Pett describes as "donkey work." They may respond to this by developing careful filing systems. They also develop idiosyncrasies that help them build momentum during the writing process: pilgrimages to the bathroom, chain smoking, taking walks, daydreaming, junk food orgies or self-flagellation.

TRAIT 8

Good writers rewrite. They love computer terminals, which permit maximum playfulness during revision. They move paragraphs around, invert word order for emphasis, find stronger verbs and occasionally purge the entire story to achieve a fresh start. Alas, they are rarely satisfied with their final stories and, burdened with imperfection, can hardly bring themselves to read their own work in the newspaper. Writing is an expression of ego, making the writer vulnerable and, at times, insufferable.

TRAIT 9

In judging their work, good writers tend to trust their ears and their feelings more than their eyes. Some stare at the screen with their lips moving, praying that the inner music will reach their fingers. Editors "look for holes in the story." Writers want to "make it sing."

TRAIT 10

Good writers love to tell stories. They are constantly searching for the human side of the news, for voices that enliven the writing. Their language reflects their interest in storytelling. Rather than talk about the five W's, they are more inclined to discuss anecdotes, scenes, chronology and narrative. During interviews, they tend to answer even the most theoretical questions with war stories, jokes and parables.

TRAIT 11

Good writers write primarily to please themselves and to meet their own exacting standards, but they also understand that writing is a transaction between writer and reader. Unlike many journalists, these writers have confidence that sophisticated work will not be lost on their readers. They treasure the reader and want to reward and protect and inform the reader and take responsibility for what the reader learns from a story.

TRAIT 12

Good writers take chances in their writing. They love the surprising and the unconventional approach to a story. They prefer failing in print on occasion because those failures are a test of their inventiveness. They love editors who tolerate experimentation but who will save them from falling on their faces. Their secret wish is to produce the best, most original piece in the newspaper every day.

TRAIT 13

Good writers are lifelong readers, mostly of novels, and they like movies. They collect story ideas and forms from other genres. They love words, names and lists.

TRAIT 14

Good writers write too long, and they know it. Unlike other journalists, who stop caring for the reader after the lead is complete, these writers use transitions and endings to keep their readers going. Their endings are so good that it is almost impossible to cut stories from the bottom. They want their stories to be "seamless" or "connected by a single thread" or "to flow." They want readers to read every word.

DON FRY: TWO PRINCIPLES FOR WRITING CLEAR SENTENCES

Stories fall apart without logically conceived paragraphs. Paragraphs deteriorate without solid, readable sentences. The foundation of good writing, then, is the sentence.

One person who recognizes and appreciates the importance of writing clear sentences is Dr. Donald Fry, associate director of the Poynter Institute for Media Studies. Fry, a former professor of English and comparative literature at the State University of New York at Stony Brook, is the author of scholarly volumes as well as popular articles. The following guidelines (through page 168), which were written by Fry, discuss how to craft clear and open sentences.

Good news prose goes down like sweet iced tea. Readers read newspaper sentences only once. This need for *steady advance* dictates that news writers construct sentences so compelling, so controlled and so clear that the reader moves easily from the first word of a story to the last. We achieve such clarity by two principles:

1 Lead the reader with open sentences.
2 Keep stuff together that belongs together.

PRINCIPLE 1: LEAD THE READER WITH OPEN SENTENCES

Many news writers believe that clarity requires short sentences. Wrong. Clarity requires *open sentences,* regardless of their length. An open sentence presents no delays, no bumps and no confusing ambiguities to the reader. We can write open sentences if we *lead the reader* through them by presenting a clear path with reliable road signs. We convince our readers that we can serve as their guides when we get to the heart of the matter, the subject and verb, as quickly as possible.

Here are some suggestions for writing open sentences.

Avoid Distracters

Avoid preceding the subject and verb with distracting dependent clauses and phrases, as in this sentence:

> When your sentence begins with dependent clauses or phrases, tending to delay the reader, especially when many such clauses intervene between the reader and the start of the thought of the sentence, and most especially with intervening material as long as this mess, then, just as you are annoyed at this sentence, the reader will regard you as a fool and stop reading your piece.

The best sentences start solidly with subject and verb:

Jones raced down the street.

Use the Passive Voice Sparingly

The passive voice should be used sparingly because it hides the agent of the action from the reader, as in this sentence:

The funds earmarked for student fellowships have been depleted.

The reader might pause and wonder who depleted the funds. The dean probably did and hid the action in the passive voice. A more honest but impolitic dean might choose the active voice:

I spent the fellowship funds to redecorate my office.

The passive voice has legitimate uses, of course, such as blurring facts the reporter cannot substantiate:

The house burned down when the kitchen curtains apparently were
accidentally set ablaze.

Ideally, good reporting solves this problem, but sometimes even the best reporters paper over the cracks in the information.

The passive also can emphasize receivers of action, such as victims:

A crippled 9-year-old girl was hit by an unidentified motorist
yesterday.

The sentence focuses on the victim but pays a price: the empty verb *was* and the need for a "by [agent]" phrase.

Let Punctuation Guide the Reader

Good writers transcend mere rules (and stylesheets) to provide a set of clear road signs. Commas tell readers what to expect next, especially in terms of clauses. An independent clause can stand alone as a sentence, but a dependent clause cannot. The conjunction *and* or *but* connects two independent clauses in a compound sentence, and the comma before the conjunction tells the reader that a second clause has begun. Notice how smoothly the long sentences flow in this paragraph so far. Back up and study them, starting with "Commas tell readers . . . " The commas kept you as a reader on the track.

On the other hand, leaving out the comma before the *and* in a compound sentence can cause confusion and disgust and chaos can result. See the problem in that last sentence? Does disgust go with *confusion,* or with *chaos* as the subject of *can result?* There is not much at stake in that sentence, but try this one:

> The mayor got a ticket for illegal parking and drunken driving and
> parking meters will rank high on his agenda.

Careful placement of the missing comma guides the reader to take *drunken driving* with *parking meters,* not with *illegal parking.* Leaving out that comma creates ambiguity, and ambiguity invites the libel lawyer.

Commas also keep items in a series together, as in this sentence:

> "The jail reports . . . including somebody's burning Styrofoam trays in
> his cell, a prisoner's throwing urine and feces at a guard and other
> inmates, and a third person who had cut both his wrists with a broken
> razor."

The careful placement of the comma before *and a third person* tells readers that the third item in the series has started. Try to sort out the various series in this badly punctuated mess:

> "When the public criticizes press coverage of bad news, it not only
> refers to the constant reporting of disturbing news, but also often
> refers to the presence of sensationalism, hype and questionable news
> judgment, and the lack of feature stories, local news and 'soft' news."

Dashes convey ambiguous punctuation signals, representing opening parentheses, a comma, colons, pauses and even quotation marks. A reader encountering a dash does not know which of these uses that dash represents at that point in the sentence. The ambiguous signal throws readers and starts them wondering, and wondering readers become wandering readers, right into the next story written by someone else. Analyze the uses of the dash in this next sentence, and try to imagine the reader's confusion at any point in trying to anticipate what might come next:

> Careless writers use dashes—represented by hyphens in typing—
> instead of more precise punctuation marks—commas, colons,
> parentheses, even quotation marks—creating the worst effect in their
> readers—confusion.

So please observe this guideline for dashes: AVOID THE DASH!

Well, one concession may be appropriate, as this sentence demonstrates:

Dashes—especially a lot of them—create for the reader—sometimes without design—a feeling—or worse—an impression—of indecisiveness—even mental illness.

Perhaps we should allow neurotics expressing their neuroses to use dashes.

PRINCIPLE 2: KEEP STUFF TOGETHER THAT BELONGS TOGETHER

The second principle of sentence clarity flows from the first: *Keep stuff together that belongs together.* We've already described the steadying effect of sentences that start with subject and verb, an effect enhanced by keeping the subject and verb side by side. Read this sentence quickly and then cover it up with your hand:

"The life of a fluffy orange kitten that was injured by a motorist on County Farm Road Wednesday afternoon ended in a brown plastic bag at the Strafford County animal shelter several hours later."

Without peeking: What was the subject of the sentence? Most people say *kitten*, but now you see the subject was *life*. This sentence loses the reader, who cannot remember the subject because of the intervening junk. In the following sentence, notice how the parenthetical material between the dashes complicates the separated subject and verb:

"Likewise, prosperity promised by project cargo—huge shipments dependent on individual overseas projects, such as the construction of King Khalid City in Saudi Arabia—fades like a mirage."

I asked the author what that sentence meant, and he had to study it to understand it himself!

The principle of keeping stuff together prevents *dangling modifiers,* phrases assigned to the wrong word, usually with unintended comic results. Try to read this sentence with a straight face:

The Palestinians released the passengers, who had held them for several weeks.

The same principle applies to verb modifiers. Consider how this sentence might rudely surprise the reader at the end:

The children visited their grandmother's house in the lovely countryside near Lexington almost never.

Or how this one might stun the Secret Service:

"President Reagan lectured the Iranians last week on not threatening American travelers on the White House lawn."

DON FRY'S PRINCIPLES IN A NUTSHELL

Many other writing tricks help clarify sentences, but the two basic principles prevent most problems. To apply them, a writer should constantly ask:

- Am I leading my reader at every point in every sentence?
- Is each item in each sentence next to the stuff it belongs with?

Remember: Write every sentence with readers in mind. They will not fail you if you do not fail them.

ROBERT GUNNING: TEN PRINCIPLES OF CLEAR WRITING

Robert Gunning's book "The Techniques of Clear Writing" is one of several that should be read by anyone who is interested in writing. The others are "The Elements of Style," by William Strunk Jr. and E. B. White; "On Writing Well," by William Zinsser; and "The Art of Readable Writing" and "A New Way to Better English," both by Rudolf Flesch. There are, of course, still others, but these form a solid nucleus. In this section, we'll concentrate on Gunning's guidelines for writers, relating them to the advice offered by Zinsser, Flesch and Strunk and White.

Gunning, a former consultant to more than 100 daily newspapers, including *The Wall Street Journal,* and to United Press International, developed what he called the *ten principles of clear writing.* The principles, which are examined in his book, are:

1 Keep sentences short, on the average.
2 Prefer the simple to the complex.
3 Prefer the familiar word.
4 Avoid unnecessary words.
5 Put action into your verbs.
6 Write the way you talk.
7 Use terms your reader can picture.
8 Tie in with your reader's experience.
9 Make full use of variety.
10 Write to express, not to impress.

These principles are straightforward. Examples and quotations from Gunning and the other writing experts, however, will bring them into even sharper focus.

1: KEEP SENTENCES SHORT, ON THE AVERAGE

Gunning wrote: "I know of no author addressing a general audience today who averages much more than 20 words per sentence and still succeeds in getting published." The key to that statement is the word *averages.* Gunning noted that "sentences must vary in length if the reader is to be saved from boredom." Indeed, don't hammer at the reader with a continuous flow of short staccato sentences. Changing the length of sentences creates variety and enhances readability.

Note the first five paragraphs of this article by Michael Allen, which was published in *The Arizona Republic* (the number of words in each sentence is in parentheses):

> ARMERO, Colombia—Five helicopters darted about like dragonflies over what had once been one of the most prosperous agricultural towns in Colombia. (20)
>
> Viewed from several thousand feet in the air, it looked as if an immense cement mixer had spilled its load in the heart of the valley's rich, green field. (29)
>
> Up close, it was a scene of unrelieved horror. (9)
>
> Very little stuck out of the soupy, gray mud: the tops of a few trees, a church steeple, glimpses of a neighborhood near the old cemetery. (26)
>
> And bodies. (2) Scores of blackened, putrefying corpses baking in the intense morning sun, a groping arm here, a blank, unseeing face there. (20)

Allen's sentences averaged 18 words. The sentences ranged, however, from 2 words to 29. The change of pace from long sentences to short ones helped to keep the story flowing.

2: PREFER THE SIMPLE TO THE COMPLEX

Gunning wrote that the emphasis in his second principle is on the word *prefer*. "The principle does not outlaw the use of complex form," he wrote. "You need both simple and complex forms for clear expression. At times the complex form is best. But if in your preferences, you use as good judgment as Mark Twain and other successful writers, you will give the simple forms more than an even break." Zinsser wrote: "Clutter is the disease of American writing. We are a society strangling in unnecessary words, circular constructions, pompous frills and meaningless jargon. . . . The secret of good writing is to strip every sentence to its cleanest components."

Variety is achieved by blending some complex sentences with a staple of simple sentences. A *simple sentence* has only one *independent clause:* The council passed the resolution. A *complex sentence* has only one independent clause and at least one *dependent clause:* This is the council member who cast the deciding vote. (*This is the council member* is an independent clause because it is a complete sentence when left standing alone. *Who cast the deciding vote* is a dependent, or subordinate, clause; it is an adjective clause, modifying *member,* a noun.)

Greta Tilley, a reporter for the *Greensboro* (N.C.) *News & Record* and a journalism graduate of the University of South Carolina, won an American Society of Newspaper Editors Distinguished Writing Award for a six-part series on life at the Dorothea Dix Hospital, a state mental institution in Raleigh. Tilley's writing was precise and vivid. Simple sentences were the staple of her writing. Through clear, well-paced writing, Tilley introduced readers to shock treatments:

RALEIGH—The clock above Anthony's head says 11 past eight.

It's morning. Anthony hasn't eaten or drunk since midnight.

He's strapped to a blue-sheeted hospital bed on wheels. Close by are two psychiatrists, two nurse anesthetists, one psychiatric nurse and two technicians.

"One-ten over 64," the psychiatric nurse says through the hiss of the blood pressure machine. She puts her fingers against Anthony's pulse.

"Sixty. After his treatment the last time he had a bit of a temp, so we need to watch that."

Anthony wears a medium Afro, a full mustache and a blue hospital gown. His tall, strong frame fills the skinny bed.

His bare feet, propped on a pillow, stick out from the end of the sheet covering his body. His eyes are half closed. A stethoscope rests on his stomach.

The technicians have just rolled him from the admissions ward, where he has lived for four months, to a small, clean room in the medical/surgery unit.

Thirty minutes before, he got an injection of atropine to dry his saliva.

In 17 minutes, 140 volts of electrical current will be shot into his brain.

This is Anthony's seventh treatment. He will have one more to go.

When the mental health center in his county sent him to Dorothea Dix Hospital, he couldn't talk, wouldn't eat and didn't respond. His chart described him as catatonic. Drugs didn't help.

Anthony's depression could be coming from a chemical abnormality or stress, or both.

The psychiatrist assigned to his case, Dr. Joe Mazzaglia, asked him to try electroshock therapy. He explained that an electrically induced grand mal seizure would release chemical substances in the brain that could jolt life back into his system.

Anthony gave a reluctant yes.

The writing in the remainder of the lengthy story was equally descriptive and powerful. The story illustrated that a careful blend of simple and complex sentences—with the emphasis on the former—is a solid formula for good writing.

3: PREFER THE FAMILIAR WORD

Gunning wrote: "Big words help you organize your thought. But in putting your message across you must relate your thoughts to the other fellow's experience. The short, easy words that are familiar to everyone do this job best." The authors of "The Elements of Style" wrote: "Avoid the elaborate, the pretentious, the coy and the cute. Do not be tempted by a twenty-dollar word when there is a ten-center handy, ready and able."

David Finkel of the *St. Petersburg* (Fla.) *Times*, in a story about a teen-ager who was entering a drug rehabilitation program, crafted a gripping lead paragraph that consisted entirely of one- or two-syllable words:

Sitting tensely in a chair, he is a young man not to be messed with, a coil of barbed wire. His mouth is in a sneer. His eyes could burn holes. His name is Paul Kulek, and he's doing his best to look as if he's in control.

A newspaper carried this wire-service lead paragraph on a national weather story published in mid-November:

> Tempestuous weather spanned the nation Tuesday as record snow and freezing temperatures swept out of the Rockies into the Plains.

Tempestuous? The Random House College Dictionary defines the adjective form as "being characterized by or subject to tempests." The dictionary defines *tempest* as "an extensive current of wind rushing with great velocity and violence, esp. one attended with rain, hail, or snow; a violent storm." *Spanned?* The dictionary defines a *span* as "the full extent, stretch, or reach of anything."

The weather map, published on the same page as the story, clearly showed that at least one-third of the country had clear skies, although temperatures were cold. Obviously, "an extensive current of wind . . . attended with rain, hail, or snow" was not blowing across "the full extent" of the United States. The weather, indeed, was tempestuous in the Rockies and Plains, but the story would have been more accurate—and understandable—had it read:

> Winter-like weather spanned the nation Tuesday as record snow and freezing temperatures swept out of the Rockies into the Plains.

4: AVOID UNNECESSARY WORDS

"The greater part of all business and journalistic writing is watered down with words that do not count," Gunning wrote. According to Gunning, such words tire readers and dull their attention.

Note this sentence:

> One of the primary aims of the extremely new master's degree program, which will offer an innovative curriculum not now available to the area's population, will be to draw them back into post-graduate education to improve their communication skills.

That sentence can be cut from 40 words to 24 without changing its meaning:

> A primary aim of the new master's degree program, which will offer a curriculum currently unavailable to area residents, is to improve communication skills.

Greg Lamm, a journalism major at the University of Florida, wasted few words as he placed his readers in the death chamber of the Florida State Prison. Lamm's article, which was published in the *Independent Florida Alligator* and which won an award in the annual William R. Hearst news writing competition, focused on the death by electrocution of a convicted killer, James

Dupree Henry. In the following portion of Lamm's account, note how he made each word, each sentence, contribute to the story:

Before Henry died, he winked and grinned nervously several times to about 30 witnesses who packed a tiny viewing room a few feet—and a picture window—away from the electric chair.

Dressed in his burial clothes, a short-sleeved white shirt and navy blue pants, Henry nodded and licked his lips as the prison electrician and an assistant strapped down his arms and legs.

His mouth was muffled with a wide leather strap that also held his head in place. A metal cap with a sponge soaked in a saline solution was then placed over Henry's freshly shaven head before his face was covered with a black hood.

After that, the two workers connected an electrode to the cap and attached another that would take the current from Henry's body through his right leg.

When some of the saline solution—used to enhance electrical conduction—ran down an exposed part of Henry's neck, one of the electricians wiped it off.

Gov. Bob Graham, on the other end of an open telephone line, told prison Superintendent Richard Dugger at 7:03 that no stay would be granted. Graham ended the conversation by saying, "God bless us all."

Henry clenched and unclenched his fists several times before the black-hooded mystery executioner engaged the electricity at 7:04, when Henry's hands shut tight. They slowly loosened during the one-minute surge, and his index finger on his left hand was almost pointed at the end.

After a four-minute examination by the prison physician and his assistant, Henry was pronounced dead.

Whether you wanted to be in the death chamber or not, Lamm's uncluttered, precise, descriptive writing pulled you there. His words made you experience the scene at the prison.

5: PUT ACTION INTO YOUR VERBS

"Strong-flavored, active verbs give writing bounce and hold a reader's attention," Gunning wrote. Use of the active voice (subject acting upon object) rather than passive voice (subject acted upon) is considered more direct and vigorous. The passive voice: *The avalanche was caused by an explosion.* The active voice: *An explosion triggered the avalanche.*

Note the strength of the verbs in this paragraph by Terry Henion, a sportswriter at the *Omaha* (Neb.) *World-Herald.*

Under a slate-gray sky, the 28-degree temperature and a 23-mph north wind combined to plummet the wind chill to minus 5 degrees. The Husker defense chilled the Cyclones, too, holding Iowa State to 137 total yards. Nebraska's offense churned out 573 total yards, including 538 on the ground.

Mark Fineman of the *Los Angeles Times* selected a particularly strong, precise verb in this paragraph:

The rebellion plunged the nation into one of the worst political crises in

its history and raised the prospect of a
military showdown between Marcos
and two of his closest aides, but Ma-
nila was calm this morning.

Partially because of the verb chosen by John Archibald of *The Birmingham*
(Ala.) *News,* readers could visualize this scene:

Birmingham-Jefferson County Tran-
sit Authority Board Chairman Bernard
Kincaid hobbled into the refurbished
board room on crutches Wednesday,
the swelling in his left foot visible beneath a thick white athletic sock.

When Associated Press writers described activity during an uprising in
China, they selected verbs carefully. Here is one example:

More than 1 million jubilant people
swarmed into central Beijing on
Wednesday to shout their support for
students who are fasting for democra-
cy, the largest show of defiance in
Communist China's 40-year history.

Here is another:

They huddled together, marched,
debated and waited restlessly for an
attack by their own army.

Note the following paragraph about the sprinter Houston McTear:

His raw speed compensated for his lack of form. His stride was brute
strength. He was aggressive in his races.

That paragraph describes McTear, but it lacks precision and strong verbs.
The best writers search diligently for the right combination of words and the
most powerful verbs. Tim Povtak of *The Orlando* (Fla.) *Sentinel* hit on that combination:

His raw speed obliterated the many
flaws in his form. His stride was brute
strength. He attacked a race and left
only scorch marks behind.

6: WRITE THE WAY YOU TALK

Reporters should work to avoid formal, stilted language, especially in leads.
Readers will appreciate it. When the Arizona Department of Public Safety

raided a home brewery, Emil Venere, a reporter for the *Tempe* (Ariz.) *Daily News Tribune,* could have written:

> Arizona Department of Public Safety officials, for the first time since 1923—four years after prohibition began—on Monday closed down a moonshine still near Gila Bend that was capable of producing 500 gallons of the tequila-like liquid a week.

Instead, Venere wrote:

> In a throwback to the days of bootleggers and speakeasies, Arizona officials raided a pig farm near Gila Bend Monday and dismantled what they claim is the biggest moonshine still ever found in the state.

Be specific. Capsulize the thrust of the story in the lead paragraph. But don't bog readers down with alphabet-soup acronyms and bulging details.

James H. Kennedy of *The Birmingham News* was conversational in this lead paragraph:

> Buddy Wesley grimaced as he looked at the mess the tornado had made of his cherished antebellum home.

7: USE TERMS YOUR READER CAN PICTURE

Gunning warned reporters to avoid "foggy" writing. A sports reporter who has played basketball and covered it for years will know, for instance, what a "box and chaser" defense is. But the reporter should not assume that all readers will. If such a term is to be used, it should be explained so that readers can understand it: "Metropolitan State will play a box and chaser defense against City College. In this defense, four team members will play a zone— they will cover a specific area of the floor, rather than guarding a particular player—while the fifth member will guard, or chase, City College's star everywhere."

Such explanations are also often needed on the business pages. Almost every day, newspapers publish stories containing references to the gross national product—the GNP. Such a term might be familiar, but it's not meaningful to many readers. It needs to be put into perspective so that readers can picture what it means:

> The Commerce Department said the gross national product—the total output of goods and services—grew at the fastest rate since a 7.1 percent increase in the second quarter of 1990.

Craig Medred of the *Anchorage* (Alaska) *Daily News* won a Distinguished Writing Award from the American Society of Newspaper Editors for his coverage of the Iditarod dogsled race from Anchorage to Nome. Medred's writing was marvelously descriptive. Readers could picture scenes he painted. One of his award-winning articles began with these paragraphs:

HAPPY RIVER GORGE—Coming down into this cleft through the Alaska Range, the Iditarod Trail is an angry serpent.

It snakes through deep snow across a steep hillside covered with birch. The trail zigzags all the way. Gravity wants the sleds to slip off the edge and tumble.

Note the first two paragraphs of this story by Medred:

McGRATH—For two days now, battered and jerry-rigged dogsleds have come trickling one by one into this community of 500 on the Kuskokwim River.

The sleds are pulled by teams of dogs fit and ready to run, but they are ridden by tired and bloodied mushers—men and women who have known the horrors of the snowless Farewell Burn.

Blaine Harden of *The Washington Post* won an ASNE Distinguished Writing Award for his articles on Africa. Few of Harden's readers had ever been in Nigeria, but the following paragraph would have enabled them to conjure up images:

Nigeria is hot, crowded and noisy. Totems of its culture are hard work and armed robbery, doctorates and tribal hatred, family loyalty and fast cars. Its people heap scorn upon themselves as corrupt, inefficient and self-destructive.

Tom Shales of *The Washington Post* showed how effective descriptive writing can be, even in obituaries:

She was the Mona Lisa of pinups—not just a seductive image, but the very image of seduction. Bright, lithe, willowy, radiant, Rita Hayworth flitted and floated through films as though suspended from wires. In the days when movies were larger than life, she was clearly and magically too beautiful to be real.

In another story that won a Distinguished Writing Award from ASNE—a story crafted on deadline—*Newsday*'s Paul Moran used vivid description to report on a racing tragedy:

A clash of two champions unfolded in magnificent fury. Two memorable female thoroughbreds: unbending will and granite courage doubled, four nostrils flared, four eyes bulging, muscles rippling rhythmically in the sunshine beneath the leather whips of frantic riders. Poetry in flight. They raced together into the stretch, everything on the line, a crowd of 51,236 cheering wildly, millions of others frozen before television screens. What was developing was the quintessential confrontation of thoroughbreds, each carrying a jockey and a share of history. What was happening was the Breeders' Cup personified, the essence of the game.

Go For Wand, sublimely brazen in the face of her greatest challenge, had taken the fight to Bayakoa in the $1 million Breeders' Cup Distaff yesterday on a long-awaited Belmont Park afternoon that was painted in sunshine and washed in tears. And while giving herself completely to the pursuit of victory, Go For Wand lost her life in the most tragic moment in racing since the immortal Ruffian gave her life to a match race on this track more than 15 years ago.

8: TIE IN WITH YOUR READER'S EXPERIENCE

"A statement cut off from context is a `figure' that simply floats about," Gunning wrote. "There must be another point of reference, a `ground' to give it stability and meaning. And you can't count on the reader's going farther than the end of his nose to construct that ground."

What does it mean to the reader if the city budget is increased by $25 million? Not much. Most readers cannot fathom $25 million. But they can understand the tax consequences that a $25 million increase will have on them as homeowners. Break the $25 million down. Tell the reader how much taxes will increase on a house valued at $100,000, on a house valued at $125,000 and so forth.

After a preliminary census count, officials of one Arizona city thought they had been shortchanged. The lead paragraph in the *Tempe Daily News Tribune* read:

> Tempe stands to lose up to $3 million if a preliminary census count of 130,000 holds up, according to city officials.

Most readers cannot relate to the impact of $3 million on an entire city, and so reporter Dave Downey used the next paragraph to help put the figure into perspective. And, to borrow Gunning's phrase, Downey saw to it that readers didn't have to go farther than the ends of their noses to comprehend the impact:

> City Manager Jim Alexander said the city could lose about $200 annually for each person not counted in the special mid-decade census being conducted in Maricopa County this fall.

When a volcano erupted in Colombia, it was difficult for most readers who had not experienced such an occurrence to imagine the devastation. Michael Allen, in the *Arizona Republic* article excerpted earlier, painted a word picture most readers could understand:

> Viewed from several thousand feet in the air, it looked as if an immense cement mixer had spilled its load in the heart of the valley's rich, green field.

The authors of "The Elements of Style" wrote: "Every writer, by the way he uses the language, reveals something of his spirit, his habits, his capacities, his bias. This is inevitable as well as enjoyable. All writing is communication; creative writing is communication through revelation—it is the Self escaping into the open. No writer long remains incognito."

Indeed, all of us put our personal brand on our writing. We work toward and nurture a style we find comfortable. Gunning wrote that style must be developed—that one "cannot be satisfied with imitation and do any job of writing well." He continued: "You must be able to size up each new situation, see how it is different, and fit the different words to it that do the job best. To do this, you need a wide knowledge of the flexibility and variety of the language."

Zinsser noted that it is important for writers to believe in their own identities and opinions. "Proceed with confidence, generating it, if necessary, by pure will power," he wrote. "Writing is an act of ego and you might as well admit it. Use its energy to keep yourself going."

Readers could feel Tim Povtak's energy flowing through his article on sprinter Houston McTear. Writing as if he were sitting in a living room telling his best friend about McTear, Povtak began his story in *The Orlando Sentinel* as follows:

It took only nine seconds for Houston McTear to make history in 1975. It took nearly 10 years for him to cope with what he had done. His sudden rise to fame was so pure and innocent. The following fall, though, was so adulterated and complex.

He was once the "world's fastest human." He later would become the world's most misguided athlete.

McTear is alive and well today, quietly plotting his grand comeback that very few really believe is possible anymore. Too many years have passed, too many other "I'm back" claims have disintegrated, for people to take him seriously.

Ten years ago, on May 9, 1975, in Winter Park, Fla., McTear ran 100 yards in 9.0 seconds during an afternoon preliminary heat in the Class AA Florida boys track meet. It stunned the track and field establishment. He tied the world record.

He had an incredible gift—the ability to run faster than anyone else—yet the care-and-maintenance instruction packet got lost in the mail. The blessing became a curse.

Track and field experts across the country lost interest in McTear long ago. They grew weary of his unkept promises. They don't know, or even care to know, about him now.

Yet things are different now, McTear says. Things have changed, he says. This one's for real, he says. "I used to be the 'world's fastest human,'" McTear says. "I can do it again. I can prove that America didn't waste time on Houston McTear."

The article went on to detail McTear's overnight burst into the national spotlight a decade earlier, to quote his high school track coach, to describe his record-setting performance, to quote one of the timers at that meet, to tell of McTear's lax training habits in his early career and to describe a drug habit that had plagued the sprinter. It was a difficult story to write; it told of developments that spanned a decade. But Povtak's style, his personal stamp on the facts, made the story flow.

10: WRITE TO EXPRESS, NOT TO IMPRESS

Gunning said it succinctly: "The chance of striking awe by means of big words is about run out in the United States." The sports broadcaster Howard Cosell might say:

> With his not-so-gallant gladiators finding themselves in the unenviable, precarious position of losing by six touchdowns, the sideline mentor, with unwavering resoluteness, dispatched his less-talented players into the fray.

But it would be better to write:

> With his team losing by six touchdowns, the coach decided to let his substitutes play.

three

Gathering Information

Reporters often check library sources for background information
before they conduct interviews and write stories.
(Frank Siteman/Picture Cube)

Written Sources

Reporters can strengthen every story they write by

consulting all available sources of information.

Sometimes, however, they do not know where to

look for information. It is important, therefore, to

have a working knowledge of newsroom and

library reference sources. Reporters should also be

familiar with federal and state access laws.

Information underlies good reporting and writing. But information must be gathered. It can be collected through interviews or observation. It can be harvested from public documents, private diaries, memos, letters, books, library statistical guides, magazines, newspapers, wastebaskets or microfilm. Information can inundate reporters. It is essential, though, that reporters know where to find information.

"I came across a quote one time that said there's an answer to every question that a journalist has, and your worth as a journalist is going to be determined by your ability to find the answer," Harry W. Stonecipher, a journalism professor at Southern Illinois University, said. "All this information is available someplace. You just have to find out how to locate it—and then make the effort to do so."

Stonecipher said that there is a tendency for journalists and journalism students to underutilize sources available to them.

"I sometimes find seniors who are not aware of basic newsroom and library sources," Stonecipher said. He sees to it that his students are introduced to these sources.

"I try to guide students to sources that should be available on the copy desk of most daily newspapers: Facts on File World News Digest, the CQ Researcher (formerly Editorial Research Reports), Current Biography, Congressional Quarterly Weekly Report and so forth," Stonecipher said. "These sources are more authoritative than news magazines or opinion journals, upon which reporters often rely for background information. Journalists need to know their way around a library as well as a newspaper morgue."

STANDARD INFORMATION SOURCES

Information gathered from volumes on library shelves or from standard references that are found in most newspaper offices can be just as valuable as information gathered from public documents, public meetings or governmental sources.

The following list is not exhaustive, but it contains valuable references for working journalists.

SOURCES IN THE NEWSROOM

Stylebooks, atlases, almanacs and thesauruses are common reference books that are found in nearly every newsroom or newspaper morgue. Reporters use them frequently. Another often-used book is the Guinness Book of World Records. It is used to provide information for stories and to answer the questions from readers that bombard newsrooms at all hours of the day.

Other newsroom sources include the following.

Clippings If time permits, always check the newspaper library or morgue to see if stories have been published on the topic or person you are assigned. Knowing the background of the person or topic will save you time during the interviewing process. You could, of course, use the interview to confirm background information or to seek elaboration of it. If your editor tells you to interview a longtime community resident about changes in city government but neglects to tell you that this source was the mayor in the 1940s, save yourself the embarrassment of the source's having to tell you.

Dictionaries   Dictionaries are consulted for correct spellings, of course, but they can also provide you with much more information. They can, among other things, provide syllabification, parts of speech, inflected forms, cross references, abbreviations, etymologies, synonyms, antonyms and various notes on usage. In addition, you can find such things as signs and symbols for astronomy, biology, chemistry, medicine, chess, music and mathematics. You can also find a directory of colleges and universities, and a basic manual of style that explains the use of the period, ellipsis, question mark, exclamation point, comma, semicolon, colon, apostrophe, quotation marks, parentheses, brackets, dash and hyphen. Some dictionaries even include proofreading symbols.

Encyclopedias   Encyclopedias provide information on almost everything from *a* (the first letter in the alphabet) to Vladimir Kosma Zworykin (a Russian-born American physicist and electronics engineer who lived from 1889 until 1982). Entries are arranged alphabetically and include cross references. The charts, maps and illustrations often provide excellent background. If you are assigned to do a story on drinking habits of students at your college or university, it would be a good idea to check an encyclopedia. You might be surprised by what you could learn about fermented beverages, Alcoholics Anonymous (A.A.), alcoholism and its effects and treatment. And if you want to try to get a grip on how much beer the average student drinks, it wouldn't hurt—again—to check the encyclopedia, where you will find such tidbits as the average yearly consumption of beer by people in the United States. (A recent entry in the World Book Encyclopedia says that the average consumption is about 24 gallons per person per year.)

Telephone directories   Telephone directories can give you more than telephone numbers. They can, for example, provide you with such things as area postal ZIP codes, street indexes and city maps. The yellow pages can be particularly valuable when searching for sources. For instance, if you are assigned to do a story on local abortion agencies, a logical starting place to line up local interviews would be the yellow pages. In the yellow pages for the Phoenix metropolitan area, there is a main subheading for "Abortion Alternatives Information" (with nine cross references listed, including "Adoption Services" and "Birth Control Centers") and a main subheading for "Abortion Information" (with eight cross references listed, including "Marriage, Family, Child and Individual Counselors" and "Clinics"). A cursory glance at the yellow pages might provide you with sources you did not know existed.

City directories   City directories, which are published by private firms, include alphabetical lists of names, addresses and telephone numbers of adult residents. They also contain street address guides, telephone number directories, ZIP codes, elementary school districts for individual addresses and information on such things as population, average income per household, home value distribution, construction permits, utilities, news media, tax bases, airlines, buses, railroads, climate and industrial sites.

State directories Called *blue books* in many states, state directories include information on the executive branch (official state rosters of elective and appointive officers, their salaries and so on), the legislative branch (rosters of officials, their districts and so forth) and the judicial branch (rosters of judges, circuits, maps and so on). These volumes also include information on things such as state schools and colleges, election returns and miscellaneous statistics.

Biographical references Standard biographical reference volumes such as Current Biography, which is published monthly except in August, are available in many newsrooms. This service provides about 30 articles in each month's edition on newsworthy living persons. The annual volumes contain about 350 biographies. The Dictionary of American Biography, another common source, contains information on distinguished Americans who are dead.

Most small- and medium-circulation newspapers limit their biographical volumes to one or two major references, but libraries have many biographical reference sources from which to choose. These range from general sources such as Biography and Genealogy Master Index, Current Biography and The New York Times Biographical Service to such specialized volumes as Who's Who in Switzerland, Who's Who in the United Nations, Current World Leaders, The International Who's Who, Who's Who in the World, Dictionary of National Biography, Who Was Who in American Art, Obituaries on File and Biography Index.

Facts on File World News Digest Published weekly, this volume summarizes, records and indexes the news. National and foreign news events are included along with information on deaths, science, sports, medicine, education, religion, crime, books, plays, films and people in the news. The index includes subjects (grain embargo, school prayer and so forth) and names of people, organizations and countries.

CQ Researcher Published four times a month, CQ Researcher deals with major contemporary news issues, presenting a balanced overview in about 6,000 words. This source is particularly valuable because of its objective approach and its footnotes, which can lead the reporter to additional sources.

SOURCES IN LIBRARIES

Public or college libraries can provide scores of useful references for reporters seeking information that is not readily available in most newsrooms.

General Information

Newspaper indexes *The New York Times, Los Angeles Times, The Washington Post* and *The Wall Street Journal,* among others, are newspapers that index news events. These indexes, which are published in bound volumes, usually contain subject and name indexes.

Miscellaneous indexes Reporters use specialized indexes when they are researching a particular topic. These indexes include, but are not limited to, the Readers' Guide to Periodical Literature, Business Periodicals Index, Social Sciences Index, General Sciences Index and the Essay and General Literature Index.

Reporters who seek book-length treatments of various subjects can consult the Subject Guide to Books in Print, which lists in-print English-language titles available from American book publishers and distributors. Additional volumes of the Subject Guide allow reporters to look up current books by both author and title. Overviews of various books can be found by using Book Review Index, Book Review Digest and various newspaper indexes.

Gale Directory of Publications and Broadcast Media This directory—formerly the Ayer Directory of Publications—provides basic information on nearly 25,000 newspapers, magazines, journals and other publications issued in the United States and Canada as well as radio stations, television stations and cable systems. Entries are arranged geographically.

Monthly Catalog of U.S. Government Publications This catalog can be helpful to the reporter who is not sure where to search for specific information. Subjects are derived from the Library of Congress Subject Headings and its supplements. The catalog consists of text and five indexes: author, title, subject, series/report number and stock number. Instructions for ordering the publications listed are also included.

American Statistics Index (ASI) ASI lists, by subject, areas in which there are federal government statistics. A counterpart, Statistical Reference Index (SRI), covers statistics gathered by organizations, university research centers and state governments.

Statistical Abstract of the United States The Statistical Abstract (SA) is a digest of statistical data that have been collected by the federal government and a variety of private agencies.

National Directory of Addresses and Telephone Numbers This directory includes sections on business and finance, government, education, religious denominations, hospitals, associations and unions, transportation and hotels, communications media and culture and recreation. It also has an alphabetical list of all names included.

National Five-Digit ZIP Code and Post Office Directory This directory, which is published by the U.S. Postal Service, provides ZIP codes for all towns and cities listed by state. ZIP codes for street listings are also included when appropriate.

Encyclopedia of Associations This encyclopedia provides information on more than 25,000 national and international organizations. Entries are arranged under 18 subject sections. Information for each entry includes address, date of founding, number of members, budget and so forth.

Gallup Poll Monthly   This source provides analytical as well as well as statistical data.

Editorials on File   Published biweekly, Editorials on File contains editorial reprints from more than 130 American newspapers. There are generally 20 to 30 editorials on each subject. Indexes for subjects are found at the end of each binder.

A Dictionary of Slang and Unconventional English   This 1,400-page dictionary contains definitions of colloquialisms, catchphrases and vulgarisms of the past five centuries.

Business Organizations, Agencies and Publications Directory   This is a guide to more than 25,000 organizations that promote, represent and serve business and industry. The volume includes such useful sections as United States diplomatic offices abroad, boards of trade, better business bureaus and labor unions.

Famous First Facts   This book includes more than 9,000 facts in American history, which are arranged alphabetically by subject (from "abdominal operation" to "zoom lens").

Physician's Desk Reference (PDR)   This source, which is published annually, is intended primarily for physicians. It includes information on more than 2,000 major pharmaceutical and diagnostic products.

The Merck Manual of Diagnosis and Therapy   The Merck Manual, which is designed primarily for practicing physicians, medical students, interns, residents and other health professionals, provides information on a broad range of medical disorders.

Familiar Quotations   Formerly Bartlett's Familiar Quotations, this book contains more than 22,500 quotations and includes an author index and an index of key words.

Emily Post's Etiquette   Emily Post's etiquette book, which was first published in 1922, provides answers to questions about a variety of things such as formal occasions, entertaining, weddings, celebrations (e.g., baby showers, graduations, anniversaries), table manners and table settings.

Encyclopedia of World Crime   A comprehensive five-volume biographical and historical encyclopedia, this source covers the fields of crime, criminology, criminal justice and law enforcement.

Other useful general references   In addition to the references discussed above, scores of other general reference sources are valuable to journalists. Cynthia Scanlon, a free-lance journalist who also works at the Phoenix, Ariz.,

Public Library, said that the following sources are helpful: Who's Who in American Politics, Facts about Presidents, Climates of the States and the Essential Guide to Prescription Drugs.

Scanlon listed the following general reference sources (with descriptions of the contents of those that are not obvious):

- *The New Address Book: How to Reach Anyone Who's Anyone.* This book provides information on how to locate more than 3,000 celebrities, corporate executives and VIPs.

- *American Hospital Association Guide to the Health Care Field.* This volume lists the addresses of hospitals and clinics throughout the United States.

- *American Library Directory.* This volume contains the names of libraries throughout the United States, listed by subject or state.

- *Chase's Annual Events.* This volume lists a full year's calendar by month.

- *Contemporary Authors.* This book contains the names, the addresses and short biographies of contemporary authors.

- *Directory of Medical Specialists.* This volume lists doctors by state or specialty.

- *Dorland's Illustrated Medical Dictionary* and *Taber's Cyclopedic Medical Dictionary.* These dictionaries define medical terms and provide an explanation of symptoms.

- *Encyclopedia of American Crime.* This source covers crime figures and crime events.

- *World Chamber of Commerce Directory.* This directory provides the addresses of chambers of commerce in cities in the 50 states and throughout the world; it also contains the addresses of the foreign embassies and consulates in the United States as well as those of the American embassies and consulates throughout the world.

- *The Official Museum Directory.* This directory contains the names of museums, listed by state and subject.

- *Places Rated Almanac.* This almanac contains ratings of cities according to their climate and terrain, housing, crimes, health care, education, transportation, arts and recreation.

- *Standard and Poor's Register.* This volume contains the names, the addresses and the telephone numbers of all officers of major corporations.

- *Acronyms, Initialisms & Abbreviations Dictionary* (also, *Reverse Acronyms, Initialisms & Abbreviations Dictionary*).

- *Standard Directory of Advertisers.* This volume contains the names of the largest advertising agencies as well as a trademark index.

- *Standard Periodical Directory.* This directory contains the names, the addresses, the telephone numbers, the circulation figures and the subscription rates of most periodicals and newsletters in the United States.

- *Symbols of America.* This volume contains information on American trademarks and the products they symbolize; according to the cover, the information includes "their history, folklore and enduring mystique."

- *Washington Information Directory.* This volume lists the addresses of almost every agency in Washington, D.C.

- *Who's Who in America* and *Webster's Biographical Dictionary.* These books contain biographical information on individuals of national and international importance.

- *World Almanac.* This volume contains information about weather, sports, world facts, awards, ambassadors to the United Nations, measurements, officials of states and countries, and so forth as well as a guide to the occurrence of full moons and a perpetual calendar. Scanlon said: "If our reference team were stranded on a desert island and could have only one reference book—this would be it. Just about anything you could imagine is probably contained in the World Almanac."

- *Almanac of Higher Education.* This volume is an annual compendium of descriptive and statistical information on higher education that is organized by state.

Harvey Sager, a reference librarian at Arizona State University who works closely with journalism and mass communication holdings, listed these additional references that could be particularly helpful to reporters:

- *Dictionary of Bias Free Usage: A Guide to Nondiscriminatory Language.* This volume offers non-biased alternatives to the many subtle, and not so subtle, reflections of gender bias, racial bias, and other biases in speech and writing.

- *Directories in Print.* This comprehensive guide to directories, with its keyword index, can help you determine if a specialized directory exists, and where you might acquire it. For example, is there a directory that lists firms owned by minorities and women? There is.

- *Directory of Corporate Affiliations.* This source helps you identify and locate the subsidiaries of a parent corporation or, conversely, to identify the parent corporation of a subsidiary.

- *Dos and Taboos Around the World.* This volume provides an overview of various customs and manners around the world, covering such diverse topics as hand gestures and gifts.

- *Dun and Bradstreet Reference Book of Corporate Managements.* Subtitled "America's Corporate Leaders," and organized by both company and personal names, these volumes give concise résumés of work history and brief biographical data for the top business leaders in the United States.

- *Dun's Business Rankings.* Companies are ranked nationally, within each state, as well as by industry; within these categories, rankings are by company revenues and by number of employees.

- *Europa World Year Book.* Included for each country is a brief overview of recent history, a description of the form of government, and information on education, defense, economic affairs, judicial system, religion, holidays and so forth; for many countries, detailed statistical tables are provided.

- *Hoover's Handbook of American Business.* Valuable for its company overviews and concise company histories, this source contains a page of useful information for each company listed. For example, it provides executives' salaries, competitors, company growth and stock performance.

- *New Book of World Rankings.* Organized into 33 chapters, this source can provide information on where nations rank in categories ranging from "Cigarette Consumption" to "Defense Expenditures as a Percentage of National Budget."

- *New York Public Library Book of How and Where to Look It Up.* A concise and useful guide for locating information regardless of its location, this book contains a useful section on key reference works as well as handy "Research Tips" for each section.

- *Open Secrets: The Dollar Power of PACs in Congress.* In addition to tracking political action committee funds, it includes charts listing campaign revenues, election spending and interest group ratings for each congressional member listed.

- *Reader's Companion to American History.* This source contains brief articles on key persons, events, concepts, issues, movements and themes that collectively reflect American history.

- *Research Centers Directory.* The university and other nonprofit research centers and organizations listed here can be excellent sources for locating the latest research finding on almost any topic.

- *Source of ZIP Code Demographics.* A rich source of demographic data on the population of the United States, organized by ZIP code, this book provides categories of data for each ZIP code that include population size, population distribution by race and sex, family size, household income, housing values and so forth.

- *Statistical Record of Women Worldwide.* Gathered from diverse sources, the statistics in this volume include such hard-to-find data as "Types of Sexual Harassment in the Military" and results of attitude and opinion surveys of women on a wide range of social issues.

- *Statistics Sources.* A guide to locating sources of statistics (through agencies, associations, compendiums and so forth) regardless of subject or national boundaries, this reference book contains a section on federal telephone contacts for acquiring statistical information.

- *Webster's Dictionary of English Usage.* Word-processing software can check spelling, but it is not a substitute for a good usage dictionary.

- *Fulltext Sources Online.* This source is one of a growing number of useful printed reference works that provides information on computer searchable data bases. It can help you identify magazines, journals, newsletters, newspapers and newswires from which articles can be searched and retrieved in full-text format with a computer. (Chapter 10 discusses electronic sources.)

Information on States

Statistical abstracts for states   State abstracts often include information on such things as geography, climate, population, vital statistics (births and deaths), health, education, labor, employment, earnings, public lands, recreation, government, law enforcement, mining, construction, housing, manufacturing, transportation, energy, communications, utilities and real estate.

The Book of the States   This reference provides information on the types of operating procedures, financing and activities of state governments. Numerous tables list all states and provide comparative information about such things as income taxes, campaign finance laws and voter turnout.

State Yellow Book   This book presents basic information on aspects of all 50 states, such as officers; major services; legislatures; supreme courts; representation in Washington, D.C.; and federal offices in each state.

Information on the Federal Government and Congress

Federal Register   Administrative rules and regulations are published in this weekday service.

U.S. Government Manual   This manual describes the functions of departments and agencies in the executive branch. It includes a bibliography of publications prepared by each.

Congressional Information Service (CIS) Index   This index provides access to contents of congressional hearings, reports and documents. It contains testimony by expert witnesses and is excellent for pro and con arguments.

Congressional Digest   This digest examines contemporary subjects being considered by Congress. It attempts to present all sides of an issue.

Congressional Directory   This directory contains short biographical sketches of all representatives (listed by state). It also lists the office and telephone numbers of members of Congress, along with the names of two principal staff members for each.

Congressional Quarterly Weekly Report   Published weekly, this source contains the voting records of members of Congress and texts of presidential press conferences and major speeches.

Congressional Record   This source contains verbatim reports of what is said on the House and Senate floors. Do not assume, however, that all statements in the Congressional Record were actually articulated on the floors. Senators and representatives can also enter materials into the Congressional Record that were not delivered on the floors of the respective Houses.

Congressional Staff Directory   Reporters often find this directory particularly valuable when gathering information on topical issues. It provides names of staff members of congressional committees and subcommittees along with nearly 3,000 staff biographies.

Guide to Congress   The subject index of this guide, published by Congressional Quarterly, includes a variety of topics on how Congress works. For example, reporters wondering about impeachment proceedings could turn to this volume for a summary of the purpose of impeachment, its history, the procedures and a chart on federal officers who have been impeached by the House.

Reporters who seek information on legal topics can consult the sources described below.

Law dictionaries   Reporters who have questions about legal terminology can consult law dictionaries. One of the most comprehensive is Black's Law Dictionary, which provides the meanings of legal terms and phrases found in statutes or judicial opinions. It also includes a guide to pronunciation.

Legal encyclopedias   Corpus Juris Secundum (C.J.S.) and American Jurisprudence 2d (Am. Jur. 2d) are excellent basic sources. Corpus Juris Secundum provides a look at American case law from the first reported case to the present. It also includes citations to such sources as treatises, form-books and law journal articles. American Jurisprudence 2d provides overviews of various aspects of law arranged alphabetically by title. Some states—such as California, Florida, New York and Texas—have their own laws published in encyclopedias. General encyclopedias include definitions of words and phrases, in addition to overviews of cases and statutory laws. Reporters who are exploring an area of the law for the first time will find encyclopedias to be excellent starting points.

Indexes to legal publications   The Index to Legal Periodicals is published monthly, except in September. Bound volumes by year can be found in law libraries and in many university libraries. The topical index is particularly helpful to reporters who need a crash course in a specific area of the law. For example, reporters doing a series of articles on fair trial versus free press in the United States could consult the subheading "Freedom of the Press" in the Index to Legal Periodicals. Under that subheading would be a long list of articles dealing with freedom of the press. The reporters could pull from the list those articles that dealt with fair trial–free press issues. This volume provides the current index to nearly 600 legal journals published in the United States, Great Britain, Ireland, Australia and New Zealand.

Federal laws   The United States Code and the United States Code Annotated contain federal statutes. Sometimes journalists know a statute only by its popular name, such as the Smith Act or the Taft-Hartley Act. In this situation, Shepard's Federal and State Acts and Cases by Popular Names is helpful because it lists acts by their popular names and provides citations to the official acts.

State laws   Each state publishes its codes. These are generally compiled under a title such as Arizona Revised Statutes or Ohio Revised Code. Reporters should familiarize themselves with the volumes of laws for their particular states.

Digests of cases   The American Digest System publishes all reported state and federal cases. The cases are arranged by subject. The U.S. Supreme Court Digest arranges high court decisions by subject.

Federal court decisions   Opinions of the U.S. Supreme Court can be found in a variety of sources, including United States Reports (the official government edition), United States Supreme Court Reports (the Lawyer's Cooperative Publishing Co. edition), Supreme Court Reporter (West Publishing Co. edition) and United States Law Week (published by the Bureau of National Affairs). Opinions of the U.S. Courts of Appeal and the U.S. Court of Appeals for the Federal Circuit can be found in the Federal Reporter series. Selected opinions of the U.S. District Courts and the U.S. Customs Court can be found in the Federal Supplement. These volumes are found in law library collections as well as in many university libraries.

Media-related court decisions   Media Law Reporter (Med. L. Rep.), published weekly since January 1977, reports almost all court cases involving press law. Media law scholar Donald Gillmor of the University of Minnesota has noted that "95 percent of cases that get even to the earliest stages of a court proceeding . . . appear in the publication, if not in official and other unofficial case reports." Media Law Reporter also publishes news notes and occasional bibliographies.

State court decisions   Some states publish volumes containing only their own state court decisions; some do not. Selected state court decisions can be found in the National Reporter System's regional volumes. The North Western Reporter, for example, contains opinions from Iowa, Michigan, Minnesota, Nebraska, North Dakota, South Dakota and Wisconsin. Several regional reports are published.

GOVERNMENT AS AN INFORMATION SOURCE

ACCESS TO FEDERAL INFORMATION: THE FREEDOM OF INFORMATION ACT

Scholars who have researched the issue of access to information have quoted from a letter James Madison once wrote:

> Knowledge will forever govern ignorance. And a people who mean to be their own governors, must arm themselves with the power knowledge gives. A popular government without popular information or the means of acquiring it, is but a prologue to a farce or a tragedy, or perhaps both.

Madison's words symbolize the philosophical bedrock of a democratic society. Sometimes, however, practices override theory. As might be expected—considering the adversarial relationship between press and government—the media would like to have access to and use certain information that the government would often prefer not to release.

Indeed, a recent report released by the Society of Professional Journalists (SPJ) noted that "media organizations across the country are experiencing a . . . sudden rise in the number of access cases." The report concluded that the increase had "resulted from news organizations' resistance to the increased closings of courtrooms and public meetings, the routine sealing of court files and the unauthorized withholding of government documents."

Bruce W. Sanford, the general counsel to SPJ, wrote in *The Quill* that "the growing pains of access law are just beginning," partially because "the boundaries of access law remain uncharted."

Background

In the early 1960s members of Congress started working on legislation that would make available, for public inspection, the records of federal departments and agencies. As a result, Congress passed the *Freedom of Information (FOI) Act* in 1966. This act unlocked doors to information that had previously been unavailable, although there were several exceptions to disclosure.

By the early 1970s members of Congress discovered the need to put teeth into the act. In 1971 a published story said that President Richard Nixon had received conflicting recommendations on the advisability of an underground nuclear test scheduled for that fall. A congresswoman sent a telegram to the president requesting immediate release of the recommendations. The request was denied.

Thirty-three members of Congress brought suit under the Freedom of Information Act. The administration said that nine of the 10 affidavits sought had been stamped "secret" by executive order. The Supreme Court upheld the right of the administration to withhold the information on that basis. Justice Byron White stated that Exemption 1 of the act blocked requests for all information classified "secret" by executive order. White added that the exemption was "intended to dispel uncertainty with respect to public access to material affecting national defense or foreign policy."

Justice William Brennan Jr. dissented in part. He said that White's majority interpretation of Exemption 1 as a "complete bar to judicial inspection of matters claimed by the executive to fall within it wholly frustrates the objective of the . . . act." Justice William O. Douglas also dissented. He contended that the executive branch should not have "carte blanche to insulate information from public scrutiny."

Congressional reaction to the majority decision was negative. Legislation was introduced to amend the act to permit, among other things, *"in-camera" inspection* of documents. A judge would then be able to examine materials in a private room or with all spectators excluded from the courtroom to determine whether documents stamped "secret" had in fact been properly classified. The implementation of faster and more efficient appeals procedures was also sought. Agencies of the executive branch lobbied against the proposals. The House, however, voted 383–8 to amend the act and later overrode President Gerald Ford's veto. The Senate then passed the bill. The legislation took effect on Feb. 19, 1975. The FOI Act was amended again in 1986.

The amendments were a tremendous help to the public—including journalists—who had felt unduly frustrated by the cavalier, wholesale designation of documents as "secret" by the executive branch. Essentially, the revised act gives "any person" access to the records of all federal agencies, unless the information sought is a clearly defined exception.

How to Use the FOI Act

If the information sought is not an exception, journalists are advised to make informal requests to the agency. This can be done by telephone. If an informal request fails to bring results, a formal written request for the records can be made. As emphasized in a booklet titled "How to Use the Federal FOI Act," "Once an FOI Act request is made, the burden is on the government to promptly release the documents or show that they are covered by one of the act's exemptions."

The agency must respond within 10 working days, though it may seek an extension if requests are backlogged. If the agency refuses to supply the information or does not respond within 10 days, the reporter can appeal to the head of the agency. If an answer is not given within 20 working days by the head of the agency, or if the agency denies the request, the reporter can file a lawsuit in federal court. If the reporter wins the lawsuit, the agency will be ordered to release the documents and to pay attorney fees and court costs. The court can also order sanctions against the government officials responsible for improperly withholding the information. Names of responsible officials are readily available, because the law specifies that any denial notification shall include "the names and titles or positions of each person responsible for the denial."

The amended FOI Act spells out the types of materials beyond its reach.

(1) (A) specifically authorized under criteria established by Executive order to be kept secret in the interest of national defense or foreign policy and (B) are in fact properly classified pursuant to such Executive order;

(2) related solely to the internal personnel rules and practices of an agency;

(3) specifically exempted from disclosure by statute . . . , provided that such statute (A) requires that the matters be withheld from the public in such a manner as to leave no discretion on the issue, or (B) establishes particular criteria for withholding or refers to particular types of matters to be withheld;

(4) trade secrets and commercial or financial information obtained from a person and privileged or confidential;

(5) inter-agency or intra-agency memorandums or letters which would not be available by law to a party other than an agency in litigation with the agency;

(6) personnel and medical files and similar files the disclosure of which would constitute a clearly unwarranted invasion of personal privacy;

(7) records or information compiled for law enforcement purposes, but only to the extent that the production of such law enforcement records or information (A) could reasonably be expected to interfere with enforcement proceedings, (B) would deprive a person of a right to a fair trial or an impartial adjudication, (C) could reasonably be expected to constitute an unwarranted invasion of personal privacy, (D) could reasonably be expected to disclose the identity of a confidential source, including a State, local, or foreign agency or authority or any private institution which furnished information on a confidential basis, and, in the case of a record or information compiled by criminal law enforcement authority in the course of a criminal investigation or by an agency conducting a lawful national security intelligence investigation, information furnished by a confidential source, (E) would disclose techniques and procedures for law enforcement investigations or prosecutions, or would disclose guidelines for law enforcement investigations or prosecutions if such disclosure

could reasonably be expected to risk circumvention of the law, or (F) could reasonably be expected to endanger the life or physical safety of any individual;

(8) contained in or related to examination, operating, or condition reports prepared by, on behalf of, or for the use of an agency responsible for the regulation or supervision of financial institutions; or

(9) geological and geophysical information and data, including maps, concerning wells.

There have been frequent and regular attempts to water down the act to make government control of information more stringent. The media and other groups have bristled at the thought of a diluted act. These groups have fought against any further moves to curtail information gathering, but the battle is ongoing.

Through the years, the FOI Act has been an effective tool for journalists seeking to secure government information. All reporters should familiarize themselves with the provisions of the act and the procedures for using it to greatest advantage.

A good starting point is to examine "How to Use the Federal FOI Act," a project of the Reporters Committee for Freedom of the Press. The booklet includes an overview of the act; the agencies covered by the act and the records that are available; a discussion of who can use the act; suggestions on informal and formal requests; guidelines on searching and copying fees; a description of ways to have fees cut or waived; suggestions on procedures for filing formal appeals; a discussion on how to file FOI Act lawsuits; and an analysis of the nine exemptions to the act. The booklet also includes a sample FOI request letter, which is reproduced on page 196.

ACCESS TO STATE INFORMATION

Legislatures have taken measures for providing access to state-level information. All states have some type of *open-records laws*; it is the responsibility of reporters to know the law in their states. Naturally, most state statutes have certain exceptions, just as the federal Freedom of Information Act does.

State Legislation: The Nebraska Public-Records Act

Open-records laws vary from state to state, but Nebraska's Public-Records Act is representative. Here are portions of the Nebraska law:

> Except as otherwise expressly provided by statute, all citizens of this state, and all other persons interested in the examination of the public records, as defined in [the next section] are hereby fully empowered and authorized to examine the same, and to make memoranda and abstracts therefrom, all free of charge, during the hours the respective offices may be kept open for the ordinary transaction of business.
>
> (1) Except where any other statute expressly provides that particular information or records shall not be made public, public records shall include all records and documents, regardless of physical form, of or belonging to this state, any county, city, village, political subdivision, or tax-supported district in this state, or any agency, branch, department, board, bureau, commission, council,

Your address
Daytime phone number
Date

Freedom of Information Office
Agency
Address

FOIA Request

Dear FOI Officer:

Pursuant to the federal Freedom of Information Act, 5 U.S.C. § 552, I request access to and copies of (here, clearly describe what you want. Include identifying material, such as names, places, and the period of time about which you are inquiring. If you think they will help to explain what you are looking for, attach news clips, reports, and other documents describing the subject of your research.)

I agree to pay reasonable duplication fees for the processing of this request in an amount not to exceed $__. However, please notify me prior to your incurring any expenses in excess of that amount.

(Suggested request for fee benefit as a representative of the news media:) As a representative of the news media I am only required to pay for the direct cost of duplication after the first 100 pages. Through this request, I am gathering information on (subject) that is of current interest to the public because (give reason). This information is being sought on behalf of (give the name of your news organization) for dissemination to the general public. (If a freelancer, provide information such as experience, publication contract, etc., that demonstrates that you expect publication.)

(Optional fee waiver request:) Please waive any applicable fees. Release of the information is in the public interest because it will contribute significantly to public understanding of government operations and activities.

If my request is denied in whole or part, I ask that you justify all deletions by reference to specific exemptions of the act. I will also expect you to release all segregable portions of otherwise exempt material. I, of course, reserve the right to appeal your decision to withhold any information or to deny a waiver of fees.

As I am making this request as a journalist (author, or scholar) and this information is of timely value, I would appreciate your communicating with me by telephone, rather than by mail, if you have questions regarding this request. I look forward to your reply within 10 business days, as the statute requires.

Thank you for your assistance.

Very truly yours,

Your signature

Sample FOI
request letter.

subunit, or committee of any of the foregoing. Data which is a public record in its original form shall remain a public record when maintained in computer files.

(2) [Sections of this law] shall be liberally construed whenever any state, county or political subdivision fiscal records, audit, warrant, voucher, invoice, purchase order, requisition, payroll, check, receipt or other record of receipt, cash or expenditure involving public funds is involved in order that the citizens of this state shall have full rights to know of, and have full access to information on the public finances of the government and the public bodies and entities created to serve them.

Any person denied any rights granted by [sections of this law] may elect to (1) file for speedy relief by a writ of mandamus in the district court within whose jurisdiction the state, county, or political subdivision officer who has custody of said public record can be served, or (2) petition the Attorney General to review the record to determine whether it may be withheld from public inspection. This determination shall be made within fifteen calendar days of the submission of the petition. If the Attorney General determines that the record may not be withheld, the public body shall be ordered to disclose the record immediately. If the public body continues to withhold the record, the person seeking disclosure may (a) bring suit in the trial court of general jurisdiction or (b) demand in writing that the Attorney General shall bring suit in the name of the state in the trial court of general jurisdiction for the same purpose. If such demand is made, the Attorney General shall bring suit within fifteen calendar days of its receipt. The requester shall have an absolute right to intervene as a full party in the suit at any time. . . .

Any person denied any rights granted by [the various sections of this law] shall receive in written form from the public body which denied the request for records at least the following information:

(a) A description of the contents of the records withheld and a statement of the specific reasons for the denial, correlating specific reasons for the denial, including citations to the particular statute and subsection thereof expressly providing the exception under [the particular section] relied on as authority for the denial.

(b) The name of the public official or employee responsible for the decision to deny request, and

(c) Notification to the requester of any administrative or judicial right of review under [a particular section of this act].

Each public body shall maintain a file of all letters of denial of request for records. This file shall be made available to any person on request.

The Nebraska law, just like the federal FOI Act, also lists the types of records that may be withheld from the public.

In addition, the law states: "Any official who shall violate the provisions of [this] act shall be subject to removal or impeachment and in addition shall be deemed guilty of a Class III misdemeanor."

In brief, then, the Nebraska law contains provisions common to many states:

- General statement about the rights of people to public records
- General statement that the law should be construed liberally in favor of persons seeking records

- Information on the appeal procedures for persons who have been denied access to records
- Information on exceptions to the types of records that can generally be obtained
- Information on penalties for officials who violate provisions of the law

It might appear that open-records laws such as those of Nebraska and other states would provide a quick, efficient right of access. Often that is the case, but it is impossible to tell how "strong" or "weak" an open-records law is until it is tested in court.

Using Open-Records Laws: A Battle in Arizona

Max Jennings, executive editor of the *Mesa Tribune,* an Arizona daily with a circulation of about 45,000, found out firsthand that merely having a state access law on the books is no guarantee that public employees will necessarily—quietly and without reservation—turn over all requests for information.

Jennings spearheaded a six-person team of reporters and editors that assembled more than 25 news stories, editorials and columns focusing on the Arizona State University athletic program. At the time, the university was under investigation by the National Collegiate Athletic Association (NCAA) for alleged violations of athletic rules. Most of the material was published during a one-week period.

The effort was substantial. Still, Jennings said that he was frustrated because the "whole story" had not been told. "We felt, despite the volumes we had written, that there was a great deal of information we did not have. We had to gain access to the NCAA documents and the ASU response" before the story could be regarded as complete.

Jennings said that his reporters made "several informal requests" to ASU officials for the NCAA documents. The university refused to turn over any materials. Jennings told the director of university relations that a suit would be filed if the records were not made available. The editor also sent a letter by certified mail to the ASU president. Jennings did not think that the president would be intimidated by the letter. "In fact, I would have been surprised had he honored the formal request," Jennings said. He was convinced that ASU, a public institution, had "hired expensive lawyers at taxpayers' expense and instructed them to stonewall" the request.

Formal requests, diplomacy and persuasion had failed. Litigation was the one remaining option. At this point, newspaper executives must decide whether to pursue information tenaciously or to sit back and rationalize that the story would not be worth the effort.

Not all newspapers—particularly small- and medium-circulation dailies with limited financial bases—choose to make the economic commitment necessary to pursue a cause in court. Public officials often realize this and gamble that their refusal to turn over what would appear to be public records will never be challenged. But Jennings, with the support of his publisher, decided to bring suit—a suit that would entail an enormous expenditure of time, money and energy. The newspaper thought it had a "50–50" chance of winning. "It was only after a great deal of thought that we decided to file suit if necessary," Jennings explained. "We were not naive about the time and expense involved. It was a last resort."

Jennings was perhaps more familiar with his state's access law than most other editors of medium-circulation dailies because of his academic background. (He had been a university professor.) "I emphasized the importance and purpose of the law in my reporting classes," he said. "That may have had something to do with my confidence in using it. I think a lot of editors of smaller newspapers don't spend a lot of time familiarizing themselves with open-meeting or open-records laws—and that is unfortunate."

Jennings said that most editors would probably want to file suit to gain access to suppressed information. "But the sad truth is," he said, "most conversations between editors and publishers concerning access to public information stop when the question of legal fees comes up. And even large organizations sometimes are reluctant to spend money fighting cases of this nature."

Bringing access cases to court is almost a matter of "idealism," Jennings said. "The tangible rewards for doing something like this [filing suit] are awfully small," he said. "The information sought, if you win in court, generally is turned over to all the media. But you can go home at night and say, 'Gee, what we did was really worthwhile, and it makes me proud to be in this business.'"

Ultimately, a Superior Court judge ordered that the documents be turned over to the media.

In its editions the morning after the documents were released, the *Mesa Tribune* published four comprehensive articles based on the new information: a summary of the NCAA charges and the ASU responses, a summary of ASU's plan to prevent future abuses, a summary of the letter sent to the NCAA by the ASU president and a reaction to the court ruling by the *Tribune*'s legal counsel.

Jennings and the media had won. But the victory was costly for Cox Arizona Publications Inc., which owns the *Mesa Tribune*. Attorney fees were substantial (they were later recovered), and Jennings had spent scores of hours in an effort to gain the information. The *Mesa Tribune* did not even get an exclusive story; all the media were given access to the documents.

"I hope we sensitized public officials in Arizona as to what the requirements of the law are—and that is to the benefit of all the citizenry, not just the media," Jennings said.

Jennings was convinced that the refusal to return phone calls, the refusal to cooperate in bringing the case to a hearing and the ultimate and unsuccessful appeal to the Arizona Supreme Court were "all part of a calculated strategy on the part of the university to deny us the record. I think it is a strategy that works most of the time for public agencies. Public officials are not using their money; they are getting paid for the time such delays consume. They have nothing to lose and everything to gain if disclosure of the documents would be embarrassing, so the strategy is to jam, stall, stonewall."

Jennings offered this advice to reporters who seek state-level documents:

- Be as aggressive as you know how to be.
- Be familiar with the access statute in your state. Type a summary of it, and carry it in your billfold.

- Don't be afraid to cite the law to public officials who want to withhold information. If this does not get results, go back to your editor and demand support from management.

"I do not want to hire a reporter who does not feel outraged at being denied a public record," Jennings said. "I want my reporters to feel a genuine sense of outrage; and, if they don't, I think they ought to practice another profession."

ACCESS TO STATE AND LOCAL MEETINGS

Open-Meeting Laws

Sharon Hartin Iorio of Wichita State University presented a paper at the Southwest Symposium for Journalism/Mass Communications at New Mexico State University that examined state open-meeting legislation. After providing an excellent overview of the historical development of the open-government concept, Iorio analyzed the major components of various state *open-meeting laws*. She found that the laws vary, but a consensus of the general content includes the following:

- Statement of purpose
- Definitions (the terms *meeting* and *open* are often defined)
- Coverage (an overview of the categories of government organizations that fall under the law)
- Notice (a requirement that the time and place of meetings should be made public)
- Minutes (a requirement that minutes be kept of meetings and that these minutes be open for public inspection)
- Sanctions (which provide avenues of enforcement of the law's component parts)

Because state open-meeting laws are not uniform, Iorio emphasized that not all statutes include the general provisions she isolated, but they are representative. Here are some of Iorio's conclusions:

It is difficult to draw any generalizations regarding the laws since they vary greatly from state to state; they are constantly being updated; they are qualified by court decisions and attorneys' general opinions; and they are affected by other legislation and state constitutional requirements.

In theory the laws have been designed to open access; in practice there often has been a disparity between the intent and application of open-meeting laws. Recurring problems involve exceptions and executive sessions which restrict access, and weak enforcement measures. . . .

Certainly state open-meeting laws today are more comprehensive and have stronger enforcement measures than did their earlier predecessors. Today all fifty states have passed open-meeting legislation, indicating a general trend toward open-meeting laws that allow greater access to government.

Some states have stronger and more specific statutes than others. It is imperative, therefore, that reporters become thoroughly acquainted with the requirements of the laws in their states.

Example: Iowa's open-meeting law   Iowa's open-meeting law is specific. It says: "Ambiguity in the construction or application of this chapter should be resolved in favor of openness." The law, which is very comprehensive, merits examination.

The Iowa law begins with important definitions. For example, it defines *governmental body* as:

A board, council, commission or other governing body expressly created by the statutes of this state or by executive order

A board, council, commission or other governing body of a political subdivision or tax-supported district in this state

A multimembered body formally and directly created by one or more boards, councils, commissions or other governing bodies subject [to the above]

Those multimembered bodies to which the state board of regents or a president of a university has delegated the responsibility for the management and control of the intercollegiate athletic programs at the state universities

An advisory board, advisory commission or task force created by the governor or the general assembly to develop and make recommendations on public policy issues

A nonprofit corporation whose facilities or indebtedness are supported in whole or in part with property tax revenue and which is licensed to conduct pari-mutuel wagering . . . or a nonprofit corporation which is a successor to the nonprofit corporation which built the facility

A nonprofit corporation licensed to conduct gambling games

The law defines a *meeting* as "a gathering in person or by electronic means, formal or informal, of a majority of the members of a governmental body where there is deliberation or action upon any matter within the scope of the governmental body's policy-making duties." Meetings, however, do not include situations in which members gather socially and do not discuss policy.

Iowa's law also provides that governmental bodies, with the exception of township trustees, "shall give notice of the time, date, and place of each meeting, and its tentative agenda." The law requires notice of at least 24 hours before the meeting, except when it is "impossible or impractical." Acknowledging that it might be necessary to hold a meeting on short notice, the law nevertheless requires that the reason for the short notice be clearly stated in the minutes.

Attention is given to closed sessions. The law provides for closed sessions "only by affirmative public vote of either two-thirds of the members of the body or all of the members present." The law spells out the only acceptable reasons for a closed session:

To review or discuss records which are required or authorized by state or federal law to be kept confidential or to be kept confidential as a condition for that governmental body's possession or continued receipt of federal funds.

To discuss application for letters patent.

To discuss strategy with counsel in matters that are presently in litigation or where litigation is imminent where its disclosure would be likely to prejudice or disadvantage the position of the governmental body in that litigation.

To discuss the contents of a licensing examination or whether to initiate licensee disciplinary investigations or proceedings if the governmental body is a licensing or examining board.

To discuss whether to conduct a hearing or to conduct hearings to suspend or expel a student, unless an open session is requested by the student or a parent or guardian of the student if the student is a minor.

To discuss the decision to be rendered in a contested case.

To avoid disclosure of specific law enforcement matters, such as current or proposed investigations, inspection or auditing techniques or schedules, which if disclosed would enable law violators to avoid detection.

To avoid disclosure of specific law enforcement matters, such as allowable tolerances or criteria for the selection, prosecution or settlement of cases, which if disclosed would facilitate disregard of requirements imposed by law.

To evaluate the professional competency of an individual whose appointment, hiring, performance or discharge is being considered when necessary to prevent needless and irreparable injury to that individual's reputation and that individual requests a closed session.

To discuss the purchase of particular real estate only where premature disclosure could be reasonably expected to increase the price the governmental body would have to pay for that property. The minutes and the tape recording of a session closed under this paragraph shall be available for public examination when the transaction discussed is completed.

The law specifies that the reason for the closed session must be provided by reference to a particular exemption, announced publicly at the open session and entered in the minutes. The body cannot discuss any business during a closed session that "does not directly relate to the specific reason announced as justification" for closure. The law also requires that "detailed minutes" be taken at the closed meeting and that the closed session be tape-recorded.

Of primary importance is the stipulation that a body must take final action in an open session "unless some other provision of the Code expressly permits such actions to be taken in closed session."

Suits to enforce the law are to be brought in the district court for the county in which the governmental body "has its principal place of business." The burden is then placed on the body "to demonstrate compliance with the requirements" of the law. If it is found that the body violated the requirements of the law, each member who participated in its violation can be fined not more than $500 but not less than $100.

The law specifies, however, that members of a body found to have violated the law shall not be assessed damages if they prove that they voted against the closed session, that they had good reason to believe that they were in compliance with the requirements of the law or that they "reasonably relied upon a decision of a court or a formal opinion of the attorney general or the attorney for the governmental body."

Iowa's law also provides for the removal from office of any official who has been assessed damages twice for violating the act.

What to Do If a Meeting Is Closed

Obviously, open-meeting laws are subject to interpretation, and not all are as carefully drawn as the Iowa statute. Still, reporters should carry copies of their states' open-meeting laws when they attend governmental sessions. If a meeting is about to be closed, the reporters should take these actions:

- Ask what section of the law is being invoked.
- If the justification appears flimsy, ask that an objection be recorded in the minutes.
- Request a delay until an editor or your medium's attorney can be called.

Reporters who are not totally familiar with the general principles of open-meeting laws as well as the specific provisions of the statutes in their states might be taken advantage of. Do not allow that to happen: Know your state's law from beginning to end.

Journalists are making greater use of computers to help them compile
and analyze statistical information.
(Photo by David Petkievicz)

Electronic Sources

Reporters are relying more extensively than ever

on information that is retrieved from data bases.

Information that would take hours to assemble

through a volume-by-volume search of a printed

index is now available in seconds to journalists

who initiate electronic searches while seated at

their personal computers.

John Naisbitt noted in "Megatrends" that "in the information society, we have systematized the production of knowledge and amplified our brainpower." To a great extent, information drives modern society. Naisbitt wrote: "Unlike other forces in the universe . . . knowledge is not subject to the law of conservation: It can be created, it can be destroyed, and most importantly it is synergetic—that is, the whole is usually greater than the sum of the parts."

Electronic data bases are the newest tools writers can use in their search for information. Many reporters, of course, will continue to gather information through meticulous checks of written sources that are housed in libraries. A new breed of reporter, though, is emerging: a journalist adept at ferreting out valuable information from electronic sources. Today's best journalists are capable of harnessing relevant information. Naisbitt wrote that "information technology brings order to the chaos of information pollution and therefore gives value to data that would otherwise be useless."

Professor Roy Halverson of Arizona State University organizes and participates in workshops that examine the intricacy and challenge of gathering information electronically. He also teaches a course in information gathering.

This chapter, written by Halverson, outlines how reporters can strengthen their stories through electronic retrieval of information.

DATA BASES AS A TOOL FOR REPORTERS

News writers gather information in three basic ways. One method is interviewing; news writers get most of their information by questioning human sources. (Steps in the interview process are covered in Chapter 11.) Another method is observation. News writers observe an event, situation or person and describe what they've observed. Yet another common method involves reading and abstracting written records. How to uncover such records held in electronic form is the subject of this chapter.

We shall consider:

- Types of electronic sources—data bases—available to news writers
- Advantages and disadvantages of electronic sources
- How to use data bases
- Sample records from two types of electronic sources
- Examples of stories written with the help of these sources

Data bases are powerful tools. Thomas L. Jacobson, a professor at State University of New York at Buffalo; and John Ullmann, assistant managing editor of the *Star Tribune*, the newspaper of the Twin Cities in Minnesota, conducted extensive research on the value and use of data bases.

Summarizing their findings, they wrote in the *Newspaper Research Journal:* "It seems fair to say that data bases can be used to support most beats, including the vast majority of kinds of stories covered on these beats. Data bases are thought to improve reporting substantially, adding depth, perspective, wider geographical coverage and better command of relevant facts."

Reporters often
spend long hours
gathering
information for
stories, from
sources ranging
from electronic data
bases to stacks of
public records.
*(Photo by
Linda Kocevar)*

TYPES OF DATA BASES

News writers have access to two major types of electronic information
sources, each of which has several variations.

1 *Full-text data bases* are electronic sources of information that are sufficient
in themselves. The actual texts of records, articles or statements are displayed on the searcher's screen.

2 *Citation data bases* are sources for sources of information. News writers
using such data bases find on their screens *citations*—information on
where to find the data—instead of the data themselves.

3 *CD-ROM* technology allows for storage of and electronic access to enormous amounts of statistical and textual information held on a single disk that looks like those played in a stereo system. The data are accessed using reading machines connected directly to news writers' computers. Archival or historical information, such as an encyclopedia or census data from an entire state, is stored on CD-ROMs.

FULL-TEXT DATA BASES

One full-text data base used by newspapers is an electronic clipping service, often called an *electronic morgue*. It's called a *morgue* because that is the term used for libraries in newspapers where "dead stories" lie until they are resurrected for use as background on current stories.

Such a service constitutes an electronic storage facility for all the stories that a newspaper or magazine has published. A computer program categorizes each story so that reporters, editors and librarians can call related stories to their screens quickly.

The traditional method for storage of stories in newspapers and magazines involved little if any technology. A hard-working librarian clipped individual stories and filed them under appropriate subjects and bylines. When key words and concepts were common to several categories of stories, multiple copies of the stories were filed and indexed. The "technology" consisted of a pair of scissors, a paste pot, file drawers and a typed index.

The new technology accomplishes the same things, except that the process is electronic.

As noted, a computer program classifies and sorts each story according to *key words* and *concepts*. Many newspapers and magazines have an electronic morgue that contains only their own stories. Others subscribe to a commercial service.

One such "morgue-type" data base is DataTimes. It offers several services in addition to electronic story filing. For example, it offers the texts from several magazines including *Time* and *Money*; the *Academic American Encyclopedia*; a movie review data base; and the PR Newswire, a series of public relations news releases. Stories from all of these are available almost instantaneously at the news writer's computer terminal.

Nexis is another full-text data base widely used by many media. It includes the full text of stories that were originally published in a variety of newspapers including *The New York Times, Chicago Tribune, Los Angeles Times, The American Banker, Christian Science Monitor, Memphis Business Journal, Business Digest of Southern Maine* and *Women's Wear Daily*. Its magazine files are also huge. *Auto Week, Computer Design, Chain Store Age, Forbes, Health, Money, People* and *Sports Illustrated* are only a few of the dozens of publications available to the news writer with a computer. Of special interest to political news writers are its files from governmental sources, such as *Congressional Honoraria Report,* and daily digests of congressional action.

Other data bases are designed for the information-hungry general user. They draw their information from newspapers, magazines, government reports, books and vast collections of other sources. The largest is CompuServe, with 500,000 members.

These data bases contain information and services to be used by anyone with a computer who craves convenience. They offer electronic mail service, news, weather, sports stories and scores, electronic shopping, electronic games, access to reference works and other services.

Many news writers use CompuServe for person-to-person communications. *Electronic mail* is a service that enables a member of CompuServe or of another data base to send messages electronically. The message is addressed to the receiver by name and number. The receiver has only to check an electronic mailbox, accessed via computer, to receive the message.

Still other commercial data bases frequently accessed by news writers offer special sorts of information. One such data base is the Dow Jones News Retrieval Service. Dow Jones is the parent company that publishes *The Wall Street Journal.* Its electronic data service offers stock and bond prices, special stories from the *Journal* and access to an encyclopedia. Like CompuServe, it is *menu-driven,* a method of access that will be discussed later in this chapter.

To get access to all this information, the searcher's computer must be attached to a telephone line with a modem, a device that translates computer-generated signals into signals that can be carried on such a line. Material thus accessible is said to be *on line.*

CITATION DATA BASES

As noted above, citation data bases are sources for sources. They offer the kind of information you would find in a footnote or a bibliographic entry, but not the text of the article itself. Two commercial data bases, DIALOG and BRS (Bibliographic Retrieval Service Inc.), are probably best-known. They hold data from hundreds of groups of periodicals and books.

In addition to commercial data bases, there is an enormous variety of electronic governmental and private holdings of value to news writers. Because of a glut of records—multiplying with the growing size and complexity of city, county, state and federal governments—more and more of those records are being kept in electronic form, and many of them are accessible to the news writer with a computer connection. The pace of "electronification" of governmental records is likely to increase with time. Because the growth is so volatile, no comprehensive catalog of such data bases is as yet available.

Industries, too, are keeping records "on line." Although most such records are closely controlled and access is difficult, some are available to news writers with permission.

CD-ROMS

Although on-line data bases are among the best sources of current information, CD-ROM technology offers special advantages for accessing certain types of information.

CD-ROM stands for *compact disk read-only memory.* The disks resemble the compact disks played in stereo systems. Instead of digitized music, however, these disks hold literary and statistical data. Their software differs slightly in that journalistic applications have extra "error detection and correction" circuitry to preserve the accuracy of the data on the disk.

CD-ROMs hold enormous amounts of information: about 650 megabytes (millions of bytes) per disk—the equivalent of 130,000 pages of typewritten text. Material on most CD-ROMs cannot be erased or changed (hence the description *read only memory*).

Much of the material needed by reporters and editors involves records that do not change with time, such as census information. CD-ROM technology offers economical and efficient access to those records.

To use CD-ROM, you need a CD-ROM player (a *reader*) compatible with your own computer and software and, of course, a disk. In addition, some computers need a special interface card to make the computer compatible with the reader.

Many news media don't purchase this equipment; instead, they use CD-ROMs available in their local libraries. Others, with a need for more frequent applications, purchase readers, software and disks appropriate to their needs.

A surprising variety of material is available on CD-ROM.

Census material is one example. In the United States, population data are gathered every 10 years. A single disk can hold data for an entire state, or even a group of states. Geographic shifts of population and changing demographics of a state's population can be a basis for news stories.

A census of economics including a census of manufacturing is taken every five years. Shifts in the manufacturing base of a state or region can make important news stories.

Education reporters might want data from ERIC (Educational Resources Information Center of the U.S. Department of Education). These data include decades of research reports on educational policy and practice, among hundreds of other topics.

Business reporters would find the Business Index valuable. An individual CD-ROM disk holds four years of data from 150 trade journals and regional business journals.

Medline provides references to biomedical information for 3,200 international journals. New disks are issued monthly, at additional cost, of course.

The vast compendia of fact and opinion known as encyclopedias also are held most efficiently on CD-ROMs.

Historic photographs and cartoons have been stored on CD-ROMs and are accessible to computer screens with the pressing of a few keys. Informational graphics such as maps can also be held on CD-ROMs. Downloaded from the disk to the computer screen, these maps can be manipulated to elucidate news stories and features.

This discussion does not cover the tremendous potential of interactive multimedia CD-ROMs. Because print media convey permanent, not transitory messages, they cannot exploit most of the power inherent in that aspect of CD-ROM technology.

Some CD-ROMs are menu-driven; others use some form of key-word search.

One obvious advantage of electronic sources is convenience; this is especially true of full-text data bases. News writers can gather a vast amount, and a great variety, of information without leaving their desks.

A second advantage, especially with commercial services, is the cross-indexing carried out by the computer. Only those articles that have the unique combination of concepts needed for the story are called to the screen. The writer is not distracted by extraneous information.

A third and obvious advantage is speed. News writers can get information in a hurry—in seconds instead of hours or days.

A fourth advantage is that electronic sources give news writers a more "global" perspective on the news. Electronic clipping files contain local stories only, although they offer convenience and speed. But commercial data bases bring to the news writer's attention information from far afield, broadening and deepening the story and thus making it more valuable.

CD-ROM technology offers some of the same advantages as on-line technology, particularly speed, convenience and cross-indexing of records. The special advantage of CD-ROMs is that they cost less to use than on-line data bases, once the equipment and disks have been purchased. There are no charges for connections or the phone line. CD-ROMs are also a cheap way to learn to use on-line data bases: the search strategies (described below) are similar.

However, electronic sources also have some significant disadvantages.

One disadvantage is cost. Access to data bases is not cheap. A very few offer their services free, but many of the most valuable cost tens to hundreds of dollars per "contact hour"—the actual amount of time (often measured in tenths of a minute) that the user's computer is connected to the host computer. A search can cost thousands of dollars.

ERIC (Educational Resources Information Center), a data base commonly used by education news writers, costs $36 per contact hour on DIALOG. The Magazine Index, a data base similar to the printed Readers' Guide to Periodical Literature, costs $90, and the European Directory of Agrochemical Products costs $312 per contact hour, all on DIALOG.

Most full-text sources are more costly per hour than citation data bases. But a news writer who is using a citation data base must journey to a library, get the original copy of a periodical or book, read it and abstract it before it can be used in the story. Full-text sources, although more costly per contact hour, are more convenient in that the data themselves pour onto the news writer's computer screen.

Data bases send information to news writers' terminals at a variety of speeds measured in *bauds*, or bits of information per second: the higher the baud rate, the higher the cost. This higher cost is offset to some extent by the fact that the searcher is connected to the host computer for a shorter period of time because information is transferred more rapidly. The commonest speeds are 300 and 1200 baud, but some transmissions are as fast as 9600.

Another disadvantage is that some data are not available in electronic form. Many government documents are still available only on paper. And not all publications are captured and put on line. Because data bases are recent innovations, data published before 1980 are seldom on line. Although some data bases are incorporating material from earlier years into their files, a considerable amount of archival data is still available only on paper.

A third disadvantage is that data bases can be difficult to use. Many were designed primarily by and for librarians, and news writers find the procedures hard to master.

Disadvantages of CD-ROMs involve the need for investment in more equipment (the reader), in software and in the disks themselves. A more serious disadvantage is that the disks are static, not dynamic. They contain information current to the time of production—no later. To get updated information, the operator must purchase a newer disk.

USING DATA BASES

ACCESSING A DATA BASE: TWO METHODS

News writers use one of two methods to access data bases. One is called the *key-word approach*, the other the *menu approach*.

The key-word method is used in formulating search statements in DIALOG, Nexis, BRS and many others. The menu method is used for CompuServe and Dow Jones News Retrieval, among others.

Method 1: Key-Word Approach

Key words are crucial words that encapsulate concepts at the heart of a research topic. To locate key words, the computer searches through every word of the headline or title and, in full-text data bases, the text of an article.

The searcher constructs a search statement with key words and connective words such as *and, or* and *not*. Some texts call these connectors "Boolean" connectors after a 19th-century English mathematician.

An example will clarify the key-word method. Suppose that the news writer wants to discover information relating to the effects on health of diesel exhaust (no small problem in narrow city streets with truck and bus traffic). The key words could be *diesel, fumes* or *exhaust* and *health*.

One of the connectors noted above is the word *or*. In the case noted here, *or* broadens the search to include citations that have either the word *fumes* or the word *exhaust*. If the searcher had used the connective word *and* between *fumes* and *exhaust*, the search process would have been narrowed to those citations that have both words.

The connector *not* excludes concepts. The search statement could say:

    fumes or exhaust, not catalytic

This statement would eliminate from the array drawn to the screen those citations that have the word *catalytic* in them.

Data bases also have additional means of refining searches. One of them is *truncation*, which is a way to expand the number of words the computer will recognize to all those that have the same root. For instance, suppose that the searcher wants to add the concept "insurance" to the diesel search. The search statement would read as follows:

diesel and exhaust or fumes and health and insur???

The three question marks would instruct the computer to uncover articles with the first four key words plus all the words with *insur* as their root. That would include *insurance, insuring* and the like.

The bases also help the searcher find the correct key words by an *expand* function, which (as the term implies) expands the root word to suggest other, associated key words. The bases also allow the searcher to specify year of publication, name of journal, author's name and other variables to shorten the search.

Using these sources involves several steps. First, the news writer must choose the correct storage bin within the data base. That's no small task, because Nexis and DIALOG, holders of many other data bases, offer literally hundreds of choices. Paperbound catalogs issued by the service guide the searcher to the proper choice—and experience helps as time goes on.

In the example below, the bin chosen was the Magazine Index in DIALOG. The Magazine Index is not unlike an electronic version of the Readers' Guide to Periodical Literature. DIALOG records include author, article title, periodical title, date of publication, page, a summary (called an *abstract*) of the article and a set of synomyms used by the indexer to identify core concepts in the article (these synonyms are called *descriptors*).

This is how the key-word strategy would work in a search for magazine articles on urban crime. DIALOG uses ? as a prompt.

Display	Explanation
? s crim???/de	The s asks for a set of references to the first key word. The root of that word is <u>crim</u>. The truncator ??? asks the computer to search for all concepts with <u>crim</u> as a root (<u>crime</u>, <u>crimes</u>, <u>criminal</u>, <u>criminality</u> and the like); de is added to the root so that the computer will search only the "descriptors"—key-word synonyms used by the indexer.

Display	Explanation
Display sl 11680 crim???/de	**Explanation** The computer tells us that there are nearly 12,000 references to <u>crim</u> and its descendants. We need to link those to the other crucial concept, <u>urban</u>.
s sl and urban/de	This is what we type to make the necessary link.
sl 11680 "crim" 4544 urban/de s2 44 sl and urban/de	The computer now gives this response. Only 44 articles show the two core concepts in their lists of descriptors.
t s2/5/1	To see the articles themselves, we must use a "type" command: t tells the computer we want something typed, s2 tells the computer we want that set of data, 5 indicates the format the citation should take and 1 says we want to see only the first and newest article citation.
11807353 DIALOG File 47:MAGAZINE INDEX *Use Format 9 for FULL TEXT*	The citation looks like this.
D.C. Mayor learns from other cities' programs.	Headline.
Pierce, Neal R.	Author.
Nation's Cities Weekly v 15 p8(1) Jan 6, 1992	Periodical name, volume number, page and date of publication.
AVAILABILITY: FULL TEXT Online	This indicates that we can get the full text of the article on-line.

Display

LINE COUNT: 00078

GEOGRAPHIC CODE: NNUSLDC

GEOGRAPHIC LOCATION:

Washington D.C.

ABSTRACT: Washington, D.C.

Mayor Sharon Pratt Dixon,

faced with governing a city

that has seen nearly 1,800

murders in four years, is

advocating tougher laws. But

she is also turning to ideas

from other cities that offer

young people from the

ghetto areas an alternative to

violence.

SIC CODE:9111

NAMED PEOPLE: Dixon, Sharon

Pratt—Planning

DESCRIPTORS: Urban youth—

Services; Mayors—Planning;

Washington D.C.—Crime.

t s2/9/1

Explanation

Further information.

If the deadline for the story is
imminent, the operator can ask
for the full text on the computer
screen by substituting 9 for 5 in
the type command. Then the
entire story, all 78 lines of it,
would flow onto the screen. Of
course, the searcher would be
connected to DIALOG for a much
longer time, and the charges
would be proportionately higher.

Method 2: Menu Approach

The key-word method for accessing a data base is subtle and complex. The
menu approach is easier to master but somewhat slower. The menu process involves working your way through progressively more precise sets of topics
and subtopics until you reach the specific information you want.

Here's how a CompuServe menu looks.

```
CompuServe      TOP
CompuServe Information Service
14:45 MST Monday 14-Sep-92
Last access: 09:34 30-Jul-92
Copyright © 1992
CompuServe Incorporated
All Rights Reserved
GO RATES for current information
CompuServe      TOP
  1 Access Basic Service
  2 Member Assistance (FREE)
  3 Communications/Bulletin Bds.
  4 News/Weather/Sports
  5 Travel
  6 The Electronic MALL/Shopping
  7 Money Matters/Markets
  8 Entertainment/Games
  9 Hobbies/Lifestyles/Education
 10 Reference
 11 Computers/Technology
 12 Business/Other Interests
```

This is how the menu approach would work in a search for information for a story on nutrition and sports.

Display

Enter Choice number !4

Explanation

The exclamation point is a "prompt," a request by CompuServe for the searcher to choose a subject.

Option 4, News/Weather/Sports, was chosen. The searcher types "4" on the computer keyboard and presses ENTER.

```
News/Weather/Sports      NEWS
BASIC NEWS SERVICES
  1 Associated Press Online
  2 Weather
```

Display	Explanation

Display

3 UK News/Sports

4 Online Today Daily Edition

EXTENDED NEWS SERVICES

5 Executive News Service ($)

6 NewsGrid US/World News

7 Sports

8 Newspaper Library

9 Hurricane Andrew

Information

10 The Business Wire

Enter Choice !7

News/Weather/Sports   SPORTS

SPORTS

1 AP Sports Wire ($)

2 Associated Press Online

3 Sports Forum

4 Motor Sports Forum

5 Sports Medicine

6 Outdoors Network

7 Sailing Forum

8 Scuba Forum

9 NCAA Collegiate Sports

Network (W)

Enter Choice !5

CompuServe   HRF-4794

Sports Medicine

1 General Aspects of Exercise

2 Nutrition and Exercise

Explanation

$ means that this option involves an extra charge to the searcher.

By pressing 7, the searcher chose to look at "Sports" material. Then ENTER was pressed.

For this story, "Sports Medicine," option 5, was the logical choice. Then ENTER was pressed.

Display

3 Some Specific Sports

© HealthNet, Ltd. 1987

Enter Choice !2

CompuServe   HRF-4668
SPORTS NUTRITION
The recent and apparently
sustained national interest in
vigorous exercise has focused
attention on the role of
nutritional factors in
performance and safety for
those who engage in rigorous
activity. The discussion of
exercise physiology addresses
some basic issues of energy
requirements. Here, the more
general relationships between
what you eat and your
performance and health will be
addressed. . . .

    . . . Athletes need not be
overly concerned about special
dietary and nutritional
requirements in most cases. The
simple principles outlined above
point out that the general diet
of most Americans is more than
adequate for the vast majority
of the exercising population,
and that special measures are
not often necessary. A prudent
diet suitable for the general
population is equally suitable

Explanation

Choosing option 2, "Nutrition
and Exercise," brought the
following story to the screen.

(The middle section of this
lengthy article has been deleted
here.)

Display	Explanation

Display

for the athlete. Except in the
most competitive environments,
no extraordinary measures are
warranted.

Last page! bye
Thank you for using
CompuServe!
Off at 14:56 MST 14-Sept-92
Connect Time = 0:11

Explanation

A signoff, ending connection
with CompuServe.

Electronic sources of information are being used with greater and greater frequency by the news media. Michael Murrie wrote in *Link-Up* in March 1988 that statistics indicate a rapid increase in newspapers' use of on-line searching. News writers themselves apparently rarely use data bases, primarily because they haven't had opportunities to develop the necessary skills. But all staff members of media with in-house electronic morgues need to master search skills.

Three researchers at the University of Minnesota—Jean Ward, Kathy Hansen and Douglas McLeod—wrote in *Journalism Quarterly*:

> News staff members generally do not have unlimited and unsupervised access to commercial electronic data base services (such as Nexis and DIALOG). For these searches news staff must request professional library search services. Yet journalists are expected to master their in-house electronic library system with minimal training and supervision. The search strategies and conceptual skills necessary for efficient use of the in-house system are as complex as those required for use of commercial systems.
>
> As more and more news writers come to their profession with knowledge and understanding of electronic data-retrieval systems, they will probably assume some of the search responsibilities now in the hands of librarians. It's hard to imagine that information-hungry reporters will allow the search process to stay in the hands of others for long.

DATA-BASE SEARCHES IN NEWS WRITING: TWO EXAMPLES

Here are two examples of how data base searches enhanced stories at the *Star Tribune,* the newspaper of the Twin Cities and an industry innovator in the use of data bases and social science methods to augment the more traditional reporting efforts.

Example 1: A Breaking Story

David Phelps, a reporter, was trying to find out how and why a local savings and loan institution had made several bad loans. It was a breaking story; and he needed the information for the next day's newspaper. In particular he needed to know about a Florida resort and condominium complex known as the Jockey Club. He knew little about the Jockey Club—only that a local S&L had sunk $20 million into it.

Librarians searched Florida publications to find data that described the club. The owner had just sold his interest and was the prime source of information. He was a California developer who no longer lived in Florida. With just his name to go on, the librarian, using a data base, located his name in a California publication; this allowed him to be tracked down with three phone calls. He provided the confirmation needed for the story about the dire financial straits of the resort and the amount funneled into it by the Minneapolis S&L.

Sylvia Frisch, the searcher, used Vu/Text. She said that the developer's name appeared in conjunction with a meeting of the city planning commission. The story appeared in a small California newspaper, and this was the only time that the developer was mentioned. Vu/Text's global search capability (a search across all its holdings, not just a single newspaper at a time) worked perfectly in tracking down obscure names and people.

Frisch, one of four professional data-base searchers at the newspaper, also used several data bases from DIALOG for general information, including Business Dateline (regional business publications in a full-text format), Trade and Industry ASAP (an index to trade and industry magazines, also in full text), Magazine Index and Magazine ASAP, Newspaper Abstracts and NEWSEARCH (which covers the last month's updates for a number of files).

Example 2: An Investigative Story

In another instance, *Star Tribune* reporters working on a yearlong project titled "Fatal Neglect" wanted to find national experts on child abuse. By using general search terms in the professional medical and social science literature, as well as the more popular periodical data bases, Frisch found the names of a number of experts who were doing the most important work in the area. The most useful sources were two faculty members at the University of Minnesota who had done a pioneering survey of adults who were physically abused as children.

John Ullmann, an assistant managing editor at the *Star Tribune*, wrote: "Sometimes the data base search is outstanding in finding sources only 20 minutes from our desk. . . . Imagine how much poorer the series might have been and how silly we would have felt if our library hadn't come across this study.

"Data-base searches take finding the answers out of the realm of serendipity and into the realm of professional information science. Reporters and editors can either get familiar with their value or find their [reporting] efforts forever falling short."

It's clear that news writers have electronic news-gathering tools of great power at their fingertips and that use of those tools by the media is growing steadily. The *Star Tribune*'s reporters used commercial data bases. As more and more governmental agencies use computer data banks to store data, their use by news writers is sure to increase.

Human Sources:
Interviews

A police officer comforts a witness to a shooting so that he can ask
her some questions. Reporters would like to interview
both the officer and the witness.
(Photo by Henri Cohen)

11

Human Sources: Interviews

An interview is the essence of a breaking news

story, a feature or an investigative story. In any

interview, a reporter must ask the right questions

with finesse at just the right time. That requires

homework, confidence and the ability to listen,

participate, observe and absorb.

An interview is an exchange of information between a reporter and a source. When a reporter asks the right questions with finesse, a source becomes a window to the news. On the other hand, a story can fail if the reporter asks the wrong questions or not enough questions, does not know how to ask questions or gives up too early on a hostile or close-lipped source.

Interviewing requires patience, confidence and an uncanny ability to listen, participate, observe and absorb. Reporters must be able to ask a question and then listen to the entire response, all the time zeroing in on the key points. Reporters who are well-prepared should be able to tell when a source is telling the truth, embellishing it or lying.

There are three stages in every interview:

1 Research
2 Setting up the interview
3 Questions and answers

Each stage requires careful attention and expertise. A shoddy job on any of the stages will show up in the final product. A thorough job on each stage will result in the best, most professional story possible.

The tone of an interview depends on whether it is for a news story, a feature or an investigative story. Those differences will be discussed later in this chapter.

DOING THE RESEARCH

The key to a successful interview is establishing rapport with the source. To do this, reporters must do their homework so that they can go into an interview knowing both the background of the source and something about the subject of the story. Sources are more likely to relax and open up when they feel that they are talking to reporters who speak with knowledge and authority. Sources often volunteer little information when they think that reporters are not asking intelligent questions or do not understand the subject.

USING THE MORGUE

Most newspapers have their own libraries—called *morgues*—in which clipping files are kept on sources and subjects. Reporters can do much of their research here. Paper clippings or computer copies of stories are generally filed under subject and reporters' bylines.

For a story on the trial of a suspect in a triple slaying more than a year ago, the reporter would first go to the morgue to read the earlier stories that were written on the slaying and on the arrest of the suspect. Some small newspapers do not have morgues. In these cases a reporter who did not cover the story originally and who does not have copies of the earlier stories would have to:

Look through bound volumes of the paper at the time of the slayings
Hope that somewhere in the office there is a file on the case
Rely on police and court officials for necessary background

Newspapers that do have morgues would have the earlier stories clipped and filed in envelopes or would have the clippings stored in a computer. The stories should be filed under the subject—such as *slayings*, the name of the suspect or the name of the victims—and the byline of the reporter who wrote the earlier stories.

Next, the reporter would scour the earlier clips for background information, making sure that facts such as spellings, dates and locations are consistent in each of the stories. If there are inconsistencies, the reporter would check with the police or court officials for corrections.

The clips would also be used to identify potential sources and to formulate questions. The prosecutors and defense attorneys may need to be interviewed before the trial begins. A story could be written on the judge, on the families of the victims and suspect or on the last time there was a triple slaying in town.

Before the trial begins, the reporter should have culled from the clips the five W's and H of the case, the names of sources and any questions that need to be asked. Doing the homework takes time, but it will help ensure that the reporter will not be lost in court or baffled or spurned by a source. Sources are much more likely to answer a reporter when the questions are formulated on the basis of facts rather than guesses.

USING THE LIBRARY

Some newspapers close their morgues to the public, which means that student reporters may not be able to use them. Check on local policies. If the local morgue is closed, the newspaper may have an index of its articles, which will make it easier to find the correct microfilm or clips at public or campus libraries. (A more complete discussion of newsroom and library sources is found in Chapters 9 and 10.) Morgues and other libraries also have a wide selection of Who's Who, encyclopedias, city directories, other reference books and indexes to material in books, magazines and major newspapers. In addition, many libraries have copies or microfilm of newspapers from other cities.

Libraries provide background information on sources and subjects; thus there is no reason to begin working on a story without being fully prepared. If nothing has been written on the source, thoroughly research the subject of the story. Look up the subject in books, after checking the library's card or on-line catalog, or in magazines, after checking the Readers' Guide to Periodical Literature. Many people have never been interviewed, but there are few subjects on which nothing has been written.

USING OTHER RESOURCES

If earlier stories have been written on a source, it is a good idea to talk to the reporters who wrote those stories. They can provide insight into a person's character and mannerisms. They will know if the person is easy or difficult to interview.

Some sources will be writers themselves. If they are, take a look at what they have written. A book or article does indeed reveal much about its author, and there is nothing like saying to a person, "I read your book" or "I read the article you wrote." Those few words can relax a source.

When preparing for an interview with someone who has never been interviewed, try to talk to some of the person's friends or professional acquaintances. Any bits of information that can be gathered before the interview will make the entire process easier; therefore, do not hesitate to call one person to ask questions about another.

SETTING UP THE INTERVIEW: GUIDELINES TO FOLLOW

Once the preliminary research has been completed, it is time to set up the interview. Here are six steps to follow, each of which will be discussed in turn:

1 If the deadline is not tight, telephone or write to the person in advance to request the interview.
2 Identify yourself as a reporter, and name the organization for which you work.
3 Establish a time and place that are convenient for the person being interviewed.
4 Tell the person the general type of information being sought. There is no need to reveal specific questions, but at least tell the source that you are doing a story on such and such and would like to ask him or her some questions. Also, tell the person approximately how long the interview will take.
5 Dress appropriately.
6 Be on time.

1: MAKE AN APPOINTMENT

For features and investigative stories, where the deadline is somewhat flexible, there is usually time to set up the interview in advance. For a breaking news story, however, reporters seldom have time to call or write in advance to arrange interviews. In this situation, time is critical, and interviews are instantaneous. If there is an explosion at a refinery outside of town, and five people are killed and nine injured, reporters will arrive on the scene almost as quickly as the fire trucks. Fire officials are interviewed. Questions are addressed to the survivors and the families of people who died. Reporters ask their questions quickly, often speaking with anyone they can get to.

In stories with less deadline pressure, setting up an interview helps curb the adversarial relationship that can exist between reporters and sources. It allows sources to prepare for the questions and to look their best. It allows reporters to be well-prepared.

Phoning or writing in advance also helps reporters get past the secretaries, public relations people and others who are on a source's payroll and who may

An antiwar
demonstration
would provide
plenty of sources
for reporters to
interview.
(Photo by T. J. Sokol)

speak for the source. To get past these people, it may be necessary to keep calling, writing or hanging around a source's office until the appointment is made. Explore every ethical avenue to arrange interviews with sources who are not interested in talking or who are well-hidden from the press by other people.

2: IDENTIFY YOURSELF

Once sources are contacted, they should be told immediately that they are talking to a reporter from a publication or broadcast medium. If the story is for a journalism class only, say so. When people know that they are being interviewed for publication or broadcast, it becomes their responsibility to control what they say.

3: CONSIDER YOUR SOURCE'S CONVENIENCE

Because sources tend to be more talkative if they are on their own turf, let them decide the time and place of the interview. Often they will ask, "When is it convenient for you?" If they do, then think of deadlines, dinner dates and growling editors or news directors. Otherwise, ride with them. Some of the best interviews take place in the middle of the night, at a gymnasium or on horseback. The point is, a reporter is stepping into someone else's world; therefore, an interview should be convenient for the source, not for the reporter.

Always be prepared for the interview before setting it up. That will avoid embarrassment when the source says, "I'll be busy later. Let's do it now."

4: DESCRIBE THE STORY

When setting up the interview, tell the source, in general terms, something about the story and how his or her information will fit into it. That will help relax the source before the questioning begins.

It is also important when setting up an interview to tell the person approximately how long the interview will take. Newsmakers are usually busy people who must budget their time. If the person will give you only a few minutes, take it. That is better than nothing. The important thing is to get the interview, because once people start talking, they often keep going past the predetermined time limit.

5: DRESS THE PART

There is no need to wear a coat and tie or high heels when covering a roundup on horseback. And do not wear a T-shirt, shorts, deck shoes or a sundress to interview the defense attorney in a murder trial. The best thing to do is to dress at the same level as the person being interviewed.

6: BE ON TIME

Once you make the appointment for the interview, keep it. If the interview is scheduled for 11 a.m., be there at 10:50. The only thing worse than coming to an interview unprepared is showing up late or out of breath. Getting to an interview early will show initiative and should impress the source. One other word of advice: Do not schedule one interview immediately after another. That way, the only person looking at a watch will be the source.

CONDUCTING THE INTERVIEW: THE QUESTIONS AND ANSWERS

During the interview, the reporter should pay particular attention to the structure of the interview, the ways in which questions are asked and the types of questions that are asked, the theme or purpose of the story, observations and note-taking. The reporter should become adept at handling hostile sources and uncommunicative sources. It is also important for reporters to understand special types of interviews, such as features and investigative stories.

Let's now consider these aspects of conducting an interview.

STRUCTURING AN INTERVIEW

Interviews follow one of two patterns that are determined by the subject matter and the type of person being interviewed. One pattern is structured like a funnel; the other, like an inverted funnel.

Funnel Interview

The *funnel interview* is the most common and the most relaxing for both the reporter and the source because the toughest and most threatening questions are saved for near the end. These interviews begin with background talk, such as:

- How long have you been with this company?
- Where were you born?
- How old are you?
- Where did you get your experience?

The background questions are followed by open-ended questions, which are followed by closed-ended questions or adversarial questions.

Funnel interviews are most useful when:

- The source is not accustomed to being interviewed.
- The length of the interview is not important.
- Particularly touchy closed-ended questions need to be asked.

By beginning with general, easy-to-answer questions, the reporter has a good chance of establishing rapport with the source. Then, once the tough questioning begins, the source is more likely to respond candidly.

Inverted-Funnel Interview

In an *inverted-funnel interview,* the key questions are asked immediately. This style of interview is used with people, such as law enforcement officers or government officials, who are experienced in fielding closed-ended or adversarial questions.

For example, when a senator voted for a controversial bill that would cost his state millions of dollars in lost federal aid, he was ready for adversarial questioning from reporters: "How could you do it?" "Don't you realize this vote might cost you your job?"

Inverted-funnel interviews are also used in breaking news stories when there is little time to ask questions.

ASKING QUESTIONS

Planning Questions

Before an interview, memorize or write down the important questions that need to be answered. Of course, the interview might take an unexpected turn and some of the questions might go unanswered, but it's still necessary to know in advance what should be covered. This is where homework is important. Questions are formulated by reading earlier clips and conducting preliminary interviews.

Additional questions will pop up during the interview. Jot them down on a note pad, and ask them at the appropriate time. Try to avoid staring at the list or reading from it. Do not check off questions one by one as they are answered. That could intimidate the source, who will begin talking to the note pad rather than to the reporter. It could prevent the eye-to-eye contact that is important in an interview.

Using Closed-Ended and Open-Ended Questions

The timing and wording of questions during an interview can affect the source's response. Some interviews require only quick questions and short, specific answers. For these, it is best to ask *closed-ended questions*, which are structured to elicit precise answers.

For instance, a reporter questioning an irascible police chief about an investigation of the kidnapping and alleged rape of teen-age girls asked such closed-ended questions as, "Do you agree with the county sheriff that the girls were raped before they were released by their kidnappers?" and "Is it true that your department did not respond to the parents' call for five hours because you believed that the girls had run away and had not been kidnapped?" By asking carefully worded questions such as these, the reporter forced the police chief to be precise.

Open-ended questions are used when a short, precise answer is not immediately necessary. Because they allow a source more time to develop an answer, open-ended questions sound less intimidating. They are a good way to break the ice and to establish rapport with a source. Examples of open-ended questions include "How would you trace your rise from a clerk to the president of the corporation?" and "In your opinion, what should the government do to reduce unemployment?" Open-ended questions give sources an opportunity to elaborate in considerably more detail than closed-ended questions do.

Two factors determine whether a reporter should use open-ended or closed-ended questions:

1 *How the subject seems to react to certain questions.* The reporter needs to gauge how the interview is going and then decide if specific, potentially threatening questions are necessary. Closed-ended questions should be reserved for the point in the interview when the source is relaxed and beginning to open up.

2 *The length of the interview.* If an important source who is rushed for time is being interviewed, get to the heart of the interview right away. Chances are that sources such as these have been interviewed many times before and are used to specific questions.

Using Personal Questions

For some reporters, asking personal questions is the toughest part of an interview. Even the most experienced reporters dread the times when they have to approach a grieving mother to ask how her son was killed or a government official to ask if the rumors of financial improprieties are true.

It is not easy asking such questions, but it is something that all reporters must do. It is also the most difficult hurdle they have to clear in an interview. Usually, though, if a personal question is asked at the right time and with sensitivity, a source will respond passionately and candidly.

"I have more trouble asking personal questions when they involve interviewing people whose children died than when they involve government officials or people in the news," said Maren Bingham, a reporter for *The Phoenix* (Ariz.) *Gazette*. "I really do feel like an intruder, as though I don't have the right to intrude on someone's tragedy."

Bingham said that before she asks personal questions, she tries to show a source that she is a professional and will get the information correct. "I try to establish trust," she said. "I try to sit and talk to them, not take notes or turn on the tape recorder. I ask general questions to try to get to know them."

Marie Dillon, an assistant metro editor at the *Palm Beach* (Fla.) *Post*, agreed that the reporter must establish rapport with the source before asking personal questions.

Dillon recalled a story she wrote after a drunken driver slammed his car into another car and killed an entire family, except for a 2-year-old boy. "I had to go interview the dead father's sister," she said. "I was worried how I was going to approach the subject. I did what I often do. I phoned first, and asked her if she had a photo of the boy we could use. That got me into her house. When I was there and she started to give me directions on where and when she wanted the photo returned, I got out my notebook to write them down. I never put it away."

For a story on teen-age suicides, Dillon had to interview the foster mother of a 13-year-old boy who shot and killed himself. Dillon said that she was nervous about asking the woman for an interview because she would have to ask many personal questions about the boy; however, once the interview began, she realized that the woman was more than willing to talk. "She turned out to be a great interview," Dillon said. "She really opened up to me. She was by herself and really needed someone to talk to."

Edie Magnus, health correspondent for CBS News, said that she, too, is uncomfortable when posing personal questions to survivors or to families of dead people. "I feel like an intruder, like a leech," she said. "When it's something that is very personal, I will preface the questions with something like 'I realize this is a touchy question' or 'I'm sorry that I have to ask you this question.'"

Bingham and Dillon said that their chief fear when asking personal questions is that sometime after the interview, sources will regret what they said and then ask that their remarks not be printed. "I find that most people do not mind answering personal questions, but they sometimes later regret it," Dillon said. She added that in cases like these, she has to weigh the worth of the source to the current story and to future stories. Bingham said: "I usually very nicely say 'too bad.' I figure that they're responsible adults, and they knew they were talking to a reporter. But I also realize that I caught them at a bad time. I try to be sympathetic."

Bingham, Dillon and Magnus offered the following guidelines for asking personal questions:

- *Do your homework.* Know something about a source before trying to enter his or her personal life.
- *Try to interview the person face to face.* It is a lot easier for a person to respond to a personal question when looking at another person, rather than speaking to a stranger on the telephone.

- *Interview in a casual setting.* If a source is relaxed, he or she is much more likely to respond candidly to personal questions.

- *Break the ice with general questions.* Sometimes it is best to begin an interview without taking notes at all or without a camera or microphone. Talk about the weather or the setting for the interview. Ask questions such as age or address. Humor—making a source smile or laugh—helps, too. There is no need to open with a joke, but smiling broadly and making a comforting comment should help put the source at ease.

- *If the interview is being taped, try not to turn the recorder on right away.* Give the source a chance to feel comfortable first.

- *Sometimes, it is easier to elicit a personal response by not asking a question at all.* Instead of asking, "How did your son die?" it might be easier to say, "Tell me about your son." Let the source talk about anything. Let the interview ramble for a while. Then later, if the source missed anything, ask more specific personal questions.

- *Preface the questions.* Sometimes, a source is more likely to answer a personal question if it is prefaced with something like "I'm sorry to bother you, but I have to ask you this question," or "I know you are busy, but I'd like to ask you this question."

- *Coax an uncooperative source.* Some sources, particularly public officials, think that by saying "no comment" they can keep something out of the newspaper or off the air. If necessary, tell the source, "We're going to use this story anyway, and your comments really will make it better."

Using Follow-Up Questions

Anyone who has seen a televised news conference has seen reporters ask *follow-up questions,* in which they rearticulate their questions or ask another question to elicit a new or a more specific response from a source. The president may be asked, "How do you plan to cut taxes?" He responds, "We'll do whatever it takes to trim taxes, including an across-the-board 10 percent decrease, but I think it will be hard to get anything through Congress." The reporter follows up immediately with, "Do you think Congress is unwilling to go along with a tax cut because of the disastrous effects it would have on the already huge federal deficit?"

The above scenario illustrates three things about the reporter who asked the two questions:

1 The reporter had done the necessary homework and asked an appropriate open-ended question.

2 The reporter listened intently to the response, realizing that the president was placing the blame on Congress, not on himself, for high taxes.

3 The reporter knew the subject well and therefore was able to interpret the response quickly and to follow it up with another appropriate question.

Of course, beginning reporters are not going to be interviewing the president on live television in front of millions of people. They are going to be talking to a variety of local sources, many of whom have never been interviewed.

But just like the president, these sources are not always going to answer a question fully, for various reasons:

- They may not understand it.
- They may ramble too much and forget it.
- They may not be qualified to answer it but try anyway.
- They may not want to answer.
- They may answer another question instead.

It is up to the reporter to make certain that each question is intelligent, brief and easy to understand. This usually eliminates the problem of a source's not understanding the question. However, the other problems may be more difficult to solve. In these cases, the reporter will need to ask follow-up questions.

Framing Questions to Fit the Story's Purpose

Reporters should know where they want their stories to go before they begin the interviewing process. Every story should have a theme or purpose. Once this purpose is determined, questions can be framed so that the interviews will help the reporter achieve it.

If a story's purpose is to show that a local politician is a crook, questions are designed so that the wrongdoing will be revealed by sources during the interview. Many of the questions will probably be adversarial.

If the purpose of the story is to show how a successful corporate president got to be where he or she is today, the questions are designed to bring out the best in the person. The questions will probably be easy to answer, seeking descriptions and anecdotes.

Example: A restaurant review   When Katherine Rodeghier, a Chicago free-lance travel writer, wrote an article on a Madison, Wis., restaurant owner, her purpose was to come up with a restaurant review with a twist. She was writing the article for *Discovery*, the travel magazine of the Allstate Motor Club.

"*Discovery* wanted something that was unusual about the restaurant, along with something about the food," Rodeghier said. "What was unusual about this restaurant was the owner."

Rodeghier's story was about 30-year-old Odessa Piper, who got her start baking bread in a commune and who later became the owner of L'Etoile, one of the finest French restaurants in Wisconsin. "The purpose of the interview was to pull from her the reasons she was a success," Rodeghier said. "I wanted background from her. She once was a hippie who ended up serving the establishment. I had met her before when I went to her restaurant for dinner with a group of travel writers, and so I already knew about her. But I needed more detail, quotes and observations."

Rodeghier, who spent four years as an education reporter and then four years as a travel editor at the *Daily Herald* in Arlington Heights, Ill., before she began free-lancing full time, first queried *Discovery* to find out if it would be interested in buying an article on Piper. In its acceptance letter, the magazine told Rodeghier that it would pay $300 plus expenses for a 1,000-word story. It would also assign a photographer.

After making the appointment for with Piper the interview, Rodeghier conducted her research. She prepared the following list of questions, which she hoped would be answered during the interview and would help her achieve her purpose:

How did you get your start in the restaurant business?

When did L'Etoile open?

What is your background? You learned to bake in a commune—when and where?

Where are you from?

How old are you?

What do you think of Madison? What attracted you here?

Do you have a published menu? May I have one?

What are your most unusual dishes? What are some of the favorites with your customers?

Where do you get your ingredients?

What is your clientele? Do you get many tourists?

What should a visitor see in Madison?

What are your prices?

What is the best time to dine here? Are reservations needed?

How many do you seat?

In any interview, a reporter may not stick to the prepared questions because there is no way of knowing in advance what direction the interview will take. The anticipated questions are a guide; and they help the reporter prepare for the interview.

In her interview with Piper, which was conducted over lunch, Rodeghier used a tape recorder and took notes. It is a challenge to eat, talk and write at the same time, but reporters must learn to do this.

By the time the 1½-hour interview was completed, Rodeghier had several pages of notes and two tapes of what was said. Here is a partial transcript of the actual interview:

Q. How did you get started in the restaurant business? (Rodeghier knew the answer to this question after her research, but by asking a background question first, she helped relax Piper and got her to talk about herself.)

A. After high school, I went to a commune and lived there for a year, and we used very basic technology. We grew almost all of our foods except our grains. Our farming efforts were not always successful that first year, and we had to rely heavily on the grains. I really did a lot of bread baking and just fell in love with it. All of us were somewhat sheltered and certainly very indulged children who grew up in nice homes and had many opportunities, and here we were out in the commune practicing things that were really rough. It was quite an adventure.

Q. What did you do when you left the commune?

A. I moved to Wisconsin to a farm outside of Madison, near my sister. I continued to grow vegetables and bake. I experimented with other things using white flour and some sugar. That prepared me for a job I took at the Ovens of Brittany, which is another fine restaurant in the city.

Q Did you have any problems in your early days of professional cooking?

A My croissants would turn out to be these horrible tough things, and the French bread would be flat. I refused to follow a recipe. I had the idea that if I was going to do this, I was going to learn about the process myself to create my own recipes, and it was very important to me for some reason. Madison didn't quite care if the French bread was kind of droopy and the croissants were hard. Madison gave me this ample opportunity to keep at it.

Rodeghier continued to ask background questions, which are important to any interview. The reporter must find out spellings, ages, addresses and other background information to make the story accurate.

Next, Rodeghier concentrated on questions about the uniqueness of Piper and L'Etoile. The reporter also made notes about the atmosphere of the restaurant, what Piper was wearing and how she spoke.

Q. Why did you go to the commune?

A. Many of the commune members were Dartmouth College students I knew. We were exploring a kind of lifestyle different from going off and taking over Dad's company.

Q. How did the commune prepare you for the restaurant business?

A. I learned a great deal of respect for food because we worked so close to the land and did live right on the edge. What we grew is what we subsisted on. I think that's the part that prepared me. At the time, I had absolutely no intention of running a restaurant. That seemed so, well, among other things, capitalistic. It seemed too indulgent for me.

In an earlier answer, Piper had mentioned a partner, something that Rodeghier did not know about. Rodeghier wanted to pursue this point:

Q. When you first opened, you had a partner. What happened?

A. In the beginning, we were equal partners. What made the partnership end is that it quickly became unequal. All the lawyers and the bankers and suppliers would talk to him. That shows how times have changed because I don't think this would necessarily happen now. Women's liberation wasn't developed then as it is now. I know a lot of women in business now. I think it's delightful. It's wonderful. My partner was interested in the limelight. Then things went wrong. Everything that could go wrong did. We lost a lot of money. I became ill. My partner was disillusioned and decided to leave. We were deep in debt. I knew I had to pick up and rebuild it and carry on. I felt an extraordinary love for the place.

These are only six of the dozens of questions that were asked during the interview. Many answers led to questions that Rodeghier had not anticipated. Near the end of the interview, Rodeghier quickly referred to her notes to ascertain whether she had asked all the questions she wanted to.

"I told her I was going to check my notes," the writer said. "I think it is important for a reporter to make sure all the questions are asked because an editor might want some very specific things covered."

When she wrote her story, Rodeghier had to condense all the information into 1,000 words, about four typewritten pages.

A key point of this story was that a former commune member had become the owner of a successful French restaurant. Rodeghier's two-paragraph contrast lead showcased that point for readers:

> When Odessa Piper was baking bread in a New Hampshire commune 10 years ago, few guessed she would one day own one of the finest gourmet restaurants in Madison, Wis.
>
> Today, at the tender age of 30, Piper has already put in more than five years as proprietor of L'Etoile, a tiny shrine to fine cuisine on Madison's star-shaped capital concourse.

Next, the writer brought readers into the restaurant. More background information would come later:

> Gourmet doesn't necessarily mean stuffy. Piper personally greets diners—among them state Supreme Court justices, legislators and members of Madison's artistic and academic communities—and recites selections from the blackboard menu.
>
> "It's an opportunity for me to talk with my clientele," says Piper. "I tell them about nouvelle cuisine without a lot of falderal. I don't want my customers to feel anxious or afraid. Unfortunately, so many people make that connection with a gourmet restaurant. Delivering the menu to them is a chance to ease their mind."

By using a direct quotation in the fourth paragraph, Rodeghier allowed one-on-one communication between the source and the reader. Establishing that source-reader relationship early in the story is important.

Rodeghier came back to the background questions in the middle of the story. Before that, she used words to paint a picture of the restaurant. She sprinkled in plenty of quotations and gave readers necessary information, such as prices. Because she had only a limited number of words in which to tell the story, she had to pare any information that was not vital. For instance, Piper told her quite a bit about the doomed partnership that started L'Etoile, but in the story Piper's statements were boiled down to one sentence:

> Through serious financial reverses, and the loss of her partner, she struggled to make L'Etoile a commercial as well as a culinary success.

By the end of the story, readers should have felt that they know Piper and how unusual she is, what she serves, how she prepares it, how much it costs, who eats it and what the atmosphere of L'Etoile is like. Rodeghier finished the story with a quotation, an effective way to end features. Piper was put in direct communication with readers:

For Piper, Madison's appeal lies in its intellectual and artistic atmosphere—its theater, dance and art openings—and its proximity to the lakes and forests of rural areas of central Wisconsin. When she takes time off from L'Etoile, she enjoys day trips to the country to bike, canoe or simply explore a small town and "find a good restaurant at the end of the day."

ESTABLISHING RAPPORT

Reporters must establish rapport with their sources as quickly as possible. That is the key to getting their questions answered. "You're like a door-to-door salesman selling yourself," said Jerry Guibor, a copy editor for the *Fresno* (Calif.) *Bee* who has been a news and sports writer in California, Oregon and Arizona. "You have to know the subject and not get bored with it. You have to know the person you are interviewing and ask intelligent questions. You have to have a good intro to stimulate the source."

Guibor said that rapport should be established as quickly as possible during an interview because most sources will not answer questions candidly until they have "warmed up" to the reporter. "To establish rapport, you have to tell them who you are and what you are doing," he said. "And you have to thank them for their time."

Here are some additional guidelines:

- *Try to conduct the interview in person.* As discussed earlier, there are times when telephone interviews are necessary, but they make establishing rapport extremely difficult. Sources are more likely to warm up to someone they can see, particularly if they have never met the reporter before.

- *Begin with general, easy-to-answer questions, if possible.* Doing so will help relax the source. Hold the adversarial questions until the end of the interview, when the source is more likely to feel comfortable.

- *Do not ask vague questions.* Ask clear, concise questions that a source can understand quickly. A source is more likely to open up when the reporter is not confused or vague.

- *Do not pull any punches.* Do not beat around the bush. Ask questions straight out. Do not ask a related, non-adversarial question in the hope that the source will respond in a certain way.

- *Avoid arguing.* Reporters have the last say when they write. "If the senior senator from your state tells you in a press conference or interview that the Earth is flat, he is to be quoted precisely," said Neil H. Mehler, a general assignment reporter for the *Chicago Tribune*. "Then, in the story or in a sidebar, it is mandatory that the reporter note that this is not the accepted belief."

- *Listen.* Let the person being interviewed feel that he or she is conversing with a friend rather than responding to a list of questions from a reporter. A reporter so wrapped up in the eloquence of his or her own questioning may ignore what the other person is saying.

- *Be open for any response.* Remember that responses to questions tend to be signals for additional questions, some that a reporter might not have thought of while preparing for the interview.

HANDLING HOSTILE AND UNCOMMUNICATIVE SOURCES

Not every source is cooperative, easy to talk to and ready to admit fault. Sources can be closed-lipped and say "no comment." They may talk only "off the record," which means that they do not want anything they say to be printed. They may be *hostile*, especially if they are asked to reveal something they do not care to share with the public. In these cases, it becomes the reporter's responsibility to try to make the source open up.

If someone does not want to comment to the press, that is his or her right. No reporter can force a person to talk. Sometimes the reporter simply must give up on a source and look for another. In these cases, an audience must be told, for instance, "The mayor refused to comment."

If a source will talk only "off the record," the reporter should take notes and should try to convince the person to allow the information to be used. Sources cannot order a reporter to take information off the record. If they could, reporters would be at their mercy. Reporters violate no ethical principles of journalism if they ignore such a command, unless they have agreed before the interview to accept the information off the record. (For a further discussion of off-the-record reporting, see Chapter 7.)

Here are some ways to persuade sources to open up, to persuade them to go on the record or to keep them from becoming hostile:

- *Do not act like a prosecuting attorney.* Avoid hostile questions. Save the tough questions for the end of the interview.
- *Be sympathetic and understanding.* This does not mean that a reporter has to be on the side of the source while writing the story, however.
- *Reason with the source.* Tell the source that using a name or comment will make the story better.
- *Genuinely try to understand the source's position.* For example, try to find a reasonable explanation for any charges against a source.
- *Repeat some of the damaging things that have been said about a source.* Often sources will open up to respond to charges against them.
- *Keep asking questions.* As long as the source does not end the interview, continue asking questions.

Rick Alm, a reporter at the *Kansas City Star*, offered some additional advice on handling hostile sources: "Do not be afraid to trade information. You can tell sources a little about what will be in the story. People don't like being interviewed cold. They want information, too. A reporter can't just take, especially in political stories. Sometimes, you have to be a conduit, trading information between sources.

"I sometimes have found that in dealing with hostile sources, it helps to say nothing. If you ask a question and the source says nothing, try saying nothing yourself. Wait until the source responds. There may be silence for 30 seconds, but if the source gives you a crumb, then you can keep asking questions."

The CBS News correspondent Edie Magnus said that she can usually anticipate before an interview when she is going to get "no comment," but she has ways to deal with this:

- She has several questions to ask. If the source does not answer the first one, she asks the second. If the source does not answer the second question, she asks the third, and so on.

- Sometimes, she shames people into answering the question. "If you ask enough questions, they may finally give in or feel bad that they are not answering any of them."

- She never badgers anyone. There is no need to keep going after one critical issue after a source has made it clear that he or she cannot or will not speak on the subject. "If the source continues to say 'no comment' after four or five questions, raise the issue in the story. 'No comment' is an answer. I can always say that when so and so was asked, he repeatedly said 'no comment.'"

MAKING AND USING OBSERVATIONS

When reporters accurately write what a source has said, the audience can "hear." When they observe and then report the source's mannerisms and surroundings, the audience can "see." Observations add *color* to stories, which means that they give an audience a clearer picture of a person or an event.

Whenever they are working on stories, reporters should keep in mind the following:

- *What is unusual—or common—about this person or place?* If a photograph were taken of the source, what would it show? How is the person dressed? New clothes? Ragged clothes? Latest fashions? How does the source look? Wrinkled face? Scars? Bushy eyebrows? Full beard? Too much makeup? Gold teeth? What are the person's mannerisms? Nervous twitch? Always winking? Never smiling? How is the office decorated? Western? Paintings? Posters? What is unusual about the person's face, hair, mouth, eyes, ears, etc.?

- *Does the source articulate well?* Is the source "comfortable" discussing this subject? Can any outside sounds be heard during the interview? Are there any pleasant or unpleasant smells? Is the source distracted?

Observations are vital to features, but they can also be effective in news stories. In a story on the conspiracy trial of 15 members of a motorcycle club charged with planning two bombings, Melinda Donnelly of the *Dallas Times Herald* used an observation in her lead:

> Jim "Sprocket" Lang has spent a lot of time hanging around the federal courthouse in Dallas lately, passing the time with racing forms from local newspapers while his comrades—allegedly some of the meanest men in Texas—sit silently in court.

Donnelly also used an observation later in the story to give readers a visual impression of some of the aging gang members:

Despite heavy security that includes an airport-type X-ray machine and two metal detectors, most visitors have little to claim but huge belt buckles or rolls of hard candy bulging from the pockets of their jeans or corduroy suits.

This news story could have been written without observations, but in using them Donnelly added color to her writing, which can help keep readers' attention.

Observations were the cornerstone of a series of articles by *The Albuquerque Tribune* that examined alcoholism in the Route 66 town of Gallup, N.M. For six days the paper devoted all or much of its front page and many inside pages to the chronic problem it called New Mexico's black eye. In one article, David Gomez, a reporter, wrote:

It's just 20 degrees, too cold for the four drunks from Chinle, Ariz., to continue living in Chinle Hole, an old boxcar embedded in the bank of the Rio Puerco wash west of downtown Gallup. The boxcar is open on one side and offers no protection from the cold.

With nowhere warmer to go, the Chinle boys—Abel Taylor, his younger brother, George, and their cousins Stanley "Danny" Draper and Kenneth Yazzie—sleep in an abandoned automobile they call "Kenny's hotel." It has been parked for months next to a tire store near the Rio West Mall.

No one ever cleans the vomit, food wrappers and wine bottles. It smells of urine and garbage.

During an interview or when covering an event, reporters make notes of their observations. Then they decide during the writing which ones are pertinent to the story. For instance, in a court trial, one of the spectators may be wearing curlers in her hair and knitting during the testimony. This is an interesting observation that is worth noting; though it may not be used in the story, it could be used to enhance a stark story:

Spectators packed the courtroom. One woman, with curlers in her hair, sat knitting while Parker admitted that he stole the words to the song.

Usually, observations are better than punctuation. There's no need to write:

People could tell that Johnson WANTED that fish to bite!!!!

Instead, use observations to let an audience decide that Johnson did indeed really want that fish to bite:

Johnson stared at the water. He was so tense that veins in his neck were bulging. While the others joked in the boat and munched on pretzels, Johnson kept his eyes on the water, waiting, one hand on his reel, the other on the handle of his rod.

Observation is something only reporters can obtain. Editors and news directors can only ask, or an audience can only wonder, "How many gold teeth did he have?" or "What was she wearing?" If these observations are not made during the reporting phase, they may be impossible to get later. That is why it is so important to take as many notes or to shoot as much videotape as possible of a source's looks, mannerisms and surroundings. Observations should not get in the way of reporting the news; they are used to enhance the news, to make an audience feel that it was there during the interview or event.

It is best to make more observations than will ever be needed in the story. Often, editors or news directors will ask for more color. This is where observation is critical. Editors and news directors do not want a reporter to say that a person is tall or old or big or young. They want the reporter to say how tall, how old, how big or how young. They may not want the story to say only that the police recruit jumped over the six-foot wall. They may want:

> The recruit ran up to the six-foot portable orange wall that had been
> rolled onto the obstacle course. He jumped up and threw one leg over
> the top. He grunted, pushed and rolled the rest of his body over.

Sometimes, observations are the first things to be cut when there is a space problem or a time problem. There will be times when editors or news directors cut the color to make a story fit a space. In cases such as these, a reporter will not be able to mention the woman in curlers or to describe the portable wall that the police recruit jumped over. This is the way daily journalism is. There simply will never be unlimited time and space to report a story.

LOGISTICS

Taking Notes

During an interview, the reporter must understand and at the same time transcribe what the speaker is saying. To do that, it is necessary to write fast. Most reporters devise some system for shortening words. Many journalists also use tape recorders, particularly in lengthy face-to-face interviews.

Using a tape recorder   By using a tape recorder, the reporter can establish and maintain eye contact with the source and can conduct the interview as if it were a conversation. But reporters who use recorders usually take notes, too. Every experienced reporter has probably lost at least one interview because of a malfunctioning recorder, which is enough to make some reporters abandon the machines altogether. Tape recorders have two other disadvantages:

- Sometimes they intimidate and inhibit a source. Some people simply do not like talking into a machine that will record everything they say. Because people choose their words more carefully when they are being taped, the interview may lack spontaneity.
- Tape recorders can waste time because the reporter has to go back and listen again and again to the recording until useful quotations are found. This problem can be eased if the reporter uses a footage meter with the recorder and makes notes of the location of pertinent comments.

The great advantage of a tape recorder is that it provides a permanent and precise record of what is said, preventing the reporter from inadvertently misquoting. It is impossible to write down everything that is said, especially in in-depth interviews, and so the recorder is useful to back up the quotations. The reporter takes notes to remember key points of the interview; and then, when it is over, the notes can be filled in by going over the tape.

"If I think the interview is going to be controversial or a source is going to come back later and question what I wrote, then I use a tape recorder," said Maren Bingham of *The Phoenix* (Ariz.) *Gazette.* "But I do not use it routinely."

Taking sufficient notes   Take copious notes, more than you will need to write the story. It is not unusual to write a two-page story from 15 pages of notes. It is better to have too many notes than not enough.

Still, there is no need to take notes on everything that is said. Listen carefully to the speaker, look for inconsistencies, formulate follow-up questions and write down only the pertinent information. And, most important, relax. Reporters run into trouble when they spend so much time frantically writing notes that they miss the meaning of what a source is saying. For example, a source might say, "Yes, I did break the law." But to get to that point, he says, "Well, all I can say is, what I mean is, gee, this is difficult for me, but yes, I did break the law." A reporter so busy trying to write down the entire quotation may miss the heart of it.

Writing faster   Even reporters using tape recorders take as many notes as they can. Some reporters learn shorthand or have their own list of abbreviations to make the job quicker. Another popular trick when taking notes is to leave the vowels out of most words. Of course, it is difficult to use this technique in the beginning, but it gets easier with practice. The source might say: "The black smoke looked like a huge mushroom cloud. I thought the area had been bombed." A reporter could write: Th blck smke lked lk a hg mshrm cld. i thght th ara hd bn bombd.

Whatever system they use, reporters go over their notes immediately after the interview to make sure that they understand them. Many reporters will stay in a room after a press conference or will sit in their cars for a while to review their notes. That is the time to insert the vowels in words, or correct errors.

Managing a note pad   When conducting an in-person interview, put the note pad and the tape recorder, if one is being used, in an inconspicuous place. The best spot for a note pad is on a reporter's lap. That makes eye contact easier and allows the person being interviewed to talk to the reporter rather than to the note pad. Eye contact is important in an interview. Neatness in taking notes is not.

Using symbols   Get into the habit of putting some type of symbol, such as a star, next to key phrases or quotations. That is a good way to identify possible leads or areas that need additional probing. Reporters facing a tight deadline often compose their stories mentally during an interview; then when it is over, they can head directly to a telephone to call in the story.

Asking for repetitions   Do not be afraid to ask the source to repeat a quotation. It is not rude or inappropriate to say: "Excuse me, but I did not get down everything you said. Can you repeat it?" It is also acceptable for a reporter to repeat a quotation to make certain that it was transcribed correctly. After all, both the source and the reporter want to make sure that a quotation is accurate.

If the person being interviewed is using confusing terms, stop the interview. A reporter can say: "I'm sorry. I do not understand that. Can you explain it better?" Doing this will make the story better and will show the person being interviewed that the reporter is conscientious.

Using the Telephone

The telephone is a valuable aid to conducting interviews. When reporters are covering breaking news near deadline, when they need to talk to a source who is out of town or when they are interviewing one of their regular sources, they almost always use the phone.

However, in many interviews, particularly when the source does not know the reporter or when there is no immediate deadline, eye contact is important. In these cases, telephone interviews are not suitable substitutes for going out into the field. Do not use the phone if:

- There is time for an eye-to-eye interview.
- The source is nervous.
- It is a breaking news story where many interviews are needed.
- Observations are important to the story.

Television reporters seldom interview over the telephone because their interviews are usually videotaped.

Here are some guidelines to follow when conducting interviews over the telephone:

- *Identify yourself carefully and fully.* This is especially important if you have never met the source. Remember, the person on the other end of the line cannot see you and will be hesitant to answer questions from a complete stranger.

- *Speak slowly and clearly.* You have to speak so that you can be understood. Over the phone, you have only your voice to persuade the source to talk to you.

- *Do things to put sources at ease.* For example, you might want to apologize for your tight deadline or for your inability to be there in person. Sometimes, it even helps to apologize for the sound of the typewriter or the computer keyboard as you take your notes.

- *Ask brief questions.* It is easy for a source to forget a detailed question or not to understand it fully when it is asked over the phone.

- *Put the telephone in a comfortable spot on your shoulder before the interview begins.* It is best to practice typing and talking at the same time before you actually interview someone for a story. That way you will not drop the phone or have to reposition it. Such fumbling may cause you to miss an important quotation, and it could make the source worry about your abilities as a reporter.

- *Type your notes.* You will soon discover that, with practice, you can type much faster than you can write in longhand.

- *Do not worry about sloppy typing.* Go over your notes as soon as possible after the interview to correct mistakes.

- *Ask permission before you tape a telephone interview.* Many states have laws forbidding a person to tape over the phone unless the other party gives permission. Be familiar with your state laws. Asking in advance will also let the source know that you are not trying anything underhanded and will prevent you from being in an embarrassing position if you have to admit that you are indeed taping the interview.

SPECIAL TYPES OF INTERVIEWS

Although the general guidelines already discussed apply to all interviews, different kinds of interviews pose different challenges for the reporter. The following sections discuss procedures for interviews for news stories, features and investigative stories.

Supplements to News Stories

In news stories, sources are generally interviewed to support or criticize the peg of the article. Of course, news stories can be made from an interview with a single source, but generally the sources of a story are supplementary to the news event itself.

The following inverted-pyramid news story from *The Dallas Morning News* illustrates how interviews are used to supplement hard news stories.

Here is the lead paragraph:

A World War II-vintage training plane crashed and burned in Abilene Monday, killing both people aboard.

This 17-word lead gave the *what* (fatal plane crash), the *who* (two people), the *where* (Abilene) and the *when* (Monday) of the story. It provided readers with the most important news. The next two paragraphs gave additional key information:

Police said the plane belonged to a member of the Confederate Air Force, a flying group that owned a seaplane that crashed a month ago, killing seven people.

Abilene police identified the dead in Monday's crash as Jake Eustace Miller, 61, of Albany, and Kimberly Brooke Pardue, 19, of Breckenridge.

In the fourth paragraph, one of the people interviewed for the story was introduced:

> Abilene police Lt. Ron Harris said he didn't know who was piloting the 1940s-era two-seat British Chipmunk when it crashed about 2:50 p.m. near Elmdale Airpark on the northeast outskirts of Abilene.

Now readers know that at least one person was interviewed for the story. What Harris said is not important enough to put in the lead, but it added useful information to the story. The next paragraph also came from Harris:

> The National Transportation Safety Board is expected to begin its investigation Tuesday, Harris said.

Later in the story, a witness to the crash—another person interviewed—was introduced:

> Tye Lawrence, an Abilene high school junior who was working on a fence about a mile from where the British trainer crashed Monday, said it appeared that the pilot was in a downward spiral and couldn't level the biplane.
>
> "At first, I thought he was just trying to do a spiral or something, then it looked like he just lost it," said Lawrence. "I just saw the plane kind of start tumbling and then it went into a nose dive and hit the ground."

As in any inverted-pyramid story, this one could have been cut from the bottom and used without the quotations and paraphrases from the people interviewed. But by including those paragraphs, readers are given additional information by named sources, which makes the story more credible and readable. As in every news story, the reporter probably interviewed more people than those who showed up in print, but because of space and time limitations, the reporter had to choose only the best quotations and paraphrases for the story.

Features

For a *feature*—an umbrella term for a variety of soft news stories—a reporter must find out as much as possible about the person being interviewed. In this type of story, the source is often a key point; therefore, the interview can make or break the final product.

Katherine Rodeghier's story on Odessa Piper illustrates how vital the person being interviewed is to a feature story. Rodeghier's feature worked because she was well-prepared and because Piper answered all the questions candidly. Without Piper, there would have been no story.

Investigative Stories

In an investigative story, it is imperative that the reporter thoroughly research both the topic and the sources before the interviewing begins. Because this type of story often entails probes that reveal wrongdoing by an agency or official, the interviews tend not to be as easy as those for news stories or features. Instead, an adversarial relationship may exist between the reporter and the source, making the interviewing process more difficult.

Investigative stories require more interviews than news stories or features, especially if the reporter is trying to expose corruption. In these stories, exhaustive interviewing of all sides of an issue is critical.

Investigative stories may deal with international topics, such as how and where terrorists receive funding to travel throughout the world; national topics, such as congressional sex scandals; or local topics, such as graft in the police department or at City Hall. Clearly, when reporters work with stories like these, sources are not going to be helpful or friendly. They may even be frightened.

For instance, when the Illinois General Assembly decided to reduce costly patronage in state government, it abolished 46 legislative study commissions, ending the jobs of 87 salaried employees and the contracts of 175 other people. When Tim Franklin and John Schrag of the *Chicago Tribune* found out that one-third of the salaried employees and some of the other people quickly landed other jobs or contracts with the state, they began an investigation to find out just how much money the state was saving.

Before they wrote their story, Franklin and Schrag had to study many things, including state records on who was hired for what jobs, how legislative study commissions operate, how patronage works in state government, how much the state was spending on the commissions and how much the people who got new jobs or contracts were being paid. They had to interview scores of people on both sides of the issue, many of whom would not enjoy being interviewed. In each of the interviews, the reporters had to back up their questions with facts they had gathered during their research.

Their story began with a summary lead:

SPRINGFIELD—About one-third of the 87 salaried employees of the defunct legislative study commissions, abolished last year to reduce costly patronage in state government, have landed new jobs or contracts with the state, a study of records shows.

The next six paragraphs detailed more of what they found during their research.

More than half of those with new jobs on the state payroll received pay raises or had their commission salaries matched. The General Assembly, which abolished the commissions, has been the single most active employer of former commission members, the study shows.

The legislature voted last spring to abolish the state's 46 study commissions, which opponents charged had become patently wasteful, unproductive and little more than havens for dozens of patronage hacks.

Thirty-nine of the commissions went out of business by the end of September, ending the jobs of 87 employees and canceling the contracts of another 175. Seven other commissions are to be phased out on March 31.

Of the 87 salaried employees who were on the now-extinct commissions last spring, 24 have gotten new jobs and 3 have signed lucrative contracts with the state, according to state records.

That means 27 of the 87 former commission employees, or 31 percent, still are drawing income from the state. Those contracts and salaries, which range from $2,400 to $40,200 annually, could cost the state $600,000 a year, records show.

Of the 262 people who either had jobs or contracts with the now-extinct commissions last spring, 49 have received new state posts or contracts that could total $1.1 million a year, records show.

In the next four paragraphs the writers introduced two of the many people they interviewed for their story. The first person criticized the rehiring of workers; the second defended it. (Note how the story puts a legislator's party and district in parentheses; *Tribune* style in this instance is not the same as Associated Press style.)

The leader of a taxpayer watchdog group said the rehiring of commission workers is a waste of state dollars that taints the well-intended commission reform plan.

"Some of these people have more lives than a cat," said Patrick Quinn, head of the Oak Park-based Coalition for Political Honesty. "They always land on their feet."

But legislative leaders who spearheaded the commission abolition plan defended the hiring of former commission workers.

"If a person is qualified and has a good work history, he should not be banned from state government just because he served on a state commission," said House Speaker Michael Madigan (D., Chicago).

By now Franklin and Schrag had set the pattern for their 35-inch investigative story. They let their readers know that they had pored over state records and had interviewed people both for and against the rehiring of state workers. They also interviewed some of the workers who were rehired. These interviews were featured in the story, along with where the people were working before and now, and their past and present salaries. Before they conducted any of the interviews, Franklin and Schrag had to make it clear to the sources that they had done their homework well and were giving the sources an opportunity to respond.

Their article is an example of a typical investigative story: It was the result of thorough research and extensive interviews. It ended with additional facts and quotations.

The architect of the commission abolition plan, House Minority Leader Lee Daniels (R., Elmhurst), said his proposal has accomplished its mission, even with the hiring of former commission workers.

"This really shows that one of the goals of the plan has been reached, and that goal was to reduce the size of state government," Daniels said. "Our job was not to eliminate good people from state government."

The Du Page County Republican also noted that even with the hiring of former commission workers, his plan is saving the state at least $6 million a year. The commission system cost the state an estimated $7.1 million in the last fiscal year, which ended June 30.

Daniels hired one former commission worker, records show. His Democratic counterpart, Madigan, hired three.

Nine other former commission workers landed jobs or contracts with other legislators or with General Assembly service agencies.

AFTER THE INTERVIEW

The more a reporter and the source talk, the better the interview and the resulting story; therefore, the reporter should try to keep the interview going as long as possible. Questions should be asked until the source stops the interview. Remember that key points for the story are often made at the end of the interview when the source is fully relaxed; therefore, keep listening intently until the interview is indeed over.

At the end of the interview, thank the source and ask, "Where can I reach you by phone if I have additional questions while I am writing the story?" That will provide quick contact if more information is needed later and will show the source that you are trying to be accurate. It also forestalls a request from the source to see the story before it is printed.

Under no circumstances should a reporter agree to show a source the story once it is written. People almost always want to retract or edit their statements once they see them on paper. If reporters are confused by something a source said, they should phone the person to ask for clarification or additional information. There is no reason to take the story to the source.

Notes should be reviewed immediately after the interview to make certain that they are clear. Many reporters type their notes after interviews to fill in empty spots. If a tape recorder was used and it malfunctioned, call the source back immediately and set up another interview.

A CHECKLIST FOR INTERVIEWS

Here are 10 important steps to follow before, during and after an interview:

1 *Do background research.* Assemble a file of stories you have written about a source or topic as well as stories by other writers. Don't forget to check Who's Who for biographical information.
2 *Schedule the interview, if possible.* If there is no tight deadline, set up the interview in advance. This will help curb the adversarial relationship that can exist between a reporter and a source.
3 *Write down questions or topics in advance.* You will be better prepared for the interview if you know the topics you want covered or the specific questions you want answered. The interview may take another path; this is fine, but you should try to cover all the topics or questions.

4 *Hide the note pad.* Sources are often intimidated if they can see a reporter's note pad. Try to keep yours in your lap or in an inconspicuous place. If you use a tape recorder, try to put it in an inconspicuous place, too. Make certain that it is functioning properly *before* the interview begins, and take along extra batteries and tape.

5 *Use shorthand or some other method to take notes quickly.*

6 *Ask for explanations.* It is not rude to ask a source to explain what he or she is saying.

7 *Observe the little things.* Observation is important in news and feature stories because it gives an audience a clearer picture of a person or an event.

8 *Be tough but fair.* Always give sources an opportunity to respond to their critics. You want your sources to know that you are trying to be fair.

9 *Keep it going.* No interview can go on forever, but the longer the better.

10 *Relax.*

Reporters conduct face-to-face interviews to gather vivid quotations
that will suppplement survey results.
(Bob Daemmich/Stock, Boston)

12

Human Sources: Surveys

During the past 20 years the media have increased

their use of surveys to gather information for

stories. The media are relying more and more on

electronic computers to assemble and analyze

huge, complicated amounts of information.

Reporters should have a working knowledge of

how to conduct surveys, interpret results and

write stories.

In a book first published in 1973, Philip Meyer alerted working reporters and editors to the feasibility and practicality of using social science methods to gather information. The methods he advocated were quantitative—the use of numbers to measure and evaluate.

The title of Meyer's book, "Precision Journalism," is appropriate. The theme that runs throughout the book is that social science research methods—methodologically sound sampling procedures and computer analysis—can be used to gather facts, leading to more precise, more accurate news stories.

Some newspapers in the United States were using straw polls to predict election outcomes in the mid-19th century. Early polling procedures were often unsophisticated and prone to error. As the mid-20th century approached, however, newspapers were increasingly publishing the results of polls. President Harry Truman's smile was wide, indeed, when he proved the polls wrong in the 1948 election. But that did not stop the media from reporting polls during ensuing decades.

Today, the survey process has grown sophisticated. Results of national polls conducted by Gallup, Harris and Roper often make the news. Even individual newspapers and electronic media are polling their audiences about local issues.

Robert Teeter, a political pollster and the head of Market Opinion Research, was quoted by *Editor & Publisher* magazine: "The publishing of polls is simply another method of reporting, a more sophisticated method of reporting than we have enjoyed in the past. It is a better and more accurate reflection than having some political reporter go out and talk to eight people in two bars and then write a story about the election."

Surveys by news media extend beyond trying to predict the outcome of elections. Newspapers practicing *precision journalism* today are polling local readers on everything from their willingness to pay higher taxes for improved highways to their support for law enforcement crackdowns on distributors of pornography.

Evans Witt, who reports on politics and polls for The Associated Press, wrote in the *Washington Journalism Review* that the media are no longer "tied to colorful, but often misleading, man-on-the-street interviews to gauge public reaction to a candidate or major news event."

But as Witt pointed out, there is a downside to the increased use of polls. "The bad news about poll proliferation is the great number of poorly done surveys, the masquerading of incompetent research under the magic word 'poll,'" Witt wrote. "News organizations often refuse to spend the money necessary to do reliable polls. But there will probably be a lot more lousy polls . . . before everyone learns that a bad poll is far worse than none at all."

Professor Gerald Stone, the former editor of *Newspaper Research Journal*, cited a polling "horror story" that occurred when a large-circulation newspaper wanted to do a survey on a coming election. "This newspaper did not have the in-house ability to do a poll story," Stone said. "So it went to a college and asked a department there to get involved in the process. The newspaper did not publish the results of the department's first election survey, choosing instead to see if the poll turned out to be accurate. The newspaper's editors found that the poll missed predicting the outcome by a long

Information
gathered from door-
to-door surveys
sometimes forms a
basis for news
stories.
*(Photo by
Shelli Wright)*

shot. That showed the editors that the newspaper was not ready to do any political polling. It was another five years before the newspaper became involved
in a precision journalism project."

The problem, of course, was that either the university researchers did not
know what they were doing or they had not been funded adequately to do a
good job. "It was probably the latter," Stone said. "It is hard for me to believe
that a school of any size does not have professors competent to conduct a representative survey for the local newspaper. The problem, of course, is convincing
newspapers that they have to spend money to carry out projects properly."

The rule is clear: news media should not attempt to conduct precision
journalism projects if they are not capable of doing so. There are a number of
dangers: The sample of people to be surveyed might not be representative of
the entire group, thus rendering inaccurate any projections based on the findings; the questions might be worded awkwardly, thus causing confusion for

the respondents; the results might be misinterpreted; and the media might not allow sufficient turnaround time to carry out the project with the care it requires.

If the dangers can be overcome, however, surveys can produce fascinating information for stories. Journalists will probably continue to make greater use of surveys to gather information. Several of the journalism schools in the United States now require courses in research methods, statistics and computer science in an effort to prepare tomorrow's journalists better for the increasingly technological field they will be entering.

CONDUCTING A SURVEY: BASIC CONSIDERATIONS

Reporters are not expected to be experts on research design or on polling procedures, but a working knowledge of these techniques is helpful. This section is not intended to cover survey research exhaustively. Books such as Meyer's "Precision Journalism" can be consulted for further information. Other sources include "Handbook of Reporting Methods," by Maxwell McCombs, Donald Shaw and David Grey; "Mass Media Research," by Roger D. Wimmer and Joseph R. Dominick; "Research Methods in Mass Communications," edited by Guido H. Stempel III and Bruce Westley; "Survey Research Methods," by Earl R. Babbie; and "How to Conduct a Readership Survey," by W. Charles Redding.

The purpose of this section is to provide a look at some basic considerations that are of value to reporters. A fictional scenario will be constructed to illustrate these basic considerations.

In this fictional example, Mike Walters covers the board of education for the *Riverdale Daily News,* an afternoon newspaper with a circulation of 15,000 published in a community of 30,000. As is often the case in communities of this size, residents have a great interest in the public schools.

A current issue has divided the townspeople. Two school board members were recently elected on the platform that modular scheduling should be eliminated in the public schools. Under modular scheduling, students attend 20 class modules of 20 minutes each day. The newly elected board members favor a return to the traditional seven-period day with each period lasting 57 minutes. During their election campaigns, these members said that modular scheduling was fine for independent, highly motivated students but that average and below-average students—the majority of those enrolled—would be served best by a traditional system.

Walters is apprehensive at the first school board meeting after the election. No one really knows what the newly elected board members might do. When it comes time for new business, one of the newcomers moves that the board mandate a return to the seven-period day. The other newcomer seconds the motion. The motion does not carry—several members object on procedural grounds—but the board does agree to hire outside consultants to measure the effectiveness of modular scheduling in Riverdale.

Walters returns to his office. He tells his editor that he would like to do some interviewing in the district to determine what community opinion is.

Walters says that he intends to station himself at various school buildings around town and interview mothers and fathers as they pick up their children after classes. He will supplement these interviews with comments from teachers, principals, the school superintendent and board members.

Walters' editor, Susan Kelly, says that these spot interviews with a limited number of district people might not paint an accurate picture of community sentiment. She suggests that a survey would provide a better picture.

Kelly says that she is familiar with survey basics, but she wants Walters to talk to a professor at Riverdale College for additional guidance. After conversations with the professor, Walters realizes that he must get to work on the project immediately. He must form questions, determine the people to be interviewed, gather data, analyze the data and then write a story on the basis of the data.

FORMULATING THE QUESTIONS

The main goal is to develop a *focal question,* one that directly addresses the primary issue to be explored. In this case, that issue is whether most residents favor modular or traditional scheduling. First, Walters writes a brief introductory statement that capsulizes the difference between modular and traditional scheduling. Now he is ready to write his focal question. Generally, it is best to structure a *closed-ended question,* one that builds an answer into the question. Walters decides on the following focal question: "The Riverdale School Board is considering changing from modular scheduling to traditional seven-period scheduling. Do you prefer modular scheduling or the traditional seven-period scheduling?"

Walters then formulates several questions, with each fitting under the broad umbrella of the focal issue. Questions are framed so that people will understand them. Leading questions should be avoided. It is imperative that questions be phrased as neutrally as possible.

Closed-ended questions are generally preferred to *open-ended questions,* such as "Which type of scheduling do you prefer in the Riverdale schools?" Because of the built-in answers, closed-ended questions are easier to code and tabulate. Open-ended questions give respondents ample opportunity to expand at length. If the respondents are not familiar with the various types of scheduling to be considered, however, they cannot answer the question precisely and their answers are thus more difficult to tabulate. Walters structures a handful of closed-ended questions to supplement the focal question. He starts with general questions, such as the number of years the respondent has lived in Riverdale, and then proceeds to specific issue-oriented questions. He reasons that this will help put the respondent at ease.

At the end of the closed-ended questions, Walters adds an open-ended query. He asks: "Do you think that the schools have generally been responsive to the individual scheduling needs of your child? Could you give me an example to support your opinion?" Open-ended questions often lead to vivid, interesting direct quotations that make excellent additions to a story which would otherwise contain only a lot of statistics based on the closed-ended questions.

TESTING THE QUESTIONS

Walters asks his editor and the college professor to look over his questions and to suggest improvements. After getting their reactions, he tests the questions on some non-editorial and editorial employees at his newspaper who have children in the public schools. Several of them have difficulty understanding the wording of one of the questions, and so Walters makes the language clearer. It is always wise to test the questions to reduce the possibility of misleading or unclear questions.

Walters is satisfied that his questions are understandable and that they will indeed help to determine what Riverdale really thinks about modular scheduling. He is ready to pose his questions. Walters writes out all the questions and makes multiple copies of them. It is important to have questions written out, to produce consistency—that is, to establish a system of asking the same question in the same way when each interview takes place.

Now, Walters must decide which people he wants to interview.

DEVELOPING THE SAMPLE

Identifying Respondents

Kelly and Walters decide that they are most interested in the opinions of parents who have children in the Riverdale schools. These are the people they want to interview. Random telephone dialing would provide a cross section of the entire community rather than only households with schoolchildren. Kelly suggests that Walters talk to the school superintendent. The district should have a list of parents, their addresses and their telephone numbers.

Walters tells the superintendent that the newspaper would like to conduct a survey to determine the opinions of parents. Walters suggests that the superintendent allow the newspaper to make *random selections* from the list of households. For the selection to be random, each household must have an equal chance of being included in the survey.

The superintendent agrees that the survey has merit, but he contends that the names cannot be released. Finally, a compromise is struck: the superintendent agrees to provide a list of addresses and telephone numbers of all households in the district. He will, however, protect the confidentiality of the parents by not providing their names. That is fine with Walters because reporters can ask names and get quotations when they conduct their interviews. Walters is pleased to get the addresses and the telephone numbers. The superintendent, of course, had no obligation to supply them. Sometimes it is difficult to get names or phone numbers for surveys. Walters considers himself fortunate.

Thirty-two hundred students are enrolled in the Riverdale schools. Because many parents have more than one child in school, however, Walters finds that 1,500 households have children enrolled. Walters does not have the time to call on all the households. The professor at Riverdale College suggests that if Walters samples 350 of the 1,500 households, the survey will be within an acceptable sampling level of confidence (See "Determining the Sampling Error," below).

The professor tells Walters not to expect all the households selected to produce usable responses. (Some people will not answer their doors or their telephones on the first call or the follow-up; and others will refuse to participate in the survey.) The professor tells Walters to expect about a 70 percent response. Thus, by randomly selecting 500 households to survey, Walters has a good chance of getting 350 usable responses.

Selecting a Random Sample

The professor then tells Walters to divide the *population*—the number of households that have children in the Riverdale schools (1,500)—by the number of households he will survey (500). In this case, Walters will call every third household. Instead of necessarily starting with the first number on the list, however, Walters puts the numbers 1, 2 and 3 in a hat. He draws 2. Thus he circles the second household on the list and every third (the *skip interval*) thereafter. He now has a systematic random sampling; on the basis of the "luck of the draw," every household on the original list had an equal chance of being included in the survey.

Determining the Sampling Error

Because not all parents of Riverdale schoolchildren will be interviewed, Walters should not report that his findings reflect precisely the opinions of the entire population. Because he is surveying only a portion, or *sample*, of the population, Walters must report the margin of error.

The professor consults a chart and tells Walters that, for a random sample of 350, the *sampling error* is 5.2 percent. (Charts that outline these figures can be found in most survey methodology books. A mathematical formula is used to compute the percentage.) In other words, the percentage of the entire population may be 5.2 percent above or below the estimate obtained from the sample of 350. For example, assume that the survey showed that 70 percent of those questioned have lived in Riverdale for more than five years. Walters would know that the true figure probably lies somewhere between 64.8 percent and 75.2 percent.

A sampling error for any survey based on random selection should be reported. A confidence interval is calculated to state the probable error because of chance variations in the sample. The most common interval is the 95 percent *level of confidence*. This means that the chances are only 5 in 100 that the true figure is not within the range found. The sampling error at the 95 percent level of confidence becomes smaller as the sample size is increased and larger as the sample size is decreased.

For example, the professor tells Walters that, if he were to randomly sample 600 parents, the sampling error would be 4 percent. That is, if he were to talk to all those 600 households, there would be only 1 chance in 20 that the true answer would vary from the results of the poll by more than 4 percentage points. Thus, nearly doubling the sample size from 350 to 600 would reduce the sampling error by only 1.2 percent (from 5.2 to 4). Therefore, the professor and Walters agree that a sample of 350 will be adequate.

Of course, determining an acceptable sampling margin of error depends on how close the researcher expects the outcome of the survey to be. In an election that promises to be extremely tight, for example, the people conducting the research would want to survey as many voters as possible to reduce the sampling margin of error. Also, it is always important to report the "don't know" responses. In close surveys, they might be the swing vote. Make sure to consider them when determining whether or not one side has a majority.

GATHERING DATA

After forming his questions and developing his sample, Walters must select the best way to gather the information. Kelly promises him that he can use eight reporters and editors to help conduct the survey. Basically, Walters can use one of three methods to gather the information: *face-to-face interviews, mailed questionnaires* and *telephone interviews*. All these methods are acceptable; choice of method depends on the situation.

Face-to-Face Interviews

Walters likes the idea of conducting face-to-face interviews. This way, the reporters conducting the interviews can probe extensively during the questioning process. Because Walters wants only parents to answer the questions, face-to-face interviewing will ensure that the respondent is not a teen-ager passing himself off as an adult.

On the other hand, Walters wants to complete the survey as quickly as possible so that he can publish the story before the school board meets in two weeks. Face-to-face interviewing will take considerable time, however, for his limited cast of reporters and editors. Walters thus realizes that the project probably cannot be completed before the next board meeting. Also, Kelly will probably question the overtime pay.

Mailed Questionnaires

Walters knows that a mailed questionnaire is relatively inexpensive, but he is concerned about the possible low rate of return. Generally, a researcher can expect about a 30 percent return on mailed questionnaires. Walters wants to get the survey completed as soon as possible. He does not want to have to conduct a follow-up survey if the response rate on the first mailing is low, and he needs at least 350 responses to keep his sampling error no higher than 5.2 percent. Thus he decides against mailed questionnaires.

Telephone Interviews

Walters finally decides that the best way to conduct the survey is by telephone. The telephone affords the luxury of follow-ups and clarification of answers, which mailed surveys are too cumbersome to handle, and it is faster than face-to-face interviewing. He realizes, of course, that telephones are used to sell everything from house siding to magazines. People often resent unsolicited telephone calls. Thus, his questions must be very clearly drafted, and he must pare them down so that they can be asked in a few minutes. He does not want to irritate the people being interviewed by asking long, irrelevant questions.

Kelly and Walters go over the questions with the eight reporters and editors who have been assigned to help conduct the survey. They decide to make their calls after 6 p.m., when working parents are more likely to be home.

The professor's estimate was accurate—500 calls result in 350 usable responses.

ANALYZING THE DATA

Walters could hand-tabulate the results, but the professor offers to show him how to computerize the data. It takes Walters about three hours to punch the data into the computer terminal. The professor programs the computer to handle the data. Once the data and the computer instructions are completed, in less than a minute the computer spits out the results. Walters is primarily interested in percentages.

Walters goes through the information, isolating percentages that he thinks will be of most interest to his readers. He turns to the printout of the survey's key question: "The Riverdale School Board is considering changing from modular scheduling to traditional seven-period scheduling. Do you prefer modular scheduling or the traditional seven-period scheduling?"

Overall, 350 persons were asked the question. The responses are as follows: modular, 210 (60 percent); traditional, 118 (34 percent); don't know, 22 (6 percent).

Next, Walters looks at the breakdown according to age. Of the 350 who responded, 70 were under age 30; 120 were between ages 30 and 39; 100 were between ages 40 and 49; and 60 were age 50 or older.

The responses:

Age	Modular	Traditional	Don't Know
Under age 30	47 (67 percent)	18 (26 percent)	5 (7 percent)
Ages 30–39	73 (61 percent)	39 (33 percent)	8 (7 percent)
Ages 40–49	65 (65 percent)	29 (29 percent)	6 (6 percent)
Ages 50 and older	25 (42 percent)	32 (53 percent)	3 (5 percent)

The percentages show that more than half of all parents polled preferred modular scheduling. In fact, 60 percent of the 350 persons surveyed said that they favored it.

With the figures in mind, Walters is ready to write his lead.

WRITING THE STORY

The Lead

Walters is careful not to overstate or to understate the significance of the figures. He determines that the most *newsworthy element* of the survey is that most of the parents favor modular scheduling. Even though the survey showed that 60 percent favor this type of scheduling, he realizes that the sampling error could lower or raise the number 5.2 percentage points. Walters decides on this safe, accurate lead:

> More than half of the parents of Riverdale schoolchildren prefer modular scheduling, a <u>Daily News</u> poll shows.

Walters continues his story with specific results of the focal question:

> Sixty percent of those surveyed said that they preferred modular scheduling; 34 percent said that they preferred traditional scheduling; and 6 percent said that they did not know.

Walters' story goes on to detail other statistical findings of the survey. He also weaves some open-ended responses into his story. He is careful, when selecting open-ended responses, to include comments from both respondents who favor modular scheduling and respondents who oppose it.

Explanatory Material: Essential Information

Walters also inserts the following into his story:

> The <u>Daily News</u> randomly interviewed 350 parents in the Riverdale School District. Telephone interviews were conducted Wednesday and Thursday evenings by <u>Daily News</u> reporters and editors.
>
> As with all sample surveys, the results of the <u>Daily News</u> poll can vary from the opinions of all school district parents because of chance variations in the sample.
>
> For a poll based on 350 interviews, the results are subject to a margin of error of 5.2 percentage points each way because of such chance variations. That is, if one could have talked to all Riverdale School District parents by telephone on Wednesday and Thursday, there is only 1 chance in 20 that the findings would vary by more than 5.2 percentage points from the results of surveys such as this one.

Walters inserted the explanatory paragraphs about the size of the sample, the survey procedures and the sampling error to keep within the guidelines suggested by the National Council on Public Polling. The Associated Press Stylebook suggests that editors and reporters consider the guidelines before using a story about a canvass of public opinion.

The guidelines, which were discussed in the *Washington Journalism Review* article by Evans Witt, include the following:

1 State who sponsored the survey.
2 Give the dates of interviewing.
3 Define the method of interviewing.
4 Describe the population interviewed.
5 Reveal the size of the sample.
6 Describe and give the size of any subsamples used in the analysis.
7 Release the wording of all questions.
8 Release the full results of the questions on which the conclusions are based.

Witt, however, put the guidelines into perspective. He wrote: "They provide the minimum information needed for a reporter—or a reader—to evaluate a poll. They do not guarantee that a poll will be competently conducted; they provide no guarantees against massive errors that could affect results."

The New York Times Manual of Style and Usage states that occasionally not all polling details can be included in a story. The manual concludes: "If there ever is a doubt, the reporter should include as much of the information as possible. The responsible editors can then decide how much should be used."

The manual also cautions that terms such as *opinion poll, poll, survey, opinion sample* and *cross section* "should be limited to truly scientific soundings of opinion. They should not be applied to stringer roundups and man-in-the-street stories by reporters."

REPORTING SURVEYS: RULES AND GUIDELINES FOR JOURNALISTS

GENERAL CONSIDERATIONS

Surveys are most commonly used at newspapers during election campaigns to measure opinions about candidates and major issues. Of course, as has been discussed, they can also be used for community issues other than elections.

Newspapers of various circulations—including student publications—can enter the arena of precision journalism relatively easily. Only those outlets that have the labor power, the expertise and the available money to do the job right, however, should base stories on precision journalism methods.

Here are some suggestions to consider when writing a story based on a survey:

- Analyze the data carefully before starting to write. Ask yourself: What findings would be of most interest to my audience?
- Make sure that you are interpreting the statistics correctly. Check with a knowledgeable editor or supervisor if you have any questions or doubts.
- Lead with the survey's most significant findings.
- Make every effort to humanize the statistics. Focus on what the statistics say about people.

- Organize the story so that readers can comprehend the most significant findings. The use of bullets (•) to outline key statistics is often an effective way to keep the story flowing while presenting a lot of information.

- Make comparisons among subgroups in the sample when appropriate (for example: male versus female, older respondents versus younger respondents, Republicans versus Democrats and so forth).

- Work in as many direct quotations from survey subjects as you can; this will help bring the numbers to life.

- Provide relevant details about the sample and the method for gathering the information.

- Devise charts to accompany the story, if that is the most efficient and understandable way to present some statistical information.

AVOIDING DISTORTIONS: JAMES SIMON'S TOP-10 FACTORS

James Simon, a veteran Associated Press journalist, is currently the assistant director of the Media Research Program in the Walter Cronkite School of Journalism and Telecommunication at Arizona State University. The Media Research Program, in conjunction with Arizona State's PBS television station, KAET-TV, regularly conducts the Cactus State Poll, a survey that measures opinions on a variety of political and social issues.

Simon noted: "Public opinion polls give reporters a chance to look at the views of the public toward an issue in the news. But the results of a survey depend largely on how it is conducted—and it can be conducted in many different ways."

Simon compiled the following list of 10 factors that can distort the outcome of polls.

Reflection versus Prediction: Polls as "Snapshots"

A poll is a snapshot of the population at a given moment. One hour after the poll is conducted, respondents may hear a television newscast on a given subject and change their views. Because survey data can have such a short shelf life, pollsters try to release their findings within days of collection.

Polls reflect; they do not predict. They can be a very good reflection of how voters feel a week before an election. In many cases, they may be a poor predictor of how a volatile electorate will feel a week later on Election Day.

Samples: Who Was Polled?

The headline is clear: Candidate Jones has a 10-point lead, with a week to go before Election Day. But in reading the story, you notice that the poll is based on interviews with 600 state *residents*, not registered voters. And you know that one-third of all state residents are not registered to vote.

Pollsters have to be careful when choosing their sampling framework to ensure that it is the right one for a given issue. The Cactus State Poll, for example, almost always uses registered voters, since so many of the surveys deal with election-season issues. But a sample of all state residents, not just voters, would be more appropriate to measure opinions on an issue such as the public's view of media ethics or any issue not headed for the ballot. When reading poll results, reporters should ask themselves: Did the pollsters go to the right people?

Attitudes and Non-Attitudes: Measuring Intensity

A pollster asks your opinion on your university's fine arts department. You don't really have a firm opinion, but the pollster presses and you say you have a generally favorable opinion. You are not lying: you may have a generally favorable opinion toward everything at the university. But in this case, you really don't have a clear attitude on the fine arts department. The pollster, if he or she takes down your view and builds it into the findings, is measuring a "non-attitude." The results won't really provide a clear picture of how you feel. Pollsters can counter this problem by asking an "intensity" question—"How strongly do you feel about the issue?"—and then focusing on those respondents who have strong feelings.

Interpretations: Evaluating Pollsters' Conclusions

In one of the Cactus State Polls in 1992, the pollsters decided to take an early look at Ross Perot, who at that point was just talking about a possible independent bid for the presidency. In an effort to gauge what impact he might have in Arizona, voters were asked whether they would consider voting for him. The result: 27 percent said they were either very likely or somewhat likely to support Perot, 49 percent said they were not very likely to support him and 24 percent said they had no opinion. Is 27 percent good or bad? Reporters often want an interpretation from the pollster, but the answer here was simply not clear. It was a high percentage for someone who at the time was barely known to the electorate. But you don't win elections with 27 percent, especially when 49 percent also said they would not consider voting for you.

There are many ways to interpret survey results. As a reporter, always ask yourself: do I agree with the pollster's interpretation?

Respondents' Answers: Considering Motivation

Most people, when called by a pollster on the telephone, are reluctant to express any socially undesirable views. They may feel a civic duty to give a politically correct answer or to say what they think the pollster wants to hear. But when they get to the privacy of the voting booth, they can act freely without any fear of what a pollster or anyone else might think.

This tendency makes it difficult to interpret poll results for issues such as whether the city should spend taxpayers' dollars to construct and operate facilities for unwed, homeless mothers with small children. Reporters should be skeptical of the validity of poll results on any issue in which there may be a socially acceptable or unacceptable response. The results on Election Day may be a lot different from the results on Polling Day.

Respondents also sometimes make up answers to questions, to avoid appearing uninformed. If a pollster asks voters if they have a favorable opinion about County Commissioner John Jones, some voters will given an opinion even though they have never heard of him.

Sources: What Questions Were Asked?

Newspapers report poll results from both non-partisan sources and sources with a vested interest in the subject. Special-interest groups routinely commission polls to help push their agendas, and such results should be judged with skepticism.

The questions that were included—and the questions that were left out—are invisible to most readers. For example, a group advocating nuclear power may include properly worded questions about the higher cost of power from fossil fuel plants, then find greater public support for cheaper nuclear power. But the survey probably would not ask any questions about public sentiment toward problems involved in disposing of radioactive waste—questions that would show less public support for nuclear power.

The lesson here: The answer received is a product of the question asked. Do the poll data do a good job of getting at the overall issue?

Neutrality and Accuracy: How Were the Questions Phrased?

Most surveys of attitudes toward abortion show general public support for a woman's right to choose. But using the phrase "innocent fetus" in such a question could produce very different results. Good surveys include the phrasing of the questions; as a reporter, you should reread the phrasing and ask yourself whether it appears neutral.

A related problem can stem from "double-barreled" questions. For example: "Do you agree or disagree with the statement, 'The United Nations is an inefficient body and the United States should leave it'?" If you agree with the first part of the sentence and not with the second, it would be impossible to give an accurate response.

As a reporter, you should examine the phrasing of survey questions very critically.

Context: In What Order Were the Questions Presented?

Appropriate phrasing of questions is not the only concern reporters should have. Pollsters usually don't release the full list of questions, which would show the *context* in which a query appeared. Again, support for abortion would be much lower if the question was preceded by a question dealing with the rights of the unborn. Most independently commissioned polls are careful with context; surveys from special-interest groups might be less inclined to be careful. Reporters always should ask for and examine the order of questions.

All polls that use a random sample are subject to potential sampling error. Poll results should specify the potential sampling error, or confidence interval, which is computed on the basis of the sample size. A survey of 1,200 respondents has a potential sampling error of 3 percent; 600 respondents, 4 percent; 377 respondents, 5 percent. Be careful in using poll data in instances where precise measurement is needed. In most cases, polls are blunt tools, not finely honed instruments.

Polls can be less than precise for a second reason. According to the rules of statistics, there is an additional 5 percent chance that the numbers will not even be within the sampling error. More optimistically, though, there is a 95 percent chance that the results will be within the sampling error.

Bottom line: Be skeptical of any poll findings where the difference is near the sampling error of the survey.

Statistical Significance: Are the Results Meaningful?

Candidate Smith is leading candidate Jones by a margin of 52 percent to 48 percent. The sampling error in the poll is 3 percent. Does Smith have a statistically significant lead?

The answer is no. The race is too close to call. The sampling error must be applied to the percentage of each candidate, not to the difference between their percentages. Smith could have anywhere from 49 percent to 55 percent of the vote. Jones could have anywhere from 45 percent to 51 percent; if it is 51 percent, then Jones is actually leading Smith. A statistically significant lead exists only when a candidate is ahead both at the high end and the low end of the sampling error.

This is a common problem. When reading poll results before writing your story, factor in the sampling error yourself to see if the analyst handled it correctly.

Simon emphasized that, because of the factors he outlined, "a healthy dose of skepticism is the best attitude to have in analyzing poll results. Reporters should insist that the pollster supply enough information to demonstrate the validity of the survey."

four

Basic Assignments

Reports are challenged to report on the human dimension of firefighters who die in arson fires and leave mourners behind.
(Ap/Wide World Photos)

13

Obituaries

When the telephone rings, most reporters hope

that it is not a funeral home calling. After all,

reporters have more important things to do than

take information for obituaries and write them. Or

so they think. The fact is, obituaries are among the

best-read items in newspapers. Many newspapers

strive not only to provide basic factual

information in their obits but to humanize them

with anecdotes and quotations.

Reporters sometimes consider writing obituaries, or obits, a fate worse than death, but the fact remains that obits—*death notices*—are highly interesting to readers.

The policy of *The Berkshire* (Mass.) *Eagle* possibly best summarizes the philosophy of many newspapers: "It is our policy to run obituaries and funeral notices involving deceased persons who have any connection at all with our circulation area. If John Jones fished here in 1937 and lived happily ever after in Tacoma, we use his obit because we deem it news, it creates goodwill (or at least it avoids creating bad will) and we try to be the paper of record for our area."

The American Society of Newspaper Editors (ASNE) certainly recognizes the value of outstanding obituary writing, as evidenced by its decision to present a Distinguished Writing Award in that category. Tom Shales of *The Washington Post* won an ASNE award for an obituary of the actor Ray Bolger. The first two paragraphs pulled readers into the story:

"I think I'll miss you most of all," Dorothy whispered in the Scarecrow's ear. We shared her sentiment. The Cowardly Lion was funny, the Tin Woodman was dear, but the Scarecrow had soul. Oz wouldn't have been the same without him. The rest of the world won't be the same without Ray Bolger, the lanky and vivacious vaudevillian who played the Scarecrow, his role of roles, in *The Wizard of Oz*.

Yesterday in Hollywood, at the age of 83, Ray Bolger died. He was the last surviving star of *The Wizard of Oz*—made in 1939 but never far from the public eye—and even if his appearances grew rare in recent years, you knew he was around, and you felt that, just like you and the kids, he might have been watching the movie during its annual telecasts.

SELECTING OBITUARIES TO PUBLISH

Most newspapers have an obit page. Depending on the circulation of the newspaper and the population of the area served, obituaries might fill a portion of the page or they might spill over to more than one page. Most newspapers publish obits—free—for every resident and former resident. Some larger-circulation newspapers obviously do not have sufficient space to publish obits of everyone who dies in their areas, but they do publish obits of as many people as they can. Some newspapers provide a list of the deceased with only basic facts such as age and date of death. Still other newspapers publish complete obituary information in classified advertising space purchased by funeral homes or by families.

In addition to obits published regularly on their designated page, newspapers occasionally carry front-page stories on the deaths of well-known people.

A national survey of 165 daily newspaper managing editors selected at random found that 94 percent of the country's dailies publish obits for all area residents and that nearly 9 in 10 of the dailies publish them free of charge.

The *New Haven* (Conn.) *Register* has a well-stated policy on the handling of obituaries. The *Register* "strives to run all obituaries submitted as quickly as possible after submission." If, in a space or time crunch, some obits must be held, the *Register*'s policy establishes the following priority system:

1   First, obituaries of people whose deaths are significant news

2   Second, obituaries in which the funerals are on the day of publication or the next day

3   Third, obituaries in which the decedent's residence and the location of the funeral are in the New Haven area as opposed to outside the region

4   Fourth, obituaries of people who formerly lived in the area but most recently lived, and will be buried, elsewhere

The *Register* even accepts "the occasional obituaries of people who never have lived in the area but have immediate family ties here or are widely known in this area." These obits, however, are kept concise, with most biographical information omitted "unless an individual is newsworthy in his or her own right."

Many newspapers are so conscious of their responsibility to publish obits that they will print an obit several days after a death if word of the death has been delayed. This often happens in the case of a person who had lived and worked in the community but had retired to another area of the country. A week after the person's death, the newspaper might receive a letter with obit information. Then, after verifying it, many papers will publish an obit beginning something like this: "Word has been received of the death of John P. Jones, 75, former Riverdale electrician, who died Oct. 25 at his home in Palm Springs, Calif."

CONTENT OF OBITUARIES

BASIC INFORMATION IN OBITS

Obits should contain certain basic information, typically including:

- Address
- Date of death
- Cause of death
- Occupation
- Accomplishments
- Time and date of services
- Visitation information
- Place of burial
- Memorial information
- Names of survivors

In addition, some smaller-circulation newspapers carry follows to obits in which pallbearers are listed.

Many newspapers, such as *The Evansville* (Ind.) *Courier,* strive to expand obits beyond this basic information. The editor, Tom Tuley, who published a study of obit practices at various newspapers in the *Editor's Exchange,* said that he had "some uneasiness about whether we are doing as good a job with obits as we should." He cited the need to find out more about the person.

"We make an effort to call people to get additional information or anecdotes," he said. "My feeling is that there is something interesting in everyone's life. We have received good responses from our readers and the families of the deceased for our efforts."

Deadlines and limited staff, of course, keep the *Courier* from expanding all obits. But Tuley said that his newspaper tries to provide interesting details about "common people," not just celebrities and public figures.

Let's look now at the basic elements in obits.

Names

Newspapers generally use the first name, middle initial and last name of the deceased. Most do not use nicknames—particularly if they sound derogatory. If the deceased was known to most people by his or her nickname, however, some newspapers will use it. For example:

> John E. "Booster" Jones, who had not missed a Riverdale High
> School home basketball game since 1947, died Wednesday in Samaritan
> Memorial Hospital after a short illness. He was 72.

Note that the nickname is set off in quotation marks; in obits, the use of parentheses indicates a maiden name. Also, if the nickname would slow the cadence of the lead sentence, save it for later. For example:

> John E. Jones, who had not missed a Riverdale High School home
> basketball game since 1947, died Wednesday in Samaritan Memorial
> Hospital after a short illness. Mr. Jones, who was known to his friends
> as "Booster," was 72.

In the above example, a *courtesy title* (Mr.) was used on second reference. Few newspapers use courtesy titles (such as Mr., Mrs., Miss, Ms. or Dr.) on second references in news stories, but many do so in obits.

Ages

Many newspaper policies mandate that the age of the deceased be printed. The *News-Journal* in Daytona Beach, Fla., has a policy that states: "Always include the age of deceased and address. If necessary (but only after having exhausted all avenues) fudge a bit and say 'in his/her 70s or 80s' or whatever. There *must be* some indication of age."

The reader should never have to use arithmetic to figure out the age of the deceased (obit writers should not merely give the date and place of birth). Reporters must be careful when computing ages. Reporters and their sources often forget to take the date of birth into account. For example, a person is born Feb. 15, 1930, and dies Feb. 1, 1990. That person would be 59, not 60. A common blunder is to merely subtract 1930 from 1990 to come up with 60.

Ages can be handled in a number of ways, including these:

- John E. Jones, 72, died Wednesday in Riverdale.
- John E. Jones died Wednesday in Riverdale. He was 72.
- John E. Jones died Wednesday in Riverdale at the age of 72.
- John E. Jones died Wednesday in Riverdale at 72 years of age.

The first two examples are preferable to the last two. In the last two examples, the extra words make the language more stilted than necessary.

Addresses

Practices vary on the use of addresses. Some newspapers use full addresses (2142 S. 168th Ave., Riverdale) while others use only the town. The policy of *The Trentonian,* for example, states: "The family, usually through the funeral director, may sometimes ask that exact addresses not be used to avoid possible burglaries. We'll go along with this request, although we usually prefer using full addresses."

Causes of Death

General policies   Policies vary on stating the cause of death in obits. The national survey of managing editors cited earlier in this chapter showed that 9 percent of the papers always publish the cause of death in obituaries. Nearly 78 percent said that they sometimes do; and 13 percent said that they never do.

The policy of the *New Haven Register,* for example, states: "If relatives do not want information disclosed concerning a particular disease, 'a long illness' or similar phrase may be used. If death is violent, however—for example, in an auto accident or a shooting—that fact should not be disguised. The rule of thumb is that if the funeral home does not volunteer a cause of death, ask. Too many times there have been attempts to slip obituaries through when the deaths were homicides or suspected homicides."

The policy of the *Fargo* (N.D.) *Forum* states: "Usually we do not specify the cause of death, but we ask the question in case we might miss an accident or death under suspicious circumstances. If an accident is involved, notify the city desk so that a news story can be prepared about the accident. Obituaries of accident victims should note that 'she died of injuries received in an auto accident Friday.' "

The Trentonian's policy also provides flexibility: "We do not insist on using the cause of death unless it involves accidental or other unusual circumstances. Where the deceased is young, we always ask the funeral director the cause of death. Where the deceased is prominent, regardless of age, try to determine whether it was a long or a short illness. We don't usually specify the type of illness unless the family requests it. Also, don't call it a 'lengthy' illness. It's short or long."

Most newspapers mention the cause of death if the person was well-known. Here are some examples taken from wire-service stories:

TOKYO (AP)—Emperor Hirohito, who held divine status until Japan's defeat in World War II and endured to reign for 62 years, died today of intestinal cancer. He was 87.

Crown Prince Akihito, 55, the emperor's oldest son, immediately became the 125th occupant of the Chrysanthemum Throne and received the imperial regalia.

Chief Cabinet Secretary Kenzo Obuchi said the emperor died at 6:33 a.m.

LOS ANGELES (AP)—Lucille Ball, the zany redhead who reigned for more than 20 years as the queen of television comedy, died today, a week after undergoing emergency heart surgery. She was 77.

The star of "I Love Lucy" and similar situation comedies that continue in syndication died of a ruptured aorta at Cedars-Sinai Medical Center, hospital spokesman Ronald Wise said.

NEW YORK (AP)—Pioneer newscaster Eric Sevareid, an eloquent heretic who thought one good word was worth a thousand pictures, died Thursday

Sevareid died of cancer at age 79.

NICOSIA, Cyprus (AP)—Iranian leader Ayatollah Ruhollah Khomeini has died 11 days after undergoing surgery for bleeding in his digestive system, the official Iranian news agency reported today. He was 86.

"The leader of the Islamic revolution and founder of the Islamic Republic, Imam Khomeini, passed away at a Tehran hospital," the Islamic Republic News Agency reported in an urgent dispatch.

EDGARTOWN, Mass. (AP)—Baseball Commissioner A. Bartlett Giamatti, who left the presidency of Yale University for the game he loved, died Friday after suffering a heart attack just five months into the sport's top job. He was 51.

Giamatti died at his weekend retreat on Martha's Vineyard eight days after he banned Cincinnati Reds Manager Pete Rose from baseball. The decision followed a six-month battle over allegations that Rose bet on his own team.

BEVERLY HILLS, Calif. (UPI)—Actor Rock Hudson, the square-jawed movie hero who played the role of the suave ladies' man for three decades, died Wednesday after a yearlong battle with AIDS—the first major celebrity known to have been felled by the disease.

In Washington, the House, acting hours after Hudson's death was announced, voted 322–107 to substantially boost the amount of federal money for the battle against AIDS. The measure provides $189.7 million for AIDS work, $70 million more than President Reagan requested and 90 percent more than is being spent this year.

Policies on suicide   One of the major problems facing newspapers is how to handle obits or news stories when suicide is the cause of death. Again, policies vary. The *Bangor* (Maine) *Daily News,* for example, stopped including that information in its obits in the early 1970s. "We feel that the obit is a permanent record which families keep, and neither they nor their descendants should have to be reminded of a suicide every time they take out the family album," said Kent H. Ward, associate managing editor. "Further, we do not run suicides as news stories unless they involve prominent people or the suicide was committed in public or in some spectacular manner. In other words, if Mr. Average Joe goes down in the privacy of his basement or out behind the barn and kills himself, we do not give it a play. And his obit would probably state that he died unexpectedly."

The *Iowa City* (Iowa) *Press Citizen*'s policy states: "If someone commits suicide, it is generally handled as an obit. But calling someone's death a suicide requires confirmation from the medical examiner."

The *New Haven Register* labels deaths as suicides or apparent suicides only if "the person taking his or her life is a public figure or the suicide takes place in full view of other people. Any statement that a death is a suicide must be attributed."

The national survey of managing editors showed that 17 percent of the newspapers always use the word *suicide* in obits if it is determined to be the cause of death; 21 percent sometimes use it; and 62 percent never use it.

The most pertinent information—name, age, address, date of death and sometimes cause of death—is placed in the lead of an obit; supplementary facts fill the remaining paragraphs. Newspaper policy and the importance of the deceased are primary factors in determining the length of obits. Generally, however, the information discussed in the following sections is provided.

Background

The extent of background information will, of course, depend on the accomplishments and the community involvement of the deceased. Many obits provide the following:

- Date and place of birth
- Names of parents
- Education
- Work experience
- Honors received
- Military background

For example:

> Dr. Johnson was born Jan. 22, 1921, in Salt Lake City, Utah, the son of Joe and Carolyn Johnson. He received his medical degree from the University of Utah.
>
> He practiced medicine in Riverdale for nearly 30 years. He was honored by the Nuckolls County Medical Association in 1993 for

outstanding contributions to the profession. He also served on the governor's blue-ribbon panel on hospital care.

Dr. Johnson, who served in World War II, is a member of the VFW, the Knights of Columbus and the Nuckolls County Cancer Society.

Newspapers normally decide on a case-by-case basis whether potentially embarrassing or sensitive information should be used in an obituary. Common sense must be exercised. An obit writer might decide, for example, that it would serve no purpose to mention that John Smith had been convicted of income tax evasion and had served a 10-month sentence in a federal penitentiary 20 years ago. However, if John Smith had been convicted in a sensational murder trial 20 years ago and was paroled only 18 months ago, that would probably merit mention in the obit.

Many writers, out of respect for the surviving family, nevertheless try to handle these references in a matter-of-fact, unemotional way that is least offensive.

Funeral Services, Visitation and Memorials

Most newspapers list the time, day and place of the funeral, the clergyman or clergywoman and the religious affiliation. Place of burial is also mentioned. For example:

> The funeral will be at 10 a.m. Wednesday in the Butler-Blatchford Funeral Home. The Rev. Silas Smith, pastor of the First Methodist Church, will officiate. Burial will be in Evergreen Cemetery.

The Findlay (Ohio) *Courier,* like many newspapers, provides details of *visitation.* Its policy states: "In addition to the hours of visitation, we will include the hours that the decedent's family will be at the funeral home, if that information is provided. For instance: 'Visitation will be held from 2–5 and 7–9 p.m. Tuesday at the funeral home. The family will be present from 4–5 p.m.'"

Policies on mention of *memorials* differ among newspapers. The policy of the *Jamestown* (N.Y.) *Post-Journal,* for example, states: "Last paragraph notes memorials, if the family suggests same. We do not use 'In lieu of flowers.' Write instead that 'The family suggests memorials be made to the Heart Fund.'"

The Findlay Courier's policy states: "We do not say 'in lieu of flowers, memorials may be made . . . ' Nor do we say that memorials 'should' be made. Simply say that 'memorials may be made to . . . ' or 'the family requests that memorials be made to . . . ' One other note: We do not say that memorials may be made to a specific person or family."

Survivors

The policy of the *Jamestown Post-Journal* concerning the listing of survivors is typical of many small- and medium-circulation newspapers. It states:

(1) List names of spouse, children, grandchildren, sisters and brothers. [Many newspapers list only the number of, but not the names of, grandchildren.] Give number of, but not names of great-grandchildren. Other distant relatives, such as nieces and nephews, aunts, uncles and cousins are named if they are the only survivors in the *Post-Journal* circulation area [many newspapers never list the names of distant relatives.]

(2) If the deceased lived with a distant relative, but is survived by someone in his immediate family, we will include that relative by noting, "Smith lived with his nephew, John Jones."

Editors will consider other special circumstances as they arise. Example: if the deceased has a lot of immediate-family survivors, but a cousin was the only one who took care of him, we will list, at the discretion of the city, regional or news editors, the cousin if the family asks us to do so. We will note, for example, that the deceased was cared for by his cousin, John Jones.

An example of a paragraph listing survivors follows:

> Survivors include his wife, the former Irene McDonald; two daughters, Susan Johnson, Evansville, Ind., and Patricia Kelly, Los Angeles; three sons, Richard, Fargo, N.D., Allan, Omaha, Neb., and William, Laramie, Wyo.; sister, Lois Folz, Cooper City, Fla.; brother, Sterling, Great Bend, Kan.; eight grandchildren; and three great-grandchildren.

A delicate situation can arise if the decedent was divorced or estranged from a spouse. The *New Haven Register* provides this advice: "Do not become embroiled in a family dispute over inclusion of the surviving individual in the obit. Tell the parties to work it out and have the funeral home supply the correct information. If, however, the relationship to the survivor is itself newsworthy, do not omit the survivor's name merely because other survivors do not like him or her."

The *Register* also takes into consideration surviving fiancés and companions: "If the decedent was engaged to be married, the fiancé or fiancée may be listed as a survivor if the decedent's family requests it. If the decedent had a live-in companion and those arranging the funeral insist the name be included, put the name at the end of the list of survivors: . . . and Mary Jones, with whom Mr. Smith resided."

Obit writers should never be surprised at requests from funeral home directors or from relatives of the deceased. With this in mind, the *Register* policy states: "Never list pets as survivors."

Newspaper policies on the range of information that might be included in an obit naturally vary. It is important, therefore, that reporters who are to write obits carefully review the policy of the newspaper. If there is no written policy, study obits from past issues. If in doubt, always consult on editor.

ORDER OF INFORMATION

The order of information presented in an obit can, of course, vary. If a person was a member of a prominent family, for example, that might be mentioned in the lead paragraph, followed by facts and accomplishments and local ties. Here are the first five paragraphs of an obit published in the *Colorado Springs (Colo.) Gazette Telegraph:*

Alfred Cowles III, 93, a member of the family associated with the Chicago Tribune for 30 years and a former resident of Colorado Springs, died Dec. 27 at his home in Lake Forest, Ill.

While a resident of Colorado Springs he founded the Cowles Commission for Research in Economics, which was moved to the University of Chicago in 1939 then to Yale in 1955, where it was renamed the Cowles Foundation for Economic Research.

He was an honorary trustee of the Colorado Springs Fine Arts Center.

Mr. Cowles was born Sept. 15, 1881, in Chicago.

His grandfather Alfred Cowles and Joseph Medill acquired the Tribune in 1855.

SOURCES OF INFORMATION

Funeral Homes

Most information for obituaries is provided to the media by funeral homes (sometimes called *mortuaries*). However, the policy of the *New Haven Register* emphasizes the need for gathering information beyond that provided by mortuaries: "In most situations the *Register* depends on funeral homes to submit obituaries. This does not mean, however, that the newspaper's position should be supine. If a prominent person or a person violently injured is known to be near death, the newspapers should check with the hospital, the public relations officer of the person's employer or a similar authority in order not to miss the news story. Information concerning funeral services may be put off until subsequent editions."

Newspaper Libraries

The *Register*'s policy also emphasizes the importance of checking the newspaper library for information for obituaries. "If anything in an obituary suggests the person may have been prominent in the New Haven area, reporters and desk editors should consider it mandatory to check the clippings in the library for background. Frequently a family, under stress, will provide inaccurate or incomplete information to a funeral home; checking the files can set this straight. If necessary, the funeral home should be called to confirm that the individual who died is the same person mentioned in the clippings."

Families

After gathering additional information from clippings and possibly from interviews with law enforcement officials, hospital officials, employers, fellow

workers and friends, calls to family members may be in order. This, of course, should be handled delicately.

Tom Tuley of *The Evansville Courier* offers this advice to reporters who are making calls to grieving family members: "The whole problem—if you can call it a problem—can be solved by the approach of the writer. The family is under great strain. But it seems to me that about 99 percent of the people we call appreciate the fact that we want to make every effort to be accurate and to include additional information. I don't think reporters should hesitate to make a call because they fear the family member will be uncomfortable." The key, of course, to a successful interview is to establish rapport with the family member and to carry on the conversation with dignity.

ENSURING ACCURACY IN OBITS

Confirming Information

Accuracy is immensely important in any news story, but inaccurate information in an obit can cause severe pain to surviving family members. Thus, it is particularly important to confirm all information gathered for obits. Because most of the facts contained in obits come from telephone calls from the mortuary, reporters should be diligent in checking names, cities and addresses in available directories. It is also wise to compute the age of the person from his or her date of birth to verify the age supplied by the mortuary. And when taking calls from the mortuary, always ask the caller to repeat any words or spellings that sound unusual.

According to the managing editor, Monroe Dodd, the *Kansas City Times* verifies all information supplied by funeral homes by calling family members. Additional information may be sought from or verified by police, coroners and other law enforcement officials. Occasionally, reporters at the *Times* will speak to business associates or close friends of the deceased if the family is vague or uncertain on some pertinent matters.

Avoiding Hoaxes

The *New Haven Register*'s policy warns reporters to confirm deaths: "An obit called in by a funeral director with whom the reporter is not familiar should be confirmed by calling back. Get the number from the phone book or long-distance information; don't trust the number the caller may just have given you. If the obit is submitted by someone other than a funeral director, call the funeral home to confirm it. If the funeral home cannot be reached, the death should be confirmed with a reliable—that word should be emphasized—second source."

Some newspapers, such as *The Trentonian* in Trenton, N.J., verify calls from mortuaries by asking for the funeral director's obit code. "If he doesn't have one," the newspaper policy states, "verify that he's a funeral director by calling back the number listed in the telephone book, no matter where in the world it is. This will hopefully eliminate the dreaded hoax, the bane of all obit writers."

OBITUARY STYLES

Routine obits at the *Chicago Tribune* and at scores of other newspapers normally follow two styles. The styles adhered to by the *Tribune* city desk are as follows: If the obit is written on the day of the death—a *same-day obit*—the fact that the person died is the lead. If the obit is written one or more days after the death—a *second-day obit*—the time of the services is the lead.

SAME-DAY OBITS

An example of an obituary written on the day of the death follows:

John E. Jones, 72, Riverdale, died Wednesday in Samaritan Memorial Hospital after a short illness. Mr. Jones was an accountant and a partner in the firm of Smith and Jones, 2020 W. Main St., until his retirement seven years ago.

Mr. Jones was a board member of the Samaritan Memorial Hospital at the time of his death.

He is survived by his wife, Mildred; two sons, John Jr. and Michael, both of Riverdale; a daughter, Mary Smith of New York; four grandchildren; a great-grandchild; two brothers; and a sister.

Mass ["services" for Protestant churches] will be said ["held"] at 9 a.m. Saturday in Resurrection Catholic [Methodist, Lutheran, etc.] Church, 1136 Central Ave. [the chapel at 1244 Kansas St., Riverdale].

SECOND-DAY OBITS

An example of an obituary that is written one or more days after the death follows:

Mass ["services"] for John E. Jones, 72, Riverdale, will be said ["held"] at 9 a.m. Saturday in Resurrection Catholic [Methodist, Lutheran, etc.] Church, 1136 Central Ave. [the chapel at 1244 Kansas St., Riverdale].

Mr. Jones, who died Wednesday in Samaritan Memorial Hospital after a short illness, was an accountant and a partner in the firm of Smith and Jones, 2020 W. Main St., until his retirement seven years ago.

Mr. Jones was a board member of Samaritan Memorial Hospital at the time of his death.

He is survived by his wife, Mildred; two sons, John Jr. and Michael, both of Riverdale; a daughter, Mary Smith of New York; four grandchildren; a great-grandchild; two brothers; and a sister.

OBITS FOR BROADCAST

Unlike most newspapers, radio and television stations do not carry obits for everyone who dies in the community, because of time limitations. Broadcasters air obits only of newsmakers. Broadcast obits are much shorter than newspaper obits, and they contain only the most important facts. A typical broadcast obit would include who died, the day of death and the person's age.

Here is a broadcast version of the Jones obit:

> A MEMBER OF THE SAMARITAN MEMORIAL HOSPITAL BOARD DIED
> TODAY AT THAT HOSPITAL AFTER A SHORT ILLNESS. DEAD IS
> JOHN E. JONES, WHO WAS 72 YEARS OLD.

This story would be used only because the death of Jones was newsworthy—he was a member of the hospital board.

To save time, broadcast reporters do not normally use the middle name or the middle initial. The exceptions are common names, such as Jones, and people known for their middle names.

Note also that broadcasters would not say, "John E. Jones, 72, Riverdale." The reason is that people don't talk this way. Saying, "Jones, who was 72 years old," is conversational.

Naturally, if the deceased is particularly newsworthy, his or her obit would be covered in greater depth. If the mayor dies, for example, he or she would receive considerably more time than a prominent local car dealer would.

Some television and radio news operations, usually those in large cities, and the networks routinely put together videotaped and audiotaped obits of the more prominent newsmakers. The taped obits are ready to use when these people die. For example, the networks have obits prepared on the president and on other major national and international figures. These obits are on audiotape for radio and videotape for television. When a person dies, reporters merely have to top the taped obit with the details of the death.

TERMINOLOGY

Editors often single out words, phrases and usages that should be considered when writing obits. A sample follows.

- *Terminology for death.* "People die—period! They don't die suddenly any more than they die slowly, although they may have died quickly after being struck in the heart with an MX missile."—Policy of *The Trentonian.*

    "Nobody dies suddenly. We all die at the same speed. Some causes of death are quicker than others, but the speed of death itself is constant. A person dies of an ailment, not from it. A person is dead on arrival at a hospital, not 'to' it. You arrive at a place, not 'to' it. Also, people are 'taken' to hospitals. If we say they are 'transported,' it sounds like they are freight."—Policy of *The Findlay Courier.*

- *Place of birth.* "Funeral directors are fond of saying that John Jones was a 'former native' of some place. Native means the place of birth, and so a person cannot be a former native."—Policy of the *Jamestown Post-Journal.*

- *Titles for ministers, pastors and priests.* Always check the AP Stylebook for proper terminology for religions and church officials.

WRITING EFFECTIVE OBITUARIES

CAPTURING THE FLAVOR OF A LIFE

Obits often fall into the standard, concise forms outlined above, but most newspapers strive to go beyond the mechanical restrictions. The policy of the *New Haven Register* makes this clear: "The obituary writer's job is not simply to report the fact of death, but also, so far as available information permits, to capture the flavor of the decedent's life. This means that, although obituary writing can be reduced to a formula, the formula never should become a straitjacket that prevents writing a better news story."

An obituary written by Belinda Brockman of *The Miami Herald,* for example, captured the qualities of an Orange Bowl official. The first three paragraphs show that obituaries can be fast-paced and descriptive:

Hal Fleming, the Orange Bowl's "Mr. Indispensable," whose nuts-and-bolts knowledge transformed Miami's New Year's celebration from a rolling rumble of floats into true majesty, died Tuesday of lymph gland cancer. He was 65.

In his 39 years with the festival, Mr. Fleming "literally developed into the closest thing that I've ever seen to an indispensable man," said Dan McNamara, executive director of the Orange Bowl Committee. "He was fantastic. My main man. We put out a lot of fires together."

Those fires were all part of turning others' creative dreams into the glitter and gold that parades down Biscayne Boulevard each New Year's Eve, or marches across the playing field each New Year's night, or races through the waterways and streets of Miami each Orange Bowl season.

Clearly, reporters who interview friends of the deceased can craft more complete, compelling obituaries.

Dave Downey, a reporter for the *Tempe* (Ariz.) *Daily News Tribune,* was assigned to write an obit on Edith S. Getz, a longtime resident for whom a local school had been named.

Downey gathered information from the mortuary and from the newspaper's clip file. But he didn't stop there. He conducted interviews with:

A former governor
Three neighbors of the deceased
A high school teacher
The wife of a former mayor

This required extra time and effort, but by conducting the interviews to supplement biographical information, Downey put together an obit that captured the flavor of the decedent's life.

Downey's first three paragraphs provided the essentials:

Edith S. Getz, 77, Arizona's second woman attorney and longtime Tempe philanthropist, died Tuesday at Friendship Village of Tempe. She had suffered a heart attack.

Getz, who lived in Tempe 53 years and ran the old Boston Store, faced adversity much of her life.

Born in Hungary, she was raised in a poor family and had to work her way through college to get a law degree.

After providing these essential facts, Downey then painted a vivid word picture of Getz based on his interviews. The obit continued:

After moving to Arizona 55 years ago and obtaining her attorney's license, she endured the sneers of male attorneys, who didn't want women invading their profession.

In later years, she endured the painful loneliness brought about by the deaths of her daughter, Barbara, and husband, Charles. And, eventually, she had to endure the decline of her own health.

"It's been kind of a dreary existence for her because she hasn't been well," said former Arizona Gov. Howard Pyle. Getz had suffered from diabetes, breast cancer and high blood pressure.

Yet, through it all, she never gave up.

"She was never bitter . . . just very kind, very soft spoken and really neat," said Mary Stewart, a neighbor. "She always put other people first and herself second."

Betty Boles, who lived across the street from Getz, said, "She was forever, until she got sick, doing something for someone."

Boles' husband, Ray, said Getz, on numerous occasions, donated money and resources to people and organizations. He recalled one instance where she gave a family $1,000 because their child had cancer.

At the same time, "she was never one to brag about what she was doing," he said.

"She was just a wonderful person," said another neighbor, Mrs. Margaret Christiansen. "She's one of those special people that come along once or twice in a lifetime."

Christiansen recalled that Getz was especially fond of children.

"She was always aware when children were around, and they were never ignored," she said.

Jean Brill, a high school teacher in Tempe for 10 years, noted that Getz donated land to build Getz School in 1970. She also donated money to the Tempe school for the handicapped that bears her name. And she made it a point to attend special school activities.

The obit went on to quote other people, to provide a summary of the organizations that she had belonged to, to list her survivors and to give information about graveside services and memorial contributions.

Downey's story clearly illustrates that it is worth the extra effort to dig through clippings and to seek out people who knew the deceased.

WRITING INTERESTING LEADS

Leads should normally contain the full name and the age of the person who has died, but other information can be added so that obits will not all read the same way. The policy of the *News-Journal*, Daytona Beach, states: "Put any interesting fact of the deceased's life in the lead, even if it is only how many years he/she lived here. Since the number of years a person had lived here is overused, dig for something else. This means the funeral home must be questioned every time it gives an obit. Occasionally, you may have to ask the director to contact the family to get something more."

Using Anecdotes and Description

The New York Times is well-known for its interesting, well-written obits. Reporters at the *Times* indeed dig deep for fascinating anecdotes and descriptive information that make their obits a pleasure to read. This is not to suggest that the media should exploit a person's death by writing eloquently about it. Rather, it should be noted that obituaries can effectively bring out the significance of the person and his or her death. That is good writing.

Note these leads of two obits published in the *Times:*

> Margaret Hamilton, the actress whose role as the cackling Wicked Witch of the West in "The Wizard of Oz" unnerved generations of children, died yesterday, apparently of a heart attack, at a nursing home in Salisbury, Conn. She was 82 years old.

> Colin Shaw Maclaren, a Scottish Highlander whose career took him from fighting Afghan tribesmen on British India's Northwest Frontier to 38 years as a reporter for *The New York Times,* died Wednesday at the Booth Memorial Medical Center in Flushing, Queens. He was 86 years old and lived in Flushing.

Not all obits, of course, are written about well-known people. But if the reporter works hard, interesting facts can be found about nearly everyone. The information might not be earth-shattering, but it can help establish an identity for the deceased.

Here is an example of a lead with interesting information about the deceased:

> John E. Jones, who had not missed a Riverdale High School home basketball game since 1947, died Wednesday in Samaritan Memorial Hospital after a short illness. He was 72.

Sometimes, if the circumstances merit, the name of the deceased can be delayed until the second paragraph:

> For the first time in more than four decades, when the Riverdale High School basketball Broncos take to the floor next season, one of their biggest fans won't be in his 10th-row midcourt seat.

John E. Jones, who had not missed a Riverdale High School home basketball game since 1947, died Wednesday in Samaritan Memorial Hospital after a short illness. He was 72.

Delayed leads on obits are the exception rather than the rule, but occasionally they are acceptable.

Emphasizing Uniqueness

John Archibald, a reporter for *The Birmingham* (Ala.) *News,* certainly recognized the potential to structure a special obituary about a retired U.S. Steel worker. After all, how many decedents are survived by 26 children? Archibald's story had an air of informality, but it was effective. The lead block of paragraphs pulled the reader inside:

It's probably appropriate that Elisha Anderson didn't come into the world alone. He had a companion, a twin.

With that kind of start, it isn't surprising that he liked children. But he never had twins of his own. He did have a few children, though.

He had 26 singles.

Anderson fathered his last child 20 years ago. He was 62 when Scotty Hill of Bessemer was born.

By the time Hill arrived, his older siblings were in their 40s. They were starting on grandchildren.

"He was getting up there by the time I was born," Hill said. "But he was a tough old guy. He was a good guy."

Anderson died March 9 after a recent stroke and other medical problems, Hill said. But he was happy with his life and his passel of children. . . .

With 25 brothers and sisters running around from Florida to Brooklyn, it's hard to keep up with all of them, Hill said.

"Is it 26?" He wasn't sure of the number. A quick rundown of names confirmed it.

There's Sara and Delorise and Cathy and Betty and Marval and Otha and Pamela and Carolyn and Teresa and Sandra and Gwendolyn and Albertina and Brenda and Gail and Joy and Justina and Jimmy and Elisha Jr. and Michael and Scotty and Thomas and Melvin and James and Marcus and Dennis and Geffery.

Wow.

Archibald went on to provide anecdotes about family reunions and to report direct quotations from neighbors. After noting that only two of the 26 children would not be in Birmingham for the funeral, Archibald provided some background on Anderson, gave details of funeral services and listed full names of all surviving children.

The obituary closed with this quotation:

"He was a nice, nice man," said Bernice Jackson, wife of Anderson's son Melvin Jackson. "He had a heap of children."

The sponsors of a championship rodeo would send press releases
to the local media before the event.
(Photo by Don B. Stevenson)

14

Press Releases

Press releases are sent to the media for two

reasons: the people who wrote them want to gain

publicity for their organizations, and they want to

reach as many people as possible. It is up to the

journalist reviewing a release to decide if it has

any interest for readers, viewers or listeners; if it

has news value; or if it is nothing more than an

attempt to gain free publicity.

In this chapter . . .

Alerts, Advisories and Releases
Evaluating Press Releases / Using Press Releases

Public Relations Work
Writing a Press Release / Working with Reporters / Going into PR: Tips and Guidelines

Each day, newspapers and broadcast outlets receive anywhere from dozens to hundreds of press releases—also called *handouts* or *news releases*. Some are worth printing or broadcasting; many are not. It is up to the journalist to:

- Decide which press releases have any local news value
- Present those with value in such a way that readers, viewers or listeners are given the most important news

Nearly every corporation, business, university, organization or political party—large or small—has one or more people whose job it is to gain the attention of the media. Many of these *public relations (PR) people* are former print or broadcast journalists or were journalism majors who planned careers in public relations. They know that much, most or all of the support their organizations will receive is linked directly to the publicity they receive from the media, and they know how to get this publicity.

Some firms and groups really do have news to release, and they help the media greatly by acting as news sources. Others are merely hoping to get their names in the newspaper or on the air without paying for an advertisement.

To get their message across, PR people telephone or visit newspapers and broadcast outlets to describe the "news," or they send press releases.

ALERTS, ADVISORIES AND RELEASES

Examples of press releases include these:

"Media alert" from the Tandy Corporation announcing a mock election by an estimated 1 million American students and parents from all 50 states and the District of Columbia

News bureau release from a state university, called "Worms and Your Pet," which discusses the dangers of internal parasites in dogs and cats

News release from the Office of Public Information of an out-of-state university telling local media that a student from their area has enrolled in the school

News release from state lottery officials announcing the winners of $89,000 in a lottery game

Release from National Frozen Food Association Inc., a trade group representing the frozen food industry, announcing that an area plant has gained, for the second consecutive year, a certificate of excellence for a sanitation program sponsored by the association

Pamphlet from a congressional candidate describing how the candidate plans to solve the problems created by public housing

Handout from a firm "specializing in effective public relations" that announces a first-anniversary celebration at a local restaurant

Announcement from the local zoo that on Thanksgiving Day the turkeys will do some gobbling of their own

Release from a company announcing the promotion of an executive

A press release would provide reporters with advance information about a ceremony to commemorate the civil rights movement of the 1960s.
(Photo by Sundi Kjenstad)

EVALUATING PRESS RELEASES

All these press releases were sent to newspapers and broadcast outlets for the same reason: the people who wrote them were hoping to gain publicity for their organizations and to reach as many people as possible. It is up to the journalist reviewing such releases to decide whether they have any interest for readers, listeners or viewers, and whether they have any news value or whether the organization is only seeking free advertisements.

Factors to Consider

There are several factors that determine whether a press release should be used or tossed into the wastebasket:

- *Does it have news value?* Is it of interest to local readers, viewers or listeners? Does it contain timely information? If so, the press release should be edited or rewritten to conform to print or broadcast style and to eliminate overuse of the name of a person or a company. Superfluous, overwritten and untimely information should be eliminated.

- *Is it trying to gain free publicity for a person, company or group?* If so, toss the release into the wastebasket or tell the PR person to check with the advertising department. Remember, though, that with careful rewriting to eliminate many of the adjectives and overuse of the name of a person or company, there could be some news value in the handout.

- *Is it worth following up, perhaps as a photograph or a story at a later time?* Many press releases simply announce a coming event. Even if they are not used in the newspaper or on the air, they may provide a good tip for later coverage.

- *Can it be trusted?* Always be leery of press releases because they may have been written by a person with little or no journalism training or by someone who does not have the same standards as a professional journalist. Remember, the purpose of a press release is to get information into print or on the air. It is up to the journalist handling the release to check the information to make certain that it is accurate and meets the medium's needs and style. For instance, the pamphlet from the congressional candidate makes some serious charges, including accusations that federal housing officials are guilty of waste and deceit. Before such allegations are printed, they should be verified, and the housing officials should be given an opportunity to respond to the candidate's charges. The release should also be checked for any missing information that, had it been included, would have changed the thrust of the release.

Which Releases Will Be Used?

Every person looking at a press release has different ideas on what is newsworthy and what is not. That is why some press releases are used and others are thrown away.

Some newspapers and some broadcast outlets—particularly the large ones—simply frown on using press releases. They may use a release as an idea for a future story or photograph, but they seldom run the release the way it is sent in. Many editors believe that all public relations people are really selling ads and that they should pay for advertising space rather than be given news space.

There is only so much news space—the *editorial news hole*—each day, and even though a press release may be of some value, there is never enough space to run all the press releases that are received. At metropolitan newspapers and broadcast outlets, the news space is taken up by staff-produced stories; there is no room for handouts. In smaller markets, however, editors may depend heavily on press releases to help fill their news space.

"For us, press releases are another source of news," said Mark Massa of the *Warrick County Press,* a weekly insert in *The Evansville* (Ind.) *Courier.* "There is no way you can know everything that is going on in the area you cover. You have to depend on people calling you or writing you. We are faced with space problems some days in that we need copy to fill extra pages. This is when the press releases come in handy, either in planting an idea in our minds or in providing a public service announcement."

Massa said that church notices are the most common press releases he receives. "Most of the churches out here show films or have evangelists, and they want to get the word out that they are showing the film or having a visitor," he added. "The press releases always talk about how fulfilling the night will be and how much fun there will be. I usually take the basic information out of it—such as the title of the film, who the star is and where and when it will be shown. I go through the release and try to find the newsworthiness in it."

There are no strict rules to follow in deciding which press releases make it into print or onto a broadcast and which ones do not. Much depends on the journalists who are looking at them. Usually, editors run press releases that they believe their readers will find interesting or that they find interesting themselves. For example, an editor who likes animals may give the handout from the zoo to a reporter to rewrite into a story; another editor may toss it into the wastebasket. A reporter whose aunt works for the county health department may think a press release from that agency is important while another reporter will ignore it.

Most press releases sent to newspapers and broadcast outlets probably contain some news value, especially if the person writing them has had any dealings with the media in the past. PR people with journalism training usually have a solid understanding of news stories and features, which means that they can produce usable copy. They know what editors and reporters like and dislike.

It is up to the journalist at the receiving end to pick the most timely and important handouts that have the most interest to a local audience. Then, on the basis of amount of time and space available, these top handouts can be converted into news stories or used as foundations for future stories.

USING PRESS RELEASES

Boiling Down a Release

Here is the press release from the zoo, announcing that turkeys are going to do some gobbling of their own. Assume that a newspaper city editor has asked for a two-paragraph story on it.

As in any press release, at the top is the name of the person to contact if there are additional questions. The words *for immediate release* tell the media that this information can be used now. All handouts give the release date. Most are "immediate," but some request a future release date.

News Release

Contact: Sandy Rodman
          Public Relations Representative
          485–0263

For Immediate Release

THANKSGIVING DAY WITH THE ANIMALS

Instead of being gobbled, the turkeys at Chicago's Brookfield Zoo will do some gobbling of their own during Thanksgiving Day with the Animals at 12:30 p.m. in the Children's Zoo.

Special food pans will be prepared to tantalize the palates of the guests of honor: the turkeys, ducks and geese. Children's Zoo visitors will be invited to help serve the holiday feast in this Thanksgiving Day celebration to be thankful for our animal friends.

Children's Zoo admission is $1 for adults, 50 cents for children (ages 3–11), and 75 cents for senior citizens and juniors (ages 12–17).

Brookfield Zoo is open from 10 a.m. to 5 p.m. Admission is free Thanksgiving Day through December 31. Located at 31st Street and First Avenue in Brookfield, the Zoo is accessible from the Stevenson and Eisenhower expressways and Interstate 294.

Find the lead   The first thing to do is to find the lead, the most important point of the story. In only two paragraphs, it is impossible to be as cute as the person who wrote this press release. Look for *who, what, where, why, when* and *how*, and then build a story around them. Not every press release contains all five of the W's or the H, but a news story can be constructed around the ones that are included, as follows:

Who: Visitors to the Children's Zoo.
What: They'll be able to feed the turkeys, ducks and geese.
Where: Brookfield Zoo.
Why: To be thankful for the animals.
When: 12:30 p.m., Thanksgiving Day.
How: With special food pans.

Once the five W's and H have been identified, the next step is to put them into a news story, in this case two paragraphs. The more space is available, the more information can be put in; however, in only two paragraphs, only the essential ingredients can be included—the five W's and the H.

Here is an example of a two-paragraph story based on the zoo's press release:

Visitors to Brookfield Zoo's Children's Zoo Thanksgiving Day will be able to help feed the turkeys, ducks and geese beginning at 12:30 p.m.

Zoo officials said that special pans of food will be prepared for the animals to show that people are thankful for their feathered friends.

With more space, such things as the zoo's hours and the admission charges could have been included. A call to the zoo could have provided a quotation or two as well as information on what will be on those special plates. But with only two paragraphs, readers will have to call the zoo—or the media—if they want additional information.

Eliminate fluff   Not all press releases are a single page long and easy to boil down to two paragraphs. For instance, the handout from the university news bureau on "Worms and Your Pet" is three pages long. It clearly seeks publicity for the veterinarians in the university's teaching hospital, but it also offers helpful tips. The trick is to *cut the fluff* and concentrate on the tips.

Some press releases are already boiled down when they are sent in because the people writing them know that a release has a better chance of being used if it reads like a news or feature story. For example, here is a press release from Ithaca Industries Inc. of Wilkesboro, N.C. It is one of the most common types of releases sent to the media: it announces a corporate promotion and was written by a public relations firm.

News Release

For Release: Immediately

Contact: Mr. Jim Waller, Ithaca Industries Inc.

(919) 667-5231

WILKESBORO, N.C.—Nicholas Wehrmann, president and chief operating officer of Ithaca Industries Inc., has been elected to the additional offices of Chairman of the Board of Directors and Chief Executive Officer, replacing Gregory B. Abbott, who resigned to pursue other business interests.

Ithaca is a leading manufacturer of hosiery, underwear and sportswear.

This release gives only the basic facts. If journalists want more, they will have to call Jim Waller. Here is a rewrite of the handout, cutting the bulky 40-word lead to a more readable 24 words:

Nicholas Wehrmann, president and chief operating officer of Ithaca Industries Inc., has been elected chairman of the board of directors and chief executive officer.

The remaining facts can be given in the second paragraph:

Wehrmann replaces Gregory B. Abbott, who resigned to pursue other business interests. Ithaca manufactures hosiery, underwear and sportswear.

Avoiding Free Ads

The following press release—on a first-anniversary celebration at a local restaurant—is a good example of a release that would probably not show up in print or on the air. Even though it is written by a firm that "specializes in effective public relations," it is nothing more than a *free ad* masked as a news release.

For Release: October 12

Please Contact: Bruce Smith Media Communications Inc.

Specializing in Effective Public Relations

(312) 337–3352

AT THE WINNETKA GRILL: A FIRST ANNIVERSARY CELEBRATION

Henry Markwood and John Stoltzmann, owners of The Winnetka Grill, 64 Green Bay Road, Winnetka, are pleased to announce a festive celebration of their restaurant's first birthday. The festivities last from November 9 (the actual birthday) through November 18. Key to the celebration is The Winnetka Grill's highly imaginative anniversary menu created, in dialogue with the owners, by Chef de Cuisine John Draz. The full menu is available at dinner, while select items will be offered on the luncheon menu as daily specials.

The Winnetka Grill Anniversary Menu

Cold Appetizers:

Grilled salmon with walnut oil

Belon oysters with malt vinegar and black pepper sauce

Country pâté with apple relish

Hot Appetizers:

Batter fried acorn squash with orange butter

Duck fois gras with wild onions

Wild mushrooms stewed with gamay and garlic

Entrées:

Grilled ribeye with shallots and thyme

Grilled pheasant with gamay and red grapes

Blackened redfish prudhomme

Grilled rockfish with gamay sauce

The Winnetka Grill's First Anniversary Wine is the Charles F. Shaw Nouveau Gamay Beaujolais, first released on the market on November 9.

This item has the same elements that would appear in any typical press release: the firm's name is mentioned more than once, the address is given, the names of the owners are listed and there is even a mention of special wine that will be released. There is only one thing missing: news value.

Remember: The fact that a press release is sent to the media does not mean that it has news value. Many releases are merely seeking free publicity for a person, business or organization.

Determining Local News Value

A few of the press releases mentioned earlier in this chapter could be interpreted as free ads: the Tandy Corporation is seeking publicity for its computers, and the National Frozen Food Association is trying to get its name into print.

Big newspapers and large broadcast outlets would probably not touch these releases, but community newspapers and radio stations may find value in them because the releases could contain news of local interest. Local people may be participating in the mock election sponsored by the Tandy Corporation; and the local firm being honored by the frozen food group may, indeed, be worthy of a story.

What lands in the wastebasket in one newsroom may be a candidate for a story in another simply because of *local news value*. The news release from the out-of-state university announcing that a student from a small town in Iowa has enrolled is probably of no value to any news operation in the country, except in that small town in Iowa. There, it may be worth a one-paragraph filler, a photograph or a story and picture. While one editor is cursing the university for wasting his or her time by submitting the release, another editor may be thanking the school for valuable information.

Example: A state lottery   Here is a release from the Colorado Lottery announcing the winners of $89,000 in a lottery game. Because it dealt only with Coloradans, it had strong local news value to media in the state.

"We send these news releases out several times a week," said Marlene Desmond, communications director of the Colorado Lottery. "They are faxed to *The Denver Post, Rocky Mountain News,* The Associated Press, United Press International and two other newspapers. They are mailed statewide."

As you read the release, try to pick out the fluff that could be easily cut.

News Release

For Immediate Release
For More Information Contact: Marlene Desmond
                                                      (303) 832-6242

PUEBLO—Luck struck Colorado Lottery players twice today as a Salida man and a Golden woman became the first and second instant winners of $89,000 in the lottery's "Surprise Package '89" game.

Mike McQuitty, 32, Salida, an equipment operator for the Rio Grande Railroad, said that he bought his lucky "Surprise Package '89" ticket this morning at the Stop and Save, 310 W. Rainbow Blvd., Salida. He said that his good fortune was enough to make him take the day off from work.

"I scratched the ticket in our morning meeting, and when I saw what I had won, I told the rest of the guys that 'I'm taking the day off,'" McQuitty said.

McQuitty said that his co-workers had no objections, and he immediately claimed the winning ticket at lottery headquarters in Pueblo.

His plans for his winnings include paying some bills and taking care of his wife and three daughters.

About 30 minutes after McQuitty claimed his prize, Schellia Wright, 40, a cosmetologist from Golden, claimed her $89,000 winning ticket at the lottery's Denver office.

Wright bought her lucky ticket last night at 7-Eleven, 980 E. 88th, Thornton.

She said that she plans on taking some time off with her husband and four children.

The "Surprise Package '89" game features the top instant prize of $89,000 and the weekly Grand Prize drawing for $1 million.

What is news and what is fluff in this handout? A reporter assigned to write a three-paragraph story based on the release will need to know. Certainly, there is much publicity in the release for the Colorado Lottery: the game's name is in three paragraphs, and the tickets are usually called "lucky." However, there is also news value in the release, especially to the media serving the towns of Salida, Golden and Thornton.

To write the three paragraphs, the reporter must first determine the five W's and H:

Who: Mike McQuitty of Salida and Schellia Wright of Golden.

What: They became the first and second instant winners of the $89,000 "Surprise Package '89" game.

Where: In Salida and Thornton.

Why: Not applicable.

When: This morning and last night.

How: They each bought instant tickets at convenience stores, scratched them and realized that they had won.

Here is how the three paragraphs could have been written:

A 32-year-old Salida man and a 40-year-old Golden woman have become the first two $89,000 instant winners in the Colorado Lottery's "Surprise Package '89" game.

Mike McQuitty, an equipment operator for the Rio Grande Railroad, and Schellia Wright, a cosmetologist, bought their tickets in convenience stores. They claimed their prizes within 30 minutes of each other.

McQuitty said that he plans to use his winnings to pay bills and to take care of his wife and three daughters. Wright said that she will take time off with her husband and four children.

The Denver Post was one of the Colorado newspapers that carried a story based on the news release. The reporter who wrote the story also interviewed a state lottery official, who provided additional information. Here are the first three paragraphs of the *Post* story, which you can compare with the release:

The Colorado Lottery's new game—Surprise Package '89—has its first $89,000 winners.

Mike McQuitty, an employee of the Rio Grande Railroad in Salida, bought two lottery tickets with the change from buying gasoline on his way to work Tuesday. He scratched off the winner while sitting in a meeting, and took the rest of the day off to drive to the lottery's headquarters in Pueblo to cash in the ticket, said Tom Kitts of the lottery.

Schellia Wright, mother of four and a Golden cosmetologist, bought her winning ticket Monday night and took it into the lottery office in Denver to cash it in. She missed being the first Surprise Package '89 big winner by about 30 minutes, Kitts said.

PUBLIC RELATIONS WORK

Most public relations professionals understand what editors and reporters look for in press releases. While they write releases to gain publicity, they also try to supply the local media with newsworthy information.

"When I arrived at Johns Hopkins, the engineering school wanted to promote the Center for Nondestructive Evaluation, a center with a big name that no one except other engineers could remember or understand," said Lisa Hooker, a science writer for the Baltimore university. "The center was worth promoting. As far as I could determine, only one other university in the country had anything comparable to the center, known as CNDE at Hopkins."

The steps that Hooker took in preparing a release on CNDE and in seeing to it that the release was placed in the media illustrate how public relations people operate each day.

Before coming to Hopkins, Hooker was a newspaper reporter. She worked at the *Huntington* (W.Va.) *Herald-Dispatch* and interned at the *Chicago Tribune*. She also worked at three newspapers while she was a journalism student at Indiana University.

In her job at Johns Hopkins, Hooker covers all the basic sciences and anything related to the science of engineering. She does not cover the medical school. "The people I'm publicizing are the scientists and engineers at Hopkins," she said. "I send information to specialized science writers at large newspapers and to the national television networks. I'm also here to publicize science at thousands of newspapers and television stations that do not have science writers but do have reporters who cover science when their newspapers or stations think it is important enough."

WRITING A PRESS RELEASE

To write about CNDE, Hooker had to follow the same steps any reporter would. First, she conducted thorough research to learn as much as she could about the center. She said: "The research behind the unexciting name was important for predicting when space shuttle parts might fail or heart pacemakers might stop. It was important because it could lead a new generation of computers capable of working together with sensors—the type of technology necessary to bring robotics from the primitive to the practical stage.

"It was also newsworthy research. For example, reporters are called upon repeatedly to write about airplane crashes in which no terrorism is involved; the airplane itself fails. Studies of why materials fail involve non-destructive testing."

Hooker said that she wrote her release much as she would write a news story. "But it was condensed," she added. "*USA Today*-style, perhaps."

Here is Hooker's release. (Although Associated Press style is to hyphenate *non* as a prefix, Hooker made it solid in *nondestructive*.)

Johns Hopkins University News

For Immediate Release

Contact: Lisa Hooker

(301) 338–7160

Everyone has seen the commercials. The ones where manufacturers throw suitcases off skyscrapers, crash cars into concrete, plunge watches to the bottom of an ocean—all to prove that their products are indestructible.

Most products in the workaday world, though, can't be crashed and burned to prove their mettle. They have to be examined in more sophisticated ways—before a hidden weakness leads to catastrophe.

The Center for Nondestructive Evaluation (CNDE) at Johns Hopkins University has developed many such techniques, designed to discover hidden flaws in everything from jet-engine turbine blades to artificial heart valves.

Recently, the center met with more than 50 health professionals to discuss ways that nondestructive evaluation can improve and even save lives.

"It's not very cost-effective to make a bunch of things and then have a majority of them rejected after the manufacturing stage," Robert Green, CNDE director, said. "And even if we make something perfect, it's going to fail sometime."

Lasers and X-rays, ultrasound and holograms help scientists test everything from heart valves to pacemakers for invisible flaws and weaknesses, Green said.

Nondestructive testing makes it possible to test sealed packages of drugs for leaks that could contaminate the contents. Surgeons can determine with lasers whether an ear surgery was successful long before the patient is aware of sounds.

"One of the beautiful aspects of nondestructive testing is its potential," Hopkins professor Jim Wagner said. "Rather than taking every 25th pacemaker and testing it for leaks, you can test every pacemaker for leaks."

Wagner, responsible for the center's research on advanced sensors, has demonstrated the benefits of nondestructive testing with heart valves. He holographically tracks the flow of blood through heart valves to study their performance and to determine when and where they are likely to fail.

Representatives of the Health Industry Manufacturers Association and the Food and Drug Administration spent Nov. 19 at Hopkins touring the labs used for CNDE's research.

Green said that the center is sponsored by 20 major corporations, which support the center in return for access to its research findings and, equally as important, its graduates.

Nondestructive evaluation of materials has become a hot topic in high-technology fields like aerospace and electronics, as scientists have shown manufacturers how to save millions of dollars in production costs by early testing.

However, transferring the technology to other fields such as medicine is now the goal of CNDE and of other scientists around the country involved in CNDE research.

Richard Johns, director of biomedical engineering at the School of Medicine, said that nondestructive testing could transform the health manufacturing industry by greatly improving the success rate of new products.

"We consider it important to disseminate what we do," he said. "We want to share ideas with industry, to solve biomedical problems through the application of engineering science."

WORKING WITH REPORTERS

When Hooker is ready to send her release, she uses her "news and information release list," which contains the names of hundreds of reporters and news media. Her list includes:

7 African reporters in the United States
24 British reporters in the United States
14 syndicated columnists
110 free-lance journalists
50 newspapers in Maryland
16 local television and radio stations
17 women's magazines

"I never pressured any reporter to write the story," she said. "Those who did write it were eager. My job, as I saw it, was to explain non-destructive evaluation in an interesting, informative way, and then let the story sell itself. That's something any good reporter does every day with editors."

The release was only one aspect of her attempt to inform reporters about the center, Hooker added. "I discussed the center in meetings with reporters, mentioned it from time to time if we were just shooting the breeze and joked about its name with them. If they laugh about something, they're more likely to remember it.

"I arranged for reporters to have lunch with CNDE professors. And I pitched it as a story idea to reporters calling on a slow day, eager for something to fill their editors' budgets."

Hooker's work paid off. She said that within several months, either CNDE or one of its professors was featured in dozens of newspapers and broadcasts. Some news media ran Hooker's release; others more typically used the release as a basis for their own staff-written stories. The story made the Associated Press and United Press International wires. It was also broadcast on Cable News Network.

One story, by Jane E. Allen, a writer for The Associated Press, began:

BALTIMORE (AP)—The Center for Nondestructive Evaluation at Johns Hopkins University is helping American firms increase their productivity and competitiveness by catching and eliminating design flaws during the manufacturing process.

"We're not only looking at things after they're finished; we look at them as they're making them," said Robert Green, director of the center. He describes the center's basic mission as improving quality control for industry.

Using $25,000 annual dues paid by each of 20 industrial firms, as well as grants and consulting fees, the center helps design ship hulls that won't leak, pacemaker batteries and heart valves that will last and gas pipelines that won't corrode easily. In addition, it can use special techniques to determine if airtight drug packaging has been tampered with.

Heather Clancy, a reporter for United Press International, wrote:

NEW YORK (UPI)—The Center for Nondestructive Evaluation at Baltimore's Johns Hopkins University likes to keep its subjects together.

Founded about four years ago, the center uses lasers, x-rays, ultrasound, heat sensors and holograms to probe anything from jet engine turbines to delicate heart pacemakers without tearing them to bits.

Professors at the Johns Hopkins center hope to avert disaster by fine-tuning products before they are put on the market.

One newspaper that gave good play to the release on CNDE was the *Baltimore Messenger*, a suburban weekly. Its story, by Charles Kupfer, began:

Professors, students and complicated contraptions fill the halls at a pioneering facility at Johns Hopkins University.

It is the Center for Nondestructive Evaluation, dedicated to testing objects for defective performance, and to building complex devices right in the first place so they won't later fail during use.

Kupfer interviewed several people at Johns Hopkins and off-campus for his 27-inch story, which included a five-column photograph of Green, the center's director.

GOING INTO PR: TIPS AND GUIDELINES

Lisa Hooker and Marlene Desmond, communications director for the Colorado Lottery, gave the following tips for people interested in becoming public relations practitioners:

- *Gain experience as a news reporter.* There is no better way of understanding what reporters and editors want.
- *Read and write.* The best PR people read newspapers and watch news shows. They know how to write in newspaper style and in broadcast style. They understand deadlines. They know how to communicate to reporters without being a bother. And they understand that reporters don't work only from 9 a.m. to 5 p.m., Monday through Friday.
- *Be a better reporter than the reporters.* Make sure that you know how to conduct careful research, always digging for more than just the basics. "It is the PR person's job to help reporters do their jobs," Desmond said. "I think a lot of time, PR people are painted as people who try to keep reporters from getting the information they need. Once you have established that reputation, you are in big trouble."
- *Never lie.* "If you lie, someone will find out and you will no longer have credibility," Hooker said. "You need to be prepared to handle the

negatives because good reporters will ask the tough questions. If they don't ask me, I won't volunteer things, but I'm not going to lie." Desmond added: "You don't have to answer a question that you are uncomfortable with or that you are not positive about. Feel free to tell them that you don't know the answer, even if there is a camera rolling. They are going to edit that. They don't expect you to know the answer to everything."

- *Pick your employer carefully.* "You should also try to work for a company where you are part of the inner circle and where your work is appreciated," Hooker said. "One of the biggest complaints reporters have is that they must deal with public relations people whom they don't trust because those people don't have the trust of the people they work for. You can do a better job if you are close to the people you are representing, people who take public relations into consideration when they make decisions."

Press Conferences and Speeches

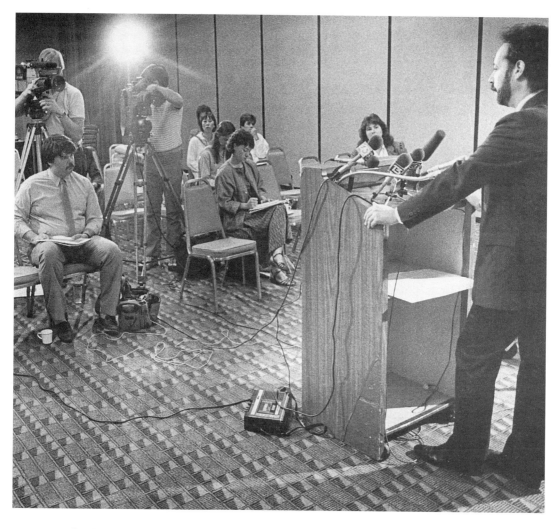

Small press conferences, such as this one in Sacramento, Calif., are held every day in cities throughout the country. Print and broadcast reporters cover the same event, all hoping that the speaker will say something newsworthy.
(Photo by Cliff Polland, The Reporter, Vacaville, Calif.)

Press Conferences and Speeches

15

Press conferences and speeches are not the same as one-on-one interviews, where a reporter has an opportunity to question and to challenge a source. People holding press conferences or giving speeches usually say just enough to get their message across to as many reporters as possible. It is up to reporters covering these public events to go beyond them to find additional newsworthy items.

11:50 a.m. The speech is to begin in 10 minutes. The hall is filling quickly. Reporters are already busy. Two reporters set up microphones and tape recorders on the lectern from where the flamboyant and world-famous trial lawyer F. Lee Bailey will make his speech.

11:58 a.m. Another reporter sets up a microphone and a tape recorder. A photographer takes readings with a light meter. Two other photographers sit in front of the lectern. Nearly all of the 1,100 seats are full.

12:08 p.m. Bailey and two others walk up to the lectern. He is introduced, quickly. The audience applauds.

12:10 p.m. Bailey begins his speech. The reporters responsible for covering Bailey's speech were ready long before he began. They knew the steps they had to follow to cover his speech adequately. Some of the reporters had also attended a press conference Bailey held 30 minutes before his speech.

PRESS CONFERENCES

Candidates, officials and other people hold press conferences for one or all of the following reasons:

- They feel an obligation to make information public.
- They want to get a message across to as many people as possible.
- They would like to be seen in newspapers and on newscasts.

A press conference is a *gang interview,* which means that every reporter present is going to get the same information. Also, people who hold press conferences usually know in advance what they want to say. They will get their message across and will not say much more, especially if they are experienced at fielding adversarial questions from reporters.

"Most press conferences are simply canned information," said Kenneth Reich, a political writer for the *Los Angeles Times.* "An experienced person holding a press conference is able to control it more than the reporters can. The person pretty much knows what he is going to say, and he does not go beyond that. Inexperienced people, or people who lose their temper, are the people who hold interesting press conferences."

THE PRESS CONFERENCE AS A MEDIA EVENT

Press conferences often make good television, which means that even on the local level they have become *media events* where both the interviewee and the reporters are in the limelight. Reich said that, in many cases, press conferences are highly stylistic shows. "Every remark is going to be 30 seconds long" to get on television, he said.

The granddaddy of press conferences is the one held by the president of the United States. It has become a major media event, staged in prime time and featuring the nation's top reporters challenging the president. It is a big show for both sides; millions of people watch every move and listen to every statement.

The presidential news conference began during Theodore Roosevelt's administration. Reporters simply gathered around the president's desk for a chat. When Herbert Hoover walked into his first meeting with the 30-member Washington press corps in his office on March 5, 1929, he reportedly said, "It seems that the whole press of the United States has given me the honor of a call this morning."

By Harry Truman's presidency, the press conference drew big crowds; 322 reporters attended his last one on Dec. 31, 1952.

Television and radio coverage of presidential press conferences began during Dwight Eisenhower's first term. In the early days of his presidency, portions of film and sound track were released for broadcast hours after the conference, a practice that gave Eisenhower's staff time to delete questions and answers they felt were potentially sensitive or embarrassing. After several months, however, the entire transcript was being released for broadcast and newsreels. Eisenhower also started the practice of having reporters identify themselves and their connections before asking questions.

Today, the presidential press conference lasts about 30 minutes and draws about 300 reporters. The president is well-coached and rehearsed on the questions most likely to come from the handful of reporters who are actually allowed to ask questions.

COVERING A PRESS CONFERENCE

Before the Conference: Preliminaries

Before a press conference begins, reporters should research the subject and the speaker thoroughly. Because they may have a chance to speak only once, reporters want to make sure that their questions are on target. Being prepared helps them find the key information in all the rhetoric.

To prepare for a press conference, reporters:

- *Read press releases announcing the conference.* Some type of press release is usually issued by an agency, organization or news bureau before a person speaks. It should give the time, date and place of the conference; provide some background information on the speaker; and tell reporters whom they can call for more information.

- *Read as many clippings as possible about the person holding the conference and about its subject.* Research should be conducted in the newsroom morgue as well as in public or university libraries.

- *Read articles or books that the interviewee has written.* Writings reveal much about their authors. People also warm up much more quickly to a reporter who tells them that he or she has read their work.

- *Talk to editors or news directors.* They will often give reporters specific questions that they want answered.

- *Talk to other reporters.* This is particularly important for reporters who have never before covered the person holding the press conference. Reporters who have covered the person before can offer helpful advice about mannerisms or types of questions that the person will or will not answer.

Advance press releases   Days before F. Lee Bailey's press conference and speech, a press release was issued by the news bureau at the university where the attorney was speaking. It said:

PRESS PREVIEW

One of the nation's top defense lawyers, F. Lee Bailey, will speak at Arizona State University on Tuesday, November 5, at noon in the Arizona Room of the ASU Memorial Union.

Bailey will discuss the problems and the inadequacies in our criminal justice system. He will also talk about some of his most famous cases and his writing.

Some of Bailey's better-known clients include kidnapped heiress Patricia Hearst, the Boston Strangler (Albert DeSalvo) and U.S. Army Captain Ernest Medina, who was charged with the mass murder of civilians at My Lai, Vietnam.

Bailey is also the author of the best-selling novel "Secrets," which tells the story of a lawyer charged with murder.

The lecture is sponsored by the Associated Students of Arizona State University Lecture Series in conjunction with the Liberal Arts College Council and the Student Bar Association.

This is the fourth lecture in the "Celebration of Diversity" series sponsored by the student association.

For more information, contact Brad Golich at the Lecture Series Office, 965–3161. Or call the News Bureau and ask for Keith Jennings.

Under no circumstances should a reporter rely solely on an advance press release for background information on a speaker. A release seldom gives enough information, and what it does give should be double-checked. For instance, the release on Bailey does not mention other books he has written, it provides only sketchy information on his clients and it does not give his age.

The advance story   A release is often used to write an *advance,* a brief story announcing a coming event. In this case, the advance would inform people that Bailey will be speaking. It could read:

F. Lee Bailey, one of the nation's top defense attorneys, will speak at noon Tuesday in the Arizona Room of Arizona State University's Memorial Union.

Bailey will discuss his most famous clients, including newspaper heiress Patricia Hearst and the Boston Strangler. He will also discuss the problems of the American justice system.

Bailey's lecture, the fourth in the "Celebration of Diversity" series, is being sponsored by the Associated Students of ASU, the Liberal Arts College Council and the Student Bar Association.

Checking written and electronic sources Much more background information on Bailey than that contained in the press release was available in the university library. It is always a good idea to check electronic sources, because much information can be found in various on-line data bases that may not be available in printed form. For example, hundreds of newspapers and the news wires are accessible electronically.

Bailey was listed in printed sources such as Biography Index, Contemporary Authors, Current Biography, *The New York Times* Index and the Readers' Guide to Periodical Literature. (Chapter 9 discusses additional sources that contain biographical information.) The library also had on file an audiotape of a Bailey interview by CBS and a copy of his 1985 book, "To Be a Trial Lawyer."

An electronic search of a newspaper index turned up numerous stories on Bailey. He also showed up in a magazine index. For example, *The Omaha World-Herald* in Nebraska reported that Bailey would be speaking at a lecture series. A story in the *Chicago Tribune* began:

> F. Lee Bailey made his name as a criminal defense attorney, but he has also made some enemies over the years suing insurance companies.
>
> His brother works for the enemy.

Here is a set of notes on Bailey, gathered during library research. The material is from Current Biography, *The New York Times* Index, Contemporary Authors and two on-line data bases.

1950 completed college preparatory training at Kimball Union Academy in New Hampshire. Entered Harvard University on a scholarship, intending to specialize in English. Left school at the end of his sophomore year to join the Naval flight training program and after 18 months transferred to the Marines as a jet pilot.

While in military service, volunteered to join 3-member legal staff at Cherry Point Marine Corps Air Station in North Carolina.

He was born in 1933.

Quoted in Saturday Evening Post, Nov. 6, 1966: "You can learn enough to practice criminal law without ever going to law school."

His experience in defending accused servicemen along with reading Lloyd Paul Stryke's "The Art of Advocacy: A Plea for the Renaissance of the Trial Lawyer" led him to pursue law as a career.

Returned to Harvard but shortly afterward transferred to Boston University Law School, which waived its requirements of three years of college because of his experience in the Marines.

Took bar exam June 1960 and was admitted to practice the following November.

Insists upon spending as much money as he feels is necessary for meticulous investigation. In his opinion, his skills in finding and analyzing facts are more than anything else responsible for his success.

Attended Chicago's Keeler Polygraph Institute.

Cases:

Pied Piper of Tucson (Charles Schmid Jr.), a loner found guilty of murdering two teenage girls.

T. Eugene Thompson, a Minnesota attorney charged with killing his wife for $1 million in insurance benefits.

Mark Fein, serving 30 years for killing a bookie.

Dr. Sam Sheppard, a Cleveland osteopath accused of killing his wife.

The Boston Strangler (Albert DeSalvo), charged with killing 13 women.

Patricia Hearst.

Punk-rock star Sid Vicious, accused of murdering his girlfriend. Vicious committed suicide before the trial began.

Chemical leak in Bhopal, India, that killed and injured thousands. It's Bailey against Union Carbide.

Established the Professional Air Traffic Controllers Organization and served as its first director.

Owns two helicopters and two airplanes. He has a remote chateau in the Bahamas. Drives flashy cars. Often called flamboyant outside the courtroom, but he never is inside.

Story in PC Week magazine reports that Bailey takes a lap-top computer with him when he travels.

He scored poorly on his exams in law school because he could not write fast enough with his left hand. He solved the problem by getting permission to use a typewriter to take tests. Typewriters favor lefties because 60 percent of the strokes are made with the left hand.

Lives on an 80-acre estate in Marshfield, a Boston suburb, with his wife and former secretary, Froma Vicki Bailey. They have a son, Scott. Bailey also has two sons from an earlier marriage, which ended in divorce.

In 1985 Federal District Judge John F. Keenan named Bailey as one of three attorneys to coordinate litigation against Union Carbide Corp. arising out of the 1984 pesticide leak in Bhopal, India.

Obviously, not all the information gathered in the library research will be used in the final story. But it can be used to help formulate questions. It also gives the reporter insight, the ability to go into the press conference and speech with a clear vision of who F. Lee Bailey is.

During the library research, a tentative list of questions to ask Bailey was assembled. This step is important because, in the heat of the press conference, it is too easy to forget the specific questions or issues. Here are the questions:

You are sharply critical of the American legal system. What are the current problems?

What solutions to these problems do you propose?

What makes you a better trial lawyer than others in your profession?

What special skills do you have that make you more successful?

You once said in an article that "you can learn enough to practice criminal law without ever going to law school." Do you still believe that today?

What do you look for in a good lawyer?

Is the Patty Hearst case an unpleasant memory for you?

You once said in an article that "the press is the only effective policy force on government." Can you comment on that?

You established PATCO more than 15 years ago. Why did you establish the organization? How did you feel when President Ronald Reagan ordered the air traffic controllers back to work during the 1981 strike?

What have been the results of lawsuits filed after the pesticide leak in Bhopal, India?

Such questions are a reporter's want list. If there is not enough time or if the interviewee concentrates on several questions or topics, much of the list will have to be abandoned.

During the Conference: The Questions and Answers

All reporters are at a press conference for the same reason: they want to ask questions that will elicit newsworthy responses. Those who have done their homework best, and those who are actually able to ask questions, will be the most successful.

Television reporters have an advantage over print reporters during a press conference because the speaker usually wants to be seen as well as heard. Hence, television reporters are more likely to control the questioning, which is usually limited in time.

Print reporters must make themselves visible and audible. First, they should arrive at the location of the press conference early enough to get a front-row seat. That will help the speaker spot them. Print reporters must also sometimes be the most vocal in the group to make certain that the speaker calls on them. This is particularly important at a large press conference where there are many reporters and the interviewee cannot answer every question. At a local press conference attended by only several reporters, an official, candidate or newsmaker will usually try to answer all of the questions.

Because of time or space limitations, reporters often attend press conferences only to obtain answers to specific questions. Their job is to challenge the speaker to provide something more than rhetoric. They all know that they cannot report everything that is said. Still, they should listen to the other questions and the answers just in case something unexpected pops up.

F. Lee Bailey agreed to hold a press conference a half-hour before his speech. Here is a transcript of the questions by various reporters and Bailey's responses.

Q. What are you here to speak about?

A. Primarily, it's directed to the law students. Litigation segment of the practice, which many are quite normally interested in today.

Q. I read an article in which you sharply criticized the legal system. Are you going to talk about that?

A. Uh huh. [Yes.] Drawbacks. I think the two primary shortcomings are cost and delays. Most civil cases take so long that by the time the remedy comes around, if it does, it's either too late or not needed.

Q. What suggestions do you have for that?

A. I think there need to be a lot of alternatives to litigation. Much greater use could be made of arbitration, mediation and conciliation. I think there is

F. Lee Bailey, a
well-known lawyer,
conducts a press
conference before
his speech.
(Photo by Rick Wiley)

some evil in the conflict between the plaintiff's and defendant's fee structures. The tendency is to string out litigation.

Q. Is that what you did when you became a litigator?

A. No. The evil is on the other side. It's the fellow being paid by the hour
who likes the delays and the case going on and on and on.

Q. What solutions do you offer?

A. Well, I don't have a quick answer to that dichotomy in fees, but I think it
needs to be addressed. We need to pay more attention to people getting
skunked unnecessarily much of the time. Inasmuch as the plaintiff system
is structured on incentive, probably that needs to be part of the defense
lawyer's motivation as well. Right now he has no incentive to get rid of
the case early if it is one that deserves to be resolved. He's simply cutting
down his gross fees.

Q. How do you feel about lawyers advertising on television and in newspapers?

A. I think within limits it's helpful to the public. It gives the public a better
understanding of the mystique of legal fees and gives a choice. Like anything else, it can be abused. There are some silly ads running around and
some that are offensive. By and large, I think the principle is sound.

Q. Do you think the public needs to be aware of how much a divorce is going
to cost?

A. Sure.

Q. Sort of like comparative shopping?

A. That's right. Competition is the only thing that keeps the price in line.

Q. What do you think of the direction that the law is taking now? More conservative?

A. With the Arizona crowd in the Supreme Court, I would say there's a lot of
pressure to try to be very conservative.

Q. With that kind of emphasis in the federal government and with some pretty important Supreme Court cases coming up, what do you think is the role of state government?

A. Well, that has a trickle-down effect. Every state judge who wants to be a federal judge knows he won't make it if his decisions are liberal. So the state judges are motivated to be more conservative so they can qualify if they manage to get suggested as a candidate to the federal bench, which in most states is more desirable than the state bench.

Q. How do you feel about your career so far?

A. There isn't much I'd change.

Q. Have you been happy with it?

A. Oh, I'd say decidedly yes within the limits of practicing what I call trouble-shooting law; that is, criminal cases and difficult civil cases. There's a lot of agony in any litigation.

Q. Concerning your most notorious trials, any comments on the Patty Hearst trial?

A. I don't think she got a fair shot, but on the other hand I don't think it made any difference because if she hadn't been hooked there she was going to be hooked in Los Angeles and we pretty well knew we were going to lose that one. Our main objective was to get her out of the murder indictment, and we did that.

Q. What role do you think the press has on a trial like that, when you are trying to separate a free press from a fair trial?

A. Normally, except under special circumstances, I feel that we can handle the press and get rid of the prejudice. In the Hearst case I can't say that we did that. The press really whipped up the public on the grounds that she was going to get away with something because she was rich. The truth is, if she hadn't have been rich, she would have never been caught up in it.

Q. I understand that when you went to Harvard that you were going to major in English.

A. I did all the way.

Q. What made you go into law?

A. Military experience. But even when I got out of the military with plans to go to law school, I still went back to Harvard and majored in English. Not many lawyers do.

Q. Why did you go into English and not law?

A. Well, originally, I wanted to be a writer. When I got back, I stayed with the English courses because the most effective advocates I bumped into in four years of watching court cases had a good command of the king's English and that seemed to be a fading phenomenon among lawyers.

Q. Do you recommend that to lawyers today?

A. Very strongly if they want to be trial lawyers.

After the Conference: Guidelines for Reporters

Once a press conference is over, reporters whose deadlines are near must head directly to telephones. They need to know their leads and how they will organize their stories even before the gang interview has ended.

Martin Luther King
III speaks to
reporters during a
press conference at
the University of
California, Davis.
King was at the
university to
participate in a
celebration honoring
his father.
*(Photo by Cliff Polland,
The Reporter,
Vacaville, Calif.)*

Reporters who phone in their news stories normally do not have a computer terminal or typewriter in front of them on which to compose a story, erase mistakes and rewrite if necessary. They must dictate a story that makes sense the first time. It also helps to have a good rewrite person on the other end of the phone to polish the rough edges, shuffle paragraphs if necessary and look up additional information.

The closer the deadline, the more quickly a reporter must pick out the news and compose the story. Most reporters, even those not under a tight deadline, begin to construct their stories during the press conference, while they are asking questions, listening and taking notes. They continually ask themselves:

- Which questions are best?
- Is the speaker answering candidly?
- What is new, and what has been said before?
- Is the speaker skirting any issues?
- What is the best lead?
- How should the story be organized?

The story's lead and organization are determined by several factors:

- *What is the most newsworthy response during the press conference?* Are the responses good enough and complete enough to be developed into a lead paragraph?
- *What are the other key points of the conference?* Would any of them make better leads? The major points covered during the conference should be rated for importance.

- *What are the editors or news directors looking for?* Do they want a specific lead or angle for the story?
- *Is a second-day lead required?* Reporters from an evening newspaper or a radio station with hourly newscasts covering a morning press conference are most likely to use a first-day summary lead. Those from morning papers or television stations with an evening newscast may use a second-day lead to avoid repeating the earlier stories.

Seldom will all the reporters covering a press conference agree on the same lead, unless the interviewee uttered something completely unexpected. They may agree on the importance of certain issues, but this does not mean that their stories will begin the same way. Five reporters at the same press conference may write five different leads because each reporter was interested only in his or her own questions and the responses to them.

Much of what Bailey said during his press conference was a rehash of what he had said before. That is not newsworthy. He did, however, talk about how state judges are motivated to be conservative and about the "Arizona crowd" in the Supreme Court; these comments would probably be of some interest to local readers. Of course, since he gave a speech after his press conference, reporters still had more information to gather before composing their stories. Solely on the basis of the press conference, however, here is how Bailey's comments could have been rated:

1 State judges are motivated to be conservative if they have ambitions to be federal judges.
2 "Arizona crowd" on the Supreme Court illustrates how judicial appointments are screened carefully to select conservatives.
3 Two primary shortcomings in the American legal system and possible solutions.
4 Advertising by lawyers.
5 Comments on Hearst.

It is possible that one or more of these five points would be dropped from the final story, either because of space limitations or, more important, because Bailey had said something more newsworthy.

SPEECHES

THE REPORTER AND THE SPEECH

Like press conferences, speeches are used to get a message across to an audience. Reporters cover a speech somewhat differently, though, because they have no control over what the speaker says.

Reporters attend a press conference to elicit responses to specific questions. They are on a hunting trip. Reporters who attend speeches, however, are there to be the eyes and ears of people who cannot attend. If they cannot get to the speaker before or after the speech, they merely digest what was said, mix it up and feed back the newsworthy material to their audience. Because no interviewing is involved and reporters cannot challenge the speaker, many of the story leads are likely to be on the same point.

Speeches are usually not organized like news stories. The speaker often builds up to a major point rather than put it at the beginning. Reporters recognize this difference. As they are listening to a speech, they are editing it, anticipating its main points and cutting out all the unnecessary information.

Reporters realize that a 30-minute speech would take up considerable space in the daily news hole if it were printed in its entirety. Metropolitan newspapers occasionally print complete speeches by the president or by other important officials, but usually they rely on their reporters to pick apart speeches and to report only the *new*, the *important* or the *unusual*.

Clever speakers are aware of the reporter's function; this means that they will make every attempt to say something new, important or unusual.

COVERING A SPEECH

Before the Speech: Preparation

As in preparing for a press conference, it is important for reporters to do their homework *before* covering a speech. Only under the most unusual circumstances, such as an extremely tight deadline, would they cover a speech without first researching the subject and the speaker. Even if the assignment is made only a short time before the speech, it is easy to go to the library or the newspaper clipping file to find out what has been written previously on the speaker or the topic of the speech.

How to prepare: Tips for reporters   Here are some tips on how to prepare for covering a speech:

- *Do your homework.* Check news clippings and written and electronic sources in libraries. Interview friends of the speaker as well as fellow reporters for background information. Go into research asking, "Who is this person?" Come out with the answer.

- *Prepare questions.* Know in advance the questions that the speaker needs to answer during the speech. If they are not answered, interview the speaker in person immediately after the speech or over the phone as soon as possible.

- *Catch the speaker early.* Every reporter covering a speech will hear the same thing; if possible, break away from the pack beforehand to obtain exclusive information. Interview the speaker over the telephone or make arrangements to see him or her just before the speech. If that is not possible, find out where the speaker will enter the room and wait there. It is sometimes possible to get in a few questions while the speaker is being introduced and before he or she walks to the podium.

Using advance texts   *Advance texts* of the speech are useful because they provide most of what the speaker will say; they also make the research phase easier.

Copies are usually available from the speaker or his or her agents before the speech. A well-known person who speaks will often have plenty of copies to hand out. A lesser-known person will probably not; reporters may have to ask to look at the speech or make copies of it.

A warning, though: Never write a story solely on the basis of an advance text. Speakers often wander from their prepared texts, adding some things and omitting others. Occasionally, they abandon the text altogether and speak off the cuff. Reporters who do not attend the speech and write stories from an advance text may end up looking foolish.

Use the advance text as a guide for doing the research and covering the speech. Follow the text during the speech, making changes in quotations and adding and deleting necessary phrases and sentences.

Using a tape recorder A tape recorder will ensure that any quotations used in a news story will be precise. Just make certain that the recorder is working properly. Keep extra batteries and tapes on hand.

Also, take notes. A tape recorder is a useful backup tool for making sure that quotations are exact. Most reporters do not rely on the recorder exclusively, however, because it takes too much time to play back the tape, take notes and then write the story. (Chapter 11 lists additional guidelines on using tape recorders.)

During the Speech: Steps to Follow

Once the speech begins, there are certain steps reporters must follow.

Take copious notes Even reporters who use tape recorders take as many notes as possible. It is impossible to transcribe the entire speech, but reporters usually take a lot more notes than they would ever need to write a story. Nearly every reporter uses shorthand or devises a personal system of speed writing.

The key here is to listen carefully for information and for quotations that can be used in the story and to write them in a notebook as quickly as possible. A tape recorder can be used as a backup for incomplete quotations.

If the speaker says something that is hard to understand, put some type of symbol in the notebook next to the confusing statement. After the speech, try to have it clarified.

When writing a direct quotation, put quotation marks around it in the notebook so that it will not be confused with a paraphrase.

Experienced reporters try to stay calm when taking notes. They know that they will often be scribbling one quotation when the speaker starts to say something else of importance. They merely quit writing the first sentence and begin the second. People are always going to speak faster than reporters can write. All a reporter can do is write down the key points and the direct quotations.

Make observations Note the speaker's clothing and mannerisms. If the speaker smokes or laughs continually or shouts at someone in the audience, make a note of this. These observations can add color to the story.

Estimate the number of people in the room. Count small crowds. For larger crowds, count the number of chairs in each row and multiply by the number of rows. Or ask a security officer for an estimate, or ask a custodian how many chairs were set up.

Listen for news   Remember that an audience does not care about old news. There has to be a reason for each story.

If the speaker says something that could make a lead or needs further development, put a star next to it in the notebook so that it can be found easily.

Listen for summaries   A speaker will usually summarize the speech, either at the beginning or at the end. Often, that summary will make the lead for a news story. Of course, reporters might disagree on what is the best lead, but they still need to know what the speaker considered the main point.

In most cases, the speaker clearly tells the audience, "I am here to talk about . . ." or "In summary, let me say . . . " Other times, summaries are masked. Listen for changes in the speaker's voice or for points repeated several times. Also, listen for topic sentences, numbered points and transitional words. These will signal major points, which could be potential leads. Good speakers are clear about the points they want to make because they want the audience to understand what they are saying.

Ask questions afterwards   When the speech has ended, it is time to ask the questions that should have been covered but were not. Try to get the speaker alone after the other reporters have left. Follow-up phone calls to the speaker may be helpful, too.

If there is time for questioning after the speech, ask for clarification of confusing points. Never be afraid to ask a speaker to repeat a quotation, explain an unclear statement or expand on any topics of the speech. Speakers will usually answer questions when they have finished talking. They know that reporters can get mixed up, and they do not want to be misquoted.

Example: A reporter's notebook   Here are the notes taken by one reporter during F. Lee Bailey's speech. Some of the sentences look incomplete; others seem to make no sense at all. However, these notes are real, and they are typical of what any reporter covering a speech would come up with.

Dark gray suit.
No vest.
Red tie.
Hair shorter than in photos.

"How many in the audience are presently law students?"
Lots of hands.
"How many expect to become law students?"
Lots of hands.
"How many are concerned there are too many lawyers?"
Lots of hands. Laughs.

There is one area where there is no difficulty in finding work. "It is greatly understaffed. That is the litigation branch." The people there aren't very good.

"The reason is because when law schools took over from the apprentice system, they improved on almost every area except one. That was litigation."

"The things that were learned from carrying a bag and being in court have pretty much been abandoned and indeed many cannot be taught in academic circles."

"Many litigation lawyers are not equipped to do battle with someone who is specially trained in that field." Most law students come to law school ill equipped for litigation.

"The reason is that in undergraduate work they have been diverted into specialties such as political science, economics, accounting, government, judicial administration, police administration. This curriculum overlooks two important tools that every litigator has got to have if he'll ever be top rank:"

(1) Consummate command of the English language. "The ability to speak and communicate persuasively in an interesting fashion so that jurors don't fall asleep and the judge doesn't fall asleep." Should be able to communicate "without resorting to notes, outlines or other crutches."

(2) Deep grounding in psychology generally, which is utilized every day in dealing with clients, opponents, witnesses, jurors, judges and so forth.

"Included in these must be courses on memory expansion. You must condition yourself to develop capacity of memory to its peak."

"Not telling the truth corrupts 90% of all litigation in the U.S. simply because the lawyers are not equipped in the art of cross examination to confront liars and expose them. To do that, one has to be able to deal without constantly diverting attention to written crutches."

Bailey is doing this lecture without notes. Practicing what he preaches?

"It is up to the trial lawyer to pick up deception, to go for the jugular and to get it. That requires a lot of homework."

"If you are not a person who enjoys doing homework and being prepared to the hilt, don't engage in litigation as a specialty. Unless you enjoy being in a pressure cooker, find a more sedentary specialty."

"Perry Mason is not a good image of a lawyer." Basically a coward.

"He's afraid of jurors and what they will do to him. He arranges in some corrupt fashion to have witnesses who are the true guilty parties and will confess in open court. This is a handy way to win lawsuits. It spares the agony of jury selection."

"I would gladly take a case without a fee if I . . . " missed the quote here.

Future bright for litigators. Computers with a search and find capability. Now necessary to take a deposition, read cases, go look for witnesses. "Data bases will make other things a flick of a switch rather than long, hard work by a paralegal summarizing long documents."

Trial lawyers can become folk heroes.

Income in later years much higher than average lawyers'.

High-risk business. Often don't get a dime for years of hard work. Sometimes get a windfall, particularly in injury and wrongful death cases.

Often the impact of outcome on the litigants is enormous. "In a criminal case the defense is a born loser. If you are innocent to begin with, and you prevail at the trial, you still are statistically guilty. When you walk out, you're much poorer and probably broke." Half your constituency will assume you are guilty and "shyster got 'em off on a technicality."

"Due process is a process that must swell or shrink with the times in which it is found. We have so . . . "

Greatest disgraces in our legal system:

Abuse of the writ. "If you are licensed to practice law, you can sue anyone who doesn't have absolute immunity and make his life miserable." The costs, particularly in civil cases, will be enormous if the litigation. . . . *Many cannot afford it.*

Delays. Average delay of 3–5 years before client ever sees courtroom. Contingency cases motivate litigator "to get our one-third or one-fourth of recovery anytime it's available." *Defense is being paid by the hour, which means in no hurry to settle the case.* "A defense lawyer who knows his client is liable and that the case should be settled for the plaintiff has two reasons to refuse to do that. No. 1 is if he settles it, his meter stops running. And when you're paid by the hour, a running meter is a symphony."

"Secondly, if he uses the greater financial clout of his client, normally an insurance company, he may wear the plaintiff out and run him out of money and settle the case for a smaller figure." "These conflicts have to be rooted out of our system. They daily plague . . ."

A key factor when defending anything is speed. You must have speed. For that you need memory. "You need to stuff memory. If you are used to cramming for exams, you have the ingredients." *Practice. Have 500 telephone numbers at your command. Give yourself a means to recognize.*

There are knocks in this business. "If you are a bad loser, stay out." *Statistically, trial lawyers lose half their cases. You perform a function. You demonstrated to the world your client was wrong even though you tried. That's a service, too.*

English justice system is superior. Solicitor evaluates claim. Writes brief for barrister. If he accepts the brief, you're in court. If not, you can try another solicitor. If he doesn't accept it, you're out. People in Britain understand the court system better than those in the U.S. "British courts are an elegant function." *They expect a tremendous ethical standard in court and they get it.* "I've never heard of a case of a corrupt British barrister or judge." *3,000 barristers responsible for all litigation for a country of 50 million.* "In England, judges have the last say. They have ultimate control over the press, something I'm not ready to advocate yet in this country."

To be an effective trial lawyer, one has to enjoy shouldering the responsibility others cannot shoulder themselves.

"No one is going to make a magician out of you. You can apprentice with the 10 best trial lawyers, and you're still just a lawyer. Perhaps a good one. If you walk into a case well prepared, you're still going to lose some cases. You have to be able to walk away from it."

If you spoke good English when you arrived here, the law will destroy it. "You have to fight that. You'll be so full of jargon. Get out of the jargon and get back on your feet. If you want to try cases you have to be streetwise."

If you defend a lot of cases plan on getting indicted, especially if you beat a lot of prosecutors. That antagonizes them.

"To be a trial lawyer, you have to keep your skirts clean. You'll be under a microscope much of the time."

"The best that justice can do is treat you as badly as your neighbor. Justice is not nice; it's consistent."

Be prepared to take it on the chin or get out.

"I learned early if I wanted to try cases, I wasn't going to learn about it in the classroom."

He spoke about an hour.

Q&A after speech:
Man asks about plea bargaining. "Plea bargaining is absolutely necessary just as settlements are necessary in the civil side. By and large the give and take of plea bargaining is necessary and appropriate. To shoot down plea bargaining is to shoot yourself in the foot.

It's unavoidable, it works and it can be corrupt. Without plea bargaining, the court system in every major city would break down in 30 days."

Woman asks, "How do we get 5 minutes of your time to discuss a case?" Bailey says his number is listed in the Boston phone book.

Man asks about military courts. Bailey says they are much better. "I was weaned in a cocoon. I got out and went to a civilian court and I was shocked by the corruption. If I had to stand trial for a crime I didn't commit, I would pick a military trial every time."

Didn't have time to answer more questions.

About 1,140 people at the speech.

After the Speech: Writing the Story

Questions to answer Before writing the story, the reporter must answer several questions:

- *What is the key point?* The answer to this question becomes the lead of the story.
- *What are the other major points?* All of them should be rated.
- *Which quotations are the best?* The reporter must look for quotations that best illustrate the speaker's points and also make the story readable.
- *Is any of this news?* Reporters who have done their homework will know if the speaker has given the same speech before.
- *When is the deadline?* If there is time, the reporter can ask more questions. Or, if the speaker has made charges, the reporter can obtain an opinion from the other side. In most speech stories, reporters simply write a brief account of what the speaker said. If there is time to interview the other side, the reporter must start the research again to find the best possible rebuttal.

Bailey made several key points during his speech. Obviously, his theme was that there are not enough good trial lawyers. He illustrated his point with some excellent quotations. He also gave advice to law students, telling them that good litigators need a consummate command of English, grounding in psychology, a good memory and the ability to go for the jugular. He said that the greatest disgraces in the American legal system are that too many lawsuits are being filed and there are too many delays. He also warned students, "If you're a bad loser, stay out." After his speech, Bailey praised plea bargaining and military courts.

There was little new in what Bailey said during his speech. He has been criticizing the lack of training of trial lawyers for years. He did make some important points and uttered some unusual quotations, which could be the basis of a story. The people who attended the speech, as well as those who wish they could have attended it, would be interested in reading a story on Bailey's appearance.

Reporters who attended the press conference before the speech would have additional information for their stories. Bailey's comments on conservatism in the American courts would still be good lead material.

Organizing the information   Most press conference stories and speech stories follow the same pattern. They are written as inverted-pyramid news stories. They begin with a terse (no more than 35 words) lead paragraph that summarizes the key points of the press conference or the speech. If the speaker is well-known, a name is used in the lead. Otherwise, a title is put in the lead to give it authority, and the speaker's name is used in the second paragraph.

After the lead, paragraphs are written in order of descending importance, but each one should contain vital information. Here is how a typical story would be organized after the lead:

- *Second paragraph.* Back up the lead with a strong quotation or paraphrase. Name the speaker if the name was not used in the lead. Give the speaker additional authority. Tell where the press conference or speech occurred and who sponsored it. Give the speaker's age.

- *Third paragraph.* Continue developing the points made in the lead, or write a transitional paragraph moving into another key point. A transitional paragraph can also introduce a set of bullets highlighting all the speaker's important points. Provide more background on the speaker. Introduce observations. Tell how many people attended the speech.

- *Fourth paragraph or the one after the bullets.* Continue developing the lead, or begin developing the bulleted items one by one. If possible, use a strong quotation to illustrate one of the key points.

- *Balance of the story.* Follow up with quotations and paraphrases. Continue to sprinkle in observations.

- *Final paragraph.* Try to end with a direct quotation, the speaker in direct communication with the reader. That will help avoid an abrupt ending and will make the reader feel that the dialogue continues even though the story has ended. Do not use an attribution such as "he concluded" in the last paragraph. Make sure that all the key points are fully developed.

The Results

Same speech, different stories   Here is one newspaper story that could have been written after Bailey's press conference and speech. This story's 27-word lead summarized Bailey's concern about growing conservatism in the courts.

The growing conservatism of the U.S. Supreme Court has trickled down to state courts, the criminal lawyer and author F. Lee Bailey said Tuesday at Arizona State University.

The second through sixth paragraphs followed with direct quotations and background. They backed up the lead:

"Every state judge who wants to be a federal judge knows he won't make it if his decisions are liberal," the 60-year-old lawyer told reporters before his speech sponsored by three student groups. "The

state judges are motivated to be more conservative so they can qualify
if they manage to get suggested as a candidate to the federal bench,
which is more desirable than the state bench."

Bailey's clients have included newspaper heiress Patricia Hearst and
the Boston Strangler. He has also written books on the legal profession
as well as a best-selling novel, "Secrets," which tells the story of a
lawyer charged with murder.

Bailey said that Chief Justice William Rehnquist and Associate
Justice Sandra Day O'Connor, two of the Supreme Court members with
ties to Arizona, illustrate judicial conservatism.

"With the Arizona crowd on the Supreme Court, I would say there is
a lot of pressure to be very conservative," he said.

O'Connor was sitting on the Arizona Court of Appeals when President
Ronald Reagan nominated her to replace a moderate. Rehnquist, who
once practiced law in Phoenix, took his seat as an associate justice in
1972, but was nominated by Reagan to be chief justice and was
confirmed in 1986.

The fourth and sixth paragraphs clarified Bailey's reference to the "Arizona crowd." During his press conference, he did not identify the people he was talking about. Their names needed to be in the story, however, because readers may wonder who they are. Such explanatory paragraphs are common to news stories.

In the seventh paragraph, the story shifted gears. A transitional phrase moved the reader from the press conference to the speech. This paragraph was a paraphrase. A direct quotation was used in the eighth paragraph to back it up. Observations were also used for the first time.

In the ninth and 10th paragraphs, Bailey defended his statements and offered a solution. The story let him develop his thoughts further in the 11th and 12th paragraphs. By ending with a direct quotation, the writer let Bailey communicate directly with readers and avoided wrapping up the story.

During his speech before approximately 1,140 people, Bailey
warned that there is a shortage of qualified trial lawyers in the United
States.

"The things that were learned from carrying a bag and being in court
have pretty much been abandoned and indeed many cannot be taught
in academic circles," he said. "Many litigation lawyers are not equipped
to do battle with someone who is specially trained in that field."

Bailey said that law students are not prepared for litigation because
their curriculum overlooks two important tools: a command of English
and a deep grounding in psychology.

Lawyers need "the ability to speak and communicate persuasively in an interesting fashion so the jurors don't fall asleep and the judge doesn't fall asleep," he said.

Bailey, who spoke without notes, added that trial lawyers must also be able to communicate "without resorting to notes, outlines and other crutches."

A good trial lawyer must "pick up deception, go for the jugular and get it," Bailey said. "That requires a lot of homework. If you are not a person who enjoys doing homework and being prepared to the hilt, don't engage in litigation as a specialty."

The reporter could have developed the story further by writing a transitional paragraph and introducing another one of Bailey's topics, but in this case a 12-paragraph story was probably adequate to summarize the press conference and speech.

Now, let's examine two actual reports of this same story.

This is how Simon Fisher of the *Tempe Daily News Tribune*, the community newspaper of the city where Arizona State University is located, approached the story:

There may be an abundance of attorneys in the United States, but there are few excellent trial lawyers who have polished their craft to perfection, one of the nation's foremost lawyers said Tuesday.

"Young lawyers will have no difficulty finding work in the litigation branch," F. Lee Bailey said. "There are people out there, but they are not very good."

Bailey, attorney for such notables as Patricia Hearst and the Boston Strangler and author of several books on defense law, urged the law students in the audience of about 500 at Arizona State University not to enter the litigation aspect of the profession unless they function well under pressure.

"One has to enjoy the responsibility others cannot handle."

Fisher's story continued for another 14 paragraphs, weaving together direct quotations and paraphrases. It ended with a quotation from Bailey, warning budding lawyers not to become corrupt:

"The worst is to wind up at age 50 and find out you won nothing but the money."

A story by Andrea Han in the *State Press*, the daily student newspaper at Arizona State University, also concentrated on Bailey's comments on trial lawyers, but it differed from Fisher's story. It began:

Trial lawyers today lack the basic training they need to confront liars on the witness stand, criminal lawyer F.

Lee Bailey said Tuesday.

Bailey, defense attorney for Patty Hearst, "Boston Strangler" Albert

DeSalvo and other famous clients, said the profession needs good lawyers who are better trained to litigate.

"Lawyers are not equipped to confront and expose liars because they have a lack of training in the science and art of cross-examination," he said.

Bailey, who spoke to a crowd of about 300 students, faculty and staff, said lawyers are "ill-equipped" to litigate because their specialties are diverted elsewhere.

This story contained another 21 paragraphs. It followed the same pattern as the other two, but it probably gave Bailey's press conference and speech too much space. Clearly, his comments on and criticisms of the judicial system could have been summarized in a dozen or so paragraphs.

Han ended her story with a direct quotation from Bailey's press conference, in which he responded to Han's question about Patricia Hearst:

> "I don't think she got a fair shot, but our main objective was to get her out of a murder indictment, and we did that," he said.

The fact that these stories on Bailey differed so much does not mean that the three reporters attended different functions. All of them got the same information. They simply approached the story differently.

Obviously, their systems for estimating the size of an audience were different. The first reporter counted the number of seats (rows times the number of chairs in one row) when he first entered the hall. Midway through the speech, he looked over his shoulder and noticed that the hall was filled. The other two reporters probably did not use that technique.

A broadcast example Radio and television reporters also covered Bailey's speech. Their stories should have reported the same major topics as the newspaper stories, but their writing would have been woven around videotape or audiotape. Also, the broadcast stories would have been shorter; there is seldom enough time in a radio or a television news broadcast for an 11-paragraph story.

Here is how Bailey's speech could have been reported in conversational broadcast style. This story would take up about 40 seconds of air time:

Announcer

STATE JUDGES ACROSS THE COUNTRY ARE SWINGING TO THE RIGHT POLITICALLY. THAT ACCORDING TO FAMED TRIAL LAWYER F. LEE BAILEY, SPEAKING TODAY AT ARIZONA STATE UNIVERSITY.

BAILEY CLAIMS THAT THE STATE COURT DECISIONS ARE

	BECOMING MORE CONSERVATIVE. THE REASON, SAYS BAILEY, IS THAT STATE JUDGES REALIZE THEY STAND NO CHANCE OF BEING APPOINTED TO THE FEDERAL BENCH IF THEY HAND DOWN LIBERAL RULINGS . . .
Sound bite	"WITH THE ARIZONA CROWD ON THE SUPREME COURT, I WOULD SAY THERE IS A LOT OF PRESSURE TO BE VERY CONSERVATIVE."
Announcer	BAILEY WAS REFERRING TO CHIEF JUSTICE WILLIAM REHNQUIST AND JUSTICE SANDRA DAY O'CONNOR. BOTH REHNQUIST AND O'CONNOR HAVE TIES TO ARIZONA.

In reality, every reporter who covered Bailey would produce a different lead and story. Those who attended the press conference would have different stories from those who attended only the speech, and vice versa. Reporters who caught Bailey alone would probably have exclusive stories.

The point is that no two reporters are the same. Most of the reporters who attended the speech wrote leads that had Bailey criticizing the American legal system, but they did not have to. As our examples show, the lead could focus on the growing conservatism of American courts.

Still, whatever point it emphasizes, every story on the press conference, the speech or both should follow the pattern of summary lead, direct quotations, paraphrases, transition, direct quotations, paraphrases and so on.

storm on the East Coast is tied to the clear weather on the West Coast some-how. A lot of stories treat weather as if it popped up out of nowhere. As a national newspaper, we want to get a national perspective."

Williams strives to be honest with his readers. "I always try to get across that a weather forecast is not an Olympian pronouncement," he said. "It is common for our stories to say that forecasters are not sure, but if certain things happen, it will rain in New York City, and if something else happens, it will snow. One thing we can do for our readers is tell them what the options are—what the atmosphere might have in store for them."

When putting together weather stories of national perspective or stories about ramifications at the local level, reporters will sometimes encounter forecasters who are reluctant to talk with them at length.

"Some forecasters are afraid that reporters will misinterpret what they say," Williams said. "Plus, the forecasters with the National Weather Service are very busy. Reporters often don't know the best times to call them. Then there's also the problem that some weather service people aren't that good at relating scientific concepts to laypeople."

USA Today has a contract with a private *weather forecasting service*—Weather Services Corp.—so that Williams is in constant touch with meteorologists. "I usually call them at least twice a day," Williams said. "But the main thing is that they are always available when we have questions. My stories are cooperative ventures between the meteorologist and me."

Readers often turn to newspapers when they want details of weather from across the country. While most television stations focus on weather forecasting, most newspapers place primary emphasis on weather coverage. Forecasts published in most newspapers are from the wire services and are based on information provided by the National Weather Service.

Naturally, most newspapers cannot devote the time and money to weather coverage that *USA Today* does. Nor can most newspapers match the sparkle and the sophistication of electronic media when it comes to weather forecasting. But most editors realize the importance of solid weather coverage.

Local readers, like others around the country, want to know how the weather will affect them. It is not enough merely to give high and low temperatures and precipitation totals. Readers also want to know, for example:

- If it is safe to travel
- If schools will be open
- If the mail will be delivered
- If planes are on time at the airport
- If fog will make it difficult to see
- If it will be bitterly cold

Readers want to know these things—and more—because their lives are affected each day by the weather. People depend on the media for this kind of information.

EXAMPLE: A SNOWSTORM IN FAIRBANKS

When a storm hits, weather coverage is particularly important at the *Daily News-Miner*, which has an evening circulation of about 17,000. Several reporters and editors play a role in gathering information when a weather story dominates the front page. This was the case when a snowstorm paralyzed Fairbanks just before a recent Christmas. The headline in Monday's editions told the story: 17.2 inches—but don't stop counting!

The story was not routine; it went beyond providing statistical information. It contained facts, figures and direct quotations from a variety of sources.

The storm was so severe that it caused a serious circulation problem. Some of the newspapers were not delivered until the following day. *News-Miner* policy states that if it is 50 degrees below zero, the carriers have the option of delivering the newspaper the next day.

The snowstorm was a major story that required extensive interviews and the gathering of factual information. It was the type of story encountered regularly at newspapers all across the United States. The straightforward opening paragraphs on the front-page story by the *Daily News-Miner* reporters John Creed and Kris Capps made it clear that the weather was wreaking havoc with travel and would probably continue to do so:

> The largest snowstorm in years is continuing to dump near-record amounts in much of Interior Alaska, causing slick roads and lots of accidents.
>
> Travel warnings are in effect, and the National Weather Service is predicting even more snow before the storm tapers off by noon Tuesday.
>
> "It ain't over yet," said weather service forecaster Paul Flatt this morning. "It's real tough to call, but we should pick up another six to 10 inches through Tuesday. This much snow is unusual in Fairbanks. It happens, but not very often."
>
> Weather officials at the airport tallied 17.2 inches of snowfall by 9 a.m. this morning—2.9 inches on Saturday, 11.5 inches Sunday and 2.8 inches by 9 a.m. today.
>
> "And it is still falling like mad," said National Weather Service meteorological technician Wayne Nelson this morning.

This lead block of paragraphs certainly provided readers with the most pertinent information: The storm was a major one; it would continue to dump snow on Fairbanks; the snow was approaching record amounts.

Had there been deaths as a result of the storm, major power outages or monetary estimates of damages, this information would probably have been included in the lead. However, in the relatively early stages of the storm, this information was not yet known.

After the lead block, the reporters focused on facts and quotations from sources in Fairbanks and in outlying areas. The story continued with information crucial and interesting to readers:

> Fairbanks International Airport remained open this morning, but traffic was slow due to snow clearing operations on the runways, said Nelson, who also does pilot briefing.
>
> "Operation is close to normal for the major airlines," Nelson said. "But for the little guys it's different. These bush pilots can't take off in this kind of stuff."

Alaska State Troopers are urging people to stay home to avoid the nasty driving conditions.

Over the weekend, both Troopers and Fairbanks city police kept busy with a string of accidents and stalled vehicles.

After the writers provided readers with information that most directly touched their daily lives, they went on to discuss the origins of the storm and to provide a summary of conditions in other towns:

According to forecasters, the snow is the result of a raging storm that originated in the North Pacific and pounded the state's western shores with high winds, snow—even rain—much of last week.

"If people think it's rough here, it's rougher in Nome and Kotzebue," said Glen Glenzer, local deputy commissioner of the Department of Transportation. He said recent flooding in Nome did not cause excessive damages, but, now "It's still blowing, still drifting there. The airports were closed occasionally (over these past few days) for zero visibility."

In Fairbanks, road-clearing crews are working around the clock to stay ahead of the storm, Glenzer said.

The story concluded with quotations from local residents, a police officer, a state trooper and managers of local towing services, who reported doing record business.

The storm continued on Monday, and so reporters and editors at the *Daily News-Miner* stayed busy gathering additional information for Tuesday's newspaper. By Tuesday, the storm was having a greater impact on the daily lives of readers and on the coffers of the government. This was apparent in the opening paragraphs of Tuesday's story, written by Kris Capps:

A near-record snowfall buried Fairbanks Monday, littering streets with stalled vehicles and taking an extra $10,000 bite out of the Department of Transportation's snow-clearing budget.

As Fairbanksans shoveled out from under 26 inches of snow this morning, forecasters warned that two to four more inches was on the way today. Another snowstorm is expected to pass through on Thursday, but forecasters don't know how much snow it will leave behind.

"This is probably about a 10-year snow," said Bob Fischer, supervising forecaster for the National Weather Service. "Storms of this magnitude are relatively rare."

Heavy snow and impassable streets prevented delivery of the U.S. mail and the Fairbanks Daily News-Miner in some rural areas. It closed some area roads, and Eilson Air Force Base was closed to all but essential personnel today.

School buses ran as scheduled, but some cut their routes short, and others stuck to main roadways, requiring children to walk there or find their own transportation.

The first five paragraphs focused on the most relevant information to readers. The story also provided these facts to aid readers:

Buses were running 15 to 30 minutes late.
Taxis were running about 30 minutes late.
Two highways were closed.

And in an additional paragraph, the newspaper advised motorists, snow-machiners and skiers "to watch for moose which are drifting from deep snow to roads, trails and railroad tracks."

GENERAL GUIDELINES FOR WEATHER STORIES

Comprehensive, complete weather stories, such as those published by the *Daily News-Miner*, are not developed simply by incorporating a few comments from local weather-service officials into a wire-service account. Reporters must diligently ferret out information from available sources. Here are some suggestions to consider when writing stories about storms:

- *Keep in constant touch with the National Weather Service bureau nearest you.* Don't wait until a major storm hits to develop sources at the bureau. If possible, visit the bureau nearest you. Get to know the forecasters. Then, when a major storm hits and you want information from the bureau, you will not be just another voice on the telephone. Other media representatives will be in touch with the bureau on days of major storms; if you have taken the time to develop sources there on less hectic days, it will pay dividends for you.

- *Keep in constant touch with the state patrol.* The state patrol can provide you with information on accidents, road conditions and the like. As is the case when working with the National Weather Service, if you have maintained ties with the state patrol throughout the year, it will be easier to get information on days of inclement weather. It is only natural for sources to be more accommodating to those journalists who check in regularly. One way to cultivate sources such as the state patrol, the National Guard, the Army Reserve, the Coast Guard and the like is to do an occasional feature story on their training or on new equipment or facilities they might have. Such stories will be of interest to your readers and will also help officials at the agencies remember you when you call on deadline and need some information from them.

- *Keep in touch with the state department of transportation or comparable agency for your area.* Officials there can keep you posted on road closings, on bridges that are out or on areas of the state where travel is not advised.

- *Keep in touch with local law enforcement agencies, such as the police and sheriff departments.*

- *Keep in touch with local agencies responsible for snow removal, storm cleanup and the like.* They can provide you with information on timetables for cleanups, how many workers are on the job, whether they are working shifts around the clock and estimated costs.

- *Interview local residents who have been caught out in the weather.* Do not limit weather stories to quotations from authorities; provide details and quotations from residents, too. Readers will appreciate and relate to the *human angle.*

- *Keep in touch with officials at local institutions, agencies and entities that are affected by the weather.*

Institutions that can be affected by weather include, but are not limited to, the following:

Schools (Will classes be held? Are buses running?)

Utility companies (What effects did the storm have on use of electricity and gas?)

Telephone companies (Did the storm down lines? Did use of telephones go up during the hours of the storm?)

Civil defense departments (Are shelters being provided for the homeless or for stranded motorists?)

National Guard, Coast Guard or Army Reserve units (Have these units been mobilized to aid residents or to help clear debris or snow? If so, how many people are involved? How long will the mobilization last?)

Post office (Is the mail being delivered? If so, are deliveries running late?)

Hospitals (Have any people been hospitalized as a result of storm-related incidents? What is their condition?)

Bus companies (Are they running on schedule?)

Airport (Are planes arriving and departing? If so, are they on schedule?)

Train depots (Are trains arriving and departing? Are they on schedule?)

Taxi companies (Are they running?)

In addition to consulting with the sources listed above, reporters might want to check weather records kept by the newspaper or by local observers. And the faculty at local colleges or universities might provide additional scientific information or background on the storm.

TYPES OF WEATHER STORIES

Several reporters and editors are often mobilized in newsrooms to help cover major storms, but on a day-to-day basis, one reporter generally assumes responsibility for routine weather coverage. It is common for new members of staffs to be assigned the task. Examples of various types of weather stories and advice on how to write them follow.

Forecasts

The wire services routinely move *state weather forecasts.* Often, reporters will use information in the wire stories to help them localize the forecasts. Generally, a call to the nearest National Weather Service station will provide sufficient information for a local angle. If a region has been hit with a storm, is in the middle of a drought or is trying to dry out after several days of rain, *local weather forecasts* are particularly pertinent to readers.

La Grande, Ore., after being hit with a "stinging combination of arctic cold, freezing rain, snow and massive power outages," looked for better days, according to *The Observer,* a 7,200-circulation daily. Brian White interviewed sources at three agencies before writing his forecast story: the National Weather Service, the county emergency services department and the U.S. Soil and Conservation Service. The opening paragraphs emphasized the uncertainty of the weather:

Even though the skies have cleared and temperatures have risen, local officials are keeping a wary eye on the weather.

Early forecasts from the National Weather Service in Pendleton this morning called for warming temperatures locally on Saturday and Sunday. At first, forecasters thought the mercury might reach the 50s in some areas, but later they revised the predicted highs to about 40.

Sudden warming after the recent heavy snowfalls is a concern, said Rich Huggins, Union County emergency services director.

"As long as it freezes at night we'll be okay," Huggins said. "But flooding is something we're watching for."

The lead block of paragraphs was carefully written. Reporters who piece together forecast stories must be particularly careful not to overstate or understate the ramifications of the weather. The next two paragraphs of White's story provided additional specifics:

Huggins has contacted shelter managers to help prepare a contingency plan in case scattered flooding problems occur over the weekend.

"We're in pretty good shape because the snow is pretty dry, but it's hard for the Weather Service to forecast locally because there's a pocket of cold air that's settled over the valley," Huggins said.

These paragraphs make it clear that flooding could occur, but the writer used good judgment in not overstating the potential danger. An overly dramatic lead could have read:

Local officials are busily preparing for scattered flooding problems that could occur locally this weekend.

That lead, though not exactly inaccurate, would sensationalize the situation. It is important for reporters to proceed cautiously with weather forecast stories. Readers should be informed as completely as possible about potential weather problems, but if there is uncertainty, it is best to seek information from several sources before rushing to print with leads that overdramatize the weather. Conversely, if hazardous weather is clearly moving into an area, that should be emphasized in a story's lead.

Readers want to know what might be in store for them today and tomorrow, but *long-term forecasts* are also important. The National Weather Service provides long-range forecasts, but reporters can go beyond these by seeking details from local or regional authorities.

Clearly, the rules that apply when putting together stories about the weather are the same as those that apply when writing other news accounts: select an appropriate lead; structure a concise, easy-to-understand first sentence; get quotations from authorities near the beginning of the story; and be sure to tell readers what they want to know—that is, how the weather will affect them.

Travel Conditions and Closings

Another basic weather story deals with travel conditions. Since many readers are constantly on the roads, they need to know how safe the roads are. Quite often, if travel conditions are poor, schools and other institutions are closed. Therefore, it is common for newspapers to publish stories that provide information on road conditions and details on closings of local institutions.

Information for these stories usually comes from the National Weather Service, from state transportation officials, from local law enforcement personnel and, in the case of school closings, from institution officials.

Jeff Boone, a reporter for *The Gleaner*, Henderson, Ky., made use of these sources in a story that he wrote. The story led with road conditions. In the fourth paragraph, the school closing was noted:

Henderson was included in a traveler's advisory on Thursday and is under a winter storm watch tonight and Saturday as the latest storm saw cold temperatures digging in and motorists digging out.

Wednesday's snow-sleet-rain storm left a covering of slush on area roads that froze as hard as concrete on Thursday, and, combined with high winds and blowing snow, made travel dangerous.

Very cold arctic air on the surface and moist southwest air in the upper atmosphere are combining to bring a winter storm to the area this weekend, said Francis Burns, a forecaster with the National Weather Service.

Hazardous road conditions and a threat of 2 to 4 inches of snow Thursday night forced officials to cancel classes today, and the coming winter storm will not make conditions any better.

Record-Breaking Weather

Newspapers routinely carry stories about record-breaking weather such as rainfall (or the lack of it) and low and high temperatures. These stories are relatively easy to write; the National Weather Service provides most of the information.

It is always hot in Phoenix during the summer months, for example, but some days are hotter than others. Stories about record-breaking heat almost write themselves. *The Arizona Republic* published a nine-paragraph story that led with record high temperatures that were recorded around the state and concluded with a forecast. Note the carefully selected verb in the lead paragraph:

Record-breaking heat cooked much of Arizona on Wednesday, with afternoon temperatures 10 to 15 degrees above normal, the National Weather Service said.

Record highs were recorded in Phoenix, Tucson, Flagstaff and Winslow.

The high in Phoenix was 108 degrees, surpassing the record for the date, 106, set last year.

The story went beyond the statistics, however. The article explained what was creating the high temperatures:

> The above-normal temperatures are due to an unusual high-pressure area that has been perched over the Southwest for the past several days, the weather service says.

The importance of the National Weather Service as a primary source cannot be stressed enough. The service is a well of information; and reporters should routinely tap it.

Unusual Weather

Many weather stories that the media disseminate each year are routine: forecasts, monthly rainfall totals, year-end summaries. It is a sure bet that reporters will be writing stories such as these. Occasionally, though, freak, unexpected weather can catch reporters—and everyone else—off guard. Such calamities as tornadoes, hurricanes and cyclones, or even natural disasters such as earthquakes, can wreak havoc.

When these events occur, reporters and editors must be ready to spring into action. Special problems develop when the weather goes berserk, when a tornado rips through town or when floodwaters inundate a community. While reporters and photographers are trying to work their way into restricted areas, editors and circulation employees face the problem of getting the newspaper to the readers. Reporters and editors should have emergency plans that can be implemented when freak weather strikes. In most cases, they need two plans, one for covering the freak weather and another for maintaining the production of the newspaper.

The *Grand Island* (Neb.) *Independent* put its newsroom emergency plan into operation when seven tornadoes devastated much of that community in south central Nebraska. Five people were killed and more than 135 were injured. The twisters caused $300 million in damage and destroyed or damaged 80 businesses and 200 houses.

The *Independent*'s emergency plan had been developed several years earlier after an airplane hijacking in Grand Island. The paper, with a circulation of 25,000, found out then that it needed plans for:

Coping with the deluge of news requests from the national media
Handling local officials
Using reporters and writers in the best way

"We kept our fastest writers in the office for the rewrites and our toughest reporters out gathering the information," the managing editor, Al Schmahl, said. "We also designated a couple of staffers to answer outside requests, providing other media with copies of what we had written and making arrangements for them to use our newsroom and darkroom."

The *Independent*'s newsroom emergency plan was put into effect long before the staff knew the seriousness of the tornadoes. In case of communication problems, two base stations were set up, one at the newspaper and the other at an assistant managing editor's house. The newspaper plant was undamaged, but it had no power or water. The staff used water from the toilets to process film. Because of the power loss, the editors decided to print the paper in York, a community about 40 miles east of Grand Island.

Every member of the staff was used to cover some aspect of the story. Schmahl became a reporter and wrote a sidebar story on the storm system and the weather bureau's role. Sportswriters helped gather information, and the family editor checked with funeral homes.

Besides spot news coverage, public service stories had to be developed to tell residents how to make certain that water was safe to drink, how long food could be kept without spoiling, how to avoid price gouging, how to cope with government bureaucracy and where to go for assistance.

Stories about people were also important. "We did articles on each of the people killed, we tramped around devastated neighborhoods to talk to victims and we looked for human interest in the hundreds of helpers who came to town for the cleanup," Schmahl said. "We just tried to tell what these tornadoes had done to people's lives." The *Independent* also let people tell their own stories in a month-long series of "Tornado Tales," which were submitted by readers affected by the twisters.

Because of damage to businesses and a weeklong loss of power, little advertising appeared in the *Independent* for the first week after the tornadoes, but the paper continued to be published.

Covering unusual weather, such as tornadoes, requires many of the same reporting procedures that are followed when writing about disasters, which are discussed more extensively beginning on page 340.

Seasonal and Year-End Stories

Newspapers regularly publish seasonal stories on the first day of winter, Groundhog Day, the first day of spring and so forth. Most are reported, with new approaches, each year. Newspapers also publish *year-end weather summaries.* Jan. 1 is traditionally a slow day for news. It is common for reporters to dig through the weather reports for the preceding 365 days and to base stories on the statistics. The statistical information, of course, is complemented with direct quotations from weather officials.

News reporters are sometimes assigned the task of writing these year-end weather stories. The assignment should not be considered unimportant busy work. Good reporters will go beyond the statistics and emphasize the human ramifications of the year's weather.

WEATHER TERMINOLOGY: AP STYLE

USA Today's Jack Williams noted that a basic knowledge of weather and an understanding of the language used to describe it are of great help in writing accurate, meaningful weather stories.

The Associated Press Stylebook and Libel Manual has a comprehensive section on weather terms—ranging from *blizzard* to *flash flood* to *hurricane watch* to *travelers' advisory* to *wind chill index*. Check the stylebook if you have any questions on proper weather terms or their meanings.

COVERING DISASTERS

Gary Washburn, the *Chicago Tribune*'s transportation writer, had just sat down for a dinner of corned beef and cabbage. His parents were visiting his home in one of the Windy City's South Side neighborhoods.

Ann Marie Lipinski, a general assignment reporter for the *Tribune,* was about ready to go home for the weekend. She was anxious to get there to feed her dog.

It was about 6:15 p.m. on a Friday, and things were slow in the newsroom. Not much was happening in the city, and the mood was relaxed because the Saturday paper is the week's smallest and not many stories get in.

ELEMENTS OF DISASTER COVERAGE

The First Bulletins

Just as Washburn and Lipinski were about to start their weekend, United Press International moved a *bulletin,* which the wire services use to alert journalists that a major story is beginning to develop. A bulletin, which does not often exceed one paragraph, is sent over the wires to newspaper and broadcast outlets.

> GRAPEVINE, Texas (UPI)—An explosion was reported Friday at Dallas-Fort Worth International Airport, and there were unconfirmed reports that a Delta jetliner had crashed on landing in a severe thunderstorm.

At about the same time, The Associated Press moved a bulletin over its broadcast wire:

> (GRAPEVINE, TEXAS)—AUTHORITIES SAY A DELTA PASSENGER PLANE CAPABLE OF CARRYING MORE THAN 200 PEOPLE HAS CRASHED NORTH OF DALLAS-FORT WORTH INTERNATIONAL AIRPORT.

Editors and news directors throughout the country saw these bulletins and immediately sprang into action. In Chicago, while one editor on the city desk went to the national editor to confirm that he wanted the Dallas story staffed, another editor watched the wires for more news from Texas. As in any disaster, print and broadcast journalists rely heavily on the wire services to supply them with news until they can get their own reporters and photographers to the scene.

When a plane
crashes, reporters
try to be on the
scene as quickly as
rescue workers.
*(Photo by Don B.
Stevenson)*

Of course, not every newspaper and broadcast outlet would send reporters to Texas to cover this story. Only those throughout Texas, as well as the television networks and the major metropolitan newspapers, would. Many newsrooms would use wire copy exclusively. Broadcast outlets, particularly radio, would use the early stories for hourly news reports or breaks into current programming. Newspapers would use the stories that move closest to their final deadlines.

Within five minutes of the first bulletin, even before there was confirmation that a jetliner had indeed crashed, Washburn got a call from the city desk telling him to get ready to go to Dallas. Lipinski was told to stand by because a major story could be developing. She immediately tried to call a friend, hoping he could take care of her dog.

Making Every Minute Count

Not long after UPI and AP sent their bulletins of a crash at Dallas–Fort Worth International Airport, Lipinski, Washburn and Val Mazzenga, a *Tribune* photographer, were on their way to O'Hare International Airport in Chicago. Neither they nor their editors knew what Dallas held for them, but they were preparing for a major story.

The three did not even know what flight they would be on. They were simply told to get to the airport—at least an hour away at this busy time of the evening—and to call the city desk for additional instructions.

"I had never been to Dallas," said Lipinski, who has worked on the *Tribune* metro staff and in its features department as a writer. "We knew nothing. We didn't know where the plane was from or how many people were aboard."

Back in the newsroom, more than a dozen reporters and editors were preparing for what would be an all-night affair. Several minutes after the bulletins moved, The Associated Press moved a 1st Lead–Writethru, the designation wire services use to tell newsrooms that this is the first complete story and that it replaces all earlier stories. In a developing disaster story such as a plane crash, where information is gathered and moved minute by minute, the wire services will move new leads, inserts to earlier stories and *writethrus* as often as they can. Within several hours of the Dallas crash, AP would move 15 writethrus on the newspaper wire; UPI would move seven.

The 1st Writethru from the AP confirmed everyone's fears:

GRAPEVINE, Texas (AP)—A Delta Air Lines jumbo jet crashed and exploded Friday during a heavy thunderstorm on its final approach to Dallas-Fort Worth International Airport, authorities said.

Local radio and television stations reported an unknown number of casualties.

Dense smoke streamed from the L-1011's charred hulk, and debris was scattered over several hundred yards just north of the airport.

One witness said that the plane bounced about five times and sent up smoke and flames. A pilot who witnessed the accident said that nothing was left of the plane.

The airplane crashed near oil storage tanks in a freight area. Ambulances raced to the scene, and firefighters spread foam. A car on Texas 114 was demolished.

This first story from AP was sketchy. Mention of casualties was put in the second paragraph because no one knew yet how many people were killed or injured, and AP was still relying on radio and television stations for its information. The AP still did not know how the plane crashed, where it was from, where it was going or why it crashed. Those important elements, and much more, would have to be reported in later stories.

The wire services also continued to move new stories over their broadcast wires. As it moved its 1st Lead–Writethru on the newspaper wire, the AP sent a similar story over the broadcast wire:

(GRAPEVINE, TEXAS)—LOCAL RADIO AND TELEVISION STATIONS IN THE DALLAS-FORT WORTH AREA ARE REPORTING MASS CASUALTIES FROM THE CRASH OF A DELTA AIR LINES PASSENGER PLANE. THE PLANE, CAPABLE OF CARRYING MORE THAN 200

PEOPLE, CRASHED NORTH OF THE DALLAS-FORTH WORTH
INTERNATIONAL AIRPORT.

WITNESSES AT THE SCENE SAY DENSE SMOKE WAS SEEN
STREAMING FROM THE AIRCRAFT FOLLOWING A TREMENDOUS
EXPLOSION. A PILOT WHO SAW THE ACCIDENT SAYS THERE'S
NOTHING LEFT OF THE PLANE.

THERE'S STILL NO WORD ON THE FLIGHT NUMBER. EMERGENCY
CREWS ARE RUSHING TO THE SCENE.

The 2nd Lead–Writethrus from AP and UPI were still unable to report the number of casualties on the airplane, but they did provide some news information. The lead paragraph of the AP's second story, for instance, was the same as in the first story, but the second paragraph was changed to update readers on casualties.

In its 2nd Lead–Writethru, UPI reported that more than 100 people were aboard the plane. It still had not confirmed the exact number, nor did it know how many people had died; but it was the first wire service to report the number of people aboard, the number of survivors, the flight number and where it originated. Here is UPI's story:

GRAPEVINE, Texas (UPI)—A Delta L-1011 with more than 100 people aboard hit two cars, crashed and exploded in a severe thunderstorm Friday at Dallas-Fort Worth International Airport, and witnesses said that there were "massive injuries."

There were at least 11 survivors, officials said, but no word on how many might have died in the fiery crash.

"Ambulances are everywhere," a witness said. "They have massive injuries."

Another witness said that the jumbo jet appeared to "nosedive" as it neared landing.

Authorities said it was believed that 147 passengers and an unknown number of crew members were on board the craft, Flight 191, originating in Fort Lauderdale, Fla.

Parkland Hospital officials in Dallas said that they received six of the injured and were alerted to "any number of people."

A witness said that about five seconds after the crash a large explosion sent flames 200 to 300 feet into the air.

"There's metal strewn all over the place," said W. J. Blankenship, a battalion chief of the Irving Fire Department.

He said that the airplane or a section of the craft apparently hit a car on Texas 114 adjacent to the airport, killing the driver.

Using Instinct

The early accounts by the wire services are typical in major breaking news stories. Coverage is based on instinct, a reporter's *nose for news*, rather than a long, carefully thought out process in which sources are cultivated. The early stories report the news as quickly as possible, and they are based on information gathered from whatever sources the reporters can get to initially. Final numbers and explanations often come hours or days later.

When reporters are able to develop a story carefully, they cultivate sources, gaining trust and ferreting out information over a period of time. In many ways a single story becomes their beat. But when they cover a fast-breaking story such as the crash of Flight 191, they must use their natural intuition and common sense to gather as much information and to make their news decisions as quickly as they can. They must react instantaneously, knowing where to go for information and knowing which witnesses, opinions, facts and figures to believe. Their intuition is based on past reporting experience.

This is why their editors sent Washburn and Lipinski to Dallas. They knew that, as transportation writer, Washburn could delve into the reasons behind the crash. His instincts would lead him to airline and federal officials investigating the crash. They knew that as a superior feature writer, Lipinski would go for the human element of the story. Her instincts would lead her to the cleanup crews, the survivors and the families.

Including the Essentials

Reporters who gather information about disasters, such as an airplane crash, strive to include essential ingredients in their stories. Each breaking story and follow-up that they write should include:

- Death count
- Number of injuries
- Condition updates from hospitals
- Update on rescue attempts
- Date of the disaster
- Time of the disaster
- Background particular to the disaster, in this case, the flight number, where the flight originated, its destination and why it was in Dallas
- Factors that led to the disaster, such as the violent weather
- Latest findings in the investigation
- Quotations from survivors
- Quotations from witnesses
- Historical significance

Coordinating Coverage

Besides sending reporters and photographers to the scene of a developing story, newspaper editors and broadcast news directors coordinate coverage inside the newsroom, which becomes even more hectic than normal when a major story breaks. Here are the various responsibilities that reporters were given in the newsroom of the *Chicago Tribune* as editors organized the coverage of Flight 191. Nearly all this activity occurred within an hour after the initial bulletin from UPI, and it illustrates what was going on in many metro newsrooms.

Orchestrating the staff   One person was assigned the task of getting Washburn, Lipinski and the photographer on the first flight to Dallas. Reservations had to be made at a hotel close to the airport. Cars had to be rented and waiting for them when they arrived in Dallas. When the three arrived at O'Hare and called the city desk, their calls were routed to this person. None of the three knew yet that the other two were also going to Dallas.

"I arrived at O'Hare at about 8:15 and called the office," Washburn said later. "I was told that I was booked on an 8:40 p.m. Delta flight, along with a fellow reporter, Ann Marie Lipinski; and a photographer, Val Mazzenga. I was informed that our first priority after arriving was to get color details of the crash."

Checking clips   Whenever coverage of a major story begins, someone has to check the files of stories written in the past about similar incidents. The clips should provide information such as the number of plane crashes this year, the worst aviation disasters, the number of crashes at Dallas–Fort Worth or any problems that Delta has been experiencing. In this story, the clips turned up a striking similarity between the crash in Texas and an air disaster in Chicago in 1979, which killed 271 people aboard the plane and two on the ground. The Chicago flight was also No. 191 and, like the plane in Dallas, had Los Angeles as its final destination. Both crashes occurred on a Friday.

There's one important thing to remember about clips: the fact that something has been in print does not mean that it is correct. Do not repeat an error. If there is doubt about something that has been reported earlier, check it out.

Checking hospitals   In any disaster, the busiest spots will probably be the local hospitals, where casualties are taken and where temporary morgues are often set up. Two reporters checked the wire stories and the Dallas phone book, making a list of hospitals where casualties could be taken. Each of the hospitals would be called regularly to find out how many people were taken there and what their condition was. Usually a reporter would ask to speak to the nursing supervisor in the emergency room, but in major stories such as this, reporters are generally transferred to a single hospital spokesperson responsible for disseminating information to the media.

Checking the coroner's office   A check of the coroner's office is always important when dealing with stories in which people have been killed. The coroner, or medical examiner, can provide information on the number and the causes of deaths.

Interviewing witnesses   Interviewing witnesses over the phone is difficult, but reporters still try. The final story will rely on reporters at the scene for interviews with witnesses, but journalists working the phones can make early contacts. In this story, one reporter started calling business numbers at the airport, hoping to find people who saw the crash.

Interviewing officials   Officials of companies, government agencies and other organizations must be interviewed as appropriate. In this story, it was of course necessary to cover Delta Air Lines. The company would need to make some type of official statement.

Checking organizations   Since the plane had crashed in a severe thunderstorm, it was important to check with the National Weather Service. Someone would have to check on how violent weather affects airplane travel. For example, can lightning strike and destroy an airplane? Can a gust of wind blow it down?

Checking the wire services   No matter how well a story is staffed, the AP, UPI and supplemental wires should be checked continually to gather additional information.

Getting the Latest Lead

The three journalists from Chicago were booked on the first flight out of O'Hare—ironically, it was on Delta Air Lines—but they would still not get to Dallas until 11 p.m., 4 hours and 55 minutes after the crash. "By the time we got to the crash site, there was not even any smoke rising," Lipinski said. "The story was already in its second phase, the cleanup operation and trying to piece together what happened. The story was still dramatic, but the original drama was already over. For that, the local press did a bang-up job."

Indeed, the media from Dallas and Fort Worth were on the story instantly. By 6:30 p.m., WFAA-TV, the ABC affiliate in Dallas, began live coverage from the airport. It continued through the evening, feeding videotape via satellite to ABC News headquarters in New York. That enabled the network to break into regular programming with bulletins. Later in the evening, ABC's "Nightline" aired a full report of the crash, including live interviews with WFAA reporters on the scene.

Five hours after the crash, there was still much news to report. The crash had already been reported; but newspaper and broadcast reporters from Texas and throughout the country still had to develop the story for Saturday editions and news shows. After initial reports of the disaster, reporters turned their attention to the cleanup operation, the names of the victims and how the disaster occurred.

By the time the AP moved its 15th Lead–Writethru to member newspapers, at 10:49 p.m. Texas time, the scope of the disaster was known. The story began:

> GRAPEVINE, Texas (AP)—A Delta Air Lines jumbo jet carrying 160 people crashed and exploded Friday during a final approach to Dallas-Fort Worth International Airport, killing about 130 people, officials said.

A few minutes earlier, the AP had moved over its broadcast wire:

> (GRAPEVINE, TEXAS)—OFFICIALS NOW SAY ABOUT 130 PEOPLE
> HAVE DIED FOLLOWING THE CRASH OF A DELTA AIR LINES JUMBO
> JET THAT CRASHED ON APPROACH AT THE DALLAS-FORT WORTH
> INTERNATIONAL AIRPORT. THERE WERE 160 PEOPLE ON BOARD
> FLIGHT 191, AND AT LEAST 34 PEOPLE WERE INJURED.

The AP's leads reported *when* and *where* the crash occurred, but they did not mention the thunderstorm. Instead, they added the *latest* key element of the story—the number of casualties. By now, reporters knew how many people were aboard. They did not have to estimate "more than 100" as UPI did in one of its earlier leads. But they still were scrambling to get the exact number of deaths. Nearly six hours after the crash, AP could only report "about 130."

UPI also moved updated stories throughout the night, but at a slower pace than AP. In its 7th Lead-Writethru, which it moved at 11:50 p.m. Texas time, UPI reported:

> GRAPEVINE, Texas (UPI)—A Delta jumbo jet carrying 161 people nosedived while trying to land during a vicious storm at Dallas-Fort Worth International Airport Friday, killing at least 122 in a fiery explosion that scattered wreckage over a half mile.

UPI's writing continued to be more colorful than the AP's, with such vivid words as "nosedived," "vicious storm" and "fiery explosion." The AP's 15th Lead–Writethru was a terse 29 words, though. UPI used 38 words in its seventh lead.

There were other differences in the leads. While the AP reported that the plane was carrying 160 people and about 130 were killed, UPI said that there were 161 aboard and at least 122 of those had died.

TWO PROBLEMS FOR REPORTERS

Problem 1: A Pitfall of Instantaneous Coverage

The wire-service leads point out a common problem in covering developing disaster stories. When scores of reporters are thrust into the middle of a major story, there is intense pressure to deliver the news faster than the competition. Because reporters are forced to go with what they've got, they are often unable to double-check each bit of information they gather.

Problem 2: Interviewing Victims' Families

One of the toughest things that a reporter has to do while covering a disaster is to interview the families of victims. At no other time does the public's right to know seem to come into such direct conflict with people's right to privacy.

Still, reporters know that by interviewing a grieving parent, spouse or child, they can add an important human element to stories that might otherwise be dominated by statistics. Professionals realize that if they handle the interviews with a great deal of sensitivity, they can offer survivors an opportunity to grieve openly and to eulogize a loved one.

Research by one reporter supports the theory that most people don't mind being interviewed during a time of grief, if they are treated with sensitivity. To fulfill the research project requirements for a master's degree in mass communication, Karen McCowan, a reporter for *The Arizona Republic* in Phoenix, sent questionnaires to 22 grieving relatives quoted in the *Republic* or in its sister paper, *The Phoenix Gazette,* after the crash of a Northwest Airlines jet at Detroit Metropolitan Airport. She also sent surveys to 26 journalists who interviewed the grieving families. People who refused to be interviewed after the crash were not surveyed.

Eleven of the grieving relatives and 15 reporters answered in-depth questions about their feelings toward the interviews. In a *Republic* article about her research, McCowan wrote that perhaps "many of the sources who refused to participate in the survey see it, like their interviews, as an invasion of privacy."

Two of the grieving relatives who responded to the survey had strong objections to being interviewed: one of them said that "privacy was more important than a story to help sell newspapers"; the other criticized the reporters' timing, saying that the first two days after the crash were "brutal." A third relative reported mixed feelings about the interviews. Eight relatives, however, said that they had not minded being interviewed. Most of these said that they wanted the public to know about their loved ones' lives, accomplishments and unexpected deaths. They also said that they saw interviews as a way to ensure accuracy in stories or to vent their emotions.

The reporters who responded to McCowan's questionnaire said that in most cases people do not mind interviews during a time of grief. "Usually, I've found that I feel much worse about asking questions than they do about answering questions," one reporter said.

All the reporters who responded said that the television interviews were most intrusive, if only because of all the equipment required. Some reporters also said that the television interviews were more exploitative emotionally because everything that the family said or did was recorded.

Three of the relatives said, however, that they found print interviews more intrusive than television interviews because of their greater length.

"Like most reporters, I dreaded having to telephone or, even worse, knock on the door of someone who had just lost a family member in a tragedy," McCowan said. "That's why I chose to do my research project on this topic.

"But my findings and personal experience have taught me that many, many people want to talk at a time like this. I think some find a great deal of comfort in the fact that they are not alone in seeing this person's death as significant."

CHRONOLOGY OF DISASTER COVERAGE: DAY BY DAY

The story of Flight 191 illustrates the chronology, or typical sequence, of coverage of disasters. Let's examine it day by day.

Reporting breaking news Saturday morning newspapers throughout the country reported the breaking news of the plane crash. Those in Dallas and Fort Worth had the most extensive coverage because the disaster occurred in their area. They were able to staff the story more quickly and with more people than other newspapers.

The entire front page of the Saturday *Dallas Times Herald* dealt with the plane crash. Two headlines and a huge photo showing smoke rising from the wreckage of the jetliner took up the top half of the page. The headlines said: "Jet crashes at D-FW" and "At least 123 dead; 27 passengers survive."

On the bottom half of the page, there was another photo and an informational graphic, showing where at the airport the crash had occurred. There were also three stories: the main piece and two sidebars. The main story, under the byline "From staff reports," reported the breaking news. It began with a 33-word summary lead that included an estimate of the casualties and a description of the crash:

> A jumbo jet carrying 161 people crashed in a spectacular fireball just north of Dallas-Fort Worth International Airport Friday evening, killing at least 122 people aboard and a motorist on the ground.

A *Times Herald* staff writer, Linda Little, wrote one of the front-page sidebars. It was about one of the survivors and, like many color stories, began as a narrative:

> Jay Slusher was in the middle seat, 42 rows back. The way he figured it, just one more stop from his wife and two children and their home in Phoenix.
>
> The 33-year-old computer programmer for American Express spent an unexpected night at St. Paul Hospital Friday. Considering what happened as his flight approached Dallas-Fort Worth International Airport, he wasn't complaining.

The other sidebar, which was written by the staff writer Maria Newman, was a hard news story dealing with the weather and its effect on the crash. It began:

> Friday started off as another blistering summer day at Dallas-Fort Worth International Airport, with little wind and the mercury rising to the 103-degree mark by 5 p.m.
>
> But just before Delta Flight 191 from Fort Lauderdale, Fla., began its approach to D-FW, a summer storm descended, sending bolts of lightning and gusts of wind up to 80 mph that officials say may have contributed to the worst air crash in Texas history.

The *Fort Worth Star-Telegram* also devoted its entire front page on Saturday to the crash. On the top half of the page, there was a five-column photo showing part of the wrecked plane and rescue workers carrying bodies from the area. The paper's main story, written by a staff writer, Gayle Reaves, was in column six, below the banner headline, "D/FW toll at least 122." Reaves used 36 words in a summary lead that reported the fiery crash, named the airline, estimated the casualties and said that the rescue attempt was continuing:

> Rescue workers were still searching for bodies early Saturday in the wreckage of a Delta Air Lines jumbo jet that went down in a fiery crash at Dallas/Fort Worth Airport, killing at least 122 people.

Reaves talked about survivors in the second paragraph:

> Delta officials said late Friday that at least 27 people—three flight attendants and 24 passengers—had survived of the 149 passengers and 12 crew members on board Flight 191 from Fort Lauderdale, Fla.

Both the *Dallas Times Herald* and *Fort Worth Star-Telegram* reported the number of deaths in their leads. That, of course, is the most important element of the story during the first day of coverage. But through careful writing, the *Star-Telegram* lead was also able to get in the rescue attempt, which the *Times Herald* saved for the second paragraph. The Fort Worth paper also put another key element of the story—the number of survivors—in the second paragraph of its main story, while the Dallas paper put it in the third paragraph.

Beating the competition   Despite the differences in how their stories were constructed, the Texas papers were far ahead of other American papers that had staff-written stories on the crash on Saturday. The *Chicago Tribune*'s story in its Saturday final edition was based on telephone interviews and wire-service accounts; its deadline passed before Washburn and Lipinski were able to phone in any information from Dallas. Its lead and second paragraph informed readers of the crash but clearly told them that it knew little else:

> GRAPEVINE, Texas—A Delta Air Lines jumbo jet carrying more than 150 people crashed and exploded Friday during a heavy thunderstorm on its final approach to Dallas-Fort Worth International Airport, killing an undetermined number of those aboard as well as at least one person on the ground.
>
> About 4 hours after the crash, at least 20 bodies had been brought to a local morgue, officials said.

Second-Day Coverage

Writing follow-up stories   As in any major developing story, reporters covering the crash of Flight 191 still had much work to do after the initial stories reported the disaster and a preliminary count of the casualties. Next, they would write *second-day stories,* follow-ups that update earlier stories and give an audience something fresh. In this story, reporters would be looking for:

A probable cause
A more exact number of casualties
Interviews with survivors
The drama of those who lost loved ones

The rush to report the breaking news was over, but by now reporters from throughout the country had descended upon Dallas, hoping to find bits of information that no other reporters found. The competition was fierce, and new elements of the story continued to surface.

Like many reporters, Washburn and Lipinski worked throughout the night. "We split up the responsibility," Lipinski said. "Gary was going to do the news, including the probable cause. I was going to do the color."

Washburn said that the two reporters began work the instant they arrived in Dallas. They had six hours before their 5 a.m. copy deadline for the first Sunday edition, which the *Tribune* and many other papers call the *bulldog.* "We landed and learned that Delta had a room for the press in the terminal," he said. "We found it and entered, baggage in hand, in the middle of a press conference being conducted by Matt Guilfoyle, Delta's Dallas marketing chief and press spokesman. We obtained a few details but not nearly enough for a comprehensive account of exactly what happened. Guilfoyle's information was still sketchy. At the end of the press conference, he said that Delta tentatively planned to hold hourly briefings and expected to have a list of the names of crash survivors later that night."

Hunting for fresh news While Washburn stayed at the terminal, Lipinski and the photographer went to the crash scene about a half mile away.

"Delta's hourly briefings did not materialize, and I tried to pick up what information I could around the terminal," Washburn said. "I interviewed a young woman who was behind the counter of a concession stand to find out how people in the terminal found out about the crash and what the reactions were. I was frustrated because so little information was available at my post initially. I hoped that Ann Marie was having better luck at the crash site."

She was. Officials of the National Transportation Safety Board were on the scene, and they were cooperative. Lipinski gathered what information she could and then went to several of the hospitals where the victims had been taken. By now, it was past midnight.

"I found families who were waiting up, waiting to hear conditions," she said. "I looked for human details and color."

Finally, Delta held a second press briefing in the terminal at about 2 a.m. "It yielded some useful details, along with a list of crash survivors," Washburn said.

The two reporters, who had been up since early Friday morning and had put in a full day's work in Chicago before going to Dallas, phoned in their notes at 5 a.m. What they had gathered was combined with notes from reporters working the phones in the newsroom. In its Sunday bulldog edition, the *Tribune* carried both a staff-generated, hard-news main story and a color sidebar.

The main story, under the double byline of Washburn and Lipinski, began:

> DALLAS—A Delta Air Lines official said Saturday that weather, rather than mechanical failure, is suspected as the reason an L-1011, wide-bodied jet crashed short of the runway at Dallas-Fort Worth International Airport here, killing about 130 people.

There was no need for Washburn and Lipinski to report simply that an airplane had crashed in Dallas. This had been done by the broadcast media within minutes after the disaster, and by the Saturday morning newspapers. Even though this was Washburn and Lipinski's first account of the disaster, the reporters had to advance the story beyond its initial phase. It had developed to the point that investigators were trying to determine the cause of the crash.

The lead revealed that, even though the story was nearly 12 hours old, the reporters still had no definite answers. Sources were still guessing about what had caused the crash; and there was still no exact body count.

The story continued:

> The dead included a motorist on a nearby highway.
>
> "We feel relatively certain it was weather-related . . . wind shear or lightning or some other disturbance in the atmosphere," said Matt Guilfoyle, district marketing manager for Delta, at an airport news conference.
>
> "I haven't heard even remote rumors that there was a problem up until the time the plane made contact with the ground short of the runway," he said.

In the first four paragraphs of the story, readers were given the information that Washburn had gathered; that is, the latest news was reported first. Lipinski's reporting efforts were revealed for the first time in the fifth paragraph, but they were used to back up the thrust of the story:

> Two passengers among the 29 passengers and 3 crew members who survived the crash Friday night of Flight 191 said they felt the plane make a sudden drop while coming in to land.

Notice how the time of the crash—Friday night—and the airplane's flight number were now pushed down to the fifth paragraph of the story. In the breaking stories, those key elements were in the leads. They were still high in the story, but they were not nearly as vital as before. By the time the Sunday bulldog hit the streets, the story would be more than a half-day old. As the story aged and developed, the early key elements would be pushed down even more.

Now the story shifted back to news gathered by Washburn inside the terminal:

Investigators said most of the survivors were in the tail section of the plane, which became separated from the rest of the fuselage as the plane exploded and broke up.

The latest news of the story was reported in the first paragraphs. Then the story did what most major developing stories do: it moved from *straight recounting of the news* to *reporting the color or human element*. This is where Lipinski's interviews at the crash scene and at the hospitals and Washburn's interviews inside the terminal became important. Mixed in with the information they gathered were quotations and data from *Tribune* reporters working in the newsroom.

Third-Day Coverage

By Saturday night, Lipinski and Washburn were exhausted. "I had gotten up at 6 a.m. Friday for a regular workday," Lipinski said. "I went to bed at 10 p.m. Saturday. I had the same clothes on Saturday night that I had come to work in on Friday morning."

Washburn added: "Though my workday was over and I had been up for more than 36 hours, I didn't feel like sleeping. I finally turned in about 11 p.m., set my alarm for 8 a.m. and awoke a little after 6."

On Sunday, many of the out-of-town reporters left Dallas. The crash was still a major story, but it was developing slowly now, and most of the media decided to rely on the wire services or the Dallas newspapers for later developments. Such a response to disaster stories is typical. National print journalists and broadcast reporters cover the breaking news and second-day stories; then they let the local press and the wire services do the rest as they devote their energies to newly developing stories.

Lipinski was one of the reporters who were told to come home. "The story was not over for Dallas or Los Angeles (the plane's final destination), but it was for Chicago," she said. "The color and drama were over by Saturday night. Everyone who was going to talk had talked. Because he is the transportation writer, Gary was told to stay in the field."

The story had entered another phase, but there was still much technical information to gather on Sunday for Monday newspapers. The drama of families arriving in Dallas, of rescue workers pulling bodies from the wreckage or of Delta officials holding press briefings was over, but there was still much news to report.

"I decided to concentrate my efforts on microbursts, a form of wind shear that, it was believed, may have caused the crash," Washburn said. "I made countless phone calls from my hotel room, but it was Sunday and difficult to find experts to interview."

At about noon, Washburn got through to the president of the Aviation Safety Institute, a non-profit watchdog organization in the aviation industry operating out of Worthington, Ohio. Washburn knew the man from previous stories and knew that he would be a good source for this one. Washburn was also able to locate, at home in Boulder, Colo., a researcher familiar with microbursts.

In the afternoon, Washburn revisited the crash site. "There, a spokesman for the transportation safety board revealed that the airport wind shear alert system sounded about 12 minutes after the Delta plane crashed," the reporter said. "This added credence to speculation about a microburst causing the accident. I went back to the hotel, wrote a piece and then dictated it. The safety board had scheduled a press conference for 8 p.m., and I would insert that into my story if it warranted it.

"More good detail surfaced at the press conference, including the fact that a tower controller told the Delta plane to 'go around' just before the crash because it was coming in too low."

The "go around" comment became the lead of most of the third-day stories, including Washburn's. His story about how the tower had told the pilot to abort the landing seconds before the crash was on top of Monday's front-page story in the *Tribune*.

Ending Coverage

By Monday, there was no reason for Washburn to stay in Dallas. There would still be developments in the story, such as the exact cause of the crash and a final death toll, but they would come later. Few newspapers or broadcast outlets would keep reporters working on stories nearly four days old. When new developments surfaced, they would be reported by the wire services, local correspondents and the local media.

Before coming home, Washburn briefed the *Tribune*'s Dallas correspondent, who had returned from an assignment in Alaska and had missed the crash of Flight 191. If anything else developed, it would be up to the correspondent to report it.

Long-Term Coverage

The story of Flight 191 would go well beyond three days. The death toll would rise to 135, the final seconds of conversation between the tower and the pilot would be released and wind shear would be blamed for the crash. All these stories would have to be reported.

Days or months later, there could be developments in this story. The fact that reporters quit working on it full time and turned their attention to other stories means only that the story of Flight 191 had slipped in priority—not that the story had ended.

Because of the rapidly changing demographics of the United States, reporters must be able to write about cultures different from their own.
(Photo by Sean Openshaw)

Multicultural Reporting

Possibly no greater challenge faces journalists in

the 1990s than providing comprehensive,

consistent, accurate, sensitive and systematic

coverage of the issues and events brought about

largely by the rapidly changing demographics of

the United States. As the staffs of media become

increasingly inclusive, they must cover, with

feeling and comprehension, a diverse society.

When Los Angeles erupted in April 1992 after a jury found four police officers not guilty in the beating of a black motorist, Rodney King, renewed attention was focused on the media's ability—or inability—to cover American cultures and neighborhoods adequately on a day-to-day, non-crisis basis.

During the 1992 convention of the American Newspaper Publishers Association, a panel of mostly minority journalists discussed media coverage of race in the United States. *Editor & Publisher* magazine summarized the thrust of the panelists' comments: "The racial violence unleashed in Los Angeles caught America by surprise because news organizations ignore the bitter racial lines dividing America, in part because they lack a minority perspective."

Today's reporters are called upon to write stories that deal with all segments of our pluralistic society; therefore, they must be sensitive to and knowledgeable about diverse racial and social groups. White reporters cannot simply report and write from the standpoint of a white person's world. White journalists need to get beyond negative stereotypes of minority groups—stereotypes that are sometimes promoted by the nation's media. And minority journalists need to become knowledgeable about the backgrounds of other cultural groups.

Indeed, within two weeks of the verdict in the King case, the *Los Angeles Times* published a massive five-section series, "Understanding the Riots," an attempt "to explain the causes and effects of the dramatic upheaval." The introduction to the series vividly set the stage for the stories that were to follow:

> Los Angeles is in flames.
>
> The date could be August, 1965, when Watts first erupted. But this is April, 1992, the verdict is in, and the eyes of the world are watching.
>
> The embers have long smoldered—urban deprivation, schools and families under pressure, racial discord, the loss of trust in leaders and institutions.
>
> And nothing but the fury of the outbursts themselves comes as much of a surprise.
>
> How did Los Angeles reach the point of crisis—again? This special section tells the city's story through the eyes of Southland residents—black and white, Asian and Latino, looter and cop.

A *New York Times*/CBS News Poll conducted after the riots found that most Americans thought it was time for a new emphasis on the problems of minorities and cities. Most respondents saw the unrest more "as a symptom of festering social needs than as a simple issue of law and order." The *Times* noted that the poll "reflected a nation still struggling with the causes of urban turmoil and the most effective response to it." More than half of the respondents said that a major roadblock to solving inner-city problems was "a lack of knowledge and understanding."

OUR CHANGING POPULATION: DEMOGRAPHICS

Very simply, the *demographics* of the United States—the density, distribution and composition of its population—are changing. Possibly, nowhere is this more apparent than in Southern California. When the *Los Angeles Times* put together its five-section series, it cited several dramatic changes over a 15-year period:

> In 1965, the population of Los Angeles was 2.5 million; 16 percent of the city's population was black; 70 percent of students in the Los Angeles Unified School District were white.

> In 1980, Los Angeles' population had grown to nearly 3 million; the city was 48 percent Anglo, 27.5 percent Latino, 17 percent black and 6 percent Asian; the schools were 28 percent Anglo, 42 percent Latino, 24 percent black and 6 percent Asian.

Clearly, journalists must become increasingly cognizant of changing demographics that have created a *culturally inclusive* society. As Barbara Vobejda of *The Washington Post* wrote in the aftermath of the rioting in Los Angeles: "Enormous social and economic changes swept over [the city] during the 1980s, including rising poverty and unemployment, and a wave of immigration that transformed the city's racial profile." The figures were certainly dramatic: more than 750,000 immigrants settled in Los Angeles during the 1980s; the 1990 census showed that nearly 40 percent of city residents were foreign-born, an increase of two-thirds over a 10-year period.

THE ROLE OF THE MEDIA: RECOMMENDATIONS OF THE KERNER COMMISSION

Thomas Winship, president of the Center for Foreign Journalists in Reston, Va., and former editor of the *Boston Globe,* noted in his column in *Editor & Publisher* magazine that journalists face major challenges in the 1990s. He wrote that "the charge to both press and politicians is to remain focused as never before on urban blight and racism in America." Winship made a plea for the media not to "duck, dance or disappear until the [political] leadership gives the same attention to the domestic urban war as we gave to the overseas Cold War."

During the past quarter-century, Winship wrote, "many metropolitan newspapers have spent untold millions on special suburban sections, with questionable bottom-line results. Yet newspapers never made a comparable commitment to the mounting rot of the inner city." He provided some suggestions for ways the media could keep "the spotlight on our city crisis over the long haul." His tips included beefing up "on-the-street coverage of the underclass in homes and barrooms, catching the everyday flavor of ghetto living." He also challenged the press to apply "investigative zeal to public housing scandals, redlining, landlord ripoffs, job training, school performance and corporate minority hiring."

Another *Editor & Publisher* article cited the concerns of Rick Rodriguez, assistant managing editor of the *Sacramento Bee,* who said that newspapers have made "no commitment to continuing coverage" of racial problems.

Rodriguez's assertion was not new. After urban rioting in the middle 1960s, President Lyndon Johnson formed the National Advisory Commission on Civil Disorders, commonly referred to as the *Kerner Commission.* The commission's report, issued in 1968, was far-ranging.

The commission noted, in examining the effect of the mass media on riots, "Our analysis had to consider also the overall treatment by the media of the Negro ghettos, community relations, racial attitudes, urban and rural poverty—day by day and month by month, year in and year out."

The commission concluded that the media, in covering Watts in 1967, did not "live up to their own professed standards" because the "totality of . . . coverage was not as representative as it should have been to be accurate." The commission found that "many of the inaccuracies of fact, tone and mood were due to the failure of reporters and editors to ask tough enough questions about official reports, and to apply the most rigorous standards possible in evaluating and presenting the news."

The commission noted particularly the role the media would play in an increasingly diverse America:

> The news media have failed to analyze and report adequately on racial problems in the United States. . . . By and large, news organizations have failed to communicate to both their black and white audiences a sense of the problems America faces and the sources of potential solutions. The media report and write from the standpoint of a white man's world. The ills of the ghetto, the difficulties of life there, the Negro's burning sense of grievance, are seldom conveyed. Slights and indignities are part of the Negro's daily life, and many of them come from what he now calls "the white press"—a press that repeatedly, if unconsciously, reflects the biases, the paternalism, the indifference of white America. This may be understandable, but it is not excusable in an institution that has the mission to inform and educate the whole of our society.

The commission painted a particularly bleak picture of the media's inability, at that time, to be responsible and sensitive to the diversity of their audience:

> Equally important, most newspaper articles and most television programming ignore the fact that an appreciable part of their audience is black. The world that television and newspapers offer to their black audience is almost totally white, in both appearance and attitude. Far too often, the press acts and talks about Negroes as if Negroes do not read the newspapers or watch television, give birth, marry, die, and go to PTA meetings. Some newspapers are beginning to make efforts to fill this void, but they have still a long way to go.

The commission also emphasized that inadequate coverage of the races and cultures making up the United States was not simply a matter of "white bias." The report stated that "many editors and news directors, plagued by shortages of staff and lack of reliable contacts and sources of information in the city, have failed to recognize the significance of the urban story and to develop resources to cover it adequately." The commission said that adequate coverage of different cultures and races "requires reporters permanently assigned to this beat." Although more than a quarter-century has elapsed, that recommendation has not been followed universally or aggressively. Some newspapers, however, are beginning to report on cultural issues with enhanced sensitivity and greater depth; and several have created "diversity beats" in response to changing demographics.

Critics are quick to point out that it has taken too long for the media to act on the major recommendation of the Kerner Commission: to diversify staffs. The report said, for example, that "the journalistic profession has been shockingly backward in seeking out, hiring, training and promoting" minorities. The report emphasized that diversifying newsrooms was essential "if the media are to report with understanding, wisdom and sympathy on the problems of the cities and the problems of the black man."

The commission was emphatic: the media needed to hire more minorities and they needed to report with greater depth and understanding on minority affairs. The report focused specifically on the plight of blacks. But the findings obviously apply to coverage of all minorities in the United States.

This chapter is not intended to tell you "everything you need to know" about multicultural coverage. Rather, its purposes are to provide an overview of the current status of multicultural reporting as seen by several scholars and journalists, and to offer a framework of suggestions on how reporters can be more cognizant of and responsive to the changing demographics of the United States.

TRENDS IN MULTICULTURAL COVERAGE

STATUS AND GOALS OF CULTURAL REPORTING AND CULTURAL SENSITIVITY: AN OVERVIEW

In this section, we give a view of today's multicultural coverage, through the eyes of journalists and scholars. This is a general discussion; mass media seminars, classes in a variety of disciplines and discussions with people from all cultural and ethnic backgrounds will help put the broad issues presented here in perspective.

Sharon Bramlett-Solomon

Sharon Bramlett-Solomon, who is a journalism professor at Arizona State University, wrote in *Journalism Educator:* "If future journalists are to understand better their culturally diverse society, and if they are to meet the challenge of improved coverage of minority Americans, training in *cultural sensitivity* is imperative."

Bramlett-Solomon wrote that in her classes "students are encouraged to see, hear, smell, taste and feel life as it is experienced by people from back-

Professor Sharon Bramlett-Solomon of Arizona State University challenges her students to understand the culturally diverse society in which they work.
(Photo by Sean Openshaw)

grounds sometimes very different from their own." Bramlett-Solomon teaches her reporting students about other cultures by giving them assignments that require them to write about worlds far removed from their own experience. For example, one student wrote about elderly people in nursing homes who have no relatives to visit them. Another wrote about two nuns studying at the university. One student reported on local Mexican and black soul food restaurants while another profiled local Hispanic and black newspaper publishers. The students were required to make at least three visits to the people they wrote about.

According to Bramlett-Solomon, cultural sensitivity training can help move journalists past stereotypes. She wrote that sensitivity training can help people learn "not to rely on long-held impressions about particular social groups. Instead, they learn the value of double-checking the validity of earlier impressions, both through their own eyes and through the eyes of participants."

Felix Gutierrez

Felix Gutierrez, a vice president of The Freedom Forum in Arlington, Va., author and former journalism professor, said that coverage of cultures is "better than it used to be but just as clearly not as good as it should be." Gutierrez said that newspapers are still playing a game of catch-up as they try to keep pace with the rapidly changing racial demographics in many communities.

Gutierrez noted that in the 1970s and 1980s, many newspapers started to target more affluent suburban readers for coverage. "That meant the newspapers didn't pay sufficient attention to the growing racial diversity in their central cities and now, in many cases, in the suburbs," he said. "Basically, you can't be the *Los Angeles Times* or *The New York Times* if you don't cover the inner city effectively. If your readers are outside of your core [of coverage] you don't represent the readers of the city that is on your masthead."

Gutierrez also stressed that striving to provide better coverage of minority affairs cannot be approached simply within a black-white context. "All groups of our society must be covered," he said. "Minority issues don't affect just blacks and whites; they cut across all groups."

Actually, because the United States is a nation of increasing diversity, the term *minority* is simply not accurate in a number of cities. "In many of our larger cities, minorities are the majorities," Gutierrez said. "We are becoming a society where almost everyone can claim to be in the minority. If you are looking to the future of the media, I think you would have to conclude that they will thrive only if they report accurately and completely on a multiracial society."

Gutierrez said that, because of the Kerner Commission report, too much attention has been placed only on hiring practices—the sheer numbers—and not enough has been devoted to improvements in coverage. "Too often both the industry and the advocacy organizations have relied on the employment numbers as the only measure of success," he said. "That might be appropriate in some industries—but, for the media, what is most important is the content—the message—and how it is being received."

Caesar Andrews

Caesar Andrews, the executive editor of a Gannett paper, the *Rockland Journal-News* in New York, said that the quest to improve coverage of minority affairs is "a movement that meanders." He elaborated: "It is one of those classic cases where the concept makes sense and the rhetoric sounds good. But the execution has not been solid. It seems that the only things that really move us are the crises—the Los Angeles outrage being a prominent case. I guess I feel that part of what it will take to fix what is wrong is for newspapers to be more forceful in pursuing coverage of people who have been previously ignored, misconstrued or simply not treated the right way. Because of the past pattern of not covering people of color and certain other groups there is almost a need to exaggerate the efforts now—to go well beyond the call of duty."

Andrews envisions a two-prong mission. First, people within the newsroom must be convinced that reporting on cultures consistently and accurately is the right thing to do. "Many journalists have a traditional mindset," he said. "Traditionally, people of color have not been part of journalism's coverage pattern. They haven't been part of what we define as news. They have had their incidents and stereotypes covered, but not their broader humanity. A lot of the efforts to turn the media mindset around have met with resistance to change, with some journalists being unwilling to alter those traditional patterns, to restructure their definition of news. So, we end up perpetuating what is wrong with coverage."

Second, Andrews said, the media must convince people in groups historically excluded from news coverage that they will be included in the future. "I've seen cases where newspaper editors have worked hard to cover all parts of the community—even doing some outstanding journalism in the process—and it goes almost totally unappreciated in certain circles," he said. "We have to better educate people inside the newsroom and we have to make the case with those people on the outside that we do care and that we want to cover them in a more complete way."

Andrews said coverage of minority affairs is better now than ever before, but it is still lacking. "More papers are talking about it now," he said. "I think editors are seeing the wisdom of a business strategy that includes covering all of these varied groups. At the same time, it is not enough yet. It is going to take more energy, more creativity, more hiring and more promoting of people of color throughout the whole range of jobs in newsrooms."

Mary Lou Fulton

Mary Lou Fulton, who edits *City Times*—a once-a-week section in the *Los Angeles Times* that focuses on central-city issues—agrees that "newspapers have neglected urban areas." She said: "The inner city should be covered as completely as we cover every other area of the county. There are 'good' community stories and there are 'tragedy' community stories. But newspapers often end up with a distorted picture of what happens in the city because we tend to respond only in times of crisis. Then we cover issues only on the surface and we don't look at the underlying causes of why the cities have evolved as they have. As a result, we don't have credibility with people in the city. Too often, the only time they see us is when there is a murder. Our new central-city edition [which was launched in 1992] will provide consistent, more complete coverage."

Fulton said that consistent coverage is the key to giving a newspaper credibility. "Minority communities should be covered as a beat," she said. "That is not to say that stories about minority issues would come exclusively from that beat. But if you are to understand a community and its history, you need a beat reporter in that area."

Fulton emphasized that each ethnic group has its own history, its own customs and traditions, its own ways of dealing with issues. "Minority communities should not be lumped together," she said. "Minorities are not all alike. In fact, there often are many divisions within each community that should be recognized along with the things they have in common.

"Very simply, we need to pay regular attention to issues that face minority groups in order to have a true understanding of what each group is all about. Newspapers need to reflect, in their stories, both the pain and the glory of all groups."

Fulton noted that most issues affect all residents of a community, "but some issues affect minorities disproportionately." For example, education is of interest to nearly all readers but, because the dropout rates of minorities are often higher, that issue is of particular relevance.

Dorothy Gilliam

Dorothy Gilliam, a *Washington Post* columnist and former associate editor of *Jet* and *Ebony* magazines, said that she worries when she hears editors say they are "tired of the sensitivity issue and are getting 'diversity burnout.'" She pointed out, "The fact of the matter is that they haven't started to truly understand some of the basic issues involved. Part of the challenge of the future is to get past the old ways and to look for new ways to approach the issue."

Gilliam said that it is imperative for newspapers to employ "a critical mass of minorities in numbers that are sufficiently reflective of the community a newspaper serves to really give an authentic voice to the various minorities in the community."

She said that one of the problems facing the United States is that diversity has not truly been recognized as an asset. "We still consider diversity to be a liability, especially in terms of race relations. The newspaper industry has to commit itself to helping this nation do a basic shift in the whole paradigm of diversity—moving from diversity as a liability to diversity as an asset."

By and large, Gilliam said that the newspaper industry, in its attempts to diversify, has merely made cosmetic changes. She said that the industry needs to put forth the same effort to diversify as it expended when it made the transition from typewriters to computer technology. "No mere Band-Aid approach would have gotten us to where we are now—in the high-tech era of satellites and pagination. Similarly, if we are going to truly meet the challenge of diversity, media will have to be leaders in this transformation. Most Americans get their information about people of color from the media, and when those images are not just negative but often false and misleading, the media are contributing to a very serious social problem."

DIVERSITY IN CULTURAL REPORTING: A COMMITMENT TO CHANGE

Clearly, reporters of the 1990s and beyond face the challenge of reporting with depth, consistency, accuracy and feeling in a nation that is culturally and ethnically diverse. This challenge must be met through diversification of media staffs as well as of coverage itself.

Diversification of Media Staffs

The impetus to diversify media staffs has accelerated in recent years. In 1978, the American Society of Newspaper Editors (ASNE) adopted its "Year 2000 Goal": achieving minority employment at daily newspapers that matches minority representation in the general population of the United States. Each year since 1978, ASNE has conducted an employment survey of the country's dailies. Progress toward the goal has been steady, though unspectacular. Still, it is highly unlikely that minority representation in newsrooms at the turn of the century will match the general population.

According to the 1992 ASNE survey,

Of the 5,121 minority journalists at American dailies, 2,604 (4.78 percent of all journalists working at daily newspapers) were black; 1,431 (2.62 percent) were Hispanic; 915 (1.68 percent) were Asian; and 171 (.31 percent) were Native Americans.

The percentage of minority professionals in newsrooms was 9.4, up seven-tenths of a percentage point from the previous year and about one-third of the way toward matching the general population. In 1978, however, minorities accounted for only 3.95 percent of newsroom forces. At the time of the Watts riots, less than 1 percent of the nation's journalists were minorities.

Of all journalists hired for their first full-time newspaper positions in 1991, 22.7 percent were minorities. Of all interns hired in 1991, 39.6 percent were minorities.

About half of the country's dailies—mainly the smaller-circulation newspapers—have no minorities on their staffs. More than 60 percent of minority journalists work at newspapers with more than 100,000 circulation.

Some newspapers have clearly been aggressive in diversifying their staffs. For example (to name a few), the *Tucson* (Ariz.) *Citizen* lists a minority staff of 26.1 percent; the *Seattle Times* lists 21.1 percent; *USA Today,* 20.8 percent; *Austin* (Texas) *American-Statesman,* 20 percent; *Washington Post,* 17 percent; and the *Los Angeles Times,* 15.7 percent.

In 1991, the overall number of newsroom professionals dropped by 2 percent while the number of minorities rose by 5 percent from the previous year.

David Hawpe, editor of *The Courier-Journal* in Louisville, Ky., and chair of ASNE's minorities committee, was quoted in the 1992 report: "We're not yet doing the kind of thing you brag about. But I do think we've made more progress and I'm happy about that. . . . Editors are determined to hold onto their gain in newsroom diversity, even when they have very little flexibility in hiring." (The inflexibility Hawpe referred to resulted from the recession and the closing of several major newspapers, which created an overall shrinking newspaper force.)

Diversification of Coverage

Many newspapers are making an increasing commitment to strengthen their coverage of minority affairs and to meet the information needs of their demographically changing readers. In 1990, David Shaw, the media critic for the *Los Angeles Times,* put together an impressive four-part series that examined multiculturalism in American newsrooms.

The lead paragraph of one of the installments was an attention-grabber:

Overt racism in the press is rare now, and some newspapers—most notably *USA Today,* others in the Gannett and Knight-Ridder chains and *The Seattle Times*—have even tried as a matter of formal policy to include people of color in the mainstream of their daily coverage. But minority journalists (and many of their white colleagues and supervisors) say the overwhelming majority of press coverage still emphasizes the pathology of minority behavior—drugs, gangs, crime, violence, poverty, illiteracy—almost to the exclusion of normal, everyday life.

Shaw wrote that "the same criticism can be made of press coverage of whites," but still the media generally cover "a much broader range of white life than of minority life."

Shaw's thoroughness in preparing the series is noteworthy. He interviewed more than 175 reporters, editors and publishers from more than two dozen newspapers across the country. Shaw cited the most common criticisms:

> The press too often engages in harmful stereotyping of African-Americans, Latinos, Asian-Americans and Native Americans.
>
> Journalists are generally ignorant of cultural differences.
>
> The press too often uses racially biased or insensitive language.
>
> The media often make unfair comparisons between different ethnic groups.
>
> The media often use unrepresentative minority "spokespersons," often "automatically lumping together all Latinos, or, in particular, all Asian-Americans as a single community, without recognizing the substantial differences in culture and language among the varied elements of those communities."

Shaw concluded that "even the most caustic critics of the press acknowledge that most white journalists mean well; it's not the intent but the results that trigger widespread criticism—and those results stem largely from ignorance, insensitivity, the absence of minority journalists from most newsrooms and, more important, the absence of minorities from most editors' offices."

As Shaw noted, Gannett Co. Inc. is among the nation's leaders in the quest for diversity in newsrooms. In 1991, Gannett—which publishes more than 80 dailies—launched NEWS 2000, a program that encourages its newspapers to improve their "content by keeping up with—and indeed anticipating—the changing needs of readers."

Mark Silverman, director of the NEWS 2000 program and former editor of the *Rockford* (Ill.) *Register Star*, outlined 10 goals for Gannett's newspapers:

1 Center on community interests.
2 Uphold First Amendment responsibilities.
3 *Require* diversity (emphasis added).
4 Utilize compelling presentation.
5 Provide information people need.
6 Evoke emotions.
7 Maintain consistency.
8 Emphasize immediacy.
9 Foster interaction with readers.
10 Anticipate change.

Regarding diversity, Silverman wrote: "Newspapers should mirror the racial, cultural, religious, economic, lifestyle and ethnic diversity of their communities. . . . Newspapers need to give all residents a public voice. What's more, newspaper staffs should mirror the diversity of their communities."

GUIDELINES FOR MEDIA AND REPORTERS

No magic formula exists that would ensure superb coverage of minority affairs and cultural issues. However, some guidelines follow.

Provide Consistent, Daily Coverage

During recent years, many newspapers have increased their coverage of minority affairs. But that coverage, for the most part, is predictable. Often, it focuses on calendar events such as Black History Month, the Chinese New Year and so forth. Many of these stories are good, but they do not put the cultures into context. "Newspapers often cover once-a-year or infrequent happenings," said Felix Gutierrez, who has written extensively on coverage of minority affairs. "Readers are given a view of the culture, but it is not a full vision. Once-a-year festivals do not provide readers with the full context of the community. The coverage should be done on a daily basis."

Mary Lou Fulton of the *Los Angeles Times* also believes that consistent coverage is the key to good cultural reporting. "Too often, newspapers assign reporters to the generic city beat," she said. "Each city, though, consists of neighborhoods that should be covered regularly by beat reporters. Most newspapers never would think of assigning just one or two reporters to cover all of suburbia. It follows that they shouldn't assign a single reporter to cover all of the inner city."

Get to Know the Communities You Cover

"You soon will realize that there are honest differences of opinion and that no one person can expect to speak for an entire race or neighborhood," Gutierrez said. "Just because you have one black source for a story doesn't mean that you have the black viewpoint. You have to go beyond tokenism when you write about communities."

Dorothy Gilliam, the *Washington Post* columnist, said that it is also important to bring people from the community to the newspapers and "really listen to them." Gilliam said that it is imperative for newspapers to have regular exchanges with the people they cover.

Develop Multicultural Links and Friendships

"It is important for students, reporters and editors to take some cross-cultural journeys," Gilliam said. "If newspapers are to cover all aspects of their communities effectively, reporters are going to have to go to places where they might initially feel uncomfortable." For example, whites might visit a black church; Hispanics might go to a function at an African-American college. "The biggest challenge will be for white Americans," Gilliam said. "They have had the luxury throughout the history of this country of telling everybody that they would have to conform to the standards that had been set. As a result, whites have become very insular."

Gutierrez pointed out that everyone has something in common with people of other cultures. "Look for ways to establish links," he said. "You might find those links in where you enjoy eating or the type of music you like."

Expand Coverage beyond the "Problem People" Perspective

"Too often minorities are depicted only as 'problem people,' people beset by problems or people causing problems for the larger society," Gutierrez said. Such stereotypes become entrenched: stories often focus only on the poor, on unwed mothers, on the unemployed. Frequently, reporters use an "up-from-the-ghetto" angle in success stories. "Minorities too often are framed within problems that they have overcome or are trying to overcome," Gutierrez said.

Mainstream Sources for All Stories

The news pages should reflect the fullness of society's cultures. Reporters should find minority sources for stories—pieces about the economy, the weather, the first day of school—and *mainstream* those sources: blend them together with all the others that make up the community.

Caesar Andrews, the executive editor of the *Rockland Journal-News*, said that journalists at *USA Today*, in particular, also understand that visual presentation makes a difference for how people perceive the newspaper. "*USA Today* works to get minorities represented in the images—the photos and graphics—as well as in the stories," he said. "But the paper takes that philosophy one step further: it not only includes people of color in the mix of stories and visuals, but it also makes sure that the stories and visuals end up in prominent places—on page 1 and other section fronts."

In mainstreaming, the burden is on reporters and editors to obtain opinions and quotes on various topics from a mix of people. "Journalists have a tendency to call people they have quoted previously, and the sources tend to be people like them," Andrews said. "All of that is a natural process. I wouldn't criticize that. But there is a great need to go beyond those natural processes, and that is what mainstreaming is all about—getting sources beyond one's natural set."

"The Gannett method of mainstreaming sources could serve as a model," Gilliam said. "All stories should contain multiple sources that reflect the *ethnic and gender mixes* of communities."

Andrews noted that, on a certain level, mainstreaming could look like a gimmick—when one gets into counting sources and faces. "With the focus in the industry on numbers, I think that plays into the perception of some that it merely is a fad," he said. "We need to look past all of that and cut to the chase—to look at the role of newspapers, the role of journalism. We need to cover all of the community. That is really what diversity and mainstreaming are about. Diversity and mainstreaming are not just about techniques. They really go to the heart of how you should cover the community."

Dawn Garcia, state editor of the *San Jose Mercury News* in California, strongly recommends that newspapers develop a master *minority source list* that can be shared by all reporters, not just those covering minority affairs. "To do this," she said, "any reporter who comes across a good source in the minority community—and not just sources who speak for minority interest groups—can type that source's name and number into an alphabetically organized computer file easily accessible to all reporters and editors. This helps reporters avoid the trouble of always using the same person as the 'spokesman for the black community,' for instance, when we all know that the black community is not monolithic.

"This also provides all reporters with a good reference for articulate minorities in many professions—professors, lawyers, union leaders, business owners, doctors, sociologists—the 'experts' that reporters so often rely on when doing daily stories. Too often, reports rely on the same white men as their 'experts,' overlooking many qualified minorities who should be portrayed in stories other than minority-issue stories."

Periodically Assess the Representativeness of Sources

During performance reviews, some editors evaluate how well reporters have diversified sources in their stories over a period of time. Reporters must be constantly reminded that a variety of sources are important in diverse communities in order to paint an accurate picture of topics.

Don't "Overcredential" Sources

If you call a source a "Latino leader," for example, make sure that the person, on the basis of his or her credentials, really is a leader. Lazy journalists who do not bother to consult multiple sources often resort to the term *leader* whether or not it is accurate.

Recognize That There Is Diversity within Cultures

Reporters should not put people under the same umbrella just because they look the same or have names that sound the same. "There are a lot of similarities among different groups in our society," Gutierrez said. "But there also are some distinctive differences among people within the same culture." Just as foreign correspondents need to be aware of the various cultures they must cover, city beat reporters should approach diversity in multicultural societies with the same level of understanding and sophistication.

Bring Your Own Perspective to the Newsroom

Andrews emphasized that journalists should not be afraid to let their special perspectives show through. "Often when people start in newsrooms there is an expectation of conformity," he said. "You are judged on how you conform to the people already in place. There is, indeed, a need to have a newsroom culture, but it should not be at the expense of killing the special qualities and perspectives of individuals. The individual has to struggle to make sure that his or her special perspective [on story ideas, for example] is not crowded out by the overriding culture of the newsroom. This advice really applies to all journalists, but it is especially important to minority journalists. Too often they are expected to think just the same as everybody else. Sometimes, then, you end up without a net gain in perspective in the newsroom."

Andrews also emphasized that once newspapers are committed to inclusivity and their reporters have a high degree of sensitivity, those newspapers must still be willing to practice hard-hitting journalism. "That means that you can't back off of things that need to be covered," he said. "Good coverage doesn't mean doing all positive stories and eliminating the so-called negative stories. I think you should cover all of the above. Some people can become a little hypersensitive about covering certain realities. That shouldn't be the case either. Covering things that aren't so good is not bad—that is part of the job. The bad part is not covering the other stuff: the achievements, accomplishments and success stories of day-to-day life."

IMPROVING COVERAGE: A CHECKLIST

Presenters at the 1992 seminar on "riot & reconstruction: covering the continuing story" distributed a checklist for improving news coverage. The tips were adapted from recommendations of *The Seattle Times'* Racial Awareness Pilot Project; Sandy Rivera, KHOU-TV, Houston; Sherrie Mazingo, a journalism professor at the University of Southern California; and Mervin Aubespin of *The Courier-Journal* in Louisville, Ky.

- Have I covered the story with sensitivity, accuracy, fairness and balance regarding all of the people involved?
- What are the likely consequences of publication? Who will be hurt and who will be helped?
- Have I sought a diversity of sources for this story?
- Am I seeking true diversity or using *tokenism* by allowing one minority person to represent a community or point of view?
- Have I allowed preconceived ideas to limit my efforts to include diversity?
- Am I flexible about the possibility that the focus of the story may change when different sources are included?
- Have I thought about using quotes from minority experts in non-traditional fields? (For example, a black lawyer, a Hispanic accountant or an Asian physician can be consulted for quotes in general stories.) Creating a minority source list is highly advisable.
- Have I spent time in minority communities and with residents to find out what people are thinking and to learn more about lifestyles, perspectives, customs, etc.?
- Have I written about achievements on their own merits, rather than as "stereotype breakers"?
- Have I guarded against allowing place names to become code words for crime?

- As I seek diversity, am I being true to my other goals as a journalist?
- Will I be able to explain my decision clearly and honestly to anyone who challenges it—and not to rationalize?

A MULTICULTURAL REPORTER AT WORK: DAWN GARCIA'S STRATEGIES

Dawn Garcia, the *San Jose Mercury News* state editor, wrote scores of minority-issue stories when she was a projects reporter for the *San Francisco Chronicle.* During her five years at the *Chronicle,* she was involved in both short- and long-term projects, about half of which involved *minority-affairs reporting.*

As a projects reporter, she was not immune from covering daily stories. "I once covered a bank robbery simply because I was the first person in the office and the editors needed someone quickly," she said. "Another time I was available to do a breaking story on a toxic spill in the Sacramento River that poisoned some of the most pristine water in California."

Garcia didn't start her career at the *Chronicle* as a projects reporter. She was hired as a general assignment reporter and quickly took on major front-page stories, including the October 1986 earthquake in El Salvador. She was selected as lead reporter to cover San Francisco Mayor Art Agnos' first two years in office before she took a short leave for a journalism fellowship in Mexico. When she returned, she joined a four-person investigative team that produced a number of award-winning projects.

The *Chronicle* does not have a minority beat per se, but as many as three reporters devote considerable time and energy specifically to covering minority affairs. One reporter, for example, covers local Asian issues while another works on articles that paint a bigger picture of Asian affairs, such as Pacific Rim stories. Garcia was never appointed "minority-affairs reporter." "But in journalism, you often gravitate toward things you are interested in, so I often did broader stories on minority affairs," she said. "That included doing stories on Mexican and Central American immigrants. I was particularly interested in those issues and I speak Spanish."

Garcia stressed that the *Chronicle's* reporting of minority affairs extends beyond stories produced by reporters who specialize in *ethnic coverage.* "Because California has such a large minority population, on a daily basis reporters who have beats completely unrelated to minority affairs still often end up doing minority-related stories," she said.

No particular organizational structure guarantees effective coverage of minority affairs. "I don't know that any newspaper has found the perfect balance yet," she said. "Newspapers still are struggling to find the best way to cover minority affairs with the proper background and perspective. The *Chronicle* setup is serviceable and it works mainly because the reporters take an interest and strive to write good stories.

"A problem you can run into when you designate a minority-beat reporter is that other reporters might hesitate to get involved in the coverage. Minority-affairs reporting can cross all kinds of beats; all reporters should be capable of and interested in doing the stories. There can be a fear that the story will be 'ghettoized' in the paper. Another problem newspapers should avoid is creating what sometimes is called the 'taco beat,' where a Hispanic reporter covers only Hispanic issues. Certainly, though, you need reporters with an understanding of ethnic communities and people who speak the language."

Garcia noted that the Asian community is particularly difficult to cover in California because it includes so many cultures. "You've got many, many languages and cultures, and no one person can handle them all. Papers have to find their way little by little as they develop effective minority-affairs coverage. I think, though, that all reporters, regardless of their beats, should have a piece of covering minority affairs. Minority-affairs reporting is as much an ongoing awareness of potential stories as it is a beat."

Garcia's minority-issue reporting has been varied and has included investigative, enterprise and daily stories. In an impressive two-part investigative series, she reported on fraud and abuse in a federal minority-business program that cheated minority businesses and made contractors rich. In an enterprise story on how Cinco de Mayo had become so popular, she eschewed the trite approach of "featurizing" the holiday in favor of examining its historical roots and the "multimillion-dollar extravaganza" marketing professionals have made it. Her daily stories on deadline covered topics such as the increasing number of undocumented, single women immigrants in the Bay Area.

Many of Garcia's stories have centered on trends and changing patterns. Even when the focus of a story is on minority affairs, the impact of the issues explored generally goes far beyond the ethnic community being examined. Changing demographics and the concomitant evolution of minority issues and concerns often have a profound impact on entire communities. Logically, then, minority-affairs stories both deserve and command attention in newspapers.

A Story on Citizenship

In one article, for example, Garcia provided an expanded interpretation of a report issued by a national Latino political organization, showing that fewer immigrants wanted to become citizens of the United States.

Garcia used a contrast lead paragraph, a vivid direct quotation and a streamlined nut graph (the "so what" peg of the story) to lure readers into her article in the *San Francisco Chronicle*:

For Marina Castillo, who fled gunfire in her native El Salvador in 1981, becoming a U.S. citizen was an important step to personal freedom. But now, as an immigration counselor in San Francisco, she finds that many newcomers are not following her path.

"Sometimes they just smile and say, 'No thanks, for me it's no different if I am a citizen or not,'" said Castillo. "They don't know the opportunities of citizenship. They think it's just safer to stay away from the INS, who could deport them if they find something wrong in their citizenship application."

Such attitudes have caught the attention of Congress and immigrant rights groups concerned that the number of legal immigrants who become citizens is lagging far behind the recent boom in immigration. According to the U.S. Census, the pool of adults who are not citizens has increased in the past decade from 6.3 million to more than 9.6 million.

Garcia then relied on statistics and quotes from several additional sources as she developed her story. She paved the way for readers with this transition paragraph:

> As the number of foreigners reaches an all-time high in the United States, this growing class of noncitizens poses long-term consequences for both the United States and the immigrants themselves.

Garcia went on to place the issue in historical perspective (in 1944, for example, 441,979 people became American citizens; in 1989, only 233,777 became citizens). She also discussed the procedures, advantages and disadvantages of seeking citizenship; and she examined the sometimes strained relationships between immigrants and the U.S. Immigration and Naturalization Service (INS).

Garcia got the idea for her story from a news release that summarized a report of the National Association of Latino Elected and Appointed Officials. One question—Why are fewer immigrants seeking citizenship?—captured her attention. She called the Washington-based organization to ask for a copy of the entire report. After digesting all the information in the report, Garcia decided to talk to officials of the organization and to groups that help immigrants who want to become citizens. She asked to meet with some of the immigrants who had sought assistance in their quest for citizenship.

"I was able to interview some immigrants in the Bay Area," she said. "It is often difficult to find people who are here illegally—or those who are legal but are not yet citizens—who are willing to be interviewed. So you sometimes can go through an organization to gain access to the people. I was able to find a few who had had experiences with INS offices. There were stories going around about people who had encountered problems with the INS. It struck me that INS might not be doing its job—it might not have been adequately helping and promoting people who wanted to become citizens."

Garcia sought to determine why people were not willing or able to become citizens—a factor that ultimately has an impact on American society. "What does it mean when we have people who are not able to vote and to exercise all their rights as citizens?" Garcia wondered. "Does it somehow take away a feeling for them of having a stake in American society? I think that question has some long-term as well as immediate consequences, and I wanted to emphasize that in my story."

When reporters develop minority-affairs stories, they need to broaden the impact. As interesting as an issue may be to the group being covered, it may not interest other readers, who might conclude erroneously that it doesn't affect them. Reporters must strive to find ways to step back, to examine the story and to convey to readers that the issue might affect more people than merely one culture or one enclave.

Garcia's story on the declining number of immigrants who were seeking citizenship was an effective combination of statistics, examples and vivid direct quotations from people in authority on both sides of the issue. "You should not merely take a press release that crosses your desk and rewrite it," she said. "Mere numbers usually don't mean much to readers. You need to insert human angles and emphasize broader perspectives."

A Story on a Changing Neighborhood

In another story published in the *Chronicle,* Garcia and Lisa Chung homed in on the fear of San Francisco Hispanics that the city's Mission District was losing its Latin flavor. Their story illustrates the impact changing demographics can have on an area. Their four-paragraph lead block culminated with the story's nut graph:

> Young Latino civic leaders in San Francisco's Mission District, for nearly 30 years the heart and soul of the Bay Area's Hispanic community, are on a crusade to preserve it as a hub of Latino culture.
>
> As Hong Kong investors, Asian grocers and bohemian artists discover the neighborhood—attracted by its sunny weather, relatively affordable housing and busy shopping districts—longtime residents are voicing fears that the district's strong Latino flavor is being diluted.
>
> Reflecting its growing diversity, the Mission District now includes San Francisco's first distinctly lesbian neighborhood along Valencia Street. With its women-oriented businesses, the area has become a cultural and social center for lesbians from throughout the city.
>
> The demographic changes in the Mission have been noted by a group of young, energetic, college-educated Latino merchants and neighborhood organizers. They say they appreciate the Mission's growing diversity, but they are organizing an effort to preserve the core of the neighborhood as a cultural mecca for Latinos.

Garcia and Chung went on to do several other things. They included several direct quotations from residents. One quotation was particularly vivid:

> "We're just trying to hold onto our turf," said Roberto Hernandez, 34, president of Mission Economic and Cultural Association and leader in the move to revitalize the Latino center of the Mission. "Our parents built the neighborhood and we, the young Chicanos, have a responsibility to preserve it."

They also explained the plans organizers had to preserve the district's culture (by developing everything from Latin-style "mercados" to Mexican art galleries), and they described how the neighborhood organizers were working with the San Francisco Convention and Visitors Bureau.

They contrasted, through description, the district today with what it had been only a few years ago. This section of the story was introduced effectively by a transition:

> Standing at 16th and Mission Streets, Hernandez can see a neighborhood vastly different from the place where he sold tamales on the church steps for youth group fund-raisers years ago.

They discussed how the changing demographics of the district "have required some adaptation by businesses trying to overcome cultural barriers," such as Asian business owners learning Spanish.

The story concluded with the following direct quote from a third-generation resident:

"It'll take a long time before you stop hearing Spanish in the Mission," he said. "We have to roll with the changes, accept them, adapt to them and make it positive for the overall well-being of San Francisco."

Garcia decided that she wanted to write the Mission District story when, after she had been reporting on the area for several years, she started to notice an increasing number of Asian businesses. "I realized that something was evolving there," she said. "At the same time, I was interviewing and talking with a number of people in the district because I had heard there was going to be a formal push to retain at least a corridor that was largely Latino in character and nature."

Garcia didn't know the Asian community as well as Chung, who was working with her. "We soon discovered that there was some animosity among both the Asian and Latino merchants," Garcia said.

When Garcia pitched the story idea to her editor, he wondered whether life was getting violent in the district. "He almost seemed disappointed when I said it was not," Garcia recalled. "This story was much more subtle. Newspapers need to get away from covering minority issues strictly from the standpoint of crime and people fighting. Different kinds of struggles need to be covered." Chung and Garcia did not want to blow the story out of proportion. Violence had not erupted, but an important shift was evolving. That development was newsworthy.

The reporters soon discovered that some merchants were starting to work together in the neighborhood—people were cooperating and "breaking away from the stereotype of conflict," Garcia said. "Some of the Asian merchants who were coming into the neighborhood realized that they had to learn at least a little Spanish to talk to their customers. Some of the Latino merchants also were trying to reach out to the Asian merchants to bring them into their organizations."

Reactions to Garcia's story on the Mission District were both positive and negative. "Whenever you do stories on minority affairs you will find they often are sensitive and difficult," Garcia said. "And as sensitive as you try to be, sometimes you write things that people might interpret differently from what you meant."

Garcia said there was a lot of good reaction. People in the Mission District often complain that they don't get written about as much as those in the middle-class and white areas of the city. Many people appreciated the fact that the story was written at all.

However, one Mission District resident, Roberto Hernandez, complained about the use of his statement concerning the need for Latinos to protect their "turf." "He said it but he didn't like it when I used that quote," Garcia said. "He said it conjured up gang images. He took a lot of heat in his community for saying that. It is a loaded word. When I wrote it I frankly didn't think someone would connect that word to gangs because the story was not about gangs. I certainly didn't think about that angle. All reporters can do, though, is reflect accurately what sources say and try to be fair."

To further complicate matters, a photo accompanied the story that showed Hernandez and some other fairly young neighborhood people who were behind the push for revitalization. They were standing together in an intersection of the district. "It was a nice photo but those in it thought it made them look too mean," Garcia said. "Some weren't smiling. That, coupled with the quote about protecting turf, conveyed to some of them that we were trying to stereotype them as young toughs trying to take over the neighborhood."

Garcia said that reporters should always be conscious of loaded words like *turf*. "It was such an appealing, strong, clear word to convey what he meant that it was a great quote," Garcia said. "But I did not think about the connection between turfs and gangs until after he pointed it out. I wrote the story because I have an interest in that area and not because I was trying to make people look like thugs. It is sometimes painful when things like that happen, but you just have to try to explain to your sources that it was not your intent."

A Story on Political Involvement

Another story written by Garcia illustrates how changes within an ethnic culture can have an impact on the larger society. Garcia began her story with a block of paragraphs that put into perspective the growing involvement of Hispanic women in politics:

In a traditionally male-dominated culture, Hispanic women are quietly emerging as political leaders, hoping to increase the political clout of the nation's 20 million Hispanics.

Although Latinas have long been the faceless workhorses in Hispanic politics—organizing fund-raisers, walking door-to-door through San Francisco's Mission District and other largely Hispanic neighborhoods to register new voters—they are now taking on new, higher-profile roles that they have been excluded from in the past.

"I think for years we have been involved in the campaigns of others, and it's our turn," said Rosario Anaya, a Bolivian native who was the first Hispanic woman in San Francisco elected to public office in 1978.

She is now running for a third term on the San Francisco Board of Education, along with another Hispanic woman, Carlota del Pontillo.

Garcia provided examples of increasing political participation by Hispanic women in California and around the country. She reported that Hispanic women are still underrepresented in politics but that "a promising cadre of Hispanic women candidates is waiting in the wings after years of work in the lower-level political trenches."

Garcia used her interviewing skills to solicit quotes from women who had become involved in politics. She intertwined the direct quotes with additional statistics and background information. She closed her story by discussing some of the obstacles that have kept Hispanic women from gaining political offices in greater numbers. The story ended with a direct quote from a candidate:

> "Some Latino men are very committed to helping Latinas get into politics, but it's hard to get others very fired up about supporting women," [the candidate] said. "There's still that traditional thinking that women aren't the power holders, and men aren't so quick to write those campaign contribution checks."

Garcia noted that journalists are sometimes afraid to write about touchy subjects such as norms within minority cultures. But she got the idea for her story on the role of Hispanic women in politics when she accompanied two of them on a voter-registration walk. The women were the "workhorses" that Garcia mentioned in the story. "They had jobs but they went out on weekends door-to-door to try to register people to vote," Garcia said. "My sense was that these women were playing the background roles that Latino women had been playing for quite a while but that some were poised to play a bigger role in politics. I hadn't seen a story on that possibility and I concluded it would be a good one."

The story was delicate. "I suppose that having the last name Garcia made me feel a little more comfortable," she said. "It helped my story in that possibly the women told me things they wouldn't have told someone else. That is, not only did many of these women feel that they were struggling to try to make it in politics, like all Latino politicians; but also, there was a sense that within Latino politics women have not come as far as they would like. I thought the story was fascinating and I wanted to get a flavor of how sensitive it was."

However, one problem for reporters with last names such as *Garcia* is having minority sources assume that the reporter will empathize with the source—to the point of being an advocate for the minority community rather than a journalist. While minority journalists are often more sensitive to the concerns of minority communities than white journalists, they often need to make it clear to their sources that they have a job to do: report the news accurately.

Garcia described her article on political participation as "pretty much a phone story"—unlike the Mission District piece, where she did a lot of walking in the streets to capture the feel of the neighborhood. "I conducted face-to-face interviews with some of the women walking door-to-door and one of the women running for office," Garcia said. "But I interviewed most of the others by phone, which is a fairly typical approach on a political story. You simply can't go flying all over to meet your sources. There is not time."

Garcia's articles illustrate how important it is to humanize stories. "You need people in your stories," she said. "Too often we talk about minorities and im-

department heads report to him. The city manager is the single best source of information in the city."

- *Management services director.* "The management services director is responsible for the budget, for setting tax rates and for adjusting the fees that the city charges for things such as turning on water. He reports directly to the city manager and then to the council. If you want numbers, he's the guy who crunches them."

- *City clerk.* "She is the right arm of the city manager. The city clerk and two assistants coordinate all the meeting schedules, keep the public records and handle the paperwork for all the boards and commissions. The office is a repository for all sorts of information and is a good source on any subject."

- *City attorney.* "The city attorney handles all legal questions for the city, writes all the ordinances and resolutions and helps lobby the legislature. He handles all claims against the city—from a garbage truck knocking a brick out of a garden wall to discrimination-in-hiring suits. He is a great source on just about everything."

- *Community development director.* "He handles all planning matters for the city. He is responsible for overseeing and approving projects to be constructed. This is a hot spot because Tempe is in the throes of a big development boom. The city led the state in industrial permits issued last year and in multifamily starts. All planning must be approved first by the council-appointed planning and zoning commission. Then most projects go to design review and finally to the city council. Projects are approved in phases, first a site plan if rezoning is required and then a final plan when building permits are ready to be issued."

- *Community services director.* "He oversees the parks, youth programs, pools, tennis courts, library, bookmobile program, museum operation and acquisition and is assisted by the parks board, the museum board, the golf board and the library board. The members of these boards are appointed by the city council."

- *Public works director.* "He heads the city's nuts and bolts departments, and so he gets the most complaints. He is responsible for keeping streets clean and in good repair, garbage collection, water and sewer treatment and traffic planning, among other things. Like all department heads, the public works director reports to the city manager."

- *Fire chief.* "The fire chief runs a paramilitary department. The fire department is not part of my city beat."

- *Police chief.* "The police department also is a paramilitary organization. The chief heads the department, which is not part of my city beat."

- *Presiding judge.* "Although the police and courts work closely together, they are very separate departments. The police enforce the law (usually city ordinances or state laws), and the courts interpret it. Police and court beats usually are separate from the city government beat, as they are at the *Tempe Daily News Tribune*. The presiding judge (also called a magistrate) pulls double duty. He not only rules on cases but hires and fires court personnel, orders stationery, schedules court time and coordinates with the police."

- *Human resources.* "This is a one-man department. He puts together benefits packages, handles insurance and does all the hiring except for the police and fire departments and department heads."

Clearly, Flynn's grasp of the system and of the people in it makes it possible for her to report quickly and comprehensively on Tempe city government. The lesson is clear: you can't report on a system until you understand it.

A DAY ON THE CITY BEAT

Flynn said that there is no typical day when covering city government. "The smaller the paper, the more your beat crosses over into others, because there just aren't enough reporters to go around," she said. "I cover some police issues, do a smattering of features, cover awards ceremonies, plus all the boards and commissions. I also cover Tempe's state legislators and Tempe's U.S. congressman. I also occasionally cover a fire, a traffic accident or a hazardous waste spill."

Flynn's hours vary, depending on the meetings she has to cover. But she's usually in the office by 9 a.m. "The first thing I do is read our paper," she said. "I get all my gripes about how my stories were treated out of the way, read the editorials in case someone asks me about them and find out what's going on in other people's beats in case I have to cover for them.

"Next, I read the competition. If I have been beaten on anything, I hustle to catch up. Fortunately, because all we cover is Tempe, we rarely get beaten on the day-to-day stuff. On some of the bigger stories, we get shelled because we don't have the resources in Washington, D.C., or Costa Rica or even the state capital."

Flynn then checks her *story budget*—a list of articles she is to work on—and her date book. "I probably do 70 percent of my work by telephone. I get on the horn and call the sources for my stories and ask them all kinds of stupid questions until I understand what they're talking about."

She likes to deal with her primary City Hall sources face to face. "It is harder for people to lie to you when you're sitting across from them," she said. "I always get better and more information in a face-to-face interview than I do on the phone."

Flynn checks in at City Hall at least twice each day—even if she has absolutely nothing to talk about. "This is a terrific way to get story ideas," she said. "It also keeps you informed of ongoing issues and lets the people know you are around."

While at City Hall, Flynn reads the agendas for posted meetings to see which ones she might sit in on and possibly write about. By midafternoon she is usually back in the office, where she writes her stories for the following day's paper. "The *Daily News Tribune* likes us to keep our stories short, and so my stories average about 12 to 15 inches," Flynn said. "Unless it is a really big issue, I never write more than 20 inches."

After she writes her stories, Flynn checks her date book for the next day's schedule and assigns art to accompany stories she is working on, particularly features. She then writes her next day's budget. Occasionally, she is home by 6 p.m. Usually, however, she is still in the office, reworking a story, rewriting or localizing wire copy and eating dinner while waiting to go to a meeting.

The Tempe City Council meets every Thursday night. The planning and zoning commission meets Tuesdays, design review meets Wednesdays and other boards compete for attention on the remaining nights. Most of the meetings do not end until 9:30 or 10 o'clock. By the time Flynn gets back to the office and writes her story for the next morning's newspaper, it is usually 11 o'clock.

"I love it, though," Flynn said. "The variety of stories is stimulating. Working for a small newspaper keeps you busy constantly, and even dull meetings seem interesting when you know what goes on behind the scenes."

CITY COUNCIL MEETINGS

An important aspect of covering city government is reporting on city council meetings. For example, one of Adrianne Flynn's primary assignments is coverage of the Tempe City Council. Let's look at her handling of this assignment.

BEFORE THE MEETING

The Agenda

Reporters who cover city council meetings should always pick up, *before* the meeting, a copy of the *agenda*—an outline of matters to be considered. The agenda for the Thursday night meetings of the Tempe City Council is available to Flynn after 5 p.m. on Tuesdays.

Here is an agenda for a Tempe City Council meeting that Flynn covered:

7:00—1. STUDIES AND SURVEYS—Mobile Home Parks—Committee Report

7:20—2. PLANNED DEVELOPMENT—Warner Ranch Village—Plan Modification UDC, SE & SWC Warner Rd/ Warner Ranch Rd

7:40—3. STUDIES AND SURVEYS—Aircraft Noise, Michael Brandman Report

8:00—4. PARKS—Tempe Soccer Club—Request for use of Diablo Stadium for Thanksgiving Tournament (Please bring booklets delivered to you)

8:15—5. ADMINISTRATION AND POLICY MANAGEMENT—Real Estate Signs, Police Enforcement

8:30—6. COMMUNITY SERVICES FACILITIES/ACTIVITIES—Latchkey Program, Mary Lou Burem

8:45—7. PARKS—Rolling Hills

9:00—8. ZONING AMENDMENT—Mixed-Use Parking Formula

9:20—9. REAL PROPERTY MANAGEMENT—Use of Parking Garage

9:30—10. ENVIRONMENT—Noise Ordinance Proposed Modification

9:40—11. PUBLIC SAFETY—Fire Truck Bid

9:45—12. STREETS—Street Name Change

9:55—Adjourn

The Pre-Meeting Story

Flynn usually reads the agenda on Tuesday night and writes a pre-meeting story on Wednesday. Because she covers the council regularly, she seldom finds an agenda item that surprises or confuses her. When this occurs, however, she calls appropriate city officials for background. Her pre-meeting stories are published in Thursday's edition.

Flynn's pre-meeting stories normally focus on what she projects to be the most important item on the agenda. After discussing this issue in the first few paragraphs of her story, Flynn uses bullets (•) to precede a synopsis of other agenda items. Her pre-meeting story this time led with the fact that a consultant would report the results of a study concerning airplane noise over Tempe.

The noise issue had been a long-running news story. Articles had been written when the consulting firm was commissioned to study the problem. Thus, it was logical that the report would be of interest to readers.

The Reporter's Preparation

Preparation is essential before covering a city council meeting. To prepare for a meeting, reporters should review the agenda and should talk to council members and other city officials about any "hidden" issues that may surface.

Flynn always does this. "Most of the issues have already been discussed at study sessions (the Tempe council meets for one hour before regular meetings)," she said. "Because reporters can attend the study sessions, most of us have ample background on the issues before they are considered formally at the regular meetings."

Reporters are not, however, allowed to attend *executive sessions* of the council (meetings at which no official action can be taken and from which members of the press and public are excluded). State laws specify the types of items that can be considered in executive sessions. Many times, when a council goes into executive session, it is to discuss personnel matters or financial matters such as the purchase of property.

Reporters can often find sources who will tell them what occurred at executive sessions on the condition that it cannot be printed or that it can be printed but not attributed. "I have a couple of good sources who trust me," Flynn said. "I can usually get them to tell me what happened during the session. If it is not of earth-shattering importance, I hold off until it comes up at a regular meeting. But by finding out about it ahead of time, I can be better prepared to deal with the issue when it does come before the public."

WRITING THE MEETING STORY

Occasionally, items will surface at council meetings that turn out to be more important than the projected primary topic. That was not the case this time, however.

An Inverted-Pyramid Story

Flynn wrote her meeting story in an inverted pyramid, with a summary lead that focused on the report on noise:

Tempe is getting most of the noise pollution and too little of the benefits from Phoenix Sky Harbor International Airport, a consultant told the City Council Thursday.

"It seems to me you deserve to have the noise levels reduced," said Sam Lane, a consultant with Michael Brandman Associates. "They are dumping their noise garbage all over you, and you're having to clean up the garbage and you're not getting paid for it."

After Flynn presented readers with the thrust of the report and a vivid direct quotation in the first two paragraphs, she provided background:

Lane's company was hired by Tempe to study the airport noise problem and to recommend technical solutions. A second consultant, Stewart Udall, is considering political solutions and will submit his report to the city within a month.

After this background paragraph, Flynn continued with more new facts from the report:

Lane said Tempe derives about 10 percent of the economic benefits from Sky Harbor while receiving about 75 percent of its noise. He said the situation will not improve without city action.

Lane said predictions made 10 years ago are far short. Sky Harbor's daily departures are now almost twice those estimates.

He said city and citizen action will "break the monopoly" that the airport and the Federal Aviation Administration have on information. He also said Sky Harbor has insulated itself and is "beholden to the airline industry, not to the general public, even though federal money has been used by them in the past."

"The cost and the benefits are not equitable," Lane said. He recommended Tempe focus on what he considered immediate solutions.

Among these solutions are to send more flights to the west over Phoenix, to require aircraft to follow the river bottom longer before turning and to reduce low-altitude approaches over Tempe.

The council will study the proposals while waiting for Udall's report. It also will wait for analysis by Tempe's Airport Noise Abatement Committee, which will consider Lane's report April 9. ANACOM will meet at 7:30 p.m. in Pyle Adult Recreation Center, 655 E. Southern.

Flynn devoted nearly half of her main meeting story to the issue of airport noise. This is common when one topic is of overriding importance. Because none of the remaining items considered by the council merited expanded treatment, Flynn employed a writing device that many reporters use when covering meetings where multiple issues are discussed. Flynn wrote:

In other action, the council:

Those transitional words opened the door for a brief discussion of other council issues. Flynn used a bullet to precede each separate item, thus providing a concise, capsulized overview of how the council treated them. Here is part of the remainder of Flynn's story to illustrate this common, punchy style:

• Reviewed the final report of the Ad Hoc Commission on Mobile Home Parks. The group was formed to give mobile home park tenants more rights through recommended changes in state and local law. It asked for more time to read the report and will make recommendations at a future meeting.

• Gave informal approval to a proposal by Universal Development Corporation to change plans for Warner Ranch Village condominiums. The company wants to make the units smaller and wants to bypass Planning and Zoning Commission approval for the change.

• Gave informal approval to a request by the community development department that confiscated illegal signs be considered non-returnable abandoned property. The signs now are locked in a city maintenance yard.

• Reviewed a proposal by the Community Services Department to run a program for latchkey children—kids that are left alone after school until their parents return from work. The report was for the council's information only.

Note that Flynn was careful to write grammatical bulleted items. Because she included the subject (*council*) in her introductory phrase (*In other action, the council:*), she started each bulleted entry with a verb.

A Broadcast Version

Broadcast reporters also cover city council meetings. Because of time limitations, their stories are not as lengthy or as detailed as newspaper accounts. Thus, broadcast reporters must work hard to capture the thrust of the meeting in a short, conversational story.

Here is a broadcast version of the Tempe City Council meeting:

DAILY FLIGHT DEPARTURES FROM PHOENIX'S SKY HARBOR INTERNATIONAL AIRPORT ARE ALMOST DOUBLE WHAT THEY WERE PROJECTED TO BE A DECADE AGO. THAT'S GOOD NEWS FOR THE PHOENIX AREA ECONOMY BUT BAD NEWS FOR TEMPE RESIDENTS WHO ARE GETTING MORE THAN THEIR SHARE OF AIRPORT NOISE.

THE TEMPE CITY COUNCIL IS LOOKING INTO THE PROBLEM. A CONSULTANT TOLD THE COUNCIL TONIGHT THAT TEMPE GETS ABOUT 10 PERCENT OF THE ECONOMIC BENEFITS OF THE AIRPORT, BUT IT RECEIVES ABOUT 75 PERCENT OF ITS NOISE.

CONSULTANT SAM LANE TOLD THE COUNCIL THE CITY WAS BEING SHORTCHANGED. LANE PUT IT THIS WAY: "THEY ARE DUMPING THEIR NOISE GARBAGE ALL OVER YOU, AND YOU'RE HAVING TO CLEAN UP THE GARBAGE, AND YOU'RE NOT GETTING PAID FOR IT."

THE COUNCIL IS WAITING ON REPORTS FROM ANOTHER CONSULTANT AND FROM A CITIZENS' COMMITTEE. POSSIBLE SOLUTIONS TO THE TEMPE NOISE PROBLEM INCLUDE HAVING THE AIRPORT DIVERT MORE TRAFFIC TO THE WEST OVER THE CITY OF PHOENIX.

AFTER THE MEETING

Writing a complete, understandable story on a city council meeting requires not only diligent preparation before the meeting but also industrious, painstaking checking of facts after the meeting.

City council meetings are often a study in chaos and confusion. To write a good story, reporters must follow up with lots of questions; and double-checking of facts is essential. For example, sometimes a vote count is in doubt and must be checked with the meeting recorder.

THE CITY BUDGET PROCESS

One of the most important tasks undertaken by a city government each year is the development and the implementation of a financial budget—and one of the most important aspects of covering city government is reporting on the budget process.

We'll now consider the budget process in Tempe, and Adrianne Flynn's coverage of it.

COVERING THE STEPS IN THE BUDGET PROCESS

In Tempe, the fiscal year runs from July 1 to June 30, but the budget process for the next fiscal year begins in late November or in early December and is spread over nearly seven months.

Here are the steps in Tempe's budget process, which are similar to those in the budget processes of other cities:

1   Individual departments compile budgets with requested increases and justification.

2   Departments submit budgets to the management services director. The management services director compiles the total requests and matches them with financial resource projections to identify the preliminary total budget targets. This preliminary budget is the basis for the city manager's recommendations, which are submitted to the city council.

3   The council sees the preliminary budget in a study session, usually an all-day affair, where major policy items are considered.

4   Management services takes the direction given by the council during the study session and incorporates it into a more formal budget proposal. Any questions at this point go back to the council in a study session for more direction.

5   After the questions or concerns are resolved, a tentative budget gets a formal hearing at a regular council session. If no objections are raised, the tentative budget is approved.

6   Once the tentative budget is approved, a second public hearing is scheduled. The tentative budget, once adopted, cannot be increased through any subsequent changes.

7 The final budget is approved by formal city council action.

8 The amount of property tax revenue to be raised is submitted to the county assessor, who sets the tax rate on the basis of the assessed valuation of property within the city limits.

9 After the tax rate is set, another public hearing is held at a council meeting. If no more questions are raised, the budget passes.

All of these steps, which vary slightly among communities, are potentially newsworthy.

DEVELOPING SOURCES OF INFORMATION

When covering the budget process for the first time, it is wise to seek the counsel of various city officials and editors or news directors. Flynn had been introduced to budgets in college, but when she was thrown head first into the budget reporting process, she went to her best sources in city government. She talked, for example, to the mayor, the city clerk, the city attorney and the management services director.

"I said, 'Look, I'm a novice, and I've had little experience in covering the budget process,'" Flynn noted. "I asked officials to explain it to me. I tried to sit down an hour or so with them. Once you understand the process, it is relatively easy to plug in the numbers."

Flynn found Tempe's management services director, Jerry Geiger, to be her best source. "He's more than a number cruncher," she said. "He's an expert on the bureaucracy. He was the key guy in showing me how the process would take place."

Geiger's role as the chief financial officer of Tempe is to prepare a budget the city manager can recommend to the council. Someone like Geiger fills this role in every community. The title for this individual varies. In larger cities, the designation is often *finance director* or *management services director*; in smaller communities, the city clerk often assumes primary responsibility for preparation of the budget.

Reporters need to identify these people and to tap them for budget information—taking full advantage of their expertise. In addition, department heads who submit their individual budget proposals to the finance directors are good sources.

"The average citizen is easily overwhelmed by the budget," Geiger said. "Most people are not totally aware of the organization of local government and of how money is gathered and spent. A budget is a series of numbers—and numbers are sometimes difficult to comprehend and write about. Numbers bore most people.

"I always try to humanize the information when I talk to reporters and other citizens. The best way to do this is to de-emphasize the numbers themselves and to concentrate instead on the level of service that the budget will provide. People want to know how the budget will affect them.

"They might want to know, for example, how many police officers will be on the streets as a result of a budget cutback or increase; they might want to know whether they will have more recreational facilities; and they might want to know if the streets they drive on will be improved. I think readers are more interested in these things than in a mass of line-item figures from a budget."

Indeed, if reporters can present budgetary information in human terms—focusing on the services citizens will receive as a result of expenditures—then the dollar figures are more easily comprehended.

Geiger warns reporters not to get totally embroiled in the figures. Numbers standing alone mean little. Naturally, reporters must have a working knowledge of budgets and of the procedures in forming them, but that is only the first step. The next and most important step is to *explain* the numbers—to tell readers *how* the dollars will affect not only their pocketbooks but their lifestyles. Good sources, like Jerry Geiger, can help them do this.

EXAMINING BUDGETS

Reporters need to know the intent of the budget—that is, the services the city intends to provide—in order to put the dollars into perspective for their readers. Budgeting is a planning process. A budget is a device through which the government entity goes on record with regard to how it will provide services to the community.

"In the old days, there was more distrust of local officials, and the focus of the media was often on line items, such as expenditures for office supplies and the like," Geiger said. "Today, however, the reporting emphasis is more on relating the dollars budgeted and spent to the services provided."

City budget managers develop a total financial program. This total financial program includes two primary types of budgets: capital budgets and operating budgets.

Capital budgets are made up of projects that are often large in magnitude, are long-range in perspective and have a physical presence. Capital budgets earmark dollars for such things as storm drains, streets, water and sewer lines and parks. The capital budget is often referred to as the "hard" budget.

Operating budgets, as the term connotes, provide details on the dollars required to finance government entities on a day-to-day basis. Operating budgets, which are known as "soft" budgets, include funds to pay the salaries of employees as well as money for the paper clips that the employees use.

The two budgets must relate. For example, money to build new parks comes from the capital budget, but money to care for the parks once they are built comes from the operating budget. For the most part, legal constraints will not permit money to be moved from capital budgets to operating budgets, or the other way around.

Tempe's total financial program for a recent fiscal year was nearly $127 million. The operating budget totaled about $95 million; and the capital budget, about $32 million.

Sources that would generate the nearly $127 million for the total financial program are shown in the illustration on page 394. A breakdown of expenditures is shown in the illustration on page 395. These two pie charts illustrate where the money comes from and where it goes. Readers can relate better to a budget the that is divided into major parts than to a staggering total of multiple millions.

Where the Money Comes From

(In Millions)

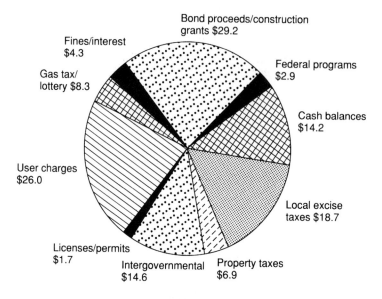

Bond proceeds/construction grants $29.2

Fines/interest $4.3

Gas tax/ lottery $8.3

Federal programs $2.9

Cash balances $14.2

User charges $26.0

Local excise taxes $18.7

Licenses/permits $1.7

Intergovernmental $14.6

Property taxes $6.9

Total $126.8 million

(1) *Bond proceeds/construction grants:* Bond proceeds to support the bonded-debt portion of the capital budget and any other anticipated construction-related grants.

(2) *User charges:* Revenue derived from user charges levied for water, wastewater, refuse, golf courses and irrigation.

(3) *Local excise:* Majority derived from city sales tax ($17.7 million). Remainder from various franchises or in lieu of tax fees.

(4) *Intergovernmental:* Includes state-shared revenues such as state sales, state income and vehicle license tax. Also includes federal revenue sharing.

(5) *Cash balances:* Represents a reduction of "carry-over" cash balances from prior years.

(6) *Gas tax/lottery:* City's share of gasoline taxes and lottery proceeds, both of which are earmarked for transportation-related purposes.

(7) *Property taxes:* Revenue generated by the city property tax rate.

(8) *Fines/interest:* Represents $1 million in traffic/parking fines plus $3.3 million in interest earned on city investments.

(9) *Federal programs:* Revenue received from federal government to support redevelopment and Section 8 housing programs.

(10) *Licenses/permits:* Building permits and business license fees.

Where the Money Goes

(In Millions)

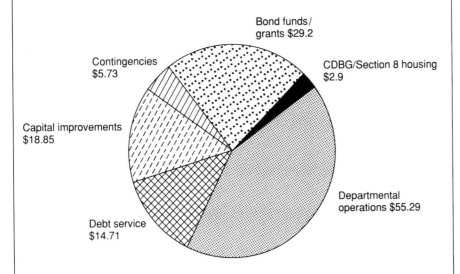

Bond funds/
grants $29.2

Contingencies
$5.73

CDBG/Section 8 housing
$2.9

Capital improvements
$18.85

Departmental
operations $55.29

Debt service
$14.71

Total $126.77 million
(discrepancy caused by rounding)

(1) *Departmental operations:* Includes day-to-day operating costs of all departments within the city. Largest single departments are public works at $25 million and police at $12 million.

(2) *Bond funds/grants:* Bond proceeds to support the bonded-debt portion of the capital budget and any other anticipated construction-related grants.

(3) *Capital improvements:* Represents participation by the city's general operating revenue in support of the capital budget.

(4) *Debt service:* Includes total principal and interest payments on all outstanding debt.

(5) *Contingencies:* Provides a contingency appropriation to meet unforeseen demands on city resources of $4.99 million and $750,000 as non-departmental expenditures.

(6) *CDBG/Section 8 housing:* Recognizes expenditures made in support of the redevelopment and Section 8 housing functions.

City budget:
Breakdown of
expenditures.

It is best for reporters to grasp the broad budget picture before ferreting out and presenting more specific information. The illustrations certainly provide a vivid view, in a general sense, of where Tempe's money comes from and where it goes.

Reporters must decide, on a case-by-case basis, which figures are relevant to readers. Don't strangle readers with numbers. Use judgment to determine which numbers are most relevant. Generally, it would be sufficient, for example, to tell readers that $18.7 million (nearly 15 percent) of the $126.8 million to be generated in Tempe will come from local excise taxes. Most of that, about $17.7 million, will come from the city sales tax. Under most circumstances, there would be little point in breaking down the total further to indicate, for example, that $125,000 of the $18.7 million will come from the cable television franchise tax. If, however, the city had been wrangling with cable television companies over the excise tax, that amount might be pertinent to a budget story.

The reporter who has been diligently following the budget process and who has kept in close touch with sources in City Hall should have a good feel for the numbers that are most relevant and important to readers.

WRITING THE BUDGET STORY

Essential Ingredients of Budget Stories

As the budget process evolves, stories will naturally emphasize different elements. Here, however, is the basic information that should be included in some or all of the stories:

- Bottom line—the total budget (for example, $126.77 million)
- Total of last year's budget (for example, $106 million)
- Percentage increase or decrease (in the above examples, the writer would report an increase of 19.6 percent)
- Breakdown of budget expenditures (which should include details on where the money will be spent—how much will go to the police department, to the city clerk's office and so forth)
- Reasons for the budget increase or decrease (for example, because of a rising crime rate, more money is needed to add 21 officers to the police department)
- Breakdown of budget revenues (report some of the primary sources of revenue: property taxes, $6.9 million; federal programs, $2.9 million; etc.)
- Details on the impact of tax increases or decreases on residents

If property taxes are being raised, for example, the reporter should not merely note that the new budget calls for a property tax rate of $1.15 per $100 of assessed valuation compared with $1.05 for the current year. Those numbers would not mean much to most readers. Instead, the reporter should put the figures into perspective. This can be done by explaining that a tax rate of $1.15 per $100 of assessed valuation equals a rate of $11.50 per $1,000. Therefore property taxes on a house assessed at $40,000 would be $460, an additional $40 a year; and taxes on a house assessed at $75,000 would be $862.50, an increase of $75. The reporter could also note, for example, that a tax increase will mean that swimming pools will be open longer hours, that new tennis courts will be built and that downtown roads will be resurfaced. Or, if appropriate, the reporter could note that, because of inflation, higher taxes are needed merely to maintain the status quo.

Property taxes are only one source of revenue for municipalities. The graph on page 394, for example, shows that Tempe needs to raise $6.9 million from property taxes, about 5.4 percent of its $126.8 million total. In some cities, property taxes account for a much larger portion of the revenues generated. School districts also rely heavily on property taxes for revenue.

The taxes that owners must pay are based on the assessed valuations of their property. Normally, assessment is only a proportion of market value. For example, if the government assesses property at 30 percent of its value, a $100,000 house would be assessed at $30,000. Levies are imposed on property values by the municipality or by the school district in order to raise the necessary money. A standard way of computing the amount is by using the *mill* as a unit of measure. A mill is $\frac{1}{10}$ of a cent. Thus, if a district must raise $1 million from property taxes, a formula is used to establish the *mill levy*. The only purpose in using the mill is to have a unit of measure smaller than one penny. In many parts of the country, the mill is no longer used as a unit of measure.

If the mill is used as a measure, the money to be raised is divided by the total assessed property value of the district. For example, if the district must raise $1 million and the total assessed property valuation of the district is $50 million, the mill levy would be determined by dividing $1 million by $50 million. This computes to 0.02—or two cents on the dollar. Because a mill is $\frac{1}{10}$ of a cent, the levy would be 20 mills. Thus, a taxpayer would have to pay $2 on every $100 in assessed value, or $20 for every $1,000 in assessed value. A home with an assessed value of $50,000, for example, would be assessed $1,000 in taxes.

A reporter may also include details on political maneuvering in a budget story. Sources in individual departments can be invaluable in ferreting out this information. For example, if the police chief is particularly upset at the finance director's unwillingness to upgrade a section of the police department's budget, this can make for an interesting angle. Interview the police chief, interview the finance director and interview the mayor. Explore and write about the controversy, if that is warranted.

Details on the input of private special-interest groups seeking city appropriations might also be appropriate. Some organizations, although they are not part of city government, can receive funds from the municipality. For example, directors of a fine arts center, a food bank or a shelter for the homeless might seek city council appropriations. During the budgeting process, these special-interest groups often become vocal because they are vying for a limited amount of money.

Details on citizens' groups that are for or against budget increases in specific areas often belong in the budget story. For example, if a group does not think that the city is doing a good job maintaining streets, it might appear before the council during the budgeting process to push for increased expenditures in this area. Reporters should analyze the motives and the effect of such a group.

In writing about city budgets and finances, reporters should also be aware of any limitations imposed by the state legislature on revenues and expenditures. "Caps" on revenue and spending can restrict the flexibility of the city council. Sometimes, though, these limitations can be overcome by a vote of the city's residents in a referendum.

Structuring a Budget Story

After Adrianne Flynn reached the point where she understood the intent of the Tempe budget and the numbers in it, she structured a story in such a way that readers would be drawn into it. She presented figures, but she was careful not to scare the readers away with an avalanche of statistics.

Tempe was in the middle of a heat wave; the temperature had exceeded 112 degrees for three consecutive days. Flynn's lead was a natural:

> It's sweltering. A dip in the pool sounds great, but every Tempe swimming hole is packed. The city's proposed $126.77 million budget hopes to change that.

Flynn's lead paragraph quickly let readers know that the city budget would affect more than their pocketbooks; it would affect their lifestyles. The story continued:

> The spending plan for the upcoming fiscal year sets aside money for a Kiwanis Park pool. And it doesn't stop there.
>
> It would establish a fourth paramedic unit, add nine holes to Rolling Hills Golf Course and help the police get the 911 emergency phone system started.
>
> On top of that, there would be no tax increase.

In the fifth paragraph, Flynn gave the total budget figures again, and then in subsequent paragraphs, she began to break them down:

> The Tempe City Council is expected to approve the $126.77 million budget Thursday, after a public hearing that day.
>
> The proposed budget is $20 million more than this year's spending plan for a city that by all estimates has grown from 136,000 to more than 150,000.
>
> Taxes should remain stable because of population and building increases and rising property values. The rate this year was $1.21 per $100 of assessed valuation, according to Management Services Director Jerry Geiger.

After presenting the essential numbers and after emphasizing how residents would be affected, Flynn explained the budget further:

> Tempe's budget has two main parts: The capital portion, which includes city construction and renovation projects and equipment purchases; and

the operations budget, for everything from salaries to telephone service.

A large chunk of the capital budget next year is for the first phase of a five-year improvements package. Storm drains will be upgraded or added, parks beefed up and streets reconstructed under the program.

After devoting the next eight paragraphs to projects that were part of the capital budget, Flynn turned to a breakdown of the operations budget. She wrote that city employees would get a 6 percent cost-of-living increase, that the police department would get 21 additional workers, that the fire department would get six new employees and that building maintenance and sanitation would each get three new workers.

Her story contained significant statistics, but the figures were presented in understandable language. When writing budget stories, a reporter should ask:

- What impact will the numbers have on readers?
- Will the budget mean that residents will receive more or fewer services?
- Will residents have to dig deeper into their pockets?
- If so, how much deeper?

Good budget stories must address people-oriented issues such as these.

Follow-Up Budget Stories

Budget stories are not necessarily limited only to the weeks or months of the formal adoption process; they can be ongoing.

For example, if the amount of money budgeted for record-keeping services in the police department provokes controversy during the approval process, it is probably worth a follow-up story. The police chief might have contended that a 50 percent increase was needed in the department's budget to keep pace with record-keeping chores. But the council might have decided that the amount budgeted for the previous fiscal year would still be adequate.

The reporter should make note of the controversy. Three months into the fiscal year, a check could be made to see if the police department is keeping up with its record-keeping demands. The reporter could, for example, determine if there is a backlog in filing and could get quotations from police officials. The reporter could also check with the city's financial director to see how many dollars the department has spent on record-keeping chores. If the department is three months into the budget period but has already used 50 percent of its allotment for the entire year, the lead for the story is apparent. Or if the reporter discovers that the police department is keeping pace with its record-keeping demands and that it has used only one-fourth of its budgeted allotment, this too would be worth a story.

Financial directors can provide updated information on expenditures by individual departments on a day-to-day basis. The important thing to remember is that budget stories should not be seen as a once-a-year chore.

GUIDELINES FOR COVERING CITY GOVERNMENT

Here are some tips for reporters covering city government:

- *Learn the system.* Check the newspaper morgue to see if stories about the hierarchy of the city government have been done. If so, these stories should provide good background. If not, consider writing such a series as one of your first major undertakings.

  A textbook can do no more than generalize about city government systems. Each system is unique. Reporters must immerse themselves totally to become familiar with the governmental structure of the city in which they work. This requires diligence, patience and concentration. Such familiarization must be accomplished quickly; reporters cannot adequately report on city government unless they thoroughly understand its structure.

- *Get to know the personalities.* It is one thing to master a city government's organizational chart; and it is quite another thing to identify the people listed on the chart who are truly significant. Once this determination has been made, reporters should get to know these people as well as possible. If the city attorney is a Boston Celtics fan, the reporter should learn about the Boston Celtics and should mention the team to the official. It might someday help the reporter get a city government story.

- *Develop reliable sources.* Many city government stories are obtained directly from people who occupy elected or appointed positions. Reporters should obviously build a network of sources from within these ranks. It is just as important, however, for reporters to develop a subnetwork of sources. Administrative assistants, secretaries and other staff members can be important sources. Reporters should choose sources wisely, cultivate them and build a bond. But they should never take advantage of their sources.

  "Be honest with your sources," Adrianne Flynn advised. "Let your sources know that you will print all the facts on both sides of an issue, no matter what, but you're not out to do a scandal sheet on every issue. Find two or three really well-informed folks on your beat whom you can find out almost anything from, and cultivate them as sources. Don't butter them up; just be forthright and get to know them as people. Be interested in their personal as well as their professional lives."

- *Be persistent.* "You catch more flies with honey than with vinegar, but if one method does not work, use the other with gusto," Flynn said. "If you want a story, you must be persistent. Call every day, every hour, if need be. Make your sources so sick of you that they'll have to talk to you just to get you off their backs. I got a great story once by waiting in a developer's office for three hours when he wouldn't return my phone calls. But I finally got to talk to him."

- *Never let friendship interfere with the job.* Reporters who cover specific beats sometimes spend as much time with officials—their sources—as they do with their personal circle of friends. It is not surprising, then, that reporters and news sources sometimes become friends. Reporters must handle this situation with care—always striving to be fair in their handling of news stories.

- *Always be prepared.* To succeed, city government reporters must know more about city government than their competition does. They must have more sources, do more homework on the issues and work longer hours. Good reporters never skim an agenda casually and write a meeting off as unimportant. Instead, they work harder to find something of value in an otherwise routine meeting.

  "It is important to know about the issues in advance," Flynn said. "Ask smart, informed questions. Know how the place operates and who can provide you with facts and figures on any given assignment."

- *Make notes of story possibilities.* Many good city government stories do not evolve from coverage of meetings. Rather, they evolve from in-depth follow-ups of news tidbits tossed out at meetings or in informal conversations with city government sources. Even if reporters are working on another story and do not have time to develop the new angle, the idea should be noted and carefully filed away for future reference.

- *Read other newspapers, and listen to radio and television news.* Reporters should not operate in a vacuum, smugly assured that their sources will keep them informed of all possible stories. Other media should be surveyed constantly. Some of the best story ideas arise from less-than-satisfactory handling of stories by other reporters.

- *Write to inform, not to impress, readers.* Develop city government stories from the standpoint of what the issue means to readers. For example, if a city intends to raise an additional $14 million in property taxes during the next fiscal year, reporters should explain what this increase means to readers as homeowners. What will the increase do to taxes on a house assessed at $50,000, at $75,000 or at $100,000? That is what is relevant to readers.

- *Use your brain.* "If you think you're so smart you can conquer the world, you're wrong," Flynn said. "Some of the littlest facts can hang you up. When they do, think your way out of it.

  "I tried once to find out when a local congressman [John McCain, who had been a prisoner of war in Vietnam and who, a decade later, had visited that country] was returning from a trip to Vietnam. I hoped to scoop the competition by meeting him at the airport. It turned out that he arrived too late for our deadline, but I found out, despite the fact that his staff was sworn to secrecy.

  "I tried the airlines and narrowed down the flights to about five possible ones that he could be on. I called the congressman's aide, but he would not tell me which flight it was. I called his wife and said, 'He's going to be on this plane at this time,' but she would not confirm it.

  "Then I called his travel agency and almost had it because a new girl in the office was going to give it to me when she suddenly had a guilt attack and checked with her supervisor.

  Finally, I called The Associated Press in New York. They relayed me to the AP bureau in Bangkok, and someone there called McCain and asked him when he was returning. He told the AP correspondent, and the correspondent told me. Because we belong to the AP, we can get all kinds of help from them. Don't be afraid to use the wire service, even when working on a local issue."

- *Do not be afraid to ask questions.* If you want to know something, ask. It is better than seeing your mistakes in print or seeing the competition get the jump on you.

Police tend to an accident victim until an ambulance arrives.
An accident with injuries is often newsworthy.
(Photo by Sean Openshaw)

19

Police and Fire

During an eight-hour shift, reporters who cover

the police and fire beats often read dozens of record

forms, interview several people, make small talk

with scores more and still find time to write

hundreds of words. That's on a routine day. If a

major story breaks, they handle that as well.

Scenes from old movies perpetuate the stereotype: police and fire reporters are booze-guzzling, cigar-chomping hacks who have difficulty stringing together complete sentences. They are devious, unscrupulous (but usually likable) fellows who gather facts, frantically call their newsrooms, always ask for rewrite and feverishly tell their sordid stories of crime. Only when they hang up the telephone and look in a mirror at their press hats and baggy pants do they return to reality: they are not really cops.

For the most part, this outdated image is disappearing. Today's police and fire reporters are likely to be well-educated men and women who do not wear baggy pants and who do know how to write. Roger Aeschliman, a law enforcement reporter for the *Topeka Capital-Journal* in Kansas, is one of this new breed.

Aeschliman, a graduate of Kansas State University, majored in journalism and political science. He took a variety of mass communication classes, including radio and television, and worked on the campus newspaper: the *Kansas State Collegian*. He served as a staff writer, as arts and entertainment editor and eventually as managing editor.

He was a midterm graduate, and so he spent the fall semester pestering Rick Dalton, managing editor of the *Capital-Journal*. "I think he decided to hire me just to get me off his back," Aeschliman said.

Aeschliman was offered a job as a staff writer two days before graduation. It was a great gift. After six months, he started filling in on the weekend police beat. He was named one of the two *Capital-Journal* law enforcement reporters as he started his second year on the job.

STAFFING POLICE AND FIRE BEATS

The size of a newspaper, television station or radio station usually determines how its reporters cover police and fire news. At newspapers with circulations of less than 20,000 and at small-market radio and television stations, one person might juggle coverage of police and fire news while reporting on all other city and county institutions (such as the mayor's office, the engineer's office, the civil defense office, the assessor's office and the clerk's office). At newspapers with larger circulations, a reporter might be responsible only for coverage of law enforcement agencies and the fire department. Large-circulation newspapers generally have more than one reporter covering the police and fire departments.

Regardless of the newspaper's circulation or the population of the community, police and fire reporters cover similar stories. Routine crime news is often played down at the major metros and by television and radio, but small-circulation dailies and weeklies generally report on all minor crime stories and accidents. Sometimes these stories are given play on the front page.

At the *Capital-Journal*, a morning newspaper with a circulation of about 70,000, there are two law enforcement reporters: Steve Fry, who works from 6 a.m. until 2:30 p.m., and Aeschliman, who works from 2:30 p.m. until 11 p.m. Both reporters work out of the *Capital-Journal*'s newsroom. At some metropoli-

404

tan papers, police reporters work out of pressrooms at the stations and are connected to their newsrooms by telephones or computers. The *Capital-Journal* publishes two editions: the 3 a.m. press run is distributed statewide; the 5 a.m. press run is distributed to Topeka residents and to residents of the immediate surrounding counties.

"I enjoy my job," Aeschliman said. "It is very exciting. Every day is different. Some days, though, can be depressing: all you see happening are bad things. That's the only drawback as I see it."

Aeschliman's days pass quickly; he spends much of his time away from the office reviewing records and talking to sources. During the late afternoon and evening hours, he routinely types into his computer terminal 50 one- or two-line items that come from police, fire or court records. These are published in the newspaper's daily record section. He also writes four or five short stories (three to 12 paragraphs) on events that merit elaboration and a longer story on a significant breaking news event or feature.

COVERING POLICE AND FIRE DEPARTMENTS

Aeschliman's primary responsibilities are coverage of the Topeka Police Department (Topeka, a city of 110,000, is the state capital); the Shawnee County Sheriff's Department; the Kansas Highway Patrol (northeast Kansas); the Kansas Turnpike Authority (which has highway patrol-type duties for northeast Kansas); the Topeka Fire Department; four Shawnee County township fire departments; and Medevac MidAmerica (the Shawnee County area ambulance).

His secondary responsibilities are the police, sheriffs' and fire departments and the ambulances of seven surrounding counties. Tertiary responsibilities include police and fire developments for the state of Kansas on weekends and evenings, if the state desk or The Associated Press does not get the story.

MASTERING ORGANIZATIONAL STRUCTURES

Before police or fire reporters can effectively cover their departments and agencies, they must master the various *organizational structures.* These structures vary among cities and states, and so textbooks can only generalize. Many structures, however, are similar to the departments that Aeschliman covers:

- *Topeka Police Department.* The chief of police is appointed by the mayor with the approval of the city council. Under the chief is a lieutenant colonel, who is second in command and in charge of personnel. Next are six majors who are division commanders of Patrol, Traffic, Detectives, Services, Administration and Topeka Emergency Communication (dispatch). Captains, lieutenants, sergeants, patrol officers and traffic officers complete the structure. There are also civilians in records, dispatch, housekeeping and so forth.

- *Shawnee County Sheriff's Department.* This department's sheriff is elected countywide, including Topeka. Three county commissioners are elected countywide, including Topeka. The sheriff is not directly responsible to the commissioners, but they control the budget.

  An undersheriff is appointed by the sheriff with the approval of the commission. The only person in the sheriff's department who holds the rank of major leads the uniformed officers. In addition, the chain of command lists captains, lieutenants, sergeants and corporals. There are eight territories. Officers do not work inside the Topeka city limits. Unlike the Topeka police, who have from 20 to 40 officers on the street at any one time, the sheriff has from three to seven officers out on patrol.

- *Topeka Fire Department.* The fire department is headed by a chief who is appointed by the mayor with the approval of the council. There are 20 assistant chiefs. Three assistant chiefs supervise each shift and live in the stations during their shifts. The firefighters work a 24-hour shift every three days. The other 11 assistant chiefs work on inspections, training and education. In the stations, captains are the leaders (there are 10 stations in Topeka), and there is a lieutenant in charge of each company. There are 17 companies active all the time and two in reserve. Topeka averages three fire calls a day. The department also responds to helicopter landings at three major hospitals about once a day and performs medical first response about six times a day.

DEVELOPING SOURCES

After reporters have a working understanding of the organizational structures of the agencies and departments they cover, sources must be developed and cultivated. Some of Aeschliman's primary sources within the Topeka Police Department, for example, are detectives, patrol and traffic officers, record keepers and high-ranking captains and majors.

In Topeka, detectives work two rotating shifts: they work mornings for two weeks and evenings for two weeks. Aeschliman figures that two or three detectives on each shift are his best sources. He does not try to gain the trust of these detectives overnight. "I start slowly in cultivating them," he said. "I use their names in feature articles or in routine stories to put them in a favorable light. After this, they often are more willing to help me with stories that are not routine."

Aeschliman always tries to determine whether sources like to see their names in print. "If I perceive that they like to see their names used, I will use them," he said. "Some sources like to provide information, but do not like to see their names in print. If that is the case, I do not overuse their names. It all depends on the person and the circumstances."

Aeschliman relies extensively on patrol and traffic officers. "They know exactly what is happening because they are close to the action," Aeschliman said. He estimated that of the 75 officers on the shift he covers, about 20 "would tell me almost anything," another 20 "would be friendly and generally helpful" and the remainder would not be as cooperative (they are the "I'm-kind-of-busy types, so please don't bother me"). "Since more than one officer usually works a case, I am not bothered much by those who don't want to be

Firefighters risk their lives when they are on the job. They make excellent sources for news or feature stories. *(Photo by Darryl Webb)*

helpful. If I am at the scene of a crime or accident and one officer tells me to stay back and not bother him, I'll go to another officer who might be helpful."

Some of Aeschliman's best sources are the keepers of records at the department. "These sources are the hardest to get, though, because they operate under strict legal requirements," Aeschliman said. "Occasionally, I try to buy them a cup of coffee or a soft drink. If you work at it long enough, you can earn their trust. After several months, I was on a first-name basis with many of them. Now, I get some good tips from them. It is always off the record, and I respect their wishes."

Aeschliman relies on upper-echelon officers—majors and captains—for information for some stories. "I find that these officers are always looking to be placed in the best possible light," he said. "I never go out of my way to write fluff pieces about them, but it is good to use their names as favorably as possible in routine stories. That way, when you are writing an unfavorable story about the department, they might be more willing to talk to you about it. If they remember you only for the bad stories, they will provide little information to you."

Aeschliman does not have the time to cultivate sources within other departments on his beat, particularly the fire department, to the extent he does at police headquarters.

"Not as many stories come out of the fire department," he said. "But I try to write a couple of nice fire prevention stories now and then. I quote the fire officials. Then, they are more willing to talk when I am covering breaking news stories."

Aeschliman realizes that coverage of hard news is his main responsibility. But he added that "writing soft features about the departments, their activities and their officers plays a big part in cultivating sources for the hard news stories."

Naturally, many of the stories police reporters write are not favorable to the department. Sometimes, the timing of a story may conflict with a police investigation. At other times, the reporter must criticize law enforcement officials for abuse of power or for other questionable activities. These stories obviously do nothing to solidify relations between the department and the reporter. Reporters, though, must overcome these obstacles. The best way is to be as fair, professional and diplomatically aggressive as possible. Officers will often respect you for handling stories fairly, even if it puts them in a bad light.

"I never try to snow my sources," Aeschliman said. "If I make a mistake, I admit it and I try to recover my credibility as best I can."

USING DEPARTMENTAL RECORDS

Reporters write many of their stories about fires, crimes, accidents, arrests and bookings after examining reports that are on file at various departments. Many times, reporters will follow up information from these reports by interviewing officials. The types of reports and the level of legal access to them vary. It is imperative that reporters fully understand reports and records that are available to them in the states and cities in which they work.

Accident Forms and Coverage of Accidents

Unrestricted access to forms   Reporters often have *unrestricted access* to some official accident forms. Aeschliman, for example, has complete unrestricted access to the Topeka Police Department's accident forms; he also has access to the accident report forms of the Kansas Department of Motor Vehicles.

However, some of the supplemental accident reports filled out by police officers are restricted—although officers will sometimes voluntarily tell reporters about information on these supplemental forms.

Information on accident forms   Accident reports vary, but the information found on the Kansas Department of Revenue Motor Vehicle Accident Report forms is representative:

- Location of accident
- Name of investigating officer
- Owner of vehicle
- Driver of vehicle
- Age and occupation of driver
- Names of passengers and witnesses
- Severity of injuries to people involved

- License number of vehicle
- Owner's liability insurance company
- Year, make, model and type of vehicle
- Damage (fixed objects, such as utility poles, as well as animals, pedestrians and so on)
- Damage to vehicle (windshield, trunk, hood and so on)
- Severity of damage to vehicle (disabling, functional and so on)
- Time authorities were notified
- Time authorities arrived at scene
- Time emergency medical service was notified
- Time emergency medical service arrived at scene
- Hospital to which injured parties were removed and by whom
- Narrative that contains the drivers' and investigating officers' opinions of what occurred
- Principal contributing circumstances (condition of the driver, condition of the vehicle, human behavior and so on)
- Driver's and pedestrian's condition before accident (ill, fatigued, apparently asleep, apparently normal, taking prescription drugs, taking illegal drugs, consuming alcohol and so on)
- Results of chemical tests
- Road surface (dry, wet, slippery and so on)
- Weather
- Light conditions
- Vehicle defects (turn lights, tires and so on)
- Visibility (vision not obscured, rain, snow, fog and so on)
- Diagram of what happened (drawing of the scene as observed; vehicles, drivers and pedestrians are normally referred to by numbers assigned in the report). The diagram includes an outline of the street and access point paths of units before and after impact, skid marks and point of impact; location of signs, traffic controls and reference points; location of other property hit or damaged; special features at the location (bridge, overpass, culvert and such); location of temporary highway conditions; and all measurements to locate the accident relative to a specific, fixed, uniquely identifiable and locatable point.

Determining newsworthiness of accidents Most small-circulation dailies and weeklies publish stories about all accidents reported to the police—no matter how minor. The *Capital-Journal*, a larger-circulation daily, does not publish stories about insignificant fender benders, but it does publish daily agate listings of all injury accidents. Each short item contains information about the location of the accident, names of people injured and condition reports from hospitals.

"Any injury reported by the police in their forms is listed as an injury in the paper," Aeschliman said. "We contact the hospital to see if the injured were seen, admitted or treated and released. In the event the police say a person was injured but no hospital has a record of the person, we write 'Police reported John Smith was possibly injured but no record of hospital treatment was found.' "

For a story to graduate from the agate listings in the *Capital-Journal* to a regular article, the victim must have been severely injured or killed, or the accident must have an interesting feature, such as a 10-car pileup in a fog or a truck jackknifing across a highway.

The *Capital-Journal* reporter said that stories about people who are seriously injured usually rate 5 to 6 inches near the classified ad pages. Stories about life-threatening injuries are often played on the second page. "Fatalities or some spectacular accident merits page 1 treatment," Aeschliman said. "Topeka, for example, sees only five to 10 fatal wrecks a year. When they occur in a city of 110,000, many readers know the victims or someone who knew the victims, and so it's news. We're also big on follow-ups. We report the victims' condition until they are out of the hospital. Occasionally, we do a feature story a year later, of the 'how life has been since' type."

Aeschliman glances through dozens of accident reports each day. Because stories will not be written about all of them, here are some key items he looks for to determine which reports are newsworthy:

- *Time and location of accident.* "The location helps to give me an idea of how many people might have seen the accident," Aeschliman said. "A minor injury accident at 8 a.m. on the freeway may be more newsworthy than a more severe injury accident at 2 a.m. on a rural gravel road."

- *Names of those involved.* "The names are necessary to obtain information about victims' condition from hospitals," Aeschliman said. "It is also important not to overlook the names of passengers, who may have been more seriously injured than the drivers. I always check the names of the vehicle owners as well. You might find that the son or daughter of a respected citizen was out joyriding. The owner's name also gives you another person to contact for more information."

- *Severity of injuries.* The Kansas form that Aeschliman works with is coded: 0 means no injury; 1 means a death; 2 means an ambulance injury; 3 means obvious but not ambulance-worthy injuries; and 4 means possible injuries. "Of all the items in a report, this one throws up the red flag for a reporter," Aeschliman said. "If the number indicates an injury, the form deserves further attention. If no injury is listed, I usually only glance at the report to see if the mayor was in an accident while driving drunk, or something like that."

- *Results of chemical tests.* Any number that appears in this box on the Kansas form shows alcohol consumption. In Kansas, any number more than 0.1 indicates that the person was legally drunk. "If the number indicates consumption, I check into it," Aeschliman said.

- *Ambulance service.* The Kansas form indicates which ambulance service arrived at the scene. "Finding out which ambulance was involved saves me time trying to find out where the injured were taken," Aeschliman said.

- *Diagram section.* "This is an important section because it gives you a quick once-over of the wreck and how it occurred," Aeschliman said. "The diagram allows you to understand the wreck and to then ask intelligent questions of the officers or the people involved."

- *Statements made by drivers.* "I often quote people involved in an accident," Aeschliman said. "But I am always careful to note that the statement was attributed to the people by the police in their report."

- *"Nuts and bolts" section that provides information on road conditions, light conditions, visibility, use of seat belts and so on.* "If properly read, this section allows you to write a story as if you were there when the crash occurred," Aeschliman said. "For example, you might write: 'The car's tires were bald and the road was slick with spilled oil, the police report said.' Also, at the *Capital-Journal,* at the risk of sounding preachy, we often use information about seat belts, such as, 'Police said that Jones might not have been injured if he had been wearing a seat belt.' "

Example: An accident story Aeschliman worked much essential information from the police report into the first three paragraphs of an accident story published in the *Capital-Journal.* He also called a hospital for a condition report. Here are his first three paragraphs:

A Grantville man was thrown from his car and died instantly in a three-car collision Friday, and the driver of another car was seriously injured.

Police said the man, Richard Bigham, 55, was westbound in the 800 block of US-24 when he lost control of his car and slid across the median broadside and into the eastbound lanes where his car was struck by two other vehicles.

Marcella Conklin, 19, Shawnee, the driver of one of the eastbound cars, was admitted to St. Francis Hospital and Medical Center for treatment of broken ribs, a broken kneecap and cuts and bruises, a hospital spokesman said. She was in serious but stable condition late Friday in the intensive care unit, the spokesman said.

The story then provided condition reports on a passenger in one of the cars and on two firefighters who had been sprayed in the eyes with hydraulic fluid while pulling people from the vehicles. Then, by attributing information to a police accident investigator, Aeschliman provided additional details on the collision:

The traffic accident happened at 3:28 p.m. at 851 E. US-24, said police accident investigator Lyndon Weddle. Bigham was westbound in the left lane when another vehicle turned west onto US-24 from Goldwater Road in front of Bigham, Weddle said.

Apparently, Bigham swerved to avoid that car, and in doing so dropped his two left side tires off the road onto the shoulder, Weddle said.

When Bigham tried to steer his car back onto the road, it went out of control on the snowy shoulder and spun broadside into the median ditch, she said.

Bigham's car slid on into the eastbound lanes of US-24, facing south, directly in front of Conklin, eastbound in the interior lane, and a third car in the exterior lane, driven by John Stein, 54, Valley Falls, Weddle said.

Standard Offense Report

LIMITED ACCESS

NAME OF AGENCY		ORI KS	KS 0890100
TOPEKA POLICE DEPT. 204 W. 5th Topeka, Kansas 66603		1. CASE NO.	0021-93

2. OFFENSE—List Most Serious First	3. OFFENSE CODE	4. DATE OF OFFENSE (MMDDYY)	5. TIME OCC.	6. DATE & TIME REPORTED
RAPE AGG. ASSAULT THEFT		1/15/93	3:25	1/15/93 10:45

7. REPORT AREA	8. TYPE OF PREMISES; CHECK IF VACANT, NOT NORMALLY IN USE ☐
	___ STREET X RESIDENCE ___ RESTAURANT
	___ COMMERCIAL ___ BANK ___ VEHICLE
	___ GAS STATION ___ PHARMACY ___ OTHER
	___ CONVENIENCE STORE ___ DRS. OFFICE

9. LOCATION OF OFFENSE

1111 Main Street

10. VICTIM'S NAME—Last, First, Middle (Firm if Business)	11. RESIDENCE ADDRESS—PHONE
Elizabeth B. Baker (not real name)	1111 Main Street

12. RACE	13. SEX	14. AGE	15. DOB (MMDDYY)	16. HT.	17. WT.	18. HAIR	19. EYES	20. OCCUPATION	21. BUSINESS ADDRESS— PHONE
W	F	17	2/15/75	5'1	105	Br	Br	student	N/A (not applicable)

CODES: V-Victim W-Witness P-Parent DC-Discovered Crime RP-Reporting Party   Check if More Names in Supplement _____

22. NAME—Last, First, Middle	23. CODE	24. RESIDENCE ADDRESS—PHONE
Mary J. Baker (not real name)	RP	1111 Main Street

25. RACE	26. SEX	27. AGE	28. DOB (MMDDYY)	29. HT.	30. WT.	31. HAIR	32. EYES	33. OCCUPATION	34. BUSINESS ADDRESS— PHONE
W	F	42	NA	NA	NA	NA	NA	housewife	NA

35. NAME—Last, First, Middle	36. CODE	37. RESIDENCE ADDRESS—PHONE

38. RACE	39. SEX	40. AGE	41. DOB (MMDDYY)	42. HT.	43. WT.	44. HAIR	45. EYES	46. OCCUPATION	47. BUSINESS ADDRESS— PHONE

48. DESCRIBE BRIEFLY HOW OFFENSE WAS COMMITTED.

Mother brought daughter to station after mother found daughter

beaten in bed. Victim Baker (not real name) reports a man entered

her window and threatened her with a knife and raped her, then

left. See Supplement 0022-93.

PROPERTY STATUS: S-Stolen RA-Recovered for your agency RO-Recovered for other agency F-Found RV-Recovered by Victim E-Evidence

49. STATUS	50. QTY	51. DESCRIPTION OF PROPERTY	52. CODE	53. MODEL-SERIAL-OWNER APPLIED NO.	54. VALUE	55. COLOR
	1	coin bank		unknown quantity change	$15-25	

56. PROPERTY DAMAGE INCURRED DURING OFFENSE	57. PROPERTY DAMAGE INCURRED DURING ARSON	58. TOTAL VALUE
X UNDER $100 ___ OVER $100	$ None	PROPERTY STOLEN $15-25

59. REPORTING OFFICER	60. DATE	61. TYPED BY	62. DATE	63. REVIEWED BY	64. DATE	65. COPIES TO:
						___ DET ___ JUVENILE ___ KBI ___ OTHER

Standard offense report form of a police department.

The story continued with additional details about the accident, a preliminary autopsy report and information about how rush-hour traffic was routed around the accident.

Aeschliman's story shows that reports can provide an abundance of details which, if gathered carefully, can be woven into a complete, understandable story.

Offense Reports and Coverage of Crimes

Limited access to forms   Reporters typically have *limited access* to police departments' forms recording crimes—that is, to standard offense reports.

For example, while Aeschliman has complete access to most accident forms, he enjoys only *limited access* to the Topeka police department's standard offense reports. Access to these is legally limited to the top half of the form's front page. (See the form on page 412; the names and the incident are not real.) Here, such information as when the alleged offense took place, where it took place, at which time it took place, the name of the victim and a brief synopsis is presented. The bottom half of the form provides information on property that might have been stolen or recovered and details about other evidence found at the scene. Also, estimates of the value of stolen property can be provided. Aeschliman does not have a legal right to the information at the bottom of the page, but quite often friendly sources within the department will grant him access.

Often, according to Aeschliman, detectives ask him to withhold some information. For example, the police might ask Aeschliman to withhold information about the theft of the coin bank described in the limited-access portion of the standard offense report. Detectives might reason that inclusion of this information in the story could tip off the suspect that the police are aware that it is missing, and this could hinder their investigation. In such instances, Aeschliman might decide to abide by their wishes.

Example: A rape story   The *Capital-Journal* seldom publishes particularly long rape stories unless the victim has severe injuries in addition to the rape itself, or the circumstances are unusual. Like many other newspapers that respect the privacy of rape victims and their families, the *Capital-Journal* never uses the person's name or address; thus, Aeschliman would observe this policy when writing a story based on the information in the form shown on page 412.

Aeschliman would lead the story this way:

A 17-year-old east Topeka girl was raped in her bed early Tuesday

by a man armed with a knife.

All this information is available from the standard offense report. But Aeschliman would not rely exclusively on information from the report to structure the remainder of his story. He would also:

Talk to the officers who investigated and filed the report

Check to see if other rapes had been reported in the area during recent weeks

Telephone the hospital for a report on the victim's condition

The remainder of the story would read like this:

> Police reported that the girl said she was beaten by the man and was threatened with a long hunting-type knife. The girl was in satisfactory condition at a local hospital Wednesday night suffering a broken nose. She was admitted for observation, a hospital spokeswoman said.
>
> According to police, this is what the girl said happened: The rape occurred at 3:25 a.m. when a man cut a window screen and then raised the window to get into her room. She woke up when the man crawled into bed with her and clamped a hand over her mouth.
>
> A detective investigating the case reported that the girl said the man held a knife to her throat and then hit her in the face and stomach several times when she tried to cry out. She said that the man raped her, threatened to kill her if she called the police and then left through the same window.
>
> Police said that the victim apparently passed out and was discovered by her mother in the morning. The woman was sleeping in an upstairs room during the attack, the detective said.
>
> The suspect was described as a white man, about 25, 5-feet-8-inches, 180 pounds. He was wearing blue jeans and a plaid shirt.

Note the attribution. Attribution is particularly important in crime stories. Readers need to know the source of the information, and it is the obligation of reporters to provide it. In the story above, for example, the reporter relied primarily on the police, who had been supplied with most of the information by the victim and the victim's mother.

A DAY ON THE POLICE AND FIRE BEAT

This section provides an overview of a typical day on the job with Roger Aeschliman. A composite day is presented to illustrate Aeschliman's thought processes and writing strategies on a variety of stories common to the police and fire beats. It is realistic in the sense that one major story dominates the day while several smaller ones need to be written and routine work still needs to be accomplished.

Firefighters stand by at the scene of a blaze just in case their help is needed again. This would be a good time to interview them. *(Photo by Sean Openshaw)*

ASSIGNMENTS: THE DAY BEGINS

At about noon, the telephone rings at Aeschliman's house. Steve Fry, the *Capital-Journal*'s police reporter for the morning shift, says: "It's going to be a big day, Rog. Can you come in an hour early? I'm all tied up with the sheriff's contract negotiations, and there's been a fatal fire."

Aeschliman reports to the office at 1:30 p.m., instead of his usual 2:30. The notes and requests to return calls piled on his desk indicate that he will probably not be going home at 11 p.m. as he normally does.

Fry has wrapped up coverage of the contract negotiations for the day; and he fills Aeschliman in on the session. The deputies approved the contract; but the county did not.

Fry then tells Aeschliman that two children were killed and their father was injured in a fire in a mobile home this morning. "That's big news anywhere," Aeschliman said.

Fry would normally have been at the scene, but he was locked up in the contract meeting, and no one on the skeleton morning staff heard the call go out on the police scanner.

Aeschliman goes to the city desk to talk to his boss, the city editor. Today, Don Marker says only one thing to him: "Do a good job on the fire story."

"On another day, he might have a news tip or a feature story idea for me," Aeschliman said. "In any case, a check-in at the city desk is vital. All the reporters clear through the city editor, and if there is something happening, he's probably going to know about it.

"Back at my desk I start calling around. I make routine checks to find out what's happening. Included are calls to the highway patrol, police traffic, patrol and detectives, the ambulance service, our sheriff, the sheriffs from the surrounding counties and the fire department."

ON-THE-SCENE COVERAGE: A MAJOR FIRE

On this day the big news comes from the fire department. The preliminary report from the inspector is fragmentary: "A mobile home fire at 245 E. 29th was reported at 10:11 a.m. The fire destroyed the structure, doing an estimated $10,000 damage. Two girls, ages 3 and 1, were killed. A man was severely burned."

"That's all I am going to get from them for the rest of the day," Aeschliman said. "It's up to me. This is the kind of story that can't wait until later. Firefighters and police change shifts soon, and witnesses have a way of disappearing. I'm going to the scene; the boss agrees."

The area is still cordoned off, and the fire chief is shuffling through the debris. He comes out to make a statement for the television crews. Again, he uses no names. The cause and origin of the fire are unknown. But he does give some details of the fire and some good quotations.

"I can use the quotes," Aeschliman said. "A door-to-door canvass is next on my list. Do you know who lived there, sir? Do you know the names of the children? Where was the mother?

"A half hour of that and I've got the names of the injured man and his wife, and I've found out that they had moved here recently from a small town north of Topeka. I've also got the name and address of a man who restrained the father from going back into the blaze to try to rescue the girls. My next stop is the witness.

"He is a shy man with children of his own. He just happened to be shopping across the street when the fire broke out. He didn't know any of the victims, but he saw what happened and he tells about it vividly. I can sure use him.

"It feels as though the day is half gone, but it's only 3:30 p.m. I check back in at the office. Nothing is new. It's time to follow up on some leads. I call the victims' hometown sheriff and ask if he's heard of the deaths. 'Sure, sure, it's the talk of the town,' he says. I tell him the names of the mother and father, and he confirms them."

The sheriff also provides the names of the girls: Shena and Kimberly.

"Now I've got the story no one else has: the victims' names and an eyewitness account of the disaster. I tell the boss, and he sends a photographer out to work up some kind of photo from the scene."

MAKING THE ROUNDS: A BURGLARY AND A PURSE SNATCHING

After Aeschliman has gathered most of the information for the fire story, he must make his regular stops on the beat. There is still a lot of day left; and he will write the major fire story later.

The *Capital-Journal* publishes a *police log* (a daily report of activity involving the department), *fire reports* and court dockets in small print. That job, tedious as it is, falls to the police reporters. Fry gets the night shift reports, and

Aeschliman picks up the morning shift reports when he makes afternoon rounds. That means checking in at the sheriff's office for traffic and offense reports. Then he goes to the police department for the same type of information. Aeschliman summarizes each report in one or two lines.

A typical item from the police blotter might read: "Fleet Service and Equipment, 1534 N. Tyler, burglary of business and theft of tools." A typical item from the fire department log might read: "7:53 p.m. Wednesday—3700 W. 29th, fire started in water heater caused by short in wiring, burned wiring and water heater, $50 loss."

"Even if the paper did not run the small print, I'd still be looking through the reports," he said. "There are important stories hidden in the pile, and you've got to find them."

On this day, he finds two that he regards as worthy of more than a mention in small print: burglary and arson at a church and the arrest of a person accused of purse snatching.

"Before leaving, I talk to detectives about the two cases," Aeschliman said. "They fill me in with enough details to make each story interesting, though short. The arrest of the purse snatcher happened after I came on duty, and from what the detectives say, it is worth getting a few quotations from the officers involved. A couple of them are at headquarters writing reports. They are friendly enough and receptive, and so we talk about it. They're both natural and open and give me good material.

"Often, the detectives try to be so precise that they sound like a boring report. That's why I like witnesses; the closer you get to the event the more accurate and more colorful the information becomes."

Aeschliman returns to his office and calls the fire department again. This time, he asks for the entire list of fire reports. He enters them quickly on his computer terminal and sends them, along with the rest of the short items for the small print, to the city desk.

It is 6:35—five minutes past deadline. "Because of the time I spent on the fire story, no one yells at me for missing the deadline," Aeschliman said.

The reporter has nearly an hour for a dinner break. But instead of eating dinner, he spends the time lifting weights at the YMCA. Now, back in the office, he is ready to write.

WRITING THE STORIES

Planning for Deadlines

Gathering the information is only half the job. A beat reporter must organize his or her time to meet deadlines. Aeschliman's next deadline is 10:15 p.m. All copy should be in, but some minor local stories do not have to be rushed. It is 7:30 p.m. Aeschliman figures that two hours and 45 minutes should be enough time to get everything written—that is, if nothing else happens.

"In addition to writing for the next deadline, I've got to monitor the scanners to keep on top of any breaking news," he said. "If everything breaks loose, some of my stories could be reassigned to another reporter or dumped entirely if something more important happens.

"For now, the boss decides that three stories—the fire, the church burglary and the purse snatching—should be written. I go to work."

Writing the Fire Story

Aeschliman always sets priorities when writing on deadline. He turns initially to his major story; on this day, it is the mobile home fire.

Developing the lead Aeschliman's first task is to develop a strong, concise, accurate lead. That takes thought.

"The deaths go first," Aeschliman said. "Everything is secondary to that. It would be good to identify the girls in the first paragraph because I know who they are and no one else does. I play around with that idea a bit, but every lead comes out extremely long. The boss suggests a simple lead: 'Two young girls were killed when a fire destroyed their mobile home Saturday.'

"That is a nice starting place, but I know I can do better," Aeschliman said. "I look through my notes and decide to go with a little extra about the injured father trying to get back in." Aeschliman writes:

> Two Topeka girls, 3 and 1 years old, died Friday in a mobile home fire, and their critically burned father had to be restrained from re-entering the inferno to try to rescue them.

"That tells the story," Aeschliman said. "The lead may be a tad long, but I like it."

Constructing the story: Ingredients Stories about fires should answer several basic questions. First, was anyone killed? Beyond that, fire stories should obviously provide additional information. Aeschliman tries to work in most of the following details:

- Identification of the dead
- Cause of death (for example, smoke inhalation, burns and so forth)
- Results of or status of autopsies
- Location of the fire
- Cause and origin of the fire
- If arson is suspected, details on leads or arrests
- Identification of the injured
- Description of the scene
- Details of treatment to the injured at the scene
- Details of where the injured were taken
- Current condition of the injured (generally obtained from hospitals)
- Time of the fire
- When the fire was reported and by whom

- Response time of the firefighters
- Length of time to get the fire under control
- Length of time the firefighters spent on the scene
- Heroics by the firefighters
- Extent of property damage (including damage to adjacent buildings)
- Estimated damage in dollars
- Insurance details
- Quotations from police and fire officials, witnesses, neighbors and so forth

"I like to use good quotes high in the story; they attract attention and keep the reader interested," Aeschliman said. "In this case, using quotes from the witness in the first paragraph would be confusing. I have to tell the readers generally about the fire, so that the quotes can be read in context. But I don't have to overdo it, and the quotes can be used about halfway through the body. The witness has a story to tell, and so I just let him. I've done rearranging to make more sense of it, and I've paraphrased when he wasn't very clear, but I try to use as much of what he said exactly the way he said it."

Aeschliman's story continues:

The girls, Shena and Kimberly Bryan, were killed in the fire at their mobile home, 245 E. 29th, lot 1, at the Crest Mobile Home Park, a fire department spokesman said.

Kenneth Bryan, father of the girls, was burned over most of his body and was taken to St. Francis Hospital and Medical Center before being trans- ferred to the burn center of the Kansas University Medical Center in Kansas City.

He was in critical condition late Friday, but hospital officials would not release further information.

His wife was not at home when the fire broke out, fire department officials said.

Providing attribution   Note that Aeschliman is careful to attribute factual information to reliable sources. Reporters should always tell readers the source of information.

Aeschliman obtained information for the first paragraphs by:

Ingenuity (scouring the neighborhood for witnesses and for background information on the family)

A telephone call to the sheriff who served the nearby small community where the family used to live (to verify the parents' names and to get the names of the girls)

Routine reporting work (talking to fire department officials at the scene and, back at the office, calling the hospital for a report on the father's condition)

Describing the scene   Aeschliman's next paragraphs provide additional details from the scene of the fire—details that the reporter would not have been able to relay to readers had he not gone to the site:

The mobile home was destroyed, with only the skeleton of charred 2-by-2 timbers still standing after the fire. The aluminum siding was mostly melted away, the strips remaining dangling and pockmarked from the heat.

The body of one girl was found in a rear bedroom, the area that had the least fire damage. Officials at the scene said she was not severely burned and probably died from smoke inhalation. The other girl was found in the front living area and was burned beyond recognition, a spokesman said.

"You had to move debris before you saw the body, and even then it was hard to tell what it was," he said.

Autopsies are pending.

Both the cause and origin of the fire are under investigation. No details as to how or where the fire began were available late Friday.

The fire was reported at 10:11 a.m. by neighbors, but Jerry Fitzgerald, 25, 2834 Topeka Ave., the first person to arrive on the scene, said the fire was burning about 15 minutes before anyone called for help.

Aeschliman strengthened his story—and earned an advantage over his competition from other newspapers and from the electronic media—by locating and interviewing Fitzgerald. His description of the scene was indeed vivid. Aeschliman's story continues:

He [Fitzgerald] said he was shopping across the street when he saw a single cloud of smoke billow skyward. Fitzgerald said he drove over right away, and when he arrived he saw Bryan run out of the front door and saw the interior of the residence explode into flames behind Bryan.

Fitzgerald tried to help Bryan, who was covered with burns. But Bryan broke away and ran around to the rear of the trailer where he wrenched open a second door in an attempt to get inside. But flames roared out at him, and Fitzgerald restrained him.

Aeschliman then incorporates some vivid direct quotations into the story:

"He tried to get back inside, so I grabbed him and another man grabbed him and pulled him back and sat him down," Fitzgerald said.

"He just kept saying that his girl was in there and for somebody to go in and get her out. I just said no way, the heat was ungodly."

The smoke pouring out was so thick "it was like you could reach out and hold it in your hand," he said.

Aeschliman then quotes Fitzgerald on how the police and the firefighters were summoned and when the ambulance arrived.

Using vivid details: A question of taste   Aeschliman's city editor objects to a vivid, gruesome quotation that the reporter uses near the end of his story. It reads:

"You could tell he [Bryan] was realizing what had happened to him. He was looking at his hands and they were bleeding, and he had shoes on and there was blood coming from the shoes. His skin was peeling off like wallpaper. And he still wanted to go into the house," he said.

"The quote graphically details the man's injuries and his feelings at the time," Aeschliman said. "I believe it has value in demonstrating the horror of a fire. It is not just sensationalism; it may scare people, but we might save a life because of the morbid paragraph."

The reporter convinces the city editor to let the quotation run. A lot of newspaper editors and reporters, however, would undoubtedly have deleted the quotation as being too gruesome. They would have reasoned that the survivors had already suffered enough and that the vivid description was not necessary to tell the story. Matters of taste often crop up. It is the reporter's job to consider his or her position carefully concerning the printing of material that could be offensive to some readers and to discuss the matter with an editor.

As Aeschliman closes his story with more details from fire department officials, a couple of fire alarms go out, but they both turn into false calls. "We don't run out on every alarm," Aeschliman said. "Fire trucks are almost always at the scene in three minutes or less, and they immediately report the extent of the fire upon arrival. We can wait three minutes to decide."

A broadcast version of the fire story   Broadcast reporters would try to introduce the fire story dramatically so that listeners could set up the scene in their minds. Because the fire was major—two young girls had died—it would receive expanded treatment. Broadcast reporters would probably supplement the story with sight or sound from the scene. Here, though, is the story written in conversational broadcast style:

TWO YOUNG TOPEKA GIRLS DIED TODAY AS THEIR CRITICALLY
BURNED FATHER HELPLESSLY WATCHED THEIR MOBILE HOME GO
UP IN FLAMES. KENNETH BRYAN WAS ABLE TO ESCAPE FROM THE
STRUCTURE SECONDS BEFORE ITS INTERIOR EXPLODED INTO A
BLAZE. A MAN WHO WAS SHOPPING ACROSS THE STREET, JERRY
FITZGERALD, SPOTTED WHAT WAS THEN SMOKE AT 245 EAST 29TH,
SPED OVER IN HIS CAR AND REACHED THE SCENE JUST AS BRYAN
WAS RUNNING OUT OF THE FRONT DOOR.

FITZGERALD SAYS BRYAN WAS COVERED WITH BURNS . . . HIS
HANDS AND FEET WERE BLEEDING . . . AND HIS SKIN WAS PEELING
OFF . . . BUT HE REFUSED ASSISTANCE AND RAN TO THE BACK OF
THE TRAILER. DESPERATELY, BRYAN ATTEMPTED TO RESCUE HIS
ONE- AND THREE-YEAR-OLD DAUGHTERS WHO WERE STILL INSIDE.
BUT TONGUES OF FIRE LEAPT OUT AT HIM AS HE WRENCHED OPEN A
DOOR. FITZGERALD AND ANOTHER MAN HAD TO RESTRAIN THE
DISTRAUGHT FATHER FROM PLUNGING INTO THE FLAMES IN
SEARCH OF DAUGHTERS SHENA AND KIMBERLY. FITZGERALD SAYS
THE SMOKE AND HEAT WERE SIMPLY TOO INTENSE FOR BRYAN TO
HAVE BEEN ABLE TO REACH THEM.

OFFICIALS SAY ONE GIRL PROBABLY DIED FROM SMOKE INHALATION . . . THE OTHER WAS BURNED BEYOND RECOGNITION. AUTOPSIES WILL BE PERFORMED. BRYAN, MEANTIME, IS IN CRITICAL CONDITION WITH BURNS OVER MOST OF HIS BODY. HE'S BEING TREATED IN KANSAS CITY AT THE BURN CENTER OF THE KANSAS UNIVERSITY MEDICAL CENTER. THE CAUSE OF THE FIRE IN LOT ONE OF THE CREST MOBILE HOME PARK IS UNKNOWN.

Note that the broadcast story quickly tells that Bryan was able to escape the fire at the last moment. The story continues from Fitzgerald's point of view. Notice also how the address is worked into the story in a way that sounds natural. By using the short action verb *sped*, listeners get a feeling of urgency.

The name of the mobile home park and the lot number are placed at the end of the story because it would have been clumsy to mention them earlier; the fast-paced rhythm of the words would have been impeded.

The story also includes the extent of Bryan's injuries. This allows listeners to sense how desperate the father was in wanting to rescue his children. Near the end of the story, which would take about one minute and 15 seconds to read, additional details about the victims are provided. That the cause of the blaze is unknown is a logical way to conclude the broadcast story.

Writing the Purse-Snatching Story

After completing the major fire story, Aeschliman is ready to write a short story about the arrest in the purse snatching. He always tries to work most of the following ingredients into his arrest stories:

- Name of the suspect arrested
- Identification (for example, address and occupation)
- Site and time of the arrest
- Name and identification of the victim of the alleged crime
- Time of the alleged crime
- Details of the alleged crime
- Details of the capture and arrest of the suspect
- Details of the booking and charges
- Details of bail
- Quotations from police officials, the victim and the suspect

One officer used the words *cornered* and *flushed out* when he was interviewed by Aeschliman. The reporter's lead reads:

> A man who police think took a purse from a woman Friday was cornered in a nearby alley and arrested when a police dog flushed him out.

Aeschliman uses direct quotations in the second and third paragraphs:

Police in the area closed in on the alleged purse snatcher and cordoned off the area of 7th and Jewell, while the police helicopter circled overhead. He was in custody "before he knew what hit him," an officer at the scene said.

The arrest was "one of those things when everybody was at the right place at the right time," one officer said. "It was very satisfying."

"The story can be told without repeated reference by name to the suspect. In this way I can identify the arrested person early in the copy block and then later in the story refer to him merely as a man," Aeschliman said. "Officers and I never say, for example, that 'John Smyth took the purse and then hid' or anything close to that. I have to be especially careful when writing my stories to avoid convicting the suspect in print. Libel is always on my mind." (See Chapter 20 on covering the courts and Chapter 28 on law for further details.)

Aeschliman's story continues:

The suspect, John C. Smyth [not his real name], 19, of Wichita, was arrested in an alley behind 704 Lindenwood and booked into Shawnee County Jail in connection with burglary and theft, officer Mike Casey said.

Note that Aeschliman says that Smyth was booked *in connection with* burglary and theft. Aeschliman is careful not to write that Smyth was booked *for* burglary and theft. Use of the word *for* would imply guilt and could be libelous.

Aeschliman goes on to provide additional details on the booking of the suspect and uses direct quotations from the officers:

Smyth remained in jail late Friday in lieu of $5,000 bond with surety.

Casey said the theft happened at 2:48 p.m. An 81-year-old woman had just gotten out of her car near 6th and Franklin when a man leaped past her, into the car, grabbed her handbag and ran away.

The woman and a witness tried to chase the suspect but stopped and phoned police. The victim was not injured.

Officer J. W. Harper was patrolling a few blocks away and on a hunch circled to 7th Street where he saw a man walking down the middle of the street. Harper said he drove to within 100 feet of the suspect before the man looked up and sprinted away down an alley.

"He pulled a vanishing act," Harper said. "I was only seconds behind him and couldn't see him, so I figured he was holed up in a garage or something."

Aeschliman then went on to describe the arrival of a police helicopter, additional officers and a police dog. He quoted Harper again: "We put so much coverage in there so fast that he [the suspect] just froze up." Aeschliman also quoted Detective Greg Halford who said that the suspect had been interrogated and that the woman's purse and money had been recovered.

Again, it is clear that reporters can add considerable spice and detail to their coverage of relatively routine events by interviewing the officers involved. Also, one sentence in this story could have alerted reporters to a follow-up article: it is not every day that an 81-year-old woman chases a 19-year-old burglary suspect.

Aeschliman emphasized that he likes to have officers tell of their participation in an event. "Detective Halford has always been good to me," he said. "He really didn't do much in the arrest, but it never hurts to stroke a few egos by putting a name in print."

Writing the Burglary Story

Aeschliman starts to work on his third story—about the church burglary—but he is interrupted by a police call concerning an accident involving an injury. He listens carefully, but when the ambulance is turned back empty, he knows that it is not a severe accident. He returns to his story and writes:

Burglars broke into Holy Name Catholic Church Friday and then set fire to an interior room, apparently in an effort to hide several thefts.

Police said the break-in happened about 2:30 p.m. at the church, 1114 W. 10th. Burglars entered the church by unknown means and ransacked the sacristy—the room where sacred utensils and vestments are kept.

Thieves took several pyxes—vessels used to carry holy water and wafers—and then set fire to the area, police said.

The Topeka Fire Department was called to the scene at 3:09 p.m. and discovered the crime, police said. A fire official said the fire was of incendiary nature and did about $350 damage to the sacristy, with smoke damage outside the room.

"My lead in the church burglary story is almost verbatim from the police report synopsis, yet that is the best, shortest way to say it," Aeschliman explained. "The second paragraph gives details. Not everyone is Catholic and knows what a sacristy is, and so I tell them. The same is true of pyxes. It doesn't do any good to write a story if you leave the reader baffled by big words or skip logical connections. Most readers aren't going to get a dictionary during their morning coffee, and so I always explain what's going on."

FINAL DEADLINE: THE DAY ENDS

Aeschliman still has unanswered questions about several stories. "As the stories are being processed, I double-check the spelling of the name of the purse-snatch suspect. It's okay. I try to run down the condition of the burned man. Nothing is new there. I try to find out how old the man is, and which child was 3 and which was 1 in the major fire story. No one who knows is available. All the family are at the hospital; officials are unsure themselves, but they do confirm (off the record) that I have the right names."

It is 10:50 p.m. The newspaper's final deadline is midnight, "but for all practical purposes, it's 11 p.m. when the boss and everyone else goes home," Aeschliman said. "I make a series of late calls to ferret out any last-minute news. Usually there's none. Tonight a detective says that narcotics officials have just finished a drug raid. It's not spectacular, and so I bounce it off the boss. He says to write it—short. Out goes the innovation, and in comes the formula":

> Three women were arrested Friday
> night and another arrest is expected in
> a cocaine ring drug bust.

Aeschliman provides additional details in the second paragraph and lists the names of those persons booked in the third paragraph. A telephone call to the jail reveals that they have been released on bond. He closes his story—and his day—with that.

SUGGESTIONS FOR BEAT REPORTERS

There is no foolproof formula for competent reporting on the police and fire beats, but here are some suggestions:

- *Develop and cultivate sources.* Get to know sources as people—not merely as officials. Hang out at the departments as much as possible. "I don't stay in the newspaper office any longer than I have to," said Aeschliman. "You can't cultivate sources sitting in the newsroom."

- *Learn how to handle hostile sources.* Reporters on the scene of investigations run the risk of being perceived as interfering with official business. Some front-line police officers and firefighters dislike talking to reporters under these circumstances. If reporters persist, they run the risk of being arrested. Officers do not have to cooperate with reporters. In these cases, begging or shouting does not usually do much good. It is best to go to fire or police supervisors, who should provide information or instruct those under them to provide it. (See Chapter 11 for additional details on how to deal with hostile sources.)

- *Know the job responsibilities of sources.* Titles can be deceiving. Know what their jobs entail.

- *Don't deceive sources.* If reporters make an error, they should admit it.

- *If a big story comes along—one that places the department in a bad light—go after it aggressively.* Work hard on the story, even if it costs you some sources. Make sure, though, that the story is important enough to justify the loss of several major sources. If it is a piddling story, think twice about whether it is worth losing valuable sources.

- *Know the territory.* Spend time driving around; get to know the streets and alleys in the community. Know where the major crime areas are. That will make it easier to write stories when the *where* element is important.

- *Learn the terminology.* The police might say that they are *interrogating an individual* who is in custody. A journalist should report, however, that the police are *questioning a suspect.* Learn the terminology and jargon, but always write understandable English for readers.

- *Be aware of the special vocabulary of an agency.* In turn, explain terms to readers. For example, the terms *one-alarm, two-alarm, three-alarm* and *four-alarm fires* can have different meanings, depending on the community. In general, more firefighters and equipment are dispatched to two-alarm fires than to one-alarm fires. More still are sent to three-alarm and four-alarm fires. The number of firefighters and equipment sent, however, depends on the size of the community and the size of the fire department. Don't assume that readers understand these terms.

- *Double-check spellings of names and streets mentioned on law enforcement department reports.* Police officers are not trained journalists. Always verify information.

- *After reading a police report in which injuries are mentioned, always check with the hospital or the morgue to update or verify the information.* If the new information conflicts, another story angle might materialize.

- *Be particularly careful when reporting arrests.* Remember always to write, for example, that John Jones was arrested *in connection with* (or *in the investigation of*) a burglary at 1122 E. Norwood. *Don't write* that Jones was arrested *for* a burglary at 1122 E. Norwood. This implies guilt.

- *Don't confuse an arrest with the filing of a charge.* A lot of suspects who are arrested are subsequently released and are never charged with a crime. Also, if someone is arrested and you report it, write a follow-up story when the person is charged or released.

- *Be leery of libel.* Journalists have the privilege of reporting most of the information on public records, but they must do so fairly and accurately. And during interviews, the fact that a police officer utters a potentially libelous statement about a suspect does not give reporters the right or the legal privilege to reiterate that statement to readers.

- *Be sure to know an organization's policy on the use of minors' names.* Some newspapers have a policy against using the names of juveniles who are involved in misdemeanors. Also, be familiar with the laws of the state that govern coverage of juvenile proceedings.

20

Courts

Reporters strive to provide vivid, accurate coverage of litigation.
(Los Angeles Daily News/Sygma)

20

Courts

Reporters covering the courts must master judicial structures, learn the terminology and write stories in understandable language. The stakes are high: reporting errors can ruin lives and can lead to additional lawsuits. Court reporting requires persistence, diligence and an eye for detail.

Mike Padgett, a court reporter for the *Mesa (Ariz.) Tribune*, vividly pointed out the perils of the job: "If you make one screwup, at the very least, you lose some credibility. At the most, you libel somebody and end up in court yourself."

Padgett started as a general assignment reporter at the 45,000-circulation daily, moved to the police and fire beats and then went on to the county government and court beats.

He follows nearly two dozen cases regularly, tracking them through the various steps in the judicial process. "It can be slow and cumbersome," he said. "But it is important to keep up with cases carefully as they move through the system."

Unlike some court reporters, Padgett is not an attorney. His college degree is in journalism, and he minored in political science. He also worked for The Associated Press and as an investigator for the Task Force on Organized Crime for the Arizona House of Representatives before he started work at the *Tribune*.

Coverage of the courts is one of the most demanding assignments a reporter can receive. During one day of testimony in a criminal trial, enough words can be spoken to fill 200 manuscript pages. From the testimony, the reporter must extract the significant points and construct a readable, concise newspaper account of perhaps fewer than 500 words. Broadcast reporters face even more stifling restrictions on words.

"The biggest challenge in court reporting is getting a grasp of the system," said Robert Rawitch, a suburban editor of the *Los Angeles Times* who covered the federal courts in that city for more than four years. "It is difficult to develop an understanding of legal procedures and jargon. You must strive diligently not to exaggerate or to underplay the importance of any happening."

Metropolitan dailies generally have more than one reporter assigned to the courts. For example, one reporter might be assigned to the federal courts, one to the state criminal courts and another to the state civil courts. In addition, some metropolitan dailies have legal affairs reporters who are not responsible for daily developments in the various court systems but who write on broader issues, such as the workings of grand juries, civil rights prosecutions of police officers, sentencing patterns of judges, unaccredited law schools and the trend toward national law firms. The largest-circulation dailies also assign a reporter to cover the Supreme Court full time in Washington, D.C.

At the *Mesa Tribune*, as at most dailies with circulations less than 100,000, one person has primary responsibility for coverage of local and state courts. The *Tribune* relies on the wire services for coverage of federal courts.

THE JUDICIAL SYSTEM

Reporters need to have a basic understanding of the judicial system, on both the federal and the state levels. To help develop that understanding, aspiring court reporters should take appropriate college courses such as law and society, public law, American national government and constitutional law. The following overview serves as a starting point.

The Supreme Court is the nation's highest court. The term of the court begins the first Monday in October and usually lasts until late June or early July. It is divided between sittings and recesses. During sittings, cases are heard and opinions announced. During recesses, the nine justices consider the business before the court and write opinions. Sittings and recesses alternate at approximately two-week intervals.

The wire services, the largest newspapers and the networks assign reporters to cover the high court regularly. Reporters who cover the Supreme Court must have a solid understanding of the law and legal procedures in addition to being capable journalists. Complex legal language filling scores of pages must be deciphered when the written opinions are distributed. The facts of the case and the significance of the holding must be grasped. Reporters often select pertinent direct quotations from the majority, concurring or dissenting opinions. For background, law school professors or practicing attorneys are sometimes consulted for an interpretation of the significance of the case or for direct quotations.

Below the Supreme Court, at the intermediate level in the *federal judicial system*, are various circuits of the U.S. Court of Appeals. At the next level are U.S. District Courts, where trials in the federal system are generally held. There are nearly 100 such courts. Each state has at least one; the more heavily populated states have more than one.

STATE JUDICIAL SYSTEMS

There are about as many types of state court systems as there are states. Usually, a *state judicial system* has three layers:

- Trial courts, where proceedings are initiated
- Intermediate courts, where appeals are first heard
- Supreme courts, which are panels of final resort

The names assigned to the courts at each of these levels vary, but generally the highest is called the *state supreme court*. The intermediate level (used by about half the states) is called an *appellate court*. Trial-level bodies, often called *superior courts*, are the highest trial courts with general jurisdiction in most states. Sometimes they are given other names; for instance, in New York the trial-level body is the Supreme Court.

Several other courts complete the various state systems. These include probate courts (which handle wills, administration of estates and guardianship of minors and incompetents); county courts (which have limited jurisdiction in civil and criminal cases); municipal courts (where cases involving less serious crimes, generally called *misdemeanors*, are heard by municipal justices or municipal magistrates); and, in some jurisdictions, justice of the peace and police magistrate courts (which have very limited jurisdiction and are the lowest courts in the judicial hierarchy). Justice courts in Arizona, for example, hear matters that involve less than $500.

TYPES OF COURT CASES

Court cases can be lumped in two divisions: criminal and civil. *Criminal cases* involve the enforcement of criminal statutes. Suits are brought by the state or by the federal government against a person charged with committing a crime such as murder or armed robbery.

Civil cases involve arriving at specific solutions to legal strife between individuals, businesses, state or local governments or agencies of government. Civil cases commonly include suits for damages arising from automobile accidents, for breach of contract and for libel.

In the next two sections, we'll look at coverage of criminal cases and civil cases.

CRIMINAL CASES

As noted, criminal cases involve the enforcement of criminal statutes. In his book "The Reporter and the Law," Lyle Denniston, a veteran Supreme Court reporter, wrote: "Crime is the main staple of legal reporting. Of course, crime alone does not make all the news on the court beat. But it does dominate the beat."

Denniston continued: "Criminal law is simply more 'newsworthy' than civil law. More often, a criminal case will have in it the ingredients of human interest, public policy and clear-cut controversy that make news. At a more fundamental level, criminal law provides the most vivid test of a community's sense of justice and morality."

THE BASIC CRIMINAL PROCESS

Criminal charges may be brought against a person through an indictment or through the filing of an information. According to Black's Law Dictionary, an *indictment* is "an accusation in writing found and presented by a grand jury . . . charging that a person has done some act or been guilty of some omission which by law is a public offense." An *information*, according to the dictionary, differs from an indictment in that it is "presented by a competent public officer [such as a prosecuting attorney] on his oath of office, instead of a grand jury on their oath."

According to "Law and the Courts," published by the American Bar Association, the steps that occur after an indictment has been returned or an information has been filed are basically as follows (naturally, these steps and the names assigned to them can vary slightly among jurisdictions; reporters need to understand the process in jurisdictions in which they work):

- The clerk of the court issues a *warrant* for the arrest of the person charged (if the person has not been arrested already). According to Black's Law Dictionary, a warrant is "a written order issued and signed by [an appropriate official], directed to a peace officer or some other person specially named, and commanding him to arrest the body of a person named in it, who is accused of an offense."

- An *arraignment,* where the charge is read to the accused, is held. The arraignment is often held in a lower court. Typically, a plea is entered. In some states, this step is referred to as an *initial appearance.*

- *Plea bargaining,* when the prosecutor negotiates with the defense lawyers over the kind of plea the suspect might enter on a specific charge, can take place at any juncture. It often takes place after the arraignment but before the preliminary hearing. At this time, the prosecutor might propose that, in exchange for a plea of guilty, the state will bring a lesser charge against the suspect. The prosecutor might propose, for example, that the state bring a charge of assault instead of a charge of aggravated assault, a more serious crime that carries a more stringent penalty. In return, the defendant would plead guilty as charged, and the state would be spared the time and the expense of further proceedings. Plea bargaining, which helps unclog the courts, is a common practice. According to Denniston's "The Reporter and the Law," the "terms of a plea bargain ordinarily will have to be disclosed in open court, and usually will be subject to some inquiry by the judge as to the advisability of the bargain." Denniston wrote that the purpose of plea bargaining "is to determine whether a trial might be avoided, and a just result reached, by encouraging a person whose guilt is not in serious doubt to plead guilty or 'no contest.'" Criminal cases often conclude through plea bargaining.

- A *preliminary hearing* is held at which the state must present evidence to convince the presiding judge that there is probable cause to believe that the defendant committed the crime he or she is being charged with. If the judge agrees that there is probable cause, he or she will order the defendant bound over for trial.

- In some states, in lieu of a preliminary hearing, a *grand jury* is convened to determine if there is probable cause that a crime has been committed and if there is probable cause that the person charged with the crime committed it. A finding of probable cause is not, however, the same as a finding of guilty. That is determined at a trial. A grand jury is so labeled because it has more members than a trial jury. The number of people who serve on a grand jury varies among jurisdictions. In Arizona, for example, 16 people are impaneled. Nine are needed for a quorum.

- A date for another arraignment is set. The second arraignment is held in a court that has jurisdiction over the case.

- The *defendant* appears at the arraignment, where the judge reads the charge and explains the defendant's rights.

- The defendant then pleads guilty or not guilty. If the defendant pleads not guilty, a trial date is set. If the defendant pleads guilty, the judge sets a date for sentencing.

- For those defendants who plead not guilty, a jury is selected.

- Once the trial is under way, opening statements by the prosecuting attorney and by the defense attorney are made.

- The prosecuting attorney presents evidence (the state's evidence is always presented first).

- The defense attorney then presents evidence.

- Final motions and closing arguments are heard.

- The judge then reads instructions to the jury.

- The jury deliberates and returns with a verdict.
- The judge enters a judgment upon the verdict.
- If the defendant is found guilty, the judge sets a date for sentencing.
- After a presentence hearing, the judge will pronounce sentence.
- The defendant, if unhappy with the verdict, may appeal to a higher court. In most states, death penalties are appealed automatically.

All these steps are potentially newsworthy. Reporters must of course be extremely careful to attribute statements to legal documents or to the person who makes the statements in court. Accurate reporting based on legal documents or statements made in court is virtually libel-proof. (See Chapter 28 for a discussion of libel defenses that include the privilege of reporting.) The source of the information should be clear to the reader. It is always sound practice to attribute information, but it is particularly important when covering litigation.

For a complete discussion of the steps in a criminal case and the role of the journalist in the process, Denniston's book "The Reporter and the Law" is an excellent source.

REPORTING CRIMINAL CASES

As stated earlier, steps in criminal proceedings can vary. To illustrate general reporting procedures, however, this section will trace the *Mesa Tribune*'s coverage of a criminal case.

The Incident

Coverage of this case started in May with a story about a missing 13-year-old girl. More than 13 months and 100 stories later, a man was convicted of murdering and raping the teen-ager.

Tonia Twichell, a police beat reporter, wrote the first story about the disappearance of the girl. It began:

> Officers combed alleys, flew over canals and poked through garbage Thursday in search of clues to the disappearance of 13-year-old Christy Fornoff who vanished Wednesday while collecting for her Tempe newspaper route.
>
> Police, dogs, Tempe's mounted patrol, a Phoenix Police helicopter, the Tempe Police ultra-light aircraft and officers in squad cars and on foot blanketed central Tempe neighborhoods and fields.
>
> After peering under every desert bush for a mile, Tempe officers closed their command post Thursday afternoon at Bekin's Van Lines, 1888 E. Broadway Road.
>
> Christy, a Connolly Junior High School seventh-grader, who turned 13 on May 3, last was seen by her mother at the Rock Point Apartment complex at 2045 S. McClintock Drive.

The story went on to say that Christy's parents were confident that she would be found. The story quoted investigating officers; it noted that Tempe police were questioning felons living in the area who had been convicted of assaults and sexually related crimes; it described the girl; and it noted that *The Arizona Republic/The Phoenix Gazette* had offered a $5,000 reward for information concerning the girl's whereabouts.

A story published the following day, also written by Twichell, contained the bad news. The summary lead told the story:

> A maintenance man discovered the body of 13-year-old Christy Fornoff—dead of asphyxia—at 5:50 a.m. Friday, wrapped in a white bedsheet behind a dumpster in the same apartment complex where she was last seen.

The second paragraph included background on the girl's disappearance and the necessary attribution for the cause of death:

> Christy, who disappeared Wednesday evening while collecting on her paper route, died of asphyxia, according to the Maricopa County Medical Examiner's Office. She was wearing the same clothing she was last seen in: blue shorts, a white pullover, white tennis shoes and a black bathing suit underneath.

The story concluded with additional background but noted that further details about the girl's death were not available because the police had ordered a blackout of all information about the slaying. In the sixth paragraph, the story mentioned the name of the maintenance man who had found the body: Don Beaty.

The *Tribune*'s police reporters and general assignment reporters continued to keep pace with developments in the slaying. One follow-up story noted that the police were making progress in the investigation, but that they declined to say whether they had any suspects or if they expected an arrest soon. Another story focused on the fact that Beaty had lost his job as maintenance man at the apartment complex. Reporter John D'Anna's story opened with a summary lead and contained background on the Fornoff slaying. It began:

> The maintenance man who found the body of 13-year-old Christy Fornoff, the Tempe newspaper carrier raped and smothered to death eight days ago, says he has lost his job because of the furor over the investigation. He also said he plans to sue.
>
> Don Beaty, 29, has worked at the Rock Point Apartments, 2045 S. McClintock Road, for eight weeks. Beaty found the girl's body behind a dumpster in the complex two days after she disappeared while collecting for her *Phoenix Gazette* route.
>
> Since then, Beaty said he has been continually harassed by Tempe police, who initially told him he was a prime suspect. Beaty said since then police have told him he is not a suspect.
>
> On Friday, the management company that owns Rock Point told Beaty he could resign or be fired because he lied about having a criminal record on his employment application. He was given until 5 p.m. Monday to move out of his apartment.

The story included several extensive direct quotations from Beaty. Beaty's name was not well known when the story appeared, but that was soon to change.

Arrest

The police reporter, Twichell, carefully crafted a summary lead when an arrest was made. The first part of her story naturally focused on:

- The fact that an arrest had been made
- Details on charges that were being requested
- Subsequent steps in the judicial process

The story began:

The 29-year-old maintenance man who found the body of 13-year-old newspaper carrier Christy Fornoff on May 11 was arrested Monday in connection with her death.

After 10 days of undercover police surveillance, Don Edward Beaty was taken to the Tempe City Jail, where he is awaiting an initial appearance today in Tempe Justice Court.

First-degree murder, robbery and sexual abuse charges are being requested by the Maricopa County Attorney's Office and Tempe police.

Beaty, who refused to talk to police and asked for a lawyer, could be released on his own recognizance after the court appearance, but probably will be ordered held on bail in the Maricopa County Jail in Phoenix.

Beaty was arrested at 4:15 p.m. in the manager's office of Rock Point Apartments, 2045 S. McClintock Drive, where he worked until Friday.

Police Chief Arthur Fairbanks refused to say what led to the Monday arrest, but other police officers said the department had been awaiting test results from the Department of Public Safety crime laboratory.

Twichell was careful to write that Beaty had been arrested *in connection with* the death of the teen-ager (some newspapers prefer to use *in suspicion of* or *in the investigation of*). Twichell did not write that Beaty was arrested *for* the death; doing so would imply guilt and could lead to a libel suit. Also note that the story said the arrest was made in connection with the *death*—not the *murder*. The AP Stylebook emphasizes that reporters should not write that a victim was murdered until someone is convicted of murder. The stylebook advises that reporters should use the words *killed* or *slain*.

Lower-Court Arraignment

The *Tribune* followed with a story about the lower-court arraignment, which is called an *initial appearance* in Arizona. In most states, an arraignment in a lower court (designations of these courts vary, but they include *police courts, municipal courts, magistrate courts* and *justice courts*) generally takes place within a specified short period after the arrest. At the arraignment, the charge is read to the accused, who then enters a plea. The plea

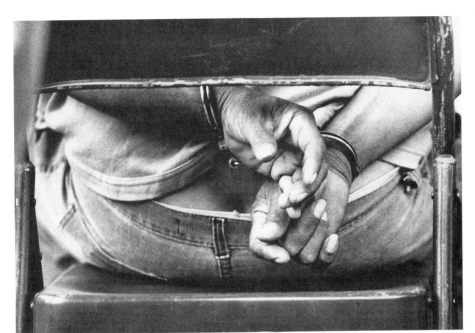

Arrests are made every day. Reporters routinely cover them, as well as subsequent steps in the judicial process. *(Photo by Sundi Kjenstad)*

normally becomes the story's lead. For the first time, the *Tribune* used in the lead paragraph the name of the accused, who by now was well-known to readers.

Donald Edward Beaty pleaded innocent to charges of first-degree murder and child molesting in the death of 13-year-old Christy Fornoff Tuesday in a heavily guarded courtroom.

After receiving phone calls threatening the 29-year-old Beaty's life, police switched courtrooms for the hearing, beefed up security and searched everyone who came to his initial appearance.

Beaty, looking disheveled after a night in Tempe City Jail, was ordered held under $685,000 bail in Maricopa County Jail in Phoenix.

Tempe Justice of the Peace Fred Ackel read Beaty the charges—which included robbery—and ordered him to appear May 31 for a preliminary hearing.

Beaty is accused of killing Fornoff after she disappeared May 9 while collecting for her *Phoenix Gazette* paper route at Rock Point Apartments, 2045 S. McClintock Drive. Beaty, who worked as a maintenance man at the apartments until Friday, found Christy's body May 11 in the complex behind a trash dumpster.

The story went on to provide attributed, documented details on Beaty's prior criminal record.

Note that the story said Beaty pleaded *innocent*. Actually, a defendant would plead *not guilty*. But newspapers long ago adopted the style of using the word *innocent* instead of the words *not guilty* to avoid the possibility that the word *not* would be inadvertently dropped from the story and thus render it inaccurate.

Preliminary Hearing or Grand Jury Proceeding

At a preliminary hearing, the judge must decide if the state's case is adequate to bring the accused to trial. The state, often without revealing all the information it has, must nevertheless present sufficient evidence to convince the judge that there is probable cause to believe that the defendant committed the crime. The state's preliminary hearing story often includes specifics on the testimony of law enforcement officers or other officials. Their testimony will probably be pivotal in deciding whether there is sufficient reason for the accused to stand trial.

As noted earlier, the procedure in some states is to bypass a preliminary hearing by referring the case to a grand jury, which will determine if there is probable cause that the person charged with the crime committed it. If the grand jury determines that there is sufficient evidence, it will return an indictment known as a *true bill.* If the grand jury decides that sufficient probability does not exist that the accused committed the crime, it will return a *no bill.*

In Arizona, both procedures are used: a preliminary hearing will sometimes be held; at other times the case is referred to a grand jury. The prosecutor can exercise either option. The Beaty case was referred to a grand jury.

The *Mesa Tribune*'s police and general assignment reporters had been covering the Beaty story to this point. Once the case went to the grand jury, however, a court reporter, Mike Padgett, took over. Grand jury proceedings are held behind closed doors. Details are given to the press if a true bill is returned. Padgett's first paragraphs were punchy and to the point:

A Maricopa County grand jury has indicted Donald Edward Beaty on charges of sexual assault and first-degree murder in the death of 13-year-old Christy Ann Fornoff of Tempe.

And a county official said Thursday tighter security will surround Beaty's arraignment next week.

Beaty, 29, was indicted by the grand jury late Wednesday. News of the indictment was not released to reporters until Thursday after Beaty received his copy, said Jane Bradley, spokeswoman for the county attorney's office.

Beaty's bond remains at $685,000. His scheduled arraignment is at 8:45 a.m. Wednesday before Maricopa County Superior Court Judge John H. Seidel.

Bradley said Seidel's courtroom is the smallest in Superior Court and easier to guard.

Higher-Court Arraignment

If the judge at the preliminary hearing decides that the evidence is sufficient, or if a grand jury returns a true bill, the accused is arraigned in a court that has jurisdiction. In Arizona, felony cases are heard in Superior Court. A *felony,* according to the American Bar Association's booklet "Law and the Courts," is "a crime of a graver nature than a misdemeanor [and generally is] an offense punishable by death or imprisonment in a penitentiary." The same source defines a *misdemeanor* generally as an offense "punishable by fine or imprisonment otherwise than in penitentiaries."

Padgett always makes an effort to sit in on the arraignment, even though most last only a few minutes. "You never know when someone—usually one of the attorneys—will come up with something newsworthy," he said. Generally, however, most arraignment stories lead with how the accused pleads to the charge. The *Tribune* story began:

Donald Edward Beaty pleaded innocent Wednesday to charges of first-degree murder and sexual assault in the slaying of Tempe newspaper carrier Christy Ann Fornoff.

At Beaty's arraignment, Superior Court Judge John Seidel scheduled a July 5 pretrial conference and a July 25 trial before Judge Rufus C. Coulter.

Both court dates are expected to be postponed by defense and prosecution motions.

Beaty, 29, remained in the Maricopa County Jail Wednesday in lieu of posting $685,000 bail.

Seidel accepted Beaty's pleas of innocent from a public defender, Mary Wisdom, who was appointed to defend Beaty.

Note that Padgett's story contains background on the circumstances that led to the arraignment. Reporters should always provide background. Background information can be developed by reviewing clippings of previous stories written about the case and by interviewing attorneys and others close to the case. Even when reports of judicial proceedings are in the news for an extended time, journalists must assume that most readers do not know the background of the case.

The Trial

Pretrial developments Before a trial, newspapers will generally publish stories that summarize past developments and inform readers of new information. The Beaty trial, for example, was delayed eight times. Naturally, the *Tribune* followed the developments closely. One of Padgett's pretrial stories focused on the pervasive publicity that the Beaty proceedings were generating.

A story by Tonia Twichell focused on Beaty's hunger strike in the county jail to protest what he alleged to be poor conditions and threatening behavior by guards.

One of Padgett's main pretrial stories discussed the issuance of a gag order. A *gag order*, which is sometimes called a *protective order*, is a judicial mandate that orders the press to refrain from disseminating specific information or that orders those associated with the trial or the investigation not to discuss the case with the press. (See Chapter 28 for a discussion of legal ramifications of the fair trial–free press issue.) Padgett's story began:

A Maricopa County Superior Court judge Friday issued a gag order and banned camera coverage of all pretrial proceedings in the Christy Ann Fornoff murder case.

On two other motions, Judge Rufus C. Coulter Jr. said he would decide later whether to ban cameras during the trial of Donald Edward Beaty, and whether it should be moved because of publicity.

The trial is scheduled to start next Wednesday, but it is expected to be reset. If it appears an unbiased jury cannot be chosen in Maricopa County, Coulter said he then would rule on defense attorney Michael A. Miller's motion to move the trial.

"But it's consistently been my policy to wait until at least an attempt has been made to select a jury," the judge said.

After providing background on the case, Padgett elaborated on the gag order. He wrote:

Since his arrest, Beaty and his attorney have granted interviews with reporters. But now the court's gag order means Beaty, Miller, police, witnesses, court staff, county prosecutors, Department of Public Safety laboratory staff and anyone else associated with the investigation cannot discuss the case with reporters.

"In the future, all information about this case will flow through (Superior Court information officer) Rob Raker," the judge said Friday.

When attorney David J. Bodney, representing the First Amendment Coalition, attempted to argue the judge's gag order and asked whether the judge would accept a written objection, the judge said he won't change his mind.

Jury selection More than six months after Beaty was arrested and arraigned, the case was ready to go to trial. A jury was selected. This generally merits a news story. Padgett wrote:

From a crowd of 150 prospective jurors, nine men and seven women were selected Tuesday to hear the first-degree murder trial of Donald Edward Beaty, the man charged in the slaying of 13-year-old Christy Ann Fornoff of Tempe.

After jury selection, defense attorney Michael A. Miller objected to public questioning of the jurors, saying they should have been interviewed in-

dividually. Maricopa County Superior Court Judge Rufus Coulter said there was no need for that.

"I'm satisfied we have a fair and impartial jury," the judge told Miller.

Beaty's trial, which is expected to last a month, is set to begin Thursday, even though attorneys still are waiting for the return of some evidence and a final scientific report.

Testimony Reporters provide gavel-to-gavel coverage of only the most important trials. Certainly the Beaty trial fell into that category for the *Mesa Tribune* and Padgett.

"I try never to miss the opening day of a trial," Padgett said. "On that day, most prosecuting attorneys are going to say, 'That guy did it and we have the evidence to back up the charge.' Once they are finished, the defense attorneys will say something like, 'The evidence is not there. My client did not do it.' They will try to shoot holes in the opening statement of the prosecutor. You want to get the opening statements down for the readers. I often use a tape recorder because I want to get as much color as possible. I also take notes. I have found, however, that tape recorders allow me to be more productive and more accurate."

Relatively minor cases might go to the jury within a day or so. Major trials, however, run much longer. Beaty's first trial lasted seven weeks (and then, after it ended in a mistrial, a second trial lasted six weeks more).

Reporters must diligently follow the testimony in long-running major trials. "You have to spend several hours each day in the courtroom," Padgett said. "It does not do much good to drop in for an hour or so, because you have no way of predicting what will happen. One hour is not enough. You simply must sit and listen. Sometimes it gets really tedious. There were days at the Beaty trial when it would be 4 p.m. and I still did not have a strong lead for the day. On several days, key testimony during the last 30 minutes of the session gave me my lead. If you are not there for the duration, you risk missing the most significant angle."

Also, reporters must often keep track of developments in less significant trials. Padgett, for example, was following the progress of other cases while he was devoting most of his time to the Beaty trial. "You often have to call the judge's secretary to keep up with other trials," Padgett said. "It is important to get to know the judge's staff—the secretary, the bailiff, the court reporter. Get to know them on a first-name basis. It helps when you have to telephone them for updates because you are tied up with a major case like Beaty's. Secretaries are very helpful. They keep the judges' schedules, and so they always know what is happening."

Reporters occasionally trade information. Padgett, however, does not like to do this because he can never be sure how accurate the information is. "I don't want to risk getting duped," he said. "If other reporters ask me for basic (non-exclusive) information, I provide it, but I always refer them to an attorney or to someone involved for verification."

There is no substitute for being in court, always looking for the most interesting, most significant developments. Without warning, for example, shouting matches can erupt. Because these spur-of-the-moment developments are often important to a story, reporters have to be alert for them. They will be difficult to reconstruct if you have to rely on secondhand information.

Attribution is also imperative when reporting key testimony. It is absolutely essential that quotations be accurate and that readers be made aware of who is making statements or articulating opinions. (See Chapter 7 for guidelines on methods and placement of attribution.) Here are the first four paragraphs from one of Padgett's stories on the trial (note how careful he was to attribute all information):

Christy Ann Fornoff, the 13-year-old girl found killed last May in an apartment parking lot, died of asphyxiation after a brief struggle, a medical expert testified Tuesday.

Dr. Heinz Karnitschnig, chief Maricopa County medical examiner, also said a lack of decomposition indicated the girl's body was kept in a cool place for nearly two days before she was found May 11 in the parking lot of the Rock Point Apartments, 2045 S. McClintock Drive. Karnitschnig said he performed the autopsy within hours after the body was found. A few bruises were found on her, but nothing to indicate there was a violent struggle before she died.

"There may have been (a struggle), but only a minimal amount of struggle," he said. "Her airway was occluded in some kind of way; either a hand was held over her or she was pushed into some permeable materials (such as a pillow)."

Karnitschnig was the fourth person to testify Tuesday in the trial of Donald Edward Beaty, charged with first-degree murder and sexual assault in the Fornoff girl's death.

Padgett also provided quotations from other testimony and closed his story with the fact that the names of 147 persons were on a list of potential witnesses.

On another day, Padgett focused on testimony from a forensic expert. Note how Padgett did not identify the expert by name—only by occupation—in the lead paragraph. That way, the lead was more streamlined and the authoritative attribution was sufficient. Here are the first three paragraphs:

> Human hairs found throughout Donald Edward Beaty's Tempe apartment exhibit "similar characteristics" to hair taken from Christy Ann Fornoff, the 13-year-old girl he is accused of slaying, a forensic expert testified Tuesday.
>
> In addition, a pubic hair taken from the girl's body is similar to Beaty's pubic hair, according to testimony of Edward Trujillo, a state Department of Public Safety laboratory technician.
>
> Trujillo said human head hair found in Beaty's apartment doorway, on the bathroom floor, on and under his living room couch, from a bed sheet found in his spare bedroom closet and from vacuumed particles from the closet are similar to the victim's head hair.

Mistrials   Padgett followed the case day by day for seven weeks. The case was sent to the jury, but the jury was unable to break a 10–2 deadlock. A mistrial was declared, and a second trial was scheduled.

About a month after the mistrial was declared, the second trial began. A new jury was in place. The second trial might be a new experience for members of the jury, but some of the testimony and evidence will be familiar to other participants in the trial and to reporters. Reporters nevertheless must stay alert for new developments. During the fifth week of the second trial, for example, Padgett's story led with a significant development. His story began:

> Saying "I didn't mean to kill her . . . I'm not the terrible man they say I am," Donald Edward Beaty confessed last December to slaying 13-year-old Christy Ann Fornoff, a jail psychiatrist testified Monday.
>
> Dr. George S. O'Connor, under a judge's orders to tell Beaty's private conversation with him, testified: "He (Beaty told me he) didn't mean to kill her. She had been making a lot of loud sounds and her mother was outside."
>
> O'Connor's testimony came in the fifth week of Beaty's second trial, and it was by far the most incriminating evidence to date in a case that has been built on circumstantial evidence.
>
> The first trial—less the psychiatrist's testimony—ended earlier this year in a hung jury.
>
> Beaty, 30, is charged with first-degree murder and sexual assault in the Fornoff girl's death. She vanished May 9 while on her newspaper route at the Rock Point Apartments, 2045 S. McClintock Drive in Tempe.

The vivid direct quotation was the natural lead. Sometimes it is best to paraphrase testimony to streamline the first paragraph. But when the quotation is extremely powerful, it is best to use it verbatim. Note also how Padgett was careful to weave background information into his story relatively high. The story continued with a discussion of the appropriateness of the psychiatrist's testimony.

Closing arguments   Padgett was in court for the closing arguments. "Just as I never want to miss opening statements, I never want to miss the closing arguments," he said.

After the closing arguments, the case goes to the jury. If the closing occurs late in the afternoon, the judge will generally instruct the jury members to return the next morning to begin deliberations.

"I always try to stay in the courtroom when the jury is locked in its room deliberating," Padgett said. "I want to be there when the jury comes out."

Verdict   The climax of a criminal trial is the verdict. There is no sacrosanct formula for writing verdict stories, but they should contain these essential ingredients:

- Outcome (was the accused found guilty or not guilty?)
- Precise charge (for example, murder)
- Length of jury deliberations
- Date of sentencing
- Range of penalties established by law
- Reactions of the defendant, the defendant's family and the defense attorneys
- Reactions of the victim or the victim's family
- Reaction of attorneys for the prosecution
- Background of the case
- Review of key testimony throughout the trial
- Possibility of appeal

Here are the first six paragraphs of Padgett's story on the verdict (note how he worked many of the key ingredients into the first part of his story):

A Maricopa County Superior Court jury deliberated less than 10 minutes Thursday before finding Donald Edward Beaty guilty of murdering and raping 13-year-old Christy Ann Fornoff of Tempe.

Beaty, 30, is scheduled to be sentenced July 22. He could face the death sentence for first-degree murder.

Defense attorney Michael Miller said he probably would appeal.

Reaction to the verdict ranged from relief by the girl's family to anger from a woman who sat behind Beaty in court and who had taken charge of having his clothes cleaned and pressed.

The victim's parents, Roger and Carol Fornoff, were not in court Thursday morning because they hadn't expected a decision so quickly. After the verdict was announced, they met with reporters in the county attorney's office.

"It's a relief for us, knowing this man has been convicted," Carol Fornoff said. "We know he won't be on the streets. He won't be doing it again."

Note that the word *murdering* is used after the conviction.

Often, the lead practically writes itself in a verdict story, but the reporter must work hard to assemble the remainder of the account. Padgett, for example, always concentrates on the reaction of the defendant. "I keep my eyes on the defendant," Padgett said. "I want the defendant's reaction—or lack of reaction. Some do not react; some almost crumble; and some will sit down and put their heads on the table."

Padgett also likes to interview spectators, lawyers and jurors. "The primary job is to get quotes from the jurors," he said. "While the trial is going, they can't talk to anyone. But once they render a verdict, they can talk to the press if they want to. I like to talk to them. I want to know what convinced them one way or the other. It also is important to talk to the attorneys. It is very hectic. You try to be in several places at the same time, but it doesn't work very well. I always try to get to the jurors first. They sometimes disappear in a hurry. I can usually get back to the lawyers."

The *Tribune* reporter always tries to interview the defendant. "It is almost impossible to get to a defendant—right away—who has been found guilty," Padgett said. "Sometimes, you might be able to get in a couple of questions walking down the hallway, but that's about it."

Padgett routinely tries to get word to the defendant—through the defense attorney or through the bailiff—that he would like to interview him or her. "If the defendant agrees to talk, you've got an exclusive," Padgett said. "The worst that can happen is that the defendant will say no."

Padgett was surprised after the Beaty trial; the defendant got word to the reporter that he would like to be interviewed. "I can't take much credit for getting the interview," Padgett said. "Beaty had not liked the coverage by some of the other newspapers, and so he called me." The *Tribune* ran the interview story on the front page with the verdict story. It began:

> "I don't care what the jury said—I know I am not guilty," Donald Edward Beaty declared shortly after a jury convicted him of first-degree murder and sexual assault in the death of 13-year-old Christy Ann Fornoff.
>
> In a jail-house interview after the verdict was returned, Beaty contended that key witnesses lied under oath, that his attorney gave up toward the end of the trial and that he had wanted to testify in his own defense.
>
> "I'm innocent, and I intend to fight it," Beaty said. "I didn't even see her that night. That's the whole deal."

The story continued with more vivid quotations.

When a jury returns a verdict late in the afternoon, broadcast reporters must scramble to put their stories together. Radio stations can air a verdict seconds after it is rendered.

A radio reporter could call in a one-sentence story:

DONALD BEATY HAS BEEN CONVICTED OF THE RAPE AND MURDER OF 13-YEAR-OLD NEWSPAPER CARRIER CHRISTY ANN FORNOFF OF TEMPE.

The reporter would then work to assemble a handful of additional facts and a direct quotation to include in a slightly expanded story for the hourly news. Television reporters would work to coordinate words with pictures for their early evening newscasts.

Here is a typical broadcast story written just minutes after the verdict and emphasizing the most important facts:

DONALD BEATY HAS BEEN CONVICTED OF THE RAPE AND MURDER OF 13-YEAR-OLD NEWSPAPER CARRIER CHRISTY ANN FORNOFF OF TEMPE. THE MARICOPA COUNTY SUPERIOR COURT JURY TOOK ONLY 10 MINUTES TO RENDER ITS VERDICT. IT CAME SO QUICKLY THAT THE VICTIM'S PARENTS WERE NOT IN THE COURTROOM TO HEAR IT. HOWEVER, MEETING WITH REPORTERS LATER, CHRISTY ANN'S MOTHER SAID SHE WAS RELIEVED AT BEATY'S CONVICTION. IN HER WORDS, "HE WON'T BE DOING IT AGAIN." THE 30-YEAR-OLD BEATY COULD BE GIVEN THE DEATH PENALTY WHEN HE IS SENTENCED JULY 22ND.

Because the case involves a person whose name had been in the news so often, Beaty is named in the lead without a phrase describing who he is. Identifying the Fornoff girl as a newspaper carrier gives the audience an indication of why she might have been around Beaty at the time she was murdered.

Broadcast reporters who write a story immediately after the verdict would choose the strongest quotation from the mother. Mrs. Fornoff's remark that "he won't be doing it again" is vivid; it capsulizes her feelings. This is particularly important in radio, a non-visual medium. Listeners could not see how the parents feel, but they could get a picture in their minds through this quotation.

The bare-boned broadcast version could be written quickly. Reporters could add details for subsequent broadcasts.

Coverage of criminal proceedings generally does not end with the verdict. There will be a presentence hearing, a sentencing and often an appeal. Let's look at these.

Presentence hearing   Padgett was in court for Beaty's presentence hearing. The lead summarized the testimony of Beaty's former wife. The story began:

The ex-wife of convicted child-murderer Donald Beaty testified Thursday that he molested several children, including his newborn daughter, and sold their son for $1,000 and a pickup.

Mary Gray said the day she returned from the hospital with their daughter, Beaty fondled the baby and "would laugh about it."

More than 50 spectators sat silently and listened intently during a presentence hearing as Gray and six others graphically described Beaty's past sexual conduct.

Their frank testimony became the only evidence presented to Superior Court Judge Rufus Coulter, who will pronounce either a life or death sentence Monday.

The damaging testimony never came to light during Beaty's first or second trial. The first ended in a hung jury.

Defense Attorney Michael A. Miller called Thursday's presentence hearing "a mud-slinging contest" by people "who don't like Don Beaty." He said he asked Beaty if he wanted to testify and Beaty said no.

In fact, no one testified for Beaty. His brother and sister in Tennessee, whose transportation to Phoenix had been paid, failed to appear. Another brother in Phoenix, Fred Beaty, who was in court, didn't testify and declined to talk to a reporter after the hearing.

Sentencing   Padgett was well-prepared to write the story of the sentencing. He had been covering the Beaty trial for months; he had background information at his fingertips; and he understood the nuances of the case. His lead was straightforward:

Donald Edward Beaty, convicted last month of the first-degree murder of 13-year-old Christy Ann Fornoff, Monday was sentenced to die in the gas chamber.

Maricopa County Superior Court Judge Rufus Coulter Jr. told Beaty he had "committed the offense in an especially heinous, cruel and depraved manner."

The death penalty will be appealed automatically.

Coulter also sentenced Beaty, 30, to the maximum term of 28 years in prison for sexually assaulting the girl.

Beaty, who has maintained his innocence, stood before the judge handcuffed and dressed in blue jail fatigues and soiled red tennis shoes. Almost imperceptibly, he began trembling after he was sentenced to death.

Appeal   Four years after Beaty was sentenced to die, the case was still in the judicial system. The *Mesa Tribune* continued to follow developments. Richard Polito's lead was to the point:

The U.S. Supreme Court on Monday rejected the appeal of Donald Edward Beaty, an apartment complex maintenance man who is on death row for the sex-slaying of 13-year-old Christy Ann Fornoff, a newspaper carrier.

The girl vanished while collecting at a Tempe apartment complex where Beaty worked.

The justices let stand rulings that Beaty received a fair trial and properly was sentenced to death.

The story went on to quote the victim's mother, who said that she was disheartened to hear that further appeals were likely. Background on the slaying followed. The story ended with this paragraph: "There has not been an execution in Arizona since 1963, and Beaty still has avenues of appeal through the federal courts."

The Aftermath

Three years after Beaty's appeal was rejected, the story continued to develop when the Fornoffs entered into a settlement in a wrongful-death suit they had brought. Lynn DeBruin's story in the *Mesa Tribune* began with these paragraphs:

Roger Fornoff says he'll never get over the murder of his youngest daughter, Christy Ann.

He and his wife, Carol Ann, still celebrate her birthday. On May 3 this year, she would have been 21.

"We stopped crying for the time being. But a song can set you off, or meeting a friend," Roger Fornoff said.

What has helped most has been talking it out in bereavement groups.

"There's a lot of need for it. People hurt," the Tempe resident said.

With that in mind, he said he and his wife hope to use part of their $1.5 million settlement from the wrongful-death suit for such programs.

The Fornoffs reached the settlement this week in their suit against the operator of the apartment complex where their 13-year-old daughter was killed . . . by maintenance man Donald Edward Beaty.

"I have to believe that (if they had done more background checks), Christy would still be alive," Fornoff said.

The Fornoffs filed suit . . . accusing Continental American Management Corp. of negligence in hiring Beaty to work at Rock Point Apartments.

The second half of DeBruin's story provided background on the case that had been in the news for nearly eight years. It also gave additional details on how the Fornoffs had devoted considerable time in recent years to calling attention to the need for schools and businesses to run sufficient checks on potential employees.

Analysis and Feature Articles on Criminal Cases

Coverage of the Beaty case by the *Mesa Tribune* illustrates that there are several newsworthy points as a case makes its way through the judicial system. The coverage often extends beyond courthouse drama. Analysis pieces and feature articles can accompany coverage of litigation. Alert reporters often pick up on items of interest to readers by keeping their eyes and ears open.

Padgett wrote several features and analysis pieces during the months of the Beaty litigation. Here are the first four paragraphs of one of Padgett's analysis pieces:

On the periphery of the testimony and drama of Donald Edward Beaty's murder trial, a quiet circus of sorts is taking place.

There is the judge's secretary who, in addition to her regular duties of supervising the judge's hectic daily calendar, is answering phone calls from prospective onlookers who ask directions to Maricopa County Superior Court in Phoenix. They ask whether parking is available, is it expensive, how is the food in the cafeteria, is the courtroom packed and show times.

They pack the courtroom and those who don't get in wait until a seat becomes available. They know the cameras are rolling, too, some even hopeful they'll get on TV. And curiously, one juror appears to take catnaps during this trial, one of the Valley's most publicized in recent years.

They come to see Beaty, the Tempe maintenance man indicted on charges of first-degree murder and sexual assault in the May 9 death of 13-year-old Christy Ann Fornoff.

Again, Padgett was careful to put background information on the case relatively high in the story. After inserting the background, Padgett provided direct quotations from sources and more observation.

Dealing with Sources on Criminal Cases

Whether they are covering major murder cases or proceedings that involve misdemeanors, reporters must develop a reliable network of sources. In addition to gaining the respect of judges and lawyers, reporters should strive to be on a first-name basis with sources such as:

- Secretaries
- Bailiffs
- Court public information officers
- Clerks
- Record-keeping personnel

These sources can help alert reporters to new cases and to developments in ongoing cases. Sources should be cultivated and never taken for granted.

Experience can help reporters deal with sources. Some attorneys and law enforcement officers, for example, crave publicity. Sometimes the information they provide is helpful. At other times they are clearly supplying less-than-essential information for their own political gain.

Experience helps reporters recognize the motives sources might have for parting with information. "Clerks are good sources because they do not have a vested interest in most cases," Robert Rawitch of the *Los Angeles Times* said. "Prosecuting attorneys and defense lawyers, although they can be helpful, do have such a vested interest. As a reporter, you must be wary of that."

Sources, particularly lawyers and judges, sometimes try to evade questions by giving rambling answers packed with legalese. Persist. Continue to repeat the question until the answer is given in understandable English.

Padgett's coverage of the Beaty proceedings illustrates the diligence and the attention to detail that are necessary when reporting on litigation. Naturally, not all the criminal cases reporters cover gain the attention that the Beaty proceedings generated. Padgett's comments on gathering information, writing stories and dealing with sources and fellow reporters apply equally, however, to covering less spectacular cases such as burglaries and assaults.

CIVIL CASES

Often, dozens of *briefs* (written reports in which lawyers set forth facts that support their positions) are filed in civil suits. Reporters must periodically check court *dockets* that record progress in specific cases. All complaints filed, motions made and other developments in a case are recorded chronologically on a docket.

In Superior Court for Los Angeles, to take one example, the average civil suit is in the system—from time of *filing* until trial or settlement—approximately four years. It is not unusual for cases to extend six or seven years. Metropolitan court systems are often short on personnel for civil cases, and legal requirements force them to give priority to criminal cases. The normal criminal cases in Superior Court for Los Angeles will generally conclude from two to four months after the arrest.

Understanding record-keeping systems is a critical element in good court coverage. Reporters in small cities do not face the crunch of cases that metropolitan reporters do, but regardless of the case load, reporters must watch dockets and calendars closely. In Superior Court for Los Angeles, the civil courts reporter for the *Los Angeles Times* is usually following the progress of more than 500 pending suits. "It is a bookkeeping nightmare," Rawitch said.

The filing system in Los Angeles' civil division of Superior Court is efficient and detailed, but Rawitch said that reporters must spend more than an hour each day checking case numbers listed on the court calendar.

THE BASIC CIVIL PROCESS

Steps taken in a civil suit vary. Procedural maneuverings can be complex and time-consuming. According to "Law and the Courts," here is the basic process:

- The *plaintiff* (the party bringing the suit) selects the proper jurisdiction (federal or state system, and the appropriate court thereof).
- The plaintiff files a *complaint* (sometimes called a *petition*) against a party (called the *defendant*). The complaint usually contains a precise set of arguments that include the damages sought. *Damages* are the estimated monetary value for the injury allegedly sustained. Of course, the filing of a complaint does not ensure that the plaintiff has a cause of action.
- The defendant is served with a *summons*, a writ informing him or her that he or she must answer the complaint.
- After a specified period, the defendant is required to file his or her *pleading*, or answer, to the plaintiff's charges.
- *Depositions* (out-of-court statements made by witnesses under oath) are taken.
- After all the pleadings have been filed, attorneys for both parties appear before a judge at a pretrial conference to agree on the undisputed facts of the case. (Often a *settlement* is reached at this point without trial.)
- If no settlement is reached, the case is scheduled for trial.
- Testimony as to the dispute is presented, and arguments are heard at the trial.
- After the arguments, the judge instructs the jury (unless the defendant has waived his or her right to a jury proceeding) on legal considerations.
- The jury goes to its room for deliberations.
- The jury returns with a verdict.

- The verdict is announced, and the judge enters a judgment upon the verdict.
- If either party is unhappy, an appeal can be made.

REPORTING CIVIL CASES

Scores of civil suits are filed each day in metropolitan jurisdictions. Certainly not all of them are newsworthy. Reporters must decide which suits are important and then must constantly check court dockets for developments. The following suit—the William Westmoreland suit—involved a well-known Army general and the Columbia Broadcasting System, and thus would clearly be considered newsworthy.

Examining a Complaint in a Civil Suit

In the Westmoreland suit, the complaint, filed in the U.S. District Court for the District of South Carolina, Greenville Division, was assigned Civil Action No. 82-2228-3.

The beginning of the complaint looked like this:

GENERAL WILLIAM C. WESTMORELAND,
United States Army (retired)
P.O. Box 1059
Charleston, South Carolina 29402
(803) 577–3156
                        Plaintiff
                        v.
COLUMBIA BROADCASTING SYSTEM, INC.,
51 West 52nd Street
New York, New York 10019
(212) 975–4321
and
VAN GORDON SAUTER, President
of CBS News
524 West 57th Street
New York, New York 10019
(212) 975–4153
and
GEORGE CRILE,
555 West 57th Street
New York, New York 10019
(212) 975–2915
and
MICHAEL WALLACE,
555 West 57th Street
New York, New York 10019
(212) 975–2997
and

SAMUEL A. ADAMS
Route 3, Box 442
Leesburg, Virginia 22075
(703) 882–3351
Defendants

COMPLAINT
(Libel, False Light)

(1) Jurisdiction herein is founded on 28 U.S.C. Sec. 1332 (a). Plaintiff and defendants are residents of different states and the amount in controversy exceeds $10,000, exclusive of interest and costs.

(2) Venue is proper in this Court under 28 U.S.C. Sec. 1391 (a).

(3) Plaintiff, General William Childs Westmoreland, United States Army, Retired, is a resident of Charleston, South Carolina. General Westmoreland was the Commander in Chief of the United States Military Assistance Command in Vietnam ("MACV") from June 1964 until June 1968. General Westmoreland was also the chief U.S. advisor to the Vietnamese military forces during the same four year period.

(4) Defendant, Columbia Broadcasting System, Inc. ("CBS"), is a corporation organized under the laws of the State of New York, whose principal place of business is located at 51 West 52nd Street, New York, New York, 10019. CBS News is a division of CBS and its principal place of business is located at 524 West 57th Street, New York, New York, 10019.

(5) Defendant Van Gordon Sauter is President of CBS News, and has been since March 1, 1982. Upon information and belief, he is a resident of the State of New York.

(6) Defendant George Crile is an employee of CBS. Defendant Crile was the producer of the CBS broadcast "The Uncounted Enemy: A Vietnam Deception" (hereinafter "the Broadcast"). Crile also participated in the Broadcast as an on and off camera interviewer. Upon information and belief he is a resident of the State of New York.

(7) Defendant Michael Wallace is an investigative reporter employed by CBS. Wallace served as narrator and interviewer for the Broadcast. Upon information and belief, he is a resident of the State of New York.

(8) Defendant Samuel A. Adams served as a paid consultant to CBS for purposes of the Broadcast, receiving $25,000 therefor, and appeared as an interviewee in the Broadcast. Upon information and belief, he is a resident of the Commonwealth of Virginia.

(9) On January 23, 1982, CBS aired the Broadcast at issue, a "CBS Report" entitled, "The Uncounted Enemy: A Vietnam Deception." The Broadcast was aired on stations WLTX-TV in Columbia, South Carolina, WBTW-TV in Florence, South Carolina, and numerous other CBS affiliates in all 50 states. The number of viewers of the Broadcast was estimated by the Nielsen Company to have been 20,041,920.

(10) The Broadcast dealt with the U.S. military's handling of intelligence regarding enemy troop strength estimates in the year prior to the 1968 Tet Offensive of the Vietnam War. The Tet Offensive began on or about January 30, 1968.

COUNT ONE
(Libel)

(11) Plaintiff adopts herein by reference paragraphs 1 through 10.

(12) On Friday, January 22, 1982, CBS placed identical full page advertisements in The Washington Post, The New York Times and upon information and belief in other newspapers across the country (hereinafter the "Advertisements"). A copy of the Advertisement which appeared in The New York Times is attached hereto as Exhibit A. The Advertisements announced a CBS Report, to be aired on January 23, 1982 and entitled, "The Uncounted Enemy: A Vietnam Deception." The Advertisements were composed of a drawing of men in uniform, seated around a conference table, with the word "Conspiracy" superimposed in large letters. The text of the Advertisement read in part:

> CBS Reports reveals the shocking decisions made at the highest level of military intelligence to suppress and alter critical information on the number and placement of enemy troops in Vietnam. A deliberate plot to fool the American public, the Congress and perhaps even the White House . . .

The complaint continued with six more paragraphs under Count One. It went on to list four additional *counts* [parts of a civil complaint claiming specific wrong done] of allegedly libelous information broadcast about Westmoreland by CBS. The complaint concluded with the following:

WHEREFORE, plaintiff, General William Childs Westmoreland respectfully prays that the Court award him the following relief:
(A) Judgment in his favor and against each defendant, and all of them, jointly and severally, in the amount of $40,000,000 compensatory damages.
(B) Judgment in his favor and against each defendant, and all of them, jointly and severally, in the amount of $80,000,000 punitive damages.
(C) Judgment in his favor for the costs of this action, including attorneys' fees.
(D) Interest on all amounts awarded.
(E) Such other relief as to the Court may deem just and proper.

JURY DEMAND
Plaintiff hereby demands trial by a jury of 12 on all issues.

Essential Ingredients of Stories on Civil Suits

A story about the Westmoreland civil suit—like all court-related articles—should contain certain essential ingredients:

- It should tell who is bringing the suit (the plaintiff).
- It should tell who is being sued (the defendant).
- It should tell when the suit was filed.
- It should identify the parties as fully as possible.
- It should provide background on the circumstances that brought about the suit.
- It should give specifics on the damages sought.
- It should give the defendants' response to the complaint.
- It should fully attribute all information. When appropriate, it should make absolutely clear to the readers that the information came from court records.

Newspapers do not cover most civil suits at every step in the judicial process. Often, a short story is written when a suit is filed, and another story is written when the suit is dismissed or settled or when there is a judgment. Some civil cases, however, because of the huge damages sought or because of the parties or issues involved, merit expanded coverage.

Example: A Suit for Damages

An example of a civil suit that did receive expanded coverage is a case filed by a Phoenix family after a natural-gas explosion in their apartment. This suit had a number of newsworthy elements: astronomical damages were sought, the defendants included public utilities and it had been a spectacular explosion.

The filing The story of the filing, which was published in *The Arizona Republic,* contained the essential items of importance. The lead paragraph focused on the damages sought:

> Members of a Phoenix family critically injured April 20 by a natural-gas explosion in their apartment have filed a $92 million suit in Maricopa County Superior Court.

The next two paragraphs provided background on the plaintiffs. The story concluded by listing the defendants, by providing details outlined in the complaint and by quoting the parties.

Developments during the suit Procedural maneuverings are extensive in complicated civil suits, but generally they are not newsworthy. As noted earlier, civil suits can drag on for years. Occasionally, however, between the filing and the conclusion of litigation, developments arise that are newsworthy and deserving of coverage. This was the case in our example.

Jeff South's story in *The Phoenix Gazette* revealed a new development:

> Because of their desperate plight, burn victims Gloria Crawley and her children will get their day in court sooner than expected.
>
> Judge James Moeller of Maricopa County Superior Court has approved a motion giving priority to the Crawleys' lawsuit in connection with an April 20 explosion that ripped through their apartment at 6565 N. 17th Ave.
>
> At the request of the Crawleys' attorney, Moeller set the case for trial next April.

The story went on to list the defendants, to provide background on the $90-million-plus suit, to explain the reasoning advanced by the Crawleys' lawyer concerning the need for the accelerated process and to explain that Mrs. Crawley's husband had died from burns 30 days after the explosion. The story also quoted from documents filed by the Crawleys' attorney, Charles Brewer:

The Crawleys' "desperate physical, financial and mental situation may become irreversible and irrecoverable" unless the case goes to trial soon, Brewer said in court documents.

The settlement   As is often the case in civil actions, the suit in our example was settled out of court. Naturally, this settlement merited a major story. Brent Whiting of *The Arizona Republic* used a straightforward lead:

> An out-of-court settlement of $8.1 million was reached Thursday in a suit filed by members of a Phoenix family critically injured last year when a natural-gas explosion ripped through their apartment.

Background on the suit was given in the next two paragraphs. Then, in the fourth and fifth paragraphs, Whiting provided details of the settlement. Note how he was careful to attribute the information.

> Charles M. Brewer, Mrs. Crawley's attorney, said the settlement will be paid by Arizona Public Service Co. and by Palo Verde Apartments Inc., owner of the 16-unit complex.
> Brewer said that under the terms of the settlement, APS and its liability-insurance carrier will pay $7.1 million, and the remaining $1 million will be paid by the carrier for the apartment owner.

A logical question naturally surfaced: had there been other civil suits in the state that involved such a large settlement? If the answer could be documented, it would probably belong in the lead. Here, it was merely an opinion that was placed lower in the story and was fully attributed:

> "This is probably the biggest settlement in Arizona history," Brewer said. "I would have liked to have tried the case, but when you have this kind of settlement offer, you have to accept it."

The story went on to provide other pertinent particulars: an update on Mrs. Crawley and her children and background on the filing.

COVERING THE COURTS: GUIDELINES FOR REPORTERS

Robert Rawitch of the *Los Angeles Times* estimated that it takes a reporter six months to a year to become attuned to covering courts in a metropolitan setting. Naturally, it does not take as long to gain a grasp of the judicial system in a non-metropolitan setting. But the job of the court reporters for big-city dailies and for community dailies or weeklies is the same: they must inform their readers accurately, in understandable language.

"The role of the court reporter is to break through the legal jargon—to translate the special role of the court to the everyday role of the reader," Rawitch said. "But just like the specialist on any beat, the court reporter must be careful—once he or she begins to feel comfortable with the system—not to lose sight of what is important to the reader."

Covering the courts involves more than reporting on procedural filings in civil suits and on spectacular criminal trials. Many good court-related stories are the result of a reporter's persistence in searching for information that can lead to in-depth stories on the workings of the judicial system or on the interaction among those involved in the system.

Following are some specific steps to follow.

- *Learn the judicial system.* Reporters need to master the intricacies of the court systems in their jurisdictions. State systems vary. Do not be afraid to ask questions. It is imperative to grasp the workings of the system.

- *Learn the record-keeping system.* Once the procedural and structural aspects of the court system are mastered, reporters need to know how to ferret out information. A knowledge of the record-keeping system is essential.

- *Provide sufficient background for the reader.* For example, even though the Beaty case was in the news for more than a year, Padgett never failed to provide a background paragraph in each story that explained how the case had started.

- *Double-check facts.* Names, ages, addresses and the specific charges should always be verified. The stakes are high. Reporters never want to make errors, but there is a monumental difference between saying that John Jones was the leading scorer for his basketball team (when he was really only the second-leading scorer) and saying that John Jones was charged with driving while intoxicated (when he was really charged with running a stop sign).

- *Use complete names and addresses or occupations.* To avoid confusion—and to head off potential lawsuits—list full names with middle initials, ages, addresses and occupations of persons charged with crimes.

- *Attribute all statements.* Never use hearsay in a court story. Carefully explain to the reader the source of all information. Information in official court documents is privileged; that is, reporters have a legal right to report their contents accurately. The privilege, however, does not extend to erroneous reporting of court documents. (See Chapter 28 for a discussion of libel defenses, including privilege of reporting.)

- *Report all relevant facts.* Search for all relevant news angles. For example, when a person is on trial for murder, a reporter could provide details on the minimum and maximum penalties as established by law, the number of murder trials in the same court during the past year and the circumstances of the arrest.

- *Don't be afraid of legal terminology.* You will encounter new legal terms regularly as you cover the courts. Rely on court personnel to give you information to supplement definitions in a source such as Black's Law Dictionary. A comprehensive dictionary of legal terms is indeed a valuable reference.

- *Write simply.* Strive to translate "legalese" into lay terms whenever possible. Reporters need an understanding of the law, but they should not forget to communicate as informed laypersons—not as lawyers.

- *Take careful notes.* Be extremely careful to take accurate notes during proceedings. When tape recorders are allowed, they provide a good backup. If notes are not clear, or if the tape recorder malfunctions, check with the official court reporter, who records verbatim the transcript of the proceedings.

- *Be alert for testimony that contradicts previous testimony or evidence.* Develop your own system for emphasizing such occurrences in your notes. As you listen to a full day of testimony, place asterisks beside such occurrences to jar your memory when you begin to write.

- *Watch for reactions (including facial expressions) of participants in a trial.* You should not play the role of amateur psychiatrist; but it is sometimes worth reporting when witnesses break down on the stand, attorneys raise their voices and spectators orally react to testimony.

- *Remember that stories can develop away from the witness stand.* Be alert for feature pieces by observing spectators and other persons associated with the proceedings.

- *Be fair.* Strive to report as objectively as possible. Remember that people involved in litigation are undergoing a traumatic experience. Do not allow prejudicial reporting to interfere with the rights of the accused. Report aggressively, but stay within ethical and legal bounds. (See Chapter 28 for a discussion of fair trial–free press issues. This discussion includes guidelines reporters can follow when covering litigation.)

Sports

In today's electronic era, sports reporters are in constant contact with their newsrooms.
(J. P. Laffont/Sygma)

21

Sports

Newspapers devote considerable space to sports

coverage. Critics sometimes refer to sports

departments as the toy departments of

newspapers. This is not necessarily the case. As

David Shaw, a media critic for the Los Angeles

Times, *wrote: "The times—and the nation's*

sports pages—they are a-changin', and it is now

no longer sufficient to write sports stories by the

numbers or by the clichés."

Lee Barfknecht, a sportswriter for the *Omaha* (Neb.) *World-Herald*, feels just as comfortable prowling the sidelines at a high school football game as he does covering one of the nation's finest college teams from the press box atop Memorial Stadium at the University of Nebraska.

Barfknecht could probably handle almost any journalistic assignment. A Phi Beta Kappa, he was graduated from the University of Nebraska with high distinction. He majored in journalism and minored in English, history and economics.

"I'm happy as a sportswriter," Barfknecht said. "I think our pages are as well-read as most other sections of the newspaper, and people often read them critically because many readers consider themselves to be sports experts."

In the early 1980s, Barfknecht was primarily responsible for high school sports coverage in the Omaha-Council Bluffs, Iowa, metropolitan area. On autumn Saturdays, though, he helped cover the Nebraska Cornhuskers. In 1985, he moved to the University of Nebraska beat exclusively. His responsibilities included coverage of all 21 varsity sports at NU.

While covering the NU beat, Barfknecht has made hundreds of round trips from Omaha to Lincoln (approximately 50 miles each way) to cover events on campus. He averages about five trips a week during the fall sports season, four trips a week during the winter and three trips a week in the spring.

The main focus of his coverage is obviously sports such as football, men's basketball, baseball and track. But in recent years, 17 of Nebraska's 21 sports programs have been ranked in the Top 20 nationally. So Barfknecht's assignments and enterprise ideas have been broad-based. He has won several Associated Press state sports writing awards and, in 1988 and 1989, he was named Nebraska sportswriter of the year.

Barfknecht got his first byline at the age of 14. His hometown weekly newspaper, the *Superior* (Neb.) *Express,* needed someone to cover American Legion baseball. "The editor was looking for someone to get the box score and to write a few paragraphs," Barfknecht said. "I was happy to volunteer. I was on the team, and so I had to be careful not to give myself too much ink."

He had to study hard to live up to his status as a Regents scholar while at Nebraska, but he also found time to work two years for the *Daily Nebraskan,* the university's student newspaper, as a sportswriter and a sports columnist. He earned a summer internship at the *World-Herald.* And when he returned to Lincoln for his final semester of school, Barfknecht continued to drive to Omaha each weekend to work the sports desk. The *World-Herald* management liked him; and upon graduation he was offered a job on the regional news desk, where he worked before moving to sports about two years later. Barfknecht enjoyed his time on the regional desk, but he jumped at the chance to return to his first love—sports writing.

SPORTS WRITING STYLES

One of the best-known American sportswriters, Grantland Rice, a Phi Beta Kappa graduate of Vanderbilt who majored in Greek and Latin, was fond of using verse. More than half a century after Rice penned his first sports stories for the *Nashville* (Tenn.) *Daily News*, he wondered in his book "The Tumult and the Shouting" why he had never gotten around to giving the score in a piece he wrote in 1901. It began:

Baker Was an Easy Mark
Pounded Hard Over Park
Selma's Infield Is a Peach
But Nashville Now Is Out of Reach
All of the Boys Go Out to Dine
And Some of Them Get Full of Wine

After their long, successful trip the locals opened up against Selma yesterday afternoon at Athletic Park, and when the shades of night had settled on the land the difference that separated the two teams had increased by some dozen points.

Throughout the whole morning a dark, lead-colored sky overhung the city, and a steady rain dripped and drizzled, only stopping in time to play the game, but leaving the field soft and slow. . . .

During the first part of this century, flowery prose like this adorned the sports pages. Today, however, sports writing styles have changed.

It is true that some writers still use such *sports writing clichés* as "flashy freshmen," "sophomore sensations," "brilliant field generals," "lanky leapers" and "diminutive, sparkplug point guards," but in general today's sports pages are filled with better, more balanced writing than ever before.

That change has been a while coming. Stanley Woodward, the sports editor of the old *New York Herald Tribune*, may have been a bit optimistic when he wrote in his book "Sports Page" (published in 1949) that the better sportswriters had started to abandon hyperbole, profuse praise and strained similes. He wrote: "The horrendous clashes of fearsome Tigers and snarling Wolverines, which usually were concluded in purple sunsets, now are taboo in the better sports departments. The sports editor doesn't mind picturesque writing if the reporter can handle it, but he no longer wishes to see his vehicle smeared with wild and indiscriminate pigments."

Woodward wrote that sportswriters should strive for the middle ground; they should avoid the *"gee whiz" school* (where athletes perform nothing but heroic feats) just as they should avoid the *"aw nuts" school* (where gifted athletes and great games are treated with near disdain).

Many of todays' sportswriters are providing readers with the high-quality coverage and writing that Woodward strived for in 1949. Woodward has theorized that World War II helped to put sports into better perspective. Writers no longer routinely extended hero status to mere athletes. A more spartan, streamlined sports writing style evolved after World War II, with an emphasis on the five W's and H—and on a horde of statistics. And that style started to give way in the 1970s and 1980s to a more balanced approach. Some of today's best sports writing certainly includes valuable statistical information and essential ingredients (who won, what the score was, who starred), but it is more literary than the bare-boned scores-and-statistics approach that held sway at many newspapers after World War II.

An examination of today's sports pages shows that clichés and hyperbole are not extinct, but they are found less frequently, and praise is not as lavish or gushing as it once was. Soft news approaches are used more frequently on stories that would once have been topped only with summary leads. Even morning newspapers are providing more analytical writing than ever before.

CONTEMPORARY SPORTS PAGES

The amount of space devoted to various sports, including women's sports, is undergoing increasing scrutiny by the nation's sports editors. The mere fact that some minor-league baseball franchises routinely received 20-inch game stories in 1960—when they were playing before relatively large crowds—does not necessarily mean that they should still be covered so extensively. Dale Bye, the executive sports editor of *The Kansas City Star* and the *Times*, made clear the need for sports editors to re-examine their philosophy of coverage. In responding to a survey question about sports reporting, Bye wrote:

> Historically, sports coverage has been defined in terms of baseball, basketball, football and golf (because all sports editors, of course, play golf). The sports boom—tennis, running, soccer, women in sports—caught most papers napping and most sports sections still have not come up with a formulaic method of handling all the information. Most obviously, sports coverage can be improved by a systematic method of giving all sports adequate coverage—coverage without ignoring any sport. Complicating the whole problem is the overall reader-interest level. You can't ignore major-league baseball on Thursday just to give rock climbing its place in the sports section. On the other hand, you can't ignore rock climbing continually by hiding behind the traditional facade of major-league baseball.

Despite attempts by sports editors to expand coverage of women's sports, in most instances women's coverage still plays a weak second fiddle to competitive men's athletics.

More newspapers are providing coverage—particularly through features—of *minor sports* such as gymnastics, volleyball, tennis, wrestling and swimming, but football, basketball, track and baseball continue to command the most space.

Local coverage is being expanded, particularly at medium- and small-circulation dailies. Some professional sports coverage is being relegated to the agate page (a page in the sports section devoted to scores and statistical information). More space is being devoted to game and feature coverage of high school athletics, recreational sports and participation sports.

The next two sections will be devoted to today's coverage of high school and college sports. Professional coverage will not be discussed, because the principles of reporting professional sports are similar to those involved in college contests. Also, it would be unusual for a sportswriter fresh from college to be assigned to a professional beat.

Gymnastics is an Olympic sport that is being covered more extensively by newspapers and television.
(Photo by Scott Troyanos)

HIGH SCHOOL SPORTS COVERAGE

Nearly all the country's daily and weekly newspapers provide readers with extensive coverage of high school sports. The prep sports beat can be viewed as the best and the worst of assignments. The *Omaha World-Herald* reporter Terry Henion, a former prep sports editor of the *Colorado Springs Gazette Telegraph* and a former sports editor of *The Hastings* (Neb.) *Tribune,* described it:

> It is a genuine pain in the neck sometimes to have to keep statistics and never get to see the game. It's a pain to listen to a wild-eyed mother question your roots because you misspelled her daughter's name in a summary. It's a pain—and somewhat frightening—to have a father scream wildly at you because you are not giving his son enough ink. It's a pain to cover six or seven games a week and rarely see your family.
>
> But it's a pleasure to watch an awkward and timid sophomore develop into a poised and polished senior. It's a pleasure to see kids play games for the fun of it without the pressure and hard sell of college and pro sports. It's a pleasure to see the smiles on their faces and in a way a pleasure to see their tears when they lose because the emotions are honest.

In the long run, Henion said, "The pleasures of covering high school sports greatly outweigh the pains, and that's why I enjoy it so much. High school sports are what sports were always meant to be: kids playing kids' games."

At high schools there is no sports information director cranking out play-by-play charts, keeping statistics and providing quotations from players after the game. The work must be done by the sports reporters, who usually find themselves walking the sideline at a football game or crammed into tight quarters at a basketball game. *Covering* a prep game is almost a misnomer, according to Henion. He thinks that *documenting* might be a better term. Henion said that the prep writer cannot always concentrate on doing what a good writer should do—answer the human interest questions that fans would ask if they had access to the locker room. Instead, reporters must keep the statistics (or rely on a 14-year-old student manager who tends to inflate his or her team's numbers), interview the coaches and players and then formulate a readable account of the game. Often the work is done under deadline pressure.

One of the best ways for a college student to gain professional journalism experience is to work as a stringer covering high school sports. A *stringer* is a part-time newspaper or broadcast correspondent who covers a specific geographical area or team for a news medium that is often located elsewhere. Sports editors of area dailies generally hire stringers during busy football and basketball seasons. Even the smallest dailies often cover at least a handful of local prep teams. By serving as stringers, young journalists get the opportunity to cover sports, write sports and occasionally see their bylines. A stint as stringer often leads to a spot on the staff.

Lee Barfknecht said that preparation for a high school game is more difficult than preparation for a college game. Before college games, mounds of releases from sports information offices provide easy access to statistics and other background. The reporter who covers a high school game, however, must generally dig up statistics and background by reviewing clippings and by talking to coaches, players or athletic directors.

Also, there is sometimes a logistical problem when covering high school sports. Barfknecht pointed out that most Omaha high schools play their games in a handful of major stadiums in the city.

"A lot of times, the coach puts the players on the bus almost immediately after the game," Barfknecht said. "You almost have to tackle them to get an interview. My strategy is to hit the losing coaches first—they tend to be the ones who want to get out of the stadium quickly. Also, by getting to them immediately after the game, you often get a very honest reaction from them."

After Barfknecht talks with the losing coach, he heads to the winning coach. "I always congratulate the coach and ask if a couple of star players can stick around for a minute to be interviewed," Barfknecht said.

The *World-Herald* sports department has no guidelines on who should be interviewed after a high school contest. Barfknecht, though, likes to gather quotations from both winning and losing coaches along with what he calls "kid quotes." "Some people think high school athletes don't have much to say," Barfknecht noted. "But sometimes they make for better interviews than college athletes."

Some high school coaches, however, prefer that reporters not talk to players after games. The wise reporter will respect those wishes. A quotation taken out of context can harm the player, the coach or the entire program. An important thing to remember when interviewing high school athletes is that these are youngsters—they are not the presumably poised athletes in college or professional programs.

As Henion said: "You're dealing with kids who usually never have felt the sting of a razor, let alone the cutting edge of a perhaps cynical and bored writer. Temperance is the word when quoting high school athletes."

COLLEGE SPORTS COVERAGE

Coverage of major college football is a choice assignment; it is also a demanding one. Barfknecht is one of four reporters who cover Nebraska Cornhusker football games for the *World-Herald*. "We arrive at the stadium about an hour and a half before the game," Barfknecht said. "We have lunch and discuss things going on in college football that day, and as game time approaches, we get our notebooks out to outline basically what we will be doing once the game starts. We don't preplan coverage too much because we don't want to limit our flexibility. We all know our basic assignments."

The four reporters watch the game from the press box. One writes the primary account of the game; one does sidebar material and the Nebraska post-game account; and one writes sidebars and covers the opposing team's locker room. The fourth reporter, the sports editor, writes an analytical column. In addition, a team of photographers in the press box shoots sequential black-and-white photos of every play. Photographers are also stationed around the field, two shooting color photos and the rest shooting black-and-white.

Even on days when Barfknecht is writing sidebars and covering the opponent's locker room, he keeps a play-by-play chronology of the game action. The sports information office provides complete play-by-play accounts at the half and after the game, but Barfknecht said that he has a better grasp of turning points and trends if he charts the games himself.

The *World-Herald* writers talk as the game progresses. "We pretty much know the writing approaches each of us will use," Barfknecht said. That way, when the four writers are scrambling to file stories after the game, there will be a minimum of duplication.

Most of the Cornhusker fans who file out of the stadium after a game probably relax and savor a victory over dinner. But the real work begins for the *World-Herald* reporters once the final gun sounds.

The first *World-Herald* sports deadline for some outstate editions (those that are delivered to counties in the western part of Nebraska) is 6:15 p.m. Games that begin at 1:30 are usually over by 4:30. Thus, the reporters have less than two hours to conduct interviews and file their stories. When starting times are moved to 2:30 or 3 o'clock to accommodate television, the deadline pressure is even more intense.

The reporter responsible for the main game story will write about 10 inches of narration on first-half highlights during the halftime. That way, after the game is over, the reporter can immediately structure a top to the story, write a transition and move directly to the second-half narration.

When the game ends, the reporters go to different areas of the stadium. "We all use tape recorders," Barfknecht said. "It is an individual decision, but we all rely strongly on them. The NU locker room is sometimes so crowded that you can't get your pen and pad out to write freely, and so we record."

The "cooling off" period for players and coaches is generally 10 minutes in the Nebraska locker room. Then the interviews begin. The writer responsible for the game story interviews the head coach; the sidebar writer interviews the Husker players. In the opponent's locker room, another *World-Herald* reporter interviews both the head coach and the players.

Within a half hour—at about 5:15—another *World-Herald* reporters are back in the press box. They strive to assemble a 25-inch game story, two side-bars and a column for the first outstate editions.

After the 6:30 p.m. deadline has been met, the reporters have 2½ hours before their next deadline.

"The writer doing the game story usually starts completely over," said Barfknecht. "All of us go back and transcribe our tapes fully. Then we try to analyze what we have. We decide how many stories we have and who and what we are going to write about."

After these decisions are made, the reporters call the Omaha newsroom, where three editors—who are assigned to the "Husker Desk"—are in a corner focusing exclusively on coordinating coverage of the Nebraska game.

"We try to let them know who and what we are going to write about so they can start gathering art and photos to supplement our stories," Barfknecht said. "Also, if any of us have ideas for the photo page (a full page of pictures that runs after every game), we pass them on to the desk. For example, if there is a great run that might be good in photographic sequence, we will suggest that. We try to keep the line open to Omaha from the NU press box as the evening wears on."

After the writers transcribe their notes, they then "sit down and sweat a lot," Barfknecht said.

Barfknecht, who normally covers the opponent's locker room, is some-times hard-pressed to write lively sidebars. "I've seen a lot of long faces and quiet players in opponents' locker rooms," Barfknecht said. Nebraska's oppo-nents have had little to cheer about. During the past decade, NU has averaged fewer than one home-game loss each year.

The day is still not over for the reporters after they meet their 9 o'clock deadline. Deadline is 10 o'clock for editions that will be distributed in the Omaha metropolitan area. The reporters take the extra 60 minutes to deter-mine if they have overlooked anything and to compile information for the fixture items: "What Others Said" (the lead paragraphs written by writers from other newspapers who covered the game) and the "Answer Box" (where some interesting tidbits about the game are placed in question-answer format).

"We usually struggle out of the press box at about 10 o'clock," Barfknecht said.

The crew then heads back to Omaha. Barfknecht does not get much rest, however. On Sunday, he prepares his agenda for the upcoming week.

WORKING WITH STATISTICS

A city hall reporter must know how to read a budget; a court reporter must know how to interpret a legal brief; a sports reporter must be able to work with statistics. Every sport has its own statistical language. Reporters do not necessarily have to be experts on each phase of every sport (although that certainly helps), but they must have a working knowledge of scoring procedures and significant statistics of the sports that they cover.

Deciphering Statistics

A portion of a *box score* for a basketball game follows:

ASU	Mn	FG	FT	Rb	At	PF	St	Tr	Pt
Deines f	22	2–7	0–1	7	0	5	0	0	4
Everett f	20	2–3	1–1	9	0	5	0	0	5
Taylor c	26	1–4	1–1	4	1	2	0	5	3
Thomson g	34	6–17	4–4	1	7	1	5	0	16
Beck g	35	4–10	5–6	7	3	4	1	2	13

The numerals listed above tell us a lot about what five players did in a basketball game. We know, for example, that these competitors play for Arizona State University. We also know how many minutes each of them played in the regulation 40-minute game, how many field goals they made (and attempted), how many free throws they made (and attempted), how many rebounds they grabbed, how many assists they had, how many personal fouls they accumulated, how many steals they made, how many turnovers they committed and the number of points they scored.

At a glance, we can tell that guards Bobby Thomson and Steve Beck were the leading scorers with 16 and 13 points, respectively. We can also tell that Thomson and Beck played most of the game; that center Jon Taylor had a rough night (he had more turnovers than he had points); that forward Warren Everett led the team in rebounds; and that Everett and forward Jim Deines both fouled out.

Team statistics are computed by adding numerals from the individuals. For example, after adding the *individual statistics* of the Arizona State substitutes to the statistics listed above, we find that in an 81–72 loss to the University of Oregon in a Pacific 10 Conference basketball game, ASU made 28 of 70 shots from the field (a frigid .400); made 16 of 20 free throws (a respectable .800); snared 44 rebounds (10 more than Oregon); had 14 assists (compared with 19 for Oregon); made 29 personal fouls (compared with 18 for Oregon); had 8 steals (compared with Oregon's 4); and committed 15 turnovers (the same as Oregon). These are significant statistics.

Sports reporters, of course, could delve deeper. They could, for example, determine how many points both teams scored within 5 feet of the basket (this might reveal which team was able to get the ball consistently deep inside the lane); they could determine which team had the most blocked shots; or they could determine how many times the lead changed hands.

Depending on available space, on readers' interest in the game or on the importance of the contest, the reporter would decide which statistics are worth mentioning in the story.

The key is this: Reporters covering basketball or any other sport must know which statistics are relevant and important. For instance, what are the magic numbers in football? For starters, there are scores by quarters, first downs, rushing yards, passing yards, return yards, passes attempted and completed, number of punts and average distances, number of fumbles and fumbles lost, number of penalties and yards penalized and time of possession. Many of these statistics are relevant for individuals also. In gymnastics, it is important to know that judges score a routine or exercise by totaling points from four areas for a maximum of 10.0. Those four areas are execution; combination; difficulty; and risk, originality and virtuosity (known as ROV).

It is not the purpose of this chapter to provide a comprehensive summary of applicable statistics for all sports. It is imperative, however, for aspiring sports reporters to realize that they must understand the statistical undercurrents of the sports they cover. If they do not, they cannot report or write intelligently.

Using Statistics Effectively

Following are suggestions for using statistics in sports writing.

- *Provide readers with statistical information that is useful for understanding the contest or its trends.*

- *Avoid being a "statistics junkie."* There is a difference between providing readers with information necessary to understand what happened at the contest and inundating them with irrelevant strings of numerals that interrupt the flow of the story.

- *Review team and individual statistics before a contest.* Preparation is a key ingredient in solid coverage of any sport. If you review team and individual statistics before a basketball game, when you write your story after the game you can note, for example, that a 22-points-per-game scorer was held to 11 points; that a team which normally makes 53 percent of its field goal attempts made a cold 37 percent; or that a team which averages 11 turnovers a game made 23. These statistical differences help put a victory or a loss into perspective.

- *Review statistics after a game for trends and turning points.* It is standard to focus on individual and team totals, but running *play-by-play charts* can help the reporter piece together important sequences in the contest. Play-by-play charts provide a chronology of a basketball game. The chart notes who scored, on what kind of shot, who fouled, who turned the ball over and what the score was at the time of the play. For example, the play-by-play chart could tell a reporter whether one team went 6 minutes and 23 seconds without scoring a field goal (while the other team was making 10 field goals) or whether one team made six consecutive field goals midway in the half without a miss. These factors will probably be worth mentioning in the game story.

GOING BEYOND STATISTICS

Reporters could put together accurate, readable game accounts merely by reviewing statistics. That, however, would not make for complete coverage of a contest. Non-statistical information—insight and information not known even by readers who might have watched the game themselves—lifts a story beyond the ordinary.

Here are some ways for sports reporters to go beyond statistics.

- *When walking the sidelines or sitting in the press area, do not focus exclusively on the field or court.* If you stalk the sidelines during a football game, you can often pick up on strategy discussed by players and coaches. If you sit in the stands or in the press box, you might notice the nervous parents of a star player.

- *Find out policies for post-game interviews.* Gaining access to players immediately after a game can sometimes be difficult, but it is often essential to complete coverage. Many coaches demand a "cool down" time of 10 to 15 minutes before the press is allowed into the locker room after a game. Many teams have developed policies in response to female sportswriters who have sought equal access to male locker rooms. Some teams have made locker rooms off limits to all reporters; these teams often provide an interview room where athletes go after they have showered and dressed. This, of course, creates delays and could cause some reporters to miss their deadlines. Most teams try to accommodate writers of both sexes. It is important, however, to know the policies of the teams being covered.

- *Talk to coaches.* Touch base with them before the event if possible. That way, you will not be a stranger in the post-contest interview. Strive to ask intelligent questions. If a team loses an opportunity to win a basketball game because of a controversial traveling call with 8 seconds remaining, don't ask the coach what the turning point of the game was.

- *Talk to players.* Do not select only the stars for interviews. Others might have some interesting insights into the game. How did the unsung offensive tackle in a football game, for example, feel after butting heads the entire game against an all-conference defensive lineman?

- *Talk to trainers.* In addition to providing you with information about specific individual injuries, trainers might pass along other useful tidbits such as the general condition of the team and whether any special conditioning drills will be conducted during the next week's practice sessions.

WRITING A SPORTS STORY

Writing for Morning Newspapers

For the most part, morning and afternoon newspapers cover the same athletic events played the night before, but the writing angles should be different. Reporters at morning (A.M.) newspapers face tight deadlines because their newspapers are printed late at night, oftentimes very close to the conclusion of the athletic event. Traditionally, morning newspapers have offered a straightforward account of the preceding night's game; although as noted earlier, even these newspapers are increasingly opting for softer analytical leads. Readers who open their morning newspapers might not know the score of the game they are interested in; thus, even when using a soft lead, writers for A.M. newspapers generally try to get the scores of games high in the stories. The reporter who covers the contest is generally rushed to meet a deadline; the story must be complete, but quite often there is not sufficient time to conduct extensive interviews or to develop an extended feature lead.

When Nebraska played a second-round National Invitation Tournament game at Ohio State, morning newspapers and the wire services could have led with a terse, to-the-point summary paragraph such as this:

> COLUMBUS, Ohio—Seven-foot center Grady Mateen scored 20 points to lead Ohio State past Nebraska 85–74 Monday night in a second-round National Invitation Tournament game.

This summary lead provides key information—*who, what, when, where, why* and *how.*

Lee Barfknecht covered the game for the *Omaha World-Herald.* He was under deadline pressure, but his newspaper had allotted space for his story. Barfknecht saved the score for the second paragraph, but being aware that many of his morning readers would be eager for details of the game, he jammed mounds of essential information into the first five paragraphs of his story:

> COLUMBUS, Ohio—Even without its steering wheel, Ohio State's basketball machine stayed on the right path long enough to run over Nebraska.
>
> "This just shows that Ohio State is a good team with or without Jay Burson," NU forward Dapreis Owens said after the Buckeyes beat the Huskers 85–74 in the second round of the National Invitation Tournament before a sellout crowd of 13,276 at St. John Arena.
>
> Owens, a freshman from Mansfield, Ohio, scored a career-high 18 points and senior guard Eric Johnson added 23. But it wasn't enough to avoid a loss that ended NU's season at 17–16.
>
> Ohio State, 19–14, played without Burson, the All Big-Ten guard who fractured a neck vertebra a month ago.
>
> But the Buckeyes made up for his 22-point average and stayed on course for a third NIT final four trip in the past four years by driving the ball inside.

Writing for Afternoon Newspapers

Sports reporters working for afternoon (P.M.) newspapers have time to write comprehensive stories that encompass not only the essential ingredients (victor, score, team records, key statistics and so on) but also a unique angle or feature lead. They therefore cannot use the standard excuse for a poorly written story—they cannot contend that they were under extreme deadline pressure. These sports reporters should analyze the games that they cover—probing deeply into the *why* and the *how* of the events—because most of their readers know the score before they open their newspapers. The reporters should combine a synopsis of the game, a statistical summary and an angle not covered in the morning newspapers or by the electronic media. The afternoon account should not be primarily a play-by-play rehash.

Barfknecht, when writing his story for the afternoon editions of the *World-Herald*, relied more extensively on direct quotations and analysis. He had more time to write his story. He conducted several post-game interviews to put the trends and the statistical accounts of the contest into better perspective. Because it was the last game of the season for the Cornhuskers, Barfknecht, in his P.M. version, chose to look ahead to the next campaign. Barfknecht once again placed the score in the second paragraph, but the first part of his story was laden with quotations.

COLUMBUS, Ohio—Danny Nee didn't sugar-coat it.

Nebraska's basketball coach told his team after Monday's season-ending 85–74 loss at Ohio State in the second round of the NIT that the Huskers' 17–16 record wasn't anything to brag about.

"Basically, I felt this team never really reached its potential," Nee said. "We could have done better."

Were there nods of agreement in the locker room to that statement?

"I don't care what they say," Nee said. "I want them to show me."

Showtime for NU's returning players apparently starts immediately.

"Coach Nee said next year starts tomorrow," forward Dapreis Owens said, "and that we can't quit working or take vacation.

"We have to work hard to get better for the years to come."

Owens, a freshman from Mansfield, Ohio, showed his stuff with a career-high 18 points plus seven rebounds, while senior guard Eric Johnson poured in 23 points. But it wasn't enough to upset the 19–14 Buckeyes before a sellout crowd of 13,276 at St. John Arena.

Providing Extensive Coverage: A College Football Game

Most sports events can be covered effectively simply by writing a single game story. This was the case for the basketball game discussed in the previous section. Some sports events, such as the Olympic Games, the Super Bowl, the World Series and major college football games, however, are of such interest and importance to readers that more than one story will be written about them. The *Omaha World-Herald*'s coverage of Nebraska football games falls into this category.

For a Nebraska–Iowa State football game, Barfknecht wrote the main story for the *World-Herald*. His 78-paragraph game story was supplemented with the following:

Column by the sports editor

Four sidebars

Scoring summary in agate type

Color photo

Four black-and-white photos scattered throughout the Sunday section

Full picture page with an additional 11 black-and-white photos

Including the essentials   Barfknecht's game story contained all the essential ingredients:

- Teams and score
- Reference to whether it was a conference or a non-conference game
- Site of the game
- When the game was played
- Key plays (who made them, which coach was responsible for calling them, etc.)
- Scoring summary
- References to star players
- Key offensive statistics (rushing and passing)
- Key defensive statistics (tackles, interceptions, fumble recoveries)
- Direct quotations by players
- Direct quotations by coaches
- Weather and its effect on the game
- Injuries and condition updates
- Results of previous games between the teams (the series record or outcomes of most recent games, whichever is most relevant)
- Overall records
- Conference records
- Reference to national rankings, if relevant
- Next games for both teams
- Historical significance, if any, of the game

Every sports fan in Nebraska probably knew the final game score before opening the Sunday *World-Herald.* Most fans had probably also listened to at least part of the game on the radio. With this in mind, Barfknecht waited until the 18th paragraph before providing narration of significant plays and scoring drives. In his lead paragraphs, he concentrated on presenting information that most readers may not have been aware of: the Husker defense held center stage in the Iowa State game. Barfknecht provided details early in his story:

AMES, Iowa—The Nebraska defense felt it owed Iowa State something for what happened a year ago in Lincoln.

Stamp that debt "PAID IN FULL," because Nebraska held Iowa State to 53 total yards in 54 offensive plays and never let the Cyclones inside the NU

37-yard line Saturday during a 44–0 victory at Cyclone Stadium.

"We were embarrassed by the way we performed last year," safety Bret Clark said.

"They just ran up and down the field on us," defensive coordinator Charlie McBride recalled.

Though Nebraska won that game 72–29, the Cyclones gained 502 total yards, the most the Blackshirts allowed all season.

But on Saturday, Iowa State did not run up the field. Or down the field. Or across the field—at least without somebody in a white jersey and red pants running next to them. The defensive effort, in allowing Iowa State 53 total yards, is Nebraska's best of the season.

If Barfknecht had been writing a single story about the game—with no accompanying sidebars focusing on star players and comments by coaches—he probably would not have placed so much emphasis on significant statistics so early in his story. But because his story was supported with thousands of additional words, he was able to focus on the staggering statistical documentation. And he did so without ruining the rhythm of his writing. It is also apparent that Barfknecht had done his homework. He was writing the story on deadline, but he was able to weave statistics, direct quotations and background efficiently into his early paragraphs.

His story continued:

Iowa State, averaging 239.2 yards a game as the Big Eight's leading passing team, was held to 37 yards in 20 pass attempts. The Cyclones could gain only 16 net yards rushing in 34 tries for an average of 0.47 yards per carry.

The statistics in the above paragraph are significant. They put the lopsided final score into perspective. Here, after all, was the conference's leading passing team—and it was totally stymied. Barfknecht's next six paragraphs further illustrate his writing ability. He carefully blended direct quotations by the Nebraska head coach with facts and figures.

A crowd of 52,919, the sixth largest in Iowa State history, saw the Huskers—ranked No. 3 by The Associated Press and No. 4 by United Press International—improve their record to 8–1 overall and 5–0 in the Big Eight. The Cyclones fall to 2–6–1 and 0–4–1.

"This is one of the better defensive games I think we've played since I've been head coach," said Tom Osborne, who took the Husker job in 1973.

"I'm not sure there may have been others that were equal to it, but this is one of the finest efforts I've seen."

It was the first shutout for Nebraska in 28 games, dating back to a 52–0 wipeout of Kansas in 1982.

It was the first shutout of an Iowa State team in 41 games, since a 35–0 loss to Nebraska in 1980.

And it was just the fifth time since 1971 that the Cyclones have been blanked—and all five have been by Nebraska.

Developing a theme Barfknecht's story went on to provide more direct quotations and to describe key plays. But his first 13 paragraphs show how a knowledgeable sports reporter can develop a theme for a contest—in this case, the defensive domination by Nebraska—by carefully culling relevant statistics to blend with quotations and description.

Not every story of a Nebraska football game will contain so much statistical information. Barfknecht said that the Iowa State–Husker game merited it. "Before the game, some comments from Husker defensive players in a Thursday feature story caught my eye. Despite a 72–29 win the year before, the players were upset that Iowa State had gained 503 yards and had scored 29 points.

"So, as the Saturday game went along, and the Nebraska defensive dominance became so apparent, I started adding up figures, compared them with last year's and checked this year's offensive and defensive averages.

"Then, in the post-game press conference, when I asked Osborne how this defensive effort ranked with others and he said, 'This is one of the better defensive games I think we've played since I've been head coach,' that convinced me to go with that angle."

Barfknecht noted that, in preparation for writing game stories, he often has two or three ideas for story angles and watches the game closely to see if any of them develop. "I want to stress, though, that I am never locked into using the ideas," Barfknecht said. "They are only broad possibilities that often end up being discarded or used only briefly in passing in a story."

Creating Effective Stories: Tips for Sportswriters

Obviously, there is no magic formula for writing sports stories, and writing approaches will always depend on the circumstances. Here, though, are some general tips:

- *Go with a summary lead if it is warranted, but you are not wedded to it.* The wire services will generally provide summary leads, and so many sportswriters strive for other approaches.

- *Avoid chronological game-story approaches.* Always lead with the most significant aspect of the contest. For example, "Chuck Johnson hit a 15-foot jump shot with three seconds left to give Grand Junction a 61–60 basketball victory over Wymore Friday night." The game story would not begin like this: "Chuck Johnson controlled the opening tip for Grand Junction, and his team went on to beat Wymore 61–60 in basketball Friday night."

- *Remember that good stories are a blend of facts, turning points, quotations, statistics and analysis.* Stories should be a careful, thoughtful blend tied together with effective transition.

- *Avoid clichés.* One-point victories, indeed, are "cliffhangers"; effective offensive line blocking often opens holes "big enough to drive the student body through"; and dominant teams often "take it to" the losers. Good writers, though, find more original descriptions.

- *Avoid "ridiculous" direct quotations.* "We whipped 'em good," has a down home ring to it, but it doesn't add much to the story.

- *Use vivid description when appropriate.* You could write, "John Jones caught the winning touchdown pass with 14 seconds left." But it might be better to write, "John Jones swerved between two defenders, stretched high in the air, cradled the ball in his left hand and pulled it to his chest for the game-winning touchdown with 14 seconds left."

- *Double-check spellings.* Particularly at high school contests, spellings listed in the official score book and on the program can be different. Find out which one is correct.

- *Do your homework.* The more background information you take with you to a contest, the easier and the faster it will be for you to write the story once the contest is over.

BEYOND THE GAME—
CONTRACTS, COURTROOMS AND BOARDROOMS

When readers turned to the sports pages two decades ago, they read primarily about heroes: high-scoring basketball players; swift, elusive running backs; and fence-rattling baseball sluggers. Those stories, of course, remain the staple of sports coverage. But on any given day, readers can also find stories such as these:

Barry Switzer resigned as Oklahoma's football coach Monday, saying he was frustrated by NCAA rules that do not "recognize the financial needs of young athletes."

Switzer, who had been under pressure since the school's football program was put on NCAA probation in December and after several players were charged early this year with crimes involving drugs, guns and sexual assault, was the fourth most successful coach in college football history. (The Associated Press)

Cal Ripkin and the Baltimore Orioles took a major step toward assuring their futures Monday night by agreeing to the biggest guaranteed contract in baseball history.

The agreement calls for the shortstop to be paid $30.5 million over the next five years and provides a $2 million option for employment for four years after his retirement. *(The Baltimore Sun)*

Charlotte Hornets owner George Shinn said he is working with local investors to come up with an offer to keep the San Francisco Giants from a possible move to Florida.

Shinn met with Mayor Frank M. Jordan, developer Walter Shorenstein and potential investors on Monday. Shinn and Jordan later took in a Giants game at Candlestick Park. (The Associated Press)

Owner Jack Kent Cooke made a $14.45 million investment in the Washington Redskins' future Tuesday by signing the team's last three holdouts— veterans Jim Lachey and Darrell Green and top draft choice Desmond Howard.

Howard, the Heisman Trophy winner, became the team's highest-paid rookie ever by signing a four-year, $5.9 million deal. Green signed a three-year, $4.5 million deal that made him the highest-paid defensive back in the NFL and Lachey signed a three-year, $4.05 million deal that made him the highest-paid offensive lineman in the league. *(The Baltimore Sun)*

Stories about strikes by players and umpires, probes by the National Collegiate Athletic Association, drug investigations, antitrust actions, franchise moves, trials and contract negotiations have not taken over the sports pages, but on some days it might seem that way.

"We're definitely seeing more coverage in these areas," said Dennis Brown, the sports news editor of *The Phoenix Gazette*. "I remember an instance when, as we approached deadline, we were looking for a story to put in an 8-inch hole. Somebody suggested that we put in the story about the Pirates being purchased and staying in Pittsburgh. Somebody else said that we could put in the story about drug allegations in the NFL. A third staffer, with a trace of a smile, suggested that we put in a 'real' sports story. We started looking through the copy, but all we could find was stuff on contracts, drugs and franchises. It's getting harder to tell if you are a sportswriter or a lawyer."

Brown said that he is not sure how extensively readers want to be informed about lawsuits, contract squabbles and drug trials. He suspects, however, that many of them prefer to read about the competitive on-the-field aspects of sports.

Still, sports pages need to provide coverage of off-the-field developments. Brown said, however, that the pendulum might have swung too far; he said that newspaper sports pages sometimes devote too much space to legal and business issues.

"We should cover these developments," Brown said. "But I think more of these stories should be handled in briefs columns unless they are really extraordinary. (*USA Today*, for example, often carries short items under the standing headline "Jurisprudence.") I'm not sure readers need to have a lengthy blow-by-blow account of where parties stand on contract negotiations. They need to know about such matters, certainly, but sports editors need to decide how many inches should be devoted to them."

Brown said that he is "depressed at times because of the overemphasis we place on the off-the-field stories."

Effective coverage of off-the-field developments is a challenge to sportswriters. It is important for them to be grounded in more than the X's and O's of particular sports.

Sportswriters need to observe the same guidelines when covering specialty areas as other newspaper or broadcast reporters do. (For an overview of court reporting, for example, see Chapter 20; for an overview of business and consumer reporting, see Chapter 24.)

"I think sportswriters definitely need to be much more informed when it comes to covering legal matters," Brown said. "For instance, we carried a story about pending lawsuits in connection with an injury that Walter Davis (a former star for the Phoenix Suns of the NBA) suffered when he slipped during an exhibition game against the Los Angeles Lakers at The Forum in Inglewood, Calif., and damaged three knee ligaments. We felt the need to take the story to the city desk so that an editor who had a better grip on that type of story could help us. We just didn't feel comfortable with it. There is nothing wrong with turning to the city side for help and advice, but sports department staffers need to be better informed in these areas."

Advanced Assignments

For Mary Gillespie of the *Chicago Sun-Times*,
feature writing is news writing with a heart.
(Courtesy of Mary Gillespie, Chicago Sun-Times)

Features

Features are not meant to deliver the news firsthand. They do contain elements of news, but their main function is to humanize, to add color, to educate, to entertain, to illuminate. They often recap major news that was reported in a previous news cycle or elsewhere in the same edition or broadcast.

For Mary Gillespie, a general assignment feature writer at the *Chicago Sun-Times*, feature writing is news writing with a heart. "News writers love the rush they get when they run out and cover a breaking news story," she said. "That's their challenge. My challenge is to grab readers and not let them go until they finish the story, to take them beyond what they may have read in the newspaper the day before."

Gillespie writes for the daily Living section of the *Sun-Times*, its main feature section. She writes anything except hard news and arts and entertainment. Her beat is wherever the story is.

She has spent a day on a barge in Lake Michigan, interviewing the men who drop buoys into harbors in preparation for the summer boating season; she has been to the Miss America pageant to find out what the contestants do before and after the contest; and she has traveled to Luxembourg to rekindle memories of the Battle of the Bulge.

"I've also written a feature on napping," she said. "Who naps, who doesn't nap. Voluntary and involuntary nappers. Famous nappers in history.

"There are an infinite number of features out there. To me, the best place to find a feature is to look at what's happening around you. Look at the news. Talk to people in the supermarket. In other words, live.

"A feature involves readers on the level of, 'This could happen to you.' You are teaching people something about themselves. You are telling them, 'Look what this did to this guy. Here's what we can learn from this.' It's like holding up a mirror."

Gillespie's first job out of college was as a news writer at the *Suburban Sun-Times*. "You have to learn your ABCs of writing news before you can write features," she said. "The two are intertwined. You should begin as a news writer, but you cannot forever evolve with *who, what, where, why* and *when,* period. The feature writer's challenge is to go farther."

FEATURES IN PRINT AND BROADCAST

HARD NEWS AND SOFT NEWS

People get up in the morning and want to know what happened since they went to bed. They read a morning newspaper or turn on the morning news. They switch their car or office radios to the news during the day to find out the latest happenings. When they get home, they turn on the evening news or read an evening newspaper for a recap of what happened during the day.

A news story can be *hard,* chronicling as concisely as possible the *who, what, where, when, why* and *how* of an event. Or it can be *soft,* standing back to examine the people, places and things that shape the world, nation or community.

Hard news events, such as school board meetings and bond elections, affect many people, and the primary job of the media is to report them as they happen. Soft news, such as the re-emerging popularity of soft-top automobiles or how people are coping with cold weather, is also reported by the media. Feature stories are often written on these soft news events.

Features: When Is Soft News Appropriate?

There is no firm line between a news story and a feature story, particularly today, when many news events are "featurized." For instance, Monday may have been the warmest day so far this year. A broadcast news story may begin: "Record heat toasted the city Monday, and there's no relief in sight." A featurized story in a newspaper may begin: "John Hilkevich did what everyone in the city wanted to do Monday. He spent the day getting a tan at the beach."

Most newspapers and broadcast news shows offer a mix: hard news stories that chronicle the significant events that occurred since the last edition, and features that:

- Profile people who made the news
- Explain events that moved or shook the news
- Analyze what is happening in the world, nation or community
- Teach an audience how to do something
- Suggest better ways to live in a complicated world
- Examine trends in constantly changing societies
- Entertain

Despite today's interest in feature stories, hard news still fills most of a newspaper's front page; a broadcast news show usually begins with several hard news stories. However, inside the newspaper and often on the lower half of the front page, the stories become softer. After the television or radio anchors report the major news of the day, they turn to features.

Today's daily media use many factors to determine what events they will report, including timeliness, proximity, consequence, the perceived interest of the audience, competition, editorial goals and even the influence of advertisers. All these factors put pressure on the media to give their audiences both news and features. Readers, viewers and listeners want hard news that tells them the *who, what, where, when, why* and *how* of events that are occurring constantly in their world, nation and community. They also want to be entertained, to smile or cry, to learn and to sit back and truly enjoy a story.

One newspaper that seems to have found a successful formula for mixing hard news and soft news is *The Wall Street Journal*. Every day, the *Journal* prints sober business and finance reports. It also has a "What's News" column that summarizes the top news stories. Mixed in with these are feature stories that center on the business world.

Sometimes, the distinction between hard and soft news is clear. When people are killed in a fire, there is *immediate news value*. The breaking stories will be written in typical inverted-pyramid form that puts the most important points at the beginning.

However, when the governor visits town just to eat chili at a favorite downtown restaurant, the writer may choose an alternative to the inverted pyramid. This is where the distinction between hard news and soft news becomes hazy. The story on the governor can be written as hard news, reporting that the governor is in town to eat chili. That could be big news in a small town. However, the story can also be written as a soft news feature, letting the governor and others explain what makes this chili and this restaurant so good. Either way, the story must be written as objectively as possible in easy-to-understand language.

Here is another situation in which the distinction is not clear-cut. A student reporter is assigned to write about the increasing burglary rate in the apartment buildings near the university. The student calls the police department, sets up an interview with the officer in charge of the burglary detail and finds out that the increase is alarming. The officer says that unless the department is given additional funding, it can do little to check the skyrocketing rate.

The reporter can handle this story as hard news and write it in inverted-pyramid form, or write it as a soft news feature. Here is an example of the inverted pyramid:

> Burglaries have increased in apartment buildings here by more than 200 percent in the last year, and police say that there is little they can do about it.
>
> "Without a bigger budget and more staff, we are powerless to reduce the wave of crime," Lt. Felix Ramirez of the burglary detail said. "The best we can do is hope witnesses will come forth and help us capture the criminals."
>
> Ramirez blamed much of the increase on a climbing unemployment rate. He said another major reason is that most apartments in the area are occupied by students, who are at school all day long.

Here is an example of the soft news feature:

> It was 5 p.m. Tuesday when Herbert V. Williamson walked in on three men who were burglarizing his apartment.
>
> Panicking, the three thieves ran out and took off in their car. Williamson called the police immediately and then started to cry as he stared at his possessions dumped on the floor.
>
> Fifteen minutes later, three men were arrested by police near the Saxton Street Mall after their car stalled. On the back seat were three paintings and hundreds of dollars worth of silver coins and clothing taken from Williamson's apartment.
>
> Williamson and the three suspects are only a small part in the city's skyrocketing burglary rate, which has increased more than 200 percent near the university in the last year. Police blame much of the increase on a rising unemployment rate, and they say that there is little they can do about it.

"Jell-O Journalism": When Is Soft News Inappropriate?

When a hard news story breaks—for example, a major development in a continuing story, a killing or a fire—it should be topped with a hard news lead. Soft leads and stories are more appropriate when a major news event is not being reported for the first time. Some editors decry an overemphasis on soft writing and refer to it as *Jell-O journalism*.

In a story on the prosecutions of a motorcycle gang for allegedly raping and beating two women in a national forest in southeastern Illinois, the *St. Louis Post-Dispatch* did not report until the 11th paragraph that the court costs could plunge a rural county into a financial crisis. The lead paragraph said:

> The two-lane road winds through the hills of Hardin County deep into the Shawnee National Forest in southeastern Illinois, carrying visitors far from the interstate highways and backward in time.

The next nine paragraphs built up to the paragraph that gave the news. Even the headline was written on the 11th paragraph. It said, "Cycle Gang Violence Jars Rural County's Budget."

There was no reason to take the reader through 10 paragraphs before giving the thrust of the story. A hard news story such as this deserved a summary lead. A soft lead would have been more appropriate on a feature on the psychological effects of the attack on the two women. And even in a feature story, the news peg should have been given in the third or fourth paragraph.

TYPES OF FEATURES

Feature is an umbrella term for a number of soft news stories that profile, humanize, add color, educate, entertain or illuminate. A feature is not meant to deliver news firsthand. It usually recaps major news that was reported in a previous news cycle. It can stand alone, or it can be a *sidebar* to the main story, the *mainbar*. A sidebar runs next to the main story or elsewhere in the same edition, providing an audience with additional information on the same topic.

Types of features include:

- Personality profiles
- Human interest stories
- Trend stories
- In-depth stories
- Backgrounders

Let's look at each of these.

Personality Profiles

A *personality profile* is written to bring an audience closer to a person in or out of the news. Interviews and observations, as well as creative writing, are used to paint a vivid picture of the person. People enjoy reading about other people, which makes a personality profile one of the most popular features in today's media.

Examples include an interview with a judge in a sensational murder trial and the story of a man in a wheelchair who has just completed a cross-country trek to raise funds for disabled children. Mary Gillespie once wrote a personality profile on her father, who was a prisoner of war during World War II. Her lead was, "I didn't expect to cry."

When the former baseball star Willie Mays appeared at a downtown Boston bookstore to autograph copies of his autobiography, "Say Hey," Alex Beam of the *Boston Globe* wrote a personality profile that was rich in observations and quotations. By the end of the story, readers knew the news of Mays' 2½-week, 10-city book tour; more important, the vivid writing offered them a snapshot of a baseball legend.

For example, here is one of the paragraphs in the story that made excellent use of observation:

> Dressed in a tan suit and sporting huge gold rings (one from the Hall of Fame and one from the 1973 World Series) on each pinky, Mays occasionally flashed his electrifying feel-good grin to two security guards hired to keep the line moving.

Every paragraph in the story revealed something about Mays' personality. Beam used one direct quotation to illustrate that Mays did not enjoy promotional tours, nor did he pay attention to worshipful comments made by fans during the book signing. The quotation's attribution also included more observations:

> "I don't listen to them," Mays said later, stretching his powerful 6-foot frame across an easy chair at the Ritz-Carlton before plunging ahead with a new round of radio and television appearances. "I don't work and play at the same time. If I talked to everyone it would take forever. The bookstore wants me to sell a lot of books and so does the publisher."

Human Interest Stories

A *human interest story* is written to show a subject's oddity or its practical, emotional or entertainment value. Examples include what Atlantic City does each year to prepare for the Miss America pageant, how to repair a washing machine and how people are surviving in the town with the nation's highest unemployment rate.

Imagine how powerful a feature story would be on an elderly man who has just found out that he has terminal cancer.
(Photo by Don B. Stevenson)

Trend Stories

A *trend story* examines people, things or organizations that are having an impact on society. Trend stories are popular because people are excited to read or hear about the latest fads. Examples include a look at summer fashions, a new religion or the language of teen-agers.

In-Depth Stories

An *in-depth story,* through extensive research and interviews, provides a detailed account well beyond a basic news story or feature. It can be a lengthy news feature that examines one topic extensively; an investigative story that reveals wrongdoing by a person, agency or institution; or a first-person article in which the writer relives a happy or painful experience.

Examples include stories on cancer and how it has affected several families, how illegal aliens get into the United States and how one rock group made it to the top while another failed.

Backgrounders

A *backgrounder*—also called an *analysis piece*—adds meaning to current issues in the news by explaining them further. These stories bring an audience up to date, explaining how this country, this organization, this person or whatever got to be where it is now.

Examples include an analysis of the state death penalty shortly after a murderer is sentenced to death or a story explaining how the university food service won its exclusive contract.

WRITING AND ORGANIZING FEATURE STORIES

Feature writers seldom use the traditional inverted-pyramid form. Instead, they may write a chronology that builds to a climax at the end, a narrative, a first-person article about one of their own experiences or a combination of these. Their stories are held together by a thread, and they often end where the lead started, with a single person or event.

Here are the steps typically followed in organizing a feature story:

- *Choose the theme.* Make sure that the theme is not too broad or too narrow.
- *Write a lead that invites an audience into the story.* A summary may not be the best lead for a feature. A two- or three-paragraph lead block may be better. The nut graph should be high in the story. Do not make readers wait until the 10th or 11th paragraph before telling them what the story is about.
- *Provide vital background information.* If appropriate, a paragraph or two of background should be placed high in the story to bring an audience up to date.
- *Write clear, concise sentences.* Sprinkle direct quotations, observations and additional background throughout the story. Paragraphs can be written chronologically or in order of importance.
- *Use a thread.* Connect the beginning, body and conclusion of the story.
- *Use transition.* Connect paragraphs with transitional words, paraphrases and direct quotations.
- *Use dialogue when possible.* Feature writers, like fiction writers, often use dialogue to keep a story moving. Of course, feature writers cannot make up dialogue; they listen for it during the reporting process. Good dialogue is like a good observation in a story. It gives readers strong mental images and keeps them attached to the writing.
- *Conclude with a quotation or another part of the thread.* A feature can trail off like a news story or it can be concluded with a climax.

We'll now consider these elements of feature writing.

FINDING THE THEME AND DEVELOPING THE STORY

Before a feature is written it should have a theme or a purpose. Writers do not simply sit down and write features. They determine the purpose of a feature —to profile someone, to teach something, to reveal something, to illuminate something—and then they do their research and organize the story to help them achieve this purpose. Each section of the story—the beginning, the body and the end—should revolve around the theme.

Writers also narrow their themes as much as possible. No one writes a feature on cancer. That would take volumes. Instead, the feature would be on the latest medicine, how certain foods reduce the risk or one person's valiant fight.

Once the theme is determined, all research, interviewing and writing should support it. Of course, something may come up during the research or interviewing process that alters the focus of the story, but writers try to stick to the original theme as much as possible.

Writers determine a theme on the basis of several factors:

- *Has the story been done before?* Writers look for something fresh or unusual. Even an old topic, such as cancer, can have a new theme.

- *The audience.* The story should be of interest to the audience. If people cannot relate to the piece, they will not read it, no matter how well-written it is.

- *Holding power.* The story has to keep the audience interested. Emotional appeal is important here. Will the story make an audience laugh or cry?

- *Worthiness.* Writers must also ask themselves (or their editors or news directors may ask them): "Is this story worth anything? Is the theme so narrow or so broad that it has no value?"

WRITING THE LEAD

As discussed in Chapter 4, possibilities for feature leads are endless. Feature writers generally write narrative, contrast, staccato, direct address or "none of the above" leads. They usually avoid summary leads because it is not necessary or practical to summarize an entire feature in a single opening paragraph.

"You can't underestimate the importance of the lead," Mary Gillespie said. "If you don't get them in the lead, you won't get them. The lead has to convey urgency, something so provocative that they'll want to read the story. You're like a carny, saying, 'Hey, don't pass me by. Stop and read me.' But you're in trouble if you can't back up your lead. You have to follow the fireworks with something just as big."

A *lead block* of two or more paragraphs often begins a feature. Rather than put the news elements of the story in the lead, the feature writer uses the first two or three paragraphs to set a mood, to arouse readers, to invite them inside. Then the news peg or the significance of the story is provided in the third or fourth paragraph, the *nut graph*. Because it explains the reason the story is being written, the nut graph—also called the *"so what" graph*—is a vital paragraph in every feature.

"Many times, I'll be sitting in an interview and I'll know the lead," Gillespie said. "I'll hear the person say something or he'll do something, and I'll think, that's great. That's the lead. Your goal in the lead is to grab readers. You're trying to tell the reader, 'I'm going to tell you a story. I'm going to tell you something you don't know. Come in here, look at this, examine this person or situation.'"

WRITING THE BODY

Between the lead and the ending, the story must be organized so that it is easy to follow and understand. The body provides vital information while it educates, entertains and emotionally ties an audience to the subject. Then, the ending will wrap up the story and come back to the lead, often with a quotation or a surprising climax.

According to Gillespie, the story's body should not jar the reader. "The middle should flush out the provocative statement in the lead. It should analyze and dig deeper. It should illuminate the lead."

Important components of the body of a feature story are background information, the thread of the story, transition, dialogue and voice.

Providing Background Information

It is essential for feature writers to provide the appropriate background information. Thus a paragraph or more of background should appear high in the story to bring the readers up to date.

The feature story described later in this chapter—James Kennedy's feature on a Native American family—is a good illustration of how to use background information.

Using a Thread

In a feature story, as in a news story, transitions, paraphrases and quotations are used to connect paragraphs and move from one area to another. Because a feature generally runs longer than a news story, it is also effective to weave a *thread* throughout the story, which connects the lead to the body and to the conclusion. This thread can be a single person, an event or a thing, and it usually highlights the theme of the story.

A feature on how people fight heart disease could begin with a 13-year-old child in a hospital bed, waiting for a heart transplant and facing the deadline of death. The body of the story would explore heart disease, how many people it affects and what is being done to help those who have it. Throughout the body of the story, the writer would keep coming back to the 13-year-old, the thread. The feature should also conclude with the child, waiting.

The same feature on heart disease could begin with an event, such as an auto accident in which a 20-year-old man dies. He is rushed to a hospital, where his heart is removed and transplanted into the chest of the 13-year-old child. The event becomes the thread. Throughout the story, the writer refers to the accident that brought death to one person and life to another.

In an in-depth series in the *Chicago Sun-Times* on the Miss America pageant, Gillespie began one story with a narrative lead block that described Ruth Booker, Miss Illinois.

It's a late-summer Sunday designed for luscious languor—bright but cool, with a silky breeze that just ruffles the luxurious old trees of West Dundee.

But as much as she loves the outdoors, 21-year-old Ruth Booker is spending this glorious day in a borrowed studio in the sleepy Fox Valley suburb, patiently being put through her paces.

By noon, she has sung "Kiss Me in the Rain" what seems like 100 times. She has been grilled on current events and made to state specific views on abortion, nuclear war and Geraldine Ferraro. She's been critiqued on her posture ("Glide!"), her eye contact (or lack of it) and the pitch of her voice (a little low, says the voice coach).

By 3 p.m., her red, white and blue outfit is rumpled, her matching high heels have long since been kicked aside and her haute couture body is momentarily draped across a folding director's chair. But Ruth Booker is still smiling. She has to. Smiling is paramount for a newly crowned Miss America, and that's what this long-legged American beauty hopes to be on Saturday night.

Booker was the story's thread. The story branched out into several areas: it was about other beauty queens from Illinois; and it was about beauty pageants in general and the Miss America pageant in particular. It was also about Booker, and because she was the thread, Gillespie used her as an example throughout.

Using Transition

Transition holds paragraphs together and allows them to flow into each other. Transition is particularly important in a long feature examining several people or events because it is the tool writers use to move subtly from one person or area to the next. Transition keeps readers from being jarred by the writing. It guides them through the story and keeps them comfortable until the end. Like the thread, it helps connect the beginning, the middle and the end of a story.

Transition can be a word or a phrase at the beginning or the end of a sentence, or it can be a sentence or a paragraph that connects other sentences or paragraphs. With transition, the writer says, "Now, reader, the writing is going to move smoothly into another area." Words commonly used as transitions include *meanwhile, therefore, sometimes, also, and, but, meantime, nevertheless* and *however*. Phrases include *at 8 p.m., in other action, despite the promises* or *in the time that followed*. Sentences include *Police gave the following account of the accident* and *The witness described how the crime occurred*.

Here is a personality profile that Gillespie wrote on the Illinois State Lottery superintendent. Try to find her transitions.

The T-shirts, posters, buttons and huge dollar-bill mural in the high-rise conference room all promise one thing—big, easy money. This is indeed the stuff of dreams, and Michael Jones feels right at home. His is the job of chief dream weaver. It's an occupation he takes seriously.

Jones is the cinema handsome, 35-year-old wunderkind superintendent of the Illinois State Lottery. In less than three years, he has upped annual lottery revenues from $334 million to more than $900 million. He's increased the number of ticket-selling agents statewide by about 5,000. Between $20 million and $21 million in dream chits are now sold every week in Illinois.

But it's not just big bucks that Jones has brought to the lottery (and thus to the general revenue fund—a sort of checking account for the state—where the currency of hope is deposited). It's also image. A higher profile. And, Jones is quick to point out, fun.

"It can be wonderful, buying a ticket and entertaining a little daily or weekly fantasy," says Jones, who admits he loves to gamble on lotteries in other states. He's especially fond of New York's Lotto game—after which ours is patterned. "I always think I'm going to win," he says with a grin that can only be described as All-American boyish. "The superintendent of the New York lottery hates me because I call him on Sunday mornings to get the winning numbers.

"But I think it's possible to overdraw the idea that people's hopes and dreams are totally tied up in winning the lottery," he adds. "I think people's hopes and dreams are probably more complex than that. The lottery is not life and death for most people; it's an escape, a fun dream that they like to believe just might come true someday."

It was "plain business sense"—which he honed in such diverse early career endeavors as managing the "late, lamented" Oakland Stompers soccer team and directing marketing for WMET radio—that led Gov. James Thompson to seek him out to oversee the lottery, Jones believes.

"I think he saw the lottery could be much more than it was, and he wanted to see it run like a business," he says. "That approach has, quite literally, paid off."

One of the key catalysts for the lottery's stunning success since Jones' arrival is his emphasis on catchy, light-hearted advertising. From prime-time TV spots to arresting L placards, impertinent Ping-Pong balls and other disarming characters and props have persuaded thousands of the previously blasé to ante up a dollar or two.

Jones works closely with Bozell and Jacobs ad agency in formulating new campaigns to convince consumers to hitch their dreams to a fame ticket. They introduced a new pitch June 18 for the latest instant game, "Pay Day."

With the fun of being lottery superintendent goes serious responsibility. "I am very careful about the lottery's image and we try to be extremely careful in explaining to people exactly what they can expect from it," he says. "Remember those ads a while back about various ways to make a million? One said, 'You can marry a millionaire,' and there were other humorous examples. But one you never saw was a guy in a funny old striped prison uniform with a ball and chain and the message, '. . . or, you could rob a bank.' That just wasn't a message we wanted to send to the public. So although it was funny, it was canned."

An Army brat, Jones grew up in various spots around the country. His high school and college years were spent in Florida, where he attended Satellite High School in the shadow of Cape Kennedy during the heyday of the space race. Now, though, he's an avowed Chicagoan. He, his wife and their 2-year-old son live on the North Side.

While he is unabashedly in love with his job, Jones says he'll not make a lifetime pursuit of it. For now, though, he says he's content in the lottery's catbird seat.

"There are still a couple more personal goals I have for the lottery that I'd like to fulfill," he says. "I've always craved work that is a challenge, and I've been very lucky so far. I can only hope that luck will continue."

Behind him, on his credenza, sits a replica of the Maltese Falcon of film fame. It was a gift from his wife, who shares his passion for movies, he says. But it also has another meaning for him.

"You have to remember at the end of the 'Maltese Falcon,' when the guy asks Bogie what the statuette is? He says, 'That's the stuff dreams are made of.' In my job and my life, it's turned out to be very appropriate."

Gillespie first used transition in the third paragraph, when she moved readers from the finances of the lottery to Jones' stamp on the lottery:

> But it's not just big bucks that Jones
> has brought to the lottery . . .

To take the reader from Jones' impression of how much fun playing the lottery can be (third through fifth paragraphs) Gillespie made her sixth paragraph transitional:

> It was "plain business sense"—which he honed in such diverse early career endeavors as managing the "late, lamented" Oakland Stompers soccer team and directing marketing and advertising for WMET radio—that led Gov. James Thompson to seek him out to oversee the lottery, Jones believes.

Gillespie began the eighth paragraph with a transitional sentence to move readers from Jones' selection as lottery chief to what he has done during his tenure:

> One of the key catalysts for the lottery's stunning success since Jones' arrival is his emphasis on catchy, light-hearted advertising.

After two paragraphs on the funny advertising, transition was used again:

> With the fun of being lottery superintendent goes serious responsibility.

In her 11th paragraph, Gillespie told readers a little about Jones' upbringing. She began with a transitional phrase:

> An Army brat, Jones grew up in various spots around the country.

Then in the 14th paragraph, Gillespie used transition to switch readers to Jones' office and the ending of the story:

> Behind him, on his credenza, sits a replica of the Maltese Falcon of film fame.

Using Dialogue

Dialogue is an important component of feature writing because it keeps readers attached to a story's key players. It helps move readers through the writing. With dialogue, the reader—like the writer—can listen in on important conversation between two or more people.

Dialogue can be sprinkled throughout a story to introduce sources or to give depth to sources who already have been introduced. The dialogue should be part of the story's flow, and it should add important information. It should not be stuck into the story merely to illustrate the reporter's skills.

Here is some dialogue near the beginning of a feature story that appeared in *Arizona Highways,* an international travel magazine. The story was about a one-room schoolhouse serving several ranch families in an isolated part of Arizona. This particular dialogue illustrated how each school day begins. It was used after the schoolteacher, Jim Hazzard, was introduced and after the story reported that the children had said the Pledge of Allegiance. Notice how the dialogue introduced sources so that attribution was not needed at the end of each quote.

"Let's talk about anything new," the teacher tells his pupils after the pledge. "Anything new happen on the creek?"

Hands jump.

"Bobby."

"I heard a bird call last night. It was real loud."

"Keith."

"I saw six cats and five dogs."

Hazzard changes the subject. "Let's have a little humor."

"Catherine."

"What's worse than a 300-pound witch?"

No response.

"Being a broom."

The pupils snicker as Hazzard calls on Jake.

"Why did the boy ghost whistle at the girl ghost?"

No answer.

"Because she was so booo-tiful."

This dialogue fit well in the story. It put readers inside the classroom with the teacher and his pupils. Of course, the writer could have described the scene by paraphrasing what happened, but the dialogue was much more effective. It added color and depth to the story.

Dialogue also helps make sources more than cardboard figures. For example, it was used effectively in an *Arizona Highways* feature on a wilderness area east of Phoenix. In this story the writer accompanied several cowboys on a three-day trail ride. Here is a portion of the dialogue between two of the sources. The first speaker is Duane Short, a cowboy who is cooking breakfast on a chilly morning. He is talking to another cowboy who is working with a horse named Popcorn.

"I hope you like my coffee. I make horseshoe coffee. It's strong enough so that if you drop a horseshoe in it, the shoe dissolves."

He glances at his friend Shaffer, still working with Popcorn. "How are you today, Lee?"

"Fine as frog's hair," Shaffer says as he clicks his tongue and cajoles Popcorn to move.

Notice how this dialogue was used with observations to reveal something more about the story's key sources. The writer could have described the scene by saying something like, *While Shaffer clicked his tongue and cajoled his horse to move, Short made coffee, which he said was so strong that "if you drop a horseshoe in it, the shoe dissolves."* There's nothing wrong with this sentence. It uses an observation to illustrate something for readers. The dialogue, however, added depth to the two cowboys and helped readers "hear" them talking.

Using Voice

Another key element that holds a feature together is *voice*, the "signature" or personal style of each writer. Yes, there is a byline on the top of the story to tell readers who the writer is, but voice inside the story allows writers to put their individual stamps on their writing. It reveals a writer's personality and subtly tells readers that this story is not by any writer; it is by this writer.

"I think if given the chance, all writers have something unique in the way they tell a story," Gillespie said. "They all bring their style, their ego and all of their baggage to whatever they do. That's the voice. Therein lies the creativity and the real challenge. There is a formula for writing feature stories, as there is for news stories. But good feature writers take the basic formula and expand it. They use their own voice. When I write a story, I want readers to say that this is Mary Gillespie writing about something, not just anyone who happened to be available to cover a story."

Remember, though, that voice should be used subtly; it is not meant to scream at readers. And it can also fall victim to an editor.

Gillespie's voice pops up whenever she writes. She did not simply call the state lottery director *handsome*—she called him *cinema handsome*. That's voice; that's Mary Gillespie drawing a conclusion and putting it into the story. When she wrote a Christmas feature about families who had to spend the holidays at home while loved ones were fighting wars or were stationed overseas, Gillespie revealed some of her personality when she wrote:

> The ache is familiar to those who remember the irony of war at Christmas—those who, while their hairlines may be beginning to recede as their bellies expand, have memories of holiday duty as sharp as blood on snow.

In his story on a championship boxing match in which the two fighters brutalized each other, the *Chicago Tribune* sportswriter Bob Verdi used voice when he said:

> You didn't just walk away from this fight; you sat in your chair awhile.

Michael Zielenziger, a writer for the *San Jose* (Calif.) *Mercury News*, clearly let his voice pop up in a story that he wrote about Warren Buffett, a major owner of Berkshire Hathaway Inc. The company is a principal investor in scores of companies, including Time Inc., Washington Post Co. and General Foods Corp.:

> There's no hint of marble, no glint of gold in Buffett's modest-size office just outside downtown Omaha. There's no stock ticker, no ornamental fountain, not even a sweeping staircase in the corporate headquarters of Berkshire Hathaway, which houses all of six people. Berkshire Hathaway doesn't even have a corporate logo.

Because voice is a subjective expression of a writer, it is often challenged by editors, who may edit it out or even insert some voice of their own. It is best used in feature stories, where writers are given more license to reveal their opinions and personality.

"Features offer potentially a far greater chance to put in voice, but you have to be careful," Gillespie said. "There's always an editor; there's always a copy desk. Every writer has a voice. You just have to find it. The only way to grab someone is if you have been grabbed."

WRITING THE CONCLUSION

A feature can trail off, like a news story, or it can end with a climax. Often, a feature ends where the lead started, with a single person or event.

Gillespie said that the ending should complete the circle and come back to the lead. "I like to end with a quote," Gillespie added. "The story then says, here's this guy, here's why he's neat, here's his final statement to the reader. By using a quote at the end, you eliminate the feeling of a chopped-off story."

In her story on the Miss America pageant, as we saw above, Gillespie began with Ruth Booker—Miss Illinois—and made Booker the story's thread. The story also ended with Booker, talking directly to the reader:

"I've learned to be thankful for my strong core when everyone is picking me apart, telling me to wear my hair up instead of down or walk differently or whatever. I've learned that the point is not so much to win; it's to grow. It's to become confident in your own abilities.

"And," she adds with a perfect runway smile, "to have a good time."

FROM START TO FINISH: AN EXAMPLE OF FEATURE WRITING

When James H. Kennedy of *The Birmingham* (Ala.) *News* wrote a human interest feature on a family of Alabama Indians moving from Texas to their native state, the story's purpose was to educate readers about one family's journey and about Native American roots in East Alabama and Georgia.

Books could be written about the migration of Indians out of Alabama in the 1700s and about how they came to live on a reservation in Livingston, Texas. Kennedy, however, narrowed his theme. His story was built around a single family, which meant that his audience could learn a part of this history by reading about some of the people who lived it. There were numerous quotations and observations in the feature, as well as a liberal dose of history.

The Beginning

Kennedy's story began with a contrast lead block:

Lloyd Sylestine had never been to Alabama until three years ago.

Yet the 59-year-old Texas native had yearned most of his life to walk on Alabama soil.

He'd dreamed of seeing its rolling hills and picturesque meadows, of strolling through its deep forests.

So last October, Sylestine, his wife Wanda and four of their six children packed up and left Texas to settle in St. Clair County.

The next three paragraphs told readers the "so what" of the story:

Sylestine is a full-blooded Alabama Indian and the grandson of a former chief of the Alabama-Coushatta Tribe in Livingston, Texas, 90 miles from Houston.

His wife—a Louisiana native—is Coushatta.

Both tribes are of Muskogean stock, and their roots run deep in East Alabama and Georgia, where they once formed the nucleus of the Creek Confederacy.

The Body

The first four paragraphs of the story invited readers inside; the next three, the nut graphs, told them the reason the story was written. A feature is often written this way. It begins with a creative lead block that entices rather than summarizes. One or more nut graphs then give the story's news peg.

After the beginning, the writer moves to the feature's body, which should entertain and educate. A news story informs people of events that have occurred within the last day or the last few hours; a feature, on the other hand, should teach them something and tie them emotionally to the subject. To do this, the body of a feature must be written so that it provides vital information and is easy and fun to read.

In the body of Kennedy's story, his readers were brought closer to the Sylestine family through quotations and observations. They also learned background information about the Indian tribes:

They started migrating westward after the English won supremacy in America over France in the 1700s, according to historians.

A large number of them ended up in Texas, where they eventually settled on a 4,600-acre reservation in Livingston. Many still live there, including Sylestine's four sisters and a brother.

In this feature, the thread was the Native American family. Throughout the story, the writer let the family members talk to the readers, explaining their difficulties in leaving the reservation:

"Ever since I was old enough to understand, I heard about Alabama and always wanted to come here," said Sylestine, who retired in 1987 because of health problems. "We love it here. The people have been very nice to us."

His only disappointment thus far has been a failure to find more "real Indians," as well as authentic Indian arts and crafts, he said.

"Everything we've seen so far—beadworks, basketry and so forth—was made in Taiwan," he said. "That's really sad. We believe in preserving our heritage."

The End

Like a news story, a feature is often concluded with a quotation, which lets the story trail off with a source talking directly to the reader. Ending with narrative is also effective. Some features build up to the conclusion, which contains an exciting or surprising climax.

Kennedy concluded his story with a direct quotation from Mrs. Sylestine, illustrating the independence and pride of the Native American family:

> "We have been independent all our lives," Mrs. Sylestine said. "My husband and I worked hard all our lives and educated our kids—we sent them all to college."

EFFECTIVE FEATURES: A CHECKLIST FOR WRITERS

Mary Gillespie gives advice to students who want to write features:

- *Know how to write news.* Learn the ABCs of digging for facts, interviewing and writing news stories under tight deadlines before trying to write features.

- *Do your homework.* Go into any story situation knowing something about the lives of the people being interviewed. Know the direction that the interview and the story should take.

- *Use observation.* Describe the house or the office, what the people are wearing, how they talk. Are they wearing wedding rings? Do they take a lot of time to answer a question? What color socks do they wear?

- *Use a tape recorder.* Taping is good because it provides a precise record of what is said. It also reveals how a person answers questions. For example, it might help a story to mention that a person took a deep breath before answering a question.

- *Do not be afraid to ask questions.* Ask as many as possible. Even fully prepared reporters sometimes have to admit their ignorance. Sometimes, a reporter will have to say, "Can you explain this all to me?"

- *Maintain a relationship with every source.* Additional questions may come up while the story is being written. At the end of the interview, ask the source where he or she can be reached.

- *Transcribe handwritten notes as soon as possible.* That will help organize thoughts and prepare an outline for the story. The longer a reporter waits to transcribe notes, the more difficult it is to do.

- *Write a rough outline first.* Then write a rough draft, revise it, write another draft, revise it and so on. Writing is all a refinement process. In the beginning, the more drafts that are written, the better.

- *Do not overwrite.* Remember, features are about people. Use quotations and paraphrases throughout the story to let sources communicate to the readers. The more talking they do, the better.

- *Polish the story.* If there is time after the story is finished, take a breather before reading it again as objectively as possible. Read the story as many times as possible before turning it in, and continue refining it.

- *Take criticism from an editor.* It is true that writers pour their hearts and souls into the stories they write, but a story is not final until the last minute. Just figure that an editor will ask for something to be rechecked or added.

"I read stuff now that I have written and that is in the paper, and I still want to tinker," Gillespie said. "I think feature writers are perfectionists. There are times when I feel that I didn't do the best job that I could have. I think that can happen when a writer doesn't have enough time or has not sufficiently understood or synthesized the information.

"You have to use all your five senses as tools when you are writing a feature. You use those five senses as a sponge, and then you go back and wring it out. It goes from mind to hand. I close my eyes, I listen to the tape and I write."

Print reporters are not the only ones doing in-depth and investigative stories.
Network as well as local broadcast reporters like the challenge of working on
stories that go well beyond routine daily news pieces or features.
(Bettye Lane/Photo Researchers)

In-Depth and Investigative Reporting

In-depth articles provide a comprehensive account

well beyond a basic news story. They can be

lengthy news features that explore one topic

extensively; investigative reports that reveal

wrongdoing by a person, agency or institution; or

first-person articles in which writers relive happy

or painful experiences. In-depths require extensive

research and interviews.

The writer Linda Witt's description of Pamela Zekman, an investigative reporter for WBBM-TV, the CBS-owned station in Chicago, is a primer for investigative journalism. In an article in *Sunday*, the weekly magazine of the *Chicago Tribune*, Witt wrote:

Still on the phone, Zekman grabs a yellow legal pad and scribbles notes. She pouts. She winces. Her soft voice echoes each facial expression, but the look in her eyes remains the same—a kind of intense delight, an adrenalin high. She is investigating the multimillion-dollar security-guard business in Illinois.

Watching her on the phone is like watching a fisherman with a big one on the hook. One minute she's reeling in, tightening the tension on the line. The next, she's giving her quarry line to run with. She plays each turning and twisting attempt to wiggle off the hook with finesse, and she loves every minute of her sport.

"But that's the point I want to make," she is saying to the owner of a security-guard company, who had hired and assigned a man to guard a printing plant without knowing that the man had been convicted of armed robbery. The state of Illinois is two years behind in running the background checks it is legally required to do on security guards—some 9,000 guards behind, Zekman will claim. She's also finding murderers, rapists, armed robbers, drug addicts and psychotics among those who have been given guns and assigned as guards to everything from hospital pharmacies to Chicago's federal buildings. "Why won't you be interviewed on that point?" she asks the security-company owner.

"There are lots of other companies involved. I have interviewed many of them," she says into the phone.

"That's exactly the point. Nobody in the state Department of Registration and Education notifies these companies even after their employees have been arrested for violent crimes. Your company is not alone.

"Hmmmmm? Uh hum. Yeah. Uh huh. Wouldn't everyone like you want some mechanism in place so you don't hire a murderer? Or if your employee is arrested for rape, somebody notifies you?

"No, a guy in your association is not somebody I can talk to . . . it didn't happen to him. It happened to you. This is television. I need *you* saying it."

Zekman hangs up. The fish got off the hook, at least temporarily. Sandy Bergo, one of three regular members of Zekman's Channel 2 Investigative Team, hands her a memo detailing the arrest record of one of the security guards in question.

"This is crazy!" Zekman explodes. "Sending a rapist to guard a women's clothing store!" She angrily punches the next number on her list into the phone.

"Hi. This is Pam." Her voice is warm, friendly. "What did you decide about an interview?" Her face shows she's resigned to a turn-down, but her voice is cordial, inviting. "Who's your attorney?" she asks, her voice suddenly flat, irritated, intimidating, a tonal slap in the face to the man on the other end of the line.

"Why am I interested in you?" An optimistic grin appears; he's taken the bait again. "Because I am interested in the problems your industry is having."

Her voice mellows. She's now conversational. This could be just a chat between old friends, but it's technique. It's a skill carefully honed in nearly 20 years as a reporter, begun in 1967 when she was one of the pioneering females at the Chicago City News Bureau, the M*A*S*H-like prep school of hard knocks that has graduated some of the city's and the nation's top reporters including Mike Royko, Walter Jacobson and Seymour Hersh.

Zekman is nibbling on one nail, and her brow is wrinkled, but her quarry can't see the concern. Instead, he hears a friend, murmuring into the phone, "Uh hum, mmmmm, uh hum. . . . Yeah, you're right."

The questions continue. Slowly, patiently, Zekman lures her prey into a net. He has lied. She has documents in front of her that contradict what he is saying. She goes round and round in circles, each time covering the same basic material. Each time he alters his story in some minute way she extracts another tiny piece of truth. Finally, even he knows he is caught and he knows that she knows it. It's tedious, this slow, careful carving away of the falsehoods, the ever-tightening circles of investigative reporting.

WHAT IS AN IN-DEPTH?

Most investigations result in in-depth articles, which—through extensive research and interviews—provide an account that goes farther than a basic news story. An in-depth can be a lengthy news feature on one topic; an investigative story that reveals wrongdoing; or a first-person article on a writer's happy or painful experience. An in-depth reports the news, and it also provides detailed information, which allows people to lead more enjoyable, safer, more profitable or better-informed lives.

Journalists have always been civic watchdogs, and this means that they have always been involved in investigations. The idea that this type of reporting is relatively new—a result of the Watergate era of the 1970s—is a misconception. So is the notion that an in-depth or investigative reporter is any different from any reporter gathering facts. In a way, all stories are investigative stories because they require research, digging, interviewing and writing. Also, all reporters are investigators who are trained to ask questions, uncover information and write the most complete story possible.

Some reporters, however, concentrate solely on investigations of wrongdoing. They deal with reporter-adversary relationships that are usually not found in beat reporting or other in-depth coverage. These reporters are trying to ferret out well-guarded information from often hostile sources.

Most American newspapers find space in the news hole each day for in-depth or investigative reports. Even local broadcast outlets are devoting an increasing amount of air time to stories that require in-depth or investigative work. The networks also devote time to in-depth reports, either on their evening newscasts or through special shows. These stories have become commonplace, running with terse accounts of news events that have occurred within the preceding 24 hours.

This increased emphasis on longer, more comprehensive stories that require extensive research and interviews gives reporters an opportunity to be more than technicians following a rigid set of guidelines. It gives them a chance to be creative, to become part of their readers' emotional lives and, sometimes, to uncover an injustice and correct it.

In-depths are choice assignments because they allow reporters to explore a topic thoroughly, learn things that most people do not have a chance to learn and tell a story without the fear of its being cut to 6 inches for a small hole on page 4. The final story may be written as hard news or as soft news. It may be one long piece that starts on the front page and jumps to one or more inside pages, or it may be a series that runs several days. Broadcast media are more likely than newspapers to run an in-depth report as a series over several days.

Assignments for in-depths are usually grueling because they require the reporter to spend days, weeks or even years investigating a topic in the library, in the courthouse and in the field, asking questions over the phone, in person and in writing. For example, the reporter Fred Schulte, an investigative team leader at the *News/Sun-Sentinel* in Fort Lauderdale, Fla., spent four years looking at Veterans Administration (VA) hospitals in general and at the one in Miami in particular. He and his newspaper also had to fight a court battle to win the right to examine medical "quality-assurance" records. His series of articles revealed excessive patient deaths during 11 years in the cardiac unit at the Miami hospital, underused facilities, botched surgical techniques, chronic staff shortages and substandard care.

Working on in-depth stories "gives you a chance to work on something you believe is worthwhile rather than working eight hours and covering routine meetings," Schulte said. "You evolve into looking for a bigger challenge than covering routine stories. Investigative reporting gives you a chance to do that. On the other hand, it's a long time between bylines. Some reporters have a short attention span, and it's difficult to stay on track for months at a time. A newspaper shouldn't try to make everyone work on in-depths. It needs to have good feature writers. It also has to have people who can cover and write a good story in three hours. Good investigative reporters can do this, too, but they do it after an investigation is announced, after their stories have run."

Of course, many reporters do not have the luxury of investigating a single topic for an extended period of time. Often, they must work on in-depths while they continue their regular beats.

GATHERING INFORMATION FOR AN IN-DEPTH STORY

An in-depth is a combination of research, interviews, observation, writing and rewriting. All of these areas require careful attention.

When Schulte wrote the first of his articles on the VA hospitals, he had to make sure that his information was precise because he was revealing wrongdoing. The reporter first heard about the problems at the VA hospital in Miami when an old man stumbled into the newsroom, saying that the hospital had scrapped its heart surgery unit two weeks before he was supposed to have heart surgery. The man said that his doctor had told him that the unit was scrapped because too many patients had died after heart surgery, according to Schulte.

When the reporter first went to the VA, the agency denied that the unit had been shut down. "I told them 'we're running a story tomorrow that 9 out of 10 patients died after heart surgery,' " Schulte said. "That opened the door. They admitted that the unit had been shut down and that 16 percent of the patients had died, more than three times the average. We ran a short story in the evening edition."

The day after that story ran, Schulte said, a Miami newspaper followed it with a story quoting a VA doctor, who claimed that the Fort Lauderdale story was inaccurate.

SMELLING A STORY

When the old man came into the *News/Sun-Sentinel* newsroom, complaining that the Miami VA hospital had scrapped its heart surgery unit two weeks before he was supposed to have an operation, Schulte did what many reporters do when they receive such a tip. He played a hunch, and in this case, it paid off.

Schulte smelled a story. He could have just as easily shrugged off the man, saying to himself, "Why should I listen to this guy or believe him?" But he had a hunch, he followed it and he ultimately wrote a hard-hitting series.

Ideally, reporters write their stories on the basis of facts that they have gathered at news events and then have synthesized. The story is there, and they go out and cover it. In reality, reporters often smell a story and chase it. They let their emotions, intuition, past experiences and gut reactions guide them in the stories they research and write. These feelings arouse reporters to begin working on a story. These feelings influence the gathering of facts, and they become the basis for what is written.

Of course, some hunches turn up nothing. Reporters do not get lucky all the time. More often than not, however, hunches do lead to stories. Experienced reporters, particularly investigative reporters, continually follow hunches. Their stories may reveal a major problem or may point out that the rumors were false.

"We all play hunches," said Jack Anderson, one of the nation's top investigative reporters who writes the syndicated "Washington Merry-Go-Round" column with Michael Binstein. "With experience you develop a certain sense of things. You learn after a while how the crooks operate. When you see a senator get up and pontificate a certain way, it raises an antenna. Many times I've said to my reporters, 'Keep your eye on this or go check this out.'"

Anderson also warned against drawing conclusions about a hunch before the reporting process is complete. "Don't make your mind up until you have the facts," he said. "I counsel my reporters never to go out to prove a story. Get the facts and then tell me what they prove."

CONDUCTING RESEARCH

Importance of Research

As in any story, the first step in writing an in-depth is to study the topic and the sources. Doing careful research is vital because research:

- *Introduces a reporter to the language of a complex topic.* That prepares the reporter to talk to specialists and helps eliminate the problem of having to ask continually, "What does this mean?" or "Can you explain that procedure to me?"

- *Introduces a reporter to people who have been sources for similar stories in the past.* Usually, if they spoke to a reporter before, they will do it again.

- *Helps a reporter formulate a list of questions.* Reporters should know what subjects they want covered and what questions they want answered. It is best to know the answers or partial answers to the questions before the interviewing even begins.

- *Provides other articles written on the same topic.* There are few major topics that have not been covered by the media at some time. There may not be any articles on the individuals involved in a story, but there is usually something about the topic.

- *Uncovers some of the good things and bad things to look for during interviews.* Careful study of records and documents can turn up much information. Much of what Schulte uncovered in his four-year investigation did not come from interviews; it came from poring over medical documents.

Sources of Information

As discussed in Chapters 9 and 10, the most common place to look for background information—clippings and reference sources—is in the newspaper morgue or the public library. The in-depth reporter often has to dig deeper than traditional morgue or library sources, however. Obscure public records often become the key to a major story.

"I almost always go to the courthouse first," Schulte said. "That is a simple way to get a ton of information. All you have to know is the names of the plaintiffs and defendants, and you can look them up in an index. You also have to know all the names of the people involved in the story. If you are doing a story on a big hospital, for instance, you should know all the key staff people. You always should know the name of the administrator. Then you can see if a suit naming the administrator has been filed."

Schulte also uses the Freedom of Information Act (see Chapter 9 for an overview of the FOI Act) to obtain necessary documents from federal agencies in his state and in Washington.

INTERVIEWING

An in-depth is not written after merely interviewing a source or two. Like the research and writing, the interviewing process for an in-depth requires extensive work.

"Talk to anyone who will talk to you," said Charlie Zdravesky of KUNM-FM radio in Albuquerque, N.M. "You never know when someone is going to have a clue that will lead you to something really big."

Zdravesky has been involved in two intermedia investigations. Along with newspaper and television reporters in New Mexico, he has studied abuses at the state prison and at the state mental hospital. In both stories, interviewing as many people as possible, both on and off the record, was critical to the success of the stories. The series of stories on the state prison was nominated for a Pulitzer Prize. Both the prison series and the mental hospital series won annual awards given by the Investigative Reporters and Editors.

Interviews with numerous
credible sources are
essential to in-depth and
investigative stories.
*(Photo by Cliff Polland, The
Reporter, Vacaville, Calif.)*

"We conducted more than 125 interviews for the state hospital story," Zdravesky said. "When we did an interview, we would ask sources if there was anyone else they knew who would talk to us about this. We talked to five sources initially, and each of them gave us three to five more names. Then the new people would give us more names. It sort of branched out like a family tree.

"After about 75 interviews, we started hearing the same thing over and over again. Then it was time to write."

Zdravesky said that throughout the interviewing process, the reporters kept hearing incriminating stories about one official of the state department which oversees the state hospital. "He was one of our last interviews," Zdravesky said. "People kept telling us how much power he had and how incompetent he was. We made sure we knew the answers to most of the questions we were going to ask him. Just like a good attorney, we didn't ask a question unless we knew the answer or part of the answer. That way, we let the source bury himself."

Zdravesky said that writing the story for radio was not much different from writing for print. "The highlights of the story were the same," he said. "The only difference was the style in which it was written. Print journalists could only report what the person had said. In radio, I was able to let the person I was interviewing actually say it himself, on tape."

The reporter said that he did a 7- or 8-minute story every night for 10 nights. "I was lucky because my news director gave me total free time to do what I wanted to do," he said.

Interviews from the Outside In

Zdravesky and the other reporters who worked on the state prison story and the mental hospital story followed the same type of interviewing process that most investigative reporters use. They used *interviews from the outside in,* much like an ever-tightening circle, from the least important to the most important players.

Instead of going to the major source first, at the bull's-eye of the circle, most investigative reporters begin at the outer rings, where people are more likely to give them information about the people in the center. For instance, in a story about a sleazy ambulance firm, most reporters would begin their interviews with former drivers for the firm, the most likely people to have an ax to grind. Then they would talk to current drivers and other officials. The last interview would be with the owner of the firm, who would be much less likely to deny wrongdoing after being presented with well-documented evidence.

"My strategy is to know everything about the person before I go in there," Schulte said. "Once you have everything, interviewing is a breeze because it is clear to the interviewee that you have done your homework. I always begin by asking questions that I know the answers to."

Smoking-Gun Interviews

John Stossel, a reporter for ABC News' "20/20," told an Investigative Reporters and Editors seminar on the special problems of interviewing for broadcast investigations that he knows the interviewee is guilty even before he conducts an interview. Instead of going into an interview to ask general questions, the reporter goes in with videotape or other evidence of wrongdoing by the interviewee and asks direct questions about a specific incident. The interviewee denies it, and the reporter then shows the incriminating evidence, hoping that the person will confirm, on camera, that he or she really is one of the bad guys.

Such an interview is called a *smoking-gun* or *shotgun interview.* "It's the best type of interview," Stossel said. "I've done all the research, and I go into the interview mad. I know the bad guy is guilty. I knew it before the interview. A hidden camera gets the bad guy doing something. Then we interview the person, and he denies everything. Then we show him the tape."

Stossel added that, to get decent television, he is also obnoxious during an interview with someone who he knows is guilty. "I ask questions such as, 'Do you sleep well at night?' or 'Are you ashamed?' " he said. "They have pat answers. They say no comment. They smile. They try to manipulate. They go into gobbledygook. I try to jar them out of that language. It seems the only way I get anything from stiffs on camera is to be a little wild."

Many reporters scorn smoking-gun interviews, for the simple reason that they believe all interviewees should be given a chance to tell their side of the story. Many editors and news directors remind their reporters that there is always a chance, no matter how small, that the interviewee may not be as guilty as all the evidence indicates; therefore, that person should have a chance to express his or her opinions on camera or in print.

"Confrontation interviews may look good on television, but they don't make it in print," Schulte said. "You don't want to do things in that sort of fashion, coming in swaggering about how bad you are. You don't want to go in there like a prosecutor.

"I prefer an informed discussion with the person, where it is clear that both of you have studied the issue sensibly. A lot of people are glad to talk to someone who shares their interest. You usually find that people are very responsive. Then as they get deeper and deeper, you can start with a little of the shotgun. You let them dig their own grave.

"If you are doing an investigation, it's really rare when the major person you need to interview is not aware that you are doing it. The person is going to be very wary, especially if you have a reputation as an investigative reporter. The more on guard these people are, the less likely they are to indict themselves. The more relaxed the tone, the more you will get. I rarely scream or yell or defend what can seem like an opinion. But at the same time, I ask the same question over and over until I get the answer that I need."

The point is, a smoking-gun interview may be useful in some cases, but it should not be used by reporters as standard operating procedure. Remember, reporters are not prosecuting attorneys. They do not interview to confirm guilt; they interview so that all sides of a story can be articulated.

Double-Checks and Triple-Checks

Reporters who work on in-depth and investigative stories do not have the same deadline pressures as reporters covering breaking or quickly developing news. They should have time to double-check and triple-check everything their sources tell them.

It is not unusual for a beat reporter or a general assignment reporter under a tight deadline to go with a single source. However, reporters working on in-depths generally have the time to develop their stories carefully, and they seldom rely on a single source. When working on in-depth articles, reporters should confirm everything three, four or more times. The general rule they follow is that *two sources are usually enough, but it is better to have more.*

An investigative reporter has to be concerned with the basics of checking and rechecking sources even more than a beat reporter, Schulte said. "My stuff gets looked at more closely than anybody else's," he added.

Confidential Sources

"I tell my reporters that a [single] confidential source is no source at all," said the syndicated columnist Jack Anderson. Of course, reporting is not always that simple. Stories are sometimes based on confidential sources. (See Chapter 7 for more on confidential sources.)

Most reporters avoid unnamed sources if they can. But there are some important stories that simply would never be reported if the daily media did not rely on confidential sources. Remember Watergate and Deep Throat, the anonymous source who was never identified but who helped bring down the presidency of Richard Nixon?

There are other examples:

> *The Dallas Morning News* reported that "a Federal Aviation Administration official who asked to remain anonymous" said he had been told that a stalled jet engine led to the crash of a Delta Air Lines jet at the Dallas–Forth Worth International Airport.

> The *San Francisco Examiner* reported that "law enforcement sources" indicated that a New York crime family was seeking a foothold in San Francisco, a city considered relatively free of traditional organized-crime activity.

> An in-depth series in *The Arizona Republic* on sex for sale used first names but no last names for many of its sources. In one article a woman named Paula said that giving good phone sex is legal, and it's safe if a person remembers to scrub the receiver with disinfectant to ward off colds and ear infections from colleagues.

Most reporters follow the same general guidelines when using confidential sources:

- During an interview, they try to talk a reluctant source into going on the record by telling him or her how important the information is to the story.
- If the source is still unwilling to talk on the record, they listen anyway because he or she can provide important information.
- They ask if the source knows of anyone who is willing to provide the same information on the record.
- If possible, they find another source who can be named.

GOING UNDERCOVER

Sometimes, while reporters are working on an in-depth article, they *go undercover* and do not tell sources for the story that they are reporters.

For example, a reporter in Chicago applied for and got a job as a guard at the state prison but never told the officials who hired him that he was a reporter. Afterwards, he wrote a first-person article. When a reporter in Albuquerque, N.M., enrolled in a local high school and then wrote a series on what goes on there, she never told school officials that she was a reporter. The *Chicago Sun-Times* once purchased a tavern in the city, renamed it the Mirage and operated it for four months with the Better Government Association, which provides investigators to work with newspaper and broadcast reporters to uncover corruption and mismanagement in government. Reporters and investigators worked as bartenders, never telling patrons who they really were.

One of the reporters involved in the Mirage investigation was Pamela Zekman, who then worked for the *Sun-Times*. When the *Sun-Times* ran its Mirage series, the stories detailed payoffs to city inspectors to ignore health and safety hazards, shakedowns by state liquor inspectors who demanded cash for silence about liquor violations, illegal kickbacks from jukebox and pinball machine operators and misconduct by public employees who loafed on the job.

The series was nominated for a Pulitzer Prize for best investigative series and was a finalist, but it was turned down because some members of the Pulitzer Board thought that reporters going underground and operating a bar as a front for a sting operation raised serious questions about journalistic ethics. Many editors and news directors continue to argue that going undercover is a deceptive practice that is not in the best interest of a news organization's credibility. They do not want their reporters to misrepresent themselves, and they will not allow this type of investigative journalism—ever.

Of course, it can also be argued that many good stories would be impossible to get if a reporter walked into a situation and quickly announced that he or she was a reporter and that everything everyone said might turn up in print. Doing this would probably have meant that the reporter in Albuquerque would not have been able to purchase drugs in a girls' rest room at the high school. The reporter in Chicago would not have been treated like all the other guards in the state prison if the officials and inmates knew he was a reporter. Certainly, the reporters who worked as bartenders at the Mirage would not have experienced extortion and payoffs.

At some newspapers and broadcast outlets, undercover journalism is practiced. Generally, however, it is a last resort, used only after editors, news directors and reporters have concluded that a story is extremely significant and that there would be no other means of obtaining it. In situations where criminal activity is being investigated, some editors and news directors contend that the end justifies the means.

William Recktenwald, the *Chicago Tribune* reporter who worked as a prison guard and who has been involved in numerous undercover investigations, agreed that reporters should avoid going undercover unless it is absolutely necessary. He gives the following advice to reporters involved in undercover work:

- Remember, the first duty of a reporter assuming another role is to do the job right and not jeopardize anyone's life. If a reporter is going to work in a nursing home, the duties of the job come before those of a journalist.

- If something is not there, do not make it up. Do not embellish. Never encourage people to break the law to help make the story.

- A reporter using a phony background should make it as close to the truth as possible. A reporter using a false name will usually use his or her real first name. That way, there is no hesitation when someone calls out the reporter's name. When filling out applications, use a real birthday and hometown and actual schools and work experience, except jobs as a reporter. It is always easy to list two years' experience when there may have been only six months. Most of the time, backgrounds are not checked. Do not lie on forms, such as a driver's license, that require an oath.

- Never break the law. The news gathering process is not protected by the First Amendment. The Ninth Circuit Court Judge Shirley Hufstedler made it clear in a 1971 court decision (*Dietemann v. Time Inc.*) that the "First

Amendment has never been construed to accord newsmen immunity from torts or crimes committed during the course of news gathering."

- Avoid *leak journalism*. Stories based on "leaks" rely too heavily on unnamed sources. Instead, rely on *enterprise journalism*. Just stay enthusiastic and work at it. Dig through those boring records. The key to success is perseverance and digging.

WRITING AN IN-DEPTH STORY

FINDING THE RIGHT LEAD

Summaries are the most common leads on investigative stories that reveal wrongdoing or break news for the first time. On other in-depths, reporters often use narrative, contrast, direct-address or other types of leads. (See Chapter 4 for a discussion of special leads.)

Summary Lead

Fred Schulte's investigation of VA hospitals took four years and involved two lawsuits before his four-day series began. Each day, the *News/Sun-Sentinel* ran a mainbar story detailing a major revelation. It also ran sidebar stories that described programs in other cities or specific cases in Miami.

Schulte's first mainbar story started with a hard summary lead, as do most in-depth investigative stories that reveal something:

> Excessive patient deaths, inept disciplining of doctors and dangerously unrestrained growth have plagued heart-surgery programs for America's veterans for more than a decade, a *News/Sun-Sentinel* investigation has found.
>
> The findings are based on Veterans Administration documents federal attorneys fought three years to suppress. The investigation is the first independent review of the $27 million-a-year heart-surgery network, run by a coterie of VA doctors who conduct their affairs in secret.

Lead Block and Nut Graph

Because an in-depth is longer than a news account and may not be delivering news firsthand, the reporter may want to paint a picture and draw readers into the story before giving them the news peg. To do that, the reporter writes a lead block. Then several paragraphs later, one or more nut graphs are used to give an audience the "so what" of the story.

Here is the lead block from an in-depth story in *The Minneapolis Star*. Its theme was the demanding, emotional life of a doctor or nurse working in a hospital emergency room, where seconds can mean the difference between life and death. The opening paragraphs were staccatos and a narrative, designed to place readers in the middle of the action immediately.

Saturday, 9:30 p.m.

"413, Code 3 to Third Avenue and Franklin. A shooting."

The Minneapolis Police Department has called the Hennepin County Medical Center's ambulance service. Owen Strandburg, a 38-year-old dispatcher, is managing the switchboard, which resembles the cockpit of an airplane. It's his job to get a two-member team of paramedics in an advanced life support ambulance to a person in need anywhere in the county as quickly as possible.

He has been told there was a shooting in front of an apartment building at Third Avenue and Franklin. He calls ambulance No. 413.

Now, it's light, siren and action. Unit 413 is en route at 9:39. Every second counts.

After painting a vivid picture for readers, the story switched to the nut graph, which was then followed by more explanatory paragraphs:

Soon, another patient will be wheeled into the medical center's emergency room and then to its stabilization room, where the critically ill are brought.

Doctors and nurses call it the stab (pronounced with a long a) room. The sign outside labels it the "Red Room." The 24 × 30-foot room is filled with gadgets only doctors understand—things with names too hard to spell or remember.

It smells clean.

In the middle of the room are two tables on wheels. Red lines are painted around them so the doctors will know the optimum area in which to work. Each of the tables—they're called hospital carts—has a blue paper cloth over it.

The only people who walk into this room are doctors, nurses and other hospital employees. Patients are wheeled in and minutes later, out, some to other parts of the hospital for treatment, others to the morgue.

The medical people who work in the stab room can, indeed, save lives. People die in their hands. Inside, it's loud and it's bloody. Outside, families scream.

USING BULLETED PARAGRAPHS TO SUMMARIZE FINDINGS

In his first story on the VA hospitals, Fred Schulte did what many writers do in the first part of an in-depth series. He used several bulleted paragraphs that summarized the major findings of the investigation:

The *News/Sun-Sentinel* found:

• Cardiac-surgery death rates are five times higher in some veterans hospitals than others—differences VA doctors cannot justify or explain.
• Death rates jumped to excessive levels 59 times at 37 VA hospitals between April 1978 and March 1982.
• VA cardiac units in four cities—including Miami—were closed after too many patients died.
• Low-use VA programs report the highest death rates. VA officials have disregarded numerous safety warnings to shut down the small units.
• Cardiac surgery is safest for veterans sent to university hospitals. VA officials are phasing out these transfers to save money.

Over the next four days, Schulte's stories delved extensively into each of these items and much more.

USING ANECDOTES AND OBSERVATIONS

Early in the emergency room story, readers knew that it was going to be about life—and death—in the emergency room, and like the patient, they were brought to the scene of the action by ambulance. Observations—"It smells clean," "Red lines are painted around them," "it's loud and it's bloody"—helped readers see the action as they read about it. Those observations, as well as anecdotes, were used throughout the story to excite, arouse and provoke readers and make them feel as though they were part of the action.

An anecdote—a short, entertaining account of a personal happening—is a valuable tool to use when writing an in-depth story or series. The simplest formula to follow when writing an anecdote is to have one of the characters in the story do something that will evoke some type of emotion from the readers. Remember, though, to stay away from cliché-filled "atmospheric" phrases, such as these:

> It was a dark and stormy night when John started the car.
>
> As the sun slowly crept over the mountain, John started his car.

It is better to use observations, such as:

> John started his red convertible, looking at the bank, waiting for her to walk out.

Or:

> John puffed on a cigarette as he started his red convertible. He stared at the bank, waiting for her to walk out.

FINDING THE THREAD

The key to a successful in-depth article is a strong thread throughout to keep readers interested. The thread may be a real-life situation, strange twists or suspense leading to a surprise ending, but it is used to keep readers interested in the entire story.

In the story on the emergency room, Saturday night was the thread that wove throughout. The article started with a Saturday night shooting, moved to statistics about emergency room care, came back to another Saturday night, went into more quotations and information on the emergency room and then ended on a Saturday night. By the end of the story, readers had been introduced to a variety of patients and doctors working on busy Saturday nights, but the readers were also told what emergency room care is all about and what doctors and nurses go through. Readers were told how much the doctors earn, how much schooling they have had and even some of the funny things that can occur in such a sad environment. The head of the emergency room was interviewed. Doctors and nurses were interviewed at work and off work.

About midway through the story, readers were brought to another Saturday night, again with staccatos:

It's winter. Another Saturday night.

Ramona Hodgeman, a 17-year-old high school senior, is walking to her home at 2813 S. Columbus Ave. from a nearby supermarket. Like always, she is taking a shortcut down the alley. While she is rounding a curve, two men come up to her. One of them has a knife. He stabs her in the chest, ripping through her breast, between her ribs, through the front of her heart and out her back. One of her lungs is torn open.

Ramona runs home, opens the front door and collapses. Her 21-year-old brother, Raymond, calls an ambulance.

As Ramona fell, the story shifted back to the hospital and to an ambulance being dispatched much as one was at the beginning of the story. Now readers were introduced to another case, more doctors and nurses and different types of medical procedures. Still, it happened on a Saturday night.

Unlike the shooting victim at the beginning of the story, Ramona lived. She was saved in the stab room.

Night after night, for weeks, the reporter and a photographer went to the emergency room. During the day, the reporter studied medical documents to learn about the procedures that doctors mentioned. Ramona would be interviewed to find out how she felt about the doctor who saved her life. The police would be interviewed to find out if suspects had been arrested in the stabbing. Throughout the story, real names were used and real cases explained so that readers could be emotionally attached to the story. Facts, figures and other often-dull statistics were given in between anecdotes and observations.

Then the story ended much the same way as it started:

The people who work in this room see it all. Drugs. Stabbings. Shootings. Murders. Suicides. Car wrecks. Burns. Scratches. Bruises.

They try to comfort the patient and the families. They want to save everyone, even when they know it's hopeless.

In a cubicle, a doctor in a green scrub suit is talking to a woman lying on a cart with the side rails pulled up.

"Why don't you want to talk to us? Are you depressed? Are you suicidal?"

A man is brought in who has overdosed on "angel dust." He's cussing. He does not want treatment. A guard is called to stand over him.

An ambulance brings in a woman, another stab room case. Her daughter stands outside, screaming, "I want to see my momma. I want to see my momma."

It's another Saturday night.

WRITING A FIRST-PERSON ARTICLE

News stories are seldom written in the first person because reporters are taught to stay out of their writing, to present both sides of a story. In the name of objectivity, reporters are trained to be intermediaries, to witness an event and then recall it in words so that readers, viewers or listeners who were not there can feel as if they were.

Unlike a hard news story written in an inverted pyramid, an in-depth meant to involve its readers in an emotional story can be effective in the first person. In these stories, the writer invites an audience into a personal experience. First-person articles can make a highly intense and personal subject much more real. Examples include, "I was an inmate at the county jail" and "I worked as a guard at the state prison."

Here is the beginning of a first-person in-depth written by a journalism student whose husband was dying of cancer. The story worked better in the first person because it allowed the writer to tell her highly personal and emotional story directly to readers. The article was purchased by *The Arizona Republic*.

I was standing at the kitchen sink washing fresh vegetables for dinner. Dennis walked in from work and said he had just heard a song on the radio that described how he felt.

"Better be good to yourself cause you're no good for anyone else," he said while he kissed me and reached around for a glass. (Dennis is in a low mood, and I had better just drift with him for a while, I thought.)

My husband Dennis is 24 years old. We've been married 2½ years, but are never sure how much longer we have together. Dennis has cancer of the soft tissue. His doctors have told us his cancer is a rare form and they can do no more than experiment with various drugs in their search for a cure. The doctors have said that the longer he goes without another growth, the greater his chances of survival.

We think the will to live is the most important factor. Somehow, this will carry us through even the lowest moods.

In this story, the writer used a lead block that put readers in the kitchen, a few minutes before dinner. Then she left the kitchen for a while to develop her story. She went back to their wedding day and mentioned the trouble Dennis had kneeling. Then she explained what they went through when they found out he had cancer. She also interviewed doctors and studied records to report the statistics on cancer of the soft tissue. Periodically, she returned to the kitchen, the thread that kept readers personally involved in her story.

While Dennis mixed a drink, he asked me, "Do you realize how short a time we've been married and how much of that time I've had cancer? I don't want you to always go through this."

We've had conversations like this before and I know what they lead to. I dropped my eyes from his and moved around him to the refrigerator.

First-person stories are powerful because, in them, a writer must relive for a mass audience a personal and sometimes painful experience. In the cancer story, the writer had to talk about her insecurities, her finances and the rest of her family. None of that was easy to do. She ended the story in the kitchen, as she and her husband were eating dinner:

The drugs and cobalt have left Dennis sterile. The doctors can't say whether it is only a temporary condition. We no longer discuss the children we would like to have. We just wait.

While Dennis ate and talked about the possibilities of investing in a home, I realized, gratefully, that he'll never give up.

IN-DEPTH REPORTING AND WRITING: STEPS TO FOLLOW

Here is a set of guidelines to follow when writing an in-depth article, from doing the research to writing the story:

- *Conduct careful and extensive research.* This phase will often produce a major story. Besides using the newspaper morgue and public libraries to find previous articles and standard resource materials, also look through as many public records and documents as possible. Always check the courthouse. Obtain relevant federal public documents by using the Freedom of Information Act if necessary.

- *Always know before an interview which questions are to be answered or which major topics are to be covered.* Be flexible enough to follow the flow of the interview when it moves away from predetermined questions, because the interview can be steered back to them later.

- *Talk to as many sources as possible.* Always confirm important information at least two times, and more if possible. Do not rely on a single source for anything.

- *Talk to off-the-record sources.* Even people who refuse to allow you to use their names can provide valuable information. Tell them how important their information is, and try to talk them into going on the record. If they still refuse, ask them if they know of a source who will go on the record.

- *Conduct investigative interviews in an ever-tightening circle.* Work from the least important to the most important players. That will make interviewing the person in the middle of the circle much easier.

- *Use the right lead.* A hard news summary lead belongs on an investigative article that reveals wrongdoing or other news firsthand. A narrative, contrast or direct-address lead or another special lead can be used on an in-depth that is not delivering news firsthand. On stories that are illuminating a previously reported news event, it is better to invite and draw readers inside before giving them the news peg.

- *Use bullets early in a lengthy article to summarize it for readers.* Don't make them search for the major points of the story.

- *Use anecdotes and observations.* They help readers become emotionally attached to a story.

- *Use a strong thread throughout the story.* Many in-depth writers begin their stories with one person or event. Then they refer to the person or event in the body and at the end of the story.

- *Consider writing a series of articles.* Instead of writing a single, extremely long story, it may be better to write a mainbar and several sidebars. A series can make a subject more palatable to an audience. Most newspapers also use informational graphics and photographs with in-depth articles.
- *Consider first-person articles.* Sometimes the most effective in-depth is written in the first person, especially if the story involves a highly personal topic. Be prepared to tell an editor or a news director all the reasons that a first-person article may be the best.

Business and Consumer News

Janice Lieberman of CNBC is one of a growing number of reporters who cover consumer news.
(Jon Simon/CNBC)

Business and Consumer News

Business and consumer reporters are specialists

who can study their complicated fields in depth

and then write about them in language that

laypeople can understand. They are hired by

newspapers and by broadcasters to cover stories

that have a major impact on the public.

Business writing and consumer writing have come of age in the American media. Most newspapers now have a daily business page or section, and more and more television and radio stations are featuring business and consumer news. Pages that once printed only stock quotations, features (free advertisements) on store openings and handouts from businesses, industries and agencies now contain sophisticated stories by writers who are specialists in business or consumer areas. Despite pressure from companies that are major advertisers, these stories often reveal unfavorable news.

REPORTERS AS SPECIALISTS

To be a good business or consumer writer, a reporter must be sufficiently informed about a complicated field to report and write on it exclusively and intelligently. The reporter must be a specialist. Many newspapers and broadcast outlets have hired such experts to cover not only business and consumer news but also the arts, architecture, medicine, legal affairs, the environment and religion.

Unlike a beat reporter, who obtains stories by making regular stops at or telephone calls to the courthouse, the police station or the county attorney's office, a specialty reporter obtains stories by cultivating and contacting a variety of experts and news sources. The beat reporter is generally concerned only with news that is occurring now; the specialty reporter is often interested in long-range stories, the roots of problems and the reasons behind the news.

BUSINESS REPORTING

The success of *The Wall Street Journal, USA Today*, other financial publications, syndicated columns on personal finances and financial reports on radio and television has shown that people are keenly interested in news from the business world. Today, business writers not only report the traditional financial news from bankers and brokers but also explain to average readers what it means and how it affects them. Business stories are regularly front-page news.

On a typical day a financial page may include news stories on a local company being purchased by a conglomerate, an airline deciding to expand its terminal space at the local airport or a trade agreement between a local company and the People's Republic of China. There may also be feature stories on people in the business world. Newspapers and broadcast outlets still use handouts, annual reports and government reports for stories, but they are also sending reporters into the field to uncover stories. This increased coverage requires reporters who are specialists in the complex field of business and who can develop contacts with many news sources.

THE BUSINESS REPORTER

As in any specialty writing, business writing is more than covering events that occurred in the last 24 hours and then reporting back to an audience. Business writers do cover breaking news such as store openings, speeches by business

leaders, corporate meetings and changes. But, like all specialists, they also sit back and analyze what something means, why it occurred and what effects it will have on an audience.

For example, if a department store in town announces that it is laying off 75 employees because of financial difficulties, business writers will report the announcement to their audiences immediately. They will also dissect the announcement to try to find the reasons behind it and what effects it will have on the future. If the company is publicly owned, the reporters will study annual reports to find out how the firm has used its revenues. They will conduct extensive interviews with company executives. Audiences—and reporters—want to know if the announcement is a harbinger of bad things to come or merely a temporary setback. Here is where specialty reporters earn their salaries, for they are hired specifically to examine events with the eyes of an expert and then write about them in easily understandable language.

The increased coverage of financial news has made business reporting more attractive to journalism students. To prepare themselves, students are studying economics and business along with journalism. They are finding out that editors are impressed by reporters who understand how the government, stock markets, money system and business world operate.

A Business Reporter at Work

Mary Beth Sammons is a business reporter who covers the business and financial worlds in Chicago and its northwestern suburbs for the *Chicago Tribune*, *Crain's Chicago Business* and other publications.

Before leaving full-time business writing to be at home with her growing family, Sammons worked full time for *Crain's Chicago Business*. She also has been a beat reporter and a business writer and columnist for *The Daily Herald* in Arlington Heights, Ill.

"I took a lot of business courses in college," Sammons said. "As a beat reporter I covered Schaumburg, the town with the most business development in our area, and much of my job was covering businesses. When there was an opening for a business writer at *The Daily Herald*, I applied for it."

During her career, Sammons has written all types of local business stories. She also has localized national and international business stories. For example, in response to the release of the monthly unemployment figures by the U.S. Labor Department, Sammons has reported the reaction from state employment experts, local business leaders and sometimes the unemployed workers themselves. That means "interviewing unemployed workers waiting in line at the local unemployment office or employers who recently had to lay off workers because of financial difficulties," Sammons said.

Sammons said she stays busy as a free-lance writer. She is the Chicago *stringer*, a person who serves as a part-time local correspondent, for *Family Circle* magazine. She writes at least one story a week for the *Chicago Tribune*, concentrating on successful businesspeople such as women who take their children with them on business trips. Her stories for *Crain's Chicago Business* are generally issue-oriented. For example, she has written about local companies complying with federal rules requiring that businesses disclose environmental impact statements in financial reports.

"When I was covering municipal government (as a beat reporter), I was always trying to find the *great* story," Sammons said. "I was always checking the people in power and looking for corruption. I had a cast of characters that I could call every day. Now the cast of people I use as sources is too big. I have to look at so many things now, such as the banking industry and the real estate industry, that I can't keep as much of a check on people. In order not to feel like an imbecile, I have to read so that I will know something about different industries."

Sammons said that the best part of writing about business is that she has the opportunity to learn about the world of finances from the people at the top. She said her work has taken her "into the office of chief executive officers and other leading personalities that most people, including the employees in their own companies, rarely meet." She added: "I meet a lot of people who are at the top of businesses, and I learn how they became successful. It is certainly an education that someone could never receive in a classroom."

Specializing in Business: Guidelines for Reporters

Sammons gives the following advice to aspiring reporters who would like to specialize in business writing:

- *Major in journalism and minor in business.* "I would encourage people to study journalism," she said. "I could go into other fields, and my writing skills could be used in any of them. People can talk for an hour, and in one minute I can pick out the key thing they say. This ability would help me in many fields."

- *Build a clip file.* "The fact that you have a degree does not mean that you have a job," Sammons said. While she was in college, Sammons served as a reporter and then as city editor for her campus daily. At various times during college, she had internships at United Press International and at a community daily. She also founded a student magazine and was its editor.

- *Don't stop learning about business.* To be successful as a speciality reporter "you have to stay with it and keep studying," Sammons said. "For business writing an M.B.A. (master's degree in business administration) could be an extra bonus. Most of all, experience counts, and you have to be able to hustle constantly."

Andrew Leckey, a financial columnist for the *Chicago Tribune* and financial editor at WLS-TV, the ABC-owned television station in Chicago, offers some additional advice to reporters who want to specialize in business writing. Leckey's nationally syndicated column, "Successful Investing," provides investment and financial advice to help readers increase their net worth.

- *Read as much financial material as possible.* Reading is important because business and economics affect many other areas requiring coverage, such as politics. Even reporters who do not want to cover business need a knowledge of annual reports and meetings, budgets, balance sheets and financial operating statements.

- *Learn how to say things simply and correctly.* Learn to cut through the jargon that people hide behind.
- *Do not fear figures and other complicated financial data.* A good solid reporter can become a competent financial reporter. A bad general reporter will probably not make it as a financial reporter. It takes homework to be able to ask the right questions; faking it will not work.
- *Remember that financial reporters can be tough.* Most newspaper managements realize now that financial reporting includes taking a hard look at businesses, even if they are major advertisers.

"Though many newspapers have increased their financial staffs in recent years, there still seems to be continuing expansion, particularly at smaller dailies," said Leckey, who has a bachelor's degree in journalism and also received a Walter Bagehot Fellowship in financial writing at Columbia University in New York. "In addition, there are countless special-interest financial publications, and television is also hiring financial reporters. The economy, the business world and what people do with their money will continue to be major stories."

THE BUSINESS STORY

Types of Business Stories

Business stories range from hard news to soft features, handouts to personal finance columns, people items to business openings. Hard news reports generally have summary leads; features have softer leads.

After the accounting firm of Arthur Andersen & Co. conducted a survey of small businesses, *The Cincinnati Enquirer* reported the results in a story that began with a summary lead, as in any hard news story:

> Small business owners believe the budget deficit is the nation's top problem, and most support spending cuts as a way of tackling it, according to a new survey by the accounting firm Arthur Andersen & Co.

Steven H. Lee, a writer for *The Dallas Morning News*, began his feature story on the effects of a Midwestern drought with a narrative lead block:

> POWESHIEK COUNTY, Iowa—It was freezing in East Central Iowa, with blustery winds sending the wind chill toward zero—usually a signal to farmer Dale Hall to finish up the year's harvest by Thanksgiving weekend.
>
> But a drought forced Hall and other farmers to complete their harvests a month ahead of time. Bundled up on his 800-acre farm, about 70 miles east of Des Moines in sparsely populated Poweshiek County, Hall invited a visitor inside where he and a calculator have been passing idle time figuring crop losses from the drought.

The wire services also report business news as part of their daily report to newspapers and broadcast outlets. When the federal government releases monthly industrial production data, The Associated Press transmits a story to its members.

> WASHINGTON (AP)—U.S. industrial production rose 0.4 percent in October, the biggest increase in three months, despite a decline in activity in the nation's oil fields, the Federal Reserve said Tuesday.

Annual Reports

A *publicly held company* is owned by investors who purchase its stock on an exchange. The value of the stock is determined by demand, what investors are willing to pay for it. A *privately,* or *closely, held company* is controlled by a family or a small group. The value of its stock, which is not traded on an exchange, is set by the owners.

Each year, a publicly held company must issue an *annual report,* which stockholders receive and may read to determine their company's financial health and find out what is in store for the future. Business reporters read the annual reports, too, because their readers include stockholders, future investors and employees of publicly held companies.

Business reporters must wade through the jargon in annual reports and synthesize it into understandable language. That is not always easy, but reporters follow certain steps. They must read between the lines to get an accurate picture of a firm's health. The personal-finance columnist and commentator Jane Bryant Quinn, in an article entitled "How to Read an Annual Report," which she wrote for the International Paper Co., suggested that the best place to begin reading a report is in the back. Many reporters follow her advice. They read the numbers after they have read and interpreted four other important sections.

Let's look at some important aspects of annual reports.

Auditor's report   The auditor's report, by independent certified public accountants, is in the back of the book, but it should be read first. It informs reporters if the annual report conforms to generally accepted accounting principles.

For example, the accounting firm of KPMG Peat Marwick wrote in the back of the 1991 annual report of PepsiCo Inc.:

> We conducted our audits in accordance with generally accepted auditing standards. . . . In our opinion, the financial statements referred to above present fairly, in all material respects, the consolidated financial position of PepsiCo Inc. and subsidiaries at December 28, 1991, and December 29, 1990, and the results of its operations and its cash flows for the years then ended in conformity with generally accepted accounting principles.

Business reporters can spot potential trouble within a company by looking for the words *subject to* in the auditor's report. According to Quinn, those words mean that the financial report is "subject to" the "company's word about a particular piece of business." They could be a signal that the reporter needs to do some more digging.

Notes to financial statements   Footnotes in the back of the annual report can also help reporters spot trouble. They should be read after the auditor's report because they explain things such as major accounting principles, deductions made on receivables, unusual charges, the interest income's effect on investments, the selling off of plants or divisions and expenses of retirement plans. All these could signal bigger stories.

Letter from the chairperson   Now reporters move to the front of the report, where the chairperson discusses the company's well-being and its goals for the next year. Quinn noted that reporters should also look for buzz words here, which could indicate trouble in the company. *To reach these goals . . . , Despite the . . .* and *Except for . . .* need to be checked carefully.

In the PepsiCo report, Wayne Calloway, chairman of the board and chief executive officer, was optimistic about his company's rapid growth, but he also admitted that the year's financial numbers were not as good as he would have liked. His comments included these:

> The quest for rapid growth keeps us hopping. It also keeps us innovating, shaking things up, breaking down barriers; all in search of new opportunities.
>
> At PepsiCo, we've increased sales and net income at an exhilarating rate of nearly 15% for 26 years. That means we've doubled our business about every five years. . . .
>
> The numbers were certainly not as good as we would have liked, somewhat below our historical trends. On a reported basis, net income and income per share were even with last year at $1.1 billion and $1.35, respectively.

Divisions and products   After the chairperson's message, an annual report turns to the firm's divisions and products. Reporters can find summaries of business during the last year as well as projections for the future.

PepsiCo's report detailed its soft drinks, snack foods and restaurants divisions.

The actual numbers   Now reporters can look at the numbers contained in the annual report's financial statements and can have a better understanding of them.

One set of numbers, the consolidated balance sheet (illustration on page 528), gives the company's *assets*—what it owns. *Current assets* are those things that can be turned into cash quickly. The balance sheet also gives *liabilities*—what the company owes. And it notes *shareholders' equity*—the difference between the total assets and all liabilities. *Current liabilities* are debts due in one year, which are paid out of current assets.

Consolidated Balance Sheet

(in millions except per share amount)
PepsiCo, Inc. and Subsidiaries
December 28, 1991 and December 29, 1990

	1991	1990
Assets		
Current Assets		
Cash and cash equivalent	$ 186.7	$170.8
Short-term investments, at cost which approximates market	1,849.3	1,644.9
	2,036.0	1,815.7
Accounts and notes receivable, less allowance: $97.5 in 1991 and $90.8 in 1990	1,481.7	1,414.7
Inventories	661.5	585.8
Prepaid expenses and other current assets	386.9	265.2
Total Current Assets	4,566.1	4,081.4
Investments in Affiliates and Other Assets	1,681.9	1,505.9
Property, Plant and Equipment, net	6,594.7	5,710.9
Goodwill and Other Intangibles, net	5,932.4	5,845.2
Total Assets	$18,775.1	$17,143.4
Liabilities and Shareholders' Equity		
Current Liabilities		
Short-term borrowings..	$228.2	$1,626.5
Accounts payable	1,196.6	1,116.3
Income taxes payable...	492.4	443.7
Other current liabilities...	1,804.9	1,584.0
Total Current Liabilities	3,722.1	4,770.5
Long-term Debt	7,806.2	5,600.1
Nonrecourse Obligation	—	299.5
Other Liabilities and Deferred Credits	631.3	626.3
Deferred Income Taxes	1,070.1	942.8
Shareholders' Equity		
Capital stock, par value 1⅔¢ per share: authorized 1,800.0 shares, issued 863.1 shares	14.4	14.4
Capital in excess of par value	476.6	365.0
Retained earnings	5,470.0	4,753.0
Currency translation adjustment...	330.3	383.2
	6,291.3	5,515.6
Less: Treasury stock, at cost: 74.0 shares in 1991, 74.7 shares in 1990	(745.9)	(611.4)
Total Shareholders' Equity..	5,545.4	4,904.2
Total Liabilities and Shareholders' Equity	$18,775.1	$17,143.4

See accompanying Notes to Consolidated Financial Statements.

Consolidated
balance sheet:
Statement of a
company's assets
and liabilities.

Consolidated Statement of Income

(in millions except per share amount)
PepsiCo, Inc. and Subsidiaries
Fifty-two weeks ended December 28, 1991, December 29, 1990 and December 30, 1989

	1991	1990	1989
Net Sales	**$19,607.9**	$17,802.7	$15,242.4
Costs and Expenses, net			
Cost of Sales	**9,395.5**	8,549.4	7,421.7
Selling, general and administrative expenses	**7,880.8**	7,008.6	5,887.4
Amortization of goodwill and other intangibles.	**208.7**	189.1	150.4
Gain on joint venture stock offering	**—**	(118.2)	—
Interest expense	**615.9**	688.5	609.6
Interest income	**(163.3)**	(182.1)	(177.2)
	17,937.6	16,135.3	13,891.9
Income from Continuing Operations Before Income Taxes	**1,670.3**	1,667.4	1,350.5
Provision for Income Taxes	**590.1**	576.8	449.1
Income from Continuing Operations	**1,080.2**	1,090.6	901.4
Discontinued Operation Charge (net of income tax benefit of $0.3)	**—**	(13.7)	—
Net Income	**$ 1,080.2**	$ 1,076.9	$ 901.4
Income (Charge) Per Share			
Continued operations	**$ 1.35**	$ 1.3	$ 1.13
Discontinued operations	**—**	(0.02)	—
Net Income Per Share	**$ 1.35**	$ 1.37	$ 1.13
Average shares outstanding used to calculate income (charge) per share	**802.5**	798.7	796.0

See accompanying Notes to Consolidated Financial Statements.

Annual report:
Statement of the
company's income
or earnings.

Another important source of numbers is the consolidated statement of income, or earnings (illustration on page 529). It shows how much money a company made or lost in the last year. The statement of income will show a company's *sales,* its cost of doing business and its *net income*—its profit or loss after taxes. Business reporters also look at *net income per share.* An increase in income per share is an indication that the company is healthy. But reporters also check the notes in the back of the report to see why the earnings per share increased. It could have happened because of budget cutbacks or the selling off of a plant, rather than because of an increase in business.

Stories on annual reports   Many newspapers run brief staff-written articles or wire stories based on reviews of annual reports. For example, the following story would be a typical one based on the PepsiCo report:

> PepsiCo reported today that its net income was $1.08 billion in 1991, up only slightly from the $1.077 billion of 1990.
>
> Sales for the soft drink, snack foods and restaurant company were $19.6 billion, compared with 1990 sales of $17.8 billion. Net income per share was $1.35, about the same as a year earlier.
>
> Besides Pepsi and other soft drinks, the firm sells Frito-Lay snack foods. It also owns Kentucky Fried Chicken, Pizza Hut and Taco Bell restaurants.
>
> In his annual statement to stockholders, Wayne Calloway, PepsiCo's chairman and chief executive officer, said the flat numbers from 1990 to 1991 "were only partially indicative of the more powerful and underlying progress we made since last year."
>
> He said sales increased 10 percent, all three divisions of the company achieved solid sales growth and the price of a share of PepsiCo stock increased 31 percent.

Quarterly Reports

Public companies also issue reports at the end of each quarter of their fiscal year. Like the annual reports, these are read carefully by business reporters. They should be read in the same way as annual reports.

Stories are also written from the quarterly reports, which provide sales and earnings information for the quarter.

Example: A Business Story from Idea to "30"

Mary Beth Sammons covers many events at Chicago's O'Hare International Airport. She said that she often noticed air express planes at the airport and decided that a story on overnight air delivery would be worthwhile. The steps she followed, from her idea to the final story, illustrate how a typical business writer operates.

"I started out knowing only a couple of names that I could pick out from television commercials, such as 'when it absolutely, positively has to be there overnight,'" Sammons said.

The research   The steps Sammons followed in her research are typical in business reporting:

- *Check the yellow pages.* Sammons said that she looked up the names of local companies and realized that there were more overnight air delivery firms than she thought.
- *Check the clips.* Sammons went to her newspaper's morgue and the public library to find out if anything had been written on the industry. There had been stories written on individual companies but nothing on the industry itself.
- *Contact professional associations.* During her research, Sammons found that there were two associations dealing with the air express industry, both of which are based in Washington, D.C. They are the Airfreight Association of America and the Air Transportation Association. She called both of them to find out which companies are the largest and to gather financial data on the firms and phone numbers and addresses.
- *Telephone or visit local companies.* Sammons said that she discovered quickly that most of the companies were not based in her area. She was told by nearly every firm that she had to call or write the public relations departments at their headquarters to get permission to interview local people.
- *Set up interviews.* Once she got permission from the companies ("Not all of them gave it") to conduct local interviews, Sammons called to set up appointments. She was able to get some data over the phone for her story, but most of the material she needed would have to come from people at the airport. As she was gathering information, Sammons also contacted local businesses that use overnight air delivery most. She asked them the advantages and disadvantages of shipping by air express. She talked to security people about what measures are taken to protect precious cargo, and she talked to customs agents about how international cargoes are handled.

The writing   "A photographer and I spent five straight days at the airport," she said. "The first day we realized that all the activity happens from midnight to 6 a.m., and so that's when we had to go there. In fact, what impressed me most while I was at the airport was all the activity at night. A businessperson can leave the office at 5 p.m., but here is all this activity late at night getting the business done. I wanted my lead to reflect that."

She said that she went with the first lead she wrote. In most cases, a reporter will change the lead several times to improve it, but Sammons said that she did not have to this time. She wrote a narrative lead block that set the stage for her readers by putting them in the middle of the nighttime activity.

Here are the story's first five paragraphs:

When most businesses are closing up shop for the night, a group of several service firms are just beginning to gear up for their busiest hours.

Hundreds of trucks, vans, station wagons and jet aircraft converge on O'Hare Airport to meet up with hundreds of workers who will labor until the pre-dawn at breakneck speed, loading, unloading, sorting and stacking. The situation is repeated at airports across the country.

The competition is hot among the companies whose employees work in close proximity to each other at O'Hare. But all have one goal in mind: to get a package or envelope to another point overnight and in a way that is economical, convenient and—most important to customers—on time.

Mention overnight air delivery and Federal Express immediately comes to mind. The Memphis-based company's funny television commercials and crisp advertising slogan, "When it absolutely, positively has to be there overnight," have brought overnight express service to the attention of even those people who never use it.

But while Federal Express may be the industry leader—growing from a tiny operation that handled a dozen packages on its first day in 1973 to one that now delivers more than 42 million packages each year—it is only one company in a very crowded field. Hundreds of firms are vying for a piece of the billion dollar industry, with more constantly entering the competition.

Sammons based her article on a combination of interviewing and observations; this is typical for business writers working on in-depths. "If I hadn't been outside, I couldn't have seen what was going on," she said. "I couldn't have interviewed the pilots, mechanics and other workers. I even got to go inside one of the planes. They're all gutted inside."

Her story included scores of quotations and paraphrases, many facts and figures and a list of who's who in the business. It ended with a look into the future by Paul Hyman, director of cargo services for the Airfreight Association of America and one of the sources she introduced earlier:

The forecast for the overnight air cargo is bright. Industry experts predict that the economic recovery will bolster the business climate and result in a fantastically high growth rate that Hyman puts at about 30 percent a year.

"There is no question that the air cargo industry will continue to grow, because the demand is there for rapid transport of business materials," Hyman said. "In fact, many companies are already starting same-day service. As long as corporations and businesses can afford to pay for air delivery, it will be a thriving industry."

Sammons wrote a lengthy story, but she still had to make cuts. Like every reporter, she writes to limited space, and she cannot get in everything she would like to.

"I had to concentrate on a description of the services rather than much of the color at the airport," she said. "I interviewed pilots who fly from New York City to Japan and back to New York City in two days, but I couldn't get that in. I also had to leave out material on security and customs measures."

TRENDS IN CONSUMER JOURNALISM

Consumer reporting has come a long way since its emergence during the 1960s and early 1970s—a period that became the era of advocacy journalism. Ralph Nader can be credited with introducing consumer reporting to the nation in 1965 with the publication of "Unsafe at Any Speed: The Designed-In Dangers of the American Automobile," in which he took on General Motors. For a long time after "Unsafe at Any Speed" appeared, consumer reporting consisted mainly of stories that compared various products or uncovered fraud in the marketplace. Reporters turned to *advocacy journalism* as consumerism and a mistrust of big business grew.

Today, consumer reporting consists of more than comparing grades of meat or prices of automobile repairs. Issues such as Interstate Commerce Commission regulations, state and local consumer protection laws and consumer rights are being covered in depth by consumer reporters at newspapers and broadcast outlets. Stories range from how and when to mail Christmas packages to an investigation that reveals the long-term dangers of using asbestos-coated material in the home. Consumer reporters are now specialists who are reporting consumer news, reasons behind the issues and long-range effects.

Another outgrowth of the consumer journalism movement of the 1960s and 1970s is the *action-line column,* which has received enthusiastic support from readers and viewers. When a news outlet offers an action-line column, people are encouraged to write or telephone to describe their problems. Then, the outlet's own reporters try to solve these problems.

Consumer reporters usually work in several specialty or general reporting areas while researching a single story. For example, a story on how to prepare for traffic court would require some police beat work, courthouse work and research into types of traffic violations, fines and sentencing. A story on the U.S. Food and Drug Administration's campaign against ineffective prescription drugs would require interviews with government officials, doctors, pharmacists and consumer advocates.

Television is well-suited for hard-hitting consumer stories because reporters can actually show children playing with dangerous toys or crop dusters spraying hazardous pesticides too close to homes. This type of reporting has become a specialty of television magazine shows such as "20/20" and "60 Minutes." Many local television stations also have consumer reporters.

Because their own staffs are not large enough to cover consumer news extensively, many small newspapers and small broadcast outlets rely on consumer stories that are supplied by the wire services. The Associated Press, United Press International and other supplementary news services supply consumer stories to thousands of newspapers and broadcast outlets throughout the United States.

SOURCES FOR CONSUMER NEWS

To gather the information for their stories, consumer reporters rely on local, state and national governmental agencies; various public action and consumer groups; corporate officials and public relations departments; economists; university professors; and stock analysts. By keeping an extensive file of sources, a consumer reporter knows whom to call as a source for a breaking news story or whom to call for background information on an important issue. Extensive sources are also important because reporters depend on them for tips.

The federal government alone offers a storehouse of information for consumer stories. First, there are the Cabinet-level departments, all of which have public affairs officers who can provide the media with information. These include the following departments:

- Agriculture
- Commerce
- Defense
- Education
- Energy
- Health and Human Services
- Housing and Urban Development
- Interior
- Justice
- Labor
- State
- Transportation
- Treasury

Besides these administrative agencies, there are independent and regulatory agencies, and sources in each of them are critical to the success of consumer reporters. These agencies include:

- U.S. Commission of Civil Rights
- Commodity Futures Trading Commission
- Consumer Product Safety Commission
- Environmental Protection Agency
- Equal Employment Opportunity Commission
- Federal Communications Commission
- Federal Deposit Insurance Corporation
- Federal Election Commission
- Federal Emergency Management Agency
- Federal Home Loan and Bank Board
- Federal Maritime Commission
- Federal Mediation and Conciliation Service

- Federal Reserve System
- Federal Trade Commission
- General Accounting Office
- General Services Administration
- Government Printing Office
- International Communication Agency
- U.S. International Trade Commission
- Interstate Commerce Commission
- Library of Congress
- National Academy of Sciences
- National Aeronautics and Space Administration
- National Archives and Records Service
- National Labor Relations Board
- National Medication Board
- National Transportation Safety Board
- Nuclear Regulatory Commission
- Occupational Safety and Health Review Commission
- Office of Personnel Management
- Postal Rate Commission
- U.S. Postal Service
- Securities and Exchange Commission
- Small Business Administration
- Veterans Administration
- Water Resources Council

Any one of these federal departments or agencies is a potential warehouse of information for consumer reporters. The key to using them effectively is to develop a *source file,* a reporter's who's who of helpful people. Beginning such a file of sources is simple. After talking to anyone from any of these agencies—or from a local or state agency—who was helpful, write that person's name, telephone number and area of expertise on an index card and put it in a permanent file. Then, whenever a call needs to be made on a story, look up the name of a source who was helpful in the past. Of course, the file should be updated and changed continually.

Because of the giant bureaucracy at every level of local, state and national government, consumer reporters need to know who the good sources are in the many areas of each department or agency. For example, the Consumer Product Safety Commission is divided into the following areas: chairperson, vice chairperson, commissioners (there are three), executive directors, directors (three), office of the secretary, office of the general counsel, associate executive directors (seven), office of congressional relations and office of media relations. Any of these people could be good sources for consumer reporters, but it is best for beginners to start by calling the office of media relations for guidance.

Many industries and large businesses rely on public relations people to handle consumers and reporters, and so it is a good idea to develop PR people as sources, too. Some are employees of the company; and others work for private public relations firms that are under contract by the company. Public relations people can be valuable contacts who are able to find key sources for reporters. They can also provide news tips and vital background information. For example, reporters who have questions about unions can call the information department for the AFL-CIO in Washington, D.C. Questions about Phillips Petroleum in particular or about the energy industry in general can usually be answered by the public information department at Phillips Petroleum in Bartlesville, Okla. The external communications department of American Airlines at the Dallas–Fort Worth airport will answer questions about the airlines industry.

Professional groups and associations also make excellent sources. They can provide information and answer questions as well as lead reporters to other sources. There are far too many such groups to try to list here, but they include:

- Aluminum Association
- American Cancer Society
- American Gas Association
- American National Metric Council
- American Railroad Foundation
- American Trucking Association
- Association of American Railroads
- Chemical Manufacturers' Association
- Electronic Industries Association
- Insurance Information Institute
- Major Appliance Consumer Action Panel
- National Association of Life Underwriters
- National Paint and Coatings Association
- Professional Insurance Agents

Telephone numbers for these associations and for others can be found in the yellow pages of metropolitan phone books under "Associations." Many such groups also run advertisements regularly in journalism trade magazines, telling reporters that they are available as sources.

Numerous local, state and national public interest and consumer groups make excellent sources. These include:

- American Civil Liberties Union
- Better Business Bureau
- Chamber of Commerce
- Common Cause
- Congress Watch

- Consumer Federation of America
- Consumers Union
- League of Women Voters
- National Consumers League
- National Council of Senior Citizens
- Public Voice for Food and Health Policy

Each year, the *American Journalism Review* (formerly *Washington Journalism Review*) publishes a "Directory of Selected News Sources," which contains hundreds of contacts at corporations, associations and unions. The directory is a valuable reference tool for consumer reporters.

THE CONSUMER REPORTER

A Consumer Reporter at Work

Despite the growth of consumer reporting, only the largest newspapers, such as *The New York Times* and the *Los Angeles Times*, cover consumer news as a specialized beat. At many newspapers, reporters who cover consumer news are financial reporters who do consumer stories in their spare time. At some newspapers, action-line columns are the only sources of consumer news.

Most broadcasters offer only superficial consumer reports, such as how to find bargains or how to shop safely. Only the networks and stations in the largest markets have consumer reporters involved in deep investigative work.

Of course, this does not mean that consumer reporting is dying. Rather, it means that consumer reporting is still in its infancy and could be a fertile area for aspiring reporters.

One reporter who covers consumer news full time is David Horowitz. He is the host, creator and executive producer of "Fight Back! With David Horowitz," a weekly consumer news television show that is syndicated nationally. He is a regular guest on talk shows. Horowitz also does nightly consumer reports on KNBC-TV, the NBC-owned television station in Los Angeles, and his newspaper column "Fight Back!" is syndicated by the Creators Syndicate. He has written two books, "Fight Back! And Don't Get Ripped Off" and "The Business of Business." Horowitz is also the host of a syndicated radio show for consumers.

"Consumer reporting cuts across every area of specialization: economics, government agencies, political science, law," Horowitz said. "This is an area in which you need to know a little about a lot of things. Your background has to carry you far enough as a reporter so that you feel comfortable covering many areas. It is easy to define an economics reporter or a political reporter, but it is not easy to define a consumer reporter."

Horowitz has been covering consumer affairs nearly 25 years. He received a bachelor's degree in journalism from Bradley University and a master's degree from the Medill School of Journalism at Northwestern University. He did post-graduate work in public law and government at Columbia University as a CBS News Fellow, one of eight selected nationally. Horowitz worked at weekly newspapers in Illinois and was a reporter for United Press

One reporter who
covers consumer
news full time is
David Horowitz—
host, creator and
executive producer
of "Fight Back! With
David Horowitz," a
weekly consumer
news television
show.
*(Photo from Western
International
Syndication)*

International before he went to KCCI-TV in Des Moines, Iowa, as a reporter
and a member of the news camera crew. He was also a writer and a producer
for ABC News in New York and later covered the Vietnam War for NBC
News. When he moved to Los Angeles for NBC, he was the network's first
racial reporting specialist. Then he became the first education specialist for the
network. "No one had anyone exclusively covering the things I covered in the
early 1960s," Horowitz said.

He said that there is not enough true consumer reporting going on today.
He said that there is a difference between covering spot news items and action-line material and the nitty-gritty investigative reporting that is required to
do effective consumer reporting. "I define a consumer reporter as a specialist
who is an investigative reporter, who has a broad knowledge and who does
nothing but cover that area," Horowitz said. "That person may do a story at
Thanksgiving on the price of turkeys, but those types of stories tend to under-
mine the whole consumer reporting area.

"The stuff we do you will very rarely see reported in a newspaper or
elsewhere because we develop our own reports from our own sources, and
we don't go through an editor. We don't use wire-service copy as a background. What we do in our office are stories we have researched ourselves."

The "we" Horowitz is referring to is about 10 people he has on his staff to help him research consumer stories and go through the thousands of pieces of mail he receives each week. He said his staff "is as large as some news departments, but it sells tickets for the network. It brings in people and ratings points."

He added: "In order to do honest consumer reporting on television, one person can't do it. You just can't go on the air when you have one story. Television will not let it happen. It is too segmented and specialized. You have to have a staff and researchers who are constantly developing material for you. The reporter must be a specialist who can be the axle of the wheel and make it turn. There are very few like that."

Horowitz is also a strong believer in internships. "Internships offer students a chance to observe and be exposed to the day-to-day workings of a news operation or specialized reporting area such as consumer affairs," he said.

Horowitz's syndicated show is a combination of entertainment, action line, spot news and hard investigative reporting. Some of it is done purely to get a reaction from the audience. The show solves viewers' problems and gives results of investigations carried out by Horowitz and his staff. It challenges commercial claims, proving or disproving that a product works the way an advertisement says it does.

"I am not a consumer advocate, because you have to be objective and unbiased on the air," he said. "I would call myself a consumer commentator. That gives me latitude for commentary as well as being a reporter."

Critics may think that Horowitz is merely an entertainer hunting for high ratings, but many agree that he is doing an admirable job of consumer reporting. He has won Emmys for investigative reporting and consumer commentary and was the first reporter to receive the U.S. Chief Postal Inspector's Award, which is given annually to the postal inspector or law enforcement officer who has uncovered mail fraud. "We have uncovered more mail fraud than some postal inspectors," Horowitz said.

He said that many stations are interested in doing more consumer reporting, and when they ask him what is needed, "I tell them they need a reporter who is interested in it and is prepared. Too many libel suits arise because reporters don't have the basic research and background. When you are dealing with products and advertisers, you leave yourself wide open. When a station has a good consumer reporter, the fear that arises from pressure from sponsors disappears. Good reporters can do anything. They can move into any area of specialization."

Horowitz has been sued a number of times for his hard-hitting shows, but most of the suits have been thrown out. "Being sued is irrelevant," he said. "Everyone is sued. Still, we have accomplished a lot of things. You know the third brake light—the collision-avoidance light—in the middle of the back window that has been standard equipment on all cars since 1986? I was the first one to do a story on this as an invention.

"We were the ones who did the first story on the use of alar on apples. It took several years before a ban on this pesticide was put into effect by the Food and Drug Administration."

Specializing in Consumer News: Guidelines for Reporters

Horowitz said that anyone interested in becoming a consumer reporter should study liberal arts and journalism in college. "When I say liberal arts, I really mean liberal arts, like home economics, where you learn about preparing and labeling food; the sciences; economics; political science."

He encouraged aspiring journalists to consider consumer reporting and added: "There is not enough consumer reporting going on. I travel across the country, and I don't see the type of benchmark in consumer affairs reporting that has been achieved in medical reporting, economics reporting or political affairs reporting. The reason for this is that it always has been looked at as a voluntary thing, like a non-profit corporation.

"While in college, if you are not sure of an area you want to get into, I would start doing general assignment stuff until you plant your feet as a journalist. Specialized reporting is where journalism is going. If you look at what's selling tickets these days, it's the White House reporter and reporters who specialize in law, medicine, entertainment—that's a hot area to be in—and economics."

Horowitz also said that there is no difference between a good print reporter and a good broadcast reporter, because they are both covering the same news. "There was a point when it was a dirty word to say *television* to a newspaper or magazine reporter," he said. "But newspapers are closing, and newspaper reporters are out on the street. Nowadays, newspaper reporters look to television as another source of income. The real purists in magazines are becoming political pundits on television. You can be a print-television-radio reporter. That's a good way to bolster your income and a much better way to make your mark as a reporter."

PREPARING FOR BUSINESS AND CONSUMER JOURNALISM: USEFUL TIPS

Here is a summary of tips for aspiring business and consumer reporters, based on the interviews with Mary Beth Sammons, Andrew Leckey and David Horowitz:

- While in college, take advanced courses in business and consumer affairs along with journalism classes. Try to get a well-rounded liberal arts education.
- Read as much about these specialized areas as possible.
- Learn the language of specialized areas.
- Learn news writing and reporting before trying to become a reporter in a specialized area.
- Try to get an internship in business journalism or consumer reporting.
- After college, take more advanced training courses.

- Don't become stereotyped as a print or broadcast journalist. A good journalist can work in any of the media.

Competent business journalists and consumer reporters are needed by newspapers, television stations and radio stations. Job opportunities also exist in public relations departments and in public and private associations and groups.

A protest by animal-rights activists would probably be covered by daily news reporters. Specialty reporters could also be involved. For example, an environmental reporter working on a series about animal rights in the United States would be interested in attending the protest.
(Paul Conklin/Monkmeyer)

Other Specialties

More than ever, print and electronic media are

hiring specialty reporters who can gather facts

about complicated subjects, synthesize the

information and then write stories that all readers

and viewers can understand. The media are

looking for journalists who are as specialized as

the experts they are covering and who are also

good reporters and news writers.

When the *Herald-Journal* of Syracuse, N.Y., needed a religion reporter, it advertised in *Editor & Publisher,* the weekly journalism trade magazine. The ad said: "We take religion reporting as seriously as City Hall coverage, and we're looking for a reporter who will do the same. Some of our hardest-edged page 1 stories come off the religion beat. We're not looking for a religion services listing clerk or someone to proselytize. We want an aggressive professional reporter who can see the potential in the beat and tap it for the outstanding journalism that's there for the taking."

When *The Patriot Ledger* in Quincy, Mass., was looking for an environment writer, its advertisement in *Editor & Publisher* said that it wanted an aggressive reporter. The advertisement added, "Experience on the beat is essential; special project work and coverage of nuclear power are major pluses."

When *The Anchorage Times* in Alaska advertised in *Editor & Publisher* for an energy reporter, it said, "We need an aggressive self-starter who can write the hard news stories about the oil industry and the issues affecting it, plus lend a soft touch for features on the people and places in the Arctic."

These advertisements, and scores of others that run in *Editor & Publisher* and in other trade magazines, have one thing in common: they are seeking aggressive reporters and writers who have an honest interest in and knowledge about a particular subject. They are looking for specialists who can gather facts on complicated subjects, synthesize the information and then write stories that readers can understand.

Broadcast outlets are also hiring more specialty reporters. Like their counterparts at newspapers, they are reporting on specialized fields ranging from law and medicine to education and fashion, from real estate and rock 'n' roll to nutrition and agriculture. And there is more: women's issues, theater, music, architecture, the media, high tech, the environment, automobiles and science. The list of specialty reporting areas is growing.

As mentioned in Chapter 24, reporters in specialized areas must be experts in complicated fields. They must be able to write about those fields exclusively and intelligently.

This chapter will examine four specialty reporting areas and the reporters who cover them. Its goal is to show how these areas are covered and how four reporters prepared themselves for their jobs. The journalists will also offer advice to students who want to become specialty reporters. There is simply not enough room to report on all of the specialty areas—that would take an entire book. The four areas discussed here—the environment, science and medicine, religion and legal affairs—are representative, however, of all areas.

ENVIRONMENT

COVERAGE OF THE ENVIRONMENT

Specialty reporters at major metropolitan newspapers and the television networks have been writing about the environment for decades. What the reporters cover has changed significantly, however. In the late 1960s and into the 1970s, environmental writing focused on the things people could see, touch and smell, such as air and water pollution. Today, much of the environmental reporting focuses on things people cannot see, such as holes in the ozone, climate changes, toxic chemicals and nuclear waste.

Although this specialty is not new, most newspapers and broadcast outlets still get their environmental stories from the wire services or from reporters covering issues on a part-time basis along with their regular beats.

As in any specialized field, environmental reporting requires expertise in complicated and highly technical areas. It also requires a reporter who can communicate with sources in areas ranging from all levels of government to the sciences.

AN ENVIRONMENTAL REPORTER IN CHICAGO

Casey Bukro, who covers the environment full time for the *Chicago Tribune,* is probably the dean of environmental reporters. He has been covering the field since 1967.

Bukro now writes for the business desk, but he began his career at the *Tribune* in 1961 as a general assignment reporter on the metropolitan desk. He then moved to the city desk as assistant day city editor. "Among my jobs was to go through the mountains of mail and make sure the right mail got to the right people," he said. "We started getting material on water pollution, and I started keeping it because there was no one to handle it. I started doing water pollution stories on a part-time basis."

In 1967 Bukro teamed with another *Tribune* reporter, Bill Jones, to produce a nine-part series on water pollution in the Great Lakes. "I took a six-month leave of absence" to work on the series, Bukro said. "Our focus was on Lake Michigan because it is right here in Chicago. Our first chore was to go to Lake Erie, which was considered to be a dead or dying lake, and see how it applied to Lake Michigan.

"In 1970 I was named environment editor. I was advertised as the first person in the country with that kind of title at a major metropolitan newspaper. There were reporters doing environment reporting, but they didn't have a title. Of course, I wasn't an editor. I was a specialist."

Bukro said that in the early days of reporting about the environment, his stories dealt mainly with pollution. "You could see the stuff," he added. "You could hear, taste and touch pollution in those days. That's why the public responded so strongly to it.

"There was heavy oil and junk in the nation's rivers. They were dangerous. There was a lot of visible stuff. There were smokestacks in Chicago producing heavy black smoke. That's all gone now. Little by little we got rid of the highly visible stuff. Now we are into the invisible stuff, the toxic stuff."

Bukro's coverage has changed over the years from dealing with immediate problems to dealing with problems that are potentially harmful in the future.

"Editors don't always like that," he said. "If you have a shooting, you can count the number of deaths. Toxic chemicals are causing deaths 20 or 30 years from now. How do you deal with that as an editor and reporter?"

Bukro said environmental reporting is a specialty, . . . "but it's my beat. That's what I spend all of my time on. I try to look for the root causes of things no matter where I have to go. I've been to the state house, I've been to city hall, I've been to the White House to cover the environment.

"It is a specialty, and not everyone covers it the same way, but I purposely cover the environment as a breaking news beat. Some people just sit back and look at the long-range stuff. I do some of that. But I treat it as a newsy beat where things are happening almost every day. When I get a block of time, I try to do a series or explanatory pieces that say what all this means. It's like juggling. You just have to find time to do it all."

Bukro's coverage of a speech during a meeting of the Society of Environmental Journalists illustrates how he covers the environment as a daily news beat. The story was written in inverted-pyramid style with a summary lead because he was reporting news firsthand. Here are the opening paragraphs:

The economic trends Americans should be looking at, says Lester Brown, president of the Worldwatch Institute, are world soil erosion and bicycle sales, not the Consumer Price Index or retail sales.

Equally important, he thinks, are the world fish catch, grain production and grain land per person.

"Our view of the world is shaped very much by economic data," Brown told the Society of Environmental Journalists recently at a meeting on the Ann Arbor campus of the University of Michigan.

Notice how Bukro used a typical inverted-pyramid form. The story used a strong lead to draw readers inside. By the end of the third paragraph, readers had been given the key points of the story: where Brown spoke and to whom. Bukro also presented plenty of environmental news in his writing, which took a look at a new book written by Brown. Bukro wrote:

The book contains some good news and bad. The bad includes:
• The world's farmers are losing about 24 million tons of topsoil a year from their croplands.
• In 1991, world population grew by a record 92 million.
• The world grain harvest has dropped 84 million tons since 1990, and grain production per person has fallen.

Grain stocks are at 66 days of world consumption, the lowest in years.
• The world fish catch fell to 97 million from 100 million tons in 1989.

"Each year now, the world's farmers are trying to feed 92 million more people with 24 million fewer tons of topsoils than they had the year before," Brown observed. "At some point, something has to give."

Bukro ended his story with comments from another source who could balance for readers the things that Brown said. Typically, news reporters do just that. They try to present all sides of a story, using as many sources as they can, and still meet their deadlines. Bukro wrote:

Brown's indicators "would be a very different system from conventional indicators," said Victor Zarnowitz, professor emeritus of economics at the University of Chicago's graduate school of business.

"Conventional indicators aim at predicting economic changes and business expansions and contractions," he said.

"Brown's system would indicate changes in something very different—changes in ecology. They would not be rivals, but complementary."

BECOMING AN ENVIRONMENTAL WRITER: TIPS FOR REPORTERS

"No kid steps out of school and goes into a beat like this," Bukro said. "You have to be a solid reporter and solid writer, and you have to know how journalism works before you get involved in a specialty. You have to know how to be a good reporter and get details. You have to be a good writer to present the details. I am dealing with scientists who use highly specialized terms. It takes years to pick up the lingo and ask intelligent questions.

"Then you have to make it into compelling reading. You don't just say what they said. You can't use their fancy terms. That's the quickest way to lose a reader. You have to take this mountain of material from highly technical people and make it into a story that a reader wants to read and can't put down."

Bukro said there will be plenty of opportunities for future reporters who want to cover the ever-changing environment. He added: "One of the things that sometimes scares me is I'm not sure we have been covering the issues that really need to be covered. If you look at journalism historically, we tend to cover conventional wisdom. How long did it take for us to see auto pollution as a real hazard? Who saw some of the problems we're having with toxic chemicals? It wasn't until this stuff slapped us in the face that we started to write about it.

"There are so many issues. The comet heading our way. Garbage. Food. Radioactive waste. These may turn out to be more of a problem than they are supposed to be. There's a lot of stuff lying around, toxic waste that already has soaked into the ground. It's a real problem. We've really messed up a lot of water. I sometimes think we don't really know yet what all these things mean together."

SCIENCE AND MEDICINE

COVERAGE OF SPECIALIZED TECHNICAL FIELDS

More than ever, people throughout the world are concerned not only about the environment but about the highly technical areas of science and medicine. They want to know why things happen the way they do or what new advancements in medicine can help them have a better quality of life.

Specialty reporters covering science and medicine are not working just for the largest newspapers and the networks. More and more newspapers and broadcast outlets are letting reporters write full time about local issues in science and medicine.

At the largest newspapers in the country, physicians are practicing journalism along with—or instead of—medicine. However, in most markets the science and medical writers are people who began as general assignment reporters and developed the specialty, or they are people who majored in science in college but had a strong interest in journalism.

A SCIENCE AND MEDICAL WRITER IN WASHINGTON

Cristine Russell, a special health correspondent for *The Washington Post* and a free-lance writer, began her career as a specialty reporter right after college. "I was a biology major in college and decided early on that I was interested in public policy and the ethical and larger consequences of science," she said. "Journalism was a good outlet for that. I edited my college newspaper and had internships during the summers. I was interested in journalism and in science from the start, and I combined the two."

Russell was fortunate. During one summer she had a fellowship at the Washington Journalism Center in the nation's capital. She explored journalism and also did a free-lance story for *The Washington Post* on the legal ramifications of cancer and the politics of the war on cancer.

"The fellowship gave me an opportunity to get hooked on Washington," said Russell, who went to college in California. She returned to the West Coast after her fellowship, but a year later she moved back to Washington to work for *Smithsonian* magazine. Next she worked for *BioScience Magazine*, a publication oriented toward a scientific audience.

In 1975 Russell went to work for the *Washington Star* as the national science and medicine correspondent. She worked there until the paper folded in 1981 and then went to work at the *Post* as a science and medical reporter. "I covered mainly medicine because there were more people at the *Post* than we had at the *Star*," she said.

At the *Post*, Russell has written breaking news, features and in-depth articles. She now does daily stories as well as long features for the *Post*'s weekly health section. "I covered a lot of news things in the 1970s and 1980s, such as the Three Mile Island nuclear accident and the environmental causes of cancer," she said. "I spent a lot of time in the 1980s on AIDS and new diseases. I've done a lot on cancer and heart disease, the two main killers in this country. I've worked on the biology of aging. I've looked at the gap between what is really a hazard or risk to the public versus the perception of what people are worried about. Recently, I have done a piece for the daily on mammograms for women in their 40s and a story on some new American Medical Association guidelines on elder abuse."

Russell said that in the more than 20 years she has been reporting on science and medicine, coverage has shifted away from stories that said, "Isn't it wonderful what science and technology can do for us," to a more skeptical look at the consequences of science, technology and medicine.

"The 1970s were the Watergate era," she added. "Journalists across the board began looking at institutions and how they function. The earlier emphasis was on glorious stories where everything went right. The 1970s became an era of raising questions about the causes of cancer, nuclear power and the worth of the space program. That increase in scrutiny has continued. Today, we are looking at the political, social and ethical consequences of science and medicine."

With the harder coverage has come greater responsibility for reporters, Russell said. "A lot of coverage of so many problems has created a public that is very worried about all of the risks it is exposed to. We participated— through our increased coverage—in making people feel more vulnerable. We have to be careful when we report about risks. If there is too much shrillness in the coverage then everything feels at risk.

"The challenge for the 1990s is to put the accomplishments and dangers in perspective for readers so that they will have a balanced view of what is happening in science and medicine. We cannot accept every advance as something over which we have to jump on the bandwagon. We don't want to be cheerleaders, but we don't want to be naysayers."

BECOMING A SCIENCE AND MEDICAL WRITER: TIPS FOR REPORTERS

Russell, a past president of the National Association of Science Writers, whose members cover science, medicine and technology, said there is no simple route to entering her specialty area. "It's not a simple time to get into journalism," she added. "I give the same advice for going into journalism in general. Go out and work at a small paper, radio or TV station and get good practical experience of how to do journalism. At the same time offer yourself to do science and medical writing on the local level."

Russell said it is important to get as much experience and as many clips as possible while in college because most newspapers and broadcast outlets do not want to be training grounds for writers. She added: "The big newspapers are looking for experienced writers, people of all ages who have done some good coverage in their own neck of the woods. Except for a major story, as a science and medical writer you have to write yourself onto page 1. Your writing has to be compelling. You can't lose the editor or readers after they have read only the first paragraph. A lot of people have the impression that they don't understand science and medicine. This makes us translators for people who speak a language that not everyone understands. We have to be highly accurate reporters and highly accurate translators or writers. We have to be storytellers."

She said science and medicine will continue to produce major stories in the next 10 years. "Because of the aging of the population, there is a lot of basic research going on in this area," Russell said. "Heart disease and cancer are going to continue to be hot topics. Brain research will be important, as will basic research about nutrition. We have covered a lot of stories and raised issues with no definitive answers. I hope there will be more answers in the next 10 years."

RELIGION

COVERAGE OF RELIGION

Religion writing—and newspapers' attitudes toward it—began to broaden and mature during the 1970s. At about the same time, journalism schools started showing more interest in religion writing, and students began considering the merits of covering religion. Still, most newspapers and broadcast outlets rely on wire services and mailings from various church denominations for much of their religion news.

Religion writing is not new. The Religious News Service was established in 1933 and has served as both a weekly and a daily service to hundreds of news media. The Associated Press and United Press International have been supplying religion news for decades.

Today, however, religion writing is gaining popularity as the media hire specialists who know the vocabulary of religion and can explain complex issues to general audiences. Besides writing hard news on a breaking story, religion reporters write features, profiles and analysis pieces. Stories range from the opening of a new synagogue to the finances of a controversial priest to an in-depth look at an evangelist. Because they are dealing with complex ideas based on a system of faith outside the realm of natural laws, religion reporters' work is demanding and at times tedious. A single story may require weeks of research, travel and interviews.

As is true of other specialties, advanced training is essential for religion reporters. This does not mean that only clergymen and clergywomen—and members of their families—can cover religion. What it does mean, however, is that students who are interested in religion reporting should take as many courses as possible in religious studies. Most colleges and universities offer such courses.

A RELIGION WRITER IN DENVER

Terry Mattingly, a religion writer for Denver's *Rocky Mountain News,* is the son of a minister. He is a graduate of Baylor University, a Southern Baptist university, where he received a bachelor's degree in journalism and history and an interdepartmental master's degree in theology, political science and history. He also has a master's degree in journalism from the University of Illinois.

Mattingly's first newspaper job was at the *Champaign-Urbana* (Ill.) *News-Gazette,* where he was a copy editor. He also wrote a column on rock 'n' roll and jazz and wrote as many religion stories as he could. Three years later, he landed a job at *The Charolotte* (N.C.) *News.* "The job was supposed to have been 75 percent religion writing and 25 percent medicine writing," Mattingly said. "They didn't think someone could write full time about religion. After three months, they changed my job description to 100 percent religion writing. I think the beat sold itself. I started writing an average of three or four stories a week, and the paper published only Monday through Friday. Charlotte is an amazing religion town."

Mattingly won the Louis Cassels Award both years he was in Charlotte. The award, in honor of the late religion writer for United Press International, is given by the Religion Newswriters Association to the top religion writers at newspapers with circulations of 50,000 or less.

In late 1984 Mattingly moved to Denver, where he has reported on the only openly gay Methodist minister in the country, the merger of a Christian liberal arts college with a fundamentalist college, the religion of Colorado's governor and a protest by local Jews against the treatment of Russian Jews. Most of his stories appear on the regular news pages, but he also writes a weekly column for the Saturday religion pages.

Although he has been lucky enough to work for papers that recognize the importance of religion writing, Mattingly said that many stories still go unreported because editors do not understand their importance. "I think the potential of religion writing has been recognized, but the institutional prejudice still exists," he said. "Editors know that they are now supposed to cover religion, but this does not mean that they want to. They still do not take religion writers seriously, and the subject of religion makes them uncomfortable. It's the Catch-22 syndrome. Editors believe, 'If this is such a good story, why don't I know about it? Why haven't I seen it in *Newsweek, Time* or the other media?'"

Mattingly said that there is still plenty of room for growth in religion writing. "Just look at the number of people involved and the amount of money involved," he said. "Look at the number of reporters and photographers from one newspaper who cover just one baseball game. At the same time, The Associated Press has one religion writer to cover the entire world."

BECOMING A RELIGION WRITER: TIPS FOR REPORTERS

"Like in any specialty reporting field, religion writing requires at least an intellectual curiosity," Mattingly said. "There are examples of people who don't have special training and who are doing a bang-up job, and there are people who do have training. There are both kinds. But to be good, they must all have at least an intellectual curiosity in their field." Here are additional tips from Mattingly:

- *Survive in the field of journalism for three to five years before becoming a specialist.* Be a good reporter first. Gain experience in writing both news stories and features.

- *Learn the language of religion.* The most difficult thing about religion writing is attempting to write about a complex, technical subject in language people can understand.

- *Take a course in religion, particularly religion in the 20th century.* Religion writing is a mix of politics and the arts. It requires an expertise in a highly technical area, and it requires an understanding of many political systems. "The United States has only one political process, but there are many political systems in the nation's churches."

- *Don't think that newspapers offer the only jobs for religion writers.* There are scores of religion publications, and most large denominations have their own newspapers, wire services and presses.

LEGAL AFFAIRS

COVERAGE OF LEGAL AFFAIRS

At most large newspapers—*The New York Times*, the *Chicago Tribune*, the *Los Angeles Times*, *The Washington Post*—and at the television networks, lawyers-turned-journalists or journalists who went back to school for a law degree are covering legal affairs. In newsrooms and journalism schools, it is no longer a rarity to see people with law degrees practicing journalism or teaching it.

There are many similarities between lawyers and journalists. Both trial lawyers and reporters start with a set of facts about some aspect of the law. They investigate those facts further and then try to communicate them convincingly—the lawyer to a jury, and the reporter to readers or viewers. "The only real difference is that a lawyer can be one-sided and journalists have to be objective," said Joseph R. Tybor, who went to law school before becoming a legal affairs writer for the *Chicago Tribune.* "I get chuckles when I tell lawyers that."

The fact that so many lawyers are practicing journalism does not prevent reporters without law degrees from understanding and writing about the law—this is being done throughout the country, too—but it does make the competition fierce in this specialty reporting area. Covering the law requires someone who is an expert at understanding complicated legal arguments, decisions and ramifications and who can put them into a language that everyone can understand.

Covering the law is no longer simply a matter of attending court trials and then writing an inverted-pyramid news story on what actions were taken. Yes, legal affairs reporters still cover spot news, but they also look behind the news and in front of the news to explore the increasingly complicated legal issues that affect people throughout the world. Those issues include entrapment, the number of racial and ethnic minorities serving on juries, recantation, the death penalty, inconsistent sentencing, the rehabilitation of inmates, incompetent lawyers and libel.

"I like to think that when I write a legal story, people don't know it's a legal story," Joseph Tybor said. "I try to stay away from the legal language. For instance, in an Illinois Appellate Court ruling in a case that dealt with the legal issue of wrongful death, I wrote a story without using the term *wrongful death suit.*

"Anyone who wants to do legal affairs reporting has to be a sound reporter and writer first. My job is to try to write about law or legal issues in a way that is understandable to non-lawyers. I am a conduit between people who consider themselves the very elite and everyday readers."

Tybor was a reporter for more than four years before he went to law school. In the summer between his sophomore and junior years at the University of Wisconsin in Madison, he got a job as an intern at The Associated Press. Midway through the internship, he was offered a full-time, permanent job as a general assignment reporter. "I covered high school sports, professional football, presidential news conferences, trials, every aspect of reporting," he said.

After spending two years at The Associated Press, Tybor was drafted into the Army. Two years later, he was back at the AP and also going to night school at De Paul University in Chicago to complete his bachelor's degree. He majored in American history and political science. Then he decided to go to law school at De Paul, at night. "I always had it in the back of my mind to go to law school, either to practice law or to do what I'm doing now," he said.

Tybor said that he intended to practice law after he got out of law school, but instead he took a job as a legal affairs writer at the *Chicago Tribune.* "The way I viewed my job from the start was that with my expertise, I could do stories that otherwise would not be done," he said. "By doing those stories, I provided insights that we wouldn't have provided." Although he is licensed to practice law in Illinois, Tybor does not because of a possible conflict of interest. He did practice it once, though, with the newspaper's support. "I got a divorce for a friend of mine in one day to show that it could be done," he said. "I did it with the newspaper's backing so that I could write about it."

Although Tybor does cover spot news, he mainly does *issues reporting.* He examines legal issues; he is not responsible for covering trials every day in city, county and federal courtrooms. Other reporters—none of whom has a law degree—cover trials.

When the Illinois Supreme Court upheld by a vote of 6–1 the death sentence of John Wayne Gacy, who had killed 33 young men and buried them under his home and in his yard, Tybor examined the decision. While most media were reporting that the high court upheld Gacy's conviction and sentence, Tybor probed deeper into the dissenting vote, which hinted that at least one of the justices was against capital punishment. Tybor's story began:

> There is a haunting inconsistency that lurks in the Illinois Supreme Court's decision upholding the conviction and death sentence of mass murderer John Wayne Gacy.
>
> Only a hint of it showed through in the one-paragraph dissent by Justice Seymour Simon that accompanied the court's 72-page opinion Wednesday, but it is clear there exists what Simon has called in the past a "deep rift" among the justices regarding the constitutionality of the 1977 death penalty under which Gacy and others have been sentenced.

Tybor said that he follows a fairly common writing formula for most of his stories. "I'll try to use an anecdotal lead in the first two or three paragraphs," he said. "Then I will use a nut graph to explain the story to readers. After that I develop the issue and pose questions. Then I bring readers back to the anecdote to bring them up to date with this particular case."

In a story on the number of minorities serving on juries, Tybor began with an anecdote about a case in New York City:

> One night some 4½ years ago, a young art student walked along a downtown Brooklyn street and withdrew $20 from an automatic bank machine. Almost immediately, he was surrounded by three black youths who pushed him into the vestibule of an apartment building and robbed him at gunpoint.

In the next two paragraphs, Tybor told readers what issue he would be examining, and how this particular case fit into it.

But this was not just another New York mugging.

It was the beginning of a type of case that some observers of the criminal justice system believe is becoming increasingly frequent, blatant and ugly: the use of race in the jury selection process to give prosecutors an edge at the trial.

After several paragraphs, in which he discussed the legal issue of excluding blacks from a jury, Tybor came back to the case in New York:

The New York case typifies the problem.

After the attack, the student, who is white, returned to his dormitory, called police and reported the crime, but nothing happened. A week later, the student called the police again and they offered to drive him around the neighborhood to look for his assailants. He didn't find them.

Three weeks after the crime, the student again called police. They drove him around the neighborhood and the student picked out a young black man, Michael McCray, as one of his assailants.

Based on that identification, McCray, who had no previous record, was charged and brought to trial. Nine white jurors voted to convict McCray and three black jurors voted to set him free—a "hung jury." Another trial date was set.

At the second trial, an all-white jury was seated. Using what were called "peremptory challenges," prosecutors were able to automatically exclude seven blacks and one Hispanic from sitting on the jury.

This time, the all-white jury convicted McCray. He was sentenced to up to six years in jail.

Now, Tybor turned to the complicated issue of peremptory challenges and how lawyers use them to sway juries in their favor. He interviewed attorneys, judges and legal experts and in a lengthy story tried to set both sides of the issue in front of his readers. At the end of the story, however, Tybor brought his readers back to New York. He ended with a quotation from Elizabeth Holtzman, the district attorney in Brooklyn who took office after McCray's prosecution and who filed a legal brief asking the Supreme Court to look at peremptory challenges:

"While the peremptory challenge is an important and traditional part of the statutory scheme for jury selection, it is not more important than the Sixth Amendment guarantee of trial by a jury drawn from a fair cross section of the community," she said in her legal brief.

"This issue is now being litigated in one state after another. . . . This court should eliminate the confusion."

BECOMING A LEGAL AFFAIRS WRITER: TIPS FOR REPORTERS

Tybor offered the following tips on covering the law:

- *Don't rely on legal knowledge.* Be a good reporter and writer first. "There are 28,000 lawyers in Chicago, and 27,990 of them cannot write."

- *Before going to law school, remember that it will take a minimum of three years, which means three years of lost reporting experience.* Also, be careful of graduating from law school thinking too much like a lawyer and writing like a lawyer.

- *Pick up the basic ways lawyers think, act and talk.* Gain this experience either by going to law school or by covering the courts and lawyers. "Lawyers like to think they're big cheese. Their tendency is to regard reporters as nothings who think they know it all. You need to convince a lawyer that you know what he is talking about. You need to know his lingo, his environment."

- *Know what legal research is all about.* Get instruction in doing legal research, which opens up a wealth of information. "Most legal decisions in this country are in a book somewhere. And every one of those legal decisions involves people. Each of them is a story. If you have the keys to legal research, you have a whole new perspective."

- *Don't look at only newspaper writing.* For example, the number of legal journals is rising. More local television stations are also turning to issues reporting, rather than simply reporting the results of court cases. Still, broadcasting is far behind newspapers. "Local television is still where newspapers used to be, reporting only what happened in the courtrooms. Print journalism is not reporting only what happened; it is trying to find out what really is happening."

Tybor said that, like any reporter, he always has to be careful of reporting something falsely or carelessly. And, like any specialty reporter, he is writing for two readers—the ordinary reader and the experts. "This means that what I write doesn't only have to be correct; it has to be almost what lawyers call 'legally precise,'" he said. "That makes me credible with lawyers and judges."

PREPARING FOR SPECIALTY JOURNALISM: USEFUL ADVICE

Here are some guidelines for those who are interested in specialty journalism:

- *Do as much general assignment reporting as possible in college.* It is better to be a general assignment reporter for a while to learn the basics of news gathering and writing before trying to sell a specialty. Specialty reporting is similar to general assignment reporting or beat reporting in that it requires a journalist who can gather facts, synthesize them and then present them in easy-to-understand language.

- *Have at least an intellectual curiosity in a specialized area.* It is possible to cover medicine without being a doctor, religion without being a minister and legal affairs without being a lawyer, but a reporter must take great interest in the specialized area he or she wants to cover. Take advanced courses in college, and read as much as possible about the field. Also, read stories by other specialty reporters.

- *Learn the language.* Remember, specialty reporters interview experts. Reporters need to know the experts' vocabulary and environment, how they think and act.

- *Don't be discouraged if there are no openings for specialty reporters at the major newspapers or networks.* Try smaller markets, where more media are realizing that they, too, need specialty reporters.

- *Consider other publications.* Specialized magazines and professional journals are always looking for experts in particular fields, especially people who also have experience as general assignment reporters. Consider working for one of these magazines or journals for a while to gain experience in a specialty reporting area. Then go to the major markets.

seven

Writing
for Radio,
Television
and the Wires

Walter Cronkite discusses the qualities of good writing with a group of college students. Cronkite always stresses that broadcast journalists must be good reporters and writers. *(Photo by Arthur Becerra)*

Broadcast Writing

Stories for broadcast are generally much shorter

than those for print; and they do not contain as

many direct quotations or as much detail. But the

same rules for clear, concise writing apply. If

anything, broadcast stories must be clearer

because the listener has only one chance to grasp

the meaning: a listener cannot go back and reread

the story the way a newspaper reader can. Stories

written for broadcast must be conversational and

easy for listeners to comprehend.

Although many of the reporting concepts are the same, writing styles for print and for broadcast differ. Wendy Black, a reporter for a radio station in Phoenix, Ariz., should know. She has written for newspapers, magazines, television and radio. She emphasizes that, whether she is writing for print or for broadcast, "my philosophy remains the same: to communicate the best way I can within the given constraints of the medium."

In radio, that translates into one of two approaches: a straight presentation of the facts in an easy-to-understand manner or the fashioning of an image with sound that allows listeners to re-create the story in their minds. In television, reporters often use motion pictures to tell part of the story and words to supplement or explain the pictures.

Black, a mass communications graduate of the University of Illinois at Chicago, has a diverse background. She has been a staff writer for the *Daily Illini* at the University of Illinois in Champaign; a stringer for WICD-TV in Champaign; an assistant news director and reporter for Chicago Audio News Service; a reporter, anchor, producer and newswriter for KTAR Radio, Phoenix; a Capitol reporter for States News Service, Washington, D.C.; a Washington stringer for Associated Press Radio; and a reporter and newscaster for KOY Radio in Phoenix. She personifies today's aggressive, competent, well-educated broadcast journalist.

"My advice to students wanting to get into broadcast reporting is the same I would give to students wanting to enter any kind of reporting: do anything," Black said. "Any job, even if it's on the periphery, should help. I've written want ads and death notices, worked as a receptionist in a radio station, checked election figures for accuracy for a news service established by the networks and been a stringer for three networks." Black's versatility illustrates that the aspiring broadcast reporter should not set a narrow career focus.

Most people attach more glamour to broadcast reporting than to print reporting. When Walter Cronkite anchored his last CBS "Evening News" program in March 1981, for example, about 18.5 million people watched. Both rival networks reported Cronkite's departure. The Associated Press said that "the final broadcast was the highlight of a day that brought Cronkite an outpouring of tribute and affection normally reserved for a national hero." Eric Sevareid, a longtime CBS News colleague, noted that Cronkite's departure received "more publicity and attention . . . than [Jimmy] Carter got leaving the presidency."

Cronkite, although a broadcast journalist, is proud of his print heritage. When he stepped down from the anchor slot, he was quoted by the AP as saying that he worried "about the truncated nature of much of broadcast journalism." As a result, he reasoned, "a whole class of people, many of whom are capable of doing only the first paragraph of a story," have emerged. But, Cronkite commented, "If you don't know what belongs in the 34th paragraph of a story, how can you know what belongs in the lead?"

Several top broadcast journalists were trained in the print field. Cronkite attended the University of Texas before going to work for the *Houston Post*. After two years there, he joined United Press and eventually became its Moscow bureau chief. Later he joined CBS.

Cronkite told Clifford Terry, who wrote an article for the *Chicago Tribune Magazine,* that at CBS he tried "to supply the principles that had long been laid down in print journalism. When I came into the business, there was a tendency toward superficiality." Even today newscasts in the electronic media do not often provide much more than headlines. Critics are quick to point out that on most 30-minute newscasts the total number of words spoken would not fill the front page of a daily newspaper. Because of time constraints, much coverage by the electronic media remains superficial.

It must be remembered, however, that television is first and foremost a visual medium and that radio is a medium of sound. Pictures and sound can convey a tremendous amount of information—often with more impact and sometimes with more accuracy than hundreds of words.

BROADCAST STYLE: GUIDELINES FOR WRITERS

Without a doubt, electronic journalism is easy for listeners or viewers to absorb; a person has to work much harder when reading than when listening or viewing. It is important, though, for reporters in the electronic media to write clearly and simply. The fact-filled lead including *who, what, why, where, when* and *how* can be a tongue twister and could cause the best newscaster to run out of breath.

Writing style for radio, as it developed through the years, became increasingly *conversational.* The rule is: Write as if you were talking to a friend. This evolution from crisp newspaper style to conversational radio style was natural.

Television writing style also evolved gradually. While it also uses conversational writing, it developed to serve a medium different from radio. For instance, when writing for television, the pauses necessary to coordinate words with video are taken into consideration. Writing is often geared to available pictures. A story on coal mining in eastern Kentucky accompanied by an aerial video of mining operations, a view of the landscape and an underground shot of a mechanical miner clawing the earth could begin like this: "Kentucky. Largest coal producer in the country . . . Eastern Kentucky . . . where most of that coal is mined . . . ."

Broadcast journalists are not as tied to stylistic detail as their print counterparts, but hundreds of stylistic and specific writing practices are widely observed. The wire services have established rules for broadcast style, and many broadcast news departments have adopted additional rules of uniformity unique to their operations. Broadcast journalists should be familiar with these guidelines.

Professor Donald E. Brown, who has taught at the University of Illinois and Arizona State University, has synthesized suggestions on stylistic practices that are followed in the broadcast industry. Practices can vary among broadcasting stations, but Brown, in his Radio and Television News Style Sheet, provides his students with guidelines on preparation of copy, use of numerals, time references, use of quotations, use of abbreviations and punctuation. Most of the guidelines listed below are drawn from Brown's style sheet.

PREPARATION OF COPY

- *Write on standard-size sheets of paper (8½ × 11 inches).* Avoid small fragments of paper, which tend to get dropped or misplaced. Do not use stiff bond paper, which is noisy when handled near a sound-sensitive microphone.

- *Triple-space all copy, and write on one side of the paper only.*

- *In the upper left-hand corner of each page, type a slug line (consisting of one or two words) that clearly identifies the story;* for example, president's speech, truckers' strike, World Series. In a newsroom where several people are employed, the writer's name should be typed below the identifying slug.

- *For radio, type lines that are approximately 70 spaces in length, with 1-inch margins on each side.* Keep the margins uniform so that lines can be counted and scripts can be timed with reasonable accuracy. Sixteen typed lines equal one minute for the average reader.

- *For television, divide the page vertically, with the left-hand side to be used for video cues.* The column at the right is for narration copy.

- *Omit datelines.* Make sure that necessary place references are incorporated in the lead of the story.

- *Use an end mark, such as # or -30-, that clearly designates the end of the story.* If a long story or roundup is not completed on one page, pencil in a long horizontal arrow in the lower right corner or write "MORE" at the bottom of the page.

- *Keep sentences and paragraphs reasonably short.* Experience shows that announcers read with more expression and emphasis when they do not get bogged down in long paragraphs. Some broadcasters prefer indenting for each new sentence.

- *Keep copy as clean as possible.* Copy that is filled with strikeovers and penciled-in words often hampers good reading on the air, and it may lead to errors in pronunciation or in fact.

- *In most instances, keep individual stories on separate pages.* Scripts can thus be quickly reorganized and late-breaking stories can be inserted at appropriate places.

- *Avoid most of the editing symbols that are used so liberally in newspaper copy.* If time does not permit retyping, completely cross out any material that is to be stricken. Print any insertions neatly and boldly so that they can be read easily at a single glance.

For example, do *not* edit broadcasting copy like this:

Block saeting, which allowed groups such as fraternites, dormitories or

campus clubs to sit together at foogtball games, was eliminaged this year

and replaceed by a general-admission policy.

For broadcast, the passage would be edited like this:

Block ~~saeting~~ seating, which allowed groups such as ~~fraternites~~ fraternities, dormitories or campus clubs to sit together at ~~foootball~~ football games, was ~~eliminaged~~ eliminated this year and ~~replaceed~~ replaced by a general-admission policy.

RULES OF STYLE

Numbers

Of all the categories customarily covered in style sheets, the section concerning numerals is perhaps of greatest importance to the beginning writer of broadcast news. Two premises should be established: First, some stories, such as those on the national budget, may have a great many large figures, and they are of such significance that they deserve intelligent coverage. (With such stories, reporters must decide which figures are of paramount importance, and they must weed out those that are not essential.) Second, a story that presents numerical information should be written in such a way that the announcer can read it easily and the listener can readily comprehend and remember it.

To facilitate the process, Brown gives the following suggestions:

- *Whenever reasonable, simplify complicated numbers.* It is often convenient and honest to use terms such as *approximately, more than, about* and *almost.*
- *Vary wording to help both the announcer and the listener.* To avoid repetition and to make trends or changes clearer, use phrases such as *dropped sharply, tumbled 40 percent, more than doubled, cut in half* and *slightly more than 15 percent.*
- *Spell out numbers under 12.* Use numerals from 12 to 999.
- *Use a hyphenated combination of numerals and words to express thousands;* for example, 35-thousand farmers. For millions, billions and trillions, hyphens are not needed to separate the numerals and the words, but the writer should precede the word by its first letter to help guard against typographical errors. For example: 21 (m) million families.
- *Translate many figures, especially large ones, into round numbers whenever feasible:* $2,001,897.46, in most cases, should be written as "slightly more than two (m) million dollars."
- *Spell out symbols for dollars and cents:* 29-dollars and 60-cents.
- *Write fractions as words, and hyphenate them:* two-thirds.
- *Remember that, in most stories, ages are not essential.* In deaths, accidents or special situations where the age is needed, do not use this common newspaper style, because it is not conversational: "Marvin Smith, 6, was honored." For broadcasting, write "Six-year-old Marvin Smith was honored."
- *For certain types of numerical information, such as automobile licenses and telephone numbers, use a hyphen to break the sequence into its component parts in the manner that they would ordinarily be read aloud:* "Illinois license number J-U-M-8-3-2."

Time References

Because the *element of immediacy* is one of the biggest assets of the broadcast media in their reporting of news, every effort should be made to give up-to-the-minute reports and to write copy in a way that makes it sound fresh and timely. With this in mind, a number of authorities have encouraged heavy usage of the present tense. Frequently, the present tense can be used effectively, but this does not justify using it when it sounds forced. For example, assume that there is a long-running strike by truckers. It would be accurate to write in the present tense: "Striking truckers are still deciding when they will return to the highways." But it would be more natural and conversational to use the *present-perfect tense* to write: "Striking truckers have not decided when they will return to the highways." The present-perfect tense is becoming the most widely used tense in broadcasting.

Some of Brown's suggestions on time references are:

- *Avoid emphasizing old time elements as much as possible.* Be wary of emphasizing such words as *last night* in lead sentences. Look for a new development and fresh approach when possible.

- *Strive to avoid undue repetition of "today."* In some instances, the day should be broken into its component parts: late this morning, this afternoon and so forth.

- *When appropriate, try to pinpoint times in terms that listeners can relate to.* It would generally be more effective, for example, to report that one lane of the freeway will be closed "during rush hours" than to report the precise time, such as from 5 p.m. until 6 p.m.

- *In capitalizing on immediacy, be alert to occasional uses of interest-catching time references.* These include "at broadcast time this noon," "within the past half-hour" and so forth. There is, however, no defense for referring to a "late bulletin" when the bulletin was transmitted an hour ago.

Quotations

The newspaper-oriented reporter shifting to broadcast writing faces an important change when quoting sources. Newspaper reporters commonly make extensive use of direct quotations. Broadcast stories should contain fewer quotations because there is no time for extended quotations, since stories are shorter. When writing for broadcast, it is usually better to summarize content briefly and understandably than to give complete verbatim quotations. Quoting presents a special problem to listeners because they cannot see the quotation marks and can become confused about who is responsible for the quotation—the newscaster or the news source. Stations know that if a speech is of paramount importance, they can broadcast it live or excerpt recorded portions. When quotations are used in broadcast copy, attribution can be handled in a number of ways. The reporter could, for example, introduce direct quotations with phrases such as "in what he called," "which she described as" or "in these words." (See Chapter 7 for a complete discussion of the use of quotations and attribution for both print and broadcast.)

Names and Titles

Most broadcasters agree that writers should never start a lead sentence for radio or television with an unfamiliar name. Without a "warmup" for the ear, it is too easy for the listener to miss the name entirely or to misunderstand it. The newspaper style "John Jones, a well-known Hill City banker, was named chairman" would become in broadcast style "A well-known Hill City banker —John Jones—today was named chairman."

Brown gives the following suggestions:

- *Titles should precede names, preparing the listener or viewer for the name to come;* for example, Massachusetts Senator Edward Kennedy.

- *If an official is well-known within a given listening area (such as the governor of the state in which the station is located), omit the first name;* for example, Governor Smith. Likewise, you can omit the first name of the president of the United States.

- *If the title is needed to put the story in perspective but it is so long that the newscaster would have difficulty running it together with the name, use two sentences;* for example, "That's according to Jerry Smith. Smith is vice president for academic affairs at the university."

- *Shorten long titles, or break them up.* Placing part of the title in front of the name and the other part after the name can be effective; for example, "Senator John Jones, the chairman of the Armed Services Committee, said that a meeting will be held soon."

Abbreviations

One principle can provide functional advice on use of abbreviations in broadcast writing: Eliminate almost all abbreviations. Even with common abbreviations such as states—Pa., for instance—there is a possibility of the announcer's making an error. And it is more than possible—in fact quite probable—that the announcer will have to hesitate while trying to make mentally sure that each abbreviation is accurately identified.

Common sense should be exercised in handling names of governmental agencies or other phrases that are sometimes conveniently identified by a series of letters. The letters Y-M-C-A and F-B-I are as easily recognized by the average listener as the more cumbersome Young Men's Christian Association and Federal Bureau of Investigation. Broadcasters place hyphens between letters to indicate pauses. A good rule is: Use only commonly known abbreviations, and write the way you want the names to be read aloud.

Punctuation

Correct punctuation for other forms of writing is also correct for broadcast news. Punctuation marks are highly valuable to the silent reader; and they are even more valuable to the person at the microphone who is striving for instantaneous interpretation, for inflections, for phrasing, for emphasis and for other qualities that will make the reading more intelligible and more interesting to the listeners.

Two somewhat unconventional punctuation practices are popular among broadcasters. First, many announcers feel that the dash is useful in setting off certain types of explanatory or identifying material. For example, "The new chairman of the budget committee—Senator Sam Smith—will make his recommendations to the entire Legislature." The second device is the use of dots as a guide for a long, dramatic pause. Often, such dots are used where a comma would naturally be placed. For instance, "He gingerly touched the flywheel of the new machine, adjusted his safety mask and reached for the switch . . . and a deafening explosion rocked the laboratory." Three dots are sufficient. Some writers will use a series of five or more dots. This, however, takes more time, is more difficult to read and serves no functional purpose.

Always remember to end a sentence with a period.

TIPS FOR BROADCAST WRITERS

In addition to stylistic considerations, broadcast journalists should always write to inform—not to impress. Professor Brown cites several taboos in broadcast writing: dialects, slang, technical terms, uncommon scientific terms and professional jargon. The last two should be translated. Also, the terms *former* and *latter* should not be used in broadcast writing. The listener cannot go back to find out what they refer to.

Brown lists three points for sentence structure in broadcast copy:

- *Avoid long separations of subjects and predicates.* Do not write, "John Jones, a resident of the Fourth Ward who was elected mayor of Riverdale by the largest margin in the city's history, will present his acceptance speech today." Instead, write, "Riverdale's new mayor, John Jones, will present his acceptance speech today. A resident of the Fourth Ward, Jones was elected by the largest margin in the city's history."

- *Break up lengthy sequences of modifiers.* Do not write, "John Jones caught a well-thrown, expertly timed, 45-yard pass from Henry Smith in Friday night's football game." If you want to emphasize what John Jones did, write: "John Jones caught a 45-yard pass from Henry Smith in Friday night's football game. The pass was well-thrown and expertly timed." If you want to emphasize the action to make a punchier lead, write: "It was well-thrown and expertly timed . . . that 45-yard pass John Jones caught from Henry Smith in Friday night's football game."

- *Avoid the common newspaper structure in which the attribution is tacked on after a quotation.* This is referred to as *dangling attribution.* Do not write, "I am going to win the election," John Jones said. Broadcasters do not use dangling attribution for two reasons: (1) people don't talk that way, and (2) the listener may think that the words are those of the broadcaster. The attribution should be handled like this for broadcast: John Jones said he will win the election, or, In these exact words, John Jones said, "I am going to win the election."

Professor Ben Silver of Arizona State University, a former CBS newsman, offers these additional tips:

- *Write conversationally.* How do you write conversationally? Talk to your typewriter or computer as you write. Talk to an audience of one or two persons when you write. Your audience may number in the thousands or even the millions, but there are rarely more than one or two people listening or watching in any one place. You are talking to one or two people driving to work. You are talking to one or two people sitting in front of the television set in the family room. The true test of broadcast writing is to read it aloud. If it sounds right, it is probably well written.

- *Broadcast copy should be written in the active voice.* In the active voice, the subject acts upon the object. Avoid the passive voice, in which the subject is acted upon. Passive voice: *The airliner was hit by the private plane.* Active voice: *The private plane crashed into the airliner.* Active voice is clearer, packs more punch and uses fewer words.

WRITING FOR RADIO

Wendy Black, a veteran reporter for radio stations in Illinois and Phoenix, is always conscious of using easy-to-understand language to draw listeners into the news stories she writes for radio. Writers for radio cannot supplement their work with photographs or motion pictures. Through their words alone, they must make listeners see the story.

CREATING PICTURES WITH WORDS

Writers do not need photos to create a picture. Black did it with words in the following story about the closing of an area near downtown Phoenix where transients had slept on the streets:

> SOME CALLED IT AN EYESORE . . . OTHERS CALLED IT HOME . . .
> THAT MAZE OF TENTS AND SPLINTERED PIECES OF WOOD MADE
> INTO SHACKS ON THE CORNER OF 9TH AVENUE AND JEFFERSON.
> BUT NO MATTER WHAT YOU CALLED IT, IT WILL BE CLOSED AT TWO
> TOMORROW BY THE COUNTY HEALTH DEPARTMENT. GONE WILL BE
> THE OLD, WRINKLED MEN WHO WARMED THEIR HANDS OVER FIRES
> IN RUSTED GARBAGE CANS AT NIGHT AND THE YOUNG, NEWLY OUT
> OF JOBS, WHO LOUNGED ON THE CHAIRS. DOWN THE BLOCK, THERE
> IS THE NEW ST. VINCENT'S SHELTER. WHILE RESPONSE HASN'T
> BEEN OVERWHELMING, THE CHARITY'S EXECUTIVE DIRECTOR, CON
> BRATTEN, IS NOT DISCOURAGED . . .

Black's last sentence above is a lead-in to an actuality, or sound bite. A *lead-in* sets up listeners so that they are mentally prepared for what follows, and it also helps to put that which follows into context. An *actuality,* also called a *sound bite,* is an excerpt from an audiotape of sources.

Here is the actuality:

"I THINK THAT WE WILL FIND . . . I'M SURE EVERY OTHER TOWN THAT HAS OPENED UP A SHELTER HAS FILLED UP WITHIN 48 HOURS WHEN IT'S BEEN FULLY OPENED."

After the actuality, Black closed the story:

BRATTEN SAYS IT APPEARS THE TENT CITY POPULATION HAS BEEN DROPPING, BUT JUST IN CASE TOO MANY PEOPLE APPEAR AT HIS SHELTER, THE SALVATION ARMY CAN HANDLE A COUPLE OF HUNDRED MORE. WENDY BLACK, K-O-Y NEWS.

Even the most dramatic of stories can be presented effectively on radio with simple, direct words and proper inflection.

PULLING LISTENERS INTO A STORY

The following is a *wrap*—a report in which a writer wraps words around one or more actualities—for the morning news. The story is about an accident that occurred the day before: Two men were asphyxiated at an interstate highway construction site in Phoenix. The lead-in ("Tragedy has struck a construction site in West Phoenix"), read by the announcer, enables listeners to flow into Black's story with understanding. Think of the lead-in to a story as a logical lead summary that capsulizes the thrust of the story. In the example below, the lead-in is followed by the introduction—or *throw line*—to the reporter.

TRAGEDY HAS STRUCK A CONSTRUCTION SITE IN WEST PHOENIX. K-O-Y'S WENDY BLACK SAYS IT TOOK TWO MEN AS ITS VICTIMS . . .

WITH AIR TANKS AND FLASHLIGHTS, FIREFIGHTERS SEARCHED THE TUNNEL. FIREMAN AFTER FIREMAN WAS FELLED BY THE DEADLY GAS AND PERHAPS THE HEAT. THE FIRE DEPARTMENT'S GORDON ROUTLEY SAYS IT WAS A STRUGGLE TO REACH THE LAST MAN IN THE TUNNEL . . .

"THEY WERE NOT ABLE TO REACH HIM UNTIL THEY HAD EXTENDED THAT AIR HOSE EIGHT HUNDRED FEET, WHICH GAVE THEM ENOUGH REACH GOING DOWN THE TUNNEL TO GET WHERE HE WAS. EVEN AT THAT, THEY WERE RUNNING OUT OF AIR BRINGING HIM BACK."

K-O-Y'S BOB SCOTT STOOD BY AS HE WAS BROUGHT OUT:
(SOUND OF HEART MASSAGE MACHINE PUMPING IN BACKGROUND)
"HE'S NOT RESPONDING . . . THE LAST . . . THE LAST ONE OUT OF THE TUNNEL. NO REFLEXES . . . A PARAMEDIC OPENED HIS EYES AND THEY STAYED OPEN. HE APPEARS TO BE DEAD."

HE WAS DEAD . . . TWO PEOPLE WERE DEAD: A 20-YEAR-OLD
CONSTRUCTION WORKER, DANIEL VAN ZANDT, AND A STATE
INSPECTOR, 26-YEAR-OLD GORDON F. WILLIS. MORE THAN TWO
DOZEN OTHER WORKERS AND FIREFIGHTERS HAD BEEN HURT.
WENDY BLACK, K-O-Y NEWS.

Good radio copy captures both the attention and the imagination of listeners. In both of Black's stories, she tried to draw a picture in the minds of the audience so that they could feel what it was like to be at the scene. The second story was taped in a news booth, not at the scene. The quiet of the announcing booth was in stark contrast to the excitement at the construction site (which was captured in the actualities) and made the presentation of the story that much more somber.

"When I am writing with a lot of detail to set up the story, I always ask myself, 'Can you *taste* it?' " Black said. Listeners who tuned in to Black's stories excerpted above would say yes.

WRITING FOR TELEVISION

Dan Fellner, an honors broadcast-journalism graduate of Arizona State University, served an internship at KPNX-TV (an NBC affiliate in Phoenix) before he received his degree. While on assignment at the county courthouse one day, Fellner looked in on the marriage license bureau. He found that it was issuing licenses at a record-breaking rate. Fellner wrote his assignment editor a note, suggesting a story on the local marriage boom. The editor liked the idea and instructed him to put the story together. A summary of statistics, while understandable when presented in the newspaper, would be hard to comprehend on television. Fellner had to explore ways to match the most relevant statistics with pictures—to conform his story to the unique medium of television.

GETTING VIDEO AND CONDUCTING INTERVIEWS

The assignment editor suggested that Fellner look in the station's film-tape library to see if there was some stock video of a wedding ceremony that could be used to illustrate the story. Fellner and a photographer then went out to shoot videotape of the rest of the story. The camera crew taped some couples waiting in line for licenses and then shot videotape of the swearing-in process that they had to go through to get the document. Interviews were conducted with some couples and three of the bureau's workers.

"I feel it is important to interview as many people as possible," Fellner said. "That way you hopefully have a greater selection of interesting sound bites to choose from when putting together the story. In this case, none of the married couples I interviewed was that interesting, so I ultimately did not include any of them in the finished product."

Reporters at KTSP-
TV in Phoenix
confer in a
newsroom located
just behind the
anchor desk.
*(Photo by Doug
Bennett)*

Fellner and the photographer then went to a bridal shop for video of practically everything in stock—from flowers to wedding gowns.

He and the photographer looked over the videotape to make sure that it was technically acceptable: it was. Fellner then reviewed the interviews and selected portions. He avoided detailed statements that exceeded 20 seconds because audiences do not sit still for a longer sound bite, unless it is particularly captivating or vivid. Instead, Fellner selected brief statements from two employees at the license bureau and one from the owner of the bridal shop.

Writing was easy.

"I just had to make sure we had the pictures to go with my words," Fellner said. "After having a producer approve the script, I went into an audio booth and cut the audiotrack for the story."

HARMONIZING WORDS AND PICTURES

The next day, the photographer edited the piece on videotape. Fellner, like many reporters, prefers to be present when his work is edited. The editing process took about an hour; then the story was ready to be aired. The words supplemented the pictures.

The total time, including the anchor lead-in, was about 1 minute, 45 seconds.

It went as follows:

Video	Audio
Anchorperson on set.	ANCHOR LEAD-IN: IF YOU THINK MARRIAGE IS A DYING INSTITUTION, YOU'RE WRONG . . . AT LEAST NOT HERE IN THE VALLEY. IN FACT, AS DAN FELLNER REPORTS, MORE VALLEY COUPLES HAVE TIED THE KNOT THIS YEAR THAN EVER BEFORE.
Couples getting their marriage licenses at the license bureau.	REPORTER: OFFICIALS AT THE COUNTY'S MARRIAGE LICENSE BUREAU SAY THEY'VE BEEN BUSY THIS YEAR. BY THE TIME THE YEAR ENDS, MORE THAN 15,000 COUPLES WILL HAVE COME INTO THEIR OFFICE TO GET A MARRIAGE LICENSE. THAT'S SUBSTANTIALLY MORE THAN ANY OTHER YEAR IN HISTORY. THIS HAS OCCURRED DESPITE A SLUGGISH ECONOMY AND A DIVORCE RATE HIGH ENOUGH TO SCARE ANY COUPLE AWAY FROM TAKING THE PLUNGE.
Sound on videotape. Bureau worker with her name superimposed on the screen.	THERE ARE ALL AGES OF PEOPLE COMING IN, AND I REALLY DON'T KNOW WHY THEY WOULD BE DOING IT NOW MORE THAN EVER. EVERY AGE HAS BEEN IN HERE SO IT MUST BE THROUGHOUT SOCIETY . . . PEOPLE ARE GETTING MARRIED.
Another interview with a bureau worker.	I THINK PEOPLE ARE TIRED OF SHORT-LIVED ROMANCES. I THINK THEY WANT SOMETHING MORE PERMANENT.

Shots of a bridal shop. Name and address supered on the screen.	VALLEY BUSINESSES, WHICH SELL ANYTHING YOU'D EVER WANT FOR A WEDDING CEREMONY, ARE BENEFITING GREATLY FROM ALL THIS. SOME SAY THIS YEAR HAS BEEN THEIR MOST PROFITABLE EVER, AND THE OUTLOOK FOR NEXT YEAR, THEY SAY, IS EVEN BETTER.
Sound on videotape. Store owner.	WE WERE REALLY SURPRISED TO FIND THAT THE MONTH OF JANUARY—WHICH IS WHAT WE'RE FIGURING RIGHT NOW—IS 50 PERCENT OVER JANUARY OF LAST YEAR, AND WE'RE ANTICIPATING WE'LL HAVE THE BIGGEST YEAR WE'VE EVER HAD IN BUSINESS.
Wedding ceremony.	(WEDDING MUSIC FROM CEREMONY UP FULL FOR SEVEN SECONDS—THEN UNDER NARRATION.) BUT WEDDING-TYPE BUSINESSES AREN'T THE ONLY ONES TO BENEFIT FROM THE MARRIAGE BOOM. IF CURRENT STATISTICS HOLD TRUE, IN A COUPLE OF YEARS THERE ARE GOING TO BE AN AWFUL LOT OF BUSY DIVORCE LAWYERS. DAN FELLNER, TV-12, ACTION NEWS.

Fellner's story is clearly written and well-organized. The pictures and the words are coordinated. Television reporters must generally work hard to do that. But only by doing so are they able to use the medium to communicate effectively with viewers.

James R. Hood and Brad Kalbfeld, who compiled and edited the Broadcast News Handbook for The Associated Press, noted: "Good writing is clear writing. The reporter's job is to tell the public what is happening and to explain—if possible—why it is happening. Above all, the story must be told in clear simple language. The more complicated the story, the more important it is that it be told clearly."

Hood and Kalbfeld recalled that broadcast writers—for radio and for television—used to do "little more than mark up newspaper copy." The AP editors said, however, that today's broadcasting copy "demands a totally different structure, a different approach and writing style."

EXAMPLE: A BROADCAST WRITING CLASS TACKLES AN ASSIGNMENT

Students in Professor Ben Silver's broadcast news writing class at Arizona State University were given the following facts taken from an Associated Press wire story. Their assignment: Look at the facts, and then write a story for broadcast.

(1) The U.S. government Tuesday issued a directive that orders airlines to tighten baggage inspections. This will apply to certain flights. It will include such steps as more physical searches of bags, and it will eliminate curbside check-in on overseas flights. The directive went into effect Tuesday.

(2) The directive came from the Federal Aviation Administration. Airlines were notified of the FAA decision by telegram. All airlines certified to fly in the United States received telegrams.

(3) The action was in response to the hijacking of Trans World Airlines Flight 847 and the suspected bombing of an Air-India jumbo jet.

(4) The directive also includes requirements that all checked baggage be matched with a traveler, or scanned by X-ray or opened. How much the new procedures will slow the movement of travelers through airports is not known. It is expected, however, that additional delays will occur. This is expected to be particularly true at busy airports.

(5) The president also received a series of options aimed at long-range improvement of security for air travelers flying abroad. Also, a House committee approved legislation intended to force upgraded security at some international airports.

(6) Among the options being considered by the White House is a call for armed sky marshals on U.S. airliners traveling in high-risk regions of the world and for improved security training for airline crews traveling those routes.

(7) The legislation approved by the White House Foreign Affairs Committee would require the president to evaluate security at foreign airports and to suspend U.S. air service to any airport that failed to meet U.S. security standards within 120 days.

One student in the class quickly seized on a solid broadcast angle: the effect of the order on passengers. The student managed to relate the story without packing too much confusing, hard-to-articulate information into it. The first paragraph follows:

TRAVELERS WHO ARE FLYING ABROAD CAN EXPECT MORE
AIRPORT DELAYS THAN USUAL BEGINNING TODAY. THE FEDERAL
AVIATION ADMINISTRATION GAVE ORDERS TO TIGHTEN BAGGAGE
INSPECTION, ELIMINATE CURBSIDE CHECK-IN ON SOME OVERSEAS
FLIGHTS AND REQUIRE BAGGAGE TO BE MATCHED WITH A
TRAVELER. THE ACTION HAS BEEN TAKEN IN RESPONSE TO THE
HIJACKING OF T-W-A FLIGHT 8-47 AND THE EXPLOSION OF AN AIR-
INDIA JUMBO JET.

Also note how the student followed broadcast style by using hyphens to break up the sequence on the TWA flight and its number.

Professor Silver had to tighten the writing of another student's story; however, that student's lead was also appropriate for broadcast. It emphasized the American reaction to the hijacking. The conversational story began:

THE HIJACKING OF T-W-A FLIGHT 8-47 AND THE SUSPECTED
BOMBING OF AN AIR-INDIA JET HAVE RESULTED IN ACTION HERE IN
THE UNITED STATES. THAT ACTION INVOLVES TIGHTENING THE
SECURITY OF AIRPORTS. THE FEDERAL GOVERNMENT HAS ORDERED
AIRLINES TO TIGHTEN BAGGAGE INSPECTIONS. THE INSPECTIONS
WILL INCLUDE STEPPED-UP PHYSICAL SEARCHES OF BAGS.
CURBSIDE CHECK-IN ON OVERSEAS FLIGHTS WILL BE ELIMINATED.
ALSO, THE DIRECTIVE REQUIRES THAT ALL CHECKED BAGGAGE BE
EITHER MATCHED WITH A TRAVELER OR SCANNED BY X-RAY OR
OPENED. THIS PROCEDURE COULD CAUSE DELAYS IN FLYING,
ESPECIALLY IN BUSY AIRPORTS.

These examples illustrate that various approaches can be taken in a broadcast story, but certain considerations are paramount: the story must be accurate, and it must tell listeners, in a conversational, easy-to-comprehend style, the impact of the action on them.

MAKING THE CONVERSION: ADVICE FROM A PRO

What is it like to make the conversion from print to broadcast journalism? Dan Fellner, who worked at a daily newspaper before landing a job as a television reporter, described it as "sort of like asking a brain surgeon to perform a heart operation. While many of the same principles apply in both areas, each requires quite different techniques and modes of operation."

Fellner took both broadcasting and print journalism courses as an undergraduate at Arizona State. He later earned a master's degree from Ohio State University. Fellner provides his perceptions of the differences between working for newspapers and working for television:

To the uninitiated, broadcast reporting might seem much easier. And in some ways it is. Reporting does not have to be as detailed. Minor facts that would be included in the bottom paragraphs of a newspaper article can be cast aside by the broadcast reporter. He or she simply does not have enough time to include them.

While working in the City Hall pressroom, covering the same stories as newspaper reporters, it would not be uncommon for me to bang out a television story in the same amount of words as their first two paragraphs. There isn't a whole lot you can say when your story is allocated 30 seconds by the 6 o'clock producer.

Another aspect of broadcast reporting that I found to be easier is interviewing. As a newspaper reporter I would write at a furious pace, trying to get enough words on paper so I could quote accurately and frequently when putting the story together. In television, the camera does all that for you. True, it is still necessary to take notes for background information. But in terms of quoting sources, all the television reporter generally has to do is look back over the videotape and select the appropriate "sound bites." It eliminates the possibility of misquoting and enables the reporter to concentrate on more important things during the interview.

But while broadcast reporting is easier in some ways, in others it is much more difficult. True, stories are usually shorter and less detailed. This, however, can make life miserable for a broadcast reporter. Deciding how to condense a complicated story into four sentences is never easy. No doubt, important points have to be omitted for the sake of time. And this can be frustrating.

While print reporters put words down on paper for people to read to themselves, broadcasters write for themselves or someone else to read out loud over the airwaves. So stories have to be put together with this in mind. Writing has to be less formal and more conversational. And sentences should be short and concise. Television anchors do not like having to read stories that leave them gasping for breath. This was perhaps the most difficult adjustment for me to make when switching from print to broadcasting. My old newspaper habits had a tendency to show up in my television stories. It was not uncommon for producers to return my scripts, telling me to cut some of the sentences in half.

Another difficult transition to make when switching from print to television reporting is the sudden importance pictures have in telling the story. The television reporter constantly has to be thinking about the visual aspects of a story. And it is imperative that his or her writing fit with what the film or videotape is showing. Sometimes semi-important parts of a story will have to be left out because there is not any suitable video with which to visualize the information. Occasionally, entire stories will be discarded for this reason. It was not uncommon for my television assignment editor to reject a story because its visual possibilities were severely limited. "That's a good story for the newspaper," he would tell me. "Let them write it."

I have found print and broadcast reporting different in many ways. Yet when it comes right down to it, basic ingredients of both are the same: the gathering and dissemination of information in an accurate, fair and interesting manner.

SUGGESTIONS FOR EFFECTIVE BROADCAST JOURNALISM

Professor Silver and Wendy Black offer the following suggestions to students who aspire to work in broadcast journalism.

Understand Technology

Broadcast journalists need to understand the production techniques and the capabilities and limitations of the equipment used in broadcast news. In radio, reporters are expected to record and edit audiotape. Reporters in small-market television news are expected to know how to use a minicam and video editing equipment.

Learn to Perform

Broadcast journalists should learn not only how to report and write but how to perform as well. After all, stories that are written are aired on news shows. Because of the emphasis on live coverage in broadcast reporting, reporters should learn to speak extemporaneously.

Emphasize the Last Sentence of a Story

Remember that the last sentence of a broadcast news item is the second most important part of the story. Only the lead is more important. The final sentence is the *wind-up line,* the "punch line." Winding up with the least important fact in a broadcast story would sound like a balloon with the air running slowly out of it. The reporter should use a summary line, a future angle or another important fact or merely repeat the main point to end the story. For example, in a story about a man pleading guilty to two counts of threatening to kill or harm the president of the Untied States, the newspaper version might end with the maximum penalties that could be assessed. That would be a logical wind-down to the story. The broadcast version, however, could end with another important, related fact, such as, "The arrest came just 10 days after another man, John Jones, was charged in connection with an attempted stabbing of the president as he was leaving a hotel in Washington, D.C."

Approach Television as a Unique Medium

Television journalists should recognize that television is a unique medium—a visual medium that can show action. Therefore, the kind and quality of visual material available for a given story frequently determine the length and position the news producer will allot to it. In fact, stories that might not otherwise be considered newsworthy may become so if they present good visual possibilities. It is not unusual for a producer to ask a reporter, "What kind of videotape do we have on the story?" One of the challenges facing the news reporter is to get motion pictures that illustrate the story.

To meet that challenge, television journalists should do two essential things:

- *Learn to think visually.* To a certain extent, this is the job of the camera crew. But it is also the reporter's responsibility. News coverage is a team effort. If there is a communication breakdown and the reporter does not let the camera crew know what will be said in the script, the reporter often winds up with a well-written story without the necessary footage to tell it visually.

- *When putting stories together for television, make sure that the words match the motion pictures.* If they do not, the words will compete with the pictures and nothing will get through to the listeners. The picture is saying one thing, and the words are saying something else. Although the words should match the picture, words should not tell viewers what they can see for themselves. Let the picture tell part of the story, and use the words as a supplement—to explain or reinforce the picture or to tell the audience what the picture does not show. Words compete with the picture when there is too much narration. Use a pause now and then to allow the natural sound and picture to tell the story without narration. Natural sound adds realism to both radio and television stories.

Approach Radio as a Unique Medium

Radio journalists need to recognize that radio is a unique medium—a medium that can make a strong appeal to the imagination. Learn to think aurally. It is very important in writing good radio copy to use sound when possible to give the listeners the proper "feel" to put the event together in their minds.

Imagine, for example, a day in which the stock market has gone wild. The Dow Jones industrials have set yet another all-time high with nearly unbelievable volume. If you have access to the floor of the New York Stock Exchange, you could start your story with copy giving all the necessary information on the session, and then you could interview one of the traders. That is all pretty pat and probably pretty boring to your listeners. Instead, you could start off with the sound of cheering at the closing bell and then present a brief montage of traders and stockholders saying what a great day it had been. Listening to the sounds would set up a picture in the minds of listeners. Then you could hit the audience with the details.

It's particularly important for radio journalists to make effective use of actualities. Remember that actualities do not have to be limited to the body of a story. A radio story can be written dramatically by beginning with an actuality or sound before starting the copy.

Newspaper reporters and editors rely on information transmitted by the wire services.
(AP/Wide World Photos)

27

Wire Services

Reporters deal with wire services—primarily The

Associated Press and United Press International—

on a daily basis. More than 2,000 journalists in

the United States work for the wire services, but

many more daily newspaper reporters and

electronic media journalists work indirectly with

the services, either by providing information to

them or by gleaning information from them.

Today's Associated Press news wires carry more copy than ever faster than ever. The A wire carries the most significant national and international news stories of the day. At the same time, stock quotations could be moving on the SelectStocks service, a legislative story on the Michigan broadcast wire, a company earnings story on the financial wire, a feature on a basketball player on the sports wire or a story datelined Kalamazoo on the state wire.

The seemingly non-stop movement of stories illustrates a wire-service principle emphasized by Joe Morris in his history of the United Press, "Deadline Every Minute":

> It is the nature of a press association that men and women scattered from St. Louis to Bombay spend their days and nights hunting not only headlines but the scraps of news that will interest readers in Centerville, Iowa, or Albany, New York, or Santa Barbara, California. There is endless routine and endless drudgery and there are times when a correspondent feels that the press association does possess certain physical assets after all—it possesses *him*. At other times, when his story skims over the wires for thousands on thousands of miles, carrying his excitement and perhaps his name into hundreds of newspapers around the world, he may feel that he is the press association. But day after day, the wires are always open, always waiting for him to produce. Day and night, on holidays and on days of disaster, the wire is always waiting.

And so it is at the hundreds of wire-service bureaus across the United States and around the world: the wire is always waiting.

THE MAJOR WIRE SERVICES

Most newspapers do not have the economic resources to hire reporters to cover developments in their state legislatures, Congress, the executive branch, the administrative agencies and scores of foreign countries. How, then, do news media in Emporia, Kan.; Casa Grande, Ariz.; Carbondale, Ill.; Tupelo, Miss.; St. Cloud, Minn.; or Ocala, Fla., provide their readers with regional, state, national and international news?

They use the wire services.

The world's oldest cooperative news-gathering service, The Associated Press, was conceived in May 1848 in New York City. Representatives of six newspapers met to find a more efficient way to gather information for stories. They decided it would be cheaper for all of them if they shared the news. Telegraph cables would be the vehicle for transmitting the information.

Costs and labor power were important considerations in that era—just as they are today. It was pure economics: substantial savings could be realized by publishers if they sent a single messenger to collect and distribute dispatches to all the newspapers involved.

The AP, as the news service was called, continued to grow during the 19th century. In the first decade of the 20th century, two of the country's most powerful publishers formed their own wire services to compete with the AP.

E. W. Scripps established the United Press Associations in 1907; William R. Hearst founded the International News Service in 1909. Over the ensuing years, others also attempted to establish wire services. One of the most interesting attempts was Transradio Press, established by the broadcasting industry in the mid-1930s in response to an effort by newspaper publishers to squeeze radio out of the national news-reporting field.

By 1958, however, only the AP, UP and INS remained, and in that year, INS and UP merged to form United Press International. Since the 1958 merger, there have been changes in ownership, but the name has remained the same. Today, then, there are two "basic" news services in the United States—the AP, which is dominant, and UPI.

Both the AP and UPI have bureaus worldwide. The AP, for example, has some combination of its 1,600 reporters, editors and photographers on duty 24 hours each day. According to a booklet published by the AP, it serves 6,000 radio and television stations and about 1,500 newspapers in the United States. In addition, it serves more than 10,000 newspaper, radio and television outlets in other countries. In 1992, the AP's newspaper members accounted for 99 percent of the daily American newspaper circulation.

The AP booklet points out that working for The Associated Press is different from working for a newspaper or broadcast outlet:

> One of the major differences . . . is the pace of work. AP staffers face constant deadlines because, unlike newspapers, there is never a final edition. Many AP bureaus operate 24 hours a day, and handle news for both newspaper and broadcast stations.
>
> Since AP has bureaus all over the world, the scope of its news coverage is wider than most newspapers. AP newspeople generally cover a wider variety of news than their newspaper counterparts.

SUPPLEMENTAL NEWS SERVICES

In addition to the AP and UPI, newspapers can subscribe to *supplemental news services.* For a fee, these supplemental services provide newspapers with materials ranging from cartoons to in-depth political analysis pieces. Scores of supplemental services are available. Small-circulation newspapers generally subscribe to only one. Some newspapers—particularly those with larger circulations—subscribe to several.

Supplemental services include the Field Newspaper Syndicate, the King Feature Syndicate, the Los Angeles Times Syndicate, the New York Times News Service, Knight-Ridder, Gannett, Cox, the Newspaper Enterprise Association, the North American Newspaper Alliance, the United Feature Syndicate and the Universal Press Syndicate.

Many supplemental services mail their material to subscribing newspapers. Their stories, which are usually not timely, are sent camera-ready—that is, they do not have to be reset in type at the newspapers. Some services, which transmit timely copy that would diminish in relevance if tied up in the mail for two or three days, contract to provide an electronic transmission vehicle to deliver material.

The New York Times News Service is among those supplemental services that provide Washington coverage, but most newspapers rely almost exclusively on the AP and UPI for Washington and foreign news. Widespread coverage of national and international affairs would be an economic impossibility for most newspapers were it not for the wire services. Each day, the wire services take people to all parts of the world for on-the-spot coverage.

HOW WIRE SERVICES OPERATE

News of assassinations, devastating hurricanes, billion-dollar budget deficits and international strife flows from wire-service facilities. News is constantly being gathered and disseminated.

FACILITIES AND STAFF

In Detroit, Charles Hill, the AP chief of bureau, and his staff gather news in a variety of ways:

- *They send reporters and photographers to the scene of a breaking story or to a neighborhood, state Capitol, school, business or sports arena or to some other place to report the news.* The AP's subscribers traditionally depended on it primarily for breaking news coverage and news features, but in recent years it has also significantly expanded its investigative and "hard-edged" reporting. In every state, the AP develops stories that go below the surface by uncovering new information or adding a perspective that gives the story more meaning to readers.

- *They monitor their member daily newspapers.* Before the news business was revolutionized by computer technology, newspapers assigned reporters or editors to telephone the AP with local stories of statewide interest. An AP staffer, in turn, had to type notes from the story as it was dictated. Newspapers in many states now transmit copy that originated locally directly from their computers to the regional AP bureau computer. These transmissions are called *electronic carbons.* A primary advantage of the computer system is that it permits news outlets to print or broadcast today's news today. Under the more cumbersome non-electronic method, by the time the story was called in, rewritten and transmitted, some outlets were beyond their deadlines. After the AP bureaus receive the electronic carbons, staffers can rewrite the stories quickly and disseminate them to member newspapers and broadcast outlets. Even in this electronic age, however, the AP staffers continue to scan the local dailies that they receive in the mail for additional story possibilities.

- *They monitor local television and radio news reports.* "Reporters at newspapers might monitor the police scanner to get story leads, but at our AP bureau we spend more time monitoring other media," Hill said. AP reporters listen to radio and television news shows, always alert for stories that could be developed further for widespread distribution.

- *They receive telephone calls from editors and news directors with news tips or requests for coverage.* Editors at newspapers and broadcast stations sometimes hear of a potential story that is beyond their geographical boundaries or labor limits. These editors often call the wire-service bureau to alert news people there to the story. Also, editors sometimes ask the AP to cover a particular story that is important to local readers or listeners. For example, a group of farmers from a small community might appear before a state legislative committee. If the local newspaper cannot send a reporter, the editor will often seek coverage assistance from the AP.

- *They receive telephone calls from news sources.* Many of the stories transmitted by the wire services are rewrites from other media sources, but some of the stories originate with bureau reporters or editors. Wire-service reporters and editors develop a network of news sources who keep them apprised of developments.

- *They carefully read their mail and commercial news release wires each day, always alert for press releases or announcements that could lead to solid news stories or features.* Going through these sources sometimes yields important news to be followed up right away. At other times it might produce tips for features or news stories to be done later.

Reporters and editors assigned to the Detroit AP bureau work in a clean, modern facility that reflects the electronic age. Hill, the chief of bureau, oversees AP operations in Michigan. A journalism graduate of the University of North Carolina at Chapel Hill, he has newspaper work in his blood; his grandfather was a journalist and college professor. Hill, who has more than 17 years of wire-service experience, heads a staff that includes a mix of veterans and newer staffers.

Of the 26 news people on the Michigan AP staff in bureaus in Detroit, Lansing, Grand Rapids, Traverse City and Washington, D.C., three journalists have worked for the AP for more than 20 years each. At the other end of the spectrum is a recent Yale graduate who had an internship in the Hartford, Conn., bureau before joining the Detroit bureau.

A common trait of wire-service reporters and editors is the ability to write quickly.

"Wire-service news people must be fast," Hill said. "We're always under deadline pressure. Many of our stories are written quickly, whether it's a story reported by telephone, picked up from a member newspaper or dictated by a reporter at the scene. For example, our stories on a presidential debate or news conference will unfold on the wire as people are still watching the event on live television. Our sportswriter at a Detroit Lions game writes the story while the game is still being played and then transmits the story moments after the end of the game so newspapers and broadcasters on deadline can use it in as many early editions or broadcasts as possible."

The AP facility in Detroit is comparable in size to the newsroom of a 20,000-circulation daily. Reporters and photographers work at desks with computer terminals in an open area. Two cubicles at the end of the room are home to two specialty writers: one covering the auto industry, one covering business news. Hill and the news editor have separate offices overlooking the newsroom.

Just off the newsroom are four darkrooms (the Detroit bureau has three photographers), but their use is dwindling because much of the photo work is now done at a computer terminal that is part of an electronic darkroom called an *AP Leaf Picture Desk*. Prints are made only rarely. Usually the photos, color as well as black-and-white, are scanned into the picture desk from negatives. There they are cropped and toned before being sent to the wire, work that used to be done in the darkroom with print-making equipment.

Nine printers that generate hard copy of stories are in a single, glassed-in room off the open newsroom. A storage room houses files, stacks of newspapers and office supplies. A lunchroom gives staffers a place to eat and relax. A conference room provides a place for meeetings or interviews. An enclosed temperature-controlled computer room is part of the area staffed by the AP Communications Department, which keeps the AP photo machines, satellite link-ups, printers and other equipment working.

Files abound. In the mail room, the counter, tables and file cabinets are adorned by 10 clipboards. They contain mandatory reading materials that range from information on how the bureau fared in head-to-head competition with other services, to memos from the AP headquarters in New York, to lists of telephone numbers of primary news sources, to directions for filing local and national sports stories.

"Because our people work different shifts, it is impossible to have everyone here together for meetings every day," Hill said. "Therefore, we use the clipboards to keep our people as informed as possible."

REWRITING FOR A WIRE SERVICE

With the coming of age of electronic carbons, cooperative efforts between newspapers and AP bureaus are easier. Stories written by reporters at member newspapers are evaluated at the regional AP bureaus for possible transmission to all members. Reporters should be pleased when the AP "picks up" their stories; this is often recognition of a solid, interesting story.

Hill noted some factors AP reporters and editors must consider when rewriting newspaper copy for widespread distribution:

- *They are writing for a state, national or international audience.* Thus, they might cut from a story the oblique local references that would be of little interest to a larger audience. Also, they might seek additional information to put the story into better perspective for a wider audience.

- *They must generally get to the heart of the story quickly.* Wire-service writers do not have the luxury of knowing how a story will be displayed by individual newspapers. Thus, summary leads are the staple of wire-service reporting for spot news stories. (See Chapter 3 for a discussion of summary leads.) Wire-service writers are less likely to use narrative and other special leads. (See Chapter 4 for a discussion of special leads and when it is most appropriate to use them.)

- *They are writing for two audiences: readers and editors.* "We first need to get the attention of editors," Hill said. "If our lead takes forever to get to the meat of the story, hurried editors working on deadline might decide that they do not have time to read the story or publish it."

- *They generally must write "shorter" than most newspaper reporters.* Enterprise and major stories naturally run longer, but wire-service staffers realize that they have to tell the story as completely as possible in as few words as possible.

Rewriting Newspaper Copy for the Newspaper Wire

Rewriting a newspaper story for AP distribution is an acquired skill that can be honed through experience.

"In many cases, rewriting a story from a member newspaper requires more than simply reorganizing it," the Minneapolis AP staffer Paula Froke said. "If the same basic story appears in more than one newspaper (for example, both in the *Star Tribune*, the newspaper of the Twin Cities, and in the *St. Paul Pioneer Press Dispatch*), then I study both versions and combine the best parts of each. This serves not only to get the most complete information but to confirm facts from story to story. Many times we also have a contribution from a broadcast member that I can work into my rewrite. In addition, I often have to use our files of previous stories to confirm information or to add details. If possible, I make phone calls to get more details or to fill any holes."

Froke spotted an excellent 1,950-word story written by Darren Carroll at *The Duluth* (Minn.) *News-Tribune.* The story, published in late September, was about roaming bears in that northern Minnesota community. It required extensive reorganizing and rewriting to boil it down to a 720-word AP story.

Here is the first part of Carroll's story:

The black bear, a local denizen since mid-summer, appears to be calling it a season.

That means relief to Duluth police dispatchers, who are no longer fielding four dozen calls a day about bears foraging in local yards and roaming local byways.

It does not mean, though, that the bruins are gone for the year, or that they are gone for good. But as winter's chill approaches, more bears will lumber toward their dens for a season's sleep.

Many bears, particularly pregnant females, are denning earlier than usual this year—probably because of the paucity of natural food.

"We've had some around here that started denning a couple of weeks ago," said David Garshelis, a Minnesota Department of Natural Resources biologist in Grand Rapids, 80 miles northwest of Duluth. "The bears that are doing the nuisance activity—the

young- to middle-age males—are still foraging."

Those bears, Garshelis said, could be out and around until late October or early November.

Hunters have been free to kill the animals since Sept. 1, when bear season opened. So far, reports indicate the bear kill is high—in some places three to four times greater than usual. That has some people—including Lynn Rogers, Ely bear researcher—worried that the state's bear population could suffer heavy losses. Last year, hunters killed 921 black bears.

An estimated 8,000 black bears roam the woodlands of Minnesota. Hundreds decamped to cities this year when capricious spring weather wreaked havoc with their dietary staples. Rogers said it was an extremely poor year for hazelnuts, cherries, dogwood berries, blueberries, Juneberries and other bear favorites.

Carroll's story went on to make an analogy with bear activity in West Yellowstone, Mont.; to provide commentary on black bear activity in previous years; and to quote several local law enforcement officers, game wardens and citizens.

After reading the story, Froke decided that it needed some perspective for readers outside of Duluth. "I liked the line about 'urban wilderness' [that Carroll mentioned near the middle of his story], and so I put that into the lead," she said. "At the same time, I noted the size of Duluth's human population. I also included a bit about the Bear Watchers Hotline [also mentioned later in Carroll's story] because that angle had gotten big play in previous stories about the bear invasion; it was something readers could relate to.

"Then I noted the cold weather to explain one of the reasons the bears were leaving. Then I added a couple of fresh quotations from a phone call to the police department the night I rewrote the story to make it more timely. At the same time, I worked in one of the amusing details of bear doings."

Here are Froke's first three paragraphs (note the use of alliteration):

DULUTH, Minn. (AP)—The black bear barrage that turned this city of 100,000 humans into an urban wilderness and prompted a 24-hour Bear Watchers Hotline is easing off, as bears distressed by the state's unseasonably cold weather retreat to their forest dens for a season's sleep.

"It started dying down a week or so ago," said officer Ralph Olson of the Duluth Police Department, which had been receiving reports of "Bear eyeing bratwurst on grill" or "Bear arguing with dogs."

"We had been getting 15 to 25 bear calls a shift, and now it's down to only a couple," Olson said Sunday.

Notice how Froke quickly got into the substance of the story. She packed her first three paragraphs with readable, to-the-point information of interest to a wide audience. Carroll, who was writing primarily for the local Duluth residents, could afford to string readers gradually into his story. Froke, who was pitching the story to both editors and readers, had to be more direct.

After constructing the first three paragraphs, Froke went into some background that she culled and rewrote from various parts of the original story. "I wanted to get it in one place [it was spread throughout Carroll's story] so that a reader unfamiliar with the 'bear blitz' would know immediately what had gone on in Duluth all summer," she said. "Then I described some more of the bear doings for those unfamiliar with the story. To do that, I had to dig into our files for some previous stories, because the source story I was working with described the bears in generalities without giving any of the specifics. I wanted to give a better picture of the havoc these animals were creating. In addition, I pointed out that the temperatures in the past week had been in the 40s and low 50s; the source story said it had been 'chilly' but wasn't specific.

"Obviously I had to leave out many of the angles that the source story—which was well-done—went into. I wished that I could have included more, but my objective here was to do an overall wrap-up on the bears' departure, speaking specifically of Duluth because that was where our previous stories had focused."

After her lead paragraphs explained the current situation, Froke inserted four paragraphs of background material. This helped to put the story into perspective for those readers who had not followed the developments throughout the summer. Notice how compact the background paragraphs are:

Thwarted in their quest for food by a poor berry and nut crop, hundreds of the estimated 8,000 bears that roam Minnesota's woodlands migrated south along the Lake Superior shore this summer and turned their sustenance search on the garbage cans and apple trees of Duluth.

As many as 70 bears rambled through the city on any given day during August and early September, said the Department of Natural Resources game warden Darrell Hanson.

The police department has handled more than 700 calls about bear antics since midsummer, and that figure doesn't include complaints received by the Minnesota State Patrol or the St. Louis County Sheriff's Department in Duluth.

The invasion prompted the Duluth Convention and Visitor's Bureau to set up a 24-hour Bear Watchers Hotline—now defunct—and an "extended bear outlook."

The remainder of Froke's story included the West Yellowstone analogy that was made in the source story along with details of the temperatures and numerous direct quotations.

Both Carroll's source story and Froke's rewrite were properly targeted to their audiences: Carroll's Duluth readers, who had been keeping up with the bear invasion developments all summer, wanted a lengthy, comprehensive piece; Froke's AP readers, many of whom were probably not familiar with the bear invasion, needed a more compact story that efficiently told them of the current situation and, at the same time, provided sufficient background to put it all into perspective.

Rewriting Newspaper Copy for the Broadcast Wire

As was discussed in Chapter 26, broadcast writing style differs from newspaper writing style. Jeff Baenen, the Minnesota AP broadcast editor, routinely rewrites newspaper stories for the broadcast wire just as he routinely rewrites broadcast stories for the newspaper wire.

Here, for example, are the first five paragraphs of a 10-paragraph news-paper wire story:

ST. PAUL (AP)—State revenue collections still show a deficit that will wipe out the $450 million "rainy day" fund by the end of the current two-year budget period, legislators have been told.

A memorandum prepared by Senate researchers said that revenues for July, August and September—the first quarter of the new fiscal year—are running "slightly ahead of expectations."

The expectations, however, were for a shortfall that would use up the rainy day fund created as a cushion for the state budget.

The research report to members of the Senate on Tuesday said that, if the present pattern continues, the $450 million budget reserve will be drawn down with the budget near balance at the biennium.

Finance Commissioner Jay Kiedrowski called the conclusions "premature."

Baenen rewrote the first paragraph to place the action at the start ("Minnesota legislators have been told . . .") and to remove the dollar figure. "This makes the news more immediate, and it prepares the listener for hearing the dollar figure," Baenen said. "I also removed the other dollar figures [which appeared later in the newspaper version], which can be confusing to hear. I also included a 'pronouncer' for the finance commissioner's name."

Here is Baenen's short, punchy, easy-to-read broadcast story:

MINNESOTA LEGISLATORS HAVE BEEN TOLD THE STATE'S "RAINY DAY" FUND MAY BE DEPLETED BY THE END OF THE CURRENT BIENNIUM.

A MEMO PREPARED BY SENATE RESEARCHERS SAYS STATE REVENUES FOR JULY, AUGUST AND SEPTEMBER—THE FIRST QUARTER OF THE NEW FISCAL YEAR—ARE "RUNNING SLIGHTLY AHEAD OF EXPECTATIONS."

HOWEVER . . . THE RESEARCHERS EXPECT A REVENUE SHORTFALL WOULD USE UP THE 450 (M) MILLION DOLLAR RESERVE FUND BY THE END OF THE CURRENT TWO-YEAR PERIOD. LEGISLATORS CREATED THE RESERVE AS A CUSHION FOR THE STATE BUDGET.

STATE FINANCE COMMISSIONER JAY KIEDROWSKI (KUH-DROW-SKEE) CALLS THE SENATE RESEARCHERS' CONCLUSIONS "PREMATURE."

Wire-service reporters and editors not only have to be fast writers capable of quickly processing materials but also have to be versatile. Baenen, for example, easily shifts gears as he moves from print style to broadcast style.

WRITING FOR THE WIRE SERVICES

Not all wire-service stories are rewrites. Reporters sometimes cover breaking news stories and write features and other enterprise pieces.

Breaking Stories

The wire services strive to be impartial gatherers of news. Staffers carry a mandate to be as objective as possible. They are instructed to be accurate and to write concisely. Wire-service staffers do not interpret the news (unless the copy is clearly marked *analysis*)—they report it. This is always sound journalistic practice, but the logic behind it in the services' early years was purely pragmatic. With hundreds of newspapers, it was imperative that the services steer clear of any political or ideological biases. If they had not maintained objectivity, the number of subscribing or member papers undoubtedly would have been reduced.

The inverted-pyramid writing style has been a staple of the newspaper wires. The most important material runs early in the story; the least important information runs at the end. This, of course, makes it easier for newspaper editors to reduce story length by cutting from the bottom.

Naturally, with the wire services always striving to meet deadlines, some copy is transmitted that is not as concise as it should be. Newspaper editors must then edit the material carefully.

In addition to updating developing stories constantly during the same cycle, the wire services also transmit separate stories for morning and afternoon newspapers. New leads, angles or writing approaches are imperative. If a story first appears in a morning newspaper, afternoon papers that subscribe to the wire obviously do not want to print the same story—even if no particularly significant new developments have occurred.

Staffers file stories on either the A.M. or the P.M. cycle. The A.M. cycle runs from about noon Eastern time until midnight; the P.M. cycle runs from midnight until noon. Copy slugged *A.M.* indicates that morning newspapers have first use of it. Copy slugged *P.M.* means that evening newspapers have first use. Copy given a BC (both cycles) designation is for use by either A.M. or P.M. papers immediately.

Writing for the A.M. cycle   The Minneapolis bureau's Betsy Henderson wrote a 16-paragraph news story for the A.M. cycle focusing on the news that a man had withdrawn his visa application after authorities determined that he had lied about his reasons for visiting the United States. The bureau's Paula Froke noted that it was logical that criticism from a gay and lesbian group was saved for the bottom of the A.M. story so that the focus would remain on the "hard news"—the action taken at the airport.

The story began:

> MINNEAPOLIS (AP)—A British citizen carrying the AIDS virus withdrew his visa application after being questioned by the Immigration and Naturalization Service at Minneapolis–St. Paul International Airport, an INS official said Wednesday.
>
> "We did have a problem with him," INS District Director Tom Schiltgen said. "He lied about the purpose of his entry" by saying he was visiting a relative. "We found him excludable from the United States."
>
> A spokeswoman for a Minneapolis gay and lesbian group said INS policy forced the man to be dishonest.
>
> Schiltgen said the man was familiar with the case of Hans Paul Verhoef, a Dutch AIDS patient detained in Minneapolis in April after immigration officials discovered the AIDS drug AZT in his luggage. Verhoef, an AIDS worker from Rotterdam, was en route to a conference on the disease in San Francisco.
>
> The INS said Verhoef, 31, could not stay in the country because he was infected with a deadly, contagious disease. Gay activists denounced the decision as ill-informed and discriminatory.

The story went on to provide additional quotations from Schiltgen, to note that the man had left the United States voluntarily and to report that authorities had decided not to press criminal charges. The story closed with direct quotations from the gay group's spokeswoman.

Writing for the P.M. cycle   By the time the P.M. cycle rolled around, the news of the withdrawal of the visa application was old, and so Henderson needed a new angle for the second-cycle lead. Froke outlined the strategy for the P.M. story: "The specifics of the INS questioning of the man and its explanation of the episode could wait in order to get the gay and lesbian group's objections higher for a fresher afternoon angle. Some details of the case had to remain high both to get the news in and to explain the story. But getting the gay and lesbian group's specific comments in the first several paragraphs provided a different perspective for afternoon readers already familiar with the basic facts of the story." Here are the first seven paragraphs of the P.M. story:

> MINNEAPOLIS (AP)—A British citizen carrying the AIDS virus was forced to lie about his reason for visiting the United States because of a federal policy regarding foreign visitors with the disease, a spokeswoman for a gay and lesbian group says.
>
> The traveler withdrew his visa application after being questioned by the Immigration and Naturalization Service at Minneapolis–St. Paul International Airport, an INS official said Wednesday.

"We did have a problem with him," INS District Director Tom Schiltgen said. "He lied about the purpose of his entry" by saying he was visiting a relative. "We found him excludable from the United States."

Federal officials recently revised their rules to allow 30-day visas for foreigners with AIDS to attend conferences or to visit relatives.

Ann DeGroot, a spokeswoman for the Gay and Lesbian Community Action Council in Minneapolis, said the federal immigration policy "forced (the man) to lie about a situation that he shouldn't have had to lie about."

DeGroot said AIDS is not a communicable disease in the way other diseases are. It is not an airborne disease. She said it was unfair of the INS to assume that AIDS-infected individuals would engage in behavior that would spread the disease.

"The policy forced a situation for (the man) of having to be dishonest in order to get a visa to come into the country."

The A.M. and P.M. versions of this story illustrate that wire-service staffers are constantly seeking and revising to update information. News often carries over from cycle to cycle; and reporters must work quickly to provide new angles on second-cycle stories.

Enterprise Stories

Keeping pace with the endless flow of breaking news naturally consumes most of the time of AP staffers, but many of them find time to get away from the office to develop enterprise stories, which normally require more research and ingenuity than routine meeting stories or rewrites.

Here, for example, are several enterprise stories that staffers at the Minneapolis AP bureau have developed:

MINNEAPOLIS (AP)—Two wreaths adorn Hubert H. Humphrey's simple monument in a lakeside cemetery. Footprints in the snow attest that the ever-optimistic senator and vice president who died 10 years ago Wednesday has not been forgotten. (By Jeff Baenen.)

LITTLE FORK, Minn. (AP)—Vast expanses of green timber stretch as far as the eye can see. The whine of chain saws punctuates the stillness in this land of woods, wolves and rugged individualists.

It's also a land of big government. Almost all of Minnesota's 16.7 million acres of commercial forests are in an arrowhead-shaped region stretching roughly north and east from Detroit Lakes to the Canadian border. More than half that land is owned by federal, state or local governments. (By Tony Kennedy.)

GLENWOOD, Minn. (AP)—When Art Groen played piano for the Blue Gordon jazz band in the 1940s and early 1950s, he didn't worry about money. He didn't have much.

Despite being blind from birth, he could manage his own income with the help of friends who accompanied him on the club circuit through the Midwest. The same was true when he played for Guy DeLeo's jazz band from 1953 to 1957 and for Blue Gordon's Seven Jolly Dutchmen old time band in the same period.

But in 1983, when Groen stood to collect a family inheritance of about $80,000 at age 58, he was pushed by his family to look for professional help. He went to court, and a local banker was appointed legal conservator to take control of Groen's finances in a stewardship role.

Nine months after the inheritance arrived, Groen was broke and had little but a color console television set to show for the money. Now advocates for the 62-year-old Ashton, Iowa, native are suing the banker for mismanagement and complaining that the court failed to have the conservator covered by an insurance bond as required by law. (By Tony Kennedy.)

MINNEAPOLIS (AP)—A two-year whale hunt by downtown redevelopers intent on cleaning up the city's most crime-ridden block will end Sunday with the final harpooning of Moby Dick's bar.

In a former life a prestigious haunt for politicians, businessmen and professional athletes, the bar has gained a reputation in the past 17 years as the core of vice on what was considered only a month ago the most decadent strip of entertainment establishments in the state.

Under a city condemnation edict, Moby Dick's will batten down the hatches for good at the close of business Sunday to await a wrecking ball that will obliterate the block. (By Tony Kennedy.)

DULUTH, Minn. (AP)—Milford Johnson stoked up the Caterpillar engine in his 30-ton fishing tug and blasted through a half-mile of ice to hit the churning open water on Lake Superior.

It's as rugged a commute to work as you're likely to find in Minnesota.

"It's got the steel hull so you can really rap it," Johnson yelled over the roar of the heaving ice. "We'll fish right up until January and come back in February."

Behind the wheel of the A.E. Clifford in his winter overalls and wool cap, the 60-year-old Johnson is a relic of an industry near its death.

When he and about 15 other aging North Shore commercial fishermen call it quits, the Minnesota waters of Lake Superior are likely to be barren of men who make a living off gill nets. (By Tony Kennedy.)

USING WIRE SERVICES

REWRITING OR LOCALIZING WIRE STORIES FOR A NEWSPAPER

Individual newspapers can rewrite or localize a wire story. When the space shuttle Columbia was circling the globe, Americans watched, hoping to be able to see the spacecraft.

UPI moved a story datelined Cape Canaveral, Fla., that began:

Hurtling through the heavens at 17,500 miles per hour, the space shuttle Columbia looks like a moving star—a speck of light visible one minute and gone the next.

Callers from around the world have deluged the Kennedy Space Center since launch time Sunday wondering when to look skyward to catch a glimpse of the shuttle.

NASA spokesman Rock Raab said the best time for viewing is shortly before the sunrise when the sun's reflection illuminates the orbiter in the darkened sky.

The story went on to list several cities around the world, giving information about the best time to see the shuttle. Included was Chicago: "visible at 4:23 a.m. moving southwest to east for four minutes at 20 degrees 450 miles distant."

When the *Chicago Tribune* received the transmission, the national desk editor asked a rewrite person to localize the story. Illinois residents, after all, were not interested in a rundown of sight times in such places as Denver, Phoenix, Perth and Tokyo. And they would probably want more details about the Chicago sighting. The rewrite person's instructions were to call Chicago's Adler Planetarium to ask where a person could stand in the city for the best sighting. The result was this story:

Chicagoans will have two chances to see the space shuttle Columbia as it hurtles through the heavens at 17,500 miles an hour on its maiden voyage.

The best sighting, according to officials from the National Aeronautics and Space Administration (NASA), will be at 4:23 a.m. Tuesday. The shuttle will be 450 miles southwest of Chicago, but will be visible for about four minutes as a shining, moving object in the darkened sky, NASA said.

To see the Columbia, turn southwest. Make a fist, point your straightened arm southwest and line up the bottom of your fist on the horizon.

Make a fist with your other hand and place it on top of the first. The Columbia should pass from right to left at the height of the top fist.

The Columbia will also be visible almost directly overhead, passing over Champaign, Ill., at 9:55 a.m. Tuesday, an Adler Planetarium spokesman said. It will be hard to see because the sky will be bright, but the sun glinting off of it will be visible for about 15 minutes.

Turn west, look for the glint overhead, and follow it east, the planetarium spokesman said.

Clearly, the wire is a two-way street. Just as the wire services best serve their readers by giving a local story more universal relevance, local news media best serve their listeners and readers by giving a national story close-to-home relevance.

COMBINING WIRE SOURCES FOR ROUNDUP STORIES

Newspaper reporters, particularly when writing roundups, often make extensive use of wire copy. If the newspaper subscribes to a particular service, it can use the copy as it sees fit. Ethically, though, attribution should be made when it is logical to do so.

For example, assume that a reporter in Wichita, Kan., is assigned to do a story on hail damage to the local wheat crop. The reporter should check wire-service copy that could be used for background or for additional information. When the reporter puts the story together, combining the local angle with wire-service information, the story could look like this:

> Southern Kansas and northern Oklahoma farmers watched helplessly as golf ball size hail pelted area wheat fields Friday.
>
> John Jones, a Wichita farmer, estimated his crop loss at 75 percent. State agriculture officials are expected to release damage figures Monday. Early estimates place total losses to county farmers in excess of $25 million, said the county extension agent Michael Johnson.
>
> Northern Kansas was also hit by the late spring storm. The Associated Press reported that hail and damaging winds near Oakley had caused "severe" damage to the maturing wheat crop.
>
> The storm weakened as it moved into south central Nebraska. No crop damage was reported there, according to United Press International.

Wichita area farmers are deciding whether to plow the damaged wheat under or to harvest what they can, a spokesman at the Emerald Elevator said.

The example above illustrates how reporters can dramatically improve stories by incorporating wire-service copy to provide complete information for readers. Wichita readers, after all, would be interested in the status of the wheat crop in other parts of the Midwest because it would have an impact on summer grain prices.

Beyond
the Writing

Journalists across the country eagerly await decisions of the Supreme Court that affect their ability to gather and report news. Chief Justice Charles Evans Hughes, when he laid the cornerstone of the Supreme Court Building on Oct. 13, 1932, noted that "the Republic endures and this is the symbol of its faith."
(Peter Gridley/FPG)

28

Law

Reporters should have a working knowledge of the

legal framework within which they operate. It is

not necessary for journalists to be authorities on

First Amendment theory, but it is essential that

they know enough about the law to report freely

and aggressively within constitutional and court-

sanctioned boundaries.

Three decades ago, when the Supreme Court considered cases that involved the mass media, reporters and editors predictably climbed onto their soapboxes and pointed majestically to the First Amendment, smugly assured that the Constitution provided them with ironclad protection to gather and print news as they wished.

Most journalists today are less confident and certainly more realistic. Lyle Denniston, a veteran Supreme Court reporter who covers legal affairs for *The Baltimore Sun,* vividly summarized what a lot of journalists think. He wrote in the *Sun:* "Reporters, editors, publishers and broadcasters can be less sure than ever before about their constitutional freedom. The law has discovered the press in a big and threatening way, and as a result the 'free press' clause is not as strongly protective as the press has thought . . . that it was."

Henry Kaufman, the general counsel for the Libel Defense Resource Center in New York, called the American climate "tumultuous" with regard to freedom of the press. He said: "There is a lot of attention being paid to journalism, the power of the press and the influence of controversial stories in a wide variety of contexts. Everything goes in cycles. We seem to be in a cycle where the public questions media methods and is less willing to question what the media are exposing."

The depth of freedom of the press indeed runs in cycles. The late Zechariah Chafee Jr., a Harvard law professor, summarized freedom of the press in the first half of the 20th century. He called the World War I years a "period of struggle and criminal prosecutions"; the 1920s a "period of growth"; the era from 1930 to 1945 a "period of achievement"; and the Cold War years a "period of renewed struggle and subtle suppressions." Freedom of the press blossomed under the liberal Earl Warren Court in the 1960s; but if there was no erosion, there was scant expansion during the 1970s and 1980s.

THE FIRST AMENDMENT AND THE PRESS

Very simply, the First Amendment does not mean literally what it says: "Congress shall make no law abridging the freedom of speech, or of the press." There are exceptions to its seemingly ironclad language. Only seven years after ratification of the First Amendment, Congress passed the Alien and Sedition Laws of 1798, designed to stifle criticism of the government. Those laws expired when the Thomas Jefferson administration took office in 1801, but more than a century later, in 1918, Congress approved another Sedition Act for basically the same reason.

In 1919 Justice Oliver Wendell Holmes wrote that "the First Amendment, while prohibiting legislation against free speech as such, cannot have been, and obviously was not, intended to give immunity for every possible use of language."

In 1942 Justice Frank Murphy wrote: "It is well understood that the right of free speech is not absolute at all times, and under all circumstances. There are certain well-defined and narrowly limited classes of speech, the prevention and punishment of which have never been thought to raise any constitutional problem."

The courts have repeatedly held that the First Amendment is not an absolute. Thus, they are constantly called upon to decide whether actions taken by the press are legally permissible. As the courts consider issues on a case-by-case basis, journalists are obligated to stay abreast of significant decisions.

A national survey reported in *Journalism Quarterly* showed that editors are increasingly cognizant of the need to keep pace with developments in communication law. Student journalists—as well as professionals—certainly need to be aware of the effects of court decisions on reporters and editors. Applicable court decisions should not be looked on as esoteric ramblings by scholarly justices; working journalists should view the decisions as fragments of wisdom that help them to function effectively—day by day.

Areas of particular concern to reporters are libel, newsroom searches, protection of sources, invasion of privacy, infliction of emotional distress and the fair trial–free press controversy. We'll examine these in turn.

LIBEL

LIBEL LAW AND LIBEL SUITS

Libel—holding someone up to public hatred, ridicule or scorn—is the communication of information that damages an individual in his or her profession, business or calling. This tort has become "politicized," according to Henry Kaufman. "Libel litigation was intended to bring about the vindication of an individual at an individual level," he said. "But it has moved into the political arena where people are vying for more power. This is a troubling development. The press, being a powerful institution itself, inherently always has been subject to this tugging and pulling within the political process. But putting libel into the political process is coercive and threatening."

Kaufman was referring to two libel suits decided in the mid-1980s: the $50 million action former Israeli Defense Minister Ariel Sharon brought against Time Inc., and the $120 million action brought by Gen. William Westmoreland against CBS. Neither public figure was able to recover monetary damages, but in both cases the media defendants were forced to spend millions of dollars to defend themselves. (These cases will be discussed in detail later in this chapter.)

Five requirements must be met before a libel action can be successfully brought against a media outlet: (1) publication (communication to a third party); (2) identification (though this is not limited to calling an individual by name); (3) harm to reputation; (4) proof of falsity; and (5) proof of fault.

William Prosser, the late dean of the Hastings College of the Law, wrote: "There is a great deal of the law of defamation which makes no sense. It contains anomalies and absurdities for which no legal writer ever has a kind word." Indeed, libel law is complex. Large-circulation newspapers have the luxury of retaining attorneys with special expertise in this area; most smaller-circulation papers retain lawyers, but they probably do not specialize in communication law. Knowing that virtually every story is potentially libelous is enough to make any reporter timid. It is imperative, therefore, that reporters have at least a basic understanding of libel law. Reporters can then free themselves from the albatross of calling an attorney—particularly one who does not specialize in communication law—every time a controversial story is written.

Lyle Denniston thinks that reporters are too dependent on attorneys. He wrote in *Quill* magazine that lawyers in the newsroom are "as much of a threat to the press as judges sitting on the bench deciding what we can print. I think you have to go hell for election with your stories and then take the consequences—and I do mean prepare to go to the slammer." Translation: Newspaper attorneys are retained to keep their newspapers out of court; the easiest way to do so is to avoid printing controversial stories.

WHAT LEADS TO LIBEL?

Most libel suits do not grow from hard-hitting, aggressive reporting of monumental importance. The majority of suits evolve from—to use the newsroom vernacular—stupid, idiotic mistakes, such as failure to copy information correctly from public records. For example, John Jones is found *not guilty* of aggravated assault, but the reporter hurriedly skims the court records and writes that Jones was found *guilty* of aggravated assault.

Bruce Sanford, a reporter-turned-attorney who represents the Society of Professional Journalists and Scripps-Howard, said at the First Amendment Survival Seminar held in Washington, D.C., that the "chief cause of libel suits is plain old unromantic carelessness." Sanford estimated that 80 percent of all libel suits flow from "the simple, routine story that nobody would have missed if it hadn't appeared in the newspaper or been broadcast." Sanford cautioned that reporters must be very careful with rewrites, condensations and summaries.

Three potential paths to libel are certain explosive words, certain categories of words and quotations. Let's consider these.

"Red Flag" Words

Sanford listed the following "red flag" words in "Synopsis of the Law of Libel and the Right of Privacy." Reporters and editors should handle these words carefully; potentially they are legally explosive and could lead to libel litigation because harm to reputation is apparent.

adulteration of products	blackguard	confidence man
adultery	blacklisted	correspondent
altered records	blackmail	corruption
ambulance chaser	blockhead	coward
atheist	booze-hound	crook
attempted suicide	bribery	deadbeat
bad moral character	brothel	deadhead
bankrupt	buys votes	defaulter
bigamist	cheats	disorderly house
	collusion	divorce
	communist (or red)	double-crosser

drug addict	intolerance	shyster
drunkard	Jekyll-Hyde personality	skunk
ex-convict	kept woman	slacker
false weights used	Ku Klux Klan	smooth and tricky
fascist	liar	sneak
fawning sycophant	mental disease	sold his influence
fool	moral delinquency	sold out to a rival
fraud	Nazi	spy
gambling house	paramour	stool pigeon
gangster	peeping Tom	stuffed the ballot
gouged money	perjurer	box
grafter	plagiarist	suicide
groveling office seeker	pockets public funds	swindle
humbug	price cutter	unethical
hypocrite	profiteering	unmarried mother
illegitimate	rascal	unprofessional
illicit relations	rogue	unsound mind
incompetent	scandalmonger	unworthy of
infidelity	seducer	credit
intemperate	sharp dealing	vice den
intimate	short in accounts	villain

Reporters can steer clear of many libel suits by scrutinizing the meaning of the words and the sentences they write. A warning bell should sound any time a reporter writes a story that contains any of the "red flag" words. In certain contexts, these words could damage a person's reputation.

Classes of Libelous Words

When writing sensitive stories, always be alert for potentially libelous statements. Libel in the state of Illinois, for example, includes these classes of words: (1) words imputing the commission of a criminal offense; (2) words that impute infection with a communicable disease of any kind which would tend to exclude one from society; (3) words that impute inability to perform, or want of integrity in the discharge of, duties of office or employment; and (4) words that prejudice a particular person in his or her profession or trade. Classes of libelous words can, of course, vary slightly among the states, but this list is representative. Following are examples of each category.

Category 1 *Words imputing the commission of a criminal offense.* Avoid statements such as this:

John Crandall was taken into custody Wednesday for murdering Sally Smith Tuesday night.

Think again. Is that really what happened? Remember to choose your words carefully. Crandall is not guilty of murder until a court says that he is. It would be better to write:

John Crandall was taken into custody Wednesday in connection with (or in the investigation of) the Tuesday night slaying of Sally Smith.

Category 2 *Words that impute infection with a communicable disease of any kind which would tend to exclude one from society.* Don't write:

> John Crandall, who was elected Wednesday to be president of the local
> chapter of the Fellowship of Christian Athletes, was treated last
> summer for a venereal disease, the Daily Bugle has learned.

Such an accusation is hardly a major scoop. There is no reason to publish it. It is an example of going out on a legal limb for the type of story that Sanford mentioned earlier: one that "nobody would have missed it if it hadn't appeared in the newspaper or been broadcast." The lesson is clear: the danger of libel constantly lurks; if you are going to tempt fate, do so with a story that is worth the risk.

Category 3 *Words that impute inability to perform, or want of integrity in the discharge of, duties of office or employment.* Don't write:

> Public school groundskeeper John Crandall is unfit by temperament
> and intelligence to adequately perform his duties, sources who wish to
> remain anonymous said Wednesday.

This lead paragraph is another example of using a verbal sledgehammer to bludgeon an ant. Why risk a suit for such a revelation? Again remember: Be aggressive when you report, but make sure that the story justifies the potential harm to your subject and to your employer's pocketbook.

Category 4 *Words that prejudice a particular person in his or her profession or trade.* Don't write:

> Attorney John Crandall, who will represent the widow in the
> embezzlement case, is the most incompetent lawyer in town, according
> to courthouse observers.

Obviously, Crandall is not going to take kindly to the accusation. Can the reporter document the charge, and is there sufficient justification for making it? The reporter who wrote the paragraph had better hope so.

The examples and suggestions outlined above illustrate one principle: Handle stories that could injure a person's reputation with care. This does not mean that you should back off of a story that should be told. But it does mean that you should choose your words carefully. Ask yourself: Am I being fair? Am I being accurate? Is this story worth the legal risk?

Remember: The reporter and the news medium are responsible for statements aired or printed—even if someone is being quoted directly or indirectly. Assume, for example, that a reporter interviews the neighbor of a man who has just been charged with murder. The neighbor says that the man is a "no-good drunken bum who beats his kids regularly and belongs to the Communist Party." The fact that the neighbor made the observation does not reduce the newspaper's level of liability; *the news medium must assume responsibility for the statement if it is used.*

As attorney Neil Rosino has pointed out, misquotations can defame not only third parties whom a speaker mentions, but also the quoted speaker. The U.S. Supreme Court ruled in 1991 that deliberate misquotations may injure reputation by attributing harmful assertions to the speaker if the misquotations result in a "material change" in the meaning intended by the speaker.

Reporters must always keep the following points in mind when using quotations.

Point 1 *The fact that information was provided by a source does not necessarily mean that it is correct.* Assume, for example, that a nurse tells a reporter that Dr. John Jones is the only physician practicing at Memorial Hospital who has been sued successfully for malpractice during the preceding year. The reporter could sit at a computer terminal and type:

> Dr. John Jones is the only physician who practices at Memorial
>
> Hospital to be sued successfully for malpractice during the past year,
>
> according to a nurse.

The lead sounds like the start of a great story. The problem is that the reporter did not verify the information. Jones had been sued, but he won his case. The nurse had him confused with another doctor. The lesson is clear: do not rely on secondhand information when printing accusations of such gravity. Check and double-check. And then go to the person who has been accused for his or her side of the story. By failing to do so, the reporter invites a libel action.

Point 2 *Beware of off-the-record tips passed along by sources, even high-ranking officials or law enforcement officers.* Always confirm potentially libelous accusations. Prefacing an accusation with the word *alleged* will not help when you get to court. Do not, for example, write:

> Police said that the alleged crook is in custody.

Instead, write:

> Police said that the man charged with the crime is in custody.

DEFENSES AGAINST LIBEL

No matter how careful a reporter is, libel suits can materialize. In this section, we'll examine defenses against libel.

If a libel suit is filed, a defendant can use a number of defenses. Some defenses are conditional: they are viable if certain conditions or qualifications are met. Others are absolute: if proven, there are no conditions or qualifications. A defense may be based on common or statutory law or on the Constitution.

Common Law and Statutory Defenses

Conditional defenses   In their book "Libel: Rights, Risks, Responsibilities," Robert H. Phelps and E. Douglas Hamilton, two authorities on libel law, discuss conditional defenses that have evolved through the common law (judge-made law based on prior court decisions) and statutory law. These defenses include the following.

Privilege of reporting   The defense known as *privilege of reporting* flows from fair and accurate reporting of official proceedings—city council meetings, state legislative sessions, congressional hearings and so forth—and the fair and accurate reporting of information contained in official documents and court records. Obviously, this defense is often cited by reporters. As emphasized, however, the defense is limited to fair and accurate reporting. Extraneous libelous matter cannot be intertwined. If, for example, during a city council meeting the mayor accuses the council president of embezzling city funds, the reporter is free to report that the charges were made—so long as the story accurately conveys what the mayor said. Any elaboration or interpretation of the mayor's remarks by the reporter would not necessarily be protected.

Many jurisdictions have extended this qualified privilege to include reporting on matters in the public interest that flow from *unofficial but open* meetings such as those taking place when citizens gather to consider construction of a nuclear waste facility or when political parties assemble to discuss pressing community issues. Check to see if this protection applies in your jurisdiction.

Fair comment and criticism   As a defense against libel, fair comment and criticism applies only when writing opinions about matters of public concern. The defense does not protect erroneous factual reporting. It must be clear that the allegedly libelous statement—whether it appears in an editorial, a book review or a personal viewpoint column—is a statement of opinion, not an expression of fact. This defense is not available to the reporter who covers an event and then writes a factual news account. However, if a reporter were to comment on the news event and offer an analysis of it in a personal column, this defense possibly could then be used.

Neutral reportage   In 1977 the 2nd U.S. Circuit Court accepted neutral reportage as a conditional defense; that is, it is defensible to report charges made by one responsible person or organization about another when both parties are involved in a public controversy. This defense has not been widely accepted, however, and at least one circuit has specifically rejected it. Where it applies, though, it makes additional protection available to the defendant in a libel suit. Check to see if it applies in your state.

The defense was cited in *Edwards* v. *National Audubon Society*. In this case, a *New York Times* reporter wrote a story concerning accusations by officials of an Audubon Society periodical, *American Birds,* that scientists who contended that the insecticide DDT did not have a negative impact on bird life were being paid to lie. The *Times* story included a short denial by some of the named scientists who had sent to the reporter extensive research material to refute the charges. The 2nd U.S. Circuit Court said that even when a newspaper seriously doubts the truth of the charges, the publication is protected under the defense of neutral reportage—objective and dispassionate reporting of the charges.

Absolute defenses   The following are absolute defenses against libel.

Statute of limitations   Statute of limitations is the most ironclad of the defenses. If a suit is brought after a specified period—in most states the statute of limitations on libel is one, two or three years—the plaintiff has no standing to sue.

Truth   Truth is an absolute defense in most states. But its practical value as a defense against libel has been considerably diminished because the burden now rests with the plaintiff to prove falsity; the burden is no longer on the defendant to prove truth.

Privilege of participant   The defense called *privilege of participant* applies to participants in official proceedings: a city council member's remarks during a meeting, the testimony of a witness during a trial, a senator speaking on the protected floor of the Senate. This, then, is not a defense reporters would generally be able to use. Reporters normally report the news—not make it.

Consent or authorization   If a reporter writes a libelous passage, calls the person in question and gets his or her permission to publish it, this defense can be used. Obviously, this situation is not likely to happen.

Self-defense or right of reply   If publicly criticized, the recipient of the criticism has a right to respond. He or she must be careful, however, to keep the response within the framework of the original accusation. For example, suppose that a newspaper's drama critic treats the opening of a play harshly. The star of the play could respond, but the privilege of response covers only a response to the original criticism. In other words, the star could not launch a salvo critical of the reviewer's home life.

Journalists would not often have occasion to use this defense.

Partial defenses   If conditional or absolute defenses (including the conditional *New York Times* actual malice defense, which will be discussed in the next section) cannot be used successfully, the defendant will probably be assessed damages. He or she can, however, cite partial defenses to mitigate the damages. Partial defenses represent good faith on the part of the defendant, and a judge can take them into consideration when levying damages. Partial defenses include publication of a retraction (a clear admission of erroneous reporting) or of facts showing that, though the newspaper erred, there was no gross negligence or ill will or that the reporter relied on a usually reliable source.

A Constitutional Defense: The Actual Malice Standard

The New York Times rule   Clearly, the reporter is not without common law and statutory defenses. However, most of these defenses are limited compared with the federal rule, commonly called the *actual malice* defense. This is a constitutional defense first articulated by the Supreme Court in 1964. In the landmark case of *New York Times Co.* v. *Sullivan,* the court nationalized the law of libel in part to provide a constitutional defense when *public officials* are plaintiffs. Suit was brought against the *Times* for publication of an advertisement in 1960 that, in essence, said that the civil rights movement in the South was being met with a wave of aggression by certain Southern officials. L. B. Sullivan, a Montgomery, Ala., commissioner, filed the suit. Portions of the advertisement were false, and under existing statutory and common law, a defendant had to prove the literal truth of the statements. The Alabama courts awarded Sullivan $500,000 in damages.

The Supreme Court, however, reversed this ruling. It held that, to collect damages, a public official—which Sullivan clearly was—would have to prove that the defendant acted with "actual malice." Justice William Brennan said that this would constitute disseminating information "with knowledge that it was false or with reckless disregard of whether it was false or not." Brennan wrote that the advertisement, "as an expression of grievance and protest on one of the major public issues of our time, would seem clearly to qualify for the constitutional protection." The media would be protected against suits brought by public officials, even when the statements were false—so long as the statements were not made with actual malice. Essentially, the case put to death the concept of seditious libel in the United States.

The conditional actual malice defense provides reporters with a primary defense to add to their arsenal of common law and statutory defenses. The condition on which the *Times* rule was based, of course, is that the publication must concern a public official. From 1964 on, the status of the plaintiff—whether public or private—has been the first consideration a defendant makes when formulating possible defenses against a libel action. In 1967 the Supreme Court said that *public figures*—in addition to public officials—also have to show actual malice to recover libel damages. The message is clear: As a reporter, you don't want to get tied up in a libel action, but if you do, there is more protection if the plaintiff is a public person.

The *Times* rule was extended again in 1971. A plurality of the court said in *Rosenbloom* v. *Metromedia* that private persons involved in events of general or public interest also have to show actual malice to recover libel damages. The press was elevated to its most protected position ever regarding libel defenses.

Gertz v. Robert Welch   In 1974, however, the press was dealt a setback. In *Gertz* v. *Robert Welch Inc.,* the court said that it had gone too far in *Rosenbloom* and that unless a libel suit plaintiff were to be awarded presumed or punitive damages, private persons involved in events of general or public interest need only prove a lower fault standard—presumably *negligence*—to receive damages. Negligence certainly would be easier to prove than actual malice, the standard still required with public officials and public figures.

In addition to stripping the press of some of the protection it had come to enjoy as a result of *Rosenbloom, Gertz* also restructured the definition of a public figure. The court said that to be categorized as a public figure, an individual must "voluntarily thrust" himself or herself into the vortex of the particular controversy that gave rise to the litigation with the intention of influencing its outcome (for example, leading a movement to recall a city council member) or must assume a role "of especial prominence" to the extent that, for all purposes, he or she is to be considered a public figure (for example, Henry Kissinger).

The court also said that each state would define the appropriate level of liability—presumably negligence—when suits were brought by non-public persons involved in events of general or public interest. Nearly 40 states have since defined negligence, but few definitions are uniform. Some states define it as "gross negligence," and others as "failure to act as a reasonable person."

Professor W. Wat Hopkins wrote in *Journalism Monographs:* "Negligence is a nebulous word. And other nebulous words—reasonable, prudent, ordinary, careful, proper—are being used to define it."

The article focused on the various standards of negligence that had been established. Hopkins concluded: "While courts may not have always agreed on the legal definition of negligence, most courts, thus far anyway, have recognized sloppy reporting. And the best protection from the finding of negligence is the elimination of sloppy reporting."

It is important that reporters check to see what definition applies in the states where they work. Some state supreme courts agreed to review cases for the sole purpose of defining the standard of liability for libel of private persons involved in public events. In reviewing such a case, for example, the Arizona Supreme Court said that negligence is "conduct which creates an unreasonable risk of harm. It is the failure to use that amount of care which a reasonably prudent person would use under like circumstances."

As emphasized earlier, with the status of the plaintiff an all-important consideration when defending against libel actions, *Gertz* took away some of the certainty editors and reporters had when deciding who might be categorized as a public figure. In *Gertz*, for example, the plaintiff was a well-known Chicago attorney who had been reasonably active in civic affairs. But the court reasoned that his reputation as a lawyer was not pervasive enough to stamp him as a public figure for all purposes; and in this particular case, he had not thrust himself to the forefront of the controversy.

Conservative libel decisions   In another far-reaching case in 1976 (*Time Inc. v. Firestone*), it became even more apparent that reporters and editors would have difficulty distinguishing between public figures and private individuals. The Supreme Court said that the wife of a prominent wealthy industrialist who held press conferences during the course of her divorce proceedings, who subscribed to a press clipping service to keep pace with articles written about her and who was well-known in Palm Beach, Fla., society was, for purposes of libel law, to be considered a private person.

In 1979 the Supreme Court continued its flow of conservative libel decisions that went against the media. The court said that to show that a defendant acted in reckless disregard for the truth, a libel plaintiff could probe the state of mind of the defendant and inquire into the "predecisional communications" between editors and reporters (*Herbert* v. *Lando*).

Justice White, who wrote the opinion for a six-member majority, said that courts have "traditionally admitted any direct or indirect evidence relevant to the state of mind of the defendant . . . necessary to defeat a conditional privilege or enhance damages." White said that he was aware of the First Amendment rights of the press but that the courts were also obligated to consider the individual's interest in his or her reputation.

Also in 1979 the court ruled that a man—a research director at a state mental hospital and an adjunct professor at a university—who had received hundreds of thousands of dollars in federal grant money was not, for libel purposes, a public figure (*Hutchinson* v. *Proxmire*). During that same term, the court held that persons who had been caught up in a criminal investigation years earlier do not automatically remain public figures for purposes of libel law application (*Wolston* v. *Reader's Digest*).

As we have seen, the press has the most protection when sued by either public officials or public figures; if the plaintiffs are so categorized, to recover damages they must prove that the defendant acted with actual malice. When plaintiffs are private persons involved in events of public concern, they must prove that the defendant acted with negligence—a less stringent standard. Reporters naturally do not want to become embroiled in libel suits. If they are, however, as we stated above, the chance of a successful defense is greater if the plaintiff is a public official or a public figure. This was apparent in two libel actions in the mid-1980s that attracted considerable attention: the *Sharon* and *Westmoreland* cases. Let's look at these.

The Sharon case   Ariel Sharon, former minister of defense for the state of Israel, brought his libel action against Time Inc., on the basis of a single paragraph in an article entitled, "The Verdict Is Guilty: An Israeli Commission Apportions the Blame for the Beirut Massacre."

While Sharon was minister of defense, Israel invaded Lebanon, hoping to eliminate Palestine Liberation Organization strongholds from which the PLO had been attacking Israel. Members of the Christian Phalangist militia—by arrangement with the Israel Defense Forces—entered Palestinian refugee camps at Sabra and Shatilla. While there, the Phalangists slaughtered hundreds of Palestinian civilians, including women and children. Israel then established a commission to determine who was responsible for the slaughter.

Time's article included a discussion of the commission's findings. *Time* said that the report was a "stinging indictment" of Sharon. Sharon based his libel claim, not on the thrust of the story, but on this paragraph:

> One section of the report, known as Appendix B, was not published at all, mainly for security reasons. That section contains the names of several intelligence agents

referred to elsewhere in the report. Time has learned that it also contains further details about Sharon's visit to the Gemayel family on the day after Bashir Gemayel's assassination. [Gemayel was Lebanon's president elect.] Sharon reportedly told the Gemayels that the Israeli army would be moving into West Beirut and that he expected the Christian forces to go into the Palestinian refugee camps. Sharon also reportedly discussed with the Gemayels the need for the Phalangists to take revenge for the assassination of Bashir, but the details of the conversation are not known.

The federal District Court for the Southern District of New York noted:

Sharon claims that this paragraph is false, both because he never discussed the need for revenge with the Gemayels and because the Commission Report contains no details of such discussion. He claims that this paragraph is defamatory both because it suggests that he instigated, encouraged, or condoned the massacres at Sabra and Shatilla, and because it suggests that the Commission had secret evidence or found secretly that he had lied when he testified that he had not known in advance that a massacre would occur.

Sharon, who was forced to resign his defense post after the commission's findings were released, said that he had visited Phalangist leaders one day before the slaughter, but he denied that he had ever discussed gaining revenge against the PLO.

Time labeled Sharon's libel action "an unprecedented case of a major foreign official suing for libel in a U.S. court over a story about his official actions." *Time*'s defense was complicated by the fact that Israel refused to turn over requested documents, for reasons of national security. This evened the odds somewhat because Sharon, as a public figure, faced the burden of showing that *Time* had acted with actual malice.

The trial attracted pervasive media attention. Federal Judge Abraham Sofaer was praised for his instructions that the jury announce its findings in stages before reaching a verdict:

First, the jury announced that the paragraph in question was defamatory. (Sharon's reputation had been tarnished.)

Next, it announced that the paragraph was false. (Appendix B made no mention of Sharon speaking of the need for revenge.)

But, after considering the third and most important point—whether *Time* had acted in reckless disregard for the truth—the jurors found for the magazine.

The Associated Press quoted Sharon's attorney, Milton Gould, who said: "The only thing we don't get is money, and the reason we don't get any money is that we're dealing with a peculiar law of actual malice which makes it almost impossible for a public figure to prove."

The AP also reported that the jury issued a statement saying that certain *Time* employees, even though they had not published the story in reckless disregard for the truth, had acted "negligently and carelessly in reporting and verifying the information which ultimately found its way" into the paragraph.

Both sides claimed victory, but one fact emerges: *Time* did not have to pay damages. The case illustrates that the protection flowing from the actual malice standard is considerable. Clearly, it is not enough for a public figure to show that a media defendant carelessly published a defamatory or false report—even when the report caused significant damage to the plaintiff's reputation. The public person must also show that the defendant published the report with a high degree of awareness of probable falsity—and that is a stringent standard to overcome.

The Westmoreland case   General William Westmoreland also discovered how difficult it is for a public figure to collect damages in a libel suit. Westmoreland, who commanded American military forces in Vietnam from 1964 to 1968, sued CBS for a documentary it had aired. The general claimed that the central theme of that program, entitled "CBS Reports—The Uncounted Enemy: A Vietnam Deception," was that he had led a conspiracy to underestimate the size of the enemy force to lend credence to his optimistic reports of American progress in the war.

CBS asked the District Court for the Southern District of New York to decide the case in its favor because it enjoyed "absolute immunity dictated by the First Amendment from a libel suit brought by a high public official challenging commentary on his performance of the duties of his office." The court refused, saying that *Sullivan* merely gave the press a "qualified immunity" to discuss public persons—that public persons could win by proving that "the defamation was published with knowledge of its falsity or in reckless disregard for its truth or falsity."

The district court said that a jury should decide the case. Ironically, after more than two months in court, a jury never did render a verdict. The lead paragraph of an article published in *Newsweek* set the scene for the rather anticlimactic conclusion of the case:

> You could almost hear the air hissing out of room 318 of federal district court in Manhattan last week. After 2½ years of litigation, nearly half a million pages of documents, reams of press coverage and 65 grinding days in court, the libel case brought by retired Gen. William C. Westmoreland against CBS deflated like the shot-out tires of an Army jeep. Only days away from going to the jury, the case was settled quietly on a Sunday afternoon.

Gen. Westmoreland and CBS issued a joint statement. CBS said that it respected Westmoreland's "long and faithful service to his country and never intended to assert, and does not believe, that General Westmoreland was unpatriotic or disloyal in performing his duties as he saw them." For his part, the general said that he respected "the long and distinguished journalistic tradition of CBS and the rights of journalists to examine the complex issues of Vietnam and to present perspectives contrary" to those he might hold.

United Press International reported the day after the discontinuance of the suit was announced that at least half of the jurors "were leaning strongly toward the network when the case came to a sudden halt."

Libel as an Economic Threat

No legal precedents were established by *Westmoreland*, but the case took its toll financially on both parties. *Editor & Publisher* magazine estimated the total cost of the case to be between $7 million and $9 million.

Judge Pierre N. Leval was quoted by the wire services at the conclusion of the case: "It may be for the best that the verdict will be left to history."

The lawyer Henry Kaufman said that, with the retreat of Westmoreland, "we hope that libel as a weapon against the press will diminish, but that remains to be seen."

The Baltimore Sun's Lyle Denniston said that the *Westmoreland* action was "really a seditious libel suit." Denniston said that the general "tried to vindicate public policy rather than personal reputation."

Many newspapers today are fearful of becoming tangled in extended, expensive libel suits—even suits they could probably eventually win. Consequently, they are approaching investigative reporting far less aggressively than in past years. The economic threat of a costly libel suit can indeed be intimidating.

Guidelines for Reporters

Following is some advice for reporters with regard to libel.

- *Be aggressive—but don't take foolish risks.* The fear of losing a libel suit probably chills the reporting process. Lyle Denniston advised reporters not to take "foolish risks" but also not to be overly cautious. "Reporters should not compromise," he said. "Journalists must take chances when reporting stories. They have to be aggressive.

  "Reporters should not consider legal ramifications as they gather information and as they write a story. They should go after the story and worry about the law later. It is a risk, but when reporters and editors operate on legal premise, they inhibit the reportorial processes.

  "If reporters follow ethical restraints, they should be within legal bounds. Reporters shouldn't try to gauge in advance what will fly legally. They aren't equipped to think legally—they inhibit themselves too much."

- *Be fair—keep an open mind.* The First Amendment scholar Marc A. Franklin of the Stanford Law School noted that reporting "involves substantial responsibility on the part of the journalist." He advised: "No reporter acts without a hypothesis. But that hypothesis must be open to change and modification continually. The reporter should not seek facts that support a strongly held hypothesis. Instead, reporters should seek as much information as will shed light on the situation. This requires an open mind, but not necessarily one that is unable to draw conclusions. If the reporter honestly concludes, after careful research and investigation, that the facts support a conclusion that is negative about someone—perhaps even defamatory—the reporter should lean over backwards to make sure that he or she has been reasonably careful in acquiring the facts and reasonably fair in considering them.

  "Reporters should recognize that the fairness with which a story is published may go a long way in avoiding the filing of a lawsuit. Working to be fair does not compromise the reporter's integrity in any way whatsoever. The point is that many subjects of defamation, though obviously unhappy, will respond to fair treatment in an article.

"This kind of press behavior is in no way inconsistent with the notion of a strong, aggressive and inquiring media."

- *Seek advice if you are unsure of your turf.* Henry Kaufman pointed out that legal rules are complex. "Reporters should take advantage of advice from legal counsel and from editors, and they should draw on what they learned in school," he said. "No matter how well-advised you are or how much you know, though, you can't completely guarantee that you are going to avoid litigation. A claim always can be filed, even if it is not meritorious. In fact, it would probably be a negative thing if the focus of reporters was on trying to guarantee a 100 percent libel-proof story. The only way to guarantee that would be to make a story completely inoffensive to public people. I don't think that would be good for journalism or in the public interest. The best thing reporters can do is to be good journalists. That means be careful and hope that you have a good lawyer if it comes down to defending the story."

Guidelines for Potential Defendants

Concern over libel actions is real enough that the New York State Newspapers Foundation, in its "Survival Kit for Reporters, Editors and Broadcasters," provided this advice for the potential defendant:

- *Be courteous and polite.* Nothing is gained by antagonizing a person who claims to have been libeled.

- *Do not admit an error when a person initially claims that he or she has been libeled.* Take advantage of the complexity of the law. Even though it is conceivable that you have libeled the person, the wrong may not be sufficient to sustain a libel suit.

- *Agree to look into the matter.* If nothing else, this will get the caller to leave you alone, at least temporarily.

- *If an attorney calls you about the potential libel, refer the call to your attorney.* Libel law is full of traps for the unwary; do not assume that you can discuss a case on an attorney's turf. The attorney probably knows the territory; you do not.

- *Notify your editor or attorney at the first mention of libel.* Reporters should not attempt to resolve the problem without proper advice or counsel.

OUTLOOK: THE MEDIA AND LIBEL IN THE 1990s

The attorney Bruce Sanford, writing in *Quill* magazine, noted that a survey conducted by the Society of Professional Journalists suggested that the media face "a changing legal climate" in the 1990s.

"While the past 20 years have been marked by almost constant libel litigation, favorable libel laws and improved libel preventive measures have caused the number of newly filed libel actions to drop steadily across the country,"

Sanford wrote. "While still concerned about large damage awards, most media attorneys believe the growing pains associated with the development of libel law have at last subsided."

NEWSROOM SEARCHES

A case decided in 1978 (*Zurcher* v. *Stanford Daily*) sent shock waves through the media. In April 1971 demonstrators seized the administrative offices of the Stanford University Hospital. After peaceful efforts to persuade the intruders to leave had failed, the police rushed one of the hospital wings. They were injured by club-wielding demonstrators. Two days later a special edition of the *Stanford Daily* was published, including photos of the altercation. The next day, the Santa Clara County district attorney's office secured a warrant for an immediate search of the *Daily*'s offices for negatives, film or pictures showing the occurrences at the hospital.

The district attorney's office, in obtaining the warrant, did not contend that any members of the *Daily* staff were suspected of criminal activity. The police searched the premises but did not open locked drawers and rooms. The lower courts held that the First Amendment precludes searches of innocent third-party newspapers except in "rare circumstances" in which authorities feel certain that the materials in question would be destroyed or removed from the premises.

On May 31, 1978, however, the Supreme Court reversed the lower court ruling, holding that neither the First nor the 14th Amendment was violated by issuance of a search warrant to obtain criminal evidence reasonably believed to be at the newspaper office. Justice Byron White said that precedent cases clearly showed that the state's interest in enforcing the law "is the same, whether the third party is innocent or not." White rejected *Stanford Daily* arguments that searches of this nature would be physically disruptive, impeding publication schedules; would cause confidential news sources to dry up; would disclose internal editorial deliberations; and would lead to self-censorship by the press.

The possibility of police ransacking newsrooms suddenly became real. Under the *Stanford Daily* ruling, authorities could show up at a newspaper's front door without warning, and could legally search the premises.

Recognizing the problem created by the *Stanford Daily* ruling, President Jimmy Carter signed a bill in 1980 that, to a certain extent, offset *Stanford Daily*. The bill prohibited federal, state and local law enforcement agencies from conducting surprise newsroom searches except under exceptional circumstances.

The bill required government officials to obtain a *subpoena*—rather than a *search warrant*—when seeking information from a person who has collected it "with a purpose to disseminate to the public a newspaper, book, broadcast or other similar form of public communication." Journalists are generally pleased with the law. Subpoenas must be issued in most cases—thus giving newspapers a chance to delay on technical grounds. Fighting subpoenas has, in fact, become a major ordeal for many American newspapers.

REPORTERS AND THEIR SOURCES

BACKGROUND

Historically, reporters have guarded the identity of anonymous sources. It is theorized that once a reporter betrays a confidential source, the reporter's other anonymous contacts will soon vanish. Why, after all, would sources who want to remain unnamed give information to reporters if the sources think that they might be betrayed?

Attorneys and police have turned to reporters for information with increasing frequency. The problem is real. To date, the Supreme Court has considered only one case that focuses on *journalists' privilege*. In 1972 the court held in a fractionated opinion that the First Amendment does not provide a testimonial privilege to reporters who have witnessed a crime if they are called upon to testify before a grand jury (*Branzburg* v. *Hayes*).

THE BRANZBURG CASE

Paul Branzburg, a reporter for the *Courier-Journal* in Louisville, Ky., had witnessed illegal drug use and had written articles about it. He was subpoenaed and asked to testify before a grand jury. He refused, claiming a First Amendment privilege. Justice Byron White, who wrote the majority decision when the case was reviewed by the Supreme Court, said that to contend that it is better to write about a crime than to do something about it is absurd. White's opinion, though not well-received by the press, did provide some hope. He emphasized that official harassment of the press in an effort to disrupt the reporter's relationship with his or her sources would not be tolerated. White also said that states were free to implement statutory laws—*shield laws*—to protect reporters.

Justice Lewis F. Powell Jr., in a concurring opinion, attempted to put *Branzburg* into perspective. He said that the ruling was "limited"; courts would still be available to reporters who think that their First Amendment rights have been violated. Furthermore, he said that the press could not be annexed as an "investigative right arm" of the government or the judiciary, and if the requested testimony was "remote," news reporters could move to quash the subpoena. The information sought had to be relevant and had to go to the heart of the issue; it could not be a fishing expedition by the authorities.

Justice Potter Stewart dissented. He proposed a three-part test to be considered whenever a reporter was asked by the government to reveal confidential information. Stewart wrote:

> [I] would hold that the government must (1) show that there is probable cause to believe that the newsman has information which is clearly relevant to a specific probable violation of law; (2) demonstrate that the information sought cannot be obtained by alternative means less destructive of First Amendment rights; and (3) demonstrate a compelling and overriding interest in the information.

Dan Cowen, a public relations practitioner, gave reporters damaging information about a political candidate who was running against one of his clients. The reporters' promise not to print Cowen's name was overridden by editors, and Cowen brought suit—successfully. *(Minneapolis Star-Tribune)*

The legal scholar Todd F. Simon of Michigan State's School of Journalism noted that "the trio of tests . . . have become the basis for decisions in many of the cases that followed *Branzburg.*" Simon said that "virtually every jurisdiction now has some form of the privilege, and most use Stewart's test." Simon noted, in fact, that the privilege is nearly absolute in civil suits in which the reporter is not a party.

Because of Justice Powell's carefully worded concurring opinion and Justice Stewart's dissent, a number of state and lower federal courts have often upheld the right of news reporters to protect their sources under certain conditions. In some circumstances, however, several lower courts have not upheld the reporter's rights. Courts consider questions of testimonial privilege on a case-by-case basis.

What if news reporters "burn" their confidential sources by revealing names? Indeed, in recent years some journalists have shown an increasing tendency to disregard promises of confidentiality when they believe that the public interest demands names of sources. The U.S. Supreme Court, though, held in *Cohen* v. *Cowles Media Co.* (1991) that the First Amendment does not immunize the press from a lawsuit if it breaks a promise of confidentiality to its sources.

SHIELD LAWS

Although the Supreme Court made it plain that the First Amendment would not provide absolute protection for journalists called to testify, it did leave the door open for states to pass laws and for state courts to fashion rules that would shield reporters from testifying. More than 40 of the states have done so. Some states have relatively stringent shield laws that provide a great deal of protection, whereas others have qualified shield laws. It is important to remember, however, that even the most stringent laws probably have some loopholes.

Nebraska has one of the country's more stringent laws. The Nebraska law is designed to ensure the free flow of news and other information to the public and to protect the reporter against direct or indirect governmental restraint or sanction. The statute states that "compelling such persons to disclose a source of information or to disclose unpublished information is contrary to the public interest and inhibits the free flow of information to the public." The law protects reporters from testifying before any federal or state judicial, legislative, executive or administrative body.

No matter how ironclad shield laws appear, however, they are subject to interpretation by the judiciary. The constitutionality of most shield laws has never been contested, and even if their constitutionality were upheld, hostile judicial interpretation could strip protection from the reporter. In essence, reporters should never assume that the law will keep them out of jail.

The Arizona shield law, for example, did not provide sufficient protection for the *Arizona Republic* investigative reporter Jerry Seper. Seper had written articles saying that a wealthy Arizona liquor distributor was under investigation by the Internal Revenue Service. Presumably, Seper had obtained this confidential information from an IRS employee. Later, the IRS officially declared the liquor distributor innocent of any wrongdoing in connection with his tax returns. Lawyers for the distributor then filed suit in federal district court in Arizona against an IRS agent who they claimed had allegedly provided Seper with the confidential information. The agent named in the suit denied that he had given information to Seper; the reporter's testimony supported the denial. Attorneys for the liquor distributor then substituted an unnamed "John Doe" as the defendant.

Seper was asked to give the name of his source; he refused, citing Arizona's shield law (which was nearly half a century old) and the First Amendment. The district judge ruled that, under *Branzburg,* Seper did not have First Amendment protection. Clearly, the information sought went to the heart of the matter and was available from no other sources. The judge also ruled that, since suit was filed in federal district court, Arizona's state shield law was not applicable. Still, Seper steadfastly refused to reveal his source.

Ultimately, the liquor distributor's lawyers requested that Seper be held in contempt of court for failure to identify sources necessary to their case. At this point, Seper invoked his Fifth Amendment right against self-incrimination. (Federal law prohibits unauthorized publication of confidential tax information.) The judge, on the basis of Seper's Fifth Amendment claim, denied the request that the reporter be held in contempt of court.

Seper was fortunate, but it was not the First Amendment or the state shield law that kept him out of jail. The case clearly illustrates that reporters cannot always depend on state laws for protection.

In addition to worrying about revealing names of confidential sources during investigations of criminal wrongdoing, reporters must also face the possibility that plaintiffs, while bringing suit for libel, will seek to identify persons who supplied the information on which the story was based. In fact, shield laws in some states specifically say that protection is not extended to journalists under these circumstances. Though shield laws might not help reporters involved in libel actions, the journalists are not without protection.

In December 1970, for example, Jack Anderson's syndicated newspaper column, "Washington Merry-Go-Round," reported that the president of the United Mine Workers (UMW), Tony Boyle, and its general counsel Ed Carey had been removing boxfuls of documents from Boyle's office. Later, Carey made an official complaint to Washington police that burglars had stolen a boxful of "miscellaneous items." Because the United Mine Workers union was under investigation by the Justice Department, Carey contended that the column had, essentially, falsely accused him of obstruction of justice.

Carey brought a libel suit against Anderson and the reporter Brit Hume. Crucial to Carey's proving that Anderson and Hume had acted in "reckless disregard for the truth"—a necessary condition to collect damages—was his showing that Anderson and Hume had obtained their information from an unreliable source. The Court of Appeals for the District of Columbia reasoned that this was a heavy burden to meet and that the identity of the source was therefore critical to Carey's claim. Hume was prepared to go to jail for contempt, fully intending not to reveal his source. However, the source, a former UMW employee, voluntarily stepped forward to testify at the jury trial. This probably saved Hume from going to jail.

Circumstances were similar in another libel suit brought against Anderson and his "Merry-Go-Round" column (*Shelton* v. *Anderson*). Turner B. Shelton, a former ambassador to Nicaragua, sought damages for a column critical of his performance as a public official. Shelton claimed that several of the allegations made against him were false. As Carey had done before him, Shelton attempted to compel Anderson to reveal confidential sources who had supplied information. Anderson supplied the names of several non-confidential sources, but he refused to supply the names of sources who had been promised anonymity. The District Court for the District of Columbia reasoned that because Shelton had made no effort to question any non-confidential sources, it could hardly be concluded that the identities of unnamed sources were essential to his case. Thus Anderson was not forced to reveal the names.

It becomes apparent, then, that the flexibility of *Branzburg* can be used to protect journalists who are asked to reveal their confidential sources, particularly when the information sought is not directly relevant to the issue or if other equally valuable sources have not been tapped.

INVASION OF PRIVACY

Reporters are finding themselves increasingly involved in *invasion of privacy* suits. Perhaps this is only logical; there is a growing concern over the lack of privacy in today's technological world. Libel has been a fear of journalists for centuries, but invasion of privacy is a relatively recent problem. Samuel Warren and Louis Brandeis, in a *Harvard Law Review* article in 1890, first contended that Americans had a right to privacy—"a right to be let alone." New York was the first state to recognize a statutory right to privacy (1903), and Georgia, in 1905, was the first state to recognize a common law right.

The late Dean Prosser of the Hastings College of the Law divided the broad area of privacy into four branches:

1 Intrusion into an individual's solitude (whether a physical intrusion or an invasion by such means as electronic surveillance or eavesdropping)
2 Appropriation of a name or a likeness for commercial gain
3 Unreasonable disclosure of embarrassing private facts
4 False light (painting a false, though not necessarily defamatory, picture of a person or event)

As with libel suits, reporters have defenses available against charges of invasion of privacy. There are no solid defenses for physical intrusion (which is akin to trespassing), although the courts have recognized "newsworthiness" as a defense for post-intrusion publication. Consent, *in writing*, and newsworthiness are viable defenses for appropriation. Newsworthiness is a defense in suits brought because of the public disclosure of embarrassing private facts. Truth and actual malice are defenses in false light suits.

The four branches of privacy are best understood by examining suits brought under each branch.

BRANCH 1: INTRUSION

The intrusion branch is illustrated by a suit brought by former U.S. Sen. Thomas Dodd of Connecticut (*Dodd* v. *Pearson*). The U.S. Court of Appeals for the District of Columbia decided the case in 1969. Four of Dodd's office workers and former employees became disenchanted with the differences between the senator's public posture and his real dealings. The employees were convinced that Dodd was converting public campaign funds to private use. They considered taking their allegations to the Senate Ethics Committee or the Federal Bureau of Investigation but decided that both institutions were capable of glossing over the alleged wrongdoing. Thus, they decided to convey their concerns to the columnists Jack Anderson and the late Drew Pearson.

Anderson met with the employees; a list of 50 "questionable practices" was drawn up. Anderson said that he would need verification of the allegations. The employees then took materials from Dodd's personal files, made copies of them and replaced the original documents. The copies were turned over to Anderson. During an 18-month period in 1966 and 1967, Anderson devoted parts of more than 120 "Washington Merry-Go-Round" columns to the Dodd story. Dodd sued. He sought $5.1 million in damages for libel and invasion of privacy. It did not take the trial court long to dispose of the libel case; as a public official, Dodd would have to show actual malice to receive damages. Because the information came from the senator's own files, it was highly unlikely that he could show that Anderson and Pearson had acted in reckless disregard for the truth.

Regarding the privacy suit, brought under the intrusion branch, the court clearly distinguished between the actual physical intrusion and the subsequent publication. The Court of Appeals for the District of Columbia struck down the privacy claim against the columnists. The court said that there were two distinct elements in most intrusion cases: trespass and publication. The court said that because Pearson and Anderson had not participated personally in the theft of the documents, they could not be held liable. Publishing the information was newsworthy and thus protected. The court made it clear that journalists would be held responsible for breaking the law—in this case, for personally participating in a theft—but that they would not be held legally responsible for publishing newsworthy information turned over to them by a third party.

A similar suit brought by A. A. Dietemann against Time Inc., illustrates a potential problem for reporters. Two reporters for *Life* magazine had posed as husband and wife while visiting the private home of Dietemann, who styled himself as a "healer" and used clay, minerals and herbs in his treatments. While Dietemann was examining a lump on the breast of the woman, the other reporter was taking photos with a concealed camera. Also, the conversation was being broadcast through a hidden microphone to authorities waiting in a car. When Dietemann was later arrested for practicing medicine without a license, *Life* carried the story and published the pictures. The trial court awarded Dietemann damages for invasion of privacy as a result of the use of the concealed microphone and camera. The 9th U.S. Circuit Court affirmed in 1971. Judge Shirley Hufstedler ruled that the "First Amendment has never been construed to accord newsmen immunity from torts or crimes committed during the course of news gathering."

The *Dodd* and *Dietemann* cases show that reporters must be aware of potential legal problems when using hidden cameras or procuring documents by illegal or unethical methods. Such awareness is important in investigative reporting.

BRANCH 2: APPROPRIATION

Appropriation is a branch of privacy that should not pose much danger to reporters. Reporters are generally dealing with newsworthy items in the public domain. Stories are written to inform the public—not for the primary purpose of reaping a financial windfall at the expense of the subject. In this area of privacy, reporters for the electronic media have more to fear than reporters for the print media. In 1977 the Supreme Court held that the First Amendment did not afford a television station the privilege of filming an entire 15-second act by the entertainer Hugo Zacchini in which he was shot from a cannon into a net some 200 feet away (*Zacchini* v. *Scripps-Howard*). Justice White emphasized that filming a performer's *entire* act posed a substantial threat to the economic value of the performance. Presumably, if the television station had aired only a *portion* of the act, it would have been legally justified.

In reality, *Zacchini* was a "right of publicity" case. A right of publicity, which has evolved through the common law, entitles a person to control the exploitation of his name or likeness. The courts have been explicit in distinguishing between appropriation and right of publicity cases like *Zacchini*. Professor Todd Simon of Michigan State noted that a news organization would seldom be liable on appropriation grounds when a private figure was somehow portrayed in news coverage. For example, if a newspaper were to publish a photo of a college student buying supplies in the bookstore before the start of classes, the student would have little chance of winning an appropriation case. "Newsworthiness looks almost like a complete defense because a 'news use' is never considered a 'commercial use,'" Simon said.

BRANCH 3: EMBARRASSING PRIVATE FACTS

Reporters could be drawn into suits brought under the embarrassing-private-facts branch. This is, at best, a hazy area. Newsworthiness, as mentioned earlier, is a defense, and the courts have been relatively liberal in applying it. Essentially, the courts use as a test whether the material violates the standards of "common decency" perceived by persons of "ordinary sensibilities."

In 1942, for example, the Missouri State Supreme Court affirmed an invasion of privacy suit against *Time* magazine, which had published a photograph of a hospitalized woman who suffered from an unusual disease (*Barber* v. *Time Inc.*). Though the woman consumed huge amounts of food, she continued to lose weight. A photographer rushed uninvited into her hospital room and took pictures without her permission. *Time* published the picture and labeled her "the starving glutton." Though the common decency test is somewhat vague, reporters clearly do not have unbridled discretion to trample the innermost feelings of their subjects.

In another case brought under this branch by William James Sidis, the 2nd U.S. Circuit Court saw things differently. Sidis, a famous child prodigy during the early part of the 20th century, was featured in a *New Yorker* article in 1937. Sidis, who was graduated from Harvard College at age 16 and was recognized as a mathematical genius, brought suit on the basis of the publication. The article told of Sidis' marvelous talents but said that instead of using them, he had reverted to a private life and the occupation of clerk. The court said that, admittedly, the article deprived Sidis of the privacy for which he obviously yearned but that nevertheless he was the object of considerable interest and discussion. The court said that his right to privacy did not render off limits press scrutiny of truthful, unexaggerated aspects of his life. Though the common decency criterion is not ironclad, one can, at least on an emotional level, discern differences between *Barber* and *Sidis* v. *F-R Publishing Corp.*

BRANCH 4: FALSE LIGHT

The false-light branch has been described as a "second cousin" to libel. Suits brought under this branch are occurring with increasing frequency. The attorney Richard Schmidt told the First Amendment Survival Seminar, "Today, in many instances, we see the movement toward actions for invasion of privacy being intermingled with defamation actions. And when you get sued, you're probably going to get sued for both."

The first privacy case involving the mass media to be heard by the Supreme Court was brought under this branch (*Time Inc.* v. *Hill*). *Life* magazine reviewed a play based on the captivity by three escaped convicts of the James Hill family in their suburban Philadelphia home in 1952. *Life*'s account included pictures of the actors in the house where the incident had taken place but from which the Hill family had moved. The play, which elevated the Hill family to the role of heroes, was adapted from a novel written about the incident. The novel added some fictionalized violence to a situation that actually had been somewhat docile, considering the circumstances. Hill brought suit for invasion of privacy. The Supreme Court held in 1967 that for a plaintiff to recover damages under the false-light privacy branch, he or she would have to prove actual malice. The *Life* article and photographs were newsworthy; they focused on the premiere of the play. Despite the lapse of time and fictionalization of the violence, Hill chose not to pursue the suit further; actual malice would have been difficult to show.

One plaintiff, however, was able to prove actual malice. In *Cantrell v. Forest City Publishing* (1974), a woman brought suit on the basis of an article in the *Cleveland Plain Dealer* that exaggerated the poverty of her family. Her husband had been killed in a bridge collapse a year earlier, and the reporter was doing a follow-up story. In an apparent effort to strengthen his story, the reporter implied that he had seen and talked to the widow. She was not, however, present when he visited her house. The court concluded that the reporter had written "calculated falsehoods" and had, indeed, acted in reckless disregard for the truth.

Reporters should guard against fictionalization techniques or attempts to exaggerate the significance of a story. Indeed, reporters must constantly consider the privacy ramifications of stories on which they are working.

INFLICTION OF EMOTIONAL DISTRESS

Professor George E. Stevens wrote in the *Newspaper Research Journal* that plaintiffs sometimes bring suits not just for one civil wrong but for two—such as libel and privacy. He noted a "new wrinkle": "Some plaintiffs are alleging an intentional or a negligent infliction of emotional distress along with other things"—such as false-light invasion of privacy.

A Supreme Court opinion handed down in 1988, however, will probably curb allegations of intentional infliction of emotional distress. The court held that the First Amendment prohibits public figures and officials from recovering damages for the tort absent a showing that the publication contained a false statement of fact that was made with actual malice. Very simply, the justices decided unanimously that emotional-distress lawsuits should be as difficult to win as libel suits when brought by public persons.

Jerry Falwell—a minister who was the founder and president of Moral Majority—had brought suit against *Hustler* magazine and its publisher, Larry Flynt, for invasion of privacy, libel and intentional infliction of emotional distress. Falwell based his suit on an advertisement that was published on the inside front cover of an issue that contained an alleged "interview" with the minister about his "first time." The *Hustler* parody portrayed Falwell and his mother as drunk and immoral. The advertisement, which contained the disclaimer "ad parody—not to be taken seriously," depicted the minister and his mother "during a drunken incestuous rendezvous . . . in an outhouse."

Not surprisingly, Falwell was outraged. He filed suit, seeking $45 million in damages. A federal jury rejected his libel and privacy claims, but did award him $200,000 in damages on the emotional-distress allegations. The 4th U.S. Circuit Court of Appeals upheld the award. The Supreme Court, however, reversed it.

Falwell had contended that the *Hustler* ad was so outrageous that it should have been distinguished from traditional political cartoons. Chief Justice William Rehnquist, who wrote the opinion, conceded that the parody was "at best a distant cousin of the political cartoons . . . and a rather poor relation at that." However, he wrote that "in the world of debate about public affairs, many things done with motives that are less than admirable are protected by the First Amendment."

The Associated Press quoted Paul McMasters, speaking for the Society of Professional Journalists; and Falwell, who reacted to the ruling.

McMasters was quoted as saying, "It's easy to stand up for nice talk from nice people, but the First Amendment protects all speech, even the outrageous."

Falwell said: "No sleaze merchant like Larry Flynt should be able to use the First Amendment as an excuse for maliciously and dishonestly attacking public figures. I'm sure the justices were holding their noses while making the ruling."

FAIR TRIAL VERSUS FREE PRESS

BACKGROUND: AN ONGOING CONFLICT

Cases involving the inherent conflict between the First Amendment rights of the press to report and the Sixth Amendment rights of the accused to a speedy and public trial by an impartial jury have surfaced with regularity during the past three decades. Such cases represent an ever-present dilemma. As early as 1807, Chief Justice John Marshall was confronted with the responsibility of seeing that Aaron Burr was not deprived of his constitutional rights during a treason trial that gained widespread public attention.

Journalists have long contended that the press is entitled to cover litigation. Reporters recognize the Sixth Amendment rights of defendants but argue that these rights can be maintained without trampling on the freedom to report. *Procedural safeguards* such as change of venue (changing the location of a trial), change of venire (transporting jurors in from another jurisdiction), sequestering jurors (keeping them away from news reports) and effective voir dire examination (questioning potential jurors to determine if they have prejudicial feelings about one of the parties) are available to judges who wish to ensure that defendants are not deprived of the judicial serenity and fairness to which they are constitutionally entitled.

Though procedural safeguards are available, they are sometimes not used. In fairness to the judiciary, however, publicity for some particularly notorious trials has been so prejudicial and so pervasive that the safeguards might not have provided sufficient protection. This was evident in some cases during the early 1960s. In *Irvin* v. *Dowd* (1961), the Supreme Court, for the first time in history, reversed and remanded a state criminal conviction because of intense prejudicial publicity. The publicity barrage leveled at Leslie Irvin in Evansville, Ind., was so intense—before Irvin had been found guilty, it even included roving man-on-the-street interviews by a radio station to determine what kind of punishment he should receive—that of 430 potential jurors examined under voir dire, about 85 percent said that they believed Irvin was guilty.

Two years later, the court considered a case in which a Lake Charles, La., station had televised, complete with sound, a sheriff securing a confession from a man accused of murder (*Rideau* v. *Louisiana*). The height of press irresponsibility, however, probably came in the trial of Dr. Sam Sheppard, who had been accused of murdering his wife (*Sheppard* v. *Maxwell*, 1966). His trial was later described by the Supreme Court as a "carnival" that rendered virtually impossible any private communication between the defendant and his attorney. Reporters jammed the 26- by 48-foot Ohio courtroom. Only 14 seats were reserved for family members. Seven of the 12 jurors had one or more Cleveland newspapers delivered to their homes; local papers cried for "justice" in front-page editorials. Not surprisingly, the high court reversed and remanded the case, contending that "bedlam reigned at the courthouse."

BALANCING CONFLICTING RIGHTS: GUIDELINES FOR THE BAR AND THE PRESS

Cases such as these that focused on media irresponsibility at its crudest brought the issue to the forefront. Shortly after *Sheppard*, the American Bar Association's Advisory Committee on Fair Trial and Free Press released its findings. The committee sought to provide guidelines that would balance the conflicting constitutional rights. Though the report was aimed primarily at lawyers, law enforcement officers and judges, it had an indirect effect on the press. Also, the committee recommended that judges use the contempt power against reporters who communicate information that could be damaging to the accused.

Several states, including Nebraska, used the ABA report as a model as lawyers, judges and journalists put their heads together in an attempt to develop guidelines for the coverage of litigation.

The Nebraska guidelines, which are drawn from the ABA report, are representative of other states. The guidelines are included in a booklet published by the Nebraska Press Association and the Nebraska Broadcasters Association.

Portions of the Nebraska Bar–Press guidelines follow:

These voluntary guidelines reflect standards which bar and news media representatives believe are a reasonable means of accommodating, on a voluntary basis, the correlative constitutional rights of free speech and free press with the right of an accused to a fair trial. They are not intended to prevent the news media from inquiring into and reporting on the integrity, fairness, efficiency and effectiveness of law enforcement, the administration of justice, or political or governmental questions whenever involved in the judicial process.

As a voluntary code, these guidelines do not necessarily reflect in all respects what the members of the bar or the news media believe would be permitted or required by law.

Information Generally Appropriate for Disclosure, Reporting

Generally, it is appropriate to disclose and report the following information:

(1) The arrested person's name, age, residence, employment, marital status and similar biographical information.

(2) The charge, its text, any amendments thereto, and, if applicable, the identity of the complainant.

(3) The amount or conditions of bail.

(4) The identity of and biographical information concerning the complaining party and victim, and if a death is involved, the apparent cause of death unless it appears that the cause of death may be a contested issue.

(5) The identity of the investigating and arresting agencies and the length of the investigation.

(6) The circumstances of arrest, including time, place, resistance, pursuit, possession of and all weapons used, and a description of the items seized at the time of arrest. It is appropriate to disclose and report at the time of seizure the description of physical evidence subsequently seized other than a confession, admission or statement. It is appropriate to disclose and report the subsequent finding of weapons, bodies, contraband, stolen property and similar physical items if, in view of the time and other circumstances, such disclosure and reporting are not likely to interfere with a fair trial.

(7) Information disclosed by the public records, including all testimony and other evidence adduced at the trial.

Information Generally Not Appropriate for Disclosure, Reporting

Generally, it is not appropriate to disclose or report the following information because of the risk of prejudice to the right of an accused to a fair trial:

(1) The existence or contents of any confession, admission or statement given by the accused, except it may be stated that the accused denies the charges made against him. This paragraph is not intended to apply to statements made by the accused to representatives of the news media or to the public.

(2) Opinions concerning the guilt, the innocence or the character of the accused.

(3) Statements predicting or influencing the outcome of the trial.

(4) Results of any examination or tests or the accused's refusal or failure to submit to an examination or test.

(5) Statements or opinions concerning the credibility or anticipated testimony of prospective witnesses.

(6) Statements made in the judicial proceedings outside the presence of the jury relating to confessions or other matters which, if reported, would likely interfere with a fair trial.

Lawyers and law enforcement personnel should not volunteer their prior criminal records of an accused except to aid in his apprehension or to warn the public of any dangers he presents. The news media can obtain prior criminal records from the public records of the courts, police agencies and other governmental agencies and from their own files. The news media acknowledge, however, that publication or broadcast of an individual's criminal record can be prejudicial, and its publication or broadcast should be considered very carefully, particularly after the filing of formal charges and as the time of the trial approaches, and such publication or broadcast should generally be avoided because readers, viewers and listeners are potential jurors and an accused is presumed innocent until proven guilty.

PRESS COVERAGE OF TRIALS

Supreme Court Decisions

Another major case involving the issue of fair trial versus free press reached the Supreme Court in 1975. Jack Murphy—who was sometimes referred to as "Murph the Surf"—was convicted in Dade County, Fla., of breaking and entering. He had a criminal background. The Florida press gave substantial coverage to his arrest and trial. Murphy sought a reversal on the basis of prejudicial publicity. The Supreme Court refused, emphasizing that prejudicial publicity is not necessarily synonymous with pervasive publicity. The majority distinguished *Murphy* from *Irvin, Rideau* and *Sheppard*. In *Murphy,* though the media coverage had been extensive, it had been responsible. Voir dire examination did not reveal pervasive hostility.

A grave threat to press coverage of criminal trials came in the autumn of 1975 when a Nebraska judge issued a *gag order*—a protective order—prohibiting the press from publishing some information from a public murder trial (*Nebraska Press* v. *Stuart*). The Reporters Committee for Freedom of the Press estimated that there had been 174 cases involving gag orders between 1967 and 1975, with 62 of the instances occurring in 1975.

Obviously, the controversy was ripe for adjudication. Among other things, a Nebraska district county judge, Hugh Stuart, prohibited the press from reporting contents of a confession that had been mentioned in open court, statements made by the accused to others, medical testimony that had been introduced at the preliminary hearing and the identity of sexual assault victims. (Six members of the Henry Kellie family of Sutherland, Neb., had been killed; some were assaulted sexually.) In addition, Stuart gagged the press from reporting the contents of the gag.

The Supreme Court in 1976 reversed the ruling, holding that though the First Amendment is not absolute, barriers to a constitutional prior restraint on the press are high. A "heavy burden" would have to be met to justify the issuance of a prior restraint on the press, and in this instance, that heavy burden had not been met. Justice Burger, in his majority opinion, criticized the trial judge for not exploring available procedural safeguards before resorting to a gag order. The majority conceded, however, that under the most extreme circumstances, some gag orders could conceivably be upheld as constitutional. In a concurring opinion, Justice William Brennan said that prior restraint could never be placed on the press in covering litigation.

Because *Nebraska Press* did not slam the door on the possibility of the press's sometimes being excluded from coverage of litigation, it was only logical that future cases would develop. In 1979 the Supreme Court held that the Sixth Amendment is for the benefit of the defendant—not the media (*Gannett* v. *DePasquale*), in a case which was such a debacle that the court was forced to correct itself only 12 months later. The majority said that the Constitution does not give the press an "affirmative right" of access to criminal trials. In a concurring opinion, Justice Burger noted that the ruling applied only to pretrial hearings. Justice William Rehnquist, however, disagreed. In his concurring opinion, he said that it applied to all stages of a public trial. Confusion prevailed. After the decision, several justices took contrasting stances during public speeches about what the decision meant. Critics of the decision contended that lower court judges would take advantage of the uncertainty of the ruling and close trials, as well as preliminary hearings, without substantial reason to believe that the press would deprive the defendant of the right to receive a fair trial.

Fortunately for the press, a case that could clarify the *DePasquale* ruling was already making its way up through the judicial system. Reporters had been denied access to a murder trial in Virginia upon the request of the defense attorney. As had been the case in *DePasquale,* the reporters present did not object to the closure. A few hours later, however, attorneys for the newspaper asked that the order be vacated. The court refused. Though the case was technically moot, the Supreme Court agreed to hear it (*Richmond Newspapers Inc.* v. *Virginia*). Exactly one year to the day after *DePasquale,* the court held that the Virginia closure was not proper. The majority said that the First Amendment guarantees the right to attend public trials, absent "overriding considerations." The 7–1 decision helped clarify the murky waters left by *DePasquale.* Though it had long been assumed, *Richmond Newspapers* was the first formal articulation by the court that the press had a right of access under the First Amendment to gather news at public trials.

In 1984, in *Press-Enterprise Co.* v. *Riverside County Superior Court,* the Supreme Court recognized the right of the public and the media to attend the voir dire examination of potential jurors. Two years later, in a case bearing the same name, the court said that, absent overriding considerations, the public and the press enjoy a First Amendment right to attend pretrial hearings. When considered in tandem, these cases certainly bring into question the continued applicability of *Gannett.* For all practical purposes, barring a "substantial probability that the defendant's right to a fair trial will be prejudiced by publicity," the public and the press enjoy an affirmative right of access to attend pretrial proceedings as well as trials.

Though the court made it clear in *Richmond Newspapers* and in both *Press-Enterprise* cases that reporters could be banned from covering public litigation only in the most extreme circumstances and that a heavy burden would be placed on the person requesting a closure to show that the defendant would otherwise be deprived of fair proceedings, reporters undoubtedly will continue to be confronted with similar situations. The rulings, however, should make judges hesitant to close public proceedings.

Closed Trials: A Statement of Objection for Reporters

In the event that a proceeding is ordered closed, several media organizations and newspapers have prepared cards for their reporters to carry. Printed on each card is a brief statement of objection that the reporter is urged to read for the court record. The Gannett group card reads:

> Your honor, I am _____, a reporter for _____, and I would like to object on behalf of my employer and the public to this proposed closing. Our attorney is prepared to make a number of arguments against closings such as this one and we respectfully ask the Court for a hearing on these issues. I believe our attorney can be here relatively quickly for the Court's convenience and he will be able to demonstrate that closure in this case will violate the First Amendment, and possibly state statutory and constitutional provisions as well. I cannot make the arguments myself, but our attorney can point out several issues for your consideration. If it pleases the Court, we request the opportunity to be heard through Counsel.

Time is clearly important to any reporter involved in closed proceedings. Editors and attorneys should be notified promptly. It is also important that reporters attempt to state on the record that they object to the closure. Of course, reporters do not have a right of access to all judicial proceedings. Grand jury proceedings and juvenile hearings are examples of judicial situations from which the press is normally barred.

Electronic Coverage in Courtrooms

As was emphasized in Chapter 26, television news teams constantly strive to coordinate pictures with words. In 1981 the Supreme Court handed down a decision that pleased broadcast journalists who had long ago advocated the televising of state court proceedings. The question that faced the court was whether, consistent with constitutional guarantees, a state could provide for radio, television and still photographic coverage of a criminal trial for public broadcast—even when the accused objected.

This was not an overnight issue. In 1937 the American Bar Association had passed Canon 35—a "suggestive code"—that banned cameras in state courtrooms. In 1952 an amendment was approved that included television cameras in the ban. Most states adopted the rationale of Canon 35. In 1972 the Code of Judicial Conduct replaced the Canons of Judicial Ethics, and Canon 35 was replaced by Section 3A(7). Rule 53 of the Federal Rules of Criminal Procedure—enacted in 1946—effectively banned cameras in federal courtrooms.

By the mid-1970s, however, some states had launched movements to allow camera coverage of state court proceedings. In 1978 a *Washington Post* survey showed that 56 percent of the lawyers, state supreme court justices and law professors favored electronic coverage of trials. About 31 percent disapproved; 13 percent were uncertain.

The only previous time the Supreme Court had considered the camera issue was in 1965 (*Estes* v. *Texas*). In that case, it held that Billy Sol Estes, who had been charged with theft, swindling and embezzlement involving the federal government, had been deprived of a fair trial because of cumbersome camera coverage of portions of it. The decision, of course, was based on the state of the technology at that time. Justice Tom Clark, who wrote the majority opinion, said that the cameras had an impact on the jurors, the quality of the testimony and the defendants. He also said that the cameras placed additional responsibilities on the judge to control the courtroom. In a concurring opinion, however, Justice John Marshall Harlan said that the door should be left open for future camera coverage as the technology became sufficiently sophisticated.

When the Supreme Court considered the question of the constitutionality of cameras in state courtrooms in January 1981, more than 20 states were experimenting or had already experimented with them.

In July 1977 two Miami Beach policemen, Noel Chandler and Robert Granger, were charged in Florida with conspiracy to commit burglary, grand larceny and possession of burglary tools. The case was widely publicized.

Chandler and Granger's counsel sought to ban electronic coverage of the trial. The judge refused. A small portion of the proceedings was broadcast. The jury returned a guilty verdict on all counts. Chandler and Granger appealed, claiming that because of the television coverage, they had been denied a fair and impartial trial. The lower courts said that they had not.

The Supreme Court voted 8–0 to affirm the lower courts. Chief Justice Warren Burger said that *Estes* did not announce a constitutional rule that all photo, radio and television coverage of criminal trials was inherently a denial of due process. Burger said, "It does not stand as an absolute ban on state experimentation with an evolving technology, which in terms of modes of mass communication, was in its relative infancy in 1964, and is, even now, in a state of continuing change."

Burger said that any criminal case "that generates a great deal of publicity presents some risks that the publicity may compromise the right of the defendant to a fair trial." Trial courts would have to be "especially vigilant to guard against any impairment of the defendant's right." Still, an "absolute ban" on camera coverage could not be justified "simply because there is a danger that, in some cases, prejudicial broadcast accounts . . . may impair the ability of jurors to decide the issue of guilt or innocence uninfluenced by extraneous matter."

Burger also talked about the Florida program. The chief justice seemed pleased with the safeguards built into it, which were similar to those of other states. The Florida guidelines provided the following: Only one television camera and technician were allowed in the courtroom; coverage had to be pooled; there could be no artificial lighting; equipment had to be placed in fixed positions; videotaping equipment had to be remote from the courtroom; film could not be changed when the court was in session; the jury could not be filmed; the judge had sole discretion to exclude coverage of certain witnesses; and the judge had discretionary power to forbid coverage whenever satisfied that it could have a "deleterious effect on the paramount right of the defendant to a fair trial."

Electronic media journalists generally regarded the *Chandler* decision as a much-deserved victory. The American Bar Association's House of Delegates in August 1982 also reacted in a positive way and repealed Section 3A(7), passed in 1972. Undoubtedly more and more states will permit cameras, microphones and recorders on an experimental or permanent basis. When the delegates repealed the section, approximately 38 states were already experimenting with electronic coverage of trials or had adopted it on a permanent basis. Today, only five states and the District of Columbia do not allow cameras in courtrooms. In 1991, several federal courts decided to permit electronic coverage of proceedings as part of a three-year experiment authorized by the U.S. Judicial Conference.

Inquiries from a reporter prompted the tennis player Arthur Ashe to hastily call a press conference to announce that he had AIDS. This episode touched off a debate over the limits of the "public's right to know."
(AP/Wide World Photos)

Ethics: Responsibility to Society

29

The First Amendment gives journalists the freedom to report and to edit, but it does not mandate responsibility in return. Society, however, is calling for journalistic accountability. In turn, national journalism organizations, individual news media and journalists have taken steps to establish acceptable codes of behavior.

Media critics constantly evaluate the role of the press as an American institution. Privately owned newspapers have understandably resisted any type of governmental control, but during recent decades critics of the press have increasingly called for codes of ethics and greater professionalism on the part of reporters.

A THEORY OF PRESS SYSTEMS

Reporters must recognize that today's society expects them to behave responsibly. This expectation fits in with the "social responsibility" theory outlined by Theodore Peterson in "Four Theories of the Press," a book he wrote more than three decades ago with Wilbur Schramm and Fred S. Siebert. Peterson wrote that "freedom carries concomitant obligations; and the press, which enjoys a privileged position under our government, is obliged to be responsible to society for carrying out certain essential functions of mass communications."

Siebert, Peterson and Schramm grouped the press systems of the world under four headings: authoritarian, Soviet Communist (which, because of its inapplicability to the American system, will not be discussed here), libertarian and social responsibility.

AUTHORITARIAN SYSTEM

In an *authoritarian system*, which is the oldest of the four, criticism of the government is not tolerated. Although most newspapers are privately owned, their content is controlled by the state through licensing or the issuance of patents. If newspapers want to be unceremoniously shut down, they criticize the government. If newspapers want to stay in business, they print what the state wants them to print. Some colonial American newspaper editors went along with the system; they were content to publish innocuous newspapers that did not offend the government or check on it. Other, more courageous colonial American journalists sought to escape suppression under the authoritarian system.

LIBERTARIAN SYSTEM

As authoritarian controls on the press were resisted, the *libertarian system* developed. Under this philosophy, humans are rational thinking beings capable of separating truth from falsehood, good from evil. Thus, newspapers must provide information on a variety of topics—particularly government—so that citizens are in a position to make enlightened decisions. This romantic concept flourished during the early 1800s and continued into the 20th century.

As might have been expected, the libertarian philosophy opened the door for unscrupulous reporters to be blatantly irresponsible. Some 19th-century American newspapers were particularly vicious. They were, however, regarded as the primary instrument for checking on the government and its officials.

SOCIAL RESPONSIBILITY THEORY

635

CHAPTER 29
ETHICS:
RESPONSIBILITY
TO SOCIETY

In reaction to perceived shortcomings of the press under the libertarian system, the Commission on Freedom of the Press was formed shortly after World War II. Made up of scholars and philosophers, it was particularly concerned about the shrinking newspaper marketplace (the number of daily newspapers had been declining since shortly after the turn of the century) and the accompanying loss of potential philosophies. The commission said that the press should exercise more responsibility; it should make a concerted effort to discuss divergent views, even if the views were not compatible with those of management. The commission said that it was the responsibility of the press not only to present diverse viewpoints but also to interpret them responsibly.

What has been called the *social responsibility theory* of the press emerged from the commission's report. According to this philosophy, everyone who wants to express views should be given access to the press, which is bound by professional ethics. Community opinion helps to keep the press in check. And if the press fails to live up to its obligations of social responsibility, the government can step in to ensure public service.

In exploring the evolution of the social responsibility theory, Peterson wrote:

> A rather considerable fraction of articulate Americans began to demand certain standards of performance from the press. . . . Chiefly of their own volition, publishers began to link responsibility with freedom. They formulated codes of ethical behavior, and they operated their media with some concern for the public good—the public good as they regarded it, at least.

Today's reporters, then, find themselves working in a libertarian system that is making increasingly strong demands for journalistic responsibility. The challenge is formidable.

The courts, however, have not been willing to impose a standard of responsibility on the press. In 1974 Chief Justice Warren Burger wrote in a court opinion: "A responsible press is an undoubtedly desirable goal, but press responsibility is not mandated by the Constitution and like so many virtues it cannot be legislated. . . . A newspaper is more than a passive receptacle or conduit for news, comment and advertising. The choice of material to go into a newspaper . . . constitutes the exercise of editorial control and judgment."

THE MEDIA AND THE PUBLIC

CRITICISM OF THE PRESS

Americans have grown increasingly outspoken in their criticism of perceived irresponsibility on the part of the news media. A national opinion poll conducted by the Public Agenda Foundation showed that the majority of Americans surveyed support laws requiring fairness in newspaper coverage of controversial stories or political races.

The message to the media is clear: society is demanding responsibility. In an article published in *Editor & Publisher*, the pollster George Gallup wrote: "The press in America is operating in an environment of public opinion that is increasingly indifferent—and to some extent hostile—to the cause of a free press in America."

Many Americans feel that journalists should exercise greater restraint in choosing stories to publish or to air. A Gallup poll showed that Americans think the media "exaggerate the news in the interest of making headlines and selling newspapers," and that the media "rush to print without first making sure all facts are correct."

Example: The Janet Cooke Episode

A dramatic episode at one of the most powerful newspapers in the United States seemed to confirm these fears. This incident, which received widespread public attention, brought concerns about journalistic excesses to the forefront.

When readers opened *The Washington Post* on Sunday morning, Sept. 28, 1980, they saw several solid, hard news stories on the front page. Most eyes, though, probably focused on a story accompanied by artwork that showed a needle piercing the thin arm of a small youngster. The all-capitals hammer headline read: "JIMMY'S WORLD." The main headline read: "8-Year-Old Heroin Addict Lives for a Fix."

The story carried the byline of Janet Cooke, a *Post* staff writer who was in her mid-20s. The lead was compelling:

> Jimmy is 8 years old and a third-generation heroin addict, a precocious little boy with sandy hair, velvety brown eyes and needle marks freckling the baby-smooth skin of his thin brown arms.

This was powerful stuff.

Miss Cooke went on to describe the "comfortably furnished home in Southeast Washington" where Jimmy lived with his mother, Andrea; and her lover, Ron. The story said that every day someone "fires up Jimmy, plunging a needle into his bony arm, sending the fourth grader into a hypnotic nod."

The story contained direct quotations from Ron and Andrea. The quotations were vivid: "I let him snort a little and, damn, the little dude really did get off," Ron was quoted as saying.

Interspersed with several direct quotations by Jimmy, Andrea and Ron were authoritative facts about the growing heroin problem in the District of Columbia; information from medical experts on the increase in the number of deaths from heroin overdoses in the district; and opinions of a social worker about the family structure of homes like Jimmy's. Names and titles of authorities were used.

The story drew to a powerful conclusion. It described Ron sliding a needle "into the boy's soft skin like a straw pushed into the center of a freshly baked cake." It ended with a direct quotation from Ron: "Pretty soon, man, you got to learn how to do this for yourself."

Before the story was published, Cooke told her editors that Jimmy existed, as did his mother and her boyfriend, but that she could not use their real names. In fact, she said that the boyfriend had threatened her life if she told anyone—and that included her editors—their real identities. Editors at the *Post* agreed to preserve their anonymity.

After publication, Washington, D.C., police tried to find Jimmy. Two weeks later, they gave up. Police Chief Burtell Jefferson was convinced that "Jimmy" did not exist. Skepticism about the story spread beyond city officials; several reporters—including Cooke's roommate—and editors at the *Post* also had doubts.

Despite these doubts about the authenticity of the article, it won a Pulitzer Prize.

Before Cooke could bask in Pulitzer glory, however, her world started to shatter. The biography she had given the *Post* said that she was a magna cum laude graduate of Vassar and that she had a master's degree from the University of Toledo. Vassar officials told the *Post* that she was not a graduate; staffers at The Associated Press in Toledo, making a routine check, found that Cooke did not have a master's degree—she had only a bachelor's degree—from the university there.

When alerted to these inaccuracies, *Post* editors started to fidget about the veracity of "Jimmy." Cooke ultimately admitted that Jimmy did not exist, that he was a composite of several drug users.

The *Post* carried a front-page story saying that the Pulitzer Prize Committee had withdrawn its feature-writing prize after Cooke "had admitted that her award-winning story was a fabrication." The story quoted the *Post* executive editor Benjamin Bradlee:

> "It is a tragedy that someone as talented and promising as Janet Cooke, with everything going for her, felt that she had to falsify the facts. The credibility of a newspaper is its most precious asset, and it depends almost entirely on the integrity of its reporters. When that integrity is questioned and found wanting, the wounds are grievous, and there is nothing to do but come clean with our readers, apologize to the Advisory Board of the Pulitzer Prizes and begin immediately on the uphill task of regaining our credibility. This we are doing."

Bradlee assigned the *Post*'s ombudsman, Bill Green, to write an account of how "Jimmy's World" came about. An *ombudsman* is a "middle person"—a theoretically objective employee of the newspaper—who listens to complaints from readers and, when they are justified, passes them on to the appropriate reporters or editors.

Green responded with a series of articles that filled nearly four full pages in a Sunday edition. Green interviewed 47 people (Cooke was not one of them) and described "the failure of a system that, in another industry, might be called 'quality control.' On newspapers, it is called editing." Green found that "Jimmy's World" made its way "through the cycle of news reporting and editing like an alien creature, unimpeded by ordinary security devices."

The ombudsman mentioned a newsroom "mythology" that leads young reporters to think that Watergate blockbusters are routine occurrences and that reporters are under heavy pressure to produce front-page copy. Green quoted Lewis Simons of the *Post*'s metro staff, who said: "Pressures are so great to produce, to go beyond excellence to the 'holy s——' story. Everyone knows that's what the editors want. The pressure is to get the incredible story, the extraordinary story."

The Gallup Organization conducted a poll for *Newsweek* magazine shortly after the Cooke episode. When asked whether this hoax was an isolated incident, 33 percent of the respondents said that reporters "often make things up."

Editor & Publisher quoted Chuck Thomas, executive editor of the *Ventura County* (Calif.) *Star-Free Press,* who wrote that it was the " 'I've Got a Secret' school of journalism inspired by Watergate that led to the ultimate anonymous quote—an entire story fabricated . . . and published."

The Cooke episode—possibly as much as any other journalistic occurrence in recent years—drew national attention to the broad issue of press responsibility. But the media have been criticized for more than fictionalization and overuse of anonymous sources. Among other things, they have also been accused of sensationalism, lack of compassion for their subjects and an inability to report objectively and accurately.

THE PRESS RESPONDS

Many newspapers have looked inward to determine, address and find solutions to the shortcomings for which they have been criticized. Some have appointed ombudsmen to see that readers' complaints are acted upon. A few metropolitan newspapers, such as the *Los Angeles Times,* have hired *media critics*—reporters who write stories about the strengths, the weaknesses and the trends of daily media coverage.

Media Critics

David Shaw, a national press reporter, has been the media critic for the *Los Angeles Times* since 1974. Shaw, who was a general assignment reporter, was asked by then-editor William H. Thomas to write in "exhaustive fashion" about the American press and the *Times.* Shaw was somewhat unsure of his turf.

But Thomas quickly cleared the air. In his book, "Journalism Today," Shaw wrote that Thomas told him that "the one thing the press covers more poorly today than anything else is the press." Shaw paraphrased Thomas: "We don't tell our readers what we do or how we do it. We don't admit our mistakes unless we're virtually forced to under threat of court action or public embarrassment. We make no attempt to explain our problems, our decisions, our fallibilities, our procedures." Thomas wanted the media critic to confront these issues directly.

Shaw wrote that his job was unique—he was to function neither as beat reporter nor as ombudsman. Thomas wanted him "to provide long, thoughtful overviews on broad issues confronting the press today, to analyze, criticize and make value judgments, to treat my own newspaper as I would any other."

Shaw's pieces are not always greeted with enthusiasm by fellow journalists who come under scrutiny, but the *Times* has been a pacesetter in media introspection.

Ombudsmen

The Washington Post has been a leader in the use of ombudsmen. Most newspapers that have ombudsmen instruct reporters and editors to respond to, not ignore, complaints or suggestions forwarded by the ombudsman. These responses take several forms—argument, agreement, disagreement, rebuttal, frustration or even anger—but the reporters and the editors must respond to the independent positions of the ombudsman. To establish rapport with these reporters and editors and to gain their respect, each ombudsman must be scrupulously fair and unbiased. It is not an easy job.

Indeed, *Editor & Publisher* noted that staffers at the *Hartford* (Conn.) *Courant* once used a photo of the newspaper's ombudsman as a dart board. The magazine quoted the ombudsman, Henry McNulty: "I think they meant it as a joke—at least I hope they did."

Naturally, friction sometimes exists between the ombudsman and the staff. In fact, some editors question the need for ombudsmen. Kent Lauer of Oklahoma State University, who surveyed 68 editors of large-circulation dailies that do not employ ombudsmen, presented his results at the 1989 annual meeting of the Organization of News Ombudsmen. He reported that about 65 percent of the editors agreed that an ombudsman's salary could be better spent on other newsroom needs.

Editor & Publisher quoted some of the respondents to Lauer's survey. For example, Ralph Langer, the executive editor of the *Dallas Morning News*, wrote: "I do not believe that an ombudsman is necessary or even desirable at a well-edited, well-managed newspaper. I believe the top editors are the reader's representatives."

Editor & Publisher conducted its own informal survey of the country's ombudsmen. Most said that they were reasonably well received in their newsrooms. The magazine quoted the *Washington Post* ombudsman Dick Harwood: "If I were disliked for doing poor work it would bother me. If I'm doing good work I'm not bothered in the slightest. It is not my perception that I am operating in a hostile environment."

The *Post* created the position of ombudsman in 1970—one year after *The Courier-Journal* in Louisville, Ky., did. Today about 30 dailies have full-time ombudsmen.

Robert J. McCloskey, a retired ambassador who for 10 years was the State Department's press spokesman, is a former ombudsman at the *Post*. According to McCloskey, an ombudsman can funnel complaints primarily in three ways: (1) go directly to the editor or reporter involved, say that an issue has been raised that should be considered and pose a possible solution; (2) write memos, which are distributed to senior editors and the publisher, outlining complaints and possible solutions; or (3) write a column outlining shortcomings and posing solutions. The column is published.

THE ETHICS OF JOURNALISM

Professors John Merrill of Louisiana State University and Ralph D. Barney of Brigham Young University, noting that journalistic ethics had received scant attention in the literature between the 1930s and the early 1970s, decided to edit a book of readings. The book, which they titled "Ethics and the Press," was published in 1975 and featured a variety of ethical topics.

Merrill said that the resurging interest in journalistic ethics at that time was a result of increasing criticism of press excesses such as leak journalism—where anonymous sources provide presumably confidential information to reporters. "A better informed, more critical, more skeptical population began to question many of the things the press does," Merrill said. "Before this time, the general public was more or less naive and trusting of the press."

Merrill put the issue of journalistic ethics into perspective in another of his books, "The Imperative of Freedom." He wrote:

> Ethics is that branch of philosophy that helps journalists determine what is right to do in their journalism; it is very much a normative science of conduct. Ethics has to do with "self-legislation" and "self-enforcement"; although it is, of course, related to law, it is of a different nature. Although law quite often stems from the ethical values of a society at a certain time (i.e., law is often reflective of ethics), law is something that is socially determined and socially enforced. Ethics, on the other hand, is personally determined and personally enforced—or should be. Ethics should provide the journalist certain basic principles or standards by which he can judge actions to be right or wrong, good or bad, responsible or irresponsible.
>
> It has always been difficult to discuss ethics; law is much easier, for what is legal is a matter of law. What is ethical transcends law, for many actions are legal, but not ethical. And there are no "ethical codebooks" to consult in order to settle ethical disputes. Ethics is primarily personal; law is primarily social. Even though the area of journalistic ethics is swampy and firm footing is difficult . . . , there are solid spots which the person may use in his trek across the difficult landscape of life.
>
> First of all, it is well to establish that ethics deals with voluntary actions. If a journalist has no control over his decisions or actions, then there is no need to talk of ethics. What are voluntary actions? Those which a journalist could have done differently had he wished. Sometimes journalists, like others, try to excuse their wrong actions by saying that these actions were not personally chosen but assigned to them—or otherwise forced on them—by editors or other superiors. Such coercion may indeed occur in some situations (such as a dictatorial press system) where the consequences to the journalist going against an order may be dire. But for an American journalist not to be able to "will" his journalistic actions—at least at the present time—is unthinkable; if he says that he is not able and that he "has to" do this-or-that, he is only exhibiting his ethical weaknesses and inauthenticity.
>
> The journalist who is concerned with ethics—with the quality of his actions—is, of course, one who wishes to be virtuous.

Merrill once said that there is often no general agreement on what is right or what is wrong. "It always boils down to an individual journalistic concept," he said. "In life, a journalist who believes that anything goes to get a story—that the ends justify the means—will apply that concept in journalism. Some

A photograph showing the body of a worker killed in a construction accident would certainly raise ethical concerns in a newsroom. Should such a picture be published? *(Photo by Irwin Daugherty)*

people, for example, believe that it is ethical to surreptitiously tape an interview; this is a personal belief. There are others, however, who believe that it is dishonest because it is not being frank or forthright with the source. Ultimately, it boils down to personal ethics—personal values applied to the work of journalism."

CODES OF ETHICS

As the growing concern about media ethics and responsibility gathered steam in the 1970s, The Associated Press Managing Editors Association, the American Society of Newspaper Editors, the Society of Professional Journalists, the National Conference of Editorial Writers and The Associated Press Sports Editors were among the groups that revised existing codes. The American Society of Newspaper Editors Statement of Principles, for example, was adopted in 1975. It replaced a code of ethics that was about a half-century old.

The *codes of ethics* developed by national groups that sincerely wished to strengthen the profession were broad statements of principle. However, Merrill wrote in "Existential Journalism": "Acting journalistically is the main thing; having a theory about journalism is another, and of much lesser import. A code of ethics hanging on the wall is meaningless; a code of ethics internalized within the journalist and guiding his actions is what is meaningful."

Merrill said that he did not know how helpful a code of ethics drawn up by a committee could be. "The codes do indicate a desire on the part of organizations to be ethical—whatever that means to them," Merrill said. "But ethics always boils right back to the individual. Ethical values are acquired all through life from a number of sources, such as church, family and friends. Reporters can't separate the ethics of journalism from the values they hold as individuals."

Although individual journalists need to assume personal responsibility for the ethical decisions that they make, it is important to examine codes of ethics that have been structured by various media organizations.

The formulation and updating of codes show an awareness by individual newspapers that ethical matters are a growing concern. A former managing editor of the no-longer-published *Washington Star*, however, contended that most codes "share a weakness—they are toothless." Charles B. Seib wrote in *presstime:*

> My belief that codes of ethics are of limited value is based on examination of a number of codes and my own experience. I have come to the conclusion that while codes have some use as broad statements of standards and as prior restraints on disgraceful conduct and bases for action in response to such conduct, their natural resting place is the back of the desk drawer.

Professor Louis W. Hodges of Washington and Lee University wrote in the "Journalism Ethics Report" of the Society of Professional Journalists (SPJ) that "codes help define what we are about."

Hodges urged SPJ members to study the code in order for the words to become "imbedded in our minds so that they shape our character and our dispositions." He said that the contents of codes "do not have to be enforced *formally* to be useful." He continued: "Informal sanctions on those who violate them can sometimes be more effective than enforcement through formal tribunals. Our society has chosen the informal route. . . . We believe that codes of conduct that individual journalists voluntarily impose upon themselves will ultimately bear good fruit."

No matter how broad some codes are, they do represent legitimate attempts by the industry to police its own ranks. The codes are often helpful—particularly to the working reporter—but journalists are regularly confronted with ethical and moral issues that must be reacted to on a case-by-case basis.

ETHICAL ISSUES

Few would argue with the assertion that journalists are more concerned than ever about the ethical ramifications of their work. Indeed, the Janet Cooke episode of more than a decade ago—when the Pulitzer Prize Committee decided to withdraw the prize it had awarded the *Post* reporter after it was learned that she had fabricated her story about an 8-year-old heroin addict—touched off a wave of discussions about ethics that continues unabated.

Scores of articles and books that focused on media ethics were published in the 1980s and early 1990s; conversations in newsrooms and at seminars about the ethics of journalism became increasingly common. Edmund B. Lambeth, a professor at the University of Missouri, wrote in his book, "Committed Journalism":

Accumulated distrust of the news media, skepticism of journalists' ethics and a resentment of media power are very nearly permanent features of the contemporary American scene. While the media themselves are not alone responsible for this state of affairs, it is past time for journalists and owners of newspapers and radio and television stations to articulate principles of performance that are publicly visible, ethically defensible and rooted clearly in a philosophic tradition that continues to justify a free press.

It has been pointed out, however, that in their well-intentioned zeal to be increasingly ethical, some journalists may avoid stories that should be brought to the attention of the public. At a Poynter Institute conference that marked the 10th anniversary of Cooke's fabricated story, Roy Peter Clark said that a "few, well-publicized ethical scandals . . . (had) prompted journalists to be overly cautious, keeping important information out of newspapers and newscasts." The institute's newsletter, "The Poynter Report," also quoted Robert M. Steele, who directs its ethics programs, as saying that "journalists must still be principled" when they make decisions but they should not be less aggressive. He also noted that the "restraint mentality has been exacerbated by the legal climate in which many newspapers failed to cover significant public policy stories out of fear of libel suits."

Do reporters adhere to the same stringent ethical standards for which they hold public officials accountable? Journalists are trained to report the first hint of governmental impropriety. Government officials, after all, have a responsibility to their constituents. Reporters should remember, however, that they too have a responsibility to their readers. Should reporters:

Jump at the chance for free movie tickets?
Stock personal libraries with review books sent out by publishers?
Look forward to gulping down free liquor from friendly sources?
Expect—and accept—small favors in return for complimentary stories?

Though the acceptance of "freebies" is often the first thing that comes to mind when discussing media ethics, the issues faced by journalists are sometimes considerably more complicated.

More than 150 editors of daily newspapers across the United States responded to two surveys that explored their opinions about and their handling of ethical issues. The first survey was conducted in the mid-1980s, the second in the early 1990s. Among other things, the editors were asked to discuss what they considered the most pressing ethical issues facing journalists. A synthesis of their responses results in the following list, which we'll examine item by item. We'll then take up an additional issue: journalistic arrogance.

- Fairness and objectivity
- Misrepresentation by reporters
- Economic pressure
- Privacy versus the public's right to know
- Conflicts of interest
- Anonymous sources
- Gifts
- Compassion versus policy

Fairness and Objectivity

Approximately one-fourth of the editors listed fairness and objectivity as the most pressing ethical issue facing journalists today. This concern far outdistanced the others.

Gilbert M. Savery, the former managing editor of the *Lincoln* (Neb.) *Journal,* explored the issue in some detail. He wrote:

> To answer the question of what I would consider to be the most pressing ethical issues facing reporters and editors today, I have to ask: "What is unethical and why should it be avoided?"
>
> Presumably when reporters or editors accept favors of magnitude, they are beholden to the donor. The question then arises as to whether that donor or his personal or corporate interests will be given more favorable treatment than other persons, businesses or institutions.
>
> Ethics, under this interpretation, translates into fairness. Therefore, the major ethical issues facing journalists today are those dealing with fair and balanced treatments of all viewpoints expressed on such issues as abortion, nuclear arms, nuclear power, a host of national issues including fiscal policy, education, religion and economics.
>
> Journalistically, the challenge is to deliver to readers, listeners and viewers a fair and balanced representation of viewpoints held by persons who differ markedly in their perceptions of what public policy should be.

Mitch Kehetian, the managing editor of *The Macomb Daily* in Michigan, said that he "cringed at some of the holes in so-called in-depth stories and the famous 'could not be reached for comment.'" He said that he worried about editors who allow the phrase "according to sources" to dominate stories. "We continue to hide behind the 'we were on deadline' excuse," Kehetian said. "That doesn't go with me. In essence: accuracy, credibility and fairness rank uppermost with me in pressing ethical issues."

Mark Baker, the managing editor of the *Shawano Evening Leader* in Wisconsin, agreed that it is imperative for reporters to write a balanced story. "Making sure a reporter provides access to all sides of a dispute—whether or not he or she agrees with the point of view rather than closing the door to those whose views or opinions are thought to be stupid, biased or just plain wrong—is important," Baker said. "Reporters, to some extent, must be like glass windows—allowing sunlight to come through with as little distortion as possible. Readers then get a true picture of the world."

Professor John Merrill of Louisiana State University, who has written extensively about journalistic ethics, wrote in *Journalism Quarterly* that acceptance of the assumption that "objective reporting is ethical reporting" raises interesting questions. He said that such acceptance would "mean that a journalist who was objective—or tried diligently to be objective—could forget about additional ethical decisions per se; for the journalist would have already entered the ethical field simply by applying technique. In short, the journalist accepting objective-reporting-as-ethics as a valid concept would have to concentrate on the technique of being objective, thereby satisfying any journalistic ethical demands which might be placed upon him."

Merrill pointed out, however, that the terms *objectivity* and *ethics* "are filled with semantic noise, and when they are brought together in tandem in this objectivity-as-ethics sense, the abstractness is greatly increased." Merrill wrote that we are "immediately aware of the intriguing question as to the possibility of ever reaching 'objective' news coverage" because of the many variables that go into the selection, writing and presentation of stories.

Misrepresentation by Reporters

Should reporters misrepresent themselves when working on stories? Yes? No? Sometimes? According to editors who responded to the surveys, this is a major ethical issue facing journalists today.

Tim Harmon, the managing editor of *The Journal-Gazette*, Fort Wayne, Ind., said that he saw ethical problems in misrepresentation "and any of the various other ways journalists foster the stereotype of the callous, get-the-story-at-any-price reporter or editor." Harmon said that journalists "don't put enough thought into how we get the information for our stories or whether we should use all of it."

Tim Wood, the managing editor of *The Weatherford* (Texas) *Democrat*, emphasized that reporters must take care to be open with sources. "Reporters must clearly identify themselves as reporters when they contact a source and make it clear that anything the source says may end up in the newspaper," he wrote. "Anyone being interviewed for publication must be aware of the purpose of the interview. Even asking vague questions without revealing the context in which the answers will be put is a practice that borders on being unethical. Sources should not be surprised when the story appears in print."

James E. Shelledy, the editor of the *Idahonian* in Moscow, Idaho, noted that it is important for reporters to allow subjects to respond "to the thrust of the story." He said, "We often seek responses to a specific question which would be answered somewhat differently if the thrust of the story were known." Shelledy said that he considered this issue to be part of the broader concern of reporter misrepresentation.

David Shaw, after conducting a non-random survey of reporters across the country, wrote in the *Los Angeles Times:* "Most journalists argue that it is unethical for a reporter to pretend he is not a reporter—or to fail to identify himself as a reporter—when interviewing someone."

Arthur C. Gorlick, the assistant managing editor of the *Seattle* (Wash.) *Post-Intelligencer*, recalled his days as a young reporter in Chicago. He was teamed with a veteran photographer to cover the shooting death of a young woman.

"The woman's family refused to talk with the press, the investigating detective told us in his office," Gorlick said. "The old photographer reached across the detective's desk, picked up the phone and dialed the reluctant family. 'I am calling from police headquarters,' he said. 'This is Jones in Lt. Smith's office. I'd like to come over and ask some questions.' It was true, but misleading. We got the interview. He got pictures. I used the material for a story and received praise from my editors for initiative, even though I was a passive partner in the deception. There is little such deception now that I am aware of, and our reporters are told we will not tolerate it. While I know of no journalists now who would openly misrepresent affiliation, some possibly will dress perhaps as a welfare recipient, say, and accept information or quotes from unsuspecting welfare recipients."

The fact remains, however, that at some metropolitan newspapers undercover journalism is occasionally practiced. Generally, it is resorted to only after editors and reporters have concluded that a story is extremely significant and that there would be no other means of obtaining it. Many journalists criticize undercover journalism, but others view it as a necessary means of gathering information, particularly when criminal activity is being investigated. In those situations, some newspaper editors and reporters contend that the ends justify the means. (See Chapter 23 for a discussion on going undercover.)

Brian Walker, the managing editor–news of *The Muncie* (Ind.) *Evening Press*, said that the issue of misrepresentation or "masquerading" by reporters is often discussed at his newspaper. "Some reporters have wanted to try it while others have been particularly sensitive about using even information given freely by sources who simply were not aware that their listeners were reporters. I oppose masquerading, but differentiate between reporters deliberately misidentifying themselves to sources and reporters accepting information or quotes from sources who didn't know their identity but simply didn't ask. The reporter's intent is important here. If the source was not intentionally misled about the reporter's identity, then the information is probably usable. If a source is willing to talk freely to someone without knowing who that someone is, then it is fair to assume that the source is speaking for public consumption."

Certainly, most editors and most reporters realize that purposeful misrepresentation to gain information should be considered only as a last resort, if ever.

Economic Pressure

Interestingly, several of the editors who participated in the survey conducted in the early 1990s tied ethical concerns to a weak economy. The majority of these comments came from editors of smaller dailies. One editor, for example, said that "the line between advertising and news becomes less clear every day; news people must keep the news untainted."

An editor of a mid-size daily wrote: "Advertorial approaches by executives outside the newsroom are my top ethical concern. More and more, papers are tying in 'stories' and photos based on advertising. We could easily mislead readers into believing that news articles can be bought. I understand a slumping newspaper economy is causing publishers to take a hard look at increasing ad revenue. We are treading on very dangerous ground."

An editor of a small-circulation daily who wrote the following comments was articulating a common theme: "With newspapers both large and small facing declining advertising revenues, I believe one area that is particularly troublesome is the relationship between editorial and advertising departments. Facing constant pressure from advertising, news departments often must decide whether to pursue a story that may put a major advertiser in a bad light. On the other hand, a story suggested by advertising, while possibly newsworthy, is—at least in my mind—immediately suspect because one wonders about the motivation behind the idea."

Historically, of course, there has been some sensitivity to the intrusion of advertising salespeople into newsrooms. But a common strain of forcefully articulated fears emerged from this survey, indicating that a sour economy has exacerbated an old problem. Many of today's editors are worrying about the ethical ramifications that ensue from the impact of revenue concerns on editorial decisions.

Critics have asserted that television, in particular, has allowed economics to influence its news programming. During recent years, the networks have aired more and more programs in which the line that separates news from entertainment has grown increasingly fuzzy.

For example, "Dateline NBC"—heralded by Ed Siegel of *The Boston Globe* as "the first successful prime-time news program in NBC's 20 years of attempting to create one"—found itself in the glare of unfavorable publicity in early 1993, when General Motors brought a defamation action against the network. This was the first such suit ever filed by GM; the charge was that NBC had rigged a truck with model rocket engines to fake a spectacular fire after a crash. The gas tanks of full-size GM trucks built from 1973 to 1987 had been mounted outside the frame and had been implicated as being susceptible to exploding in flames.

Michael Gartner, the president of NBC News, who later resigned, conceded that "sparking devices" had been used. At first Gartner said that the broadcast was nevertheless "fair and accurate." The next day, however, NBC admitted error, apologized and settled the case out of court, now saying that the use of devices was a "bad idea from start to finish."

The "Dateline" anchors, Jane Pauley and Stone Phillips, told a prime-time television audience, "We deeply regret that we included the inappropriate demonstration." They issued an apology to their viewers as well as to GM.

Appearing on NBC's "Meet the Press," Bob Woodward of *The Washington Post* described the apology as a "full grovel." In his column in *USA Today,* Al Neuharth compared NBC's handling of the story to methods employed during the era of "yellow journalism" ushered in by the publisher William R. Hearst at the turn of the 20th century. "You fake the fire, and we'll stretch the story, NBC in effect told a so-called 'safety' group that rigged the wreck," Neuharth wrote. According to Neuharth, NBC had settled the case because its lawyers "realized their jig would be up before a jury."

Clearly, newsrooms are not immune from economic pressures. Perhaps Siegel of *The Boston Globe* said it best: "Any news organization can be victimized by an unethical reporter or producer. It's unclear, however, whether the reverse is true in [the GM] case—whether reporters and producers were victimized by a network that was less interested than the others in saying that news had a mission aside from making money."

Privacy versus the Public's Right to Know

We have all seen the scenes on television or read the stories in the newspaper: a man has just died in a traffic accident caused by a drunken driver. The victim's widow, barely able to compose herself, is confronted by reporters who want to know how she feels and whether there should be stiffer sentences for people found guilty of driving while intoxicated.

To what extent should reporters invade privacy in an effort to get a story? Wickliffe R. Powell, the managing editor of *The Daily Independent* in Ashland, Ky., said that he thinks this issue becomes most sensitive when interviews are sought with "people who are thrust into the public eye because of circumstances beyond their own control."

In April 1992, one of the world's best-known athletes, the tennis player Arthur Ashe, was talking to a reporter for *USA Today* who had been a friend in high school. The reporter's primary purpose, though, was not to talk about old times. Rather, he asked Ashe to respond to the rumor that he had AIDS. Ashe, who asked also to speak to the newspaper's executive editor for sports, did not confirm the rumor. Because Ashe didn't confirm the rumor and because of its policy not to use unnamed sources, *USA Today* did not publish the story.

But the conversations spurred Ashe to hastily call a press conference for the following day to make public what a small circle of friends already knew: the former tennis star did indeed have AIDS. Ashe thought he had contracted the disease through tainted blood during an operating-room transfusion nearly a decade earlier; he died of it in February 1993.

Just before the press conference, when *USA Today* journalists were able to confirm what Ashe intended to announce, they immediately prepared a story for the newspaper's international edition and for the Gannett News Service.

As one would expect, reaction to the story and its handling was strong and emotional. *USA Today* created a special telephone line to receive calls. Hundreds of readers made their feelings known; most of them were critical.

Debra Gersh, writing in *Editor & Publisher* magazine, assembled reactions that had been published in the media and solicited opinions from a sample of journalists. The lead on her story was compelling: "The media found out last week that the boundaries of good journalism are not as clear as the service line on a tennis court."

Included in her story were some excerpts from a column Ashe had written for *The Washington Post:*

> I know there are tradeoffs in life. I understand that the press has a watchdog role in the maintenance of our freedoms and to expose corruption. But the process whereby news organizations make distinctions seems more art than science.
>
> I wasn't then, and I am not now, comfortable with being sacrificed for the sake of the "public's right to know."

Gersh went on to quote journalists who were outraged at what they perceived to be an invasion of Ashe's privacy. For example, DeWayne Wickham, a columnist for *USA Today* and Gannett News Service, wrote that Ashe "deserves the same privacy considerations this newspaper routinely gives rape victims."

Gersh also quoted Jonathan Yardley of *The Washington Post*, who wrote: "We tell ourselves that we are serving the public; but the bloodthirstiness and competitiveness with which we pursue our quarries are evidence enough that we are in search of nothing more noble than headlines."

Other journalists, though most of them admitted to feeling uneasy about the situation, said that the media had no choice but to write the story once the rumor was circulating and had been confirmed.

Does the public always have a right to know? What do you think?

Conflicts of Interest

Mike Foley of the *St. Petersburg* (Fla.) *Times* sees conflicts of interest as a major ethical issue facing journalists. Foley said that these conflicts—real or perceived—can involve such things as club memberships, friendships and even a spouse's political involvements.

Reporters and editors cannot be expected to live like hermits or to develop no friendships. But friendships can pose potential problems. Arthur C. Gorlick, the assistant managing editor of the *Seattle Post-Intelligencer*, called these problems "cronyism." He said: "It seems manifested in many ways at various levels of news organizations. Reporters, editors and publishers establish friendships with many of the people involved with things news organizations are expected to report about fairly. It is difficult for reporters or editors to maintain the impression of being impartial in a news report about a legislator if they have been socializing the previous evening or have a weekend golf date. It is difficult for journalists to function easily in reporting about a business leader knowing the publisher has invited the business leader to join the board of a civic fund-raising effort, however good the cause."

Reporters can also feel an ethical squeeze when they are asked to write newsletters for organizations to which they belong. Media policies vary with regard to the level of outside involvement their reporters and editors can have. New reporters should familiarize themselves with the codes of ethics of organizations for which they work.

Anonymous Sources

"The anonymous source—its use or misuse—is an issue of growing concern for us and other newspapers, particularly as it relates to the issue of newspaper credibility and public confidence in the media," said William T. Newill, the editor of the *Burlington* (N.J.) *County Times*. "There are times when it is absolutely necessary to guarantee anonymity in exchange for vital information. But the process has been abused by politicians and reporters up and down the system to the point where readers must certainly believe that the anonymous sources quoted in so many stories are none other than the reporters themselves. And who can blame our readers for thinking that way?"

The Janet Cooke episode, discussed earlier in this chapter, illustrates the ultimate danger in using anonymous quotations: if not even editors are told of the sources' identities, news media can be duped into running fabricated stories.

A national survey of managing editors of daily newspapers, reported in *Journalism Quarterly*, found that nearly 90 percent of the respondents agreed that editors at *The Washington Post* were negligent in failing to verify Cooke's story before publishing it. Still, it is interesting to note that 73 percent agreed that a fabricated story written by one of their own reporters could conceivably make its way into print.

More than four-fifths of the editors said that their newspapers had published staff-written articles based on unnamed sources. The survey also found that a majority of the editors felt that the press generally overuses unidentified sources in stories, that the use of unnamed sources leads to more distortion or hyperbolic statements in stories and that newspaper editors in the future will scrutinize more carefully stories that rely on unnamed sources.

Newspaper policies on the use of unnamed sources vary, but most prohibit publication of material in which the identity of sources is not shared with at least one key editor. A sampling of policies and an extended discussion of the use of anonymous sources can be found in Chapter 7 and Chapter 23.

Gifts

Presumably all editors and reporters agree that is it unethical to accept any gift of value from a news source. Some editors contend that it is unethical to accept any gifts—period. There are, however, some gray areas.

Tim Wood of *The Weatherford Democrat* said: "Accepting gifts usually is a judgment call. For example, several organizations bring food to our office during the holiday season. Is it unethical to accept this food? The food has little monetary value. Turning it down could be interpreted as an insult. The people who give us the food don't expect anything in return. However, if an organization wanted to treat the staff to a nice dinner at a local restaurant, that would be a different matter."

Many of the national and individual newspaper codes deal with the matter of gifts. The code of the Society of Professional Journalists says that "nothing of value should be accepted." The Associated Press Sports Editors' code says: "Gifts of insignificant value—a calendar, pencil, key chain or such—may be accepted if it would be awkward to refuse or return them. All other gifts should be declined. A gift that exceeds token value should be returned immediately with an explanation that it is against policy. If it is impractical to return it, the gift should be donated to a charity by your company." *The Washington Post*'s code says: "We accept no gifts from news sources. Exceptions are minimal (tickets to cultural events to be reviewed) or obvious (invitations to meals). Occasionally, other exceptions might qualify. If in doubt, consult the executive editor or the managing editor or his deputy."

Codes also often address the matter of free travel. The code of the *Chicago Sun-Times* says: "As a general principle, we will continue to pay for all travel. If an exception is required, a decision will be made on the merits of each case, with the understanding that conditions of any free travel are to be fully explained in connection with the subsequent news coverage."

The issue of free travel usually surfaces in sports departments. The AP Sports Editors' code addresses this question: "The basic aim for members of this organization and their staffs is a pay-your-own-way standard. It is acceptable to travel on charter flights operated by teams and organizations, but the newspaper should insist on being billed."

Mitch Kehetian of *The Macomb Daily* in Michigan said that he thinks too much attention is given to accepting a lunch or dinner because he has "too much faith in the journalists of today to insinuate that they could be bought off with a Big Boy burger."

The biggest problem for reporters at smaller newspapers, according to Kehetian, is dealing with "informational trips." Reporters and editors are often offered trips by groups such as the National Guard, which might provide transportation to training exercises at a summer camp. "The downtown dailies have unlimited sources, and can preach ethics at accepting such offers—but small daily staffers, and more so at weekly levels, find that the free offer is the only way of getting the story," Kehetian said. "That's sometimes the price for good ethics. In most cases, however, questionable examples are resolved by maintaining an open discussion line in the newsroom and always stressing that it is in the best interest of the reporter's professional integrity and, in the general run, that of the newspaper."

Compassion versus Policy

Reporters and editors of smaller dailies and weeklies are most likely to encounter those ticklish, awkward day-to-day situations when a subscriber, acquaintance or friend walks in the front door of the newsroom and asks, for example, that his or her name be kept out of the court news.

Most journalists have been threatened with, "Do you want to be responsible for the consequences if you print this story?" Such threats occur with frequency, but even veteran reporters never grow completely calloused to them.

It is not uncommon for court reporters—particularly those who work for smaller newspapers—to be confronted by people charged with criminal offenses. It is surprising how many of them have relatives with heart trouble or other medical problems—conditions that would quickly worsen if a story were published. Most reporters have received telephone calls from ministers or other community leaders urging that a drunken-driving story not be printed because of the disastrous effects such a story would have on the family of the accused. Sometimes, policies are in place to handle such matters. At other times, reporters or editors must make individual decisions.

"The real ethical issues are the hard choices faced in reporting day-to-day news," said Bill Williams, the editor of *The Paris* (Tenn.) *Post-Intelligencer.* "Do I publish the name of the rape victim? Do I wait until the defendant appears in court before publishing news of the arrest? Do I allow the mayor to provide information off the record? Does my birth column list illegitimate children?"

Williams told of an incident that occurred at his newspaper. It illustrates that, particularly in small-town journalism, editors are sometimes darned if they do and darned if they don't.

"The child of divorced parents won an honor," he said. "The mother reported the information, and we identified the child with her mother's name. The father called to object, said he was proud of the kid, too, even though the mother had custody, and he wanted to be identified as the father. So we ran a correction. The mother stormed in [subscribers don't have to get by security guards at small dailies and weeklies], said the father was a louse who had forfeited any claim. The child had subsequently been adopted by the stepfather, she said, and he should be identified as the father. I agreed with her that the guy was a louse, but I said he was still the biological father and we didn't see that we had any choice. She slapped me in the face and stalked out. That's how I 'solved' the issue."

T. J. Hemlinger, the editor of the *Hartford City* (Ind.) *News-Times*, said that, at his small-town (population 7,600) newspaper, staffers don't face some of the ethical problems encountered by larger newspapers. " 'Free travel' [for us] means riding a bus to the state capital with the Farm Bureau members to attend the state convention. Our ethics questions are: Should we run a picture of a suicide victim covered by a sheet, or a picture of someone injured in a traffic accident? Should we run a picture of a woman who probably is mentally ill as she goes into court to face charges of murdering her 9-month-old infant? My answers are all 'yes,' by the way."

Thad Poulson, the editor of the *Daily Sitka Sentinel* in Alaska, said: "We are regularly asked, by acquaintances and strangers alike, to 'keep my name out of the paper' in connection with the police news we publish. We often would prefer to comply, but we never do. Everyone on the staff, editorial and in other departments, knows that exceptions cannot be made even for employees of the newspaper."

Policies often provide ironclad rules for journalists, but it is clear that sometimes difficult decisions must be made on the spot. As Professor Merrill pointed out, ethics involves personal values. Journalists must decide what, under the circumstances, is the correct course of action.

Journalistic Arrogance

Editors who were surveyed spoke at length on some of the ethical issues discussed above. In their continuous effort to be responsible to their readers, their sources and themselves, however, reporters and editors also need to consider the issue of journalistic arrogance.

David Shaw, the national press reporter for the *Los Angeles Times*, touched on the issue of journalistic arrogance in an article he wrote for the magazine of the Society of Professional Journalists' national convention.

Shaw described one of the characters in Irving Wallace's novel "The Almighty": "The protagonist . . . is a power-mad, megalomaniacal, second-generation newspaper publisher who makes such observations as, 'There's not enough hard news around, exclusive news. Usually, my competitors have the same thing to sell that I have. But we here want our news alone. Since it's not around, we might have to invent some of it.' "

Shaw noted that this hyperbolic view is held by a lot of people who read novels and watch movies about newspapers. Still, Shaw said that the press likes to point majestically to the First Amendment, claiming that it "separates us from other institutions in our society." He wrote: "Like lawyers—and doctors and politicians and athletes and movie stars and everyone else I know—we don't like to be criticized."

The *Los Angeles Times* reporter said that "the arrogance of the press may be one of the greatest problems we, as an institution, face today." Shaw said that he was convinced "that the press must be held morally accountable to itself and to the society it serves." He said that it was important for the press to tell the public what it does and why—and, when necessary, to admit its mistakes.

IN CONCLUSION: THE JOURNALIST'S RESPONSIBILITY

Clearly, there are no absolute or certain answers to many of the ethical questions that regularly confront journalists. As Professor Merrill noted, "Ethics has to do with 'self-legislation' and 'self-enforcement.'" Merrill vividly summarized the issue of ethics and journalism in his book "The Imperative of Freedom": "When we enter the area of journalistic ethics, we pass into a swampland of philosophical speculation where eerie mists of judgment hang low over a boggy terrain. In spite of the unsure footing and poor visibility, there is no reason not to make the journey. In fact, it is a journey well worth taking for it brings the matter of morality to the individual person; it forces the journalist, among others, to consider his basic principles, his values, his obligations to himself and to others. It forces him to decide for himself how he will live, how he will conduct his journalistic affairs, how he will think of himself and of others, how he will think, act and react to the people and issues surrounding him.

"Ethics has to do with duty—duty to self and/or duty to others. It is primarily individual or personal even when it relates to obligations and duties to others."

Journalists bear an awesome responsibility to themselves and to their audience; this they should never forget.

Appendixes

Associated Press Style Rules

Here is a summary of the major rules from The Associated Press Stylebook and Libel Manual. These rules are only a sampling of what can be found in the stylebook, which you should also have.

Abbreviations and acronyms The notation *abbrev* is used in this book to identify the abbreviated form that may be used for a word in some contexts.

A few universally recognized abbreviations are required in some circumstances. Some others are acceptable depending on the context. But in general, avoid alphabet soup. Do not use abbreviations or acronyms which the reader would not quickly recognize.

Guidance on how to use a particular abbreviation or acronym is provided in entries alphabetized according to the sequence of letters in the word or phrase.

Some general principles:

BEFORE A NAME: Abbreviate the following titles when used before a full name outside direct quotations: *Dr., Gov., Lt. Gov., Mr., Mrs., Rev., the Rev., Sen.* and certain military designations listed in the **military titles** entry. Spell out all except *Dr., Mr., Mrs.* and *Ms.* when they are used before a name in direct quotations.

AFTER A NAME: Abbreviate *junior* or *senior* after an individual's name. Abbreviate *company, corporation, incorporated* and *lim-*

ited when used after the name of a corporate entity.

WITH DATES OR NUMERALS: Use the abbreviations *A.D., B.C., a.m., p.m., No.* and abbreviate certain months when used with the day of the month.

Right: *In 450 B.C.; at 9:30 a.m.; in room No. 6; on Sept. 16.*

Wrong: *Early this a.m. he asked for the No. of your room.* The abbreviations are correct only with figures.

Right: *Early this morning he asked for the number of your room.*

IN NUMBERED ADDRESSES: Abbreviate *avenue, boulevard* and *street* in numbered addresses: *He lives on Pennsylvania Avenue. He lives at 1600 Pennsylvania Ave.*

Addresses Use the abbreviations *Ave., Blvd.* and *St.* only with a numbered address: *1600 Pennsylvania Ave.* Spell them out and capitalize when part of a formal street name without a number: *Pennsylvania Avenue.* Lowercase and spell out when used alone or with more than one street name: *Massachusetts and Pennsylvania avenues.*

All similar words (*alley, drive, road, terrace,* etc.) always are spelled out. Capitalize them when part of a formal name without a number; lowercase when used alone or with two or more names.

Always use figures for an address number: *9 Morningside Circle.*

Spell out and capitalize *First* through *Ninth* when used as street names; use figures with two letters for *10th* and above: *7 Fifth Ave., 100 21st St.*

Abbreviate compass points used to indicate directional ends of a street or quadrants of a city in a numbered address; *222 E. 42nd St., 562 W. 43rd St., 600 K St. N.W.* Do not abbreviate if the number is omitted: *East 42nd Street, West 43rd Street, K Street Northwest.*

Capitalization   In general, avoid unnecessary capitals. Use a capital letter only if you can justify it by one of the principles listed here.

Many words and phrases, including special cases, are listed separately in this book. Entries that are capitalized without further comment should be capitalized in all uses.

If there is no relevant listing in this book for a particular word or phrase, consult Webster's New World Dictionary. Use lowercase if the dictionary lists it as an acceptable form for the sense in which the word is being used.

As used in this book, *capitalize* means to use uppercase for the first letter of a word. If additional capital letters are needed, they are called for by an example or a phrase such as *use all caps.*

Some basic principles:

PROPER NOUNS: Capitalize nouns that constitute the unique identification for a specific person, place or thing: *John, Mary, America, Boston, England.*

Some words, such as the examples just given, are always proper nouns. Some common nouns receive proper noun status when they are used as the name of a particular entity: *General Electric, Gulf Oil.*

PROPER NAMES: Capitalize common nouns such as *party, river, street* and *west* when they are an integral part of the full name for a person, place or thing: *Democratic Party, Mississippi River, Fleet Street, West Virginia.*

Lowercase these common nouns when they stand alone in subsequent references: *the party, the river, the street.*

Lowercase the common noun elements of names in all plural uses: *the Democratic and Republican parties, Main and State streets, lakes Erie and Ontario.*

POPULAR NAMES: Some places and events lack officially designated proper names but have popular names that are the effective equivalent: *the Combat Zone* (a section of downtown Boston), *the Main Line* (a group of Philadelphia suburbs), *the South Side* (of Chicago), *the Badlands* (of North Dakota), *the Street* (the financial community in the Wall Street area of New York).

The principle applies also to shortened versions of the proper names for one-of-a-kind events: *the Series* (for the World Series), *the Derby* (for the Kentucky Derby). This practice should not, however, be interpreted as a license to ignore the general practice of lowercasing the common noun elements of a name when they stand alone.

DERIVATIVES: Capitalize words that are derived from a proper noun and still depend on it for their meaning: *American, Christian, Christianity, English, French, Marxism, Shakespearean.*

Lowercase words that are derived from a proper noun but no longer depend on it for their meaning: *french fries, herculean, manhattan cocktail, malapropism, pasteurize, quixotic, venetian blind.*

SENTENCES: Capitalize the first word in a statement that stands as a sentence.

In poetry, capital letters are used for the first words of some phrases that would not be capitalized in prose.

COMPOSITIONS: Capitalize the principal words in the names of books, movies, plays, poems, operas, songs, radio and television programs, works of art, etc.

TITLES: Capitalize formal titles when used immediately before a name. Lowercase formal titles when used alone or in constructions that set them off from a name by commas.

Use lowercase at all times for terms that are job descriptions rather than formal titles.

Comma The following guidelines treat some of the most frequent questions about the use of commas.

For more detailed guidance, consult "The Comma" and "Misused and Unnecessary Commas" in the Guide to Punctuation section in the back of Webster's New World Dictionary.

IN A SERIES: Use commas to separate elements in a series but do not put a comma before the conjunction in a simple series: *The flag is red, white and blue. He would nominate Tom, Dick or Harry.*

Put a comma before the concluding conjunction in a series, however, if an integral element of the series requires a conjunction: *I had orange juice, toast, and ham and eggs for breakfast.*

Use a comma also before the concluding conjunction in a complex series of phrases: *The main points to consider are whether the athletes are skillful enough to compete, whether they have the stamina to endure the training, and whether they have the proper mental attitude.*

WITH EQUAL ADJECTIVES: Use commas to separate a series of adjectives equal in rank. If the commas could be replaced by the word *and* without changing the sense, the adjectives are equal: *a thoughtful, precise manner; a dark, dangerous street.*

Use no comma when the last adjective before a noun outranks its predecessors because it is an integral element of a noun phrase, which is the equivalent of a single noun: *a cheap fur coat* (the noun phrase is *fur coat*); *the old oaken bucket; a new, blue spring bonnet.*

WITH INTRODUCTORY CLAUSES AND PHRASES: A comma normally is used to separate an introductory clause or phrase from a main clause: *When he had tired of the mad pace of New York, he moved to Dubuque.*

The comma may be omitted after short introductory phrases if no ambiguity would result: *During the night he heard many noises.*

But use the comma if its omission would slow comprehension: *On the street below, the curious gathered.*

WITH CONJUNCTIONS: When a conjunction such as *and, but* or *for* links two clauses that could stand alone as separate sentences, use a comma before the conjunction in most cases: *She was glad she had looked, for a man was approaching the house.*

As a rule of thumb, use a comma if the subject of each clause is expressly stated: *We are visiting Washington, and we also plan a side trip to Williamsburg. We visited Washington, and our senator greeted us personally.* But no comma when the subject of the two clauses is the same and is not repeated in the second: *We are visiting Washington and plan to see the White House.*

The comma may be dropped if two clauses with expressly stated subjects are short. In general, however, favor use of a comma unless a particular literary effect is desired or it would distort the sense of a sentence.

INTRODUCING DIRECT QUOTES: Use a comma to introduce a complete, one-sentence quotation within a paragraph: *Wallace said, "She spent six months in Argentina and came back speaking English with a Spanish accent."* But use a colon to introduce quotations of more than one sentence.

Do not use a comma at the start of an indirect or partial quotation: *He said his victory put him "firmly on the road to a first-ballot nomination."*

BEFORE ATTRIBUTION: Use a comma instead of a period at the end of a quote that is followed by attribution: *"Rub my shoulders," Miss Cawley suggested.*

Do not use a comma, however, if the quoted statement ends with a question mark or exclamation point: *"Why should I?" he asked.*

WITH HOMETOWNS AND AGES: Use a comma to set off an individual's hometown when it is placed in apposition to a name: *Mary Richards, Minneapolis, and Maude Findlay, Tuckahoe, N.Y., were there.* However, the use of the word *of* without a comma between the individual's name and the city name generally is preferable: *Mary Richards of Minneapolis and Maude Findlay of Tuckahoe, N.Y., were there.*

If an individual's age is used, set it off by commas: *Maude Findlay, 48, Tuckahoe, N.Y., was present.* The use of the word *of* eliminates the need for a comma after the hometown if a state name is not needed: *Mary Richards, 36, of Minneapolis and Maude Findlay, 48, of Tuckahoe, N.Y., attended the party.*

NAMES OF STATES AND NATIONS USED WITH CITY NAMES: *His journey will take him from Dublin, Ireland, to Fargo, N.D., and back. The Selma, Ala., group saw the governor.*

Use parentheses, however, if a state name is inserted within a proper name: *The Huntsville (Ala.) Times.*

WITH YES AND NO: *Yes, I will be there.*

IN DIRECT ADDRESS:

Mother, I will be home late. No, sir, I did not do it.

SEPARATING SIMILAR WORDS: Use a comma to separate duplicated words that otherwise would be confusing: *What the problem is, is not clear.*

IN LARGE FIGURES: Use a comma for most figures higher than 999. The major exceptions are: street addresses (*1234 Main St.*), broadcast frequencies (*1460 kilohertz*), room numbers, serial numbers, telephone numbers and years (*1976*).

PLACEMENT WITH QUOTES: Commas always go inside quotation marks.

Courtesy titles In general, do not use the courtesy titles *Miss, Mr., Mrs. or Ms.* with first and last names of the person: *Betty Ford, Jimmy Carter.*

Do not use *Mr.* in any reference unless it is combined with *Mrs.*: *Mr. and Mrs. John Smith, Mr. and Mrs. Smith.*

On sports wires, do not use courtesy titles in any reference unless needed to distinguish among persons of the same last name.

On news wires, use courtesy titles for women on second reference, following the woman's preference. Some guidelines:

MARRIED WOMEN: The preferred form on first reference is to identify a woman by her own first name and her husband's last name: *Susan Smith.* Use Mrs. on the first reference only if a woman requests that her husband's first name be used or her own first name cannot be determined: *Mrs. John Smith.*

On second reference, use *Mrs.* unless a woman identified by her own first name prefers *Ms., Ms. Hills*; or no title: *Carla Hills, Mrs. Hills, Hills.*

If a married woman is known by her maiden last name, precede it by *Miss* on second reference unless she prefers *Ms.*: *Jane Fonda, Miss Fonda, Ms. Fonda*; or no title, *Jane Fonda or Fonda.*

UNMARRIED WOMEN: For women who have never been married, use *Miss* or *Ms.* or no title before a woman's last name, depending on her preference.

For divorced women and widows, the normal practice is to use *Mrs.* or no title, if she prefers. But if a woman returns to the use of her maiden name, use *Miss, Ms.* or no title, if she prefers it.

MARITAL STATUS: If a woman prefers *Ms.* or no title, do not include her marital status in a story unless it is clearly pertinent.

Dates Always use Arabic figures, without *st, nd, rd* or *th.*

Directions and regions In general, lowercase, *north, south, northeast, northern,* etc. when they indicate compass direction; capitalize these words when they designate regions.

Some examples:

COMPASS DIRECTION: *He drove west. The cold front is moving east.*

REGIONS: *A storm system that developed in the Midwest is spreading eastward. It will bring showers to the East Coast by morning and to the entire Northeast by late in the day.*

Warm temperatures will prevail throughout the Western states.

The North was victorious. The South will rise again. Settlers from the East went west in search of new lives. The customs of the East are different from those of the West. The Northeast depends on the Midwest for its food supply.

She has a Southern accent. He is a Northerner. Nations of the Orient are opening doors to Western businessmen. The candidate developed a Southern strategy. She is a Northern liberal.

The storm developed in the South Pacific. Leaders of Western Europe met leaders of Eastern Europe to talk about supplies of oil from Southeast Asia.

WITH NAMES OF NATIONS: Lowercase unless they are part of a proper name or are used to designate a politically divided nation: *northern France, eastern Canada, the western United States.*

But: *Northern Ireland, East Germany, South Korea.*

WITH STATES AND CITIES: The preferred form is to lowercase compass points when they describe a section of a state or city: *western Texas, southern Atlanta.*

But capitalize compass points:

—When part of a proper name: *North Dakota, West Virginia.*

—When used in denoting widely known sections: *Southern California, the South Side of Chicago, the Lower East Side of New York.* If in doubt, use lowercase.

IN FORMING PROPER NAMES: When combining with another common noun to form the name for a region or location: *the North Woods, the South Pole, the Far East, the Middle East, the West Coast* (the entire region, not the coastline itself), *the Eastern Shore, the Western Hemisphere.*

Doctor Use *Dr.* in first reference as a formal title before the name of an individual who holds a doctor of medicine degree: *Dr. Jonas Salk.*

The form *Dr.,* or *Drs.* in the plural construction, applies to all first-reference uses before a name, including direct quotations.

If appropriate in the context, *Dr.* also may be used on first reference before the names of individuals who hold other types of doctoral degrees. However, because the public frequently identifies *Dr.* only with physicians, care should be taken to assure that the individual's specialty is stated in first or second reference. The only exception would be a story in which the context left no doubt that the person was a dentist, psychologist, chemist, historian, etc.

In some instances it also is necessary to specify that an individual identified as *Dr.* is a physician. One frequent case is a story reporting on joint research by physicians, biologists, etc.

Do not use *Dr.* before the names of individuals who hold honorary doctorates.

Do not continue the use of *Dr.* in subsequent references.

House of representatives Capitalize when referring to a specific governmental body: *The U.S. House of Representatives, the Massachusetts House of Representatives.*

Capitalize shortened references that delete the words *of Representatives: the U.S. House, the Massachusetts House.*

Retain capitalization if *U.S.* or the name of a state is dropped but the reference is to a specific body:

BOSTON (AP)—The House has adjourned for the year.

Lowercase plural uses: *the Massachusetts and Rhode Island houses.*

Apply the same principles to similar legislative bodies such as *the Virginia House of Delegates.*

Hyphen Hyphens are joiners. Use them to avoid ambiguity or to form a single idea from two or more words.

Some guidelines:

AVOID AMBIGUITY: Use a hyphen whenever ambiguity would result if it were omitted: *The president will speak to small-business men.* (*Businessmen* normally is one word. But *The president will speak to small businessmen* is unclear.)

Others: *He recovered his health. He recovered the leaky roof.*

COMPOUND MODIFIERS: When a compound modifier—two or more words that express a single concept—precedes a noun, use hyphens to link all the words in the compound except the adverb *very* and all adverbs that end in *ly: a first-quarter touchdown, a bluish-green dress, a full-time job, a well-known man, a better-qualified woman, a know-it-all attitude, a very good time, an easily remembered rule.*

Many combinations that are hyphenated before a noun are not hyphenated when they occur after a noun: *The team scored in the first quarter. The dress, a bluish green, was attractive on her. She works full time. His attitude suggested that he knew it all.*

But when a modifier that would be hyphenated before a noun occurs instead after a form of the verb *to he,* the hyphen usually must be retained to avoid confusion: *The man is well-known. The woman is quick-witted. The children are soft-spoken. The play is second-rate.*

The principle of using a hyphen to avoid confusion explains why no hyphen is required with *very* and *ly* words. Readers can expect them to modify the word that follows. But if a combination such as *little-known man* were not hyphenated, the reader could logically be expecting *little* to be followed by a noun, as in *little man.* Instead, the reader encountering *little known* would have to back up mentally and make the compound connection on his own.

TWO-THOUGHT COMPOUNDS:
serio-comic, socio-economic.

COMPOUND PROPER NOUNS AND ADJECTIVES: Use a hyphen to designate dual heritage: *Italian-American, Mexican-American.*

No hyphen, however, for *French Canadian* or *Latin American.*

AVOID DUPLICATED VOWELS, TRIPLED CONSONANTS: Examples: *anti-intellectual, pre-empt, shelllike.*

WITH NUMERALS: Use a hyphen to separate figures in odds, ratios, scores, some fractions and some vote tabulations.

When large numbers must be spelled out, use a hyphen to connect a word ending in *y* to another word: *twenty-one, fifty-five,* etc.

SUSPENSIVE HYPHENATION: The form: *He received a 10- to 20-year sentence in prison.*

Legislative titles

FIRST REFERENCE FORM: Use *Rep., Reps., Sen.* and *Sens.* as formal titles before one or more names in regular text. Spell out and capitalize these titles before one or more names in a direct quotation. Spell out and lowercase *representative* and *senator* in other uses.

Spell out other legislative titles in all uses. Capitalize formal titles such as *assemblyman, assemblywoman, city councilor, delegate,* etc., when they are used before a name. Lowercase in other uses.

Add *U.S.* or *state* before a title only if necessary to avoid confusion: *U.S. Sen. Herman Talmadge spoke with state Sen. Hugh Carter.*

FIRST REFERENCE PRACTICE: The use of a title such as *Rep.* or *Sen.* in first reference is normal in most stories. It is not mandatory, however, provided an individual's title is given later in the story.

SECOND REFERENCE: Do not use legislative titles before a name on second reference unless they are part of a direct quotation.

CONGRESSMAN, CONGRESSWOMAN: *Rep.* and *U.S. Rep.* are the preferred first-reference forms when a formal title is used before the name of a U.S. House member. The words *congressman* or *congresswoman*, in lowercase, may be used in subsequent references that do not use an individual's name, just as *senator* is used in references to members of the Senate.

Congressman and *congresswoman* should appear as capitalized formal titles before a name only in direct quotation.

Legislature Capitalize when preceded by the name of a state: *the Kansas Legislature.*

Retain capitalization when the state name is dropped but the reference is specifically to that state's legislature:

TOPEKA, Kan. (AP)—Both houses of the Legislature adjourned today.

Capitalize *legislature* in subsequent specific references and in such constructions as: *the 100th Legislature, the state Legislature.*

Although the word *legislature* is not part of the formal, proper name for the lawmaking bodies in many states, it commonly is used that way and should be treated as such in any story that does not use the formal name.

If a given context or local practice calls for the use of a formal name such as *Missouri General Assembly,* retain the capital letters if the name of the state can be dropped, but lowercase the word *assembly* if it stands alone. Lowercase *legislature* if a story uses it in a subsequent reference to a body identified as a general assembly.

Lowercase *legislature* when used generically: *No legislature has approved the amendment.*

Use *legislature* in lowercase for all plural references: *The Arkansas and Colorado legislatures are considering the amendment.*

In 49 states the separate bodies are a *senate* and a *house* or *assembly.* The *Nebraska Legislature* is a unicameral body.

Military titles   Capitalize a military rank when used as a formal title before an individual's name.

See the lists that follow to determine whether the title should be spelled out or abbreviated in regular text. Spell out any title used before a name in a direct quotation.

On first reference, use the appropriate title before the full name of a member of the military.

In subsequent references, do not continue using the title before a name. Use only the last name of a man. Use *Miss, Mrs., Ms.* or no title before the last name of a woman depending on her preference.

Spell out and lowercase a title when it is substituted for a name: *Gen. John J. Pershing arrived today. An aide said the general would review the troops.*

In some cases, it may be necessary to explain the significance of a title: *Army*

Sgt. Maj. John Jones described the attack. Jones, who holds the Army's highest rank for enlisted men, said it was unprovoked.

In addition to the ranks listed, each service has ratings such as *machinist, radarman, torpedoman,* etc., that are job descriptions. Do not use any of these designations as a title on first reference. If one is used before a name in a subsequent reference, do not capitalize or abbreviate it.

ABBREVIATIONS: The abbreviations, with the highest ranks listed first:

MILITARY TITLES

Rank	Usage before a name

ARMY

Commissioned Officers

general	Gen.
lieutenant general	Lt. Gen.
major general	Maj. Gen.
brigadier general	Brig. Gen.
colonel	Col.
lieutenant colonel	Lt. Col.
major	Maj.
captain	Capt.
first lieutenant	1st Lt.
second lieutenant	2nd Lt.

Warrant Officers

chief warrant officer	Chief Warrant Officer
warrant officer	Warrant Officer

Enlisted Personnel

sergeant major of the Army	Army Sgt. Maj.
command sergeant major	Command Sgt. Maj.
staff sergeant major	Staff Sgt. Maj.
first sergeant	1st Sgt.
master sergeant	Master Sgt.
platoon sergeant	Platoon Sgt.
sergeant first class	Sgt. 1st Class
specialist seven	Spec. 7
staff sergeant	Staff Sgt.
specialist six	Spec. 6
sergeant	Sgt.

specialist five	Spec. 5
corporal	Cpl.
specialist four	Spec. 4
private first class	Pfc.
private 2	Pvt. 2
private 1	Pvt. 1

NAVY, COAST GUARD

Commissioned Officers

admiral	Adm.
vice admiral	Vice Adm.
rear admiral	Rear Adm.
commodore	Commodore
captain	Capt.
commander	Cmdr.
lieutenant commander	Lt. Cmdr.
lieutenant	Lt.
lieutenant junior grade	Lt. j.g.
ensign	Ensign

Warrant Officers

| chief warrant officer | Chief Warrant Officer |
| warrant officer | Warrant Officer |

Enlisted Personnel

master chief petty officer	Master Chief Petty Officer
senior chief petty officer	Senior Chief Petty Officer
chief petty officer	Chief Petty Officer
petty officer first class	Petty Officer 1st Class
petty officer second class	Petty Officer 2nd Class
petty officer third class	Petty Officer 3rd Class
seaman	Seaman
seaman apprentice	Seaman Apprentice
seaman recruit	Seaman Recruit

MARINE CORPS

Ranks and abbreviations for commissioned officers are the same as those in the Army. Warrant officer ratings follow the same system used in the Navy. There are no specialist ratings.

Others

sergeant major	Sgt. Maj.
master gunnery sergeant	Master Gunnery Sgt.
master sergeant	Master Sgt.
first sergeant	1st Sgt.
gunnery sergeant	Gunnery Sgt.
staff sergeant	Staff Sgt.
sergeant	Sgt.
corporal	Cpl.
lance corporal	Lance Cpl.
private first class	Pfc.
private	Pvt.

AIR FORCE

Ranks and abbreviations for commissioned officers are the same as those in the Army.

Enlisted Designations

chief master sergeant of the Air Force	Chief Master Sgt. of the Air Force
senior master sergeant	Senior Master Sgt.
master sergeant	Master Sgt.
technical sergeant	Tech. Sgt.
staff sergeant	Staff Sgt.
sergeant	Sgt.
senior airman	Senior Airman
airman first class	Airman 1st Class
airman	Airman
airman basic	Airman

PLURALS: Add *s* to the principal element in the title: *Majs. John Jones and Robert Smith; Maj. Gens. John Jones and Robert Smith; Specs. 4 John Jones and Robert Smith.*

RETIRED OFFICERS: A military rank may be used in the first reference before the name of an officer who has retired if it is relevant to a story. Do not however, use the military abbreviation *Ret.*

Instead, use *retired* just as *former* would be used before the title of a civilian: *They invited retired Army Gen. John Smith.*

FIREFIGHTERS, POLICE OFFICERS: Use the abbreviations listed here when a military-style title is used before the name of a firefighter or police officer outside a direct quotation. Add *police* or *fire* before the title if needed for clarity: *police Sgt. William Smith, fire Capt. David Jones.*

Spell out titles such as *detective* that are not used in the armed forces.

Months Capitalize the names of months in all uses. When a month is used with a specific date, abbreviate only *Jan., Feb., Aug., Sept., Oct., Nov.* and *Dec.* Spell out when using alone, or with a year alone.

When a phrase lists only a month and a year, do not separate the year with commas. When a phrase refers to a month, day and year, set off the year with commas.

EXAMPLES: *January 1972 was a cold month. Jan. 2 was the coldest day of the month. His birthday is May 8. Feb. 14, 1987, was the target date.*

Numerals A number is a figure, letter, word or group of words expressing a number.

Roman numerals use letters *I, V, X, L, C, D* and *M.* Use Roman numerals for wars and to show personal sequence for animals and people: *World War II, Native Dancer II, King George VI, Pope John XXIII.*

Arabic numerals use the figures *1, 2, 3, 4, 5, 6, 7, 8, 9* and *0.* Use Arabic forms unless Roman numerals are specifically required.

The figures *1, 2, 10, 101,* etc. and the corresponding words—*one, two, ten, one hundred one,* etc.—are called cardinal numbers. The term ordinal number applies to *1st, 2nd, 10th, 101st, first, second, tenth, one hundred first,* etc.

Follow these guidelines in using numerals:

LARGE NUMBERS: When large numbers must be spelled out, use a hyphen to connect a word ending in *y* to another word; do not use commas between other separate words that are part of one number: *twenty; thirty; twenty-one; thirty-one; one hundred forty-three; one thousand one hundred fifty-five; one million two hundred seventy-six thousand five hundred eighty-seven.*

SENTENCE START: Spell out a numeral at the beginning of a sentence. If necessary, recast the sentence. There is one exception—a numeral that identifies a calendar year.

Wrong: *993 freshmen entered the college last year.*

Right: *Last year 993 freshmen entered the college.*

Right: *1976 was a very good year.*

CASUAL USES: Spell out casual expressions: *A thousand times no! Thanks a million. He walked a quarter of a mile.*

PROPER NAMES: Use words or numerals according to an organization's practice: *20th Century-Fox, Twentieth Century Fund, Big Ten.*

FIGURES OR WORDS?: For ordinals:

—Spell out *first* through *ninth* when they indicate sequence in time and location—*first base, the First Amendment, he was first in line.* Starting with *10th,* use figures.

—Use *1st, 2nd, 3rd, 4th,* etc. when the sequence has been assigned in forming names. The principal examples are geographic, military and political designations such as *1st Ward, 7th Fleet* and *1st Sgt.*

SOME PUNCTUATION AND USAGE EXAMPLES:
—*Act 1, Scene 2*
—*a 5-year-old girl*
—*DC 10* but *747B*
—*a 5–4 court decision*
—*2nd District Court*
—*the 1970s, the '70s*
—*The House voted 230–205.* (Fewer than 1,000 votes)
—*5 cents, $1.05, $650,000, $2.45 million*
—*No. 3 choice,* but *Public School 3*
—*0.6 percent, 1 percent, 6.5 percent*
—*a pay increase of 12 percent to 15 percent*
Or: *a pay increase of between 12 percent and 15 percent*
Also: *from $12 million to $14 million*
—*a ratio of 2-to-1, a 2–1 ratio*
—*a 4–3 score*
—*(212) 262-4000*
—*minus 10, zero, 60 degrees*

OTHER USES: For uses not covered by these listings: Spell out whole numbers below 10, use figures for 10 and above.

Typical examples: *The woman has three sons and two daughters. He has a fleet of 10 station wagons and two buses.*

IN A SERIES: Apply the appropriate guidelines: *They had 10 dogs, six cats and 97 hamsters. They had four four-room houses, 10 three-room houses and 12 10-room houses.*

Party affiliation   Let relevance be the guide in determining whether to include a political figure's party affiliation in a story.

Party affiliation is pointless in some stories, such as an account of a governor accepting a button from a poster child.

It will occur naturally in many political stories.

For stories between these extremes, include party affiliation if readers need it for understanding or are likely to be curious about what it is.

FORM FOR U.S. HOUSE MEMBERS: The normal practice for U.S. House members is to identify them by party and state. In contexts where state affiliation is clear and home city is relevant, such as a state election roundup, identify representatives by party and city: *U.S. Reps. Thomas P. O'Neill Jr., D-Cambridge, and Margaret Heckler, R-Wellesley.* If this option is used, be consistent throughout the story.

FORM FOR STATE LEGISLATORS: Short-form listings showing party and home city are appropriate in state wire stories. For trunk wire stories, the normal practice is to say that the individual is a *Republican* or *Democrat*. Use a short-form listing only if the legislator's home city is relevant.

Periods   Follow these guidelines:

END OF DECLARATIVE SENTENCE: *The storybook is finished.*

END OF A MILDLY IMPERATIVE SENTENCE: *Shut the door.*

Use an exclamation point if greater emphasis is desired: *Be careful!*

END OF SOME RHETORICAL QUESTIONS: A period is preferable if a statement is more a suggestion than a question: *Why don't we go.*

END OF AN INDIRECT QUESTION: *He asked what the score was.*

INITIALS: *John F. Kennedy, T.S. Eliot.* (No space between *T.* and *S.*, to prevent them from being placed on two lines in typesetting.)

Abbreviations using only the initials of a name do not take periods: *JFK, LBJ.*

ENUMERATIONS: After numbers of letters in enumerating elements of a summary: *1. Wash the car. 2. Clean the basement.* Or: *A. Punctuate properly. B. Write simply.*

PLACEMENT WITH QUOTATION MARKS: Periods always go inside quotation marks.

Plurals   Follow these guidelines in forming and using plural words:

MOST WORDS: Add *s: boys, girls, ships, villages.*

WORDS ENDING IN CH, S, SH, SS, X AND Z: Add *es: churches, lenses, parishes, glasses, boxes, buzzes.* (*Monarchs* is an exception.)

WORDS ENDING IN IS: Change *is* to *es: oases, parentheses, theses.*

WORDS ENDING IN Y: If *y* is preceded by a consonant or *qu*, change *y* to *i* and add *es: armies, cities, navies, soliloquies.* (See proper names below for an exception.)

Otherwise add *s: donkeys, monkeys.*

WORDS ENDING IN O: If *o* is preceded by a consonant, most plurals require *es: buffaloes, dominoes, echoes, heroes, potatoes.* But there are exceptions: *pianos.*

WORDS ENDING IN F: Change *f* to *v* and add *es: leaves, selves.*

LATIN ENDINGS: Latin-root words ending in *us* change *us* to *i: alumnus, alumni.*

Most ending in *a* change to *ae: alumna, alumnae* (*formula, formulas* is an exception).

Those ending in *on* change to *a: phenomenon, phenomena.*

Most ending in *um* add *s: memorandums, referendums, stadiums.* Among those that still use the Latin ending: *addenda, curricula, media.*

Use the plural that Webster's New World lists as most common for a particular sense of a word.

FORM CHANGE: *man, men; child, children; foot, feet; mouse, mice;* etc.

Caution: When *s* is used with any of these words it indicates possession and must be preceded by an apostrophe: *men's, children's,* etc.

WORDS THE SAME IN SINGULAR AND PLURAL: *corps, chassis, deer, moose, sheep,* etc.

The sense in a particular sentence is conveyed by the use of a singular or plural verb.

WORDS PLURAL IN FORM, SINGULAR IN MEANING: Some take singular verbs: *measles, mumps, news.* Others take plural verbs: *grits, scissors.*

COMPOUND WORDS: Those written solid add *s* at the end: *cupfuls, handfuls, tablespoonfuls.*

For those that involve separate words or words linked by a hyphen, make the most significant word plural:

—Significant word first: *adjutants general, aides-de-camp, attorneys general, courts-martial, daughters-in-law, passers-by, postmasters general, presidents-elect, secretaries general, sergeants major.*

—Significant word in the middle: *assistant attorneys general, deputy chiefs of staff.*

—Significant word last: *assistant attorneys, assistant corporation councils, deputy sheriffs, lieutenant colonels, major generals.*

WORDS AS WORDS: Do not use *'s:* His speech had too many ifs, ands and buts. (Exception to Webster's New World.)

PROPER NAMES: Most ending in *es* or *z* add *es: Charleses, Joneses, Gonzalezes.*

Most ending in *y* add *s* even if preceded by a consonant: *the Duffys, the Kennedys, the two Germanys, the two Kansas Citys.* Exceptions include *Alleghenies* and *Rockies.*

For others, add *s: the Carters, the McCoys, the Mondales.*

FIGURES: Add *s: The custom began in the 1920s. The airline has two 727s. Temperatures will be in the low 20s. There were five size 7s.* (No apostrophes, an exception to Webster's New World guideline under "apostrophe.")

SINGLE LETTERS: Use *'s: Mind your p's and q's. He learned the three R's and brought home a report card with four A's and two B's. The Oakland A's won the pennant.*

MULTIPLE LETTERS: Add *s: She knows her ABCs. I gave him five IOUs. Four VIPs were there.*

Possessives   Follow these guidelines:

PLURAL NOUNS NOT ENDING IN S: Add *'s: the alumni's contributions, women's rights.*

PLURAL NOUNS ENDING IN S: Add only an apostrophe: *the churches' needs, the girls' toys, the horses' food, the ships' wake, states' rights, the VIPs' entrance.*

NOUNS PLURAL IN FORM, SINGULAR IN MEANING: Add only an apostrophe: *mathematics' rules, measles' effects.* (But see INANIMATE OBJECTS below.)

Apply the same principle when a plural word occurs in the formal name of a singular entity: *General Motors' profits, the United States' wealth.*

NOUNS THE SAME IN SINGULAR AND PLURAL: Treat them the same as plurals, even if the meaning is singular: *one corps' location, the two deer's tracks, the lone moose's antlers.*

SINGULAR NOUNS NOT ENDING IN S: Add *'s: the church's needs, the girl's toys, the horse's food, the ship's route, the VIP's seat.*

Some style guides say that singular nouns ending in *s* sound such as *ce, x* and *z* may take either the apostrophe alone or *'s.* See SPECIAL EXPRESSIONS below, but otherwise, for consistency and ease in remembering a rule, always use *'s* if the word does not end in the letter *s: Butz's policies, the fox's den, the justice's verdict, Marx's theories, the prince's life, Xerox's profits.*

SINGULAR COMMON NOUNS ENDING IN S: Add *'s* unless the next word begins with *s: the hostess's invitation, the hostess' seat; the witness's answer, the witness' story.*

SINGULAR PROPER NAMES ENDING IN S: Use only an apostrophe: *Achilles' heel, Agnes' book, Ceres' rites, Descartes' theories, Dick-*

ens' novels, Euripides' dramas, Hercules' labors, Jesus' life, Jules' seat, Kansas' schools, Moses' law, Socrates' life, Tennessee Williams' plays, Xerxes' armies.

SPECIAL EXPRESSIONS: The following exceptions to the general rule for words not ending in *s* apply to words that end in an *s* sound and are followed by a word that begins with *s: for appearance' sake, for conscience' sake, for goodness' sake.* Use *'s* otherwise: *the appearance's cost, my conscience's voice.*

PRONOUNS: Personal, interrogative and relative pronouns have separate forms for the possessive. None involve an apostrophe: *mine, ours, your, yours, his, hers, its, theirs, whose.*

Caution: If you are using an apostrophe with a pronoun, always double-check to be sure that the meaning calls for a contraction: *you're, it's, their's, who's.*

Follow the rules listed above in forming the possessives of other pronouns: *another's idea, others' plans, someone's guess.*

COMPOUND WORDS: Applying the rules above, add an apostrophe or *'s* to the word closest to the object possessed: *the major general's decision, the major generals' decisions, the attorney general's request.*

Also: *anyone else's attitude, John Adams Jr.'s father, Benjamin Franklin of Pennsylvania's motion.* Whenever practical, however, recast the phrase to avoid ambiguity: *the motion by Benjamin Franklin of Pennsylvania.*

JOINT POSSESSION, INDIVIDUAL POSSESSION: Use a possessive form after only the last word if ownership is joint: *Fred and Sylvia's apartment, Fred and Sylvia's stocks.*

Use a possessive form after both words if the objects are individually owned: *Fred's and Sylvia's books.*

DESCRIPTIVE PHRASES: Do not add an apostrophe to a word ending in *s* when it is used primarily in a descriptive sense: *citizens band radio, a Cincinnati Reds infielder; a teachers college, a Teamsters request, a writers guide.*

Memory Aid: The apostrophe usually is not used if *for* or *by* rather than *of* would

be appropriate in the longer form: *a radio band for citizens, a college for teachers, a guide for writers, a request by the Teamsters.*

An *'s* is required, however, when a term involves a plural word that does not end in *s: a children's hospital, a people's republic, the Young Men's Christian Association.*

DESCRIPTIVE NAMES: Some governmental, corporate and institutional organizations with a descriptive word in their names use an apostrophe; some do not. Follow the user's practice: *Actors Equity, Diners Club, the Ladies' Home Journal, the National Governors' Association, the Veterans Administration.*

QUASI POSSESSIVES: Follow the rules above in composing the possessive form of words that occur in such phrases as a *day's pay, two weeks' vacation, three days' work, your money's worth.*

Frequently, however, a hyphenated form is clearer: *a two-week vacation, a three-day job.*

DOUBLE POSSESSIVE: Two conditions must apply for a double possessive—a phrase such as *a friend of John's*—to occur: 1. The word after *of* must refer to an animate object, and 2. The word before *of* must involve only a portion of the animate object's possessions.

Otherwise, do not use the possessive form on the word after *of: The friends of John Adams mourned his death.* (All the friends were involved.) *He is a friend of the college.* (Not *college's,* because college is inanimate).

Memory Aid: This construction occurs most often, and quite naturally, with the possessive forms of personal pronouns: *He is a friend of mine.*

INANIMATE OBJECTS: There is no blanket rule against creating a possessive form for an inanimate object, particularly if the object is treated in a personified sense. See some of the earlier examples, and note these: *death's call, the wind's murmur.*

In general, however, avoid excessive personalization of inanimate objects, and give preference to an *of* construction when it fits the makeup of the sentence. For example, the earlier mentioned references to *mathematics' rules* and *measles' effects* would better be phrased: *the rules of mathematics, the effects of measles.*

Quotation marks The basic guidelines for open-quote marks (") and close-quote marks ("):

FOR DIRECT QUOTATIONS: To surround the exact words of a speaker or writer when reported in a story:
"I have no intention of staying," he replied.
"I do not object," he said, "to the tenor of the report."
Franklin said, "A penny saved is a penny earned."
A speculator said the practice is "too conservative for inflationary times."

RUNNING QUOTATIONS: If a full paragraph of quoted material is followed by a paragraph that continues the quotation, do not put close-quote marks at the end of the first paragraph. Do, however, put open-quote marks at the start of the second paragraph. Continue in this fashion for any succeeding paragraphs, using close-quote marks only at the end of the quoted material.

If a paragraph does not start with quotation marks but ends with a quotation that is continued in the next paragraph, do not use close-quote marks at the end of the introductory paragraph if the quoted material constitutes a full sentence. Use close-quote marks, however, if the quoted material does not constitute a full sentence. For example: *He said, "I am shocked and horrified by the incident.*
"I am so horrified, in fact, that I will ask for the death penalty." But:
He said he was "shocked and horrified by the incident."
"I am so horrified, in fact, that I will ask for the death penalty," he said.

DIALOGUE OR CONVERSATION: Each person's words, no matter how brief, are placed in a separate paragraph, with quotation marks at the beginning and the end of each person's speech:

"Will you go?"
"Yes."
"When?"
"Thursday."

NOT IN Q-AND-A: Quotation marks are not required in formats that identify questions and answers by *Q* and *A*.

NOT IN TEXTS: Quotation marks are not required in full texts, condensed texts or textual excerpts.

IRONY: Put quotation marks around a word or words used in an ironical sense: *The "debate" turned into a free-for-all.*

UNFAMILIAR TERMS: A word or words being introduced to readers may be placed in quotation marks on first reference:
Broadcast frequencies are measured in "kilohertz."
Do not put subsequent references to *kilohertz* in quotation marks.

AVOID UNNECESSARY FRAGMENTS: Do not use quotation marks to report a few ordinary words that a speaker or writer has used:
Wrong: *The senator said he would "go home to Michigan" if he lost the election.*
Right: *The senator said he would go home to Michigan if he lost the election.*

PARTIAL QUOTES: When a partial quote is used, do not put quotation marks around words that the speaker could not have used.
Suppose the individual said, *"I am horrified at your slovenly manners."*
Wrong: *She said she "was horrified at their slovenly manners."*
Right: *She said she was horrified at their "slovenly manners."*
Better when practical: Use the full quote.

QUOTES WITHIN QUOTES: Alternative between double quotation marks ("or") and single marks ('or'):
She said, *"I quote from his letter, 'I agree with Kipling that "the female of the species is more deadly than the male," but the phenomenon is not an unchangeable law of nature,' a remark he did not explain."*

Use three marks together if two quoted elements end at the same time: *She said, "He told me, 'I love you.'"*

PLACEMENT WITH OTHER PUNCTUATION: Follow these long-established printers' rules:

—The period and the comma always go within the quotation marks.

—The dash, the semicolon, the question mark and the exclamation point go within the quotation marks when they apply to the quoted matter only. They go outside when they apply to the whole sentence.

Semicolon   In general, use the semicolon to indicate a greater separation of thought and information than a comma can convey but less than the separation that a period implies.

The basic guidelines:

TO CLARIFY A SERIES: Use semicolons to separate elements of a series when individual segments contain material that also must be set off by commas:

He leaves a son, John Smith of Chicago; three daughters, Jane Smith of Wichita, Kan., Mary Smith of Denver, and Susan, wife of William Kingsbury of Boston; and a sister, Martha, wife of Robert Warren of Omaha, Neb.

Note that the semicolon is used before the final *and* in such a series.

TO LINK INDEPENDENT CLAUSES: Use a semicolon when a coordinating conjunction such as *and, but* or *for* is not present: *The package was due last week; it arrived today.*

If a coordinating conjunction is present, use a semicolon before it only if extensive punctuation also is required in one or more of the individual clauses: *They pulled their boats from the water, sandbagged the retaining walls and boarded up the windows; but even with these precautions, the island was hard-hit by the hurricane.*

Unless a particular literary effect is desired, however, the better approach in these circumstances is to break the independent clauses into separate sentences.

PLACEMENT WITH QUOTES: Place semicolons outside quotation marks.

Senate   Capitalize all specific references to governmental legislative bodies, regardless of whether the name of the nation or state is used: *the U.S. Senate, the Senate; the Virginia Senate, the state Senate, the Senate.*

Lowercase plural uses: *the Virginia and North Carolina senates.*

The same principles apply to foreign bodies.

Lowercase references to non-governmental bodies: *The student senate at Yale.*

State names   Follow these guidelines:

STANDING ALONE: Spell out the names of the 50 U.S. states when they stand alone in textual material. Any state name may be condensed, however, to fit typographical requirements for tabular material.

EIGHT NOT ABBREVIATED: The names of eight states are never abbreviated in datelines or text: *Alaska, Hawaii, Idaho, Iowa, Maine, Ohio, Texas* and *Utah.*

Memory Aid: Spell out the names of the two states that are not part of the continental United States and of the continental states that are five letters or fewer.

ABBREVIATIONS REQUIRED: Use the state abbreviations listed at the end of this section:

—In conjunction with the name of a city, town, village or military base in most datelines.

—In conjunction with the name of a city, county, town, village or military base in text. See examples in punctuation section below.

—In short-form listings of party affiliation: *D-Ala., R-Mont.* See **party affiliation** for details.

The abbreviations, which also appear in the entries for each state, are:

Ala.	Ga.	Mich.
Ariz.	Ill.	Minn.
Ark.	Ind.	Miss.
Calif.	Kan.	Mo.
Colo.	Ky.	Mont.
Conn.	La.	Neb.
Del.	Md.	Nev.
Fla.	Mass.	N.H.

N.J.	Ore.	Vt.
N.M.	Pa.	Va.
N.Y.	R.I.	Wash.
N.C.	S.C.	W.Va.
N.D.	S.D.	Wis.
Okla.	Tenn.	Wyo.

PUNCTUATION: Place one comma between the city and the state name, and another comma after the state name, unless ending a sentence or indicating a dateline: *He was traveling from Nashville, Tenn., to Austin, Texas, en route to his home in Albuquerque, N.M. She said Cook County, Ill., was Mayor Daley's stronghold.*

MISCELLANEOUS: Use *New York state* when necessary to distinguish the state from New York City.

Use *state of Washington* or *Washington state* when necessary to distinguish the state from the District of Columbia. (*Washington State* is the name of a university in the state of Washington.)

Time element Use *today, this morning, this afternoon, tonight,* etc., as appropriate in stories for afternoon editions. Use the day of the week elsewhere.

Use *Monday, Tuesday,* etc., for days of the week within seven days before or after the current date.

Use the month and figure for dates beyond this range.

Avoid such redundancies as *last Tuesday* or *next Tuesday.* The past, present or future tense used for the verb usually provides adequate indication of which *Tuesday* is meant: *He said he finished the job Tuesday. She will return on Tuesday.*

Avoid awkward placements of the time element, particularly those that suggest the day of the week is the object of a transitive verb: *The police jailed Tuesday.* Potential remedies include the use of the word *on,* rephrasing the sentence or placing the time element in a different sentence.

Titles In general, confine capitalization to formal titles used directly before an individual's name.

The basic guidelines:

LOWERCASE: Lowercase and spell out titles when they are not used with an individual's name: *The president issued a statement. The pope gave his blessing.*

Lowercase and spell out titles in constructions that set them off from a name by commas: *The vice president, Nelson Rockefeller, declined to run again. Paul VI, the current pope, does not plan to retire.*

COURTESY TITLES: See the courtesy titles entry for guidelines on when to use *Miss, Mr., Mrs.* and *Ms.*

The forms *Mr., Mrs., Miss* and *Ms.* apply both in regular text and in quotations.

FORMAL TITLES: Capitalize formal titles when they are used immediately before one or more names: *Pope Paul, President Washington, Vice Presidents John Jones and William Smith.*

A formal title generally is one that denotes a scope of authority, professional activity or academic accomplishment so specific that the designation becomes almost as much an integral part of an individual's identity as a proper name itself.

Other titles serve primarily as occupational descriptions: *astronaut John Glenn, movie star John Wayne, peanut farmer Jimmy Carter.*

A final determination on whether a title is formal or occupational depends on the practice of the governmental or private organization that confers it. If there is doubt about the status of a title and the practice of the organization cannot be determined, use a construction that sets the name or the title off with commas.

ABBREVIATED TITLES: The following formal titles are capitalized and abbreviated as shown when used before a name outside quotations: *Dr., Gov., Lt. Gov., Rep., Sen.* and certain military ranks listed in the **military titles** entry. Spell out all except *Dr.* when they are used in quotations.

All other formal titles are spelled out in all uses.

ROYAL TITLES: Capitalize *king, queen,* etc., when used directly before a name.

TITLES OF NOBILITY: Capitalize a full title when it serves as the alternate name for an individual.

PAST AND FUTURE TITLES: A formal title that an individual formerly held, is about to hold or holds temporarily is capitalized if used before the person's name. But do not capitalize the qualifying word: *former President Ford, deposed King Constantine, Attorney General-designate Griffin B. Bell, acting Mayor Peter Barry.*

LONG TITLES: Separate a long title from a name by a construction that requires a comma: *Charles Robinson, undersecretary for economic affairs, spoke.* Or: *The undersecretary for economic affairs, Charles Robinson, spoke.*

UNIQUE TITLES: If a title applies only to one person in an organization, insert the word *the* in a construction that uses commas: *John Jones, the deputy vice president, spoke.*

Women Women should receive the same treatment as men in all areas of coverage. Physical descriptions, sexist references, demeaning stereotypes and condescending phrases should not be used.

To cite some examples, this means that:

—Copy should not assume maleness when both sexes are involved, as in *Jackson told newsmen* or in *the taxpayer . . . he* when it easily can be said *Jackson told reporters* or *taxpayers . . . they.*

—Copy should not express surprise that an attractive woman can be professionally accomplished, as in: *Mary Smith doesn't look the part but she's an authority on . . .*

—Copy should not gratuitously mention family relationships where there is no relevance to the subject, as in: *Golda Meir, a doughty grandmother, told the Egyptians today . . .*

—Use the same standards for men and women in deciding whether to include specific mention of personal appearance or marital and family situation.

In other words, treatment of the sexes should be even-handed and free of assumptions and stereotypes. This does not mean that valid and acceptable words such as *mankind* or *humanity* cannot be used. They are proper.

Codes of Ethics

B

SPJ'S CODE OF ETHICS

The Society of Professional Journalists adopted the following code:

> The Society of Professional Journalists believes the duty of journalists is to serve the truth.
>
> We believe the agencies of mass communication are carriers of public discussion and information, acting on their constitutional mandate and freedom to learn and report the facts.
>
> We believe in public enlightenment as the forerunner of justice, and in our Constitutional role to seek the truth as part of the public's right to know the truth.
>
> We believe those responsibilities carry obligations that require journalists to perform with intelligence, objectivity, accuracy and fairness.
>
> To these ends, we declare acceptance of the standards of practice here set forth:

I. Responsibility

The public's right to know of events of public importance and interest is the overriding mission of the mass media. The purpose of distributing news and enlightened opinion is to serve the general welfare. Journalists who use their professional status as representatives of the public for selfish or other unworthy motives violate a high trust.

II. Freedom of the Press

Freedom of the press is to be guarded as an inalienable right of people in a free society. It carries with it the freedom and the responsibility to discuss, question and challenge actions and utterances of our government and of our public and private institutions. Journalists uphold the right to speak unpopular opinions and the privilege to agree with the majority.

673

III. Ethics

Journalists must be free of obligation to any interest other than the public's right to know the truth.

(1) Gifts, favors, free travel, special treatment or privileges can compromise the integrity of journalists and their employers. Nothing of value should be accepted.

(2) Secondary employment, political involvement, holding public office and service in community organizations should be avoided if it compromises the integrity of journalists and their employers. Journalists and their employers should conduct their personal lives in a manner that protects them from conflict of interest, real or apparent. Their responsibilities to the public are paramount. That is the nature of their profession.

(3) So-called news communications from private sources should not be published or broadcast without substantiation of their claims to news values.

(4) Journalists will seek news that serves the public interest, despite the obstacles. They will make constant efforts to assure that the public's business is conducted in public and that public records are open to public inspection.

(5) Journalists acknowledge the newsman's ethic of protecting confidential sources of information.

(6) Plagiarism is dishonest and unacceptable.

IV. Accuracy and Objectivity

Good faith with the public is the foundation of all worthy journalism.

(1) Truth is our ultimate goal.

(2) Objectivity in reporting the news is another goal that serves as the mark of an experienced professional. It is a standard of performance toward which we strive. We honor those who achieve it.

(3) There is no excuse for inaccuracies or lack of thoroughness.

(4) Newspaper headlines should be fully warranted by the contents of the articles they accompany. Photographs and telecasts should give an accurate picture of an event and not highlight an incident out of context.

(5) Sound practice makes clear distinction between news reports and expressions of opinion. News reports should be free of opinion or bias and represent all sides of an issue.

(6) Partisanship in editorial comment that knowingly departs from the truth violates the spirit of American journalism.

(7) Journalists recognize their responsibility for offering informed analysis, comment and editorial opinion on public events and issues. They accept the obligation to present such material by individuals whose competence, experience and judgment qualify them for it.

(8) Special articles or presentations devoted to advocacy or the writer's own conclusions and interpretations should be labeled as such.

V. Fair Play

Journalists at all times will show respect for the dignity, privacy, rights and well-being of people encountered in the course of gathering and presenting the news.

(1) The news media should not communicate unofficial charges affecting reputation or moral character without giving the accused a chance to reply.

(2) The news media must guard against invading a person's right to privacy.

(3) The media should not pander to morbid curiosity about details of vice and crime.

(4) It is the duty of news media to make prompt and complete correction of their errors.

(5) Journalists should be accountable to the public for their reports and the public should be encouraged to voice its grievances against the media. Open dialogue with our readers, viewers and listeners should be fostered.

VI. Pledge

Adherence to this code is intended to preserve and strengthen the bond of mutual trust and respect between American journalists and the American people. The Society shall—by programs of education and other means—encourage individual journalists to adhere to these tenets, and shall encourage journalistic publications and broadcasters to recognize their responsibility to frame codes of ethics in concert with their employees to serve as guidelines in furthering these goals. (Adopted 1926; revised 1973, 1984, 1987)

THE LOS ANGELES TIMES' CODE OF ETHICS

Guidelines established by national organizations, though helpful, are inherently vague. Recognizing this, individual newspapers have formulated more concrete policies.

In 1982 William F. Thomas, who then was editor of the *Los Angeles Times*, distributed to members of the editorial staff this code:

> Members of the Times staff are being offered increasing opportunities these days to use their expertise for outside publications or the electronic media. These offers can bring career enhancement and personal satisfaction, and we do not seek to discourage either.
>
> But, to try to avoid embarrassment or conflicts with your responsibilities to the Times, and to answer questions which arise from time to time, here are some general guidelines to confirm and clarify our existing practices.
>
> Since they are general, possibly the most important of them is the recommendation that any question of definition or applicability can be settled by a discussion of specifics. So if the slightest doubt is sparked by any situation, talk it over with a supervisor.

Outside Writing

(1) No articles for competing publications.

(2) No articles for business or trade publications, or any others which might fit the category of house organs, by writers or editors involved in coverage of their special areas.

(3) No paid sports scoring.

(4) No record or book jacket reviews which have not been published in The Times, with rare exceptions.

Gifts

(1) Shun gifts from news sources or subjects of coverage, except those gifts of insignificant value.

(2) Books or records received for review should not be sold by staffers.

Junkets

(1) Within the bounds of common sense and civil behavior, staffers should not accept free transportation or reduced rate travel, or free accommodations or meals. Exceptions can occur in such areas as political coverage, when convenience or access to news sources dictates. Again: if there are any questions, ask.

Meals

(1) As before, common sense and good manners should guide. A meal or a drink with a news source may be perfectly acceptable with the understanding that they will be reciprocated at company expense when appropriate.

(2) A staffer in most cases may accept a meal ticket when covering a political or civic event.

Tickets, Admission

(1) Staff members covering a sports or entertainment event can accept admission or preferred or press box seating. When attending an event upon which you will not report, but is judged by a supervisor to be useful to your work, pay the price and submit an expense report.

(2) In all other situations, ask.

Business Dealing

(1) Staff members may not enter into a business relationship with their news sources.

(2) Staff members with investments or stockholdings in corporations should avoid making news decisions that involve these corporations. If it is impossible to avoid them, these potential conflicts should be disclosed to a supervisor.

Political Activities

(1) Staff members should not take part in political or governmental activities they may be called upon to cover, or whose coverage they supervise.

(2) No staff member should work for pay in any political campaign or organization.

(3) Only in cases where there is no possibility of conflict should a staff member run for public office or assist in a political campaign or organization.

(4) If a staff member has a close relative or personal friend working in a political campaign or organization, the staffer should refrain from covering or making news judgments about that campaign or organization.

Broadcasting and Other Outside Appearances

(1) All such appearances for pay should be carefully examined from the aspect of possible conflicts and embarrassment to yourself or the newspaper. In general, regularly scheduled appearances or those under any other circumstances which might confuse the staffer's primary identification as a Times person should be avoided.

We all recognize that these are sensitive areas with many possible sets of governing circumstances. Again, if anything raises a question in your minds, bring it to your supervisors.

Glossary

A wire Main news wire of The Associated Press and United Press International that transmits the most significant national and international stories of the day. The wire is sometimes written as **AAA** or **Aye.**

Absolute defenses In libel suits, defenses that, if proven, are viable with no conditions or qualifications. For example, under the statute of limitations, suit must be brought within a specified period or the plaintiff has no standing to sue.

Abstracts Brief summaries of articles or books that are contained in some computer reference searches.

Accident forms Reports available in police stations that outline the circumstances surrounding accidents investigated by the department. Larger-circulation newspapers generally cover only spectacular accidents. Smaller-circulation dailies and weeklies routinely report all accidents, no matter how minor.

Action-line column Consumer-oriented column that helps people solve their problems. People write or call to describe their problems, and a reporter tries to solve them.

Active voice Term describing the verb form used when the subject of a sentence acts upon an object. For example: *The mayor denied the charge.* Active voice is generally preferred in journalistic writing because it is more vigorous than passive voice (see page 689).

Actual malice Fault standard in libel law, first articulated by the Supreme Court in 1964, that must be met by plaintiffs who are public officials or public figures. Such plaintiffs must prove that the information was communicated "with knowledge that it was false or with reckless disregard of whether it was false or not."

Actuality Audiotape excerpt, sometimes called a **soundbite,** that is inserted in a broadcast news story.

Add Each subsequent page of a story written on hard copy. For example, the second page of a story is the first add, the third page is the second add and so forth. When wire copy is electronically transmitted, an add is additional information to a story that is filed under the same key word as the original story.

Advance Story announcing a coming event.

Advance text A copy of the speech a

source is expected to deliver. Reporters use advance texts to help them prepare for covering speeches. They do not write stories from advance texts, however, because speakers often wander from their prepared remarks.

Advocacy journalism News writing in which a reporter defends or maintains a proposal or a cause.

Agate Type size smaller than regular text type; agate is generally 6 points or 7 points. (A **point** is ½nd of an inch.) Sports statistics and public-record items are commonly set in agate.

Agenda Outline of matters to be considered by a government body.

A.M. Morning newspaper.

A.M. cycle Morning newspapers usually report news that breaks on the A.M. cycle, generally the time from noon to midnight.

Analysis piece Feature story, also called a **backgrounder,** that adds meaning to current issues in the news by explaining them further.

Anchor On-camera person who reads the script for a broadcast news show. Some anchors write their own scripts; some read only what reporters and other off-camera newspeople have written.

Annual report Report issued by a public company and sent to its stockholders, informing them of the company's financial health and what is in store for the future.

Anonymous sources People who are willing to provide information on the condition that their names not be used in the story.

AP members Newspapers and broadcast stations that receive news from The Associated Press (see next column), a not-for-profit cooperative.

Appropriation Type of invasion of privacy that involves using someone's name or likeness for commercial gain.

Area editor See **state editor**.

Arraignment Step in the judicial process involving the reading of the charge to the accused. The arraignment is often held in a lower court, where a plea is typically entered.

Assets What a company owns. A company's assets are listed in its report to stockholders.

Assignment editor Editor who coordinates all assignments in a broadcast newsroom. He or she makes assignments, keeps track of crews in the field, makes follow-up calls for reporters and takes incoming calls.

Associated Press Generally referred to as the **AP,** the world's oldest cooperative news-gathering service.

Attribution Telling readers the source of information.

Authoritarian (press) system System in which criticism of the government is forbidden. Most newspapers in countries that operate under this philosophy are privately owned, but their content is controlled by the state through licensing or the issuance of patents.

"Aw nuts" school Premise subscribed to by some sports reporters that even great games and gifted athletes should be treated with near disdain.

B wire News wire of The Associated Press and United Press International that transmits national and international news of secondary importance.

Background Sentences in a news story that explain important elements. Background can explain something technical or provide details that were reported in earlier stories.

Backgrounder See **analysis piece**.

Banner Headline that stretches across a newspaper page.

Baud Measure of speed of data transmission .

Beat reporter Reporter who covers a specific geographic or subject area each day. Beats include police and fire; county and federal courts; and city, county and state governments.

Body Portion of a news story or a feature between the lead and the conclusion. The body should keep readers interested in the story and hold them until the conclusion.

Bold face Dark type that is thicker and blacker than ordinary text type. Also: **boldface caps,** which are capital letters set in type blacker than ordinary type. Bold face or boldface caps are often used for bylines.

Box score Statistical summary for various sports.

Breaking news News that is available for publication and that reporters try to cover as quickly as possible.

Brief Written report in which a lawyer sets forth facts that support his or her position.

Brightener Short, often humorous story that emphasizes quirks in the news. Brighteners are used to give an audience a break from hard news. They allow people to sit back and smile.

Broadcast producer Person who puts a broadcast news show together. He or she chooses which stories will be broadcast, in what order they will appear, how long they will be and in what production style they will be (how much videotape of a scene, how many interviews, etc.).

Broadcast wire News wire of The Associated Press and United Press International that transmits stories written in a shorter, more conversational style than those transmitted for print media.

Bulldog Newspaper's first edition of the day.

Bulletin Priority designation used by wire services. A bulletin contains at least one publishable paragraph but not more than two; it alerts newsrooms that a major story is developing.

Bullets Bold dots that introduce and highlight items in a news story or a feature.

Bureau Geographically removed extension of a news medium's headquarters. The Associated Press, for example, has its headquarters in New York, but it has bureaus in every state and in scores of foreign countries.

Buried lead Term for a news story's most important point when it is not in the opening paragraph, where it belongs.

Byline Line, usually at the top of a story, that names the author.

Capital budget Sometimes called a "hard" budget, the capital budget provides the dollars for government projects that are often large and long-range and have a physical presence, such as storm drains, streets and parks.

Caps Media shorthand reference to capital letters.

Change of venue Moving a trial to another location to reduce the possibility that prejudicial opinions, emotions and publicity will deprive the accused of a fair, impartial hearing.

Citation Information found on a data base that tells the searcher where an article, news story, report or document can be found. A citation usually contains name of author, title of article, title of publication in which it appeared, volume number, date and page number. It may also include a summary of the article's contents.

Citation data base Electronic storage facility accessible by computers connected to it with telephone lines. It contains citations, or information that indicates where an article or document can be found.

City editor Editor who runs the city (or metropolitan) desk and is in charge of city-side general assignment, beat and specialty reporters. The city editor makes certain that news in the city (or metropolitan area) is covered and that as many local stories as possible get into each edition.

Civil case Case that involves arriving at specific solutions to legal strife between individuals, businesses, state or local governments or agencies of government. Civil cases include suits for breach of contract and for libel.

Closed-ended question Question that is structured to elicit a short, precise answer. Reporters often ask closed-ended questions that require only "yes" or "no" responses. Sometimes, such questions have answers built into them. For example: *John Johnson and Bill Blodgett are candidates for mayor. Which of these candidates will you vote for?*

Clutter lead Awkward and difficult-to-understand lead that contains too many elements.

Codes of ethics Guidelines for journalists developed by national groups and by some individual news media. Codes often cover matters such as responsibilities of journalists, use of unnamed sources, accuracy, objectivity, misrepresentation by reporter, acceptance of gifts and favors from sources, political activities that journalists should or should not take part in and business dealings that could present conflicts of interest.

Color Observations, narrative or anecdotes in a story that give an audience a clearer picture of a person or an event.

Column inch Measure of space in a newspaper; a column inch is one column wide and one inch deep. Stories are often measured in column inches.

Commission government Municipal government system in which a committee of city leaders assumes both executive and legislative functions.

Complaint In law, a document that is filed by a plaintiff against a defendant in a civil suit. The complaint usually contains a precise set of arguments against the defendant.

Complete direct quotation Source's exact words, set off by quotation marks.

Complex sentence Sentence that has only one independent clause and at least one dependent clause. For example, *Johnson is the coach who will be elected to the hall of fame. Johnson is the coach* is an independent clause because it would make complete sense when left standing alone; *who will be elected to the hall of fame* is a dependent, or subordinate, clause (it does not make sense standing alone).

Composing room Production area of a newspaper where each edition's pages are put together according to an editor's instructions on layout sheets.

Computer reference services Services provided by many libraries to search for information via computer. The search is similar to a volume-by-volume search of a printed index, except that the requested information is returned electronically.

Conditional defense Defense against libel suits that involves certain conditions or qualifications. For example, privilege of reporting may be used as a defense when reporting information from official proceedings, public documents and court proceedings. This defense is limited, however, to *fair* and *accurate* reporting that does not intertwine extraneous, libelous matter.

Contrast lead Lead that compares or contrasts one person or thing with one or more other people or things.

Conversational style Less formal, less stilted style of writing for broadcast than is normally found in print media.

"Cooling off" period Relatively short time, generally 10 or 15 minutes, set aside by coaches after a game during which the locker room is off limits to reporters who seek interviews with players.

Cop shop Old-time journalism term for *police station* that is still used today by many reporters.

Copy Written material produced by journalists.

Copy desk Desk inside a newsroom where copy editors process copy written by journalists and then write headlines.

Copy editor Editor who checks stories to make certain that they follow proper style, usage, spelling and grammar rules. The copy editor also makes certain that a story is well-organized and not libelous. After editing the story, the copy editor writes a headline for it.

Copy paper Paper on which a story is typed. Copy paper is often newsprint trimmed to 8½ by 11 inches.

Correction Material that corrects something in a previously disseminated story.

Correspondent Journalist who contributes news stories to a medium that is located elsewhere. Metropolitan newspapers, for example, normally have correspondents stationed in the nation's capital as well as in countries around the world.

Council-manager government Municipal government system in which the city manager controls the administrative apparatus of the city. The main source of government expertise is the city manager, a trained professional adept at administering a community's affairs.

Counts In law, parts of a complaint or indictment claiming a specific wrong done.

Courtesy titles Titles such as Mr., Mrs. or Miss that precede names. Most newspapers limit courtesy titles to second references in obituaries.

Criminal case Case that involves the enforcement of a criminal statute. Actions are brought by the state or federal government against an individual charged with committing a crime, such as murder or armed robbery.

Criss-cross directory Directory that lists a city's residents by names and addresses. By looking up an address in the directory, a reporter can find the identity and phone number of the person at the address.

Crop Mark on a photograph or other piece of art indicating that it will not be used full frame. Art is cropped to eliminate unneeded material or to make it fit into a predetermined hole.

Cultural sensitivity Awareness of and sensitivity to the manifestations and structures of diverse cultures and their people.

Culturally inclusive Term describing newsrooms where reporters, editors and photographers with various racial, linguistic or religious ties work together to cover diverse communities.

Current assets Those things owned by a company that can be turned into cash quickly.

Current liabilities Debts of a company that are due in one year. Current liabilities are paid out of current assets.

Cursor Flashing light on a computer screen that indicates where the next character would appear.

Cut Another term for a printed photograph or some other piece of art. Stories are also *cut, trimmed* or *sliced*.

Cutline Copy accompanying a photograph or other piece of art that explains what is occurring or being shown.

Damages In law, the monetary value of an injury allegedly sustained through the unlawful act or negligence of another.

Dangling modifiers Grammatical errors that occur when a phrase used to begin a sentence is not followed by a subject, or when the subject is not correctly connected to the phrase or modifier. For example: *By working diligently, the job was accomplished.*

Dateline Opening line of an out-of-town story that gives the place of origin.

Death notice Story or listing of information about someone who has died. Many newspapers consider death notices and **obituaries** synonymous

Defendant Party against whom a lawsuit is brought.

Demographics Distribution, density, size and composition of a population.

Dependent clause Clause that would not make complete sense if left standing alone. For example: *John studies hard before he takes a test.* The clause *before he takes a test* is dependent upon *John studies hard* in order to make sense. It cannot be left standing alone.

Deposition Out-of-court statement made by a witness under oath.

Direct-address lead Lead that communicates directly with an audience by including the word *you.*

Docket Court record that documents progress in a specific case. All complaints filed, motions made and other developments in a case are recorded chronologically.

Double truck Story or advertisement that covers two facing pages of a newspaper or magazine, including the **gutter** (the space down the center of the two pages).

Dummy Mock-up of a newspaper or magazine page that has advertisements with specific sizes keyed in. News stories, features and photographs are laid out around the ads.

Dupe Abbreviation for *duplicate* and a designation for a carbon copy of a story.

Editor Person in charge of the editorial function of a newspaper. The role of the editor changes depending on the size of the newspaper.

Editorial news hole Space on a newspaper page that does not contain an advertisement and is reserved for stories or art. The ads are laid out on the page first; the editorial news hole consists of the remaining column inches.

Electronic camera Computerized camera that uses no film. Instead, pictures are recorded on a video floppy disk that resembles a computer floppy disk.

Electronic carbons Designation by The Associated Press for the transmission of stories directly from newspapers' computers to regional AP bureaus.

Electronic mail Facility for exchanging messages using central computer storage. A writer can type a message on a computer and then store it in a central electronic file accessible only by the addressee. The remote computers and central file are connected by telephone lines.

Electronic morgue Electronic storage facility that holds clippings of published stories for instant retrieval.

Electronic storage bin Computer disks and other electronic devices that store data accessible from remote terminals.

Element of immediacy Asset of the broadcast media that allows them to give up-to-the-minute reports and to write copy in a way that makes it sound fresh and lively.

Enterprise journalism Stories that require reporters to go beyond their daily routine. For example, a police reporter routinely writes stories from accident logs. An enterprise story would examine why a particular intersection has more accidents than any other in the city and would require multiple sources, statistical information and extensive quotations.

Ethnic coverage Reporting on the trends, events and issues of particular ethnic groups, people who have ties of ancestry, culture, nationality or language that distinguish them from the majority in society.

Executive producer Person who runs a television newsroom. He or she is responsible for story content, reading and editing reporters' scripts, long-range planning and scheduling, and countless other decisions. At smaller stations, the executive producer may also make assignments and decide the layout of each news show.

Executive session Meeting at which no official actions can be taken by government officials and from which members of the press and public are excluded.

False light Type of invasion of privacy that involves painting a false, though not necessarily defamatory, picture of a person or event.

Feature story Story that analyzes the news; entertains; or describes people, places or things in or out of the news.

Federal judicial system Branch of the federal government that is responsible for interpreting the law. The Supreme Court is the nation's highest court.

Feeds Program content sent to a television station via satellite, microwave or land lines from a network's headquarters or from another station.

Felony Serious crime for which punishment is normally imprisonment in a penitentiary.

Field producer Person who directs broadcast reporters and photographers in the field. At many stations the reporter is also the field producer. In some operations, however, a separate field producer directs the news gathering.

Filing In law, the formal lodging of a complaint in a civil action.

Filler Short story of less importance that is used to fill a small open space on a newspaper page.

Financial editor Editor in charge of handling business news. Most newspapers have a business page or section each day, and many have a staff of financial reporters who cover local businesses.

Financial wire News wire of The Associated Press that transmits business news stories, some stock tables and other market data.

Fire reports Daily reports of activity involving the fire department.

Five W's and H Six primary elements of a news story: *who, what, where, when, why* and *how.*

Flash Top-priority designation used by wire services. It usually contains only a few words and may not be a complete sentence. A classic flash: *DALLAS (AP)— Kennedy shot.*

Floppy disk Portable storage device that is inserted into a computer's disk drive.

Fluff Superfluous, overwritten and untimely information from a press release.

Focal point Thrust of a summary lead. A reporter determines the focal point of the lead by choosing which of the five W's and H (see above) to emphasize.

Focal question Primary question in a survey directly addressing the main issue. Other survey questions flow from this umbrella query.

Follow Sometimes referred to as a **second-day story,** a second or later story written about a newsworthy event. A follow provides the latest news in the lead or early in the story, but it also repeats the major news that was reported earlier.

Follow-up question Rearticulated or new question that a reporter asks to elicit a new or more specific response.

Foreign editor Editor who supervises reporters who cover news events outside the United States.

Fragmentary quotations Extremely small parcels of the precise words of a source that are spread throughout a sentence or paragraph. Fragmentary quotations look confusing when set in type and should generally not be used.

Free ad Information in a press release that is clearly of no news value and tries to seek free publicity for a person, business or organization.

Freedom of Information Act Generally referred to as the **FOI Act,** the law that provides for access to federal materials that are not statutorily exempt.

Free-lance To produce news stories for several publications, none of which is a full-time employer.

Frequency distribution In surveys, the percentage of responses to each question.

Full-text data base Electronic storage facility accessible by computers connected to it with telephone lines. It contains the entire text of an article or document.

Funnel interview Most common type of interview, in which the reporter begins with non-threatening background and open-ended questions. The toughest questions, those that may put the source on the spot, are saved for near the end of the interview.

Gag order Judicial mandate, sometimes called a **protective order,** that requires the press to refrain from disseminating specific information or that restricts those associated with the trial or investigation from discussing the case with the press.

Gang interview Press conference in which every reporter is given the same information and the source refuses to meet with reporters individually.

Gatekeepers People who make news decisions. Editors and reporters, on a story-by-story basis, decide what items to include and what angles to emphasize.

"Gee whiz" school Premise of some sports stories that athletes perform nothing but heroic feats.

General assignment reporter Reporter who covers a breaking news story or a feature that has been assigned by an editor. A general assignment reporter does not cover a specific beat.

Grand jury Jury of citizens convened to determine if there is probable cause that a crime has been committed and that the person charged with the crime committed it. A grand jury is so labeled because it has more members than a trial jury.

Graph Media shorthand for *paragraph*. Also spelled **graf.**

Graphics editor Editor who serves as a liaison between reporters, editors, photographers, artists and designers to coordinate the production of maps, charts, diagrams, illustrations and other informational graphics that accompany stories.

Guild Union of journalists formed to bargain collectively over such things as wages and benefits. For example, many newspaper journalists belong to the Newspaper Guild.

Handout Another term for **news release** or **press release.** Corporations, businesses, universities, organizations and political parties send handouts to alert the media to something they are doing.

Hard copy Product of a story composed on a typewriter or printed out from a computer.

Hard news Events that are timely and are covered almost automatically by print and electronic media. A speech by a ranking public official is an example.

Hardware Physical components of a computer such as terminal, cables, disk drives and so forth.

Head sheet Paper on which a headline is written or typed. Computerized newsrooms no longer use head sheets.

Hoax Deceptive or fraudulent story. An example is a call or letter that dupes a newspaper or broadcast station into disseminating an obituary for someone who has not died or does not exist.

Hostile source Uncooperative, close-lipped source who does not want to talk to reporters.

Hourglass style Style of writing in which the major news of a story is reported in the first few paragraphs and then a transitional paragraph introduces a chronology of the events of the story.

House ad Advertisement that promotes a publication.

Human angle Approach to a story that readers can relate to. The human angle is common on weather-related stories that reporters write to emphasize how the weather will affect people.

Human interest story Feature story that shows a subject's oddity or emotional or entertainment value.

Hyperbolic adjectives Overused references (most common in sports writing) that stretch beyond controlled, accurate description. Phrases such as *phenomenal freshman, sensational sophomore* and *game of the century* are examples.

Immediate news value Term descriptive of a breaking story, such as a fire, an accident or an election, that reporters try to cover as quickly as possible.

Immediate release Line at the top of a press release informing the media that the information it contains can be used immediately.

In-camera inspection Judge's examination of materials in a private room or with all spectators excluded from the courtroom.

Independent clause Clause that makes complete sense when left standing alone. For example: *John studies hard before he takes a test.* The clause *John studies hard* could stand alone; it expresses a complete thought.

In-depth story Story that, through extensive research and interviews, provides a detailed account well beyond a basic news story. An in-depth story can be a lengthy news feature that examines one topic extensively; an investigative story that reveals wrongdoing by a person, an agency or an institution; or a first-person article in which the writer relives a happy or painful experience.

Indictment Written accusation by a grand jury charging that a person has committed a public offense.

Indirect quotation Paraphrase of a source's statement that retains its meaning. Attribution must be provided.

Individual statistics Data compiled for each player in an athletic contest. For example, field goals made, free throws made, fouls, rebounds and total points are important individual statistics for basketball players.

Information In law, a written accusation, presented by a public officer such as a prosecuting attorney instead of a grand jury, that charges a person with committing a public offense.

Initial appearance Step in the judicial process at which the charge is read to the accused. In most states, this is referred to as an **arraignment.**

Insert Copy that is placed, or inserted, into a story to make the story more complete or to clarify what has been written already.

Interview from the outside in (See **outside-in interview.**)

Intrusion Type of invasion of privacy in which the defendant intrudes upon an individual's solitude, either physically or by electronic eavesdropping.

Invasion of privacy Legal wrong against what has evolved in the 20th century as the right "to be let alone." There are four types of invasion: intrusion, appropriation, public disclosure of embarrassing private facts and false light.

Inverted-funnel interview Type of interview in which the key questions, often the toughest, are asked immediately. This style of interview is used when sources are experienced in fielding closed-ended or adversarial questions or when there is little time to ask questions.

Inverted pyramid Traditional news writing form in which the key points of a story are put in the opening paragraph and the news is stacked in the following paragraphs in order of descending importance.

Issues reporting Reporting that examines complex matters of interest rather than simply providing the *who, what, where, when, why* and *how* of a newsworthy event.

Italics Type that slants to the right *like this.*

"Jell-O journalism" News reporting that overemphasizes soft writing, which is decried by some editors.

Journalists' privilege Assertion that journalists have a privilege, under certain conditions, not to reveal information sought by a court or grand jury. No such absolute privilege exists.

Jump To continue a story from one newspaper page to another.

Kerner Commission National commission appointed by President Lyndon B. Johnson and headed by Otto Kerner (then governor of Illinois) to study the effect of the mass media on riots. The official name of the group was the National Advisory Commission on Civil Disorders.

Key-word approach Method of selecting data for the holdings in a data base. It involves writing a computer command citing concepts and terms central to the research topic.

Kid quotes In sports writing, quotations gathered from junior-high and high-school athletes.

Lay out To position stories and art elements on a newspaper page. A **layout,** or **dummy,** is an editor's plan of how the page will look when it is printed.

Lead Opening paragraph of a story.

Lead-in In broadcast writing, a sentence or phrase that sets listeners up so that they are mentally prepared for what follows. For example, *Reporting from the scene of the fire, Tom Johnson describes . . .*

Lead block Multiparagraph lead that builds up to the major point of the story.

Leak journalism Reliance on "leaks" from unnamed sources to construct a story. Most editors and news directors discourage this practice.

Level of confidence In a random-sample survey, the probable error because of chance variations. The most common interval is the 95 percent level of confidence. This means that the probability is only 5 in 100 that the true answer is not within the range found.

Liabilities What a company owes. A company lists its liabilities in its reports to stockholders.

Libel Legal offense of publishing or broadcasting a story that damages a person's reputation by holding him or her up to public ridicule, hatred or scorn.

Libertarian (press) system Developed in the United States beginning early in the 19th century. A system in which the media flood the marketplace with information so that citizens can make enlightened decisions. The press is regarded as a primary instrument for checking on the government and its officials.

Lifestyle editor Person, also called the **features editor,** who leads what is usually a newspaper's main features section. The section may include articles by lifestyle writers, a food editor, an entertainment writer, a drama critic, a television writer and other reviewers and critics.

Limited access Designation for police reports that cannot be examined in their entirety, under all circumstances, by members of the public or journalists.

Localizing Putting a local emphasis on a story with broader ramifications. For example, if a wire-service report datelined Washington mentions a local or state official in the body of the story, the local newspaper may rework the story to move the local reference to the top of the story.

Local news value Characteristic of a story of particular interest to local readers, viewers or listeners.

Local weather forecasts Stories that discuss and predict weather for a local area.

Lower case Small letters of type, in contrast to capital letters.

Mainbar Main story in a group of articles about the same topic in a single edition of a newspaper.

Mainframe Powerful central computer to which other computers are connected. The mainframe usually holds a system's software.

Mainstreaming Practice at newspapers of citing and quoting in stories a variety of sources that represent and reflect the ethnic and gender mixes of communities.

Makeup editor Person who dummies (lays out) pages of a newspaper.

Managing editor Top editor in most newspaper newsrooms. This editor makes certain that the paper is out on time each day and that costs are kept within a budget. The managing editor is responsible for hiring and firing newsroom personnel and is usually involved in selecting stories, photos and graphics.

Masthead Box that appears inside a newspaper, often on the editorial page, identifying its top executives.

Mayor-council government Municipal government system in which the mayor can be categorized as "weak" or "strong," depending on the powers assigned to the position. In a "strong" mayor system, the mayor has the power to draw up budgets and to make and administer policy. In a "weak" mayor system, the mayor is, in essence, the chairperson of the city council, with most managerial functions divided among other elected officials and the council.

Media critic Reporter who writes stories about the strengths and weaknesses of and trends in daily media coverage. David Shaw of the *Los Angeles Times* is probably the best known. Also called a **press critic.**

Media event News occurrence, such as a presidential press conference, in which both the interviewee and the reporters are in the limelight.

Memorials Gifts in honor of a person who has died. In obituaries, most newspapers note when families suggest memorials to a specific cause or organization.

Menu approach Method of selecting data from the holdings in a data base. The searcher gets computer access to a generic list of topics from which one is chosen. That action brings a second list of subtopics to the computer screen from which, again, one is chosen. This process continues until the precise information is uncovered.

Meteorologist Person trained in the science of weather and climate. Metropolitan-area television and radio stations often employ meteorologists to provide weather forecasts and news.

Mill levy Tax imposed on property values by a municipality or school district in order to raise necessary money. The **mill** is the unit of measure (¹/₁₀ of a cent) used by municipalities and school districts in computing property taxes.

Minor sports Non-revenue-producing sports such as gymnastics, volleyball, cross country and swimming.

Minority affairs reporting Reporting on the trends, events and issues of people who are not part of the larger, more dominant group in a given society.

Minority source list List of names of minority people in a variety of professions and capacities, developed at media outlets to help reporters find sources for stories that reflect the ethnic mixes of communities.

Misdemeanor Crime considered less serious than a felony. Punishment is normally a fine or imprisonment in a facility other than a penitentiary.

Modem Short for *modulator-demodulator*. Device that translates computer-generated signals into signals that telephone lines can transmit.

More Word written at the end of a page to indicate that another page follows.

Morgue Common name for a newspaper library where clippings files and reference books are kept. Reporters do much of their research in the morgue. Stories (clips) are generally filed under subject and reporters' bylines.

Mugshot Head-only photograph of a source. One-column mugshots of primary sources often accompany news stories. They are used to show readers what the sources look like, as well as to break up long stretches of gray type.

Multiple-element lead Lead, also called a **double-barreled lead,** that gives two or more of the primary elements of a news story equal rating and that informs an audience immediately that more than one major event is occurring.

Nameplate Name of a newspaper on the front page; also called the **flag.**

Narrative lead Lead that uses narrative to draw people into a story by putting them in the middle of the action. A narrative lead is the most popular on features and non-breaking news stories.

National editor Editor who supervises reporters covering news events in cities other than the city in which the newspaper is published.

Negligence Fault standard in libel law articulated by the Supreme Court in 1974 that can vary from state to state. In some states, the level of liability is "gross negligence"; in others, it is "failure to act as a reasonable person" when gathering information for and writing a story.

Net income Company's profit or loss after taxes.

Net income per share How much each share of a public company earned in a quarter or for the year.

New lead Updated information that replaces the original lead. The wire services, during a 12-hour cycle, are constantly transmitting new leads to developing stories.

News director Top person in a television newsroom. He or she reports to a station manager or a general manager or both and does many of the jobs that a managing editor of a newspaper does. The news director is responsible for what goes on the air, the newsroom budget and the hiring and firing of most reporters and other personnel.

News editor Editor who decides which news appears in the newspaper and where. This editor is in charge of the copy desk, where makeup editors and copy editors work.

News hole Number of column inches available for news.

News huddle Daily meeting of a newspaper's editors, also called a **doping session,** a **news conference,** an **editors' meeting** or an **editorial conference.** In this meeting the editors discuss and then decide which of the top foreign, national, state and local stories and photographs will make it into the paper.

News mix Combination of hard news stories and feature pieces. The news mix can also include a blend of longer and shorter local, regional, national and international stories.

News peg Sentence or paragraph linking a story to a news occurrence.

News release See **handout.**

News story Write-up or broadcast piece that chronicles the *who, what, where, when, why* and *how* of timely occurrences.

Newsworthy element Peg of a story that should often be reported in the lead paragraph. In stories based on survey research, for example, the most significant statistical finding would be the newsworthy element that belongs in the lead.

No bill Finding returned by a grand jury if it determines that a sufficient probability does not exist that the accused committed the crime with which he or she is being charged.

Nose for news Reporter's instinct, which is used to gather information and to make news decisions as quickly as possible.

Nut graph Explanatory paragraph, also called a **"so-what" paragraph,** that follows the introductory lead block and explains the significance of a story.

Obit Common journalism term for **obituary,** a story about someone who has died.

Objective verbs of attribution Verbs of attribution such as *said* or *added* that reporters can use when quoting sources, to avoid interjecting personal feelings or perceptions about the way the source sounded.

Observation What a reporter sees, hears, smells, tastes or touches while working on a story. Observations add color to news stories and features.

Off the record Agreement reached by a reporter and a source before an interview that disallows use of the material revealed. Often, reporters refuse to accept information off the record, choosing instead to try to obtain it from another source.

Ombudsman "Middle person," or theoretically objective employee of a newspaper, who listens to complaints from readers and, when they are justified, passes them on to appropriate reporters or editors. About 30 newspapers employ ombudsmen.

On background Agreement reached by a reporter and a source before an interview that the material can be used, but attribution by name cannot be provided.

On deep background Agreement reached by a reporter and a source before an interview that the material can be used, but not in direct quotations and not accompanied by attribution.

On line Connected. Information held in computer memory that is available to searchers using computers remote from the memory unit is said to be "on line."

On the record Agreement reached by a reporter and a source before an interview that the material can be used, complete with the name of the source and identification.

Op-ed page Page that runs next to an editorial page, giving readers a mix of opinion columns and illustrations.

Open-ended question Question that is structured to allow a source time to develop an answer. Open-ended questions are a good way to break the ice between a reporter and a source because they give the source time to expand at length. For example: *What do you think about the quality of sports coverage in your local daily?*

Open-meeting laws Statutes in all 50 states that provide for public access to meetings of government bodies. The laws are not uniform, and all list exceptions to access.

Open-records laws Statutes that provide for access to state-level information. Most of these statutes, which also list specific exceptions to access to public records, specify that the laws should be construed liberally in favor of people seeking the records.

Open sentences Clearly constructed sentences that present no confusing ambiguities to the reader. Open sentences normally contain a straight subject-verb sequence and are seldom introduced with distracting dependent clauses and phrases.

Operating budget Sometimes called the "soft" budget, the operating budget provides dollars required to finance government entities on a day-to-day basis. One of the largest components of operating budgets is salaries.

Organizational structures Chains of command that outline the titles and duties of executives and employees. Beat reporters, for example, must master the organizational structures of the agencies they cover.

Outside-in interview Technique, used by investigative reporters, of interviewing acquaintances, associates and friends of a source first, before going to the source. By the time the reporter is ready to interview the source, he or she is well-armed with information and already knows many of the answers to critical questions.

Pagination Layout process in which stories, photographs, graphics, cutlines and headlines are assembled electronically on a computer screen.

Paper of record Newspaper that offers comprehensive, straightforward news accounts of what happened in the world, nation, state and community since the last edition. A paper of record is also a source for future historical reference.

Paraphrase Sentence or sentences providing the essence of what a source said, but not in the source's precise words.

Partial defense Defense, sometimes called a **mitigating factor,** that can be employed against libel suits if conditional or absolute defenses cannot be used successfully. Partial defenses, such as publication of a retraction, represent good faith on the part of the defendant and can be taken into consideration when damages are assessed.

Partial quotation Specific portions of a lengthier complete direct quotation that are reported and set off by quotation marks.

Passive voice Term describing the verb form used when the subject of a sentence is acted upon by the object. For example: *The child was hit by the car.* Passive voice should be used in news writing only when the person or thing receiving the action is more important than the person or thing doing the acting.

Personal computer Stand-alone computer that can be used for a variety of functions, including the input of stories. Material produced on a personal computer (PC) can be stored in the computer's built-in storage device, which is called its *hard disk,* or on a portable storage device called a *floppy disk.*

Personality profile Feature story that brings an audience closer to a person in or out of the news. Interviews, observations and creative writing are used to paint a vivid picture of the person.

Petition In law, a document that asks a court to take a particular action.

Photo editor Editor who supervises a newspaper's photographers. This editor may also write the captions that run with photographs.

Plaintiff Party who is bringing a lawsuit.

Planning editor Also called a **metropolitan editor,** the person who is in charge of long-term planning in a broadcast newsroom. The planning editor coordinates coverage of future events, such as trials or elections.

Play-by-play charts Tables produced at sports events such as football and basketball games to help reporters piece together important sequences in the contests. In basketball, for example, the chart would note who scored, on what kind of shot and what the score was at the time of the play.

Plea bargaining Negotiation between the prosecutor and defense lawyers over the kind of plea a suspect might enter on a specific charge. Prosecutors often propose that, in exchange for a plea of guilty, the state would bring a lesser charge against the suspect.

Pleadings In law, a written statement by all the parties setting forth assertions, denials and contentions.

P.M. Evening newspaper.

P.M. cycle Evening newspapers usually report news that breaks on the P.M. cycle, generally the time from midnight to noon.

Police log Daily report of activity involving the police department.

Population In surveys, the total number of subjects in the group to be studied. For example, in a survey conducted to find out where local high school seniors will attend college, the population would be all seniors in all local high schools.

Precision journalism Use of social science research methods—such as methodologically sound sampling procedures and computer analysis—to gather facts, leading to more precise, accurate news stories.

Preliminary hearing Step in the judicial process at which the state must present evidence to convince the presiding judge that there is probable cause to believe that the defendant committed the crime with which he or she is being charged.

Press critic See **media critic.**

Privately held company Also called a **closely held company,** a privately held company is a firm controlled by a family or small group. The value of the company's stock, which is not traded on an exchange, is set by the owners.

Procedural safeguards Steps, such as a change of venue, available to judges who want to ensure that defendants are not deprived of the judicial serenity and fairness to which they are constitutionally entitled.

Proof Copy of a typeset story.

Proofreader Person who reads a proof of a story to ensure that it is set the way the editors wanted and that it is free of typographical errors.

Public disclosure of embarrassing private facts Type of invasion of privacy that involves communicating information not of public concern in violation of standards of "common decency" perceived by persons of "ordinary sensibilities."

Public figure In libel cases, a person who has "voluntarily thrust" himself or herself into the vortex of a particular controversy to resolve that controversy, or a person who has assumed a role "of especial prominence" to the extent that, for all purposes, he or she is to be considered a public figure.

Publicly held company Company owned by investors who purchase its stock on an exchange.

Public official In libel cases, a government employee who has substantial responsibility for or control over the conduct of governmental affairs.

Public relations people People who work for public relations (PR) firms and whose job it is to gain media attention for the businesses, organizations, people or institutions that they represent.

Public relations wire Wire over which news releases and other public relations transmissions are sent to wire-service bureaus and to other news outlets that subscribe to it.

Queue File in a newsroom computer system. Stories and other information are stored in and pulled out of queues.

Question lead Lead that asks a question. The key to writing a question lead is to answer the question as quickly as possible.

Quote lead Lead that allows a central character to begin a news story or a feature by talking directly to the audience. The quotation may be the most powerful one in the story, or it may set the tone for what is to follow.

Rambling quotations Long, drawn-out direct quotations that journalists should avoid when possible by paraphrasing or by using indirect quotations.

Random selection Process by which each entity in a group has an equal chance of being selected.

Release date Date at the beginning of a press release or a wire story that informs the media of the earliest time that they can use the information. Many press releases are stamped *for immediate release,* which means that the information can be used as soon as it is received.

Religious News Service Supplemental news service established in 1933 to supply religion stories to news outlets.

Same-day obits Obituaries, written on the day of a person's death, in which the lead paragraph reports that the person has died.

Sample Portion of a population being studied. For example, in a survey conducted to find out where local high school seniors will attend college, a news medium might question one out of every 10 students.

Sampling error Margin of error that should be reported in all stories based on random-sample surveys. A mathematical formula is used to compute the percentage. An error margin of 5 percent, for example, means that the result could vary 5 percentage points either way because of chance variations in the sample.

Scanner Multichannel radio that monitors police and fire dispatches.

Search warrant Court document issued in the name of the state that directs a law enforcement officer to search specified premises.

Second-day obits Obituaries, written one or more days after a person dies, in which the lead paragraph features the time of services.

Second-day story Follow-up story written after the breaking news has been reported.

Settlement In law, an agreement reached by the parties, often before the case goes to trial.

Shareowners' equity Difference between a company's total assets and its liabilities.

Shield laws Statutes (existing in about half the states) that allow journalists and other specified people who are questioned by grand juries or under other circumstances to protect their sources under certain conditions.

Shotgun interview See **smoking-gun interview.**

Sidebar Story that runs with a mainbar. A sidebar isolates a person, place or thing usually mentioned in a mainbar and further explains, examines or illustrates it.

Simple sentence Sentence that has only one independent clause. For example: *The high jumper won.*

Skip interval In random selections from a list, every nth entry. E.g., if 10 names are to be chosen from a list of 100, the skip interval is 10. If the fourth name on the list is the first chosen, every 10th name thereafter would be chosen.

Slot editor Person who supervises copy editors. The slot editor distributes stories to copy editors and then checks their editing and headlines.

Slug One- or two-word label on a story. The slug identifies a story and keeps it separate from other stories.

Smelling a story In reporting a story, letting emotions, intuition, past experiences and gut reactions be a guide in gathering information.

Smoking-gun interview Question-and-answer session (also called a **shotgun interview**) in which a reporter, armed with videotape or other evidence of wrongdoing, asks direct questions about specific incidents. When the source denies any wrongdoing, the reporter shows the incriminating evidence in the hope that the source will admit guilt.

Social responsibility theory Philosophy, which emerged as a theory in the United States in the post-World War II years, that all views should be disseminated through the media, which are bound by professional ethics. The theory holds that if the press fails to live up to its obligations to present diverse views and to interpret them responsibly, the government can step in to ensure public service.

Soft news Events that are usually not considered immediately important or timely to a wide audience. Many of these events still merit coverage. A math fair at an elementary school or a faculty member's prize-winning rose garden might be covered as soft news, for example.

Software Program that tells the computer how to carry out specific functions such as word processing.

Soundbite See **actuality.**

Source Written material or a person that a reporter uses for information.

Source file File a reporter keeps of names, phone numbers, addresses and the expertise of useful sources.

Specialty reporter Reporter who covers breaking news stories or features in a highly specialized area, such as transportation, energy, education, religion, aviation, the arts and legal affairs. Like the sources they cover, specialty reporters must be experts in a particular field.

Spending caps Limitations imposed by government bodies on revenue or expenditure. Such caps can sometimes be overcome by a referendum.

Sports editor Editor in charge of sportswriters and the desk people who process their copy. The sports editor often writes a column.

Sports writing clichés Phrases, such as *brilliant field generals* and *sparkplug guards,* often overused by reporters.

Spot news News event covered by reporters as it is occurring.

Staccato lead Lead made up of a short burst of phrases that carry readers into a story by dangling some of its key elements in front of them. It is meant to tease readers and to set the mood for the story.

Standard offense forms Forms available at police and sheriff's departments, providing information such as when the alleged offense took place, where it occurred, the names of any victims and a brief synopsis of what reportedly happened.

State editions Issues of a metropolitan daily newspaper that have earlier deadlines than other editions and are delivered to counties and towns outside the metropolitan area.

State editor Person who supervises reporters covering communities and areas outside the city in which the newspaper is published; alternatively called the **area** or **suburban editor.**

State judicial systems Third branch of government for each of the 50 states. State judicial systems usually have three layers: trial courts, intermediate courts and supreme courts.

State news only (SNO) wire News wire that carries virtually all of the state news and sports produced by The Associated Press or United Press International for a particular state.

State weather forecasts Stories that discuss and predict weather for a state.

Steady advance Term used to describe writing that flows smoothly and logically. Sentences are constructed in such a way that readers glide efficiently from the first word to the last.

Story budget List of stories that have been written or are to be written. Individual reporters sometimes keep their own budgets. The wire services move international, national and state budgets that contain overviews of the most important stories on each day's cycles.

Stringer Part-time newspaper or broadcast correspondent who covers a specific subject or geographical area for a news medium often located elsewhere.

Sub Substitute. Reporters are often asked to write subs, which may provide later information or which may be better written than the original material.

Subpoena Court order for an individual to give testimony or to supply documents.

Suburban editor See **state editor.**

Summary lead Terse opening paragraph that provides the gist of a story and lets readers decide right away if they are interested enough in the story to continue.

Summons In law, a writ informing a person that an action has been filed against him or her in court and that he or she must answer the complaint.

Supplemental news services Services more limited in scope and resources than

The Associated Press and United Press International. Supplemental services, for a fee, provide news media with materials ranging from cartoons to in-depth political analysis. An example is the Newspaper Enterprise Association.

Survivors Persons who live after the death of someone closely related to them. In obituaries, most newspapers list names of surviving spouses, children, sisters, brothers and parents.

Team statistics Data computed by totaling individual statistics for sports contests. For example, if a team used eight basketball players in a game and each accumulated three fouls, the team total would be 24.

Text type Type in which newspaper stories are set. Text type is generally 8-, 9-, or 10-point. (One point equals $\frac{1}{72}$ inch.)

-30- Symbol used to indicate that a story has ended.

Thread Common element, usually a narrative about a person or event, that is intertwined throughout a story to connect the beginning, body and conclusion.

Throw line In broadcast writing, an introduction to the reporter. For example: *KFAB's John Johnson reports from the scene . . .*

Tight pages Pages on which there are so many advertisements that comparatively little space is available for news stories and features.

Time element The *when* of a news story. Generally, the time element is included in the lead paragraph.

Tokenism Practice, which should be avoided, of quoting or citing in stories a single minority person who ostensibly represents the point of view of an entire community or group.

Tort In civil law, a wrongful act committed against a person or against his or her property.

Transition Word, phrase, sentence or paragraph that ushers an audience from one area of a story to another. Transition alerts an audience that a shift or change is coming.

Transitional paragraph Paragraph that shifts readers smoothly from one area of a story to another.

Trend story Type of feature story that examines people, things or organizations having an impact on society.

True bill Indictment returned by a grand jury if it determines that there is probable cause that a person charged with a crime committed it and should stand trial for it.

Truncation Means of using root words plus extra symbols to broaden a computer key-word search of a data base. For example, **report???** in a command would elicit articles with key words such as *reporter, reportage* and *reporting.*

Turn word Transitional word that moves readers from one area to another. Some of the most common turn words are *now, today, but* and *meanwhile.*

Typo Typographical error.

Undercover journalism Type of reporting in which the journalist does not reveal to a source that he or she is working on a story.

United Press International Privately held corporation formed in 1958 when United Press and International News Service merged; generally referred to as **UPI.**

Unrestricted access Term for unlimited availability of police reports to members of the public or to journalists. The types of reports permitted unrestricted access vary among cities and states, but accident reports are often unrestricted.

UPI clients (subscribers) Newspapers and broadcast stations that receive news from United Press International (see above). These news media are called *clients* because UPI, unlike the AP, is a private corporation.

User friendly Term for a computer that is easy to use and that requires little training by anyone using it.

Video display terminal Computer terminal at which a reporter "inputs" (types) a story. A video display terminal, or **VDT,** is normally connected to a publication's mainframe computer.

Verdict Decision of a trial jury after it has considered the directions given to it by the judge and after it has weighed the evidence presented.

Visitations Hours established for viewing a decedent at a funeral home. Most newspapers provide details about visitation in obituaries.

Visuals Non-word elements of a printed page, including photographs, illustrations and graphics.

Voice "Signature" or personal style of every writer. Using voice in a story allows writers to put an individual stamp on their work. Voice reveals a reporter's personality and subtly tells readers that this story is not by any writer, but by *this* writer.

Voice track Words of a television reporter that accompany an anchor's words and the videotape.

Warrant Writ issued by a magistrate or by another appropriate official to a law enforcement officer, directing that officer to arrest a person and to bring him or her before a court to answer a charge.

Weather forecasting services Sources of information for journalists working on weather-related stories. The National Weather Service is a primary source, although some larger newspapers and television stations also contract with private weather forecasting services.

Wide-open pages Pages on which there are few or no advertisements.

Wind-up line In broadcast writing, the final sentence or "punch line" of a story. The last sentence can be a summary line, a future angle or merely a repetition of the main point of the story.

"Words in your mouth" technique Method used occasionally by journalists when interviewing inarticulate or tight-lipped sources. For instance, the reporter asks: *Did you feel ecstatic when you won the race?* and the source says, *Yes*. The journalist reports: *Jones said that he felt ecstatic when he won the race.*

Wrap In preparing a broadcast story, to place a reporter's words around one or more actualities.

Writethru Designation used by wire services to tell newsrooms that a story replaces all earlier stories on the same news event.

Year-end weather summaries Stories routinely published by newspapers on Jan. 1 that recap the weather for the previous year and present the most relevant statistics, such as rainfall amounts.

Chapter 1 Pages 5–6: W. D. Wigglesworth. 6–7: Charles Hill. 8: Ann Nykanen. 9–10: Patrice Bingham. 10: M. K. Glassner. 11: Ted Murphy. 11–12: Charles Kelly. 12–13: Brian Brainerd. 14: Kym Fox. 21, 24: Ann Nykanen.

Chapter 2 36–37: Bill Mock. 37, 39–40: Ron Jenkins. 44, 46: David Dixon. 45: Reprinted with permission of *The Gleaner*. 46, 48: David Yarnold. 47: Reprinted with permission of the *San Jose Mercury News*. 48, 50–52, 54: Dale Peskin and Beth Valone. 49, 53: Reprinted with permission of *The Detroit News*.

Chapter 4 85, 96: *Chicago Tribune*. 87: *Mohave Valley News*, Bullhead City, Ariz.

Chapter 5 100–103: Mark Eissman. 102–105: *Chicago Tribune*. 110–111: Roy Peter Clark. 112: Reprinted from the *Philadelphia Inquirer*, Jan. 9, 1985, by permission. 114–117: Julie Carey.

Chapter 6 122–128: Judi Villa.

Chapter 7 139–140: Edward Sylvester. 140–141: The Associated Press; used by permission of The Associated Press. 143: *Tempe* (Ariz.) *Daily News Tribune*. 154–156: Ben Silver.

Chapter 8 160–163: Reprinted with permission from the *Washington Journalism Review*. 164–168: Copyright © 1985 by Don Fry; reprinted with permission. 168– 178: Adapted from Robert Gunning, "The Technique of Clear Writing," rev. ed. (New York: McGraw-Hill,

1968); used with permission of the Gunning-Mueller Clear Writing Institute, Inc. 169: Reprinted with permission of *The Arizona Republic*. 170: Greta Tilley, *Greensboro* (N.C.) *News and Record*. 172: *Independent Florida Alligator*. 177: *The Orlando Sentinel*.

Chapter 9 182: Harry W. Stonecipher. 196: FOI Service Center; a joint project of the Reporters Committee for Freedom of the Press and the Society of Professional Journalists. 198–200: Max Jennings. 200: Copyright © 1986 by Sharon Hartin Iorio.

Chapter 11 231–232, 242: Maren S. Bingham. 231–232: Marie C. Dillon. 231–232, 238–239: Edie Magnus. 233–237: Katherine Rodeghier. 237: Jerry Guibor. 237: Neil H. Mehler. 238: Rick Alm. 239–240: Reprinted with permission of *The Dallas Morning News*. 246–248: *Chicago Tribune*.

Chapter 12 252, 260–261: Reprinted with permission from the *Washington Journalism Review*. 252–253: Gerald C. Stone. 262–265: James Simon.

Chapter 13 270: *Berkshire Eagle*. 270–271, 273, 275, 277–279, 282: *New Haven* (Conn.) *Register*. 271–272, 279: Tom Tuley. 272, 284: *News-Journal*, Daytona Beach, Fla. 273, 279, 281: *Trentonian*, Trenton, N.J. 273: *Fargo* (N.C.) *Forum*. 275: Kent Ward. 276, 281: *Findlay* (Ohio) *Courier*. 276, 282: *Jamestown* (N.Y.) *Post-Journal*. 278: Reprinted with permission of the *Colorado Springs Gazette Telegraph*. 283: Reprinted

with permission of the *Tempe* (Ariz.) *Daily News Tribune*. 285: Reprinted with permission of *The Birmingham* (Ala.) *News*.

Chapter 14 290–291: Mark S. Massa. 295, 301–302: Marlene Desmond. 297–298, 300–302: Lisa S. Hooker.

Chapter 15 324: Reprinted with permission of the *Tempe* (Ariz.) *Daily News Tribune*. 324–325: *State Press*, Arizona State University.

Chapter 16 330–331: Jack Williams. 332–333: *Fairbanks* (Alaska) *Daily News-Miner*. 335–336: *The Observer*, Le Grande, Ore. 337: *The Gleaner*, Henderson, Ky. 337–338: Reprinted with permission of *The Arizona Republic*. 338–339: Al Schmahl. 342, 346, 353: Ann Marie Lipinski. 342–343: The Associated Press; used by permission of The Associated Press. 343: Reprinted with permission of United Press International, Inc. 345, 351, 353–354: Gary Washburn. 348: Karen McCowan.

Chapter 17 362–363, 368–370: Felix Gutierrez. 363–364, 369–371: Caesar Andrews. 364, 368: Mary Lou Fulton. 364–365, 368–369: Dorothy Gilliam. 370, 372–379: Dawn Garcia. 373–378: © *San Francisco Chronicle*; Reprinted by permission.

Chapter 18 382–383, 385–388, 392, 400–401: Adrianne Flynn. 388–390, 398–399: Reprinted with permission of the *Tempe* (Ariz.) *Daily News Tribune*. 392–395: Jerry Geiger, Management Services Director, Tempe, Ariz.

Chapter 19 404–411, 414–421, 423–425: Roger Aeschliman. 411, 418–420, 422–425: Reprinted with permission of the *Topeka* (Kan.) *Capital-Journal*.

Chapter 20 430, 438–441, 443–444: Michael Padgett. 431: Description of state court systems from a chart in "Mass Communication Law," 5th ed., by Donald M. Gillmor, Jerome A. Barron, Todd F. Simon and Herbert H. Terry, West Publishing Co., 1990. 434–447: *Mesa* (Ariz.) *Tribune*. 453: The Associated Press; used by permission of The Associated Press. 455–456: Reprinted with permission of *The Arizona Republic*. 455–456: Reprinted with permission of *The Phoenix Gazette*.

Chapter 21 462, 466–468, 476: Lee Barfknecht. 463: From "The Tumult and the Shouting," by Grantland Rice; published by A. S. Barnes; copyright, 1954. 465–466: Terry Henion. 472–475: Reprinted with permission of the *Omaha* (Neb.) *World-Herald*. 478: Dennis Brown.

Chapter 22 482, 489–490, 495–496,498–499: Mary D. Gillespie. 491–492: News Group Chicago, Inc., 1985; articles by Mary Gillespie; with permission of the *Chicago Sun-Times*. 496–498: Reprinted with permission of *The Birmingham* (Ala.) *News*.

Chapter 23 502–503: *Chicago Tribune*. 504–506, 509: Fred Schulte. 506–508: Charles Zdravesky. 511–512: William Recktenwald. 513, 515: Reprinted with permission from *The Minneapolis Star and Tribune*. 513: News & Sun-Sentinel Company. 516–517: Reprinted with permission of *The Arizona Republic*.

Chapter 24 523–524, 530–532: Mary Beth Sammons. 524–525: Andrew Leckey. 537–540: David Horowitz.

Chapter 25 545–547: Casey J. Bukro. 546–547, 553–554: *Chicago Tribune*. 548–549: Cristine Russell. 550–551: Terry Mattingly. 552–555: Joseph R. Tybor.

Chapter 26 560, 569, 576–577: Wendy Black. 562–567: Donald E. Brown. 567, 573–574, 576–577 : Ben Silver. 567–569: KOY Radio, Phoenix, Ariz. 569–570, 575–576: Dan Fellner. 571–572: KPNX-TV, Phoenix, Ariz. 573: The Associated Press; used by permission of The Associated Press.

Chapter 27 580: Excerpt from "Deadline Every Minute," by Joe Morris, copyright © 1957 by Joe Alex Morris; reprinted by permission of Doubleday & Company, Inc. 582–585: Charles Hill. 585–587,

590: Paula Froke. 585: Reprinted with permission of *The Duluth* (Minn.) *News-Tribune*. 586–588, 590–593: The Associated Press; used by permission of The Associated Press. 594: *Chicago Tribune*.

Chapter 28 600, 602, 613: Lyle Denniston. 600–601: Henry R. Kaufman. 602–603: From "Synopsis of the Law of Libel and the Right of Privacy," by Bruce W. Sanford; used with permission of Scripps-Howard Newspapers. 613–614: Marc A. Franklin. 614: New York State Newspapers Foundation.

Chapter 29 636–638: Reprinted by permission from *Journalism Quarterly*, Autumn 1982. 640–641, 653: John C. Merrill. 642–643, 646–647: Reprinted with permission of *Newspaper Research Journal*, Winter/Spring 1992. 644–646, 648–652: *Nebraska Newspaper*, publication of the Nebraska Press Association.

Appendix A Portions of The Associated Press Stylebook are used by permission of The Associated Press.

Appendix B 673–675: Society of Professional Journalists. 675–676: Reprinted with permission of the author, William F. Thomas, *Los Angeles Times*.

697

698

700

701

705

711

713

714